THE DECLINE AND FALL OF THE ROMAN EMPIRE

THE DECLINE AND FALL OF THE ROMAN EMPIRE

EDWARD GIBBON

Abridged and with an Introduction by
Frank C. Bourne

Tess Press

CONTENTS

List of Maps   ix

Preface   xi

Introduction   xiii

I   THE EXTENT AND MILITARY FORCE OF THE EMPIRE IN THE AGE OF THE ANTONINES   1

II   OF THE UNION AND INTERNAL PROSPERITY OF THE ROMAN EMPIRE IN THE AGE OF THE ANTONINES   16

III (96–180 A.D.) OF THE CONSTITUTION OF THE ROMAN EMPIRE IN THE AGE OF THE ANTONINES   35

IV   (180–193 A.D.) THE CRUELTY, FOLLIES, AND MURDER OF COMMODUS—ELECTION OF PERTINAX—HIS ATTEMPTS TO REFORM THE STATE—HIS ASSASSINATION BY THE PRÆTORIAN GUARDS   47

V   (193–197 A.D.) PUBLIC SALE OF THE EMPIRE TO DIDIUS JULIANUS BY THE PRÆTORIAN GUARDS—CLODIUS ALBINUS IN BRITAIN, PESCENNIUS NIGER IN SYRIA, AND SEPTIMIUS SEVERUS IN PANNONIA, DECLARE AGAINST THE MURDERERS OF PERTINAX—CIVIL WARS AND VICTORY OF SEVERUS OVER HIS THREE RIVALS—RELAXATION OF DISCIPLINE—NEW MAXIMS OF GOVERNMENT   61

VI   (208–235 A.D.) THE DEATH OF SEVERUS—TYRANNY OF CARACALLA—USURPATION OF MACRINUS—FOLLIES OF ELAGABALUS—VIRTUES OF ALEXANDER SEVERUS—LICENTIOUSNESS OF THE ARMY   74

VII (235–248 A.D.) THE ELEVATION AND TYRANNY OF MAXIMIN—REBELLION IN AFRICA AND ITALY, UNDER THE AUTHORITY OF THE SENATE—CIVIL WARS AND SEDITIONS—VIOLENT DEATHS OF MAXIMIN AND HIS SON, OF MAXIMUS AND BALBINUS, AND OF THE THREE GORDIANS—USURPATION AND SECULAR GAMES OF PHILIP   90

VIII (248–268 A.D.) THE EMPERORS DECIUS, GALLUS, ÆMILIANUS, VALERIAN, AND GALLIENUS—THE GENERAL IRRUPTION OF THE BARBARIANS—THE THIRTY TYRANTS   101

IX   (268–275 A.D.) REIGN OF CLAUDIUS—DEFEAT OF THE GOTHS—VICTORIES, TRIUMPH, AND DEATH OF AURELIAN   122

X (275–285 A.D.) CONDUCT OF THE ARMY AND SENATE AFTER THE DEATH OF AURELIAN—REIGNS OF TACITUS, PROBUS, CARUS, AND HIS SONS 138

XI (285–313 A.D.) THE REIGN OF DIOCLETIAN AND HIS THREE ASSOCIATES, MAXIMIAN, GALERIUS, AND CONSTANTIUS— GENERAL RE-ESTABLISHMENT OF ORDER AND TRAN- QUILLITY—THE NEW FORM OF ADMINISTRATION— ABDICATION AND RETIREMENT OF DIOCLETIAN AND MAXIMIAN 152

XII (305–324 A.D.) TROUBLES AFTER THE ABDICATION OF DIOCLETIAN—DEATH OF CONSTANTIUS—ELEVATION OF CONSTANTINE AND MAXENTIUS—SIX EMPERORS AT THE SAME TIME—DEATH OF MAXIMIAN AND GALERIUS— VICTORIES OF CONSTANTINE OVER MAXENTIUS AND LICINIUS—REUNION OF THE EMPIRE UNDER THE AUTHORITY OF CONSTANTINE 166

XIII THE PROGRESS OF THE CHRISTIAN RELIGION— SENTIMENTS, MANNERS, NUMBERS, AND CONDITIONS OF THE PRIMITIVE CHRISTIANS 186

XIV (180–313 A.D.) THE CONDUCT OF THE ROMAN GOVERN- MENT TOWARDS THE CHRISTIANS, FROM THE REIGN OF NERO TO THAT OF CONSTANTINE 231

XV (300–500 A.D.) FOUNDATION OF CONSTANTINOPLE— POLITICAL SYSTEM OF CONSTANTINE AND HIS SUCCESSORS—MILITARY DISCIPLINE—THE PALACE—THE FINANCES 262

XVI (324–353 A.D.) CHARACTER OF CONSTANTINE—GOTHIC WAR—DEATH OF CONSTANTINE—DIVISION OF THE EMPIRE AMONG HIS THREE SONS—PERSIAN WAR—TRAGIC DEATHS OF CONSTANTINE THE YOUNGER AND CONSTANS—USURPATION OF MAGNENTIUS—CIVIL WAR—VICTORY OF CONSTANTIUS 287

XVII (351–360 A.D.) CONSTANTIUS SOLE EMPEROR—ELEVATION AND DEATH OF GALLUS—DANGER AND ELEVATION OF JULIAN—SARMATIAN AND PERSIAN WARS—VICTORIES OF JULIAN IN GAUL 304

XVIII (306–438 A.D.) THE PROGRESS AND EFFECTS OF THE CONVERSION OF CONSTANTINE—LEGAL ESTABLISHMENT AND CONSTITUTION OF THE CHRISTIAN OR CATHOLIC CHURCH 320

XIX (312–362 A.D.) PERSECUTION OF HERESY—THE SCHISM OF THE DONATISTS—THE ARIAN CONTROVERSY—ATHANASIUS— DISTRACTED STATE OF THE CHURCH AND EMPIRE UNDER CONSTANTINE AND HIS SONS—TOLERATION OF PAGANISM 330

XX   (360–361 A.D.) JULIAN IS DECLARED EMPEROR BY THE LEGIONS
OF GAUL—HIS MARCH AND SUCCESS—THE DEATH OF
CONSTANTIUS—CIVIL ADMINISTRATION OF JULIAN 351

XXI   (351–363 A.D.) THE RELIGION OF JULIAN—UNIVERSAL
TOLERATION—HE ATTEMPTS TO RESTORE AND REFORM
THE PAGAN WORSHIP—HIS ARTFUL PERSECUTION OF THE
CHRISTIANS—MUTUAL ZEAL AND INJUSTICE 366

XXII (314–390 A.D.) RESIDENCE OF JULIAN AT ANTIOCH—HIS
SUCCESSFUL EXPEDITION AGAINST THE PERSIANS—
PASSAGE OF THE TIGRIS—THE RETREAT AND DEATH OF
JULIAN—ELECTION OF JOVIAN—HE SAVES THE ROMAN
ARMY BY A DISGRACEFUL TREATY 375

XXIII (343–384 A.D.) THE GOVERNMENT AND DEATH OF JOVIAN—
ELECTION OF VALENTINIAN, WHO ASSOCIATES HIS
BROTHER VALENS, AND MAKES THE FINAL DIVISION OF
THE EASTERN AND WESTERN EMPIRES—CIVIL AND
ECCLESIASTICAL ADMINISTRATION—BRITAIN—THE EAST—
THE DANUBE—DEATH OF VALENTINIAN—HIS TWO SONS,
GRATIAN AND VALENTINIAN II, SUCCEED TO THE
WESTERN EMPIRE 393

XXIV (365–395 A.D.) PROGRESS OF THE HUNS FROM CHINA TO
EUROPE—FLIGHT OF THE GOTHS—DEFEAT AND DEATH
OF VALENS—GRATIAN INVESTS THEODOSIUS WITH THE
EASTERN EMPIRE—PEACE AND SETTLEMENT OF THE
GOTHS 415

XXV   (340–397 A.D.) CHARACTER, ADMINISTRATION, AND PENANCE,
OF THEODOSIUS—DEATH OF THEODOSIUS 442

XXVI (378–420 A.D.) FINAL DESTRUCTION OF PAGANISM—
INTRODUCTION OF THE WORSHIP OF SAINTS AND RELICS
AMONG THE CHRISTIANS 451

XXVII (395–408 A.D.) REVOLT OF THE GOTHS—THEY PLUNDER
GREECE—TWO GREAT INVASIONS OF ITALY BY ALARIC AND
RADAGAISUS—THEY ARE REPULSED BY STILICHO—
THE GERMANS OVERRUN GAUL—USURPATION OF
CONSTANTINE IN THE WEST—DISGRACE AND DEATH OF
STILICHO 460

XXVIII (408–449 A.D.) INVASION OF ITALY BY ALARIC—ROME IS THRICE
BESIEGED, AND AT LENGTH PILLAGED, BY THE GOTHS—
DEATH OF ALARIC—THE GOTHS EVACUATE ITALY—FALL OF
CONSTANTINE—GAUL AND SPAIN ARE OCCUPIED BY THE
BARBARIANS—INDEPENDENCE OF BRITAIN 481

XXIX (423–455 A.D.) DEATH OF HONORIUS—VALENTINIAN III
EMPEROR OF THE WEST—ADMINISTRATION OF HIS
MOTHER PLACIDIA—AËTIUS AND BONIFACE—CONQUEST
OF AFRICA BY THE VANDALS 504

XXX   (376–453 A.D.) THE CHARACTER, CONQUESTS, AND COURT OF
       ATTILA, KING OF THE HUNS—DEATH OF THEODOSIUS THE
       YOUNGER—ELEVATION OF MARCIAN TO THE EMPIRE OF
       THE EAST 513

XXXI   (419–455 A.D.) INVASION OF GAUL BY ATTILA—HE IS
       REPULSED BY AËTIUS AND THE VISIGOTHS—ATTILA
       INVADES AND EVACUATES ITALY—DEATHS OF ATTILA,
       AËTIUS, AND VALENTINIAN THE THIRD 522

XXXII (430–490 A.D.) SACK OF ROME BY GENSERIC, KING OF THE
       VANDALS—HIS NAVAL DEPREDATIONS—SUCCESSION OF
       THE LAST EMPERORS OF THE WEST, MAXIMUS, AVITUS,
       MAJORIAN, SEVERUS, ANTHEMIUS, OLYBRIUS, GLYCERIUS,
       NEPOS, AUGUSTULUS—TOTAL EXTINCTION OF THE
       WESTERN EMPIRE—REIGN OF ODOACER, THE FIRST
       BARBARIAN KING OF ITALY 540

XXXIII (305–712 A.D.) MONASTICISM—CONVERSION OF THE
       BARBARIANS TO CHRISTIANITY AND ARIANISM 564

XXXIV (449–582 A.D.) REIGN AND CONVERSION OF CLOVIS—HIS
       VICTORIES OVER THE VISIGOTHS—ESTABLISHMENT OF
       THE FRENCH MONARCHY IN GAUL—LAWS OF THE
       BARBARIANS—STATE OF THE ROMANS—THE VISIGOTHS OF
       SPAIN—CONQUESTS OF BRITAIN BY THE SAXONS 571

XXXV   BYZANTIUM—EXTENT AND NATURE—THEODORA—THE
       FACTIONS OF THE CIRCUS—THE TRISAGION RIOTS—
       THE EASTERN EMPIRE IN THE TENTH CENTURY—THE
       SIEGE AND FALL OF CONSTANTINOPLE 595

XXXVI EPILOGUE—PROSPECT OF THE RUINS OF ROME IN
       THE FIFTEENTH CENTURY—FOUR CAUSES OF DECAY
       AND DESTRUCTION—EXAMPLE OF THE COLISEUM—
       RENOVATION OF THE CITY—CONCLUSION OF THE WHOLE
       WORK 647

       List of Roman Emperors 659

       Index 667

MAPS

*Based on original drawings
by Jane Fraser and Louis Weeks III*

THE ROMAN EMPIRE AT FULLEST EXTENT IN SECOND
CENTURY A.D. 2

THE ROMAN EMPIRE IN THE FOURTH CENTURY A.D. SHOWING
THE DIOCESES 263

THE MEDITERRANEAN WORLD TOWARD THE END OF THE FIFTH
CENTURY A.D. 541

PREFACE

The purpose of this abridgment is to make easily and inexpensively available one of the world's few great historians. To do this the enormous bulk of *The Decline and Fall* necessitates the most rigorous exclusion. Because this edition is prepared for members of Western Civilization the editor has selected those portions that are strictly related to the decline and fall of the Western Empire and that furnish a continuous account of that Empire from the second century A.D. to the establishment of the Gothic kingdom in Italy in the fifth century. These are drawn from the first thirty-eight chapters of the work. Considerations of space have also dictated the reluctant omission of Gibbon's footnotes. The reader must be assured that these are monuments to his industry and intellectual integrity, but they frequently are given in French, Greek, or Latin and they are not generally necessary to the understanding of the lucid text. While the chapters are numbered continuously, the numbers of the original chapters are given in parentheses for those readers who may wish to refer to the unabridged edition.

Chapter 35 of this text consists of selections from five chapters of the second half of the original work and illustrates the spirit and nature of the Byzantine Empire and Gibbon's attitude toward it. It concludes with his magnificent account of the Turkish conquest of Constantinople in 1453. Chapter 36 is an epilogue, an account, drawn from Gibbon's last chapter, of the state of Rome in his own day.

FRANK C. BOURNE

Princeton, New Jersey

INTRODUCTION

Edward Gibbon was born May 8, 1737, in Putney, Surrey. He came from a family of gentlemen of moderate means that could be traced back to Kent for at least six generations. The family had a number of important connections by marriage, most prominent of which were the Actons. Edward's grandfather, also an Edward Gibbon, had been involved in the great South Sea scheme, and he was fined heavily by the indignant public. But he had astutely concealed sufficient capital to re-establish himself comfortably, although the family continued to deplore what was considered the injustice of a decreased fortune. He had disapproved of his only son's marriage to Judith Porten, and though there had been finally a grudging consent, our Gibbon was not born in time to complete the reconciliation and insure a more favorable will for his father: for the old gentleman died in December 1736.

Gibbon was a sickly youth, unable to participate in the sports of other boys, but early he became a voracious reader, especially in the library of his Grandfather Porten. He speaks of the dynasties of the ancient Orient as being his "top and cricket ball." Largely due to his ill health, ventures at two secondary schools were not productive, but he continued his self-improvement by omnivorous reading. This he did under the kindly eye of a maiden aunt who fostered him after his mother's death, which occurred when he was about ten years of age.

With the very one-sided education that resulted, he was sent up to Oxford by his father to Magdalen College in 1752 "with erudition and ignorance." He was terribly disappointed in finding that this was not, as he had imagined, a community of scholars, but rather of wastrels and gossips Pursuing his own interests there, his reading and logic convinced him of the truth of Catholic dogma. He became a convert and sent home a proud and sincere declaration of his new faith. His father was furious: not only was such conversion dangerous, but its object would be cut off from all political future in England.

His father thereupon sent him packing off to Lausanne in Switzerland to the care of a Calvinist minister, M. Daniel Pavilliard. Here he continued his studies in Latin, French, history, and geography; and also under the gentle direction of M. Pavilliard he came to argue himself out of his Romanism, and he was re-entered into a Protestant congregation in December 1754. While in Lausanne Gibbon became enamored of the belle of the town, one Suzanne Curchod, and when he finally was recalled to England in 1758 he sought permission to marry her. But his father was violently opposed to the match, and Gibbon broke off the affair. Suzanne later married extremely well, however, and became Mme. Necker, wife of Louis XVI's minister of finance. After a number of years' lapse an old love affair was renewed as a firm friendship which lasted until Gibbon's death.

The elder Mr. Gibbon's attitude toward Suzanne Curchod seems at least a little ungracious when one realizes that he himself remarried during his son's absence without bothering to inform his son, and that he had called him home precisely in time to per-suade him to sign off certain entailed portions of the family estate in order to relieve his own financial embarrassment. These embarrassments continued, in fact, throughout the rest of the elder Gibbon's life; and it is to his son's credit that he was always generous, self-denying, and forbearing in respect to his father's un-deniable financial irresponsibility. In fact, Gibbon's thoughtfulness, patience, and genuine unselfish devotion to his family—his father, stepmother, and Aunt Hester—to his best Swiss friend, Deyverdun, and best British friends, the Holroyds, are among his most note-worthy characteristics.

His first literary venture was finished in 1759, though not published until 1761. This, his *L'Essai sur l'Etude de la Littérature*, he had commenced in Lausanne but finished at home. It was a defense of the importance and utility of ancient literature, and though a slender work, it was well received abroad.

The dangers of a French invasion of England in 1759 caused both the elder and younger Gibbon to volunteer to serve in the militia for the defense of the country. Though the likelihood of invasion largely disappeared in 1759, they both were called up in 1760 with the rank of major and captain respectively, and Gibbon served conscientiously for two and one-half years. He rose from captain to the rank of lieutenant colonel, and by carefully doing well his own work and that of a great number of incompetents he came to appreciate many of the problems of supply and support that someday would occupy him; and he could surmise, "the discipline and evolutions of a modern battalion gave me a clearer notion of the phalanx and the legions, and the captain of the Hampshire grenadiers (the reader may smile) has not been useless to the historian of the Roman empire."

At the end of his military service Gibbon convinced his father of the need to return to the Continent and to complete his training by travel. Setting out in January of 1763 he first visited Paris, where his first literary effort was known and where its language and erudition both were much appreciated. After a few months of sightseeing, salons, and mild flirtations in Paris, Gibbon proceeded to his old haunts in Lausanne, where he settled down for nearly a year to a round of social activity and of study preparatory to a tour of Italy.

In April 1764 he started out. Geneva, Turin, Milan, Parma, Bologna, and Florence: in each of these places there was sightseeing and leisurely social intercourse with a few French and Italian acquaintances, with such resident Englishmen as each place already contained, and with the bevies of young English gentlemen who also were trooping through on the Grand Tour. Then he moved rapidly on through Pisa, Leghorn, and Siena to Rome. His emotion and excitement here were intense. He plunged into sight-seeing, investigation, and reflection. It was during these activities that the idea of his great work was born:

> ... It was at Rome, on the 15th of October 1764, as I sat musing amid the ruins of the Capitol, while the barefooted friars were singing vespers in the temple of Jupiter, that the idea of writing the decline and fall of the city first started to my mind. But my original plan was circumscribed to the decay of the city rather than of the empire, and though my reading and reflections began to point toward that object, some years elapsed, and several avocations intervened, before I was seriously engaged in the execution of that laborious work.

There was a side-trip to Naples early in 1765, and the return to England came by June of that year.

In the next few years Gibbon was busied by a variety of preoccupations, though a number of these were accessory to his life's work. In 1768 and 1769 he brought out, with his Swiss friend Deyverdun, the *Mémoires Littéraires de la Grande-Bretagne* in which English literary and other cultural progress was reported to the Continent. In 1770 his father died, and he was able soon after to settle in lodgings in London that were conducive to study and a participation in the social, political, and intellectual interchanges of the day. In 1774 he received a seat in Parliament representing the pocket borough of Liskeard procured for him by Edward Eliot, the husband of a cousin. In 1775 he became a member of The Literary Club, where between 1775 and 1778 he occasionally dined and talked with Sir Joshua Reynolds, Sam Johnson, Boswell, Fox, Garrick, Burke, Adam Smith, and Sheridan. His parliamentary career was surely undistinguished, but his political and literary connections did reward him in 1779 with a seat on the Board of Trade and Plantations, which he held until 1782, and the salary from this helped to tide him over a number of difficult years.

Meanwhile research for his great work had been going on for some time, though his correspondence over the earlier years of preparation holds very few allusions to it—a reference to a devotion to his studies in 1773, in 1774 a hope that another year would see some product of his labor, and in 1775 a definite statement of the work's nature and of his desire that it should appear in 1776. The first volume did indeed appear in February of 1776. It was an instantaneous success and went through three editions in fifteen months. Enthusiasm was so great, and the praise of men like Robertson, Hume, and Walpole so unequivocal, that it was an established success before those persons annoyed by the last two chapters, which treated Christianity, had had an opportunity to marshal an attack.

Work on succeeding volumes was interspersed by attendance at lectures on anatomy and chemistry, and by a trip to Paris from May to November 1777. One attack on his veracity in his account of the early Church forced him to publish a *Vindication*, but thereafter he preferred to remain silent and left to others the defense of his honesty and accuracy. In 1781 there appeared the second and third volumes, which completed his account of the fall of the empire in the West.

After the loss of his position with the Board of Trade his financial situation became more precarious and his parliamentary life more tedious. In 1783 therefore he gave up his seat in Parliament and carried out a project that would be both economical and pleasant: to settle down with his old Swiss friend Deyverdun at the latter's house, La Grotte, in Lausanne. Here the two old bachelors lived pleasantly and sociably together, each pursuing his own interests and work. Here Gibbon completed *The Decline*, and reported in his *Autobiography*:

. . . It was on the day, or rather, night, of the 27th of June 1787, between the hours of eleven and twelve, that I wrote the last lines of the last page in a summerhouse in my garden. After laying down my pen I took several turns in a *berceau*, or covered walk of acacias, which commands a prospect of the country, the lake, and the mountains. The air was temperate, the sky was serene, the silver orb of the moon was reflected from the waters, and all nature was silent. I will not dissemble the first emotions of joy on the recovery of my freedom, and perhaps the establishment of my fame. But my pride was soon humbled, and a sober melancholy was spread over my mind, by the idea that I had taken my everlasting leave of an old and agreeable companion, and that whatsoever may be the future fate of my *History*, the life of the historian must be short and precarious.

In 1787 he returned to London to prepare for the publication which took place on his fifty-first birthday in 1788. His trip to England was a round of tribute and applause, but he returned to Lausanne in July. Deyverdun's health was rapidly failing and he died of apoplexy in 1789. Gibbon arranged for the use of La Grotte for the rest of his life, however, and he remained in Lausanne studying, enjoying society, flirting a little, and writing and rewriting his memoirs.

In 1793 he hastily returned to England, however, at the news of the death of Lady Sheffield, wife of his best friend John Holroyd, Lord Sheffield. His own health had long caused concern among his friends, for he had developed a hydrocele, which had become more and more noticeable, but which he refused to treat. Finally in late 1793 he underwent a number of tappings to remove the fluid; in January of 1794 his condition became rapidly worse, and he died, attended only by his valet, on the sixteenth of that month. He was buried in the tomb of his friends the Holroyds in Fletching Church.

After the publication of *The Decline and Fall* in 1788 Gibbon clearly was not entirely at ease with his new-found freedom and he toyed with a number of projects. The only literary monument of the period, however, is his *Autobiography*. Indeed, he left six different versions, or partially completed versions, of this effort; and his friend John Holroyd fashioned from these the official version that appeared after his death. This is not only an important human document for understanding Gibbon, his outlook, training, and methods, but also it emphasizes how much Gibbon's style in *The*

Decline and Fall is supremely Gibbon's own, and how completely he is part of the eighteenth century.

The Decline and Fall bids fair to be permanent on the Western scene. Gibbon is the only Western historian whose work is more than 100 years old and yet continues to be read regularly by the nonspecialized educated public. His permanence can perhaps be classed, then, with Herodotus and Thucydides in Greece, and with Tacitus among the Romans. Why is this so?

For one thing, the greatness of the subject arrests the attention and fires the imagination and tragic sympathy of the spectator. For here he finds himself at once introduced into the situation for which man most fondly has wished, when most civilized men were peacefully united in "the period in the history of the world, during which the condition of the human race was most happy and prosperous." And yet men lost this grace, and always with dark suspicion or sickening fear wonder why. And, further, for Western man there is here a peculiar fascination: for out of the death-throes of the Western Empire were born Europe's nations, while out of the Eastern Empire's tardy fall came sparks that lit Europe's lamps of humanism and science.

It is difficult to imagine the amount of literature that Gibbon controlled. He had read voluminously all his life—the ancient authors, church fathers, medieval tracts, collections of laws and inscriptions, critical studies—and he seems to have forgotten almost nothing. His prodigious energy and diligence are perhaps best illustrated by his early self-training at Lausanne:

> . . . In my French and Latin translations I adopted an excellent method which, from my own success, I would recommend to the imitation of students. I chose some classic writer, such as Cicero and Vertot, the most approved for purity and elegance of style. I translated, for instance, an epistle of Cicero into French; and after throwing it aside till the words and phrases were obliterated from my memory, I retranslated my French into such Latin as I could find, and then compared each sentence of my imperfect version with the ease, the grace, the propriety of the Roman orator.
>
> A similar experiment was made on some pages of the *Révolutions* of Vertot: I turned them into Latin, returned them after a sufficient interval into my own French, and again scrutinized the resemblance or dissimilitude of the copy and the original.

This care was transferred to his composition of *The Decline and Fall*:

> . . . Three times did I compose the first chapter, and twice the
> second and third, before I was tolerably satisfied with their effect.
> In the remainder of the way I advanced with a more equal and
> easy pace. But the fifteenth and sixteenth chapters have been
> reduced, by three successive revisals, from a large volume to their
> present size, and they might still be compressed without any loss
> of facts or sentiments.

His thoroughness and industry are attested by the full and meticulous documentation given in the footnotes of the original and
unabridged editions, his honesty by the reluctant confession of his
most severe critics after they have studied his documentation, and
his candor by his own free admission of uncertainty where primary
sources were lacking and the secondary sources equivocal or
unreliable.

Despite the wealth of detail, *The Decline and Fall* does not have
the character of a series of reigns or episodes casually connected. As
Lucretius managed to make an account of atomism an epic of the
rise and fall of life, so Gibbon's pages seem a great panorama of a
people's fate. This is partly due no doubt to the variety of his theme,
but it is also due to his style and composition: to the evenness and
stateliness of the flow of his prose, and to the art of the construction.
His paragraphs are models of clarity and unity, and he tells us that
he always had completely composed them in his mind before setting
them to paper. But, further, they follow each other with a logic so
undeniable that there is no sense of juncture or change.

Intertwined with the sweep of the narrative are the themes of
decline. They are not itemized or set apart for emphasis or diag-
nosis. But after each makes its original and often casual appearance it intrudes more and more often and more and more vigorously: the irresponsibility of militarization, the self-betrayal of
barbarization, the dissipation of energy by the sectarians. And they
grow in violent and mutually fortified energy to the crash, a crash
the more thunderous because the body itself was overlarge. The
crescendos and the climax had been played out by the end of
the Western Empire: little wonder that the mad parodies on these
themes in the Eastern Empire have seemed to be long drawn out
and to compose a less compelling afterpiece.

The artist in Gibbon had seen the black of the monk against the white of the temple and could not resist the contrast. As soon as the churchmen could catch their breaths in the tide of applause greeting the first volume, the attack began on chapters fifteen and sixteen, which concluded that portion and which treated the development of the early Church. Cries of atheism were belied by the facts of his life and by his privately expressed views on religion. And the careful critics, even the clerical ones, had to dispute the charges of intellectual dishonesty irresponsibly made by some of the outraged. To those who resent the two chapters and the recurrences of their tone and implications with great frequency and frankness throughout the work there is left the charge of malice. And this is just.

But to Gibbon the malice and the ironic tone were completely justified: the internal bickerings of the Christians did weaken his world state, though he was candid enough to add that the conversion of the barbarians softened the fall; and the ironic tone might well be dictated by a still formidable religious power in England. An unequivocal statement of his judgment ran the risk of the Church's own Blasphemy Act of 1697–1698, and he must have known that Thomas Woolston had died in prison in 1731 for publishing his *Discourses on the Miracles of Our Saviour.* The churchmen could, therefore, only blame themselves for what they called his insidious, unfair, sneering methods. His tone was his shield, while for a sword he had facts so substantially accurate that they disarmed his opponents as devastatingly as they once did Verres for Cicero.

Chapters fifteen and sixteen are important and command our attention because they are witty and readable and yet meticulous accounts of the early Church and its fortunes. And they are monuments to the use of irony in historiography and possibly in satire. But their real importance is that in them Gibbon first insisted on making the history of the Christian Church a natural phenomenon, a part of secular history. This is matter-of-fact treatment of the five "secondary" causes for the growth of the Church insured. From now on a study of the religious disposition, practices, and experience of a given people must be included in any responsible account of them.

Another important factor in the decline was the barbarians. Gibbon saw them originally as a small danger, but as one that constantly increased as the Romans temporized in respect to them, while at the same time weakening themselves by internal dissension. The internal dissension was partly due to the religious schisms; yet when the Empire, weakened by these schisms, fell, the fall was softened, for exiled schismatics had converted many of the barbarians before they crossed the frontiers. This was not an unadulterated benefit, however, for then these barbarian Christians also were heretical, and sectarian disputes sometimes proved more deadly than racial or cultural differences. In any case, the indifferent masses, a confident and venal soldiery, weakened frontiers, purchased peace, mercenary troops, and abandoned provinces: these acted and reacted on one another, intertwined, were swollen, and rushed headlong into deluge and death.

And yet Gibbon did not assert that the changes in the Roman people were solely due to their religious quarrels or their policies toward the barbarians. Their largeness, if not their eminence, was fatal. He seemed to sense almost a biological limitation on an effective organization:

> ... But the decline of Rome was the natural and inevitable effect
> of immoderate greatness. Prosperity ripened the principle of decay;
> the causes of destruction multiplied with the extent of conquest;
> and as soon as time or accident had removed the artificial supports,
> the stupendous fabric yielded to the pressure of its own weight.

In his later years Gibbon appears to have surmised that the seeds of decline were sown much earlier than he had indicated in his work: perhaps in the civil wars or tyrannies of the first century A.D. And further reflection might have suggested that the poison and the infirmity were coterminous with the acquisition and enjoyment of other men's estates. Gibbon certainly did not analyze beyond improvement or suggest beyond addition the causes for the decline of the Roman Empire. But he collected and ordered the evidence with an industry and perception that have been unequaled, and he described the event with a clarity, grace, and power that none since have rivaled.

Gibbon is a child of the eighteenth century in more than his rational approach to religion. His manner, outlook, and standards all mirror that age. He had devoured both earlier and contemporary literature in his youth, and his method reflects the influence of earlier and careful historians such as Abbé de la Bléterie and Giannone. Montesquieu, Diderot, and Hume are on his lips, and their freedom of investigation illumined the path of his own researches. And he made full and grateful use of the monographs, pamphlets, and books of inquiry and travel that the age produced.

His language has the balance, polish, and finish of England's Augustans. The symmetry, terseness, and vigor of his summaries or judgments give them an epigrammatic and inevitable air: "But the Romans, after the fall of the republic, combated only for the choice of masters. Under the standard of a popular candidate for empire, a few enlisted from affection, some from fear, many from interest, none from principle." He had a consummate control of the adverb, adjective, and epithet, and with these he caught, fixed, summarized, and damned. This power can be seen in so typical a passage as some remarks on the miseries of the monks of Egypt (the italics are mine):

> . . . Even sleep, *the last refuge of the unhappy*, was *rigorously* measured: the *vacant* hours of the monk *heavily* rolled along, without business or pleasure; and, before the close of each day, he had repeatedly *accused* the *tedious* progress of the sun. In this *comfortless* state, superstition still *pursued and tormented* her *wretched* votaries. The *repose* which they had sought in the cloister was *disturbed* by *tardy repentance, profane doubts*, and *guilty desires*; and, while they considered each *natural* impulse as an *unpardonable* sin, they *perpetually trembled* on the edge of a flaming and bottomless abyss. From the *painful* struggles of disease and despair, the unhappy victims were sometimes *relieved by madness or death*; and, in the sixth century, a hospital was founded at Jerusalem for a small portion of the austere penitents who were deprived of their senses.

His text is logical and lucid: "the luminous page of Gibbon," said Sheridan, though he later tried to emend his tribute to "voluminous." And he knew full well how to lighten the march of the narrative with the leisurely aside and the telling anecdote. The exclamation and sigh of Emperor Julian as he assumed his duties, "O Plato, Plato, what a task for a philosopher!" fixes forever in the mind the character and tragic dilemma of that laborious prince. While Gibbon's footnotes attest his industry and honesty, they surely are not needed to clarify the text. They are, rather, the asides, the amplifications, the conversation of a witty and cultured eighteenth-century man. It has been mischievously suggested that Gibbon lived his sex life in his footnotes. It is true that both in his text and in his footnotes he appreciated the humor of Nature's greatest joke on humanity. And he addressed himself to this subject with the wit and wisdom of a man of the world, and of one that had a greater facility and greater sensibility in expressing himself than most. No doubt his obvious relish in such pursuits could scandalize dear Mr. Thomas Bowdler, who contrived a maidenly version of *The Decline and Fall*; but who would wish to lose, for example, his characterization of the younger Gordian?

> . . . His manners were less pure, but his character was equally amiable with that of his father. Twenty-two acknowledged concubines, and a library of sixty-two thousand volumes, attested the variety of his inclinations, and from the productions which he left behind him, it appears that the former as well as the latter were designed for use rather than ostentation.

And Gibbon enjoyed the optimism that is characteristic of the eighteenth century. It is not that he was deceived about man's nature, of whose improvement he could say, "but the power of instruction is seldom of much efficacy, except in those happy dispositions where it is almost superfluous." And he took a cool and judicious view of human institutions as well:

> . . . The influence of the clergy, in an age of superstition, might be usefully employed to assert the rights of mankind; but so intimate is the connection between the throne and the altar, that the banner of the church has very seldom been seen on the side of the people. A martial nobility and stubborn commons, possessed of arms, tenacious of property, and collected into constitutional assemblies, form the only balance capable of preserving a free constitution against enterprises of an aspiring prince.

Amusingly enough, a well-known editor of Gibbon, Oliphant Smeaton, saw fit to append a footnote to the first sentence of this statement: "Gibbon's remark here is wholly incorrect" But *he* did not see fit to document *his* dictum. Further, Gibbon was not deceived by the nature of history, which he describes as "little more than the register of the crimes, follies, and misfortunes of mankind," nor did he expect any rapid change of the human element therein: he could describe the historian as

Surrounded with imperfect fragments, always concise, often
obscure, and sometimes contradictory, he is reduced to collect,
to compare, and to conjecture: and though he ought never
to place his conjectures in the rank of facts, yet the knowledge
of human nature, and of the sure operation of its fierce and
unrestrained passions, might, on some occasions, supply the want
of historical materials.

In observing Europe's rapid progress in the arts of armament he
ruefully observed, "If we contrast the rapid progress of this mischievous discovery with the slow and laborious advances of reason, science, and the arts of peace, a philosopher, according to his temper,
will laugh or weep at the folly of mankind." And though his own work
might encompass weighty issues, basic trends, and the grandest pageants, he was conscious too of a certain inconsequence in history:
"and, if we are more deeply affected by the ruin of a palace than by
the conflagration of a cottage, our humanity must have formed a very
erroneous estimate of the miseries of human life." Yet with these
qualifications he did believe in the existence and ultimate triumph
of rational and disciplined man. His analysis is simple and moving:

> There are two very natural propensities which we may distinguish
> in the most virtuous and liberal dispositions, the love of pleasure
> and the love of action. If the former is refined by art and learn-
> ing, improved by the charms of social intercourse, and corrected
> by a just regard to economy, to health, and to reputation, it is
> productive of the greatest part of the happiness of private life.
> The love of action is a principle of a much stronger and more
> doubtful nature. It often leads to anger, to ambition, and to
> revenge; but when it is guided by the sense of propriety and
> benevolence, it becomes the parent of every virtue, and, if those
> virtues are accompanied with equal abilities, a family, a state, or
> an empire may be indebted for their safety and prosperity to the
> undaunted courage of a single man. To the love of pleasure we
> may therefore ascribe most of the agreeable, to the love of action
> we may attribute most of the useful and respectable, qualifications.
> The character in which both the one and the other should
> be united and harmonized would seem to constitute the most
> perfect idea of human nature.

And he thought that the progress of rational man toward that
end was constant, though laborious. He asserted that the world

could never again be barbarized as the Romans allowed it to be, for political and military expansion would depend wholly on technological superiority, and advance in technology could only be made by people who cared deeply for the arts and sciences. Whatever qualifications our own experiences may suggest to this judgment, we may draw some comfort from the cool and disinterested optimism of this eighteenth-century man concerning the twenty-fourth century: after a leisurely digression on the possible identification of the comet that appeared in 531 A.D. in the reign of Justinian with Halley's Comet of 1680 A.D, and on the current theories of the periodicity of that body, he observes,

> At the eighth period, in the year two thousand three hundred and fifty-five, their calculations may perhaps be verified by the astronomers of some future capital in the Siberian or American wilderness.

Gibbon was a man with a standard, a standard that included industry, integrity, tolerance, and reason, and that was necessary for reasonable government both public and private. This standard he applied so steadily and judiciously to a dark and universal human problem that rational men ever since have been attracted and will be attracted to his tale of the tragic flaws that encompassed the ruin of the Roman people.

I

THE EXTENT AND MILITARY FORCE OF THE EMPIRE IN THE AGE OF THE ANTONINES

In the second century of the Christian era, the Empire of Rome comprehended the fairest part of the earth, and the most civilised portion of mankind. The frontiers of that extensive monarchy were guarded by ancient renown and disciplined valour. The gentle but powerful influence of laws and manners had gradually cemented the union of the provinces. Their peaceful inhabitants enjoyed and abused the advantages of wealth and luxury. The image of a free constitution was preserved with decent reverence: the Roman senate appeared to possess the sovereign authority, and devolved on the emperors all the executive powers of government. During a happy period (A.D. 98–180) of more than fourscore years, the public administration was conducted by the virtue and abilities of Nerva, Trajan, Hadrian, and the two Antonines. It is the design of this, and of the two succeeding chapters, to describe the prosperous condition of their empire; and afterwards from the death of Marcus Antoninus, to deduce the most important circumstances of its decline and fall; a revolution which will ever be remembered, and is still felt by the nations of the earth.

The principal conquests of the Romans were achieved under the republic; and the emperors, for the most part, were satisfied with preserving those dominions which had been acquired by the policy of the senate, the active emulation of the consuls, and the martial enthusiasm of the people. The seven first centuries were filled with a rapid succession of triumphs; but it was reserved for Augustus to relinquish the ambitious design of subduing the whole earth, and to introduce a spirit of moderation into the public councils. Inclined to peace by his temper and situation, it was easy for him to discover that Rome, in her present exalted situation, had much less to hope than to fear from the chance of arms; and that, in the prosecution of remote wars, the undertaking became every day more difficult, the event more doubtful, and the possession more

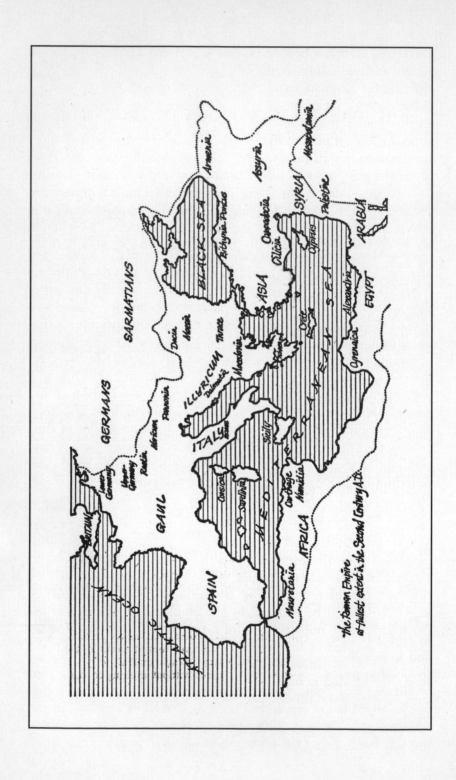

The Roman Empire at fullest extent in the Second Century A.D.

precarious, and less beneficial. The experience of Augustus added weight to these salutary reflections, and effectually convinced him that, by the prudent vigour of his counsels, it would be easy to secure every concession which the safety or the dignity of Rome might require from the most formidable Barbarians. Instead of exposing his person and his legions to the arrows of the Parthians, he obtained, by an honourable treaty, the restitution of the standards and prisoners which had been taken in the defeat of Crassus.

His generals, in the early part of his reign, attempted the reduction of Æthiopia and Arabia Felix. They marched near a thousand miles to the south of the tropic; but the heat of the climate soon repelled the invaders, and protected the unwarlike natives of those sequestered regions. The northern countries of Europe scarcely deserved the expense and labour of conquest. The forests and morasses of Germany were filled with a hardy race of barbarians, who despised life when it was separated from freedom; and though, on the first attack, they seemed to yield to the weight of the Roman power, they soon, by a signal act of despair, regained their independence, and reminded Augustus of the vicissitude of fortune. On the death of that emperor, his testament was publicly read in the senate. He bequeathed, as a valuable legacy to his successors, the advice of confining the empire within those limits, which Nature seemed to have placed as its permanent bulwarks and boundaries; on the west the Atlantic ocean; the Rhine and Danube on the north; the Euphrates on the east; and towards the south, the sandy deserts of Arabia and Africa.

Happily for the repose of mankind, the moderate system recommended by the wisdom of Augustus, was adopted by the fears and vices of his immediate successors. Engaged in the pursuit of pleasure, or in the exercise of tyranny, the first Cæsars seldom showed themselves to the armies, or to the provinces; nor were they disposed to suffer, that those triumphs which *their* indolence neglected should be usurped by the conduct and valour of their lieutenants. The military fame of a subject was considered as an insolent invasion of the Imperial prerogative; and it became the duty, as well as interest, of every Roman general, to guard the frontiers intrusted to his care, without aspiring to conquests which might have proved no less fatal to himself than to the vanquished barbarians.

The only accession which the Roman empire received, during the first century of the Christian era, was the province of Britain.

In this single instance the successors of Cæsar and Augustus were persuaded to follow the example of the former, rather than the precept of the latter. The proximity of its situation to the coast of Gaul seemed to invite their arms; the pleasing, though doubtful intelligence, of a pearl fishery, attracted their avarice; and as Britain was viewed in the light of a distinct and insulated world, the conquest scarcely formed any exception to the general system of continental measures. After a war of about forty years, undertaken by the most stupid, maintained by the most dissolute, and terminated by the most timid of all the emperors, the far greater part of the island submitted to the Roman yoke.

Such was the state of the Roman frontiers, and such the maxims of Imperial policy, from the death of Augustus to the accession of Trajan. That virtuous and active prince had received the education of a soldier, and possessed the talents of a general. The peaceful system of his predecessors was interrupted by scenes of war and conquest; and the legions, after a long interval, beheld a military emperor at their head. The first exploits of Trajan were against the Dacians, the most warlike of men, who dwelt beyond the Danube, and who, during the reign of Domitian, had insulted with impunity the Majesty of Rome. To the strength and fierceness of barbarians, they added a contempt for life, which was derived from a warm persuasion of the immortality and transmigration of the soul. Decebalus, the Dacian king, approved himself a rival not unworthy of Trajan; nor did he despair of his own and the public fortune, till, by the confession of his enemies, he had exhausted every resource both of valour and policy. This memorable war, with a very short suspension of hostilities, lasted five years; and as the emperor could exert, without control, the whole force of the state, it was terminated by an absolute submission of the barbarians. The new province of Dacia, which formed a second exception to the precept of Augustus, was about 1300 miles in circumference. Its natural boundaries were the Dniester, the Teyss [Theiss modern form], or Tibiscus, the Lower Danube, and the Euxine Sea. The vestiges of a military road may still be traced from the banks of the Danube to the neighbourhood of Bender, a place famous in modern history, and the actual frontier of the Turkish and Russian empires.

Trajan was ambitious of fame; and as long as mankind shall continue to bestow more liberal applause on their destroyers than on their benefactors, the thirst of military glory will ever be the vice of the most exalted characters. The praises of Alexander, transmitted by a succession of poets and historians, had kindled a dangerous emulation in the mind of Trajan. Like him the Roman emperor undertook an expedition against the nations of the east, but he lamented with a sigh, that his advanced age scarcely left him any hopes of equalling the renown of the son of Philip. Yet the success of Trajan, however transient, was rapid and specious. The degenerate Parthians, broken by intestine discord, fled before his arms. He descended the river Tigris in triumph, from the mountains of Armenia to the Persian gulf. He enjoyed the honour of being the first, as he was the last, of the Roman generals, who ever navigated that remote sea. His fleets ravaged the coasts of Arabia; and Trajan vainly flattered himself that he was approaching towards the confines of India. Every day the astonished senate received the intelligence of new names and new nations, that acknowledged his sway. They were informed that the kings of Bosphorus, Colchos, Iberia, Albania, Osrhoene, and even the Parthian monarch himself, had accepted their diadems from the hands of the emperor; that the independent tribes of the Median and Carduchian hills had implored his protection; and that the rich countries of Armenia, Mesopotamia, and Assyria, were reduced into the state of provinces. But the death of Trajan soon clouded the splendid prospect; and it was justly to be dreaded, that so many distant nations would throw off the unaccustomed yoke, when they were no longer restrained by the powerful hand which had imposed it.

It was an ancient tradition, that when the Capitol was founded by one of the Roman kings, the god Terminus (who presided over boundaries, and was represented according to the fashion of that age by a large stone) alone, among all the inferior deities, refused to yield his place to Jupiter himself. A favourable inference was drawn from his obstinacy, which was interpreted by the augurs as a sure presage that the boundaries of the Roman power would never recede. During many ages, the prediction, as it is usual, contributed to its own accomplishment. But though Terminus had resisted the majesty of Jupiter, he submitted to the authority of the emperor Hadrian. The resignation of all the eastern conquests of Trajan was the first measure of his reign. He restored to the Parthians the election of an independent sovereign, withdrew the Roman garrisons from the provinces of Armenia, Mesopotamia, and Assyria, and, in compliance with the precept of Augustus, once more established the Euphrates as the frontier of the empire.

Censure, which arraigns the public actions and the private motives of princes, has ascribed to envy a conduct which might be attributed to the prudence and moderation of Hadrian. The various character of that emperor, capable, by turns, of the meanest and the most generous sentiments, may afford some colour to the suspicion. It was, however, scarcely in his power to place the superiority of his predecessor in a more conspicuous light, than by thus confessing himself unequal to the task of defending the conquests of Trajan.

The martial and ambitious spirit of Trajan formed a very singular contrast with the moderation of his successor. The restless activity of Hadrian was not less remarkable, when compared with the gentle repose of Antoninus Pius. The life of the former was almost a perpetual journey; and as he possessed the various talents of the soldier, the statesman, and the scholar, he gratified his curiosity in the discharge of his duty. Careless of the difference of seasons and of climates, he marched on foot, and bare-headed, over the snows of Caledonia, and the sultry plains of the Upper Egypt; nor was there a province of the empire which, in the course of his reign, was not honoured with the presence of the monarch. But the tranquil life of Antoninus Pius was spent in the bosom of Italy; and, during the twenty-three years that he directed the public administration, the longest journeys of that amiable prince extended no farther than from his palace in Rome to the retirement of his Lanuvian Villa.

Notwithstanding this difference in their personal conduct, the general system of Augustus was equally adopted and uniformly pursued by Hadrian and by the two Antonines. They persisted in the design of maintaining the dignity of the empire, without attempting to enlarge its limits. By every honourable expedient they invited the friendship of the barbarians; and endeavoured to convince mankind that the Roman power, raised above the temptation of conquest, was actuated only by the love of order and justice. During a long period of forty-three years their virtuous labours were crowned with success; and if we except a few slight hostilities that served to exercise the legions of the frontier, the reigns of Hadrian and Antoninus Pius offer the fair prospect of universal peace. The Roman name was revered among the most remote nations of the earth. The fiercest barbarians frequently submitted their differences to the arbitration of the emperor; and we are informed by a contemporary historian, that he had seen ambassadors who were refused the honour which they came to solicit, of being admitted into the rank of subjects.

The terror of the Roman arms added weight and dignity to the moderation of the emperors. They preserved peace by a constant preparation for war; and while justice regulated their conduct, they announced to the nations on their confines that they were as little disposed to endure as to offer an injury. The military strength, which it had been sufficient for Hadrian and the elder Antoninus to display, was exerted against the Parthians and the Germans by the emperor Marcus. The hostilities of the barbarians provoked the resentment of that philosophic monarch, and, in the prosecution of a just defence, Marcus and his generals obtained many signal victories, both on the Euphrates and on the Danube. The military establishment of the Roman empire, which thus assured either its tranquillity or success, will now become the proper and important object of our attention.

In the purer ages of the commonwealth, the use of arms was reserved for those ranks of citizens who had a country to love, a property to defend, and some share in enacting those laws, which it was their interest, as well as duty, to maintain. But in proportion as the public freedom was lost in extent of conquest, war was gradually improved into an art, and degraded into a trade. The legions themselves, even at the time when they were recruited in the most distant provinces, were supposed to consist of Roman citizens. That distinction was generally considered either as a legal qualification or as a proper recompense for the soldier; but a more serious regard was paid to the essential merit of age, strength, and military stature. In all levies, a just preference was given to the climates of the North over those of the South: the race of men born to the exercise of arms was sought for in the country rather than in cities; and it was very reasonably presumed, that the hardy occupations of smiths, carpenters, and huntsmen, would supply more vigour and resolution than the sedentary trades which are employed in the service of luxury. After every qualification of property had been laid aside, the armies of the Roman emperors were still commanded, for the most part, by officers of a liberal birth and education; but the common soldiers, like the mercenary troops of modern Europe, were drawn from the meanest, and very frequently from the most profligate, of mankind.

That public virtue which among the ancients was denominated patriotism, is derived from a strong sense of our own interest in the preservation and prosperity of the free government of which we are members. Such a sentiment, which had rendered the legions of the republic almost invincible, could make but a very feeble impression on the mercenary servants of a despotic prince; and it became necessary to supply that defect by other motives, of a different, but not less forcible nature; honour and religion. The peasant, or mechanic, imbibed the useful prejudice that he was advanced to the more dignified profession of arms, in which his rank and reputation would depend on his own valour; and that, although the prowess of a private soldier must often escape the notice of fame, his own behaviour might sometimes confer glory or disgrace on the company, the legion, or even the army, to whose honours he was associated. On his first entrance into the service, an oath was administered to him, with every circumstance of solemnity. He promised never to desert his standard, to submit his own will to the commands of his leader, and to sacrifice his life for the safety of the emperor and the empire. The attachment of the Roman troops to their standards was inspired by the united influence of religion and of honour. The golden eagle, which glittered in the front of the legion, was the object of their fondest devotion; nor was it esteemed less impious than it was ignominious, to abandon that sacred ensign in the hour of danger. These motives, which derived their strength from the imagination, were enforced by fears and hopes of a more substantial kind. Regular pay, occasional donatives, and a stated recompense, after the appointed time of service, alleviated the hardships of the military life, whilst, on the other hand, it was impossible for cowardice or disobedience to escape the severest punishment. The centurions were authorised to chastise with blows, the generals had a right to punish with death; and it was an inflexible maxim of Roman discipline, that a good soldier should dread his officers far more than the enemy. From such laudable arts did the valour of the Imperial troops receive a degree of firmness and docility, unattainable by the impetuous and irregular passions of barbarians.

We have attempted to explain the spirit which moderated, and the strength which supported, the power of Hadrian and the Antonines. We shall now endeavour, with clearness and precision, to describe the provinces once united under their sway, but, at present, divided into so many independent and hostile states.

Spain, the western extremity of the empire, of Europe, and of the ancient world, has, in every age, invariably preserved the same natural limits; the Pyrenæan mountains, the Mediterranean, and the Atlantic Ocean. That great peninsula, at present so unequally divided between two sovereigns, was distributed by Augustus into three provinces, Lusitania, Bætica, and Tarraconensis. The kingdom of Portugal now fills the place of the warlike country of the Lusitanians; and the loss sustained by the former, on the side of the East, is compensated by an accession of territory towards the North. The confines of Grenada and Andalusia correspond with those of ancient Bætica. The remainder of Spain, Gallicia and the Asturias, Biscay and Navarre, Leon and the two Castilles, Murcia, Valencia, Catalonia, and Arragon, all contributed to form the third and most considerable of the Roman governments, which, from the name of its capital, was styled the province of Tarragona. Of the native barbarians, the Celtiberians were the most powerful, as the Cantabrians and Asturians proved the most obstinate. Confident in the strength of their mountains, they were the last who submitted to the arms of Rome, and the first who threw off the yoke of the Arabs.

Ancient Gaul, as it contained the whole country between the Pyrenees, the Alps, the Rhine, and the Ocean, was of greater extent than modern France. To the dominions of that powerful monarchy, with its recent acquisitions of Alsace and Lorraine, we must add the duchy of Savoy, the cantons of Switzerland, the four electorates of the Rhine, and the territories of Liege, Luxemburg, Hainault, Flanders, and Brabant. When Augustus gave laws to the conquests of his father, he introduced a division of Gaul equally adapted to the progress of the legions, to the course of the rivers, and to the principal national distinctions, which had comprehended above an hundred independent states. The sea-coast of the Mediterranean, Languedoc, Provence, and Dauphiné, received their provincial appellation from the colony of Narbonne. The government of Aquitaine was extended from the Pyrenees to the Loire. The country between the Loire and the Seine was styled the Celtic Gaul, and soon borrowed a new denomination from the celebrated colony of Lugdunum, or Lyons. The Belgic lay beyond the Seine, and in more ancient times had been bounded only by the Rhine; but a little before the age of Cæsar the Germans, abusing their superiority of valour, had occupied a considerable portion of the Belgic territory. The Roman conquerors very eagerly embraced so flattering a circumstance, and the Gallic frontier of the Rhine, from Basil to Leyden, received the pompous names of the Upper and the Lower Germany. Such, under the reign of the Antonines, were the six provinces of Gaul; the Narbonnese, Aquitaine, the Celtic, or Lyonnese, the Belgic, and the two Germanies.

We have already had occasion to mention the conquest of Britain, and to fix the boundary of the Roman province in this island. It comprehended all England, Wales, and the Lowlands of Scotland, as far as Dumbarton and Edinburgh. Before Britain lost her freedom, the country was irregularly divided between thirty tribes of barbarians, of whom the most considerable were the Belgæ in the West, the Brigantes in the North, the Silures in South Wales, and the Iceni in Norfolk and Suffolk. As far as we can either trace or credit the resemblance of manners and language, Spain, Gaul, and Britain were peopled by the same hardy race of savages. Before they yielded to the Roman arms, they often disputed the field, and often renewed the contest. After their submission they constituted the western division of the European provinces, which extended from the columns of Hercules to the wall of Antoninus and from the mouth of the Tagus to the sources of the Rhine and Danube.

Before the Roman conquest, the country which is now called Lombardy was not considered as a part of Italy. It had been occupied by a powerful colony of Gauls, who, settling themselves along the banks of the Po, from Piedmont to Romagna, carried their arms and diffused their names from the Alps to the Apennine. The Ligurians dwelt on the rocky coast, which now forms the republic of Genoa. Venice was yet unborn; but the territories of that state, which lie to the east of the Adige, were inhabited by the Venetians. The middle part of the peninsula that now composes the duchy of Tuscany and the ecclesiastical state, was the ancient seat of the Etruscans and Umbrians; to the former of whom Italy was indebted for the first rudiments of civilised life. The Tiber rolled at the foot of the seven hills of Rome, and the country of the Sabines, the Latins, and the Volsci, from that river to the frontiers of Naples, was the theatre of her infant victories. On that celebrated ground the first consuls deserved triumphs; their successors adorned villas, and *their* posterity have erected convents. Capua and Campania possessed the immediate territory of Naples; the rest of the kingdom was inhabited by many warlike nations, the Marsi, the Samnites, the Apulians, and the Lucanians; and the sea-coasts had been covered by the flourishing colonies of the Greeks. We may remark, that when Augustus divided Italy into eleven regions, the little province of Istria was annexed to that seat of Roman sovereignty.

The European provinces of Rome were protected by the course of the Rhine and the Danube. The latter of those mighty streams, which rises at the distance of only thirty miles from the former, flows above thirteen hundred miles, for the most part, to the south-east, collects the tribute of sixty navigable rivers, and is, at length, through six mouths, received into the Euxine, which appears scarcely equal to such an accession of waters. The provinces of the Danube soon acquired the general appellation of Illyricum, or the Illyrian frontier, and were esteemed the most warlike of the empire; but they deserve to be more particularly considered under the names of Rhætia, Noricum, Pannonia, Dalmatia, Dacia, Mæsia, Thrace, Macedonia, and Greece.

The province of Rhætia, which soon extinguished the name of the Vindelicians, extended from the summit of the Alps to the banks of the Danube; from its source, as far as its conflux with the Inn. The greatest part of the flat country is subject to the elector of Bavaria; the city of Augsburg is protected by the constitution of the German empire; the Grisons are safe in their mountains, and the country of Tyrol is ranked among the numerous provinces of the house of Austria.

The wide extent of territory, which is included between the Inn, the Danube, and the Save; Austria, Styria, Carinthia, Carniola, the Lower Hungary, and Sclavonia, was known to the ancients under the names of Noricum and Pannonia. In their original state of independence, their fierce inhabitants were intimately connected. Under the Roman government they were frequently united, and they still remain the patrimony of a single family. They now contain the residence of a German prince, who styles himself Emperor of the Romans, and form the centre, as well as strength, of the Austrian power. It may not be improper to observe, that if we except Bohemia, Moravia, the northern skirts of Austria, and a part of Hungary, between the Theiss and the Danube, all the other dominions of the House of Austria were comprised within the limits of the Roman empire.

Dalmatia, to which the name of Illyricum more properly belonged, was a long but narrow tract between the Save and the Adriatic. The best part of the sea-coast, which still retains its ancient appellation, is a province of the Venetian state, and the seat of the little republic of Ragusa. The inland parts have assumed the

Sclavonian names of Croatia and Bosnia; the former obeys an Austrian governor, the latter a Turkish pasha; but the whole country is still infested by tribes of barbarians, whose savage independence irregularly marks the doubtful limit of the Christian and Mahometan power.

After the Danube had received the waters of the Theiss and the Save, it acquired, at least among the Greeks, the name of Ister. It formerly divided Mæsia and Dacia, the latter of which, as we have already seen, was a conquest of Trajan, and the only province beyond the river. If we inquire into the present state of those countries, we shall find that, on the left hand of the Danube, Temeswar and Transylvania have been annexed, after many revolutions, to the crown of Hungary; whilst the principalities of Moldavia and Wallachia acknowledge the supremacy of the Ottoman Porte. On the right hand of the Danube, Mæsia, which, during the middle ages, was broken into the barbarian kingdoms of Servia and Bulgaria, is again united in Turkish slavery.

The appellation of Roumelia, which is still bestowed by the Turks on the extensive countries of Thrace, Macedonia, and Greece, preserves the memory of their ancient state under the Roman empire. In the time of the Antonines, the martial regions of Thrace, from the mountains of Hæmus and Rhodope, to the Bosphorus and the Hellespont, had assumed the form of a province. Notwithstanding the change of masters and of religion, the new city of Rome, founded by Constantine on the banks of the Bosphorus, has ever since remained the capital of a great monarchy. The kingdom of Macedonia, which, under the reign of Alexander, gave laws to Asia, derived more solid advantages from the policy of the two Philips; and with its dependencies of Epirus and Thessaly, extended from the Ægean to the Ionian Sea. When we reflect on the fame of Thebes and Argos, of Sparta and Athens, we can scarcely persuade ourselves that so many immortal republics of ancient Greece were lost in a single province of the Roman empire, which, from the superior influence of the Achæan league, was usually denominated the province of Achaia.

Such was the state of Europe under the Roman emperors. The provinces of Asia, without excepting the transient conquests of Trajan, are all comprehended within the limits of the Turkish power. But, instead of following the arbitrary divisions of despotism and ignorance, it will be safer for us, as well as more agreeable, to observe the indelible characters of nature. The name of Asia Minor is attributed with some propriety to the peninsula, which, confined betwixt the Euxine and the Mediterranean, advances from the Euphrates towards Europe. The most extensive and flourishing district, westward of Mount Taurus and the river Halys, was dignified by the Romans with the exclusive title of Asia. The jurisdiction of that province extended over the ancient monarchies of Troy, Lydia, and Phrygia, the maritime countries of the Pamphylians, Lycians, and Carians, and the Grecian colonies of Ionia, which equalled in arts, though not in arms, the glory of their parent. The kingdoms of Bithynia and Pontus possessed the northern side of the peninsula from Constantinople to Trebizond. On the opposite side, the province of Cilicia was terminated by the mountains of Syria: the inland country, separated from the Roman Asia by the river Halys, and from Armenia by the Euphrates, had once formed the independent kingdom of Cappadocia. In this place we may observe that the northern shores of the Euxine, beyond Trebizond in Asia, and beyond the Danube in Europe, acknowledged the sovereignty of the emperors, and received at their hands either tributary princes or Roman garrisons. Budzak, Crim Tartary, Circassia, and Mingrelia, are the modern appellations of those savage countries.

Under the successors of Alexander, Syria was the seat of the Seleucidæ, who reigned over Upper Asia, till the successful revolt of the Parthians confined their dominions between the Euphrates and the Mediterranean. When Syria became subject to the Romans, it formed the eastern frontier of their empire; nor did that province, in its utmost latitude, know any other bounds than the mountains of Cappadocia to the north, and towards the south the confines of Egypt, and the Red Sea. Phœnicia and Palestine were sometimes annexed to, and sometimes separated from, the jurisdiction of Syria. The former of these was a narrow and rocky coast; the latter was a territory scarcely superior to Wales, either in fertility or extent. Yet Phœnicia and Palestine will for ever live in the memory of mankind, since America, as well as Europe, has received letters from the one, and religion from the other. A sandy desert alike destitute of wood and water skirts along the doubtful confine of Syria, from the Euphrates to the Red Sea. The wandering life of the Arabs was inseparably connected with their independence; and wherever, on some spots less barren than the rest, they ventured to form any settled habitation, they soon became subjects to the Roman empire.

The geographers of antiquity have frequently hesitated to what portion of the globe they should ascribe Egypt. By its situation that celebrated kingdom is included within the immense peninsula of Africa; but it is accessible only on the side of Asia, whose revolutions, in almost every period of history, Egypt has humbly obeyed. A Roman præfect was seated on the splendid throne of the Ptolemies; and the iron sceptre of the Mamalukes is now in the hands of a Turkish pasha. The Nile flows down the country, above five hundred miles from the tropic of Cancer to the Mediterranean, and marks, on either side, the extent of fertility by the measure of its inundations. Cyrene, situate towards the west, and along the sea-coast, was first a Greek colony, afterwards a province of Egypt, and is now lost in the desert of Barca.

From Cyrene to the ocean, the coast of Africa extends above fifteen hundred miles; yet so closely is it pressed between the Mediterranean and the Sahara, or sandy desert, that its breadth seldom exceeds fourscore or an hundred miles. The eastern division was considered by the Romans as the more peculiar and proper province of Africa. Till the arrival of the Phœnician colonies, that fertile country was inhabited by the Libyans, the most savage of mankind. Under the immediate jurisdiction of Carthage, it became the centre of commerce and empire; but the republic of Carthage is now degenerated into the feeble and disorderly states of Tripoli and Tunis. The military government of Algiers oppresses the wide extent of Numidia, as it was once united under Massinissa and Jugurtha: but in the time of Augustus, the limits of Numidia were contracted; and, at least, two-thirds of the country acquiesced in the name of Mauritania, with the epithet of Cæsariensis. The genuine Mauritania, or country of the Moors, which, from the ancient city of Tingi, or Tangier, was distinguished by the appellation of Tingitana, is represented by the modern kingdom of Fez. Sallè, on the Ocean, long infamous for its piratical depredations, was noticed by the Romans, as the extreme object of their power, and almost of their geography. A city of their foundation may still be discovered near Mequinez, the residence of the barbarian whom we condescend to style the Emperor of Morocco; but it does not appear that his more southern dominions, Morocco itself, and Segelmessa, were ever comprehended within the Roman province. The western parts of Africa are intersected by the branches of Mount Atlas, a name so idly celebrated by the fancy of poets; but which is now diffused over the immense ocean that rolls between the ancient and the new continent.

Having now finished the circuit of the Roman empire, we may observe, that Africa is divided from Spain by a narrow strait of about twelve miles, through which the Atlantic flows into the Mediterranean. The columns of Hercules, so famous among the ancients, were two mountains which seemed to have been torn asunder by some convulsion of the elements; and at the foot of the European mountain the fortress of Gibraltar is now seated. The whole extent of the Mediterranean Sea, its coasts, and its islands, were comprised within the Roman dominion. Of the larger islands, the two Baleares, which derive their name of Majorca and Minorca from their respective size, are subject at present, the former to Spain, the latter to Great Britain. It is easier to deplore the fate, than to describe the actual condition, of Corsica. Two Italian sovereigns assume a regal title from Sardinia and Sicily. Crete, or Candia, with Cyprus, and most of the smaller islands of Greece and Asia, have been subdued by the Turkish arms; whilst the little rock of Malta defies their power, and has emerged, under the government of its military Order, into fame and opulence.

This long enumeration of provinces, whose broken fragments have formed so many powerful kingdoms, might almost induce us to forgive the vanity or ignorance of the ancients. Dazzled with the extensive sway, the irresistible strength, and the real or affected moderation of the emperors, they permitted themselves to despise, and sometimes to forget, the outlying countries which had been left in the enjoyment of a barbarous independence; and they gradually usurped the licence of confounding the Roman monarchy with the globe of the earth. But the temper, as well as knowledge, of a modern historian requires a more sober and accurate language. He may impress a juster image of the greatness of Rome, by observing that the empire was above two thousand miles in breadth, from the wall of Antoninus and the northern limits of Dacia, to mount Atlas and the tropic of Cancer; that it extended, in length, more than three thousand miles from the Western Ocean to the Euphrates; that it was situated in the finest part of the Temperate Zone, between the twenty-fourth and fifty-sixth degrees of northern latitude; and that it was supposed to contain above sixteen hundred thousand square miles, for the most part of fertile and well-cultivated land.

II

OF THE UNION AND INTERNAL PROSPERITY OF THE ROMAN EMPIRE IN THE AGE OF THE ANTONINES

It is not alone by the rapidity, or extent of conquest, that we should estimate the greatness of Rome. The sovereign of the Russian deserts commands a larger portion of the globe. In the seventh summer after his passage of the Hellespont, Alexander erected the Macedonian trophies on the banks of the Hyphasis. Within less than a century, the irresistible Zingis, and the Mogul princes of his race, spread their cruel devastations and transient empire from the sea of China to the confines of Egypt and Germany. But the firm edifice of Roman power was raised and preserved by the wisdom of ages. The obedient provinces of Trajan and the Antonines were united by laws and adorned by arts. They might occasionally suffer from the partial abuse of delegated authority; but the general principle of government was wise, simple, and beneficent. They enjoyed the religion of their ancestors, whilst in civil honours and advantages they were exalted, by just degrees, to an equality with their conquerors.

I. The policy of the emperors and the senate, as far as it concerned religion, was happily seconded by the reflections of the enlightened, and by the habits of the superstitious, part of their subjects. The various modes of worship, which prevailed in the Roman world, were all considered by the people, as equally true; by the philosopher, as equally false; and by the magistrate, as equally useful. And thus toleration produced not only mutual indulgence, but even religious concord.

The superstition of the people was not embittered by any mixture of theological rancour; nor was it confined by the chains of any speculative system. The devout polytheist, though fondly attached to his national rites, admitted with implicit faith the different religions of the earth. Fear, gratitude, and curiosity, a dream or an omen, a singular disorder, or a distant journey, perpetually disposed him to multiply the articles of his belief, and to enlarge the list of his protectors. The thin texture of the Pagan mythology was interwoven with various but not discordant materials. As soon as it was allowed that sages and heroes, who had lived, or who had died for the benefit of their country, were exalted to a state of power and immortality, it was universally confessed that they deserved, if not the adoration, at least the reverence of all mankind. The deities of a thousand groves and a thousand streams possessed, in peace, their local and respective influence; nor could the Roman who deprecated the wrath of the Tiber, deride the Egyptian who presented his offering to the beneficent genius of the Nile. The visible powers of Nature, the planets, and the elements, were the same throughout the universe. The invisible governors of the moral world were inevitably cast in a similar mould of fiction and allegory. Every virtue, and even vice, acquired its divine representative; every art and profession its patron, whose attributes, in the most distant ages and countries, were uniformly derived from the character of their peculiar votaries. A republic of gods of such opposite tempers and interest required, in every system, the moderating hand of a supreme magistrate, who, by the progress of knowledge and flattery, was gradually invested with the sublime perfections of an Eternal Parent, and an Omnipotent Monarch. Such was the mild spirit of antiquity, that the nations were less attentive to the difference than to the resemblance of their religious worship. The Greek, the Roman, and the Barbarian, as they met before their respective altars, easily persuaded themselves, that under various names, and with various ceremonies, they adored the same deities. The elegant mythology of Homer gave a beautiful, and almost a regular form, to the polytheism of the ancient world.

The philosophers of Greece deduced their morals from the nature of man, rather than from that of God. They meditated, however, on the Divine Nature, as a very curious and important speculation; and in the profound inquiry, they displayed the strength and weakness of the human understanding. Of the four most celebrated schools, the Stoics and the Platonists endeavoured to reconcile the jarring interests of reason and piety. They have left us the most sublime proofs of the existence and perfections of the first cause; but, as it was impossible for them to conceive the creation of matter, the workman in the Stoic philosophy was not sufficiently distinguished from the work; whilst, on the contrary, the spiritual God of Plato and his disciples resembled an idea rather than a substance. The opinions of the Academics and Epicureans were of a less religious cast; but whilst the modest science of the former induced them to doubt, the positive ignorance of the latter urged them to deny, the providence of a Supreme Ruler. The spirit of inquiry, prompted by emulation, and supported by freedom, had divided the public teachers of philosophy into a variety of contending sects; but the ingenuous youth who, from every part, resorted to Athens, and the other seats of learning in the Roman empire, were alike instructed in every school to reject and to despise the religion of the multitude. How, indeed, was it possible, that a philosopher should accept, as divine truths, the idle tales of the poets, and the incoherent traditions of antiquity; or, that he should adore, as gods, those imperfect beings whom he must have despised, as men! Against such unworthy adversaries, Cicero condescended to employ the arms of reason and eloquence; but the satire of Lucian was a much more adequate, as well as more efficacious weapon. We may be well assured, that a writer conversant with the world would never have ventured to expose the gods of his country to public ridicule, had they not already been the objects of secret contempt among the polished and enlightened orders of society.

Notwithstanding the fashionable irreligion which prevailed in the age of the Antonines, both the interests of the priests and the credulity of the people were sufficiently respected. In their writings and conversation, the philosophers of antiquity asserted the independent dignity of reason; but they resigned their actions to the commands of law and of custom. Viewing, with a smile of pity and indulgence, the various errors of the vulgar, they diligently practised the ceremonies of their fathers, devoutly frequented the temples of the gods; and sometimes condescending to act a part on the theatre of superstition, they concealed the sentiments of an Atheist under the sacerdotal robes. Reasoners of such a temper were scarcely inclined to wrangle about their respective modes of faith, or of worship. It was indifferent to them what shape the folly of the multitude might choose to assume; and they approached, with the same inward contempt, and the same external reverence, the altars of the Libyan, the Olympian, or the Capitoline Jupiter.

It is not easy to conceive from what motives a spirit of persecution could introduce itself into the Roman councils. The magistrates could not be actuated by a blind, though honest bigotry, since the magistrates were themselves philosophers; and the schools of Athens had given laws to the senate. They could not

be impelled by ambition or avarice, as the temporal and ecclesiastical powers were united in the same hands. The pontiffs were
chosen among the most illustrious of the senators; and the office
of Supreme Pontiff was constantly exercised by the emperors themselves. They knew and valued the advantages of religion, as it is
connected with civil government. They encouraged the public
festivals which humanise the manners of the people. They
managed the arts of divination, as a convenient instrument of policy;
and they respected as the firmest bond of society, the useful
persuasion that, either in this or in a future life, the crime of perjury is most assuredly punished by the avenging gods. But whilst
they acknowledged the general advantages of religion, they were
convinced that the various modes of worship contributed alike to
the same salutary purposes; and that, in every country, the form of
superstition, which had received the sanction of time and experience, was the best adapted to the climate and to its inhabitants.
Avarice and taste very frequently despoiled the vanquished nations
of the elegant statues of their gods, and the rich ornaments of their
temples; but, in the exercise of the religion which they derived
from their ancestors, they uniformly experienced the indulgence,
and even protection, of the Roman conquerors. The province of
Gaul seems, and indeed only seems, an exception to this universal
toleration. Under the specious pretext of abolishing human sacrifices, the emperors Tiberius and Claudius suppressed the dangerous
power of the Druids, but the priests themselves, their gods and
their altars, subsisted in peaceful obscurity till the final destruction
of Paganism.

Rome, the capital of a great monarchy, was incessantly filled
with subjects and strangers from every part of the world, who all
introduced and enjoyed the favourite superstitions of their native
country. Every city in the empire was justified in maintaining the
purity of its ancient ceremonies; and the Roman senate, using
the common privilege, sometimes interposed, to check this inundation of foreign rites. The Egyptian superstition, of all the most
contemptible and abject, was frequently prohibited; the temples of
Serapis and Isis demolished and their worshippers banished from
Rome and Italy. But the zeal of fanaticism prevailed over the cold
and feeble efforts of policy. The exiles returned, the proselytes
multiplied, the temples were restored with increasing splendour,
and Isis and Serapis at length assumed their place among the
Roman deities. Nor was this indulgence a departure from the old

maxims of government. In the purest ages of the commonwealth, Cybele and Æsculapius had been invited by solemn embassies; and it was customary to tempt the protectors of besieged cities, by the promise of more distinguished honours than they possessed in their native country. Rome gradually became the common temple of her subjects; and the freedom of the city was bestowed on all the gods of mankind.

II. The narrow policy of preserving, without any foreign mixture, the pure blood of the ancient citizens, had checked the fortune, and hastened the ruin, of Athens and Sparta. The aspiring genius of Rome sacrificed vanity to ambition, and deemed it more prudent, as well as honourable, to adopt virtue and merit for her own wheresoever they were found, among slaves or strangers, enemies or barbarians. During the most flourishing era of the Athenian commonwealth, the number of citizens gradually decreased from about thirty to twenty-one thousand. If, on the contrary, we study the growth of the Roman republic, we may discover, that, notwithstanding the incessant demands of wars and colonies, the citizens, who, in the first census of Servius Tullius, amounted to no more than eighty-three thousand, were multiplied, before the commencement of the social war, to the number of four hundred and sixty-three thousand men, able to bear arms in the service of their country. When the allies of Rome claimed an equal share of honours and privileges, the senate indeed preferred the chance of arms to an ignominious concession. The Samnites and the Lucanians paid the severe penalty of their rashness; but the rest of the Italian states, as they successively returned to their duty, were admitted into the bosom of the republic, and soon contributed to the ruin of public freedom. Under a democratical government, the citizens exercise the powers of sovereignty; and those powers will be first abused, and afterwards lost, if they are committed to an unwieldy multitude. But when the popular assemblies had been suppressed by the administration of the emperors, the conquerors were distinguished from the vanquished nations, only as the first and most honourable order of subjects; and their increase, however rapid, was no longer exposed to the same dangers. Yet the wisest princes, who adopted the maxims of Augustus, guarded with the strictest care the dignity of the Roman name, and diffused the freedom of the city with a prudent liberality.

Till the privileges of Romans had been progressively extended to all the inhabitants of the empire, an important distinction was preserved between Italy and the provinces. The former was esteemed the centre of public unity, and the firm basis of the constitution. Italy claimed the birth, or at least the residence, of the emperors and the senate. The estates of the Italians were exempt from taxes, their persons from the arbitrary jurisdiction of governors. Their municipal corporations, formed after the perfect model of the capital, were entrusted, under the immediate eye of the supreme power, with the execution of the laws. From the foot of the Alps to the extremity of Calabria, all the natives of Italy were born citizens of Rome. Their partial distinctions were obliterated, and they insensibly coalesced into one great nation, united by language, manners, and civil institutions, and equal to the weight of a powerful empire. The republic gloried in her generous policy, and was frequently rewarded by the merit and services of her adopted sons. Had she always confined the distinction of Romans to the ancient families within the walls of the city, that immortal name would have been deprived of some of its noblest ornaments. Virgil was a native of Mantua; Horace was inclined to doubt whether he should call himself an Apulian or a Lucanian: it was in Padua that an historian was found worthy to record the majestic series of Roman victories. The patriot family of the Catos emerged from Tusculum; and the little town of Arpinum claimed the double honour of producing Marius and Cicero, the former of whom deserved, after Romulus and Camillus, to be styled the Third Founder of Rome; and the latter, after saving his country from the designs of Catiline, enabled her to contend with Athens for the palm of eloquence.

The provinces of the empire (as they have been described in the preceding chapter) were destitute of any public force, or constitutional freedom. In Etruria, in Greece, and in Gaul, it was the first care of the senate to dissolve those dangerous confederacies, which taught mankind, that as the Roman arts prevailed by division, they might be resisted by union. Those princes, whom the ostentation of gratitude or generosity permitted for a while to hold a precarious sceptre, were dismissed from their thrones as soon as they had performed their appointed task of fashioning to the yoke the vanquished nations. The free states and cities which had embraced the cause of Rome, were rewarded with a nominal alliance, and insensibly sunk into real servitude. The public authority was everywhere exercised by the ministers of the senate and of the emperors, and that authority was absolute, and without control.

But the same salutary maxims of government, which had secured the peace and obedience of Italy, were extended to the most distant conquests. A nation of Romans was gradually formed in the provinces, by the double expedient of introducing colonies, and of admitting the most faithful and deserving of the provincials to the freedom of Rome.

"Wheresoever the Roman conquers, he inhabits," is a very just observation of Seneca, confirmed by history and experience. The natives of Italy, allured by pleasure or by interest, hastened to enjoy the advantages of victory; and we may remark, that about forty years after the reduction of Asia, eighty thousand Romans were massacred in one day, by the cruel orders of Mithridates. These voluntary exiles were engaged, for the most part, in the occupations of commerce, agriculture, and the farm of the revenue. But after the legions were rendered permanent by the emperors, the provinces were peopled by a race of soldiers; and the veterans, whether they received the reward of their service in land or in money, usually settled with their families in the country where they had honourably spent their youth. Throughout the empire, but more particularly in the western parts, the most fertile districts, and the most convenient situations, were reserved for the establishment of colonies; some of which were of a civil, and others of a military nature. In their manners and internal policy, the colonies formed a perfect representation of their great parent; and they were soon endeared to the natives by the ties of friendship and alliance, they effectually diffused a reverence for the Roman name, and a desire, which was seldom disappointed, of sharing, in due time, its honours and advantages. The municipal cities insensibly equalled the rank and splendour of the colonies; and in the reign of Hadrian, it was disputed which was the preferable condition, of those societies which had issued from, or those which had been received into the bosom of Rome. The right of Latium, as it was called, conferred on the cities to which it had been granted a more partial favour. The magistrates only, at the expiration of their office, assumed the quality of Roman citizens; but as those offices were annual, in a few years they circulated round the principal families. Those of the provincials who were permitted to bear arms in the legions; those who exercised any civil employment; all, in a word, who performed any public service, or displayed any personal talents, were rewarded with a present, whose value was continually diminished by the increasing liberality of the emperors. Yet even, in the age of the Antonines, when the freedom of the city had been bestowed on the greater number of their subjects, it was still accompanied with very solid advantages. The bulk of the people acquired, with that title, the benefit of the Roman laws, particularly in the interesting articles of marriage, testaments, and inheritances; and the road of fortune was open to those whose pretensions were seconded by favour or merit. The grandsons of the Gauls, who had besieged Julius Cæsar in Alesia, commanded legions, governed provinces, and were admitted into the senate of Rome. Their ambition, instead of disturbing the tranquillity of the state, was intimately connected with its safety and greatness.

So sensible were the Romans of the influence of language over national manners, that it was their most serious care to extend, with the progress of their arms, the use of the Latin tongue. The ancient dialects of Italy, the Sabine, the Etruscan, and the Venetian, sunk into oblivion; but in the provinces, the east was less docile than the west to the voice of its victorious preceptors. This obvious difference marked the two portions of the empire with a distinction of colours, which, though it was in some degree concealed during the meridian splendour of prosperity, became gradually more visible as the shades of night descended upon the Roman world. The western countries were civilised by the same hands which subdued them. As soon as the barbarians were reconciled to obedience, their minds were opened to any new impressions of knowledge and politeness. The language of Virgil and Cicero, though with some inevitable mixture of corruption, was so universally adopted in Africa, Spain, Gaul, Britain, and Pannonia, that the faint traces of the Punic or Celtic idioms were preserved only in the mountains, or among the peasants. Education and study insensibly inspired the natives of those countries with the sentiments of Romans; and Italy gave fashions as well as laws to her Latin provincials. They solicited with more ardour, and obtained with more facility, the freedom and honours of the state; supported the national dignity in letters and in arms; and, at length, in the person of Trajan, produced an emperor whom the Scipios would not have disowned for their countryman. The situation of the Greeks was very different from that of the Barbarians. The former had been long since civilised and corrupted. They had too much taste to relinquish their language, and too much vanity to adopt any foreign institutions. Still preserving the prejudices after they had lost the virtues of their ancestors, they affected to despise the unpolished manners of the

Roman conquerors, whilst they were compelled to respect their superior wisdom and power. Nor was the influence of the Grecian language and sentiments confined to the narrow limits of that once celebrated country. Their empire, by the progress of colonies and conquest, had been diffused from the Hadriatic to the Euphrates and the Nile. Asia was covered with Greek cities, and the long reign of the Macedonian kings had introduced a silent revolution into Syria and Egypt. In their pompous courts those princes united the elegance of Athens with the luxury of the East, and the example of the court was imitated, at an humble distance, by the higher ranks of their subjects. Such was the general division of the Roman empire into the Latin and Greek languages. To these we may add a third distinction for the body of the natives in Syria, and especially in Egypt. The use of their ancient dialects, by secluding them from the commerce of mankind, checked the improvements of those barbarians. The slothful effeminacy of the former, exposed them to the contempt; the sullen ferociousness of the latter, excited the aversion of the conquerors. Those nations had submitted to the Roman power, but they seldom desired or deserved the freedom of the city; and it was remarked that more than two hundred and thirty years elapsed after the ruin of the Ptolemies before an Egyptian was admitted into the senate of Rome.

It is a just though trite observation, that victorious Rome was herself subdued by the arts of Greece. Those immortal writers who still command the admiration of modern Europe, soon became the favourite object of study and imitation in Italy and the western provinces. But the elegant amusements of the Romans were not suffered to interfere with their sound maxims of policy. Whilst they acknowledged the charms of the Greek, they asserted the dignity of the Latin tongue, and the exclusive use of the latter was inflexibly maintained in the administration of civil as well as military government. The two languages exercised at the same time their separate jurisdiction throughout the empire: the former as the natural idiom of science; the latter as the legal dialect of public transactions. Those who united letters with business were equally conversant with both; and it was almost impossible, in any province, to find a Roman subject of a liberal education, who was at once a stranger to the Greek and to the Latin language.

It was by such institutions that the nations of the empire insensibly melted away into the Roman name and people. But there still remained, in the centre of every province and of every family, an unhappy condition of men who endured the weight, without sharing the benefits, of society. In the free states of antiquity the domestic slaves were exposed to the wanton rigour of despotism. The perfect settlement of the Roman empire was preceded by ages of violence and rapine. The slaves consisted, for the most part, of barbarian captives, taken in thousands by the chance of war, purchased at a vile price, accustomed to a life of independence, and impatient to break and to revenge their fetters. Against such internal enemies, whose desperate insurrections had more than once reduced the republic to the brink of destruction, the most severe regulations, and the most cruel treatment, seemed almost justified by the great law of self-preservation. But when the principal nations of Europe, Asia, and Africa, were united under the laws of one sovereign, the source of foreign supplies flowed with much less abundance, and the Romans were reduced to the milder but more tedious method of propagation. In their numerous families, and particularly in their country estates, they encouraged the marriage of their slaves. The sentiments of nature, the habits of education, and the possession of a dependent species of property, contributed to alleviate the hardships of servitude. The existence of a slave became an object of greater value, and though his happiness still depended on the temper and circumstances of the master, the humanity of the latter, instead of being restrained by fear, was encouraged by the sense of his own interest. The progress of manners was accelerated by the virtue or policy of the emperors; and by the edicts of Hadrian and the Antonines, the protection of the laws was extended to the most abject part of mankind. The jurisdiction of life and death over the slaves, a power long exercised and often abused, was taken out of private hands, and reserved to the magistrates alone. The subterraneous prisons were abolished; and, upon a just complaint of intolerable treatment, the injured slave obtained either his deliverance, or a less cruel master.

The number of subjects who acknowledged the laws of Rome, of citizens, of provincials, and of slaves, cannot now be fixed with such a degree of accuracy, as the importance of the object would deserve. We are informed that when the emperor Claudius exercised the office of censor, he took an account of six million nine hundred and forty-five thousand Roman citizens, who, with the proportion of women and children, must have amounted to about twenty millions of souls. The multitude of subjects of an inferior rank was uncertain and fluctuating. But, after weighing with attention every circumstance which could influence the balance, it seems probable that there existed, in the time of Claudius, about twice as many provincials as there were citizens, of either sex, and of every age; and that the slaves were at least equal in number to the free inhabitants of the Roman world. The total amount of this imperfect calculation would rise to about one hundred and twenty millions of persons; a degree of population which possibly exceeds that of modern Europe, and forms the most numerous society that has ever been united under the same system of government.

Domestic peace and union were the natural consequences of the moderate and comprehensive policy embraced by the Romans. If we turn our eyes towards the monarchies of Asia, we shall behold despotism in the centre, and weakness in the extremities; the collection of the revenue, or the administration of justice, enforced by the presence of an army; hostile barbarians established in the heart of the country, hereditary satraps usurping the dominion of the provinces, and subjects inclined to rebellion, though incapable of freedom. But the obedience of the Roman world was uniform, voluntary, and permanent. The vanquished nations, blended into one great people, resigned the hope, nay even the wish, of resuming their independence, and scarcely considered their own existence as distinct from the existence of Rome. The established authority of the emperors pervaded without an effort the wide extent of their dominions, and was exercised with the same facility on the banks of the Thames, or of the Nile, as on those of the Tiber. The legions were destined to serve against the public enemy, and the civil magistrate seldom required the aid of a military force. In this state of general security, the leisure as well as opulence both of the prince and people were devoted to improve and to adorn the Roman empire.

We have computed the inhabitants and contemplated the public works of the Roman empire. The observation of the number and greatness of its cities will serve to confirm the former, and to multiply the latter. It may not be unpleasing to collect a few scattered instances relative to that subject, without forgetting, however, that from the vanity of nations and the poverty of language, the vague appellation of city has been indifferently bestowed on Rome and upon Laurentum. I. *Ancient* Italy is said to have contained eleven hundred and ninety-seven cities; and for whatsoever era of antiquity the expression might be intended, there is not any reason to believe the country less populous in the age of the Antonines than in that of Romulus. The petty states of Latium were contained within the metropolis of the empire, by whose superior influence they had been attracted. Those parts of Italy which have so long languished under the lazy tyranny of priests and viceroys, had been afflicted only by the more tolerable calamities of war; and the first symptoms of decay which *they* experienced were amply compensated by the rapid improvements of the Cisalpine Gaul. The splendour of Verona may be traced in its remains: yet Verona was less celebrated than Aquileia or Padua, Milan or Ravenna. II. The spirit of improvement had passed the Alps, and been felt even in the woods of Britain, which were gradually cleared away to open a free space for convenient and elegant habitations. York was the seat of government; London was already enriched by commerce; and Bath was celebrated for the salutary effects of its medicinal waters. Gaul could boast of her twelve hundred cities; and though, in the northern parts, many of them, without excepting Paris itself, were little more than the rude and imperfect townships of a rising people; the southern provinces imitated the wealth and elegance of Italy. Many were the cities of Gaul, Marseilles, Arles, Nismes, Narbonne, Thoulouse, Bourdeaux, Autun, Vienna, Lyons, Langres, and Treves, whose ancient condition might sustain an equal, and perhaps advantageous comparison with their present state. With regard to Spain, that country flourished as a province, and has declined as a kingdom. Exhausted by the abuse of her strength, by America, and by superstition, her pride might possibly be confounded, if we required such a list of three hundred and sixty cities, as Pliny has exhibited under the reign of Vespasian. III. Three hundred African cities had once acknowledged the authority of Carthage, nor is it likely that their numbers diminished under the administration of the emperors: Carthage itself rose with new splendour from its ashes; and that capital, as well as Capua and Corinth, soon recovered all the advantages which can be separated from independent sovereignty. IV. The provinces of the east present the contrast of Roman magnificence with Turkish barbarism. The ruins of antiquity scattered over uncultivated fields, and ascribed, by ignorance, to the power of magic, scarcely afford a shelter to the oppressed peasant or wandering Arab. Under the reign of the Cæsars, the proper Asia alone contained five hundred populous cities, enriched with all the gifts of nature, and adorned with all the refinements of art. Eleven cities of Asia had once disputed the honour of dedicating a temple to Tiberius, and their respective merits were examined by the senate. Four of them were immediately rejected as unequal to the burden; and among these was Laodicea, whose splendour is still displayed in its ruins. Laodicea collected a very considerable revenue from its flocks of sheep, celebrated for the fineness of their wool, and had received, a little before the contest, a legacy of above four hundred thousand pounds by the testament of a generous citizen. If such was the poverty of Laodicea, what must have been the wealth of those cities, whose claim appeared preferable, and particularly of Pergamus, of Smyrna, and of Ephesus, who so long disputed with each other over the titular primacy of Asia. The capitals of Syria and Egypt held a still superior rank in the empire: Antioch and Alexandria looked down with disdain on a crowd of dependent cities, and yielded, with reluctance, to the majesty of Rome itself.

All these cities were connected with each other, and with the capital, by the public highways, which issuing from the Forum of Rome, traversed Italy, pervaded the provinces, and were terminated only by the frontiers of the empire. If we carefully trace the distance from the wall of Antoninus to Rome, and from thence to Jerusalem, it will be found that the great chain of communication, from the north-west to the south-east point of the empire, was drawn out to the length of four thousand and eighty Roman miles. The public roads were accurately divided by mile-stones, and ran in a direct line from one city to another, with very little respect for the obstacles either of nature or private property. Mountains were perforated, and bold arches thrown over the broadest and most rapid streams. The middle part of the road was raised into a terrace which commanded the adjacent country, consisted of several strata of sand, gravel, and cement, and was paved with large stones, or in some places, near the capital, with granite. Such was the solid construction of the Roman highways, whose firmness has not entirely yielded to the effort of fifteen centuries. They united the subjects of the most distant provinces by an easy and familiar intercourse; but their primary object had been to facilitate the marches of the legions; nor was any country considered as completely subdued, till it had been rendered, in all its parts, pervious to the arms and authority of the conqueror. The advantage of receiving the earliest intelligence, and of conveying their orders with celerity, induced the emperors to establish throughout their extensive dominions, the regular institution of posts. Houses were everywhere erected at the distance only of five or six miles; each of them was constantly provided with forty horses, and by the help of these relays it was easy to travel an hundred miles in a day along the Roman roads. The use of the posts was allowed to those who claimed it by an Imperial mandate; but though originally intended for the public service, it was sometimes indulged to the business or conveniency of private citizens. Nor was the communication of the Roman empire less free and open by sea than it was by land. The provinces surrounded and inclosed the Mediterranean; and Italy, in the shape of an immense promontory, advanced into the midst of that great lake. The coasts of Italy are, in general, destitute of safe harbours; but human industry had corrected the deficiencies of nature; and the artificial port of Ostia, in particular, situate at the mouth of the Tiber, and formed by the emperor Claudius, was a useful monument of Roman greatness. From this port, which was only sixteen miles from the capital, a favourable breeze frequently carried vessels in seven days to the columns of Hercules, and in nine or ten, to Alexandria in Egypt.

Whatever evils either reason or declamation have imputed to extensive empire, the power of Rome was attended with some beneficial consequences to mankind; and the same freedom of intercourse which extended the vices, diffused likewise the improvements of social life. In the more remote ages of antiquity, the world was unequally divided. The east was in the immemorial possession of arts and luxury; whilst the west was inhabited by rude and warlike barbarians, who either disdained agriculture, or to whom it was totally unknown. Under the protection of an established government, the productions of happier climates, and the industry of more civilised nations, were gradually introduced into the western countries of Europe; and the natives were encouraged, by an open and profitable commerce, to multiply the former, as well as to improve the latter. It would be almost impossible to enumerate all the articles, either of the animal or the vegetable reign, which were successively imported into Europe, from Asia and Egypt; but it will not be unworthy of the dignity, and much less of the utility, of an historical work, slightly to touch on a few of the principal heads. 1. Almost all the flowers, the herbs, and the fruits, that grow in our European gardens, are of foreign extraction, which, in many cases, is betrayed even by their names: the apple was a native of Italy, and when the Romans had tasted the richer flavour of the apricot, the peach, the pomegranate, the citron, and the orange, they contented themselves with applying to all these new fruits the common denomination of apple, discriminating them from each other by the additional epithet of their country. 2. In the time of Homer, the vine grew wild in the island of Sicily, and most probably in the adjacent continent; but it was not improved by the skill, nor did it afford a liquor grateful to the taste, of the savage inhabitants. A thousand years afterwards, Italy could boast, that of the fourscore most generous and celebrated wines, more than two-thirds were produced from her soil. The blessing was soon communicated to the Narbonnese province of Gaul; but so intense was the cold to the north of the Cevennes, that, in the time of Strabo, it was thought impossible to ripen the grapes in those parts of Gaul. This difficulty, however, was gradually vanquished; and there is some reason to believe, that the vineyards of Burgundy are as old as the age of the Antonines. The olive, in the western world, followed the progress of peace, of which it was considered as the symbol. Two centuries after the foundation of Rome, both Italy and Africa were strangers to that useful plant; it was naturalised in those countries; and at length carried into the heart of Spain and Gaul. The timid errors of the ancients, that it required a certain degree of heat, and could only flourish in the neighbourhood of the sea, were insensibly exploded by industry and experience. The cultivation of flax was transported from Egypt to Gaul, and enriched the whole country, however it might impoverish the particular lands on which it was sown. 3. The use of artificial grasses became familiar to the farmers both of Italy and the provinces, particularly the Lucerne, which derived its name and origin from Media. The assured supply of wholesome and plentiful food for the cattle during winter, multiplied the number of the flocks and herds, which in their turn contributed to the fertility of the soil. To all these improvements may be added an assiduous attention to mines and fisheries, which, by employing a multitude of laborious hands, serve to increase the pleasures of the rich, and the subsistence of the poor. The elegant treatise of Columella describes the advanced state of the Spanish husbandry, under the reign of Tiberius; and it may be observed, that those famines which so frequently afflicted the infant republic, were seldom or never experienced by the extensive empire of Rome. The accidental scarcity, in any single province, was immediately relieved by the plenty of its more fortunate neighbours.

Agriculture is the foundation of manufactures; since the productions of nature are the materials of art. Under the Roman empire, the labour of an industrious and ingenious people was variously, but incessantly employed, in the service of the rich. In their dress, their table, their houses, and their furniture, the favourites of fortune united every refinement of conveniency, of elegance, and of splendour, whatever could soothe their pride or gratify their sensuality. Such refinements, under the odious name of luxury, have been severely arraigned by the moralists of every age; and it might perhaps be more conducive to the virtue, as well as happiness, of mankind, if all possessed the necessities, and none of the superfluities, of life. But in the present imperfect condition of society, luxury, though it may proceed from vice or folly, seems to be the only means that can correct the unequal distribution of property. The diligent mechanic, and the skilful artist, who have obtained no share in the division of the earth, receive a voluntary tax from the possessors of land; and the latter are prompted, by a sense of interest, to improve those estates, with whose produce they may purchase additional pleasures. This operation, the particular effects of which are felt in every society, acted with much more diffusive energy in the Roman world. The provinces would soon have been exhausted of their wealth, if the manufactures and commerce of luxury had not insensibly restored to the industrious subjects the sums which were exacted from them by the arms and authority of Rome. As long as the circulation was confined within the bounds of the empire, it impressed the political machine with a new degree of activity, and its consequences, sometimes beneficial, could never become pernicious.

But it is no easy task to confine luxury within the limits of an empire. The most remote countries of the ancient world were ransacked to supply the pomp and delicacy of Rome. The forests of Scythia afforded some valuable furs. Amber was brought over land from the shores of the Baltic to the Danube; and the barbarians were astonished at the price which they received in exchange for so useless a commodity. There was a considerable demand for Babylonian carpets and other manufactures of the East; but the most important and unpopular branch of foreign trade was carried on with Arabia and India. Every year, about the time of the summer solstice, a fleet of an hundred and twenty vessels sailed from Myos-hormos, a port of Egypt, on the Red Sea. By the periodical assistance of the Monsoons, they traversed the ocean in about forty days. The coast of Malabar, or the island of Ceylon, was the usual term of their navigation, and it was in those markets that the merchants from the more remote countries of Asia expected their arrival. The return of the fleet of Egypt was fixed to the months of December or January; and as soon as their rich cargo had been transported on the backs of camels, from the Red Sea to the Nile, and had descended that river as far as Alexandria, it was poured, without delay, into the capital of the empire. The objects of oriental traffic were splendid and trifling; silk, a pound of which was esteemed not inferior in value to a pound of gold; precious stones, among which the pearl claimed the first rank after the diamond; and a variety of aromatics, that were consumed in religious worship and the pomp of funerals. The labour and risk of the voyage was rewarded with almost incredible profit; but the profit was made upon Roman subjects, and a few individuals were enriched at the expense of the Public. As the natives of Arabia and India were contented with the productions and manufactures of their own country, silver, on the side of the Romans, was the principal, if not the only instrument of commerce. It was a complaint worthy of the gravity of the senate, that in the purchase of female ornaments, the wealth of the state was irrevocably given away to foreign and hostile nations. The annual loss is computed, by a writer of an inquisitive but censorious temper, at upwards of eight hundred thousand pounds sterling. Such was the style of discontent, brooding over the dark prospect of approaching poverty. And yet, if we compare the proportion between gold and silver, as it stood in the time of Pliny, and as it was fixed in the reign of Constantine, we shall discover within that period a very considerable increase. There is not the least reason to suppose that gold was become more scarce; it is therefore evident that silver was grown more common; that whatever might be the amount of the Indian and Arabian exports, they were far from exhausting the wealth of the Roman world; and that the produce of the mines abundantly supplied the demands of commerce.

Notwithstanding the propensity of mankind to exalt the past, and to depreciate the present, the tranquil and prosperous state of the empire was warmly felt, and honestly confessed, by the provincials as well as Romans. "They acknowledged that the true principles of social life, laws, agriculture, and science, which had been first invented by the wisdom of Athens, were now firmly established by the power of Rome, under whose auspicious influence the fiercest barbarians were united by an equal government and common language. They affirm, that with the improvement of arts, the human species was visibly multiplied. They celebrate the increasing splendour of the cities, the beautiful face of the country, cultivated and adorned like an immense garden; and the long festival of peace, which was enjoyed by so many nations, forgetful of their ancient animosities, and delivered from the apprehension of future danger." Whatever suspicions may be suggested by the air of rhetoric and declamation, which seems to prevail in these passages, the substance of them is perfectly agreeable to historic truth.

It was scarcely possible that the eyes of contemporaries should discover in the public felicity the latent causes of decay and corruption. This long peace, and the uniform government of the Romans, introduced a slow and secret poison into the vitals of the empire. The minds of men were gradually reduced to the same level, the fire of genius was extinguished, and even the military spirit evaporated. The natives of Europe were brave and robust, Spain, Gaul, Britain, and Illyricum supplied the legions with excellent soldiers, and constituted the real strength of the monarchy. Their personal valour remained, but they no longer possessed that public courage which is nourished by the love of independence, the sense of national honour, the presence of danger, and the habit of command. They received laws and governors from the will of their sovereign, and trusted for their defence to a mercenary army. The posterity of their boldest leaders was contented with the rank of citizens and subjects. The most aspiring spirits resorted to the court or standard of the emperors; and the deserted provinces, deprived of political strength or union, insensibly sunk into the languid indifference of private life.

The love of letters, almost inseparable from peace and refinement, was fashionable among the subjects of Hadrian and the Antonines, who were themselves men of learning and curiosity. It was diffused over the whole extent of their empire; the most northern tribes of Britons had acquired a taste for rhetoric; Homer as well as Virgil were transcribed and studied on the banks of the Rhine and Danube; and the most liberal rewards sought out the faintest glimmerings of literary merit. The sciences of physic and astronomy were successfully cultivated by the Greeks; the observations of Ptolemy and the writings of Galen are studied by those who have improved their discoveries and corrected their errors; but if we except the inimitable Lucian, this age of indolence passed away without having produced a single writer of original genius, or who excelled in the arts of elegant composition. The authority of Plato and Aristotle, of Zeno and Epicurus, still reigned in the schools; and their systems, transmitted with blind deference from one generation of disciples to another, precluded every generous attempt to exercise the powers, or enlarge the limits, of the human mind. The beauties of the poets and orators, instead of kindling a fire like their own, inspired only cold and servile imitations: or if any ventured to deviate from those models, they deviated at the same time from good sense and propriety. On the revival of letters, the youthful vigour of the imagination, after a long repose, national emulation, a new religion, new languages, and a new world, called forth the genius of Europe. But the provincials of Rome, trained by a uniform artificial foreign education, were engaged in a very unequal competition with those bold ancients, who, by expressing their genuine feelings in their native tongue, had already occupied every place of honour. The name of Poet was almost forgotten; that of Orator was usurped by the sophists. A cloud of critics, of compilers, of commentators, darkened the face of learning, and the decline of genius was soon followed by the corruption of taste.

The sublime Longinus, who in somewhat a later period, and in the court of a Syrian queen, preserved the spirit of ancient Athens, observes and laments this degeneracy of his contemporaries, which debased their sentiments, enervated their courage, and depressed their talents. "In the same manner," says he, "as some children always remain pigmies, whose infant limbs have been too closely confined; thus our tender minds, fettered by the prejudices and habits of a just servitude, are unable to expand themselves, or to attain that well-proportioned greatness which we admire in the ancients; who living under a popular government, wrote with the same freedom as they acted." This diminutive stature of mankind, if we pursue the metaphor, was daily sinking below the old standard, and the Roman world was indeed peopled by a race of pygmies; when the fierce giants of the north broke in, and mended the puny breed. They restored a manly spirit of freedom; and after the revolution of ten centuries, freedom became the happy parent of taste and science.

III

(96–180 A.D.) OF THE CONSTITUTION OF THE ROMAN EMPIRE IN THE AGE OF THE ANTONINES

The obvious definition of a monarchy seems to be that of a state, in which a single person, by whatsoever name he may be distinguished, is intrusted with the execution of the laws, the management of the revenue, and the command of the army. But, unless public liberty is protected by intrepid and vigilant guardians, the authority of so formidable a magistrate will soon degenerate into despotism. The influence of the clergy, in an age of superstition, might be usefully employed to assert the rights of mankind; but so intimate is the connection between the throne and the altar, that the banner of the church has very seldom been seen on the side of the people. A martial nobility and stubborn commons, possessed of arms, tenacious of property, and collected into constitutional assemblies, form the only balance capable of preserving a free constitution against enterprises of an aspiring prince.

From what has been already observed in the first chapter of this work, some notion may be formed of the armies and provinces thus intrusted to the ruling hand of Augustus. But as it was impossible that he could personally command the legions of so many distant frontiers, he was indulged by the senate, as Pompey had already been, in the permission of devolving the execution of his great office on a sufficient number of lieutenants. In rank and authority these officers seemed not inferior to the ancient proconsuls; but their station was dependent and precarious. They received and held their commissions at the will of a superior, to whose *auspicious* influence the merit of their action was legally attributed. They were the representatives of the emperor. The emperor alone was the general of the republic, and his jurisdiction, civil as well as military, extended over all the conquests of Rome. It was some satisfaction, however, to the senate, that he always delegated his power to the members of their body. The Imperial lieutenants were of consular or prætorian dignity; the legions were commanded by senators, and the præfecture of Egypt was the only important trust committed to a Roman knight.

Within six days after Augustus had been compelled to accept so very liberal a grant, he resolved to gratify the pride of the senate by an easy sacrifice. He represented to them, that they had enlarged his powers, even beyond that degree which might be required by the melancholy condition of the times. They had not permitted him to refuse the laborious command of the armies and the frontiers; but he must insist on being allowed to restore the more peaceful and secure provinces, to the mild administration of the civil magistrate. In the division of the provinces, Augustus provided for his own power, and for the dignity of the republic. The proconsuls of the senate, particularly those of Asia, Greece, and Africa, enjoyed a more honourable character than the lieutenants of the emperor, who commanded in Gaul or Syria. The former were attended by lictors, the latter by soldiers. A law was passed that wherever the emperor was present, his extraordinary commission should supersede the ordinary jurisdiction of the governor; a custom was introduced, that the new conquest belonged to the Imperial portion; and it was soon discovered that the authority of the *Prince*, the favourite epithet of Augustus, was the same in every part of the empire.

In return for this imaginary concession, Augustus obtained an important privilege, which rendered him master of Rome and Italy. By a dangerous exception to the ancient maxims, he was authorised to preserve his military command, supported by a numerous body of guards, even in time of peace, and in the heart of the capital. His command, indeed, was confined to those citizens who were engaged in the service by the military oath; but such was the propensity of the Romans to servitude, that the oath was voluntarily taken by the magistrates, the senators, and the equestrian order, till the homage of flattery was insensibly converted into an annual and solemn protestation of fidelity.

Although Augustus considered a military force as the firmest foundation, he wisely rejected it, as a very odious instrument of government. It was more agreeable to his temper, as well as to his policy, to reign under the venerable names of ancient magistracy, and artfully to collect, in his own person, all the scattered rays of civil jurisdiction. With this view, he permitted the senate to confer upon him, for his life, the powers of the consular and tribunitian offices, which were, in the same manner, continued to all his successors. The consuls had succeeded to the kings of Rome, and represented the dignity of the state. They superintended the ceremonies of religion, levied and commanded the legions, gave audience to foreign ambassadors, and presided in the assemblies both of the senate and people. The general control of the finances was intrusted to their care; and though they seldom had leisure to administer justice in person, they were considered as the supreme guardians of law, equity, and the public peace. Such was their ordinary jurisdiction; but whenever the senate empowered the first magistrate to consult the safety of the commonwealth, he was raised by that degree above the laws, and exercised, in the defence of liberty, a temporary despotism. The character of the tribunes was, in every respect, different from that of the consuls. The appearance of the former was modest and humble; but their persons were sacred and inviolable. Their force was suited rather for opposition than for action. They were instituted to defend the oppressed, to pardon offences, to arraign the enemies of the people, and, when they judged it necessary, to stop, by a single word, the whole machine of government. As long as the republic subsisted, the dangerous influence, which either the consul or the tribune might derive from their respective jurisdiction, was diminished by several important restrictions. Their authority expired with the year in which they were elected; the former office was divided between two, the latter among ten persons; and, as both in their private and public interest they were averse to each other, their mutual conflicts contributed, for the most part, to strengthen rather than to destroy the balance of the constitution. But when the consular and tribunitian powers were united, when they were vested for life in a single person, when the general of the army was, at the same time, the minister of the senate, and the representative of the Roman people, it was impossible to resist the exercise, nor was it easy to define the limits, of his Imperial prerogative.

To these accumulated honours, the policy of Augustus soon added the splendid as well as important dignities of supreme pontiff, and of censor. By the former he acquired the management of the religion, and by the latter a legal inspection over the manners and fortunes, of the Roman people. If so many distinct and independent powers did not exactly unite with each other, the complaisance of the senate was prepared to supply every deficiency by the most ample and extraordinary concessions. The emperors, as the first ministers of the republic, were exempted from the obligation and penalty of many inconvenient laws: they were authorised to convoke the senate, to make several motions in the same day, to recommend candidates for the honours of the state, to enlarge the bounds of the city, to employ the revenue at their discretion, to declare peace and war, to ratify treaties; and by a most comprehensive clause, they were empowered to execute whatsoever they should judge advantageous to the empire, and agreeable to the majesty of things private or public, human or divine.

When all the various powers of executive government were committed to the *Imperial magistrate*, the ordinary magistrates of the commonwealth languished in obscurity, without vigour, and almost without business. The names and forms of the ancient administration were preserved by Augustus with the most anxious care. The usual number of consuls, prætors, and tribunes, were annually invested with their respective ensigns of office, and continued to discharge some of their least important functions. Those honours still attracted the vain ambition of the Romans; and the emperors themselves, though invested for life with the powers of the consulship, frequently aspired to the title of that annual dignity, which they condescended to share with the most illustrious of their fellow-citizens. In the election of these magistrates, the people, during the reign of Augustus, were permitted to expose all the inconveniences of a wild democracy. That artful prince, instead of discovering the least symptom of impatience, humbly solicited their suffrages for himself or his friends, and scrupulously practised all the duties of an ordinary candidate. But we may venture to ascribe to his councils, the first measure of the succeeding reign, by which the elections were transferred to the senate. The assemblies of the people were for ever abolished, and the emperors were delivered from a dangerous multitude, who, without restoring liberty, might have disturbed, and perhaps endangered, the established government.

The face of the court corresponded with the forms of the administration. The emperors, if we except those tyrants whose capricious folly violated every law of nature and decency, disdained that pomp and ceremony which might offend their countrymen, but could add nothing to their real power. In all the offices of life they affected to confound themselves with their subjects, and maintained with them an equal intercourse of visits and entertainments. Their habit, their palace, their table, were suited only to the rank of an opulent senator. Their family, however numerous or splendid, was composed entirely of their domestic slaves and freedmen. Augustus or Trajan would have blushed at employing the meanest of the Romans in those menial offices, which, in the household and bed-chamber of a limited monarch, are so eagerly solicited by the proudest nobles of Britain.

The deification of the emperors is the only instance in which they departed from their accustomed prudence and modesty. The Asiatic Greeks were the first inventors, the successors of Alexander the first objects, of this servile and impious mode of adulation. It was easily transferred from the kings to the governors of Asia; and the Roman magistrates very frequently were adored as provincial deities, with the pomp of altars and temples, of festivals and sacrifices. It was natural that the emperors should not refuse what the proconsuls had accepted: and the divine honours which both the one and the other received from the provinces, attested rather the despotism than the servitude of Rome. But the conquerors soon imitated the vanquished nations in the arts of flattery; and the imperious spirit of the first Cæsar too easily consented to assume, during his lifetime, a place among the tutelar deities of Rome. The milder temper of his successor declined so dangerous an ambition, which was never afterwards revived, except by the madness of Caligula and Domitian. Augustus permitted indeed some of the provincial cities to erect temples to his honour, on condition that they should associate the worship of Rome with that of the sovereign; he tolerated private superstition, of which he might be the object; but he contented himself with being revered by the senate and people in his human character, and wisely left to his successor the care of his public deification. A regular custom was introduced, that on the decease of every emperor who had neither lived nor died like a tyrant, the senate by a solemn decree should place him in the number of the gods: and the ceremonies of his Apotheosis were blended with those of his funeral. This legal, and, as it should seem, injudicious profanation, so abhorrent to our stricter principles, was received with a faint murmur, by the easy nature of polytheism; but it was received as an institution, not of religion, but of policy. We should disgrace the virtues of the Antonines, by comparing them with the vices of Hercules or Jupiter. Even the character of Cæsar or Augustus were far superior to those of the popular deities. But it was the misfortune of the former to live in an enlightened age, and their actions were too faithfully recorded to admit of such a mixture of fable and mystery, as the devotion of the vulgar requires. As soon as their divinity was established by law, it sunk into oblivion, without contributing either to their own fame, or to the dignity of succeeding princes.

The tender respect of Augustus for a free constitution which he had destroyed, can only be explained by an attentive consideration of the character of that subtle tyrant. A cool head, an unfeeling heart, and a cowardly disposition, prompted him, at the age of nineteen, to assume the mask of hypocrisy, which he never afterwards laid aside. With the same hand, and probably with the same temper, he signed the proscription of Cicero, and the pardon of Cinna. His virtues, and even his vices, were artificial; and according to the various dictates of his interest, he was at first the enemy, and at last the father, of the Roman world. When he framed the artful system of the Imperial authority, his moderation was inspired by his fears. He wished to deceive the people by an image of civil liberty, and the armies by an image of civil government.

During a long period of two hundred and twenty years, from the establishment of this artful system to the death of Commodus, the dangers inherent to a military government were, in a great measure, suspended. The soldiers were seldom roused to that fatal sense of their own strength, and of the weakness of the civil authority, which was, before and afterwards, productive of such dreadful calamities. Caligula and Domitian were assassinated in their palace by their own domestics; the convulsions which agitated Rome on the death of the former, were confined to the walls of the city. But Nero involved the whole empire in his ruin. In the space of eighteen months, four princes perished by the sword; and the Roman world was shaken by the fury of the contending armies. Excepting only this short, though violent, eruption of military licence, the two centuries from Augustus to Commodus passed away unstained with civil blood, and undisturbed by revolutions. The emperor was elected by *the authority of the senate*, and *the consent of the soldiers*. The legions respected their oath of fidelity; and it requires a minute inspection of the Roman annals to discover three inconsiderable rebellions, which were all suppressed in a few months, and without even the hazard of a battle.

In elective monarchies, the vacancy of the throne is a moment big with danger and mischief. The Roman emperors, desirous to spare the legions that interval of suspense, and the temptation of an irregular choice, invested their designed successor with so large a share of present power, as should enable him, after their decease, to assume the remainder, without suffering the empire to perceive the change of masters. Thus Augustus, after all his fairer prospects had been snatched from him by untimely deaths rested his last hopes on Tiberius, obtained for his adopted son the censorial and tribunitian powers, and dictated a law by which the future prince was invested with an authority equal to his own, over the provinces and the armies. Thus Vespasian subdued the generous mind of his eldest son. Titus was adored by the eastern legions, which, under his command, had recently achieved the conquest of Judæa. His power was dreaded, and, as his virtues were clouded by the intemperance of youth, his designs were suspected. Instead of listening to such unworthy suspicions, the prudent monarch associated Titus to the full powers of the Imperial dignity; and the grateful son ever approved himself the humble and faithful minister of so indulgent a father.

The good sense of Vespasian engaged him indeed to embrace every measure that might confirm his recent and precarious elevation. The military oath, and the fidelity of the troops, had been consecrated by the habits of an hundred years, to the name and family of the Cæsars; and although that family had been continued only by the fictitious rite of adoption, the Romans still revered, in the person of Nero, the grandson of Germanicus, and the lineal successor of Augustus. It was not without reluctance and remorse that the Prætorian Guards had been persuaded to abandon the cause of the tyrant. The rapid downfall of Galba, Otho, and Vitellius, taught the armies to consider the emperors as the creatures of *their* will, and the instruments of *their* licence. The birth of Vespasian was mean; his grandfather had been a private soldier, his father a petty officer of the revenue; his own merit had raised him, in an advanced age, to the empire; but his merit was rather useful, than shining, and his virtues were disgraced by a strict and even sordid parsimony. Such a prince consulted his true interest by the association of a son, whose more splendid and amiable character might turn the public attention from the obscure origin to the future glories of the Flavian house. Under the mild administration of Titus, the Roman world enjoyed a transient felicity, and his beloved memory served to protect, above fifteen years, the vices of his brother Domitian.

Nerva had scarcely accepted the purple from the assassins of Domitian before he discovered that his feeble age was unable to stem the torrent of public disorders, which had multiplied under the long tyranny of his predecessor. His mild disposition was respected by the good; but the degenerate Romans required a more vigorous character, whose justice should strike terror into the guilty. Though he had several relations, he fixed his choice on a stranger. He adopted Trajan, then about forty years of age, and who commanded a powerful army in the Lower Germany; and immediately, by a decree of the senate, declared him his colleague and successor in the empire. It is sincerely to be lamented, that whilst we are fatigued with the disgustful relation of Nero's crimes and follies, we are reduced to collect the actions of Trajan from the glimmerings of an abridgment, or the doubtful light of a panegyric. There remains, however, one panegyric far removed beyond the suspicion of flattery. Above two hundred and fifty years after the death of Trajan, the senate, in pouring out the customary acclamations on the accession of a new emperor, wished that he might surpass the felicity of Augustus, and the virtue of Trajan.

We may readily believe, that the father of his country hesitated whether he ought to intrust the various and doubtful character of his kinsman Hadrian with sovereign power. In his last moments, the arts of the empress Plotina either fixed the irresolution of Trajan, or boldly supposed a fictitious adoption; the truth of which could not be safely disputed, and Hadrian was peaceably acknowledged as his lawful successor. Under his reign, as has been already mentioned, the empire flourished in peace and prosperity. He encouraged the arts, reformed the laws, asserted military discipline, and visited all his provinces in person. His vast and active genius was equally suited to the most enlarged views, and the minute details of civil policy. But the ruling passions of his soul were curiosity and vanity. As they prevailed, and as they were attracted by different objects, Hadrian was, by turns, an excellent prince, a ridiculous sophist, and a jealous tyrant. The general tenor of his conduct deserved praise for its equity and moderation. Yet in the first days of his reign, he put to death four consular senators, his personal enemies, and men who had been judged worthy of empire; and the tediousness of a painful illness rendered him, at last, peevish and cruel. The senate doubted whether they should pronounce him a god or a tyrant; and the honours decreed to his memory were granted to the prayers of the pious Antoninus.

The caprice of Hadrian influenced his choice of a successor. After revolving in his mind several men of distinguished merit, whom he esteemed and hated, he adopted Ælius Verus, a gay and voluptuous nobleman, recommended by uncommon beauty to the lover of Antoninus. But while Hadrian was delighting himself with his own applause, and the acclamations of the soldiers, whose consent had been secured by an immense donative, the new Cæsar was ravished from his embraces by an untimely death. He left only one son. Hadrian commended the boy to the gratitude of the Antonines. He was adopted by Pius; and, on the accession of Marcus, was invested with an equal share of sovereign power. Among the many vices of this younger Verus he possessed one virtue; a dutiful reverence for his wiser colleague, to whom he willingly abandoned the ruder cares of empire. The philosophic emperor dissembled his follies, lamented his early death, and cast a decent veil over his memory.

As soon as Hadrian's passion was either gratified or disappointed, he resolved to deserve the thanks of posterity, by placing the most exalted merit on the Roman throne. His discerning eye easily discovered a senator about fifty years of age, blameless in all the offices of life, and a youth of about seventeen, whose riper years opened the fair prospect of every virtue: the elder of these was declared the son and successor of Hadrian, on condition, however, that he himself should immediately adopt the younger. The two Antonines (for it is of them that we are now speaking) governed the Roman world forty-two years, with the same invariable spirit of wisdom and virtue. Although Pius had two sons, he preferred the welfare of Rome to the interest of his family, gave his daughter Faustina in marriage to young Marcus, obtained from the senate the tribunitian and proconsular powers, and with a noble disdain, or rather ignorance of jealousy, associated him to all the labours of government. Marcus, on the other hand, revered the character of his benefactor, loved him as a parent, obeyed him as his sovereign, and, after he was no more, regulated his own administration by the example and maxims of his predecessor. Their united reigns are possibly the only period of history in which the happiness of a great people was the sole object of government.

Titus Antoninus Pius has been justly denominated a second Numa. The same love of religion, justice, and peace, was the distinguishing characteristic of both princes. But the situation of the latter opened a much larger field for the exercise of those virtues. Numa could only prevent a few neighbouring villages from plundering each other's harvests. Antoninus diffused order and tranquillity over the greatest part of the earth. His reign is marked by the rare advantage of furnishing very few materials for history; which is, indeed, little more than the register of the crimes, follies, and misfortunes of mankind. In private life, he was an amiable as well as a good man. The native simplicity of his virtue was a stranger to vanity or affectation. He enjoyed with moderation the conveniences of his fortune, and the innocent pleasures of society: and the benevolence of his soul displayed itself in a cheerful serenity of temper.

The virtue of Marcus Aurelius Antoninus was of a severer and more laborious kind. It was the well-earned harvest of many a learned conference, of many a patient lecture, and many a midnight lucubration. At the age of twelve years he embraced the rigid system of the Stoics, which taught him to submit his body to his mind, his passions to his reason; to consider virtue as the only good, vice as the only evil, all things external as things indifferent. His meditations, composed in the tumult of a camp, are still extant; and he even condescended to give lessons of philosophy in a more public manner than was perhaps consistent with the modesty of a sage, or the dignity of an emperor. But his life was the noblest commentary on the precepts of Zeno. He was severe to himself, indulgent to the imperfections of others, just and beneficent to all mankind. He regretted that Avidius Cassius, who excited a rebellion in Syria, had disappointed him, by a voluntary death, of the pleasure of converting an enemy into a friend; and he justified the sincerity of that sentiment, by moderating the zeal of the senate against the adherents of the traitor. War he detested, as the disgrace and calamity of human nature; but when the necessity of a just defence called upon him to take up arms, he readily exposed his person to eight winter campaigns on the frozen banks of the Danube, the severity of which was at last fatal to the weakness of his constitution. His memory was revered by a grateful posterity, and above a century after his death, many persons preserved the image of Marcus Antoninus, among those of their household gods.

If a man were called to fix the period in the history of the world, during which the condition of the human race was most happy and prosperous, he would, without hesitation, name that which elapsed from the death of Domitian to the accession of Commodus. The vast extent of the Roman empire was governed by absolute power, under the guidance of virtue and wisdom. The armies were restrained by the firm but gentle hand of four successive emperors, whose characters and authority commanded involuntary respect.

The forms of the civil administration were carefully preserved by Nerva, Trajan, Hadrian, and the Antonines, who delighted in the image of liberty, and were pleased with considering themselves as the accountable ministers of the laws. Such princes deserved the honour of restoring the republic had the Romans of their days been capable of enjoying a rational freedom.

The labours of these monarchs were overpaid by the immense reward that inseparably waited on their success; by the honest pride of virtue, and by the exquisite delight of beholding the general happiness of which they were the authors. A just, but melancholy reflection embittered, however, the noblest of human enjoyments. They must often have recollected the instability of a happiness which depended on the character of a single man. The fatal moment was perhaps approaching, when some licentious youth, or some jealous tyrant, would abuse, to the destruction, that absolute power which they had exerted for the benefit of their people. The ideal restraints of the senate and the laws might serve to display the virtues, but could never correct the vices, of the emperor. The military force was a blind and irresistible instrument of oppression; and the corruption of Roman manners would always supply flatterers eager to applaud, and ministers prepared to serve the fear or the avarice, the lust or the cruelty, of their masters.

These gloomy apprehensions had been already justified by the experience of the Romans. The annals of the emperors exhibit a strong and various picture of human nature, which we should vainly seek among the mixed and doubtful characters of modern history. In the conduct of those monarchs we may trace the utmost lines of vice and virtue; the most exalted perfection, and the meanest degeneracy of our own species. The golden age of Trajan and the Antonines had been preceded by an age of iron. It is almost superfluous to enumerate the unworthy successors of Augustus. Their unparalleled vices, and the splendid theatre on which they were acted, have saved them from oblivion. The dark unrelenting Tiberius, the furious Caligula, the feeble Claudius, the profligate and cruel Nero, the beastly Vitellius, and the timid inhuman Domitian, are condemned to everlasting infamy. During fourscore years (excepting only the short and doubtful respite of Vespasian's reign) Rome groaned beneath an unremitting tyranny, which exterminated the ancient families of the republic, and was fatal to almost every virtue, and every talent, that arose in that unhappy period.

The division of Europe into a number of independent states, connected, however, with each other, by the general resemblance of religion, language, and manners, is productive of the most beneficial consequences to the liberty of mankind. A modern tyrant, who should find no resistance either in his own breast, or in his people, would soon experience a gentle restraint from the example of his equals, the dread of present censure, the advice of his allies, and the apprehension of his enemies. The object of his displeasure, escaping from the narrow limits of his dominions, would easily obtain, in a happier climate, a secure refuge, a new fortune adequate to his merit, the freedom of complaint, and perhaps the means of revenge. But the empire of the Romans filled the world, and when that empire fell into the hands of a single person, the world became a safe and dreary prison for his enemies. The slave of Imperial despotism, whether he was condemned to drag his gilded chain in Rome and the senate, or to wear out a life of exile on the barren rock of Seriphus, or the frozen banks of the Danube, expected his fate in silent despair. To resist was fatal, and it was impossible to fly. On every side he was encompassed with a vast extent of sea and land, which he could never hope to traverse without being discovered, seized, and restored to his irritated master. Beyond the frontiers, his anxious view could discover nothing, except the ocean, inhospitable deserts, hostile tribes of barbarians, of fierce manners and unknown language, or dependent kings, who would gladly purchase the emperor's protection by the sacrifice of an obnoxious fugitive. "Wherever you are," said Cicero to the exiled Marcellus, "remember that you are equally within the power of the conqueror."

IV

(180–193 A.D.) THE CRUELTY, FOLLIES, AND MURDER OF COMMODUS—ELECTION OF PERTINAX—HIS ATTEMPTS TO REFORM THE STATE—HIS ASSASSINATION BY THE PRÆTORIAN GUARDS

The mildness of Marcus, which the rigid discipline of the Stoics was unable to eradicate, formed, at the same time, the most amiable, and the only defective, part of his character. His excellent understanding was often deceived by the unsuspecting goodness of his heart. Artful men, who study the passions of princes, and conceal their own, approached his person in the disguise of philosophic sanctity, and acquired riches and honours by affecting to despise them. His excessive indulgence to his brother, his wife, and his son, exceeded the bounds of private virtue, and became a public injury, by the example and consequences of their vices.

Faustina, the daughter of Pius and the wife of Marcus, has been as much celebrated for her gallantries as for her beauty. The grave simplicity of the philosopher was ill calculated to engage her wanton levity, or to fix that unbounded passion for variety, which often discovered personal merit in the meanest of mankind. The Cupid of the ancients was, in general, a very sensual deity; and the amours of an empress, as they exact on her side the plainest advances, are seldom susceptible of much sentimental delicacy. Marcus was the only man in the empire who seemed ignorant or insensible of the irregularities of Faustina; which, according to the prejudices of every age, reflected some disgrace on the injured husband. He promoted several of her lovers to posts of honour and profit, and during a connection of thirty years, invariably gave her proofs of the most tender confidence, and of a respect which ended not with her life. In his Meditations, he thanks the gods, who had bestowed on him a wife, so faithful, so gentle, and of such a wonderful simplicity of manners. The obsequious senate, at his earnest request, declared her a goddess. She was represented in her temples, with the attributes of Juno, Venus, and Ceres; and it was decreed, that on the day of their nuptials, the youth of either sex should pay their vows before the altar of their chaste patroness.

The monstrous vices of the son have cast a shade on the purity of the father's virtues. It has been objected to Marcus, that he sacrificed the happiness of millions to a fond partiality for a worthless boy; and that he chose a successor in his own family, rather than in the republic. Nothing, however, was neglected by the anxious father, and by the men of virtue and learning whom he summoned to his assistance, to expand the narrow mind of young Commodus, to correct his growing vices, and to render him worthy of the throne, for which he was designed. But the power of instruction is seldom of much efficacy, except in those happy dispositions where it is almost superfluous. The distasteful lesson of a grave philosopher was in a moment obliterated by the whispers of a profligate favourite; and Marcus himself blasted the fruits of this laboured education, by admitting his son, at the age of fourteen or fifteen, to a full participation of the Imperial power. He lived but four years afterwards; but he lived long enough to repent a rash measure, which raised the impetuous youth above the restraint of reason and authority.

Most of the crimes which disturb the internal peace of society are produced by the restraints which the necessary, but unequal, laws of property have imposed on the appetites of mankind, by confining to a few the possession of those objects that are coveted by many. Of all our passions and appetites, the love of power is of the most imperious and unsociable nature, since the pride of one man requires the submission of the multitude. In the tumult of civil discord, the laws of society lose their force, and their place is seldom supplied by those of humanity. The ardour of contention, the pride of victory, the despair of success, the memory of past injuries, and the fear of future dangers, all contribute to inflame the mind, and to silence the voice of pity. From such motives almost every page of history has been stained with civil blood; but these motives will not account for the unprovoked cruelties of Commodus, who had nothing to wish and everything to enjoy. The beloved son of Marcus succeeded (A.D. 180) to his father, amidst the acclamations of the senate and armies, and when he ascended the throne the happy youth saw round him neither competitor to remove nor enemies to punish. In this calm elevated station it was surely natural that he should prefer the love of mankind to their detestation, the mild glories of his five predecessors, to the ignominious fate of Nero and Domitian.

Yet Commodus was not, as he has been represented, a tiger born with an insatiate thirst of human blood, and capable, from his infancy, of the most inhuman actions. Nature had formed him of a weak, rather than a wicked, disposition. His simplicity and timidity rendered him the slave of his attendants, who gradually corrupted his mind. His cruelty, which at first obeyed the dictates of others, degenerated into habit, and at length became the ruling passion of his soul.

Upon the death of his father, Commodus found himself embarrassed with the command of a great army, and the conduct of a difficult war against the Quadi and Marcomanni. The servile and profligate youths whom Marcus had banished, soon regained their station and influence about the new emperor. They exaggerated the hardships and dangers of a campaign in the wild countries beyond the Danube; and they assured the indolent prince, that the terror of his name and the arms of his lieutenants would be sufficient to complete the conquest of the dismayed barbarians; or to impose such conditions as were more advantageous than any conquest. By a dexterous application to his sensual appetites, they compared the tranquillity, the splendour, the refined pleasures of Rome, with the tumult of a Pannonian camp, which afforded neither leisure nor materials for luxury. Commodus listened to the pleasing advice; but whilst he hesitated between his own inclination and the awe which he still retained for his father's counsellors, the summer insensibly elapsed, and his triumphal entry into the capital was deferred till the autumn. His graceful person, popular address, and imagined virtues, attracted the public favour; the honourable peace which he had recently granted to the barbarians diffused an universal joy; his impatience to revisit Rome was fondly ascribed to the love of his country; and his dissolute course of amusements was faintly condemned in a prince of nineteen years of age.

During the three first years of his reign, the forms, and even the spirit, of the old administration were maintained by those faithful counsellors, to whom Marcus had recommended his son, and for whose wisdom and integrity Commodus still entertained a reluctant esteem. The young prince and his profligate favourites revelled in all the licence of sovereign power; but his hands were yet unstained with blood; and he had even displayed a generosity of sentiment, which might perhaps have ripened into solid virtue. A fatal incident decided his fluctuating character.

One evening (A.D. 183), as the emperor was returning to the palace through a dark and narrow portico in the amphitheatre, an assassin, who waited his passage, rushed upon him with a drawn sword, loudly exclaiming, *The senate sends you this.* The menace prevented the deed; the assassin was seized by the guards, and immediately revealed the authors of the conspiracy. It had been formed, not in the state, but within the walls of the palace. Lucilla, the emperor's sister, and widow of Lucius Verus, impatient of the second rank, and jealous of the reigning empress, had armed the murderer against her brother's life. She had not ventured to communicate the black design to her second husband Claudius Pompeianus, a senator of distinguished merit and unshaken loyalty; but among the crowd of her lovers (for she imitated the manners of Faustina), she found men of desperate fortunes and wild ambition, who were prepared to serve her more violent as well as her tender passions. The conspirators experienced the rigour of justice, and the abandoned princess was punished, first with exile, and afterwards with death.

But the words of the assassin sunk deep into the mind of Commodus, and left an indelible impression of fear and hatred against the whole body of the senate. Those whom he had dreaded as importunate ministers, he now suspected as secret enemies. The Delators, a race of men discouraged, and almost extinguished, under the former reigns, again became formidable, as soon as they discovered that the emperor was desirous of finding disaffection and treason in the senate. That assembly, whom Marcus had ever considered as the great council of the nation, was composed of the most distinguished of the Romans; and distinction of every kind soon became criminal. The possession of wealth stimulated the diligence of the informers; rigid virtue implied a tacit censure of the irregularities of Commodus; important services implied a dangerous superiority of merit; and the friendship of the father always insured the aversion of the son. Suspicion was equivalent to proof; trial to condemnation. The execution of a considerable senator was attended with the death of all who might lament or revenge his fate; and when Commodus had once tasted human blood, he became incapable of pity or remorse.

Pestilence and famine contributed to fill up the measure of the calamities of Rome. The first could be only imputed to the just indignation of the gods; but (A.D. 189) a monopoly of corn, supported by the riches and power of the minister, was considered as the immediate cause of the second. The popular discontent, after it had long circulated in whispers, broke out in the assembled circus. The people quitted their favourite amusements for the more delicious pleasure of revenge, rushed in crowds towards a palace in the suburbs, one of the emperor's retirements, and demanded, with angry clamours, the head of the public enemy. Cleander, who commanded the Prætorian guards, ordered a body of cavalry to sally forth, and disperse the seditious multitude. The multitude fled with precipitation towards the city; several were slain, and many more were trampled to death: but when the cavalry entered the streets, their pursuit was checked by a shower of stones and darts from the roofs and windows of the houses. The foot guards who had been long jealous of the prerogatives and insolence of the Prætorian cavalry, embraced the party of the people. The tumult became a regular engagement, and threatened a general massacre. The Prætorians, at length, gave way, oppressed with numbers; and the tide of popular fury returned with redoubled violence against the gates of the palace, where Commodus lay, dissolved in luxury, and alone unconscious of the civil war. It was death to approach his person with the unwelcome news. He would have perished in this supine security, had not two women, his elder sister Fadilla, and Marcia, the most favoured of his concubines, ventured to break into his presence. Bathed in tears, and with dishevelled hair, they threw themselves at his feet; and with all the pressing eloquence of fear, discovered to the affrighted emperor, the crimes of the minister, the rage of the people, and the impending ruin, which, in a few minutes, would burst over his palace and person. Commodus started from his dream of pleasure, and commanded that the head of Cleander should be thrown out to the people. The desired spectacle instantly appeased the tumult; and the son of Marcus might even yet have regained the affection and confidence of his outraged subjects.

But every sentiment of virtue and humanity was extinct in the mind of Commodus. Whilst he thus abandoned the reins of empire to these unworthy favourites, he valued nothing in sovereign power, except the unbounded licence of indulging his sensual appetites. His hours were spent in a seraglio of three hundred beautiful women, and as many boys, of every rank, and of every province; and, wherever the arts of seduction proved ineffectual, the brutal lover had recourse to violence. The ancient historians have expatiated on these abandoned scenes of prostitution, which scorned every restraint of nature or modesty; but it would not be easy to translate their too faithful descriptions into the decency of modern language. The intervals of lust were filled up with the basest amusements. The influence of a polite age, and the labour of an attentive education, had never been able to infuse into his rude and brutish mind the least tincture of learning; and he was the first of the Roman emperors totally devoid of taste for the pleasures of the understanding. Nero himself excelled, or affected to excel, in the elegant arts of music and poetry; nor should we despise his pursuits had he not converted the pleasing relaxation of a leisure hour into the serious business and ambition of his life. But Commodus, from his earliest infancy, discovered an aversion to whatever was rational or liberal, and a fond attachment to the amusements of the populace; the sports of the circus and amphitheatre, the combats of gladiators, and the hunting of wild beasts. The masters in every branch of learning, whom Marcus provided for his son, were heard with inattention and disgust; whilst the Moors and Parthians, who taught him to dart the javelin and to shoot with the bow, found a disciple who delighted in his application, and soon equalled the most skilful of his instructors, in the steadiness of the eye, and the dexterity of the hand.

The servile crowd, whose fortune depended on their master's vices, applauded these ignoble pursuits. The perfidious voice of flattery reminded him that by exploits of the same nature, by the defeat of the Nemæn lion, and the slaughter of the wild boar of Erymanthus, the Grecian Hercules had acquired a place among the gods, and an immortal memory among men. They only forgot to observe, that, in the first ages of society, when the fiercer animals often dispute with man the possession of an unsettled country, a successful war against those savages is one of the most innocent and beneficial labours of heroism. In the civilised state of the Roman empire, the wild beasts had long since retired from the face of man, and the neighbourhood of populous cities. To surprise them in their solitary haunts, and to transport them to Rome, that they might be slain in pomp by the hand of an emperor, was an enterprise equally ridiculous for the prince, and oppressive for the people. Ignorant of these distinctions, Commodus eagerly embraced the glorious resemblance, and styled himself (as we still read on his medals) the *Roman Hercules*. The club and the lion's hide were placed by the side of the throne, amongst the ensigns of sovereignty; and statues were erected, in which Commodus was represented in the character, and with the attributes, of the god, whose valour and dexterity he endeavoured to emulate in the daily course of his ferocious amusements.

Elated with these praises, which gradually extinguished the innate sense of shame, Commodus resolved to exhibit, before the eyes of the Roman people, those exercises, which till then he had decently confined within the walls of his palace, and to the presence of a few favourites. On the appointed day, the various motives of flattery, fear, and curiosity, attracted to the amphitheatre an innumerable multitude of spectators: and some degree of applause was deservedly bestowed on the uncommon skill of the Imperial performer. Whether he aimed at the head or heart of the animal, the wound was alike certain and mortal. With arrows, whose point was shaped into the form of a crescent, Commodus often intercepted the rapid career, and cut asunder the long bony neck of the ostrich. A panther was let loose; and the archer waited till he had leaped upon a trembling malefactor. In the same instant the shaft flew, the beast dropped dead, and the man remained unhurt. The dens of the amphitheatre disgorged at once a hundred lions; a hundred darts from the unerring hand of Commodus laid them dead as they ran raging around the *Arena*. Neither the huge bulk of the elephant, nor the scaly hide of the rhinoceros, could defend them from his stroke. Ethiopia and India yielded their most extraordinary productions; and several animals were slain in the amphitheatre, which had been seen only in the representations of art, or perhaps of fancy. In all these exhibitions, the securest precautions were used to protect the person of the Roman Hercules from the desperate spring of any savage; who might possibly disregard the dignity of the emperor, and the sanctity of the god.

But the meanest of the populace were affected with shame and indignation when they beheld their sovereign enter the lists as a gladiator, and glory in a profession which the laws and manners of the Romans had branded with the justest note of infamy. He chose the habit and arms of the *Secutor*, whose combat with the *Retiarius* formed one of the most lively scenes in the bloody sports of the amphitheatre. The *Secutor* was armed with an helmet, sword, and buckler; his naked antagonist had only a large net and a trident; with the one he endeavoured to entangle, with the other to dispatch, his enemy. If he missed the first throw, he was obliged to fly from the pursuit of the *Secutor,* till he had prepared his net for a second cast. The emperor fought in this character seven hundred and thirty-five times. These glorious achievements were carefully recorded in the public acts of the empire; and that he might omit no circumstance of infamy, he received from the common fund of gladiators, a stipend so exorbitant, that it became a new and most ignominious tax upon the Roman people. It may be easily supposed that in these engagements the master of the world was always successful: in the amphitheatre his victories were not often sanguinary; but when he exercised his skill in the school of gladiators, or his own palace, his wretched antagonists were frequently honoured with a mortal wound from the hand of Commodus, and obliged to seal their flattery with their blood. He now disdained the appellation of Hercules. The name of Paulus, a celebrated Secutor, was the only one which delighted his ear. It was inscribed on his colossal statues, and repeated in the redoubled acclamations of the mournful and applauding senate. Claudius Pompeianus, the virtuous husband of Lucilla, was the only senator who asserted the honour of his rank. As a father, he permitted his sons to consult their safety by attending the amphitheatre. As a Roman, he declared, that his own life was in the emperor's hands, but that he would never behold the son of Marcus prostituting his person and dignity. Notwithstanding his manly resolution, Pompeianus escaped the resentment of the tyrant, and with his honour had the good fortune to preserve his life.

Commodus had now attained the summit of vice and infamy. Amidst the acclamations of a flattering court, he was unable to disguise, from himself, that he had deserved the contempt and hatred of every man of sense and virtue in his empire. His ferocious spirit was irritated by the consciousness of that hatred, by the envy of every kind of merit, by the just apprehension of danger, and by the habit of slaughter, which he contracted in his daily amusements. History has preserved a long list of consular senators sacrificed to his wanton suspicion, which sought out, with peculiar anxiety, those unfortunate persons connected, however remotely, with the family of the Antonines, without sparing even the ministers of his crimes or pleasures. His cruelty proved at last fatal to himself. He had shed with impunity the noblest blood of Rome: he perished as soon as he was dreaded by his own domestics. Marcia his favourite concubine, Eclectus his chamberlain, and Lætus his Prætorian præfect, alarmed by the fate of their companions and predecessors, resolved to prevent the destruction which every hour hung over their heads, either from the mad caprice of the tyrant, or the sudden indignation of the people. Marcia seized the occasion of presenting a draught of wine to her lover, after he had fatigued himself with hunting some wild beasts. Commodus retired to sleep; but whilst he was labouring with the effects of poison and drunkenness, a robust youth, by profession a wrestler, entered his chamber, and strangled him without resistance. The body was secretly conveyed out of the palace, before the least suspicion was entertained in the city, or even in the court, of the emperor's death. Such was the fate of the son of Marcus, and so easy was it to destroy a hated tyrant, who, by the artificial powers of government, had oppressed, during thirteen years, so many millions of subjects, each of whom was equal to their master in personal strength and personal abilities.

The measures of the conspirators were conducted with the deliberate coolness and celerity which the greatness of the occasion required. They resolved instantly to fill the vacant throne with an emperor whose character would justify and maintain the action that had been committed. They fixed on Pertinax, præfect of the city, an ancient senator of consular rank, whose conspicuous merit had broke through the obscurity of his birth, and raised him to the first honours of the state. He had successively governed most of the provinces of the empire; and in all his great employments, military as well as civil, he had uniformly distinguished himself by the firmness, the prudence, and the integrity of his conduct. He now remained almost alone of the friends and ministers of Marcus; and when, at a late hour of the night, he was awakened with the news, that the chamberlain and the præfect were at his door, he received them with intrepid resignation, and desired they would execute their master's orders. Instead of death, they offered him the throne of the Roman world. During some moments he distrusted their intentions and assurances. Convinced at length of the death of Commodus, he accepted the purple with a sincere reluctance, the natural effect of his knowledge both of the duties and of the dangers of the supreme rank.

Lætus conducted without delay his new emperor to the camp of the Prætorians, diffusing at the same time through the city a seasonable report that Commodus died suddenly of an apoplexy; and that the virtuous Pertinax had *already* succeeded to the throne. The guards were rather surprised than pleased with the suspicious death of a prince whose indulgence and liberality they alone had experienced; but the emergency of the occasion, the authority of their præfect, the reputation of Pertinax, and the clamours of the people, obliged them to stifle their secret discontents, to accept the donative promised of the new emperor, to swear allegiance to him, and with joyful acclamations and laurels in their hands to conduct him to the senate-house, that the military consent might be ratified by the civil authority.

This important night was now far spent; with the dawn of day, and (A.D. 193, 1st January) the commencement of the new year, the senators expected a summons to attend an ignominious ceremony. In spite of all remonstrances, even of those of his creatures, who yet preserved any regard for prudence or decency, Commodus had resolved to pass the night in the gladiators' school, and from thence to take possession of the consulship, in the habit and with the attendance of that infamous crew. On a sudden, before the break of day, the senate was called together in the temple of Concord, to meet the guards, and to ratify the election of a new emperor. For a few minutes they sat in silent suspense, doubtful of their unexpected deliverance, and suspicious of the cruel artifices of Commodus; but when at length they were assured that the tyrant was no more, they resigned themselves to all the transports of joy and indignation. Pertinax, who modestly represented the meanness of his extraction, and pointed out several noble senators more deserving than himself of the empire, was constrained by their dutiful violence to ascend the throne, and received all the titles of Imperial power, confirmed by the most sincere vows of fidelity. The memory of Commodus was branded with eternal infamy. The names of tyrant, of gladiator, of public enemy, resounded in every corner of the house. They decreed in tumultuous votes, that his honours should be reversed, his titles erased from the public monuments, his statues thrown down, his body dragged with a hook into the stripping-room of the gladiators, to satiate the public fury; and they expressed some indignation against those officious servants who had already presumed to screen his remains from the justice of the senate. But Pertinax could not refuse those last rites to the memory of Marcus, and the tears of his first protector Claudius Pompeianus, who lamented the cruel fate of his brother-in-law, and lamented still more that he had deserved it.

These effusions of impotent rage against a dead emperor, whom the senate had flattered when alive with the most abject servility, betrayed a just but ungenerous spirit of revenge. The legality of these decrees was however supported by the principles of the Imperial constitution. To censure, to depose, or to punish with death, the first magistrate of the republic, who had abused his delegated trust, was the ancient and undoubted prerogative of the Roman senate; but that feeble assembly was obliged to content itself with inflicting on a fallen tyrant that public justice, from which, during his life and reign, he had been shielded by the strong arm of military despotism.

Pertinax found a nobler way of condemning his predecessor's memory; by the contrast of his own virtues with the vices of Commodus. On the day of his accession, he resigned over to his wife and son his whole private fortune; that they might have no pretence to solicit favours at the expense of the state. He refused to flatter the vanity of the former with the title of Augusta; or to corrupt the inexperienced youth of the latter by the rank of Cæsar. Accurately distinguishing between the duties of a parent and those of a sovereign, he educated his son with a severe simplicity, which, while it gave him no assured prospect of the throne, might in time have rendered him worthy of it. In public, the behaviour of Pertinax was grave and affable. He lived with the virtuous part of the senate (and in a private station, he had been acquainted with the true character of each individual), without either pride or jealousy; considered them as friends and companions, with whom he had shared the dangers of the tyranny, and with whom he wished to enjoy the security of the present time. He very frequently invited them to familiar entertainments, the frugality of which was ridiculed by those who remembered and regretted the luxurious prodigality of Commodus.

To heal, as far as it was possible, the wounds inflicted by the hand of tyranny, was the pleasing, but melancholy, task of Pertinax. The innocent victims, who yet survived, were recalled from exile, released from prison, and restored to the full possession of their honours and fortunes. The unburied bodies of murdered senators (for the cruelty of Commodus endeavoured to extend itself beyond death) were deposited in the sepulchres of their ancestors; their memory was justified, and every consolation was bestowed on their ruined and afflicted families. Among these consolations, one of the most grateful was the punishment of the Delators; the common enemies of their master, of virtue, and of their country. Yet even in the inquisition of these legal assassins, Pertinax proceeded with a steady temper, which gave everything to justice, and nothing to popular prejudice and resentment.

The finances of the state demanded the most vigilant care of
the emperor. Though every measure of injustice and extortion had
been adopted, which could collect the property of the subject into
the coffers of the prince; the rapaciousness of Commodus had
been so very inadequate to his extravagance, that, upon his death,
no more than eight thousand pounds were found in the exhausted
treasury, to defray the current expenses of government, and to
discharge the pressing demand of a liberal donative, which the
new emperor had been obliged to promise to the Prætorian
guards. Yet under these distressed circumstances, Pertinax had the
generous firmness to remit all the oppressive taxes invented by
Commodus, and to cancel all the unjust claims of the treasury;
declaring, in a decree of the senate, "that he was better satisfied
to administer a poor republic with innocence, than to acquire
riches by the ways of tyranny and dishonour." Economy and
industry he considered as the pure and genuine sources of wealth;
and from them he soon derived a copious supply for the public
necessities. The expense of the household was immediately
reduced to one half. All the instruments of luxury, Pertinax
exposed to public auction, gold and silver plate, chariots of a singular construction, a superfluous wardrobe of silk and embroidery,
and a great number of beautiful slaves of both sexes; excepting
only, with attentive humanity, those who were born in a state of
freedom, and had been ravished from the arms of their weeping
parents. At the same time that he obliged the worthless favourites
of the tyrant to resign a part of their ill-gotten wealth, he satisfied
the just creditors of the state, and unexpectedly discharged the
long arrears of honest services. He removed the oppressive restrictions which had been laid upon commerce, and granted all the
uncultivated lands in Italy and the provinces to those who would
improve them; with an exemption from tribute, during the term
of ten years.

Such an uniform conduct had already secured to Pertinax the
noblest reward of a sovereign, the love and esteem of his people.
Those who remembered the virtues of Marcus were happy to contemplate in their new emperor the features of that bright original;
and flattered themselves that they should long enjoy the benign
influence of his administration. A hasty zeal to reform the corrupted
state, accompanied with less prudence than might have been
expected from the years and experience of Pertinax, proved fatal to
himself and to his country. His honest indiscretion united against

him the servile crowd, who found their private benefit in the public disorders, and who preferred the favour of a tyrant to the inexorable equality of the laws.

Amidst the general joy, the sullen and angry countenance of the Prætorian guards betrayed their inward dissatisfaction. They had reluctantly submitted to Pertinax; they dreaded the strictness of the ancient discipline, which he was preparing to restore; and they regretted the licence of the former reign. Their discontents were secretly fomented by Lætus their præfect, who found, when it was too late, that this new emperor would reward a servant, but would not be ruled by a favourite. On the third day of his reign the soldiers seized on a noble senator, with a design to carry him to the camp, and to invest him with the Imperial purple. Instead of being dazzled by the dangerous honour, the affrighted victim escaped from their violence, and took refuge at the feet of Pertinax. A short time afterwards Sosius Falco, one of the consuls of the year, a rash youth, but of an ancient and opulent family, listened to the voice of ambition; and a conspiracy was formed during a short absence of Pertinax, which was crushed by his sudden return to Rome, and his resolute behaviour. Falco was on the point of being justly condemned to death as a public enemy, had he not been saved by the earnest and sincere entreaties of the injured emperor; who conjured the senate, that the purity of his reign might not be stained by the blood even of a guilty senator.

These disappointments served only to irritate the rage of the Prætorian guards. On the twenty-eighth of March, eighty-six days only after the death of Commodus, a general sedition broke out in the camp, which the officers wanted either power or inclination to suppress. Two or three hundred of the most desperate soldiers marched at noon-day, with arms in their hands and fury in their looks, towards the Imperial palace. The gates were thrown open by their companions upon guard; and by the domestics of the old court, who had already formed a secret conspiracy against the life of the too virtuous emperor. On the news of their approach, Pertinax, disdaining either flight or concealment, advanced to meet his assassins, and recalled to their minds his own innocence, and the sanctity of their recent oath. For a few moments they stood in silent suspense, ashamed of their atrocious design, and awed by the vulnerable aspect and majestic firmness of their sovereign, till at length the despair of pardon reviving their fury, a barbarian of the country of Tongres levelled the first blow against Pertinax, who was instantly dispatched with a multitude of wounds. His head separated from his body, and placed on a lance, was carried in triumph to the Prætorian camp, in the sight of a mournful and indignant people, who lamented the unworthy fate of that excellent prince, and the transient blessings of a reign, the memory of which could serve only to aggravate their approaching misfortunes.

V

(193–197 A.D.) PUBLIC SALE OF THE EMPIRE TO DIDIUS JULIANUS BY THE PRÆTORIAN GUARDS—CLODIUS ALBINUS IN BRITAIN, PESCENNIUS NIGER IN SYRIA, AND SEPTIMIUS SEVERUS IN PANNONIA, DECLARE AGAINST THE MURDERERS OF PERTINAX—CIVIL WARS AND VICTORY OF SEVERUS OVER HIS THREE RIVALS—RELAXATION OF DISCIPLINE—NEW MAXIMS OF GOVERNMENT

The Prætorians had violated the sanctity of the throne, by the atrocious murder of Pertinax; they dishonoured the majesty of it, by their subsequent conduct. The camp was without a leader, for even the Præfect Lætus, who had excited the tempest, prudently declined the public indignation. Amidst the wild disorder Sulpicianus, the emperor's father-in-law, and governor of the city, who had been sent to the camp on the first alarm of mutiny, was endeavouring to calm the fury of the multitude, when he was silenced by the clamorous return of the murderers, bearing on a lance the head of Pertinax. Though history has accustomed us to observe every principle and every passion yielding to the imperious dictates of ambition, it is scarcely credible that, in these moments of horror, Sulpicianus should have aspired to ascend a throne polluted with the recent blood of so near a relation, and so excellent a prince. He had already begun to use the only effectual argument, and to treat for the Imperial dignity; but the more prudent of the Prætorians, apprehensive that, in this private contract, they should not obtain a just price for so valuable a commodity, ran out upon the ramparts; and, with a loud voice, proclaimed that the Roman world was to be disposed of to the best bidder by public auction.

This infamous offer, the most insolent excess of military licence, diffused an universal grief, shame, and indignation throughout the city. It reached at length the ears of Didius Julianus, a wealthy senator, who, regardless of the public calamities, was indulging himself in the luxury of the table. His wife and his daughter, his freedmen and his parasites, easily convinced him that he deserved the throne, and earnestly conjured him to embrace so fortunate an opportunity. The vain old man (A.D. 193, March 28th) hastened to the Prætorian camp, where Sulpicianus was still in treaty with the guards; and began to bid against him from the foot of the rampart. The unworthy negotiation was transacted by faithful emissaries, who passed alternately from one candidate to the other, and acquainted each of them with the offers of his rival. Sulpicianus had already promised a donative of five thousand drachms (above one hundred and sixty pounds) to each soldier; when Julian, eager for the prize, rose at once to the sum of six thousand two hundred and fifty drachms, or upwards of two hundred pounds sterling. The gates of the camp were instantly thrown open to the purchaser; he was declared emperor, and received an oath of allegiance from the soldiers, who retained humanity enough to stipulate that he should pardon and forget the competition of Sulpicianus.

It was now incumbent on the Prætorians to fulfil the conditions of the sale. They placed their new sovereign, whom they served and despised, in the centre of their ranks, surrounded him on every side with their shields, and conducted him in close order of battle through the deserted streets of the city. The senate was commanded to assemble; and those who had been the distinguished friends of Pertinax, or the personal enemies of Julian, found it necessary to affect a more than common share of satisfaction at this happy revolution. After Julian had filled the senate-house with armed soldiers, he expatiated on the freedom of his election, his own eminent virtues, and his full assurance of the affections of the senate. The obsequious assembly congratulated their own and the public felicity; engaged their allegiance, and conferred on him all the several branches of the Imperial power. From the senate Julian was conducted, by the same military procession, to take possession of the palace. The first objects that struck his eyes were the abandoned trunk of Pertinax and the frugal entertainment prepared for his supper. The one he viewed with indifference; the other with contempt. A magnificent feast was prepared by his order, and he amused himself till a very late hour with dice, and the performances of Pylades, a celebrated dancer. Yet it was observed, that after the crowd of flatterers dispersed, and left him to darkness, solitude, and terrible reflection, he passed a sleepless night; revolving most probably in his mind his own rash folly, the fate of his virtuous predecessor, and the doubtful and dangerous tenure of an empire, which had not been acquired by merit, but purchased by money.

He had reason to tremble. On the throne of the world he found himself without a friend, and even without an adherent. The guards themselves were ashamed of the prince whom their avarice had persuaded them to accept; nor was there a citizen who did not consider his elevation with horror, as the last insult on the Roman name. The nobility whose conspicuous station and ample possessions exacted the strictest caution, dissembled their sentiments, and met the affected civility of the emperor with smiles of complacency and professions of duty. But the people, secure in their numbers and obscurity, gave a free vent to their passions. The streets and public places of Rome resounded with clamours and imprecations. The enraged multitude affronted the person of Julian, rejected his liberality, and conscious of the impotence of their own resentment, they called aloud on the legions of the frontiers to assert the violated majesty of the Roman empire.

The public discontent was soon diffused from the centre to the frontiers of the empire. The armies of Britain, of Syria, and of Illyricum, lamented the death of Pertinax, in whose company, or under whose command, they had so often fought and conquered. They received with surprise, with indignation, and perhaps with envy, the extraordinary intelligence that the Prætorians had disposed of the empire by public auction; and they sternly refused to ratify the ignominious bargain. Their immediate and unanimous revolt was fatal to Julian, but it was fatal at the same time to the public peace; as the generals of the respective armies, Clodius Albinus, Pescennius Niger, and Septimius Severus, were still more anxious to succeed than to revenge the murdered Pertinax. Their forces were exactly balanced. Each of them was at the head of three legions, with a numerous train of auxiliaries; and however different in their characters, they were all soldiers of experience and capacity.

Clodius Albinus, governor of Britain, surpassed both his competitors in the nobility of his extraction, which he derived from some of the most illustrious names of the old republic. But the branch from whence he claimed his descent was sunk into mean circumstances, and transplanted into a remote province. It is difficult to form a just idea of his true character. Under the philosophic cloak of austerity, he stands accused of concealing most of the vices which degrade human nature. But his accusers are those venal writers who adored the fortune of Severus, and trampled on the ashes of an unsuccessful rival. Virtue, or the appearances of virtue, recommended Albinus to the confidence and good opinion of Marcus; and his preserving with the son the same interest which he had acquired with the father, is a proof, at least that he was possessed of a very flexible disposition. The favour of a tyrant does not always suppose a want of merit in the object of it; he may, without intending it, reward a man of worth and ability, or he may find such a man useful to his own service. It does not appear that Albinus served the son of Marcus, either as the minister of his cruelties, or even as the associate of his pleasures. He was employed in a distant honourable command, when he received a confidential letter from the emperor, acquainting him of the treasonable designs of some discontented generals, and authorising him to declare himself the guardian and successor of the throne, by assuming the title and ensigns of Cæsar. The governor of Britain wisely declined the dangerous honour, which would have marked him for the jealousy, or involved him in the approaching ruin, of Commodus. He courted power by nobler, or, at least, by more specious arts. On a premature report of the death of the emperor, he assembled his troops; and, in an eloquent discourse, deplored the inevitable mischiefs of despotism, described the happiness and glory which their ancestors had enjoyed under the consular government, and declared his firm resolution to reinstate the senate and people in their legal authority. This popular harangue was answered by the loud acclamations of the British legions, and received at Rome with a secret murmur of applause. Safe in the possession of this little world, and in the command of an army less distinguished indeed for discipline than for numbers and valour, Albinus braved the menaces of Commodus, maintained towards Pertinax a stately ambiguous reserve, and instantly declared against the usurpation of Julian. The convulsions of the capital added new weight to his sentiments, or rather to his professions of patriotism. A regard to decency induced him to decline the lofty titles of Augustus and Emperor; and he imitated perhaps the example of Galba, who, on a similar occasion, had styled himself the Lieutenant of the senate and people.

Personal merit alone had raised Pescennius Niger from an obscure birth and station to the government of Syria; a lucrative and important command, which in times of civil confusion gave him a near prospect of the throne. Yet his parts seem to have been better suited to the second than to the first rank; he was an unequal rival, though he might have approved himself an excellent lieutenant, to Severus, who afterwards displayed the greatness of his mind by adopting several useful institutions from a vanquished enemy. In his government, Niger acquired the esteem of the soldiers, and the love of the provincials. His rigid discipline fortified the valour and confirmed the obedience of the former, whilst the voluptuous Syrians were less delighted with the mild firmness of his administration, than with the affability of his manners, and the apparent pleasure with which he attended their frequent and pompous festivals. As soon as the intelligence of the atrocious murder of Pertinax had reached Antioch, the wishes of Asia invited Niger to assume the Imperial purple and revenge his death. The legions of the eastern frontier embraced his cause; the opulent but unarmed provinces from the frontiers of Æthiopia to the Hadriatic cheerfully submitted to his power; and the kings beyond the Tigris and the Euphrates congratulated his election, and offered him their homage and services. The mind of Niger was not capable of receiving this sudden tide of fortune; he flattered himself that his accession would be undisturbed by competition, and unstained by civil blood; and whilst he enjoyed the vain pomp of triumph, he neglected to secure the means of victory. Instead of entering into an effectual negotiation with the powerful armies of the west, whose resolution might decide, or at least must balance, the mighty contest; instead of advancing without delay towards Rome and Italy, where his presence was impatiently expected, Niger trifled away in the luxury of Antioch those irretrievable moments which were diligently improved by the decisive activity of Severus.

The country of Pannonia and Dalmatia, which occupied the space between the Danube and the Hadriatic, was one of the last and most difficult conquests of the Romans. In the defence of national freedom, two hundred thousand of these barbarians had once appeared in the field, alarmed the declining age of Augustus, and exercised the vigilant prudence of Tiberius at the head of the collected force of the empire. The Pannonians yielded at length to the arms and institutions of Rome. Their recent subjection, however, the neighbourhood, and even the mixture, of the uncon-quered tribes, and perhaps the climate, adapted, as it has been observed, to the production of great bodies and slow minds, all con-tributed to preserve some remains of their original ferocity, and under the tame and uniform countenance of Roman provincials, the hardy features of the natives were still to be discerned. Their warlike youth afforded an inexhaustible supply of recruits to the legions stationed on the banks of the Danube, and which, from a perpetual warfare against the Germans and Sarmatians, were deservedly esteemed the best troops in the service.

The Pannonian army was at this time commanded by Septimius Severus, a native of Africa, who, in the gradual ascent of private honours, had concealed his daring ambition, which was never diverted from its steady course by the allurements of pleasure, the apprehension of danger, or the feelings of humanity. On the first news of the murder of Pertinax, he assembled his troops, painted in the most lively colours the crime, the insolence, and the weakness of the Prætorian guards, and animated the legions to arms and to revenge. He concluded (and the peroration was thought extremely eloquent) with promising every soldier about four hundred pounds; an honourable donative, double in value to the infamous bribe with which Julian had purchased the empire. The acclamations of the army immediately saluted Severus with the names of Augustus, Pertinax, and Emperor; and he (A.D. 193, April 13th) thus attained the lofty station to which he was invited, by conscious merit and a long train of dreams and omens, the fruitful offspring either of his superstition or policy.

The new candidate for empire saw and improved the peculiar advantage of his situation. His province extended to the Julian Alps, which gave an easy access into Italy; and he remembered the saying of Augustus, That a Pannonian army might in ten days appear in sight of Rome. By a celerity proportioned to the greatness of the occasion, he might reasonably hope to revenge Pertinax, punish Julian, and receive the homage of the senate and people, as their lawful emperor, before his competitors, separated from Italy by an immense tract of sea and land, were apprised of his success, or even of his election. During the whole expedition he scarcely allowed himself any moments for sleep or food; marching on foot, and in complete armour, at the head of his columns, he insinuated himself into the confidence and affection of his troops, pressed their diligence, revived their spirits, animated their hopes, and was well satisfied to share the hardships of the meanest soldier, whilst he kept in view the infinite superiority of this reward.

The wretched Julian had expected, and thought himself prepared, to dispute the empire with the governor of Syria; but in the invincible and rapid approach of the Pannonian legions, he saw his inevitable ruin. The hasty arrival of every messenger increased his just apprehensions. He was successively informed that Severus had passed the Alps; that the Italian cities, unwilling or unable to oppose his progress, had received him with the warmest professions of joy and duty; that the important place of Ravenna had surrendered without resistance, and that the Hadriatic fleet was in the hands of the conqueror. The enemy was now within two hundred and fifty miles of Rome; and every moment diminished the narrow span of life and empire allotted to Julian.

He attempted, however, to prevent, or at least to protract, his ruin. He implored the venal faith of the Prætorians, filled the city with unavailing preparations for war, drew lines round the suburbs, and even strengthened the fortifications of the palace; as if those last intrenchments could be defended without hope of relief against a victorious invader. Fear and shame prevented the guards from deserting his standard; but they trembled at the name of the Pannonian legions, commanded by an experienced general, and accustomed to vanquish the barbarians on the frozen Danube. They quitted, with a sigh, the pleasures of the baths and theatres, to put on arms, whose use they had almost forgotten, and beneath the weight of which they were oppressed. The unpractised elephants, whose uncouth appearance, it was hoped, would strike terror into the army of the north, threw their unskilful riders; and the awkward evolutions of the marines, drawn from the fleet of Misenum, were an object of ridicule to the populace; whilst the senate enjoyed, with secret pleasure, the distress and weakness of the usurper.

Every motion of Julian betrayed his trembling perplexity. He insisted that Severus should be declared a public enemy by the senate. He intreated that the Pannonian general might be associated to the empire. He sent public ambassadors of consular rank to negotiate with his rival; he dispatched private assassins to take away his life. He designed that the Vestal virgins, and all the colleges of priests, in their sacerdotal habits, and bearing before them the sacred pledges of the Roman religion, should advance, in solemn procession, to meet the Pannonian legions; and, at the same time, he vainly tried to interrogate, or to appease, the fates, by magic ceremonies, and unlawful sacrifices.

Severus, who dreaded neither his arms nor his enchantments, guarded himself from the only danger of secret conspiracy, by the faithful attendance of six hundred chosen men, who never quitted his person or their cuirasses, either by night or by day, during the whole march. Advancing with a steady and rapid course, he passed, without difficulty, the defiles of the Apennine, received into his party the troops and ambassadors sent to retard his progress, and made a short halt at Interamnia, about seventy miles from Rome. His victory was already secure; but the despair of the Prætorians might have rendered it bloody; and Severus had the laudable ambition of ascending the throne without drawing the sword. His emissaries, dispersed in the capital, assured the guards, that provided they would abandon their worthless prince, and the perpetrators of the murder of Pertinax, to the justice of the conqueror, he would no longer consider that melancholy event as the act of the whole body. The faithless Prætorians, whose resistance was supported only by sullen obstinacy, gladly complied with the easy conditions, seized the greatest part of the assassins, and signified to the senate that they no longer defended the cause of Julian. That assembly, convoked by the consul, unanimously acknowledged Severus as lawful emperor, decreed divine honours to Pertinax, and pronounced a sentence of deposition and death against his unfortunate successor. Julian was conducted into a private apartment of the baths of the palace, and (A.D. 193, June 2) beheaded as a common criminal, after having purchased, with an immense treasure, an anxious and precarious reign of only sixty-six days. The almost incredible expedition of Severus, who, in so short a space of time, conducted a numerous army from the banks of the Danube to those of the Tiber, proves at once the plenty of provisions produced by agriculture and commerce, the goodness of the roads, the discipline of the legions, and the indolent subdued temper of the provinces.

The first cares of Severus were bestowed on two measures, the one dictated by policy, the other by decency; the revenge, and the honours, due to the memory of Pertinax. Before the new emperor entered Rome, he issued his commands to the Prætorian guards, directing them to wait his arrival on a large plain near the city, without arms, but in the habits of ceremony, in which they were accustomed to attend their sovereign. He was obeyed by those haughty troops, whose contrition was the effect of their just terrors. A chosen part of the Illyrian army encompassed them with levelled spears. Incapable of flight or resistance, they expected their fate in silent consternation. Severus mounted the tribunal, sternly reproached them with perfidy and cowardice, dismissed them with ignominy from the trust which they had betrayed, despoiled them of their splendid ornaments, and banished them, on pain of death, to the distance of an hundred miles from the capital. During the transaction, another detachment had been sent to seize their arms, occupy their camp, and prevent the hasty consequences of their despair.

The funeral and consecration of Pertinax was next solemnised with every circumstance of sad magnificence. The senate, with a melancholy pleasure, performed the last rites to that excellent prince, whom they had loved, and still regretted. The concern of his successor was probably less sincere. He esteemed the virtues of Pertinax, but those virtues would for ever have confined his ambition to a private station. Severus pronounced his funeral oration with studied eloquence, inward satisfaction, and well-acted sorrow; and by this pious regard to his memory, convinced the credulous multitude that *he alone* was worthy to supply his place. Sensible, however, that arms, not ceremonies, must assert his claim to the empire, he left Rome at the end of thirty days, and, without suffering himself to be elated by this easy victory, prepared to encounter his more formidable rivals.

Both Niger and Albinus were discovered and put to death in their flight from the field of battle. Their fate excited neither surprise nor compassion. They had staked their lives against the chance of empire, and suffered what they would have inflicted; nor did Severus claim the arrogant superiority of suffering his rivals to live in a private station. But his unforgiving temper, stimulated by avarice, indulged a spirit of revenge where there was no room for apprehension. The most considerable of the provincials, who, without any dislike to the fortunate candidate, had obeyed the governor under whose authority they were accidentally placed, were punished by death, exile, and especially by the confiscation of their estates. Many cities of the east were stript of their ancient honours, and obliged to pay, into the treasury of Severus, four times the amount of the sums contributed by them for the service of Niger.

Till the final decision of the war, the cruelty of Severus was, in some measure, restrained by the uncertainty of the event, and his pretended reverence for the senate. The head of Albinus, accompanied with a menacing letter, announced to the Romans, that he was resolved to spare none of the adherents of his unfortunate competitors. He was irritated by the just suspicion, that he had never possessed the affections of the senate, and he concealed his old malevolence under the recent discovery of some treasonable correspondences. Thirty-five senators, however, accused of having favoured the party of Albinus, he freely pardoned; and, by his subsequent behaviour, endeavoured to convince them that he had forgotten, as well as forgiven, their supposed offences. But, at the same time, he condemned forty-one other senators, whose names history has recorded; their wives, children, and clients, attended them in death, and the noblest provincials of Spain and Gaul were involved in the same ruin. Such rigid justice, for so he termed it, was, in the opinion of Severus, the only conduct capable of ensuring peace to the people, or stability to the prince; and he condescended slightly to lament, that, to be mild, it was necessary that he should first be cruel.

The true interest of an absolute monarch generally coincides with that of his people. Their numbers, their wealth, their order, and their security, are the best and only foundations of his real greatness; and were he totally devoid of virtue, prudence might supply its place, and would dictate the same rule of conduct. Severus considered the Roman empire as his property, and had no sooner secured the possession, than he bestowed his care on the cultivation and improvement of so valuable an acquisition. Salutary laws, executed with inflexible firmness, soon corrected most of the abuses with which, since the death of Marcus, every part of the government had been infected. In the administration of justice, the judgments of the emperor were characterised by attention, discernment, and impartiality; and whenever he deviated from the strict line of equity, it was generally in favour of the poor and oppressed; not so much indeed from any sense of humanity, as from the natural propensity of a despot, to humble the pride of greatness, and to sink all his subjects to the same common level of absolute dependence. His expensive taste for building, magnificent shows, and above all a constant and liberal distribution of corn and provisions, were the surest means of captivating the affection of the Roman people. The misfortunes of civil discord were obliterated. The calm of peace and prosperity was once more experienced in the provinces; and many cities, restored by the munificence of Severus, assumed the title of his colonies, and attested by public monuments their gratitude and felicity. The fame of the Roman arms was revived by that warlike and successful emperor, and he boasted with a just pride, that, having received the empire oppressed with foreign and domestic wars, he left it established in profound, universal, and honourable peace.

Although the wounds of civil war appeared completely healed, its mortal poison still lurked in the vitals of the constitution. Severus possessed a considerable share of vigour and ability; but the daring soul of the first Cæsar, or the deep policy of Augustus, were scarcely equal to the task of curbing the insolence of the victorious legions. By gratitude, by misguided policy, by seeming necessity, Severus was induced to relax the nerves of discipline. The vanity of his soldiers was flattered with the honour of wearing gold rings; their ease was indulged in the permission of living with their wives in the idleness of quarters. He increased their pay beyond the example of former times, and taught them to expect, and soon to claim, extraordinary donatives on every public occasion of danger or festivity. Elated by success, enervated by luxury, and raised above the level of subjects by their dangerous privileges, they soon became incapable of military fatigue, oppressive to the country, and impatient of a just subordination. Their officers asserted the superiority of rank by a more profuse and elegant luxury. There is still extant a letter of Severus, lamenting the licentious state of the army, and exhorting one of his generals to begin the necessary reformation from the tribunes themselves; since, as he justly observes, the officer who has forfeited the esteem, will never command the obedience, of his soldiers. Had the emperor pursued the train of reflection, he would have discovered that the primary cause of this general corruption might be ascribed, not indeed to the example, but to the pernicious indulgence, however, of the commander in chief.

The Prætorians, who murdered their emperor and sold the empire, had received the just punishment of their treason; but the necessary, though dangerous, institution of guards, was soon restored on a new model by Severus, and increased to four times the ancient number. Formerly these troops had been recruited in Italy; and as the adjacent provinces gradually imbibed the softer manners of Rome, the levies were extended to Macedonia, Noricum, and Spain. In the room of these elegant troops, better adapted to the pomp of courts than to the uses of war, it was established by Severus, that from all the legions of the frontiers, the soldiers most distinguished for strength, valour, and fidelity, should be occasionally draughted; and promoted, as an honour and reward, into the more eligible service of the guards. By this new institution, the Italian youth were diverted from the exercise of arms, and the capital was terrified by the strange aspect and manners of a multitude of barbarians. But Severus flattered himself that the legions would consider these chosen Prætorians as the representatives of the whole military order; and that the present aid of fifty thousand men, superior in arms and appointments to any force that could be brought into the field against them, would for ever crush the hopes of rebellion, and secure the empire to himself and his posterity.

The command of these favoured and formidable troops soon became the first office of the empire. As the government degenerated into military despotism, the Prætorian Præfect, who in his origin had been a simple captain of the guards, was placed, not only at the head of the army, but of the finances, and even of the law. In every department of administration he represented the person and exercised the authority of the emperor. The first Præfect who enjoyed and abused this immense power was Plautianus, the favourite minister of Severus. His reign lasted above ten years, till the marriage of his daughter with the eldest son of the emperor, which seemed to assure his fortune, proved the occasion of his ruin. The animosities of the palace, by irritating the ambition and alarming the fears of Plautianus, threatened to produce a revolution, and obliged the emperor, who still loved him, to consent with reluctance to his death. After the fall of Plautianus an eminent lawyer, the celebrated Papinian, was appointed to execute the motley office of Prætorian Præfect.

Till the reign of Severus, the virtue and even the good sense of the emperors had been distinguished by their zeal or affected reverence for the senate, and by a tender regard to the nice frame of civil policy instituted by Augustus. But the youth of Severus had been trained in the implicit obedience of camps, and his riper years spent in the despotism of military command. His haughty and inflexible spirit could not discover, or would not acknowledge, the advantage of preserving an intermediate power, however imaginary, between the emperor and the army. He disdained to profess himself the servant of an assembly that detested his person and trembled at his frown; he issued his commands, where his request would have proved as effectual; assumed the conduct and style of a sovereign and a conqueror, and exercised, without disguise, the whole legislative as well as the executive power.

The victory over the senate was easy and inglorious. Every eye and every passion was directed to the supreme magistrate, who possessed the arms and treasure of the state; whilst the senate, neither elected by the people, nor guarded by military force, nor animated by public spirit, rested its declining authority on the frail and crumbling basis of ancient opinion. The fine theory of a republic insensibly vanished, and made way for the more natural and substantial feelings of monarchy. As the freedom and honours of Rome were successively communicated to the provinces, in which the old government had been either unknown, or was remembered with abhorrence, the tradition of republican maxims was gradually obliterated. The Greek historians of the age of the Antonines observe with a malicious pleasure, that although the sovereign of Rome, in compliance with an obsolete prejudice, abstained from the name of king, he possessed the full measure of regal power. In the reign of Severus, the senate was filled with polished and eloquent slaves from the eastern provinces, who justified personal flattery by speculative principles of servitude. These new advocates of prerogative were heard with pleasure by the court, and with patience by the people, when they inculcated the duty of passive obedience, and descanted on the inevitable mischiefs of freedom. The lawyers and the historians concurred in teaching, that the Imperial authority was held, not by the delegated commission, but by the irrevocable resignation of the senate; that the emperor was freed from the restraint of civil laws, could command by his arbitrary will the lives and fortunes of his subjects, and might dispose of the empire as of his private patrimony. The most eminent of the civil lawyers, and particularly Papinian, Paulus, and Ulpian, flourished under the house of Severus; and the Roman jurisprudence having closely united itself with the system of monarchy, was supposed to have attained its full maturity and perfection.

The contemporaries of Severus, in the enjoyment of the peace and glory of his reign, forgave the cruelties by which it had been introduced. Posterity, who experienced the fatal effects of his maxims and example, justly considered him as the principal author of the decline of the Roman empire.

VI

(208–235 A.D.) THE DEATH OF SEVERUS—
TYRANNY OF CARACALLA—USURPATION OF
MACRINUS—FOLLIES OF ELAGABALUS—
VIRTUES OF ALEXANDER SEVERUS—LICEN-
TIOUSNESS OF THE ARMY

Two sons, Caracalla and Geta, were the fruit of *Severus'* marriage, and the destined heirs of the empire. The fond hopes of the father, and of the Roman world, were soon disappointed by these vain youths, who displayed the indolent security of hereditary princes; and a presumption that fortune would supply the place of merit and application. Without any emulation of virtue or talents, they discovered, almost from their infancy, a fixed and implacable antipathy for each other. Their aversion, confirmed by years, and fomented by the arts of their interested favourites, broke out in childish, and gradually in more serious, competitions; and, at length, divided the theatre, the circus, and the court, into two factions; actuated by the hopes and fears of their respective leaders. The prudent emperor endeavoured, by every expedient of advice and authority, to allay this growing animosity. The unhappy discord of his sons clouded all his prospects, and threatened to overturn a throne raised with so much labour, cemented with so much blood, and guarded with every defence of arms and treasure. With an impartial hand he maintained between them an exact balance of favour, conferred on both the rank of Augustus, with the revered name of Antoninus; and for the first time the Roman world beheld three emperors. Yet even this equal conduct served only to inflame the contest, whilst the fierce Caracalla asserted the right of primo-geniture, and the milder Geta courted the affections of the people and the soldiers. In the anguish of a disappointed father, Severus foretold that the weaker of his sons would fall a sacrifice to the stronger; who, in his turn, would be ruined by his own vices.

In these circumstances the intelligence of a war in Britain and of an invasion (A.D. 208) of the province by the barbarians of the

North, was received with pleasure by Severus. Though the vigilance of his lieutenants might have been sufficient to repel the distant enemy, he resolved to embrace the honourable pretext of withdrawing his sons from the luxury of Rome, which enervated their minds and irritated their passions; and of inuring their youth to the toils of war and government. Notwithstanding his advanced age (for he was above threescore), and his gout, which obliged him to be carried in a litter, he transported himself in person into that remote island, attended by his two sons, his whole court, and a formidable army. He immediately passed the walls of Hadrian and Antoninus, and entered the enemy's country, with a design of completing the long-attempted conquest of Britain. He penetrated to the northern extremity of the island without meeting an enemy. But the concealed ambuscades of the Caledonians, who hung unseen on the rear and flanks of his army, the coldness of the climate, and the severity of a winter march across the hills and morasses of Scotland, are reported to have cost the Romans above fifty thousand men. The Caledonians at length yielded to the powerful and obstinate attack, sued for peace, and surrendered a part of their arms, and a large tract of territory. But their apparent submission lasted no longer than the present terror. As soon as the Roman legions had retired, they resumed their hostile independence. Their restless spirit provoked Severus to send a new army into Caledonia, with the most bloody orders, not to subdue but to extirpate the natives. They were saved by the death of their haughty enemy.

The declining health and last illness of Severus inflamed the wild ambition and black passions of Caracalla's soul. Impatient of any delay or division of empire, he attempted, more than once, to shorten the small remainder of his father's days, and endeavoured, but without success, to excite a mutiny among the troops. The old emperor had often censured the misguided lenity of Marcus, who, by a single act of justice, might have saved the Romans from the tyranny of his worthless son. Placed in the same situation, he experienced how easily the rigour of a judge dissolves away in the tenderness of a parent. He deliberated, he threatened, but he could not punish; and this last and only instance of mercy was more fatal to the empire than a long series of cruelty. The disorder of his mind irritated the pains of his body; he wished impatiently for death, and hastened the instant of it by his impatience. He expired (A.D. 211, February 4th) at York in the sixty-fifth year of his life, and in the

eighteenth of a glorious and successful reign. In his last moments
he recommended concord to his sons, and his sons to the army.
The salutary advice never reached the heart, or even the understanding, of the impetuous youths; but the more obedient troops,
mindful of their oath of allegiance, and of the authority of their
deceased master, resisted the solicitations of Caracalla, and proclaimed both brothers emperors of Rome. The new princes soon
left the Caledonians in peace, returned to the capital, celebrated
their father's funeral with divine honours, and were cheerfully
acknowledged as lawful sovereigns, by the senate, the people, and
the provinces. Some pre-eminence of rank seems to have been
allowed to the elder brother; but they both administered the empire
with equal and independent power.

This latent civil war already distracted the whole government,
when a scheme was suggested that seemed of mutual benefit to the
hostile brothers. It was proposed, that since it was impossible to reconcile their minds, they should separate their interest, and divide
the empire between them. The conditions of the treaty were already
drawn with some accuracy. It was agreed that Caracalla, as the
elder brother, should remain in possession of Europe and the
western Africa; and that he should relinquish the sovereignty of
Asia and Egypt to Geta, who might fix his residence at Alexandria
or Antioch, cities little inferior to Rome itself in wealth and greatness; that numerous armies should be constantly encamped on
either side of the Thracian Bosphorus, to guard the frontiers of the
rival monarchies; and that the senators of European extraction
should acknowledge the sovereign of Rome, whilst the natives of
Asia followed the emperor of the East. The tears of the empress
Julia interrupted the negotiation, the first idea of which had filled
every Roman breast with surprise and indignation. The mighty
mass of conquest was so intimately united by the hand of time and
policy, that it required the most forcible violence to rend it asunder.
The Romans had reason to dread that the disjoined members
would soon be reduced by a civil war under the dominion of
one master; but if the separation was permanent, the division of
the provinces must terminate in the dissolution of an empire whose
unity had hitherto remained inviolate.

Had the treaty been carried into execution, the sovereign of
Europe might soon have been the conqueror of Asia; but Caracalla
obtained an easier though a more guilty victory. He artfully listened
to his mother's entreaties, and consented (A.D. 212, 27th February)

to meet his brother in her apartment, on terms of peace and reconciliation. In the midst of their conversation, some centurions, who had contrived to conceal themselves, rushed with drawn swords upon the unfortunate Geta. His distracted mother strove to protect him in her arms; but, in the unavailing struggle, she was wounded in the hand, and covered with the blood of her younger son, while she saw the elder animating and assisting the fury of the assassins. As soon as the deed was perpetrated, Caracalla, with hasty steps, and horror in his countenance, ran towards the Prætorian camp as his only refuge, and threw himself on the ground before the statues of the tutelar deities. The soldiers attempted to raise and comfort him. In broken and disordered words he informed them of his imminent danger and fortunate escape; insinuating that he had prevented the designs of his enemy, and declared his resolution to live and die with his faithful troops. Geta had been the favourite of the soldiers; but complaint was useless, revenge was dangerous, and they still reverenced the son of Severus. Their discontent died away in idle murmurs, and Caracalla soon convinced them of the justice of his cause, by distributing in one lavish donative the accumulated treasures of his father's reign. The real *sentiments* of the soldiers alone were of importance to his power or safety. Their declaration in his favour, commanded the dutiful *professions* of the senate. The obsequious assembly was always prepared to ratify the decision of fortune; but as Caracalla wished to assuage the first emotions of public indignation, the name of Geta was mentioned with decency, and he received the funeral honours of a Roman emperor. Posterity, in pity to his misfortune, has cast a veil over his vices. We consider that young prince as the innocent victim of his brother's ambition, without recollecting that he himself wanted power, rather than inclination, to consummate the same attempts of revenge and murder.

It had hitherto been the peculiar felicity of the Romans, and in the worst of times their consolation, that the virtue of the emperors was active, and their vice indolent. Augustus, Trajan, Hadrian, and Marcus, visited their extensive dominions in person, and their progress was marked by acts of wisdom and beneficence. The tyranny of Tiberius, Nero, and Domitian, who resided almost constantly at Rome, or in the adjacent villas, was confined to the senatorial and equestrian orders. But Caracalla was the common enemy of mankind. He left (A.D. 213) the capital (and he never returned to it) about a year after the murder of Geta. The rest of his reign was spent in the several provinces of the empire, particularly those of the East, and every province was by turns the scene of his rapine and cruelty. The senators, compelled by fear to attend his capricious motions, were obliged to provide daily entertainments at an immense expense, which he abandoned with contempt to his guards; and to erect, in every city, magnificent palaces and theatres, which he either disdained to visit, or ordered to be immediately thrown down. The most wealthy families were ruined by partial fines and confiscations, and the great body of his subjects oppressed by ingenious and aggravated taxes. In the midst of peace, and upon the slightest provocation, he issued his commands, at Alexandria in Egypt, for a general massacre. From a secure post in the temple of Serapis, he viewed and directed the slaughter of many thousand citizens, as well as strangers, without distinguishing either the number or the crime of the sufferers; since, as he coolly informed the senate, *all* the Alexandrians, those who had perished and those who had escaped, were alike guilty.

The wise instructions of Severus never made any lasting impression on the mind of his son, who, although not destitute of imagination and eloquence, was equally devoid of judgment and humanity. One dangerous maxim, worthy of a tyrant, was remembered and abused by Caracalla, "To secure the affections of the army, and to esteem the rest of his subjects as of little moment." But the liberality of the father had been restrained by prudence, and his indulgence to the troops was tempered by firmness and authority. The careless profusion of the son was the policy of one reign, and the inevitable ruin both of the army and of the empire. The vigour of the soldiers, instead of being confirmed by the severe discipline of camps, melted away in the luxury of cities. The excessive increase of their pay and donatives exhausted the state to enrich the military order, whose modesty in peace, and service in war, is best secured by an honourable poverty. The demeanour of Caracalla was haughty and full of pride; but with the troops he forgot even the proper dignity of his rank, encouraged their insolent familiarity, and, neglecting the essential duties of a general, affected to imitate the dress and manners of a common soldier.

It was impossible that such a character, and such a conduct as that of Caracalla, could inspire either love or esteem; but as long as his vices were beneficial to the armies, he was secure from the danger of rebellion. A secret conspiracy, provoked by his own jealousy, was fatal to the tyrant. The Prætorian præfecture was divided between two ministers. The military department was intrusted to Adventus, an experienced rather than an able soldier; and the civil affairs were transacted by Opilius Macrinus, who, by his dexterity in business, had raised himself, with a fair character, to that high office. But his favour varied with the caprice of the emperor, and his life might depend on the slightest suspicion, or the most casual circumstance. Malice or fanaticism had suggested to an African, deeply skilled in the knowledge of futurity, a very dangerous prediction, that Macrinus and his son were destined to reign over the empire. The report was soon diffused through the province; and when the man was sent in chains to Rome, he still asserted, in the presence of the Præfect of the city, the faith of his prophecy. That magistrate, who had received the most pressing instructions to inform himself of the *successors* of Caracalla, immediately communicated the examination of the African to the Imperial court, which at that time resided in Syria. But, notwithstanding the diligence of the public messengers, a friend of Macrinus found means to apprise him of the approaching danger. The emperor received the letters from Rome; and as he was then engaged in the conduct of a chariot-race, he delivered them unopened to the Prætorian Præfect, directing him to dispatch the ordinary affairs, and to report the more important business that might be contained in them. Macrinus read his fate, and resolved to prevent it. He inflamed the discontents of some inferior officers, and employed the hand of Martialis, a desperate soldier, who had been refused the rank of centurion. The devotion of Caracalla prompted him to make a pilgrimage from Edessa to the celebrated temple of the Moon at Carrhæ. He (A.D. 217, 8th March) was attended by a body of cavalry; but having stopped on the road for some necessary occasion, his guards preserved a respectful distance, and Martialis approaching his person under a pretence of duty, stabbed him with a dagger. The bold assassin was instantly killed by a Scythian archer of the Imperial guard. Such was the end of a monster whose life disgraced human nature, and whose reign accused the patience of the Romans. The grateful soldiers forgot his vices, remembered only his partial liberality, and obliged the senate to prostitute their own dignity and that of religion by granting him a place among the gods.

After the extinction of the house of Severus, the Roman world remained three days without a master. The choice of the army (for the authority of a distant and feeble senate was little regarded) hung in an anxious suspense; as no candidate presented himself whose distinguished birth and merit could engage their attachment and unite their suffrages. The decisive weight of the Prætorian guards elevated the hopes of their præfects, and these powerful ministers began to assert their *legal* claim to fill the vacancy of the Imperial throne. Adventus, however, the senior præfect, conscious of his age and infirmities, of his small reputation, and his smaller abilities, resigned the dangerous honour to the crafty ambition of his colleague Macrinus, whose well-dissembled grief removed all suspicion of his being accessory to his master's death. The troops neither loved nor esteemed his character. They cast their eyes around in search of a competitor, and at last yielded with reluctance to his promises of unbounded liberality and indulgence. A short time after his accession (A.D. 217, March 11th) he conferred on his son Diadumenianus, at the age of only ten years, the Imperial title and the popular name of Antoninus. The beautiful figure of the youth, assisted by an additional donative, for which the ceremony furnished a pretext, might attract, it was hoped, the favour of the army, and secure the doubtful throne of Macrinus.

The authority of the new sovereign had been ratified by the cheerful submission of the senate and provinces. They exulted in their unexpected deliverance from a hated tyrant, and it seemed of little consequence to examine into the virtues of the successor of Caracalla. But as soon as the first transports of joy and surprise had subsided, they began to scrutinise the merits of Macrinus with a critical severity, and to arraign the hasty choice of the army. It had hitherto been considered as a fundamental maxim of the constitution, that the emperor must be always chosen in the senate, and the sovereign power, no longer exercised by the whole body, was always delegated to one of its members. But Macrinus was not a senator. The sudden elevation of the Prætorian præfects betrayed the meanness of their origin; and the equestrian order was still in possession of that great office, which commanded with arbitrary sway the lives and fortunes of the senate. A murmur of indignation was heard, that a man whose obscure extraction had never been illustrated by any signal service, should dare to invest himself with the purple, instead of bestowing it on some distinguished senator, equal in birth and dignity to the splendour of the Imperial station.

As soon as the character of Macrinus was surveyed by the sharp eye of discontent, some vices, and many defects, were easily discovered. The choice of his ministers was in many instances justly censured, and the dissatisfied people, with their usual candour, accused at once his indolent tameness and his excessive severity.

His rash ambition had climbed a height where it was difficult to stand with firmness, and impossible to fall without instant destruction. Trained in the arts of courts, and the forms of civil business, he trembled in the presence of the fierce and undisciplined multitude, over whom he had assumed the command; his military talents were despised, and his personal courage suspected; a whisper that circulated in the camp, disclosed the fatal secret of the conspiracy against the late emperor, aggravated the guilt of murder by the baseness of hypocrisy, and heightened contempt by detestation. To alienate the soldiers, and to provoke inevitable ruin, the character of a reformer was only wanting: and such was the peculiar hardship of his fate, that Macrinus was compelled to exercise that invidious office. The prodigality of Caracalla had left behind it a long train of ruin and disorder; and if that worthless tyrant had been capable of reflecting on the sure consequences of his own conduct, he would perhaps have enjoyed the dark prospect of the distress and calamities which he bequeathed to his successors.

The empress Julia had experienced all the vicissitudes of fortune. From an humble station she had been raised to greatness, only to taste the superior bitterness of an exalted rank. she was doomed to weep over the death of one of her sons, and over the life of the other. The cruel fate of Caracalla, though her good sense must have long taught her to expect it, awakened the feelings of a mother and of an empress. Notwithstanding the respectful civility expressed by the usurper towards the widow of Severus, she descended with a painful struggle into the condition of a subject, and soon withdrew herself by a voluntary death from the anxious and humiliating dependence. Julia Mæsa, her sister, was ordered to leave the court and Antioch. She retired to Emesa with an immense fortune, the fruit of twenty years' favour, accompanied by her two daughters, Soæmias and Mamæa, each of whom was a widow, and each had an only son. Bassianus, for that was the name of the son of Soæmias, was consecrated to the honourable ministry of high priest of the Sun; and this holy vocation, embraced either from prudence or superstition, contributed to raise the Syrian youth to the empire of Rome. A numerous body of troops was stationed at Emesa; and, as the severe discipline of Macrinus had constrained them to pass the winter encamped, they were eager to revenge the cruelty of such unaccustomed hardships. The soldiers, who resorted in crowds to the temple of the Sun, beheld with veneration and delight the elegant dress and figure of a young Pontiff: they recognised, or they thought that they recognised, the features of Caracalla, whose memory they now adored. The artful Mæsa saw and cherished their rising partiality, and readily sacrificing her daughter's reputation to the fortune of her grandson, she insinuated that Bassianus was the natural son of their murdered sovereign. The sums distributed by her emissaries with a lavish hand silenced every objection, and the profusion sufficiently proved the affinity, or at least the resemblance, of Bassianus with the great original. The young Antoninus (for he had assumed and polluted that respectable name) was (A.D. 218, May 16) declared emperor by the troops of Emesa, asserted his hereditary right, and called aloud on the armies to follow the standard of a young and liberal prince, who had taken up arms to revenge his father's death and the oppression of the military order.

The Sun was worshipped at Emesa, under the name of Elagabalus, and under the form of a black conical stone, which, as it was universally believed, had fallen from heaven on that sacred place. To this protecting deity, Antoninus, not without some reason, ascribed his elevation to the throne. The display of super-stitious gratitude was the only serious business of his reign. The triumph of the God of Emesa over all the religions of the earth, was the great object of his zeal and vanity: and the appellation of Elagabalus (for he presumed as pontiff and favourite to adopt that sacred name) was dearer to him than all the titles of Imperial greatness. In a solemn procession through the streets of Rome, the way was strewed with gold dust; the black stone, set in precious gems, was placed on a chariot drawn by six milk-white horses richly caparisoned. The pious emperor held the reins, and, supported by his ministers, moved slowly backwards, that he might perpetually enjoy the felicity of the divine presence. In a magnif-icent temple raised on the Palatine Mount, the sacrifices of the god of Elagabalus were celebrated with every circumstance of cost and solemnity. The richest wines, the most extraordinary victims, and the rarest aromatics, were profusely consumed on his altar. Around the altar a chorus of Syrian damsels performed their lascivious dances to the sound of barbarian music, whilst the gravest personages of the state and army, clothed in long Phœnician tunics, officiated in the meanest functions, with affected zeal and secret indignation.

To this temple, as to the common centre of religious worship, the Imperial fanatic attempted to remove the Ancilia, the Palladium, and all the sacred pledges of the faith of Numa. A crowd of inferior deities attended in various stations the majesty of the god of Emesa; but his court was still imperfect, till a female of distinguished rank was admitted to his bed. Pallas had been first chosen for his comfort; but as it was dreaded lest her warlike terrors might affright the soft delicacy of a Syrian deity, the Moon, adored by the Africans under the name of Astarte, was deemed a more suitable companion for the Sun. Her image, with the rich offerings of her temple as a marriage portion, was transported with solemn pomp from Carthage to Rome, and the day of these mystic nuptials was a general festival in the capital and throughout the empire.

A rational voluptuary adheres with invariable respect to the temperate dictates of nature, and improves the gratifications of sense by social intercourse, endearing connections, and the soft colouring of taste and the imagination. But Elagabalus (I speak of the emperor of that name), corrupted by his youth, his country, and his fortune, abandoned himself to the grossest pleasures with ungoverned fury, and soon found disgust and satiety in the midst of his enjoyments. The inflammatory powers of art were summoned to his aid: the confused multitude of women, of wines, and of dishes, and the studied variety of attitudes and sauces, served to revive his languid appetites. New terms and new inventions in these sciences, the only ones cultivated and patronised by the monarch, signalised his reign, and transmitted his infamy to succeeding times. A capricious prodigality supplied the want of taste and elegance; and whilst Elagabalus lavished away the treasures of his people in the wildest extravagance, his own voice and that of his flatterers applauded a spirit and magnificence unknown to the tameness of his predecessors. To confound the order of seasons and climates, to sport with the passions and prejudices of his subjects, and to subvert every law of nature and decency, were in the number of his most delicious amusements. A long train of concubines, and a rapid succession of wives, among whom was a vestal virgin, ravished by force from her sacred asylum, were insufficient to satisfy the impotence of his passions. The master of the Roman world affected to copy the dress and manners of the female sex, preferred the distaff to the sceptre, and dishonoured the principal dignities of the empire by distributing them among his numerous lovers; one of whom was publicly invested with the title and authority of the emperor's, or, as he more properly styled himself, of the empress's husband.

The licentious soldiers, who had raised to the throne the dissolute son of Caracalla, blushed at their ignominious choice, and turned with disgust from that monster, to contemplate with pleasure the opening virtues of his cousin Alexander the son of Mamæa. The crafty Mæsa, sensible that her grandson Elagabalus must inevitably destroy himself by his own vices, had provided another and surer support of her family. Embracing a favourable moment of fondness and devotion, she had persuaded the young emperor to adopt Alexander, and to invest him (A.D. 221) with the title of Cæsar, that his own divine occupations might be no longer interrupted by the care of the earth. In the second rank that amiable prince soon acquired the affections of the public, and excited the tyrant's jealousy, who resolved to terminate the dangerous competition, either by corrupting the manners, or by taking away the life, of his rival. His arts proved unsuccessful; his vain designs were constantly discovered by his own loquacious folly, and disappointed by those virtuous and faithful servants whom the prudence of Mamæa had placed about the person of her son. In a hasty sally of passion, Elagabalus resolved to execute by force what he had been unable to compass by fraud, and by a despotic sentence degraded his cousin from the rank and honours of Cæsar. The message was received in the senate with silence, and in the camp with fury. The Prætorian guards swore to protect Alexander, and to revenge the dishonoured majesty of the throne. The tears and promises of the trembling Elagabalus, who only begged them to spare his life, and to leave him in the possession of his beloved Hierocles, diverted their just indignation; and they contented themselves with empowering their præfects to watch over the safety of Alexander, and the conduct of the emperor.

It was impossible that such a reconciliation should last, or that even the mean soul of Elagabalus could hold an empire on such humiliating terms of dependence. He soon attempted, by a dangerous experiment, to try the temper of the soldiers. The report of the death of Alexander, and the natural suspicion that he had been murdered, inflamed their passions into fury, and the tempest of the camp could only be appeased by the presence and authority of the popular youth. Provoked at this new instance of their affection for his cousin, and their contempt for his person, the emperor ventured to punish some of the leaders of the mutiny. His unseasonable severity proved instantly fatal to his minions, his mother, and himself. Elagabalus was (A.D. 222, 10th March) massacred by the indignant Prætorians, his mutilated corpse dragged through the streets of the city, and thrown into the Tiber. His memory was branded with eternal infamy by the senate; the justice of whose decree has been ratified by posterity.

In the room of Elagabalus, his cousin Alexander was raised to the throne by the Prætorian guards. His relation to the family of Severus, whose name he assumed, was the same as that of his predecessor; his virtue and his danger had already endeared him to the Romans, and the eager liberality of the senate conferred upon him, in one day, the various titles and powers of the Imperial dignity. But as Alexander was a modest and dutiful youth, of only seventeen years of age, the reins of government were in the hands of two women, of his mother Mamæa, and of Mæsa, his grandmother. After the death of the latter, who survived but a short time the elevation of Alexander, Mamæa remained the sole regent of her son and of the empire.

In every age and country, the wiser, or at least the stronger, of the two sexes, has usurped the powers of the state, and confined the other to the cares and pleasures of domestic life. In hereditary monarchies, however, and especially in those of modern Europe, the gallant spirit of chivalry, and the law of succession, have accustomed us to allow a singular exception; and a woman is often acknowledged the absolute sovereign of a great kingdom, in which she would be deemed incapable of exercising the smallest employment, civil or military. But as the Roman emperors were still considered as the generals and magistrates of the republic, their wives and mothers, although distinguished by the name of Augusta, were never associated to their personal honours; and a female reign would have appeared an inexpiable prodigy in the eyes of those primitive Romans, who married without love, or loved without delicacy and respect. The haughty Agrippina aspired, indeed, to share the honours of the empire, which she had conferred on her son; but her mad ambition, detested by every citizen who felt for the dignity of Rome, was disappointed by the artful firmness of Seneca and Burrhus. The good sense, or the indifference, of succeeding princes, restrained them from offending the prejudices of their subjects; and it was reserved for the profligate Elagabalus, to discharge the acts of the senate, with the name of his mother Soæmias, who was placed by the side of the consuls, and subscribed, as a regular member, the decrees of the legislative assembly. Her more prudent sister, Mamaea, declined the useless and odious prerogative, and a solemn law was enacted, excluding women for ever from the senate, and devoting to the infernal gods, the head of the wretch by whom this sanction should be violated. The substance, not the pageantry, of power was the object of Mamæa's manly ambition. She maintained an absolute and lasting empire over the mind of her son, and in his affection the mother could not brook a rival. Alexander, with her consent, married the daughter of a Patrician; but his respect for his father-in-law, and love for the empress, were inconsistent with the tenderness or interest of Mamæa. The Patrician was executed on the ready accusation of treason, and the wife of Alexander driven with ignominy from the palace, and banished into Africa.

Notwithstanding this act of jealous cruelty, as well as some instances of avarice, with which Mamæa is charged; the general tenor of her administration was equally for the benefit of her son and of the empire. With the approbation of the senate, she chose sixteen of the wisest and most virtuous senators, as a perpetual council of state, before whom every public business of moment was debated and determined. The celebrated Ulpian, equally distin-guished by his knowledge of, and his respect for, the laws of Rome, was at their head; and the prudent firmness of this aristocracy restored order and authority to the government. As soon as they had purged the city from foreign superstition and luxury, the remains of the capricious tyranny of Elagabalus, they applied them-selves to remove his worthless creatures from every department of public administration, and to supply their places with men of virtue and ability. Learning, and the love of justice, became the only recommendations for civil offices. Valour, and the love of discipline, the only qualifications for military employments.

In the civil administration of Alexander, wisdom was enforced by power, and the people, sensible of the public felicity, repaid their benefactor with their love and gratitude. There still remained a greater, a more necessary, but a more difficult enterprise; the reformation of the military order, whose interest and temper, con-firmed by long impunity, rendered them impatient of the restraints of discipline, and careless of the blessings of public tranquillity. In the execution of his design the emperor affected to display his love, and to conceal his fear, of the army. The most rigid economy in every other branch of the administration, supplied a fund of gold and silver for the ordinary pay and the extraordinary rewards of the troops. In their marches he relaxed the severe obligation of carrying seventeen days' provision on their shoulders. Ample magazines were formed along the public roads, and as soon as they entered the enemy's country, a numerous train of mules and camels waited on their haughty laziness. As Alexander despaired of correcting the luxury of his soldiers, he attempted, at least, to direct it to objects at martial pomp and ornament, fine horses splendid armour, and shield enriched with silver and gold. He shared whatever fatigues he was obliged to impose, visited, in person, the sick and wounded, preserved an exact register of their services and his own gratitude, and expressed, on every occasion, the warmest regard for a body of men, whose welfare, as he affected to declare, was so closely connected with that of the state. By the most gentle arts he laboured to inspire the fierce multitude with a sense of duty, and to restore at least a faint image of that discipline to which the Romans owed their empire over so many other nations, as warlike and more powerful than themselves. But his prudence was vain, his courage fatal, and the attempt towards a reformation served only to inflame the ills it was meant to cure.

The Prætorian guards were attached to the youth of Alexander. They loved him as a tender pupil, whom they had saved from a tyrant's fury, and placed on the Imperial throne. That amiable prince was sensible of the obligation, but as his gratitude was restrained within the limits of reason and justice, they soon were more dissatisfied with the virtues of Alexander, than they had ever been with the vices of Elagabalus. Their præfect, the wise Ulpian, was the friend of the laws and of the people, he was considered as the enemy of the soldiers, and to his pernicious counsels every scheme of reformation was imputed. Some trifling accident blew up their discontent into a furious mutiny; and a civil war raged, during three days, in Rome, whilst the life of that excellent minister was defended by the grateful people. Terrified, at length, by the sight of some houses in flames, and by the threats of a general conflagration, the people yielded with a sigh, and left the virtuous, but unfortunate, Ulpian to his fate. He was pursued into the Imperial palace, and massacred at the feet of his master, who vainly strove to cover him with the purple, and to obtain his pardon from the inexorable soldiers. Such was the deplorable weakness of government, that the emperor was unable to revenge his murdered friend and his insulted dignity, without stooping to the arts of patience and dissimulation. The lenity of the emperor confirmed the insolence of the troops; the legions imitated the example of the guards, and defended their prerogative of licentiousness with the same furious obstinacy. The administration of Alexander was an unavailing struggle against the corruption of his age. In Illyricum, in Mauritania, in Armenia, in Mesopotamia, in Germany, fresh mutinies perpetually broke out; his officers were murdered, his authority was insulted, and his life at last sacrificed to the fierce discontents of the army.

The dissolute tyranny of Commodus, the civil wars occasioned by his death, and the new maxims of policy introduced by the house of Severus, had all contributed to increase the dangerous power of the army, and to obliterate the faint image of laws and liberty that was still impressed on the minds of the Romans. This internal change, which undermined the foundations of the empire, we have endeavoured to explain with some degree of order and perspicuity. The personal characters of the emperors, their victories, laws, follies, and fortunes, can interest us no farther than as they are connected with the general history of the Decline and Fall of the monarchy. Our constant attention to that great object will not suffer us to overlook a most important edict of Antoninus Caracalla, which communicated to all the free inhabitants of the empire the name and privileges of Roman citizens. His unbounded liberality flowed not, however, from the sentiments of a generous mind; it was the sordid result of avarice. Inattentive, or rather averse, to the welfare of his people, he found himself under the necessity of gratifying the insatiate avarice, which he had excited in the army. Of the several impositions introduced by Augustus, the twentieth on inheritances and legacies was the most fruitful, as well as the most comprehensive. As its influence was not confined to Rome or Italy, the produce continually increased with the gradual extension of the ROMAN CITY. The new citizens, though charged, on equal terms, with the payment of new taxes, which had not affected them as subjects, derived an ample compensation from the rank they obtained, the privileges they acquired, and the fair prospect of honours and fortune that was thrown open to their ambition. But the favour which implied a distinction, was lost in the prodigality of Caracalla, and the reluctant provincials were compelled to assume the vain title, and the real obligations, of Roman citizens. Nor was the rapacious son of Severus contented with such a measure of taxation, as had appeared sufficient to his moderate predecessors.

Instead of a twentieth, he exacted a tenth of all legacies and inheritances; and during his reign (for the ancient proportion was restored after his death) he crushed alike every part of the empire under the weight of his iron sceptre.

When all the provincials became liable to the peculiar impositions of Roman citizens, they seemed to acquire a legal exemption from the tributes which they had paid in their former condition of subjects. Such were not the maxims of government adopted by Caracalla and his pretended son. The old as well as the new taxes were, at the same time, levied in the provinces. It was reserved for the virtue of Alexander to relieve them in a great measure from this intolerable grievance, by reducing the tributes to a thirtieth part of the sum exacted at the time of his accession. It is impossible to conjecture the motive that engaged him to spare so trifling a remnant of the public evil; but the noxious weed, which had not been totally eradicated, again sprang up with the most luxuriant growth, and in the succeeding age darkened the Roman world with its deadly shade. In the course of this history, we shall be too often summoned to explain the land-tax, the capitation, and the heavy contributions of corn, wine, oil, and meat, which were exacted from the provinces for the use of the court, the army, and the capital.

As long as Rome and Italy were respected as the centre of government, a national spirit was preserved by the ancient, and insensibly imbibed by the adopted, citizens. The principal commands of the army were filled by men who had received a liberal education, were well instructed in the advantages of laws and letters, and who had risen, by equal steps, through the regular succession of civil and military honours. To their influence and example we may partly ascribe the modest obedience of the legions during the two first centuries of the Imperial history.

But when the last enclosure of the Roman constitution was trampled down by Caracalla, the separation of professions gradually succeeded to the distinction of ranks. The more polished citizens of the internal provinces were alone qualified to act as lawyers and magistrates. The rougher trade of arms was abandoned to the peasants and barbarians of the frontiers, who knew no country but their camp, no science but that of war, no civil laws, and scarcely those of military discipline. With bloody hands, savage manners, and desperate resolutions, they sometimes guarded, but much oftener subverted, the throne of the emperors.

VII

(235–248 A.D.) THE ELEVATION AND TYRANNY OF MAXIMIN — REBELLION IN AFRICA AND ITALY, UNDER THE AUTHORITY OF THE SENATE — CIVIL WARS AND SEDITIONS — VIOLENT DEATHS OF MAXIMIN AND HIS SON, OF MAXIMUS AND BALBINUS, AND OF THE THREE GORDIANS — USURPATION AND SECULAR GAMES OF PHILIP

Maximin, though born on the territories of the empire, descended from a mixed race of barbarians. His father was a Goth, and his mother of the nation of the Alani. He displayed, on every occasion, a valour equal to his strength; and his native fierceness was soon tempered or disguised by the knowledge of the world. Under the reign of Severus and his son, he obtained the rank of centurion, with the favour and esteem of both those princes, the former of whom was an excellent judge of merit. Gratitude forbade Maximin to serve under the assassin of Caracalla. Honour taught him to decline the effeminate insults of Elagabalus. On the accession of Alexander he returned to court, and was placed by that prince in a station useful to the service and honourable to himself. The fourth legion, to which he was appointed tribune, soon became, under his care, the best disciplined of the whole army. With the general applause of the soldiers, who bestowed on their favourite hero the names of Ajax and Hercules, he was successively promoted to the first military command; and had not he still retained too much of his savage origin, the emperor might perhaps have given his own sister in marriage to the son of Maximin.

Instead of securing his fidelity, these favours served only to inflame the ambition of the Thracian peasant, who deemed his fortune inadequate to his merit, as long as he was constrained to acknowledge a superior. Though a stranger to real wisdom, he was not devoid of a selfish cunning, which showed him that the emperor had lost the affection of the army, and taught him to improve their discontent to his own advantage. It is easy for faction and calumny to shed their poison on the administration of the best of princes, and to accuse even their virtues, by artfully confounding them with those vices to which they bear the nearest affinity. The troops listened with pleasure to the emissaries of Maximin. They blushed at their own ignominious patience, which, during thirteen years, had supported the vexatious discipline imposed by an effeminate Syrian, the timid slave of his mother and of the senate. It was time, they cried, to cast away that useless phantom of the civil power, and to elect for their prince and general a real soldier, educated in camps, exercised in war, who would assert the glory, and distribute among his companions the treasures, of the empire. A great army was at that time assembled on the banks of the Rhine, under the command of the emperor himself, who, almost immediately after his return from the Persian war, had been obliged to march against the barbarians of Germany. The important care of training and reviewing the new levies was intrusted to Maximin. One day (A.D. 235, March 19), as he entered the field of exercise, the troops, either from a sudden impulse or a formed conspiracy, saluted him emperor, silenced by their loud acclamations his obstinate refusal, and hastened to consummate their rebellion by the murder of Alexander Severus.

The former tyrants, Caligula and Nero, Commodus and Caracalla, were all dissolute and inexperienced youths, educated in the purple, and corrupted by the pride of empire, the luxury of Rome, and the perfidious voice of flattery. The cruelty of Maximin was derived from a different source, the fear of contempt. Though he depended on the attachment of the soldiers, who loved him for virtues like their own, he was conscious that his mean and barbarian origin, his savage appearance, and his total ignorance of the arts and institutions of civil life, formed a very unfavourable contrast with the amiable manners of the unhappy Alexander. He remembered that, in his humbler fortune, he had often waited before the door of the haughty nobles of Rome, and had been denied admittance by the insolence of their slaves. He recollected too the friendship of a few who had relieved his poverty, and assisted his rising hopes. But those who had spurned, and those who had protected the Thracian, were guilty of the same crime, the knowledge of his original obscurity. For this crime many were put to death; and by the execution of several of his benefactors, Maximin published, in characters of blood, the indelible history of his baseness and ingratitude.

As long as the cruelty of Maximin was confined to the illustrious senators, or even to the bold adventurers, who in the court or army expose themselves to the caprice of fortune, the body of the people viewed their sufferings with indifference, or perhaps with pleasure. But the tyrant's avarice, stimulated by the insatiate desires of the soldiers, at length attacked the public property. Every city of the empire was possessed of an independent revenue, destined to purchase corn for the multitude, and to supply the expenses of the games and entertainments. By a single act of authority, the whole mass of wealth was at once confiscated for the use of the Imperial treasury. The temples were stripped of their most valuable offerings of gold and silver, and the statues of gods, heroes, and emperors, were melted down and coined into money. These impious orders could not be executed without tumults and massacres, as in many places the people chose rather to die in the defence of their altars, than to behold in the midst of peace their cities exposed to the rapine and cruelty of war. The soldiers themselves, among whom this sacrilegious plunder was distributed, received it with a blush; and, hardened as they were in acts of violence, they dreaded the just reproaches of their friends and relations. Throughout the Roman world a general cry of indignation was heard, imploring vengeance on the common enemy of human kind; and at length, by an act of private oppression, a peaceful and unarmed province was driven into rebellion against him.

The procurator of Africa was a servant worthy of such a master, who considered the fines and confiscations of the rich as one of the most fruitful branches of the Imperial revenue. An iniquitous sentence had been (A.D. 237, April) pronounced against some opulent youths of that country, the execution of which would have stripped them of far the greater part of their patrimony. In this extremity, a resolution that must either complete or prevent their ruin, was dictated by despair. A respite of three days, obtained with difficulty from the rapacious treasurer, was employed in collecting from their estates a great number of slaves and peasants, blindly devoted to the commands of their lords, and armed with the rustic weapons of clubs and axes. The leaders of the conspiracy, as they were admitted to the audience of the procurator, stabbed him with the daggers concealed under their garments, and, by the assistance of their tumultuary train, seized on the little town of Thysdrus, and erected the standard of rebellion against the sovereign of the Roman empire. They rested their hopes on the hatred of mankind against Maximin, and they judiciously resolved to oppose to that detested tyrant, an emperor whose mild virtues had already acquired the love and esteem of the Romans, and whose authority over the province would give weight and stability to the enterprise. Gordianus, their proconsul, and the object of their choice, refused, with unfeigned reluctance, the dangerous honour, and begged with tears that they would suffer him to terminate in peace a long and innocent life, without staining his feeble age with civil blood. Their menaces compelled him to accept the Imperial purple, his only refuge indeed against the jealous cruelty of Maximin; since, according to the reasoning of tyrants, those who have been esteemed worthy of the throne deserve death, and those who deliberate have already rebelled.

The family of Gordianus was one of the most illustrious of the Roman senate. On the father's side, he was descended from the Gracchi; on his mother's, from the emperor Trajan. A great estate enabled him to support the dignity of this birth, and, in the enjoyment of it, he displayed an elegant taste and beneficent disposition. When he reluctantly accepted the purple, he was above fourscore years old; a last and valuable remains of the happy age of the Antonines, whose virtues he revived in his own conduct and celebrated in an elegant poem of thirty books. With the venerable proconsul, his son, who had accompanied him into Africa as his lieutenant, was likewise declared emperor. His manners were less pure, but his character was equally amiable with that of his father. Twenty-two acknowledged concubines, and a library of sixty-two thousand volumes, attested the variety of his inclinations, and from the productions which he left behind him, it appears that the former as well as the latter were designed for use rather than ostentation. The Roman people acknowledged in the features of the younger Gordian the resemblance of Scipio Africanus, recollected with pleasure that his mother was the grand-daughter of Antoninus Pius, and rested the public hope on those latent virtues which had hitherto, as they fondly imagined, lain concealed in the luxurious indolence of a private life.

As soon as the Gordians had appeased the first tumult of a popular election, they removed their court to Carthage. They were received with the acclamations of the Africans, who honoured their virtues, and who, since the visit of Hadrian, had never beheld the majesty of a Roman emperor. But these vain acclamations neither strengthened nor confirmed the title of the Gordians. They were induced by principle, as well as interest, to solicit the approbation of the senate; and a deputation of the noblest provincials was sent, without delay, to Rome, to relate and justify the conduct of their countrymen, who, having long suffered with patience, were at length resolved to act with vigour. The letters of the new princes were modest and respectful, excusing the necessity which had obliged them to accept the Imperial title; but submitting their election and their fate to the supreme judgment of the senate.

The inclinations of the senate were neither doubtful nor divided. The birth and noble alliances of the Gordians had intimately connected them with the most illustrious houses of Rome. While the cause of the Gordians was embraced with such diffusive ardour, the Gordians themselves (A.D. 237, 3rd July) were no more. The feeble court of Carthage was alarmed with the rapid approach of Capelianus, governor of Mauritania, who, with a small band of veterans, and a fierce host of barbarians, attacked a faithful but unwarlike province. The younger Gordian sallied out to meet the enemy at the head of a few guards, and a numerous undisciplined multitude, educated in the peaceful luxury of Carthage. His useless valour served only to procure him an honourable death, in the field of battle. His aged father, whose reign had not exceeded thirty-six days, put an end to his life on the first news of the defeat. Carthage, destitute of defence, opened her gates to the conqueror, and Africa was exposed to the rapacious cruelty of a slave, obliged to satisfy his unrelenting master with a large account of blood and treasure.

The fate of the Gordians filled Rome with just, but unexpected terror. The senate convoked in the temple of Concord, affected to transact the common business of the day; and seemed to decline, with trembling anxiety, the consideration of their own and the public danger. A silent consternation prevailed on the assembly, till a senator, of the name and family of Trajan, awakened his brethren from their fatal lethargy. He represented to them, that the choice of cautious dilatory measures had been long since out of their power; that Maximin, implacable by nature, and exasperated by injuries, was advancing towards Italy, at the head of the military force of the empire; and that their only remaining alternative was either to meet him bravely in the field, or tamely to expect the tortures and ignominious death reserved for unsuccessful rebellion.

"We have lost," continued he, "two excellent princes; but unless we desert ourselves, the hopes of the republic have not perished with the Gordians. Many are the senators, whose virtues have deserved, and whose abilities would sustain, the Imperial dignity. Let us elect two emperors, one of whom may conduct the war against the public enemy, whilst his colleague remains at Rome to direct the civil administration. I cheerfully expose myself to the danger and envy of the nomination, and give my vote in favour of Maximus and Balbinus. Ratify my choice, conscript fathers, or appoint, in their place, others more worthy of the empire." The general apprehension silenced the whispers of jealousy; the merit of the candidates was universally acknowledged; and the house resounded with the sincere acclamations, of "long life and victory to the emperors Maximus and Balbinus. You are happy in the judgment of the senate; may the republic be happy under your administration!"

When the troops of Maximin, advancing in excellent order, arrived at the foot of the Julian Alps, they were terrified by the silence and desolation that reigned on the frontiers of Italy. The villages and open towns had been abandoned on their approach by the inhabitants, the cattle was driven away, the provisions removed, or destroyed, the bridges broke down, nor was anything left which could afford either shelter or give subsistence to an invader. Such had been the wise orders of the generals of the senate, whose design was to protract the war, to ruin the army of Maximin by the slow operation of famine, and to consume his strength in the sieges of the principal cities of Italy, which they had plentifully stored with men and provisions from the deserted country. Aquileia received and withstood the first shock of the invasion. The streams that issue from the head of the Hadriatic gulf, swelled by the melting of the winter snows, opposed an unexpected obstacle to the arms of Maximin. At length, on a singular bridge, constructed with art and difficulty of large hogsheads, he transported his army to the opposite bank, rooted up the beautiful vineyards in the neighbourhood of Aquileia, demolished the suburbs, and employed the timber of the buildings in the engines and towers, with which on every side he attacked the city. The walls, fallen to decay during the security of a long peace, had been hastily repaired on this sudden emergency; but the firmest defence of Aquileia consisted in the constancy of the citizens; all ranks of whom, instead of being dismayed, were animated by the extreme danger, and their knowledge of the tyrant's unrelenting temper.

The people of Aquileia had scarcely experienced any of the common miseries of a siege, their magazines were plentifully supplied, and several fountains within the walls assured them of an inexhaustible resource of fresh water. The soldiers of Maximin were, on the contrary, exposed to the inclemency of the season, the contagion of disease, and the horrors of famine. The open country was ruined, the rivers filled with the slain, and polluted with blood. A spirit of despair and disaffection began to diffuse itself among the troops; and as they were cut off from all intelligence, they easily believed that the whole empire had embraced the cause of the senate, and that they were left as devoted victims to perish under the impregnable walls of Aquileia. The fierce temper of the tyrant was exasperated by disappointments, which he imputed to the cowardice of his army; and his wanton and ill-timed cruelty, instead of striking terror, inspired hatred and a just desire of revenge. A party of Prætorian guards, who trembled for their wives and children in the camp of Alba, near Rome, executed the sentence of the senate. Maximin, abandoned by his guards, was (A.D. 238, April) slain in his tent, with his son (whom he had associated to the honours of the purple), Anulinus the præfect, and the principal ministers of his tyranny.

It is easier to conceive than to describe the universal joy of the Roman world on the fall of the tyrant, the news of which is said to have been carried in four days from Aquileia to Rome. The return of Maximus was a triumphal procession, his colleague and young Gordian went out to meet him, and the three princes made their entry into the capital, attended by the ambassadors of almost all the cities of Italy, saluted with the splendid offerings of gratitude and superstition, and received with the unfeigned acclamations of the senate and people, who persuaded themselves that a golden age would succeed to an age of iron. The conduct of the two emperors correspond with these expectations. They administered justice in person; and the rigour of the one was tempered by the other's clemency. The oppressive taxes with which Maximin had loaded the rights of inheritance and succession were repealed, or at least moderated. Discipline was revived, and with the advice of the senate many wise laws were enacted by their imperial ministers, who endeavoured to restore a civil constitution on the ruins of military tyranny. "What reward may we expect for delivering Rome from a monster?" was the question asked by Maximus, in a moment of freedom and confidence. Balbinus answered it without hesitation. "The love of the senate, of the people, and of all mankind." "Alas!" replied his more penetrating colleague, "Alas! I dread the hatred of the soldiers, and the fatal effects of their resentment." His apprehensions were but too well justified by the event.

When the senate elected two princes, it is probable that, besides the declared reason of providing for the various emergencies of peace and war, they were actuated by the secret desire of weakening by division the despotism of the supreme magistrate. Their policy was effectual, but it proved fatal both to their emperors and to themselves. The jealousy of power was soon exasperated by the difference of character. Maximus despised Balbinus as a luxurious noble, and was in his turn disdained by his colleague as an obscure soldier. Their silent discord was understood rather than seen; but the mutual consciousness prevented them from uniting in any vigorous measures of defence against their common enemies of the Prætorian camp. The whole city was (A.D. 238, July 15) employed in the Capitoline games, and the emperors were left almost alone in the palace. On a sudden they were alarmed by the approach of a troop of desperate assassins. Ignorant of each other's situation or designs, for they already occupied very distant apartments, afraid to give or to receive assistance, they wasted the important moments in idle debates and fruitless recriminations. The arrival of the guards put an end to the vain strife. They seized on these emperors of the senate, for such they called them with malicious contempt, stripped them of their garments, and dragged them in insolent triumph through the streets of Rome, with a design of inflicting a slow and cruel death on those unfortunate princes. The fear of a rescue from the faithful Germans of the Imperial guards, shortened their tortures; and their bodies, mangled with a thousand wounds, were left exposed to the insults or to the pity of the populace.

In the space of a few months, six princes had been cut off by the sword. Gordian, who had already received the title of Cæsar, was the only person that occurred to the soldiers as proper to fill the vacant throne. They carried him to the camp, and unanimously saluted him Augustus and Emperor. His name was dear to the senate and people; his tender age promised a long impunity of military licence; and the submission of Rome and the provinces to the choice of the Prætorian guards, saved the republic, at the expense indeed of its freedom and dignity, from the horrors of a new civil war in the heart of the capital.

As the third Gordian was only nineteen years of age at the time of his death, the history of his life, were it known to us with greater accuracy than it really is, would contain little more than the account of his education, and the conduct of the ministers, who by turns abused or guided the simplicity of his inexperienced youth. Immediately after his accession, he fell into the hands of his mother's eunuchs, that pernicious vermin of the East, who, since the days of Elagabalus, had infested the Roman palace. By the artful conspiracy of these wretches, an impenetrable veil was drawn between an innocent prince and his oppressed subjects, the virtuous disposition of Gordian was deceived, and the honours of the empire sold without his knowledge, though in a very public manner, to the most worthless of mankind. We are ignorant by what fortunate accident the emperor escaped from this ignominious slavery, and devolved his confidence on a minister whose wise counsels had no object except the glory of his sovereign and the happiness of the people. It should seem that (A.D. 240) love and learning introduced Misitheus to the favour of Gordian. The young prince married the daughter of his master of rhetoric, and promoted his father-in-law to the first offices of the empire.

The life of Misitheus had been spent in the profession of letters, not of arms; yet such was the versatile genius of that great man, that, when (A.D. 242) he was appointed Prætorian Præfect, he discharged the military duties of his place with vigour and ability. The Persians had invaded Mesopotamia, and threatened Antioch. By the persuasion of his father-in-law, the young emperor quitted the luxury of Rome, opened, for the last time recorded in history, the temple of Janus, and marched in person into the East. On his approach with a great army, the Persians withdrew their garrisons from the cities which they had already taken, and retired from the Euphrates to the Tigris. Gordian enjoyed the pleasure of announcing to the senate the first success of his arms, which he ascribed with a becoming modesty and gratitude to the wisdom of his father and Præfect. During the whole expedition, Misitheus watched over the safety and discipline of the army; whilst he prevented their dangerous murmurs by maintaining a regular plenty in the camp, and by establishing ample magazines of vinegar, bacon, straw, barley, and wheat, in all the cities of the frontier. But the prosperity of Gordian expired with Misitheus, who died of a flux, not without very strong suspicions of poison. Philip, his successor (A.D. 243) in the præfecture, was an Arab by birth, and consequently, in the earlier part of his life, a robber by profession. His rise from so obscure a station to the first dignities of the empire, seems to prove that he was a bold and able leader. But his boldness prompted him to aspire to the throne, and his abilities were employed to supplant, not to serve, his indulgent master. The minds of the soldiers were irritated by an artificial scarcity, created by his contrivance in the camp; and the distress of the army was attributed to the youth and incapacity of the prince. It is not in our power to trace the successive steps of the secret conspiracy and open sedition, which were at length fatal to Gordian. A sepulchral monument was erected to his memory on the spot where (A.D. 244, March) he was killed, near the conflux of the Euphrates with the little river Aboras. The fortunate Philip, raised to the empire by the votes of the soldiers, found a ready obedience from the senate and the provinces.

On his return from the East to Rome, Philip, desirous of obliterating the memory of his crimes, and of captivating the affections of the people, solemnized (A.D. 248, April 21) the secular games with infinite pomp and magnificence. Since their institution or revival by Augustus, they had been celebrated by Claudius, by Domitian, and by Severus, and were now renewed the fifth time, on the accomplishment of the full period of a thousand years from the foundation of Rome. Since Romulus, with a small band of shepherds and outlaws, fortified himself on the hills near the Tiber, ten centuries had already elapsed. During the first four ages, the Romans, in the laborious school of poverty, had acquired the virtues of war and government; by the vigorous exertion of those virtues, and by the assistance of fortune, they had obtained, in the course of the three succeeding centuries, an absolute empire over many countries of Europe, Asia, and Africa. The last three hundred years had been consumed in apparent prosperity and internal decline. The nation of soldiers, magistrates, and legislators, who composed the thirty-five tribes of the Roman people, was dissolved into the common mass of mankind and confounded with the millions of servile provincials, who had received the name without adopting the spirit of Romans. A mercenary army, levied among the subjects and barbarians of the frontier, was the only order of men who preserved and abused their independence. By their tumultuary election, a Syrian, a Goth, or an Arab, was exalted to the throne of Rome, and invested with despotic power over the conquests and over the country of the Scipios.

The limits of the Roman empire still extended from the Western Ocean to the Tigris, and from Mount Atlas to the Rhine and the Danube. To the undiscerning eye of the vulgar, Philip appeared a monarch no less powerful than Hadrian or Augustus had formerly been. The form was still the same, but the animating health and vigour were fled. The industry of the people was discouraged and exhausted by a long series of oppression. The discipline of the legions, which alone, after the extinction of every other virtue, had propped the greatness of the state, was corrupted by the ambition, or relaxed by the weakness, of the emperors. The strength of the frontiers, which had always consisted in arms rather than in fortifications, was insensibly undermined; and the fairest provinces were left exposed to the rapaciousness or ambition of the barbarians, who soon discovered the decline of the Roman empire.

In 226 A.D. a Parthian monarchy in the East was replaced by a Persian one under Artaxerxes I (226–241) or Ardashir. The ambitions of this prince to restore his realm to the confines of the ancient Persian Empire were bolstered by the resurrection of the nationalistic and fanatical religion of Zoroastrianism. This led to centuries of more embittered conflict between Rome and Persia, which broke out in 232 A.D.

Simultaneously the perils of the northern frontier were increasing. Here the barbarous tribes of Germany, through their poverty, bravery, obsession with honor, and primitive virtues and vices, were a constant source of anxiety. Rome's early policy had been to keep them divided by fostering inter-tribal squabbles. But now, when Roman military discipline was being corrupted and the Roman government distracted, the energetic pressure of the northern barbarians became extremely dangerous.

VIII

(248–268 A.D.) THE EMPERORS DECIUS, GALLUS, ÆMILIANUS, VALERIAN, AND GALLIENUS—THE GENERAL IRRUPTION OF THE BARBARIANS— THE THIRTY TYRANTS

From the great secular games celebrated by Philip to the death of the emperor Gallienus there elapsed (A.D. 248–268) twenty years of shame and misfortune. During that calamitous period every instant of time was marked, every province of the Roman world was afflicted by barbarous invaders and military tyrants, and the ruined empire seemed to approach the last and fatal moment of its dissolution. The confusion of the times, and the scarcity of authentic memorials, oppose equal difficulties to the historian, who attempts to preserve a clear and unbroken thread of narration. Surrounded with imperfect fragments, always concise, often obscure, and sometimes contradictory, he is reduced to collect, to compare, and to conjecture: and though he ought never to place his conjectures in the rank of facts, yet the knowledge of human nature, and of the sure operation of its fierce and unrestrained passions, might, on some occasions, supply the want of historical materials.

There is not, for instance, any difficulty in conceiving that the successive murders of so many emperors had loosened all the ties of allegiance between the prince and people; that all the generals of Philip were disposed to imitate the example of their master; and that the caprice of armies, long since habituated to frequent and violent revolutions, might any day raise to the throne the most obscure of their fellow-soldiers. History can only add that the rebellion against the emperor Philip broke out in the summer of the year two hundred and forty-nine, among the legions of Mæsia; and that a subaltern officer, named Marinus, was the object of their seditious choice. Philip was alarmed. He dreaded lest the treason of the Mæsian army should prove the first spark of a general conflagration. Distracted with the consciousness of his guilt and of his danger, he communicated the intelligence to the senate. A gloomy silence prevailed, the effect of fear, and perhaps of disaffection: till at length Decius, one of the assembly, assuming a spirit worthy of his noble extraction, ventured to discover more intrepidity than the emperor seemed to possess. He treated the whole business with contempt, as a hasty and inconsiderate tumult, and Philip's rival as a phantom of royalty, who in a very few days would be destroyed by the same inconstancy that had created him. The speedy completion of the prophecy inspired Philip with a just esteem for so able a counsellor: and Decius appeared to him the only person capable of restoring peace and discipline to an army whose tumultuous spirit did not immediately subside after the murder of Marinus. Decius who long resisted his own nomination, seems to have insinuated the danger of presenting a leader of merit to the angry and apprehensive minds of the soldiers; and his prediction was again confirmed by the event. The legion of Mæsia forced their judge to become (A.D. 249) their accomplice. They left him only the alternative of death or the purple. His subsequent conduct, after that decisive measure, was unavoidable. He conducted or followed his army to the confines of Italy, whither Philip, collecting all his force to repel the formidable competitor whom he had raised up, advanced to meet him. The Imperial troops were superior in number; but the rebels formed an army of veterans, commanded by an able and experienced leader. Philip was either killed in the battle or put to death a few days afterwards at Verona. His son and associate in the empire was massacred at Rome by the Prætorian guards; and the victorious Decius, with more favourable circumstances than the ambition of that age can usually plead, was universally acknowledged by the senate and provinces. It is reported that, immediately after his reluctant acceptance of the title of Augustus, he had assured Philip, by a private message, of his innocence and loyalty, solemnly protesting that, on his arrival in Italy, he would resign the imperial ornaments and return to the condition of an obedient subject. His professions might be sincere. But in the situation where fortune had placed him it was scarcely possible that he could either forgive or be forgiven.

The emperor Decius had employed a few months in the works of peace and the administration of justice, when (A.D. 250) he was summoned to the banks of the Danube by the invasion of the GOTHS. This is the first considerable occasion in which history mentions that great people, who afterwards broke the Roman power, sacked the Capitol, and reigned in Gaul, Spain, and Italy. So memorable was the part which they acted in the subversion of the Western empire that the name of GOTHS is frequently but improperly used as a general appellation of rude and warlike barbarism.

The Goths were now in possession of the Ukraine, a country of considerable extent and uncommon fertility, intersected with navigable rivers, which, from either side, discharge themselves into the Borysthenes; and interspersed with large and lofty forests of oaks. The plenty of game and fish, the innumerable bee-hives, deposited in the hollows of old trees, and in the cavities of rocks, and forming, even in that rude age, a valuable branch of commerce, the size of the cattle, the temperature of the air, the aptness of the soil for every species of grain, and the luxuriancy of the vegetation, all displayed the liberality of Nature, and tempted the industry of man. But the Goths withstood all these temptations, and still adhered to a life of idleness, of poverty, and of rapine.

The Scythian hordes, which, towards the east, bordered on the new settlements of the Goths, presented nothing to their arms except the doubtful chance of an unprofitable victory. But the prospect of the Roman territories was far more alluring; and the fields of Dacia were covered with rich harvests, sown by the hands of an industrious, and exposed to be gathered by those of a warlike, people. It is probable that the conquests of Trajan maintained by his successors, less for any real advantage than for ideal dignity, had contributed to weaken the empire on that side. The new and unsettled province of Dacia was neither strong enough to resist, nor rich enough to satiate, the rapaciousness of the barbarians. As long as the remote banks of the Dniester were considered as the boundary of the Roman power, the fortifications of the Lower Danube were more carelessly guarded, and the inhabitants of Mæsia lived in supine security, fondly conceiving themselves at an inaccessible distance from any barbarian invaders. The irruptions of the Goths, under the reign of Philip, fatally convinced them of their mistake. The king, or leader, of that fierce nation traversed with contempt the province of Dacia, and passed both the Dniester and the Danube without encountering any opposition capable of retarding his progress. The relaxed discipline of the Roman troops betrayed the most important posts where they were stationed, and the fear of deserved punishment induced great numbers of them to enlist under the Gothic standard. The various multitude of barbarians appeared, at length, under the walls of Marcianopolis, a city built by Trajan in honour of his sister, and at that time the capital of the second Mæsia. The inhabitants consented to ransom their lives and property by the payment of a large sum of money, and the invaders retreated back into their deserts, animated, rather than satisfied, with the first success of their arms against an opulent but feeble country. Intelligence was soon transmitted to the emperor Decius that Cniva, king of the Goths, had passed the Danube a second time, with more considerable forces; that his numerous detachments scattered devastation over the province of Mæsia, whilst the main body of the army, consisting of seventy thousand Germans and Sarmatians, a force equal to the most daring achievements, required the presence of the Roman monarch, and the exertion of his military power.

Decius found (A.D. 250) the Goths engaged before Nicopolis, on the Jatrus, one of the many monuments of Trajan's victories. On his approach they raised the siege, but with a design only of marching away to a conquest of greater importance, the siege of Philippopolis, a city of Thrace, founded by the father of Alexander, near the foot of mount Hæmus. Decius followed them through a difficult country, and by forced marches; but when he imagined himself at a considerable distance from the rear of the Goths, Cniva turned with rapid fury on his pursuers. The camp of the Romans was surprised and pillaged, and, for the first time, their emperor fled in disorder before a troop of half-armed barbarians. After a long resistance, Philippopolis, destitute of succour, was taken by storm. A hundred thousand persons are reported to have been massacred in the sack of that great city. Many prisoners of consequence became a valuable accession to the spoil; and Priscus, a brother of the late emperor Philip, blushed not to assume the purple under the protection of the barbarous enemies of Rome. The time, however, consumed in that tedious siege enabled Decius to revive the courage, restore the discipline, and recruit the numbers of his troops. He intercepted several parties of Carpi, and other Germans, who were hastening to share the victory of their countrymen, intrusted the passes of the mountains to officers of approved valour and fidelity; repaired and strengthened the fortifications of the Danube, and exerted his utmost vigilance to oppose either the progress or the retreat of the Goths. Encouraged by the return of fortune, he anxiously waited for an opportunity to retrieve, by a great and decisive blow, his own glory and that of the Roman arms.

The high-spirited barbarians preferred death to slavery. An obscure town of Mæsia, called Forum Terebronii, was the scene of the battle. The Gothic army was drawn up in three lines, and, either from choice or accident, the front of the third line was covered by a morass. In the beginning of the action, the son of Decius, a youth of the fairest hopes, and already associated to the honours of the purple, was slain by an arrow, in the sight of his afflicted father; who, summoning all his fortitude, admonished the dismayed troops that the loss of a single soldier was of little importance to the republic. The conflict was terrible; it was the combat of despair against grief and rage. The first line of the Goths at length gave way in disorder; the second, advancing to sustain it, shared its fate; and the third only remained entire, prepared to dispute the passage of the morass, which was imprudently attempted by the presumption of the enemy. "Here the fortune of the day turned, and all things became adverse to the Romans: the place deep with ooze, sinking under those who stood, slippery to such as advanced; their armour heavy, the waters deep; nor could they wield, in that uneasy situation, their weighty javelins. The barbarians, on the contrary, were enured to encounters in the bogs, their persons tall, their spears long, such as could wound at a distance." In the morass the Roman army, after an ineffectual struggle, was irrecoverably lost; nor could the body of the emperor ever be found. Such was the fate of Decius, in the fiftieth year of his age; an accomplished prince, active in war, and affable in peace; who, together with his son, has deserved to be compared, both in life and death, with the brightest examples of ancient virtue.

This fatal blow humbled, for a very little time, the insolence of the legions. They appear to have patiently expected, and submissively obeyed, the decree of the senate, which regulated the succession to the throne. From a just regard for the memory of Decius, the Imperial title was (A.D. 251, Dec.) conferred on Hostilianus, his only surviving son; but an equal rank, with more effectual power, was granted to Gallus, whose experience and ability seemed equal to the great trust of guardian to the young prince and the distressed empire. The first care of the new emperor was to deliver the Illyrian provinces from the intolerable weight of the victorious Goths. He (A.D. 252) consented to leave in their hands the rich fruits of their invasion, an immense booty, and, what was still more disgraceful, a great number of prisoners of the highest merit and quality. He plentifully supplied their camp with every convenience that could assuage their angry spirits, or facilitate their so much wished-for departure; and he even promised to pay them annually a large sum of gold, on condition they should never afterwards infest the Roman territories by their incursions.

The dangerous secret of the wealth and weakness of the empire had been revealed to the world. New swarms of barbarians, encouraged (A.D. 253) by the success, and not conceiving themselves bound by the obligation, of their brethren, spread devastation through the Illyrian provinces, and terror as far as the gates of Rome. The defence of the monarchy, which seemed abandoned by the pusillanimous emperor, was assumed by Æmilianus, governor of Pannonia and Mæsia; who rallied the scattered forces, and revived the fainting spirits of the troops. The barbarians were unexpectedly attacked, routed, chased, and pursued beyond the Danube. The victorious leader distributed as a donative the money collected for the tribute, and the acclamations of the soldiers proclaimed him emperor on the field of battle. Gallus, who, careless of the general welfare, indulged himself in the pleasures of Italy, was almost in the same instant informed of the success of the revolt and of the rapid approach of his aspiring lieutenant. He advanced to meet him as far as the plains of Spoleto. When the armies came in sight of each other, the soldiers of Gallus compared the ignominious conduct of their sovereign with the glory of his rival. They admired the valour of Æmilianus; they were attracted by his liberality, for he offered a considerable increase of pay to all deserters. The murder of Gallus, and of his son Volusianus, put an end to the civil war; and the senate (A.D. 253, May) gave a legal sanction to the rights of conquest. The letters of Æmilianus to that assembly displayed a mixture of moderation and vanity. He assured them that he should resign to their wisdom the civil administration; and, contenting himself with the quality of their general, would in a short time assert the glory of Rome, and deliver the empire from all the barbarians both of the North and of the East.

If the new monarch possessed the abilities, he wanted the time necessary to fulfil these splendid promises. Less than four months intervened between his victory and his fall. He had vanquished Gallus: he sunk under the weight of a competitor more formidable than Gallus. That unfortunate prince had sent Valerian, already distinguished by the honourable title of censor, to bring the legions of Gaul and Germany to his aid. Valerian executed that commission with zeal and fidelity; and as he arrived too late to save his sovereign, he resolved to revenge him. The troops of Æmilianus, who still lay encamped in the plains of Spoleto, were awed by the sanctity of his character, but much more by the superior strength of his army; and as they were now become as incapable of personal attachment as they had always been of constitutional principle, they (A.D. 253, Aug.) readily imbrued their hands in the blood of a prince who had so lately been the object of their partial choice. The guilt was theirs, but the advantage of it was Valerian's; who obtained the possession of the throne by the means indeed of a civil war, but with a degree of innocence singular in that age of revolutions; since he owned neither gratitude nor allegiance to his predecessor whom he dethroned.

Valerian was about sixty years of age when he was invested with the purple, not by the caprice of the populace, or the clamours of the army, but by the unanimous voice of the Roman world. In his gradual ascent through the honours of the state, he had deserved the favour of virtuous princes, and had declared himself the enemy of tyrants. His noble birth, his mild but unblemished manners, his learning, prudence, and experience, were revered by the senate and people; and if mankind (according to the observation of an ancient writer) had been left at liberty to choose a master, their choice would most assuredly have fallen on Valerian. Perhaps the merit of this emperor was inadequate to his reputation; perhaps his abilities, or at least his spirit, were affected by the languor and coldness of old age. The consciousness of his decline engaged him to share the throne with a younger and more active associate: the emergency of the times demanded a general no less than a prince; and the experience of the Roman censor might have directed him where to bestow the Imperial purple, as the reward of military merit. But instead of making a judicious choice, which would have confirmed his reign and endeared his memory, Valerian, consulting only the dictates of affection or vanity, immediately invested with the supreme honours his son Gallienus, a youth whose effeminate vices had been hitherto concealed by the obscurity of a private station. The joint government of the father and the son subsisted about seven, and the sole administration of Gallienus continued about eight, years (A.D. 253–268). But the whole period was one uninterrupted series of confusion and calamity. As the Roman empire was at the same time, and on every side, attacked by the blind fury of foreign invaders, and the wild ambition of domestic usurpers, we shall consult order and perspicuity by pursuing not so much the doubtful arrangement of dates as the more natural distribution of subjects. The most dangerous enemies of Rome, during the reigns of Valerian and Gallienus, were, 1. The Franks; 2. The Alemanni; 3. The Goths; and 4. The Persians. Under these general appellations we may comprehend the adventures of less considerable tribes, whose obscure and uncouth names would only serve to oppress the memory and perplex the attention of the reader.

The Romans had long experienced the daring valour of the people of Lower Germany. The union of their strength threatened Gaul with a more formidable invasion, and required the presence of Gallienus, the heir and colleague of imperial power. Whilst that prince, and his infant son Salonius, displayed, in the court of Treves, the majesty of the empire, its armies were ably conducted by their general Posthumus, who, though he afterwards betrayed the family of Valerian, was ever faithful for the great interest of the monarchy. The treacherous language of panegyrics and medals darkly announces a long series of victories. Trophies and titles attest (if such evidence can attest) the fame of Posthumus, who is repeatedly styled The Conqueror of the Germans, and the saviour of Gaul.

But a single fact, the only one indeed of which we have any distinct knowledge, erases, in a great measure, these monuments of vanity and adulation. The Rhine, though dignified with the title of Safeguard of the provinces, was an imperfect barrier against the daring spirit of enterprise with which the Franks were actuated. Their rapid devastations stretched from the river to the foot of the Pyrenees: nor were they stopped by those mountains. Spain, which had never dreaded, was unable to resist, the inroads of the Germans. During twelve years, the greatest part of the reign of Gallienus, that opulent country was the theatre of unequal and destructive hostilities. Tarragona, the flourishing capital of a peaceful province, was sacked and almost destroyed, and so late as the days of Orosius, who wrote in the fifth century, wretched cottages, scattered amidst the ruins of magnificent cities, still recorded the rage of the barbarians. When the exhausted country no longer supplied a variety of plunder, the Franks seized on some vessels in the ports of Spain, and transported themselves into Mauritania. The distant province was astonished with the fury of these barbarians, who seemed to fall from a new world, as their name, manners, and complexion were equally unknown on the coast of Africa.

In the reign of the emperor Caracalla, an innumerable swarm of Suevi appeared on the banks of the Mein, and in the neighbourhood of the Roman provinces, in quest either of food, of plunder, or of glory. The hasty army of volunteers gradually coalesced into a great and permanent nation, and as it was composed from so many different tribes, assumed the name of Alemanni, or *All-men*; to denote at once their various lineage and their common bravery. The latter was soon felt by the Romans in many a hostile inroad. The Alemanni fought chiefly on horseback; but their cavalry was rendered still more formidable by a mixture of light infantry, selected from the bravest and most active of the youth, whom frequent exercise had enured to accompany the horsemen in the longest march, the most rapid charge, or the most precipitate retreat.

This warlike people of Germans had been astonished by the immense preparations of Alexander Severus; they were dismayed by the arms of his successor, a barbarian equal in valour and fierceness to themselves. But still hovering on the frontiers of the empire, they increased the general disorder that ensued after the death of Decius. They inflicted severe wounds on the rich provinces of Gaul; they were the first who removed the veil that covered the feeble majesty of Italy. A numerous body of the Alemanni penetrated across the Danube, and through the Rhætian Alps, into the plains of Lombardy, advanced as far as Ravenna, and displayed the victorious banners of barbarians almost in sight of Rome. The insult and the danger rekindled in the senate some sparks of their ancient virtue. Both the emperors were engaged in far distant wars, Valerian in the East and Gallienus on the Rhine. All the hopes and resources of the Romans were in themselves. In this emergency, the senators resumed the defence of the republic, drew out the Prætorian guards, who had been left to garrison the capital, and filled up their numbers by enlisting into the public service the stoutest and most willing of the Plebeians. The Alemanni, astonished with the sudden appearance of an army more numerous than their own, retired into Germany laden with spoil; and their retreat was esteemed as a victory by the unwarlike Romans.

When Gallienus received the intelligence that his capital was delivered from the barbarians, he was much less delighted than alarmed with the courage of the senate, since it might one day prompt them to rescue the public from domestic tyranny as well as from foreign invasion. His timid ingratitude was published to his subjects in an edict which prohibited the senators from exercising any military employment, and even from approaching the camps of the legions. But his fears were groundless. The rich and luxurious nobles, sinking into their natural character, accepted, as a favour, this disgraceful exemption from military service; and as long as they were indulged in the enjoyment of their baths, their theatres, and their villas, they cheerfully resigned the more dangerous cares of empire to the rough hands of peasants and soldiers.

The Goths, in their new settlement of the Ukraine, soon became masters of the northern coast of the Euxine: to the south of that inland sea were situated the soft and wealthy provinces of Asia Minor, which possessed all that could attract, and nothing that could resist, a barbarian conqueror. With the acquisition of a superfluous waste of fertile soil, the conquerors obtained the command of a naval force, sufficient to transport their armies to the coast of Asia. The fleet of the Goths, leaving the coast of Circassia on the left hand, first appeared before Pityus, the utmost limits of the Roman provinces; a city provided with a convenient port and fortified with a strong wall. Here they met with a resistance more obstinate than they had reason to expect from the feeble garrison of a distant fortress. They were repulsed; and their disappointment seemed to diminish the terror of the Gothic name. As long as Successianus, an officer of superior rank and merit, defended that frontier, all their efforts were ineffectual; but as soon as he was removed by Valerian to a more honourable but less important station, they resumed the attack of Pityus; and, by the destruction of that city, obliterated the memory of their former disgrace.

Circling round the eastern extremity of the Euxine Sea, the navigation from Pityus to Trebizond is about three hundred miles. The course of the Goths carried them in sight of the country of Colchis, so famous by the expedition of the Argonauts, and they even attempted, though without success, to pillage a rich temple at the mouth of the river Phasis. Trebizond, celebrated in the retreat of the Ten Thousand as an ancient colony of Greeks, derived its wealth and splendour from the munificence of the emperor Hadrian, who had constructed an artificial port on a coast left destitute by nature of secure harbours. The city was large and populous; a double enclosure of walls seemed to defy the fury of the Goths, and the usual garrison had been strengthened by a reinforcement of ten thousand men. But there are not any advantages capable of supplying the absence of discipline and vigilance. The numerous garrison of Trebizond, dissolved in riot and luxury, disdained to guard their impregnable fortifications. The Goths soon discovered the supine negligence of the besieged, erected a lofty pile of fascines, ascended the walls in the silence of the night, and entered the defenceless city sword in hand. A general massacre of the people ensued, whilst the affrighted soldiers escaped through the opposite gates of the town. The most holy temples, and the most splendid edifices, were involved in a common destruction. The booty that fell into the hands of the Goths was immense: the wealth of the adjacent countries had been deposited in Trebizond, as in a secure place of refuge. The number of captives was incredible, as the victorious barbarians ranged without opposition through the extensive province of Pontus. The rich spoils of Trebizond filled a great fleet of ships that had been found in the port. The robust youth of the sea-coast were chained to the oar; and the Goths, satisfied with the success of their first naval expedition, returned in triumph to their new establishments in the kingdom of Bosphorus.

The second expedition of the Goths was undertaken with greater powers of men and ships; but they steered a different course, and, disdaining the exhausted provinces of Pontus, followed the western coast of the Euxine, passed before the wide mouths of the Borysthenes, the Dniester, and the Danube, and increasing their fleet by the capture of a great number of fishing barks, they approached the narrow outlet through which the Euxine Sea pours its waters into the Mediterranean, and divides the continents of Europe and Asia. The garrison of Chalcedon was encamped near the temple of Jupiter Urius, on a promontory that commanded the entrance of the Strait; and so dreaded were the invasions of the barbarians, that this body of troops surpassed in number the Gothic army. But it was in numbers alone that they surpassed it. They deserted with precipitation their advantageous post, and abandoned the town of Chalcedon, most plentifully stored with arms and money, to the discretion of the conquerors. Whilst they hesitated whether they should prefer the sea or land, Europe or Asia, for the scene of their hostilities, a perfidious fugitive pointed out Nicomedia, once the capital of the kings of Bithynia, as a rich and easy conquest. He guided the march, which was only sixty miles from the camp of Chalcedon, directed the resistless attack, and partook of the booty; for the Goths had learned sufficient policy to reward the traitor whom they detested. Nice, Prusa, Apamaea, Cius, cities that had sometimes rivalled, or imitated, the splendour of Nicomedia, were involved in the same calamity, which, in a few weeks, raged without control through the whole province of Bithynia. Three hundred years of peace, enjoyed by the soft inhabitants of Asia, had abolished the exercise of arms and removed the apprehension of danger. The ancient walls were suffered to moulder away, and all the revenue of the most opulent cities was reserved for the construction of baths, temples, and theatres.

When we are informed that the third fleet, equipped by the Goths in the ports of Bosphorus, consisted of five hundred sail of ships, our ready imagination instantly computes and multiplies the formidable armament; but as we are assured, by the judicious Strabo, that the piratical vessels used by the barbarians of Pontus and the Lesser Scythia were not capable of containing more than twenty-five or thirty men, we may safely affirm that fifteen thousand warriors, at the most, embarked in this great expedition. Impatient of the limits of the Euxine, they steered their destructive course from the Cimmerian to the Thracian Bosphorus. When they had almost gained the middle of the Straits, they were suddenly driven back to the entrance of them, till a favourable wind springing up the next day carried them in a few hours into the placid sea, or rather lake, of the Propontis. Their landing on the little island of Cyzicus was attended with the ruin of that ancient and noble city. From thence issuing again through the narrow passage of the Hellespont, they pursued their winding navigation amidst the numerous islands scattered over the Archipelago, or the Ægean Sea. The assistance of captives and deserters must have been very necessary to pilot their vessels and to direct their various incursions, as well on the coast of Greece as on that of Asia. At length the Gothic fleet anchored in the port of Piræus, five miles distant from Athens, which had attempted to make some preparations for a vigorous defence. Cleodamus, one of the engineers employed by the emperor's orders to fortify the maritime cities against the Goths, had already begun to repair the ancient walls fallen to decay since the time of Sylla. The efforts of his skill were ineffectual, and the barbarians became masters of the native seat of the muses and the arts. But while the conquerors abandoned themselves to the licence of plunder and intemperance, their fleet, that lay with a slender guard in the harbour of Piræus, was unexpectedly attacked by the brave Dexippus, who, flying with the engineer Cleodamus from the sack of Athens, collected a hasty band of volunteers, peasants as well as soldiers, and in some measure avenged the calamities of his country.

But this exploit, whatever lustre it might shed on the declining age of Athens, served rather to irritate than to subdue the undaunted spirit of the northern invaders. A general conflagration blazed out at the same time in every district of Greece. Thebes and Argos, Corinth and Sparta, which had formerly waged such memorable wars against each other, were now unable to bring an army into the field, or even to defend their ruined fortifications. The rage of war, both by land and by sea, spread from the eastern point of Sunium to the western coast of Epirus. The Goths had already advanced within sight of Italy, when the approach of such imminent danger awakened the indolent Gallienus from his dream of pleasure. The emperor appeared in arms; and his presence seems to have checked the ardour, and to have divided the strength, of the enemy. Naulobatus, a chief of the Heruli, accepted an honourable capitulation, entered with a large body of his countrymen into the service of Rome, and was invested with the ornaments of the consular dignity, which had never before been profaned by the hands of a barbarian. Great numbers of the Goths, disgusted with the perils and hardships of a tedious voyage, broke into Mæsia, with a design of forcing their way over the Danube to their settlements in the Ukraine. The wild attempt would have proved inevitable destruction if the discord of the Roman generals had not opened to the barbarians the means of an escape. The small remainder of this destroying host returned on board their vessels; and measuring back their way through the Hellespont and the Bosphorus, ravaged in their passage the shores of Troy, whose fame, immortalised by Homer, will probably survive the memory of the Gothic conquests.

Another circumstance is related of these invasions, which might deserve our notice, were it not justly to be suspected as the fanciful conceit of a recent sophist. We are told that in the sack of Athens the Goths had collected all the libraries, and were on the point of setting fire to this funeral pile of Grecian learning, had not one of their chiefs, of more refined policy than his brethren, dissuaded them from the design; by the profound observation that as long as the Greeks were addicted to the study of books, they would never apply themselves to the exercise of arms. The sagacious counsellor (should the truth of the fact be admitted) reasoned like an ignorant barbarian. In the most polite and powerful nations, genius of every kind has displayed itself about the same period; and the age of science has generally been the age of military virtue and success.

The new sovereigns of Persia, Artaxerxes and his son Sapor, had triumphed over the house of Arsaces. Of the many princes of that ancient race, Chosroes, king of Armenia, had alone preserved both his life and his independence. He defended himself by the natural strength of his country; by the perpetual resort of fugitives and malcontents; by the alliance of the Romans, and, above all, by his own courage. Invincible in arms, during a thirty years' war, he was at length assassinated by the emissaries of Sapor, king of Persia. The patriotic satraps of Armenia, who asserted the freedom and dignity of the crown, implored the protection of Rome in favour of Tiridates the lawful heir. But the son of Chosroes was an infant, the allies were at a distance, and the Persian monarch advanced towards the frontier at the head of an irresistible force. Young Tiridates, the future hope of his country, was saved by the fidelity of a servant, and Armenia continued above twenty-seven years a reluctant province of the great monarchy of Persia. Elated with this easy conquest, and presuming on the distresses or the degeneracy of the Romans, Sapor obliged the strong garrisons of Carrhæ and Nisibis to surrender, and spread devastation and terror on either side of the Euphrates.

The loss of an important frontier, the ruin of a faithful and natural ally, and the rapid success of Sapor's ambition, affected Rome with a deep sense of the insult as well as of the danger. Valerian flattered himself that the vigilance of his lieutenants would sufficiently provide for the safety of the Rhine and of the Danube; but he resolved, notwithstanding his advanced age, to march in person to the defence of the Euphrates. During his progress through Asia Minor, the naval enterprises of the Goths were suspended, and the afflicted province enjoyed a transient and fallacious calm. He passed the Euphrates, encountered the Persian monarch near the walls of Edessa, was (A.D. 260) vanquished and taken prisoner by Sapor. The particulars of this great event are darkly and imperfectly represented; yet by the glimmering light which is afforded us, we may discover a long series of imprudence, of error, and of deserved misfortunes on the side of the Roman emperor. He reposed an implicit confidence in Macrinus, his Prætorian præfect. That worthless minister rendered his master formidable only to the oppressed subjects, and contemptible to the enemies of Rome. By his weak or wicked counsels, the Imperial army was betrayed into a situation where valour and military skill were equally unavailing. The vigorous attempt of the Romans to cut their way through the Persian host was repulsed with great slaughter; and Sapor, who encompassed the camp with superior numbers, patiently waited till the increasing rage of famine and pestilence had ensured his victory. The licentious murmurs of the legions soon accused Valerian as the cause of their calamities; their seditious clamours demanded an instant capitulation. An immense sum of gold was offered to purchase the permission of a disgraceful retreat. But the Persian, conscious of his superiority, refused the money with disdain; and detaining the deputies, advanced in order of battle to the foot of the Roman rampart, and insisted on a personal conference with the emperor. Valerian was reduced to the necessity of intrusting his life and dignity to the faith of an enemy. The interview ended as it was natural to expect. The emperor was made a prisoner, and his astonished troops laid down their arms. In such a moment of triumph, the pride and policy of Sapor prompted him to fill the vacant throne with a successor entirely dependent on his pleasure. Cyriades, an obscure fugitive of Antioch, stained with every vice, was chosen to dishonour the Roman purple; and the will of the Persian victor could not fail of being ratified by the acclamations, however reluctant, of the captive army.

The Imperial slave was eager to secure the favour of his master by an act of treason to his native country. He conducted Sapor over the Euphrates, and by the way of Chalcis to the metropolis of the East. So rapid were the motions of the Persian cavalry that, if we may credit a very judicious historian, the city of Antioch was surprised when the idle multitude was fondly gazing on the amusements of the theatre. The splendid buildings of Antioch, private as well as public, were either pillaged or destroyed, and the numerous inhabitants were put to the sword, or led away into captivity. The tide of devastation was stopped for a moment by the resolution of the high priest of Emesa. Arrayed in his sacerdotal robes, he appeared at the head of a great body of fanatic peasants, armed only with slings, and defended his god and his property from the sacrilegious hands of the followers of Zoroaster. But the ruin of Tarsus, and many other cities, furnishes a melancholy proof that, except in this single instance, the conquest of Syria and Cilicia scarcely interrupted the progress of the Persian arms.

At the time when the East trembled at the name of Sapor, he received a present not unworthy of the greatest kings; a long train of camels laden with the most rare and valuable merchandises. The rich offering was accompanied with an epistle, respectful but not servile, from Odenathus, one of the noblest and most opulent senators of Palmyra. "Who is this Odenathus" (said the haughty victor, and he commanded that the presents should be cast into the Euphrates), "that he thus insolently presumes to write to his lord? If he entertains a hope of mitigating his punishment let him fall prostrate before the foot of our throne with his hands bound behind his back. Should he hesitate, swift destruction shall be poured on his head, on his whole race, and on his country." The desperate extremity to which the Palmyrenian was reduced called into action all the latent powers of his soul. He met Sapor; but he met him in arms. Infusing his own spirit into a little army collected from the villages of Syria and the tents of the desert, he hovered round the Persian host, harassed their retreat, carried off part of the treasure, and, what was dearer than any treasure, several of the women of the Great King; who was at last obliged to repass the Euphrates with some marks of haste and confusion. By this exploit, Odenathus laid the foundations of his future fame and fortunes. The majesty of Rome, oppressed by a Persian, was protected by a Syrian or Arab of Palmyra.

The voice of history, which is often little more than the organ of hatred or flattery, reproaches Sapor with a proud abuse of the rights of conquest. We are told that Valerian, in chains, but invested with the Imperial purple, was exposed to the multitude, a constant spectacle of fallen greatness; and that whenever the Persian monarch mounted on horseback, he placed his foot on the neck of a Roman emperor. Notwithstanding all the remonstrances of his allies, who repeatedly advised him to remember the vicissitude of fortune, to dread the returning power of Rome, and to make his illustrious captive the pledge of peace, not the object of insult, Sapor still remained inflexible. When Valerian sunk under the weight of shame and grief, his skin, stuffed with straw, and formed into the likeness of a human figure, was preserved for ages in the most celebrated temple of Persia; a more real monument of triumph than the fancied trophies of brass and marble so often erected by Roman vanity. The tale is moral and pathetic, but the truth of it may very fairly be called in question. The letters still extant from the princes of the East to Sapor are manifest forgeries;

nor is it natural to suppose that a jealous monarch should, even in the person of a rival, thus publicly degrade the majesty of kings. Whatever treatment the unfortunate Valerian might experience in Persia, it is at least certain that the only emperor of Rome who had ever fallen into the hands of the enemy languished away his life in hopeless captivity.

The emperor Gallienus, who had long supported with impatience the censorial severity of his father and colleague, received the intelligence of his misfortunes with secret pleasure and avowed indifference. "I knew that my father was a mortal," said he, "and since he has acted as becomes a brave man, I am satisfied." Whilst Rome lamented the fate of her sovereign, the savage coldness of his son was extolled by the servile courtiers as the perfect firmness of a hero and a stoic. It is difficult to paint the light, the various, the inconstant character of Gallienus, which he displayed without constraint, as soon as he became sole possessor of the empire. In every art that he attempted his lively genius enabled him to succeed; and as his genius was destitute of judgment, he attempted every art except the important ones of war and government. He was a master of several curious but useless sciences, a ready orator and elegant poet, a skilful gardener, an excellent cook, and most contemptible prince. When the great emergencies of the state required his presence and attention, he was engaged in conversation with the philosopher Plotinus, wasting his time in trifling or licentious pleasures, preparing his initiation to the Grecian mysteries, or soliciting a place in the Areopagus of Athens. His profuse magnificence insulted the general poverty; the solemn ridicule of his triumphs impressed a deeper sense of the public disgrace. The repeated intelligence of invasions, defeats, and rebellions, he received with a careless smile; and singling out, with affected contempt, some particular production of the lost province, he carelessly asked whether Rome must be ruined unless it was supplied with linen from Egypt and Arras cloth from Gaul? There were, however, a few short moments in the life of Gallienus when, exasperated by some recent injury, he suddenly appeared the intrepid soldier and the cruel tyrant; till satiated with blood, or fatigued by resistance, he insensibly sunk into the natural mildness and indolence of his character.

At a time when the reins of government were held with so loose a hand, it is not surprising that a crowd of usurpers should start up in every province of the empire against the son of Valerian. It was probably some ingenious fancy, of comparing the thirty tyrants of Rome with the thirty tyrants of Athens, that induced the writers of the Augustan History to select that celebrated number, which has been gradually received into a popular appellation. But in every light the parallel is idle and defective. What resemblance can we discover between a council of thirty persons, the united oppressors of a single city, and an uncertain list of independent rivals, who rose and fell in irregular succession through the extent of a vast empire? Nor can the number of thirty be completed, unless we include in the account the women and children who were honoured with the Imperial title. The reign of Gallienus, distracted as it was, produced only nineteen pretenders to the throne: Cyriades, Macrianus, Balista, Odenathus, and Zenobia in the east; in Gaul, and the western provinces, Posthumus, Lollianus, Victorinus and his mother Victoria, Marius, and Tetricus. In Illyricum and the confines of the Danube, Ingenuus, Regillianus, and Aureolus; in Pontus, Saturninus; in Isauria, Trebellianus, Piso in Thessaly; Valens in Achaia; Æmilianus in Egypt; and Celsus in Africa. To illustrate the obscure monuments of the life and death of each individual would prove a laborious task, alike barren of instruction and of amusement. We may content ourselves with investigating some general characters that most strongly mark the condition of the times and the manners of the men, their pretensions, their motives, their fate, and the destructive consequences of their usurpation.

It is sufficiently known that the odious appellation of *Tyrant* was often employed by the ancients to express the illegal seizure of supreme power, without any reference to the abuse of it. Several of the pretenders, who raised the standard of rebellion against the emperor Gallienus, were shining models of virtue, and almost all possessed a considerable share of vigour and ability. Their merit had recommended them to the favour of Valerian, and gradually promoted them to the most important commands of the empire. The generals, who assumed the title of Augustus, were either respected by their troops for their able conduct and severe discipline, or admired for valour and success in war, or beloved for frankness and generosity. The field of victory was often the scene of their election; and even the armourer Marius, the most contemptible of all the candidates for the purple, was distinguished however by intrepid courage, matchless strength, and blunt honesty. His mean and recent trade cast indeed an air of ridicule on his elevation; but his birth could not be more obscure than was that of the greater part of his rivals, who were born of peasants and enlisted in the army as private soldiers.

The lieutenants of Valerian were grateful to the father, whom they esteemed. They disdained to serve the luxurious indolence of his unworthy son. The throne of the Roman world was unsupported by any principle of loyalty; and treason against such a prince might easily be considered as patriotism to the state. Yet if we examine with candour the conduct of these usurpers, it will appear that they were much oftener driven into rebellion by their fears than urged to it by their ambition. They dreaded the cruel suspicions of Gallienus; they equally dreaded the capricious violence of their troops. If the dangerous favour of the army had imprudently declared them deserving of the purple, they were marked for sure destruction; and even prudence would counsel them to secure a short enjoyment of empire, and rather to try the fortune of war than to expect the hand of an executioner. When the clamour of the soldiers invested the reluctant victims with the ensigns of sovereign authority, they sometimes mourned in secret their approaching fate. "You have lost," said Saturninus on the day of his elevation, "you have lost a useful commander, and you have made a very wretched emperor."

The apprehensions of Saturninus were justified by the repeated experience of revolutions. Of the nineteen tyrants who started up under the reign of Gallienus, there was not one who enjoyed a life of peace or a natural death. As soon as they were invested with the bloody purple, they inspired their adherents with the same fears and ambition which had occasioned their own revolt. Encompassed with domestic conspiracy, military sedition, and civil war, they trembled on the edge of precipices, in which, after a longer or shorter term of anxiety, they were inevitably lost. The precarious monarchs received, however, such honours as the flattery of their respective armies and provinces could bestow; but their claim, founded on rebellion, could never obtain the sanction of law or history. Italy, Rome, and the senate constantly adhered to the cause of Gallienus, and he alone was considered as the sovereign of the empire.

The rapid and perpetual transitions from the cottage to the throne and from the throne to the grave, might have amused an indifferent philosopher; were it possible for a philosopher to remain indifferent amidst the general calamities of human kind. The election of these precarious emperors, their power and their death, were equally destructive to their subjects and adherents. The price of their fatal elevation was instantly discharged to the troops, by an immense donative, drawn from the bowels of the exhausted people. However virtuous was their character, however pure their intentions, they found themselves reduced to the hard necessity of supporting their usurpation by frequent acts of rapine and cruelty. When they fell, they involved armies and provinces in their fall. There is still extant a most savage mandate from Gallienus to one of his ministers, after the suppression of Ingenuus, who had assumed the purple in Illyricum. "It is not enough," says that soft but inhuman prince, "that you exterminate such as have appeared in arms: the chance of battle might have served me as effectually. The male sex of every age must be extirpated; provided that, in the execution of the children and old men, you can contrive means to save our reputation. Let every one die who has dropped an expression, who has entertained a thought against me, against *me*, the son of Valerian, the father and brother of so many princes. Remember that Ingenuus was made emperor: tear, kill, hew in pieces. I write to you with my own hand, and would inspire you with my own feelings." Whilst the public forces of the state were dissipated in private quarrels, the defenceless provinces lay exposed to every invader. The bravest usurpers were compelled, by the perplexity of their situation, to conclude ignominious treaties with the common enemy, to purchase with oppressive tributes the neutrality or services of the barbarians, and to introduce hostile and independent nations into the heart of the Roman monarchy. Such were the barbarians, and such the tyrants, who, under the reigns of Valerian and Gallienus, dismembered the provinces, and reduced the empire to the lowest pitch of disgrace and ruin, from whence it seemed impossible that it should ever emerge.

Our habits of thinking so fondly connect the order of the universe with the fate of man, that this gloomy period of history has been decorated with inundations, earthquakes, uncommon meteors, preternatural darkness, and a crowd of prodigies fictitious or exaggerated. But a long and general famine was a calamity of a more serious kind. It was the inevitable consequence of rapine and oppression, which extirpated the produce of the present, and the hope of future harvests. Famine is almost always followed by epidemical diseases, the effect of scanty and unwholesome food. Other causes must however have contributed to the furious plague, which, from the year two hundred and fifty to the year two hundred and sixty-five, raged without interruption in every province, every city, and almost every family, of the Roman empire. During some time five thousand persons died daily in Rome; and many towns, that had escaped the hands of the barbarians, were entirely depopulated.

We have the knowledge of a very curious circumstance, of some use perhaps in the melancholy calculation of human calamities. An exact register was kept at Alexandria, of all the citizens entitled to receive the distribution of corn. It was found that the ancient number of those comprised between the ages of forty and seventy had been equal to the whole sum of claimants, from fourteen to fourscore years of age, who remained alive after the reign of Gallienus. Applying this authentic fact to the most correct tables of mortality, it evidently proves that above half the people of Alexandria had perished; and could we venture to extend the analogy to the other provinces, we might suspect that war, pestilence, and famine had consumed, in a few years, the moiety of the human species.

IX

(268–275 A.D.) REIGN OF CLAUDIUS—DEFEAT OF THE GOTHS—VICTORIES, TRIUMPH, AND DEATH OF AURELIAN

Under the deplorable reigns of Valerian and Gallienus the empire was oppressed and almost destroyed by the soldiers, the tyrants, and the barbarians. It was saved by a series of great princes, who derived their obscure origin from the martial provinces of Illyricum. Within a period of about thirty years, Claudius, Aurelian, Probus, Diocletian and his colleagues, triumphed over the foreign and domestic enemies of the state, re-established, with the military discipline, the strength of the frontiers, and deserved the glorious title of Restorers of the Roman world.

The removal of an effeminate tyrant made way for a succession of heroes. The indignation of the people imputed all their calamities to Gallienus, and the far greater part were, indeed, the consequence of his dissolute manners and careless administration. He was even destitute of a sense of honour, which so frequently supplies the absence of public virtue; and as long as he was permitted to enjoy the possession of Italy, a victory of the barbarians, the loss of a province, or the rebellion of a general, seldom disturbed the tranquil course of his pleasures. At length a considerable army, stationed on the Upper Danube, invested with the Imperial purple their leader Aureolus, who, disdaining a confined and barren reign over the mountains of Rhætia, passed the Alps, occupied Milan, threatened Rome, and challenged Gallienus to dispute in the field the sovereignty of Italy. The emperor, provoked by the insult, and alarmed by the instant danger, suddenly exerted that latent vigour which sometimes broke through the indolence of his temper. Forcing himself from the luxury of the palace, he appeared in arms at the head of his legions, and advanced beyond the Po to encounter his competitor. At a late hour of the night, but while the emperor still protracted the pleasures of the table, an alarm was suddenly given that Aureolus, at the head of all his forces, had made a desperate sally from the town; Gallienus, who was never deficient in personal bravery, started from his silken couch, and, without allowing himself time either to put on his armour or to assemble his guards, he mounted on horseback and rode full speed towards the supposed place of the attack. Encompassed by his declared or concealed enemies, he soon, amidst the nocturnal tumult, received a mortal dart from an uncertain hand. Before he expired, a patriotic sentiment rising in the mind of Gallienus induced him to name a deserving successor, and it was his last request that the Imperial ornaments should be delivered to Claudius, who then commanded a detached army in the neighbourhood of Pavia. The report at least was diligently propagated, and the order cheerfully obeyed by the conspirators, who had already agreed to place Claudius on the throne. On the first news of the emperor's death the troops expressed some suspicion and resentment, till the one was removed and the other assuaged by a donative of twenty pieces of gold to each soldier. They then ratified the election and acknowledged the merit of their new sovereign.

In the arduous task which Claudius had undertaken of restoring the empire to its ancient splendour, it was first necessary to revive among his troops a sense of order and obedience. With the authority of a veteran commander, he represented to them that the relaxation of discipline had introduced a long train of disorders, the effects of which were at length experienced by the soldiers themselves; that a people ruined by oppression, and indolent from despair, could no longer supply a numerous army with the means of luxury, or even of subsistence; that the danger of each individual had increased with the despotism of the military order, since princes who tremble on the throne will guard their safety by the instant sacrifice of every obnoxious subject. The emperor expatiated on the mischiefs of a lawless caprice, which the soldiers could only gratify at the expense of their own blood, as their seditious elections had so frequently been followed by civil wars, which consumed the flower of the legions either in the field of battle or in the cruel abuse of victory. He painted in the most lively colours the exhausted state of the treasury, the desolation of the provinces, the disgrace of the Roman name, and the insolent triumph of rapacious barbarians. It was against those barbarians, he declared, that he intended to point the first effort of their arms. Tetricus might reign for a while over the West, and even Zenobia might preserve the dominion of the East. These usurpers were his personal adversaries, nor could he think of indulging any private resentment till he had saved an empire whose impending ruin would, unless it was timely prevented, crush both the army and the people.

The various nations of Germany and Sarmatia who fought under the Gothic standard had already collected an armament more formidable than any which had yet issued from the Euxine. By the most signal victories he delivered the empire from this host of barbarians, and was distinguished by posterity under the glorious appellation of the Gothic Claudius. The imperfect historians of an irregular war do not enable us to describe the order and circumstances of his exploits; but, if we could be indulged in the allusion, we might distribute into three acts this memorable tragedy. I. The decisive battle was fought near Naissus, a city of Dardania. The legions at first gave way, oppressed by numbers and dismayed by misfortunes. Their ruin was inevitable, had not the abilities of their emperor prepared a seasonable relief. A large detachment, rising out of the secret and difficult passes of the mountains, which by his order they had occupied, suddenly assailed the rear of the victorious Goths. The favourable instant was improved by the activity of Claudius. He revived the courage of his troops, restored their ranks, and pressed the barbarians on every side. Fifty thousand men are reported to have been slain in the battle of Naissus. Several large bodies of barbarians, covering their retreat with a movable fortification of waggons, retired, or rather escaped, from the field of slaughter. II. We may presume that some insurmountable difficulty—the fatigue, perhaps, or the disobedience, of the conquerors—prevented Claudius from completing in one day the destruction of the Goths. The war was diffused over the provinces of Mæsia, Thrace, and Macedonia, and its operations drawn out into a variety of marches, surprises and tumultuary engagements, as well by sea as by land. When the Romans suffered any loss, it was commonly occasioned by their own cowardice or rashness; but the superior talents of the emperor, his perfect knowledge of the country, and his judicious choice of measures as well as officers, assured on most occasions the success of his arms. The immense booty, the fruit of so many victories, consisted for the greater part of cattle and slaves. A select body of the Gothic youth was received among the Imperial troops; the remainder was sold into servitude; and so considerable was the number of female captives that every soldier obtained as his share two or three women. A circumstance from which we may conclude that the invaders entertained some designs of settlement as well as of plunder; since even in a naval expedition they were accompanied by their families. III. The loss of their fleet, which was either taken or sunk, had intercepted the retreat of the Goths. A vast circle of Roman posts, distributed with skill, supported with firmness, and gradually closing towards a common centre, forced the barbarians into the most inaccessible parts of Mount Hæmus, where they found a safe refuge, but a very scanty subsistence. During the course of a rigorous winter, in which they were besieged by the emperor's troops, famine and pestilence, desertion and the sword, continually diminished the imprisoned multitude. On the return of spring nothing appeared in arms except a hardy and desperate band, the remnant of that mighty host which had embarked at the mouth of the Dniester.

The pestilence which swept away such numbers of the barbarians at length proved fatal to their conqueror. After a short but glorious reign of two years, Claudius expired at Sirmium, amidst the tears and acclamations of his subjects. In his last illness he convened the principal officers of the state and army, and in their presence recommended Aurelian, one of his generals, as the most deserving of the throne, and the best qualified to execute the great design which he himself had been permitted only to undertake. The virtues of Claudius, his valour, affability, justice, and temperance, his love of fame and of his country, place him in that short list of emperors who added lustre to the Roman purple. Those virtues, however, were celebrated with peculiar zeal and complacency by the courtly writers of the age of Constantine, who was the great-grandson of Crispus, the elder brother of Claudius. The voice of flattery was soon taught to repeat that the gods, who so hastily had snatched Claudius from the earth, rewarded his merit and piety by the perpetual establishment of the empire in his family.

The reign of Aurelian lasted only four years and about nine months; but every instant of that short period was filled by some memorable achievement. He put an end to the Gothic war, chastised the Germans who invaded Italy, recovered Gaul, Spain, and Britain out of the hands of Tetricus, and destroyed the proud monarchy which Zenobia had erected in the East on the ruins of the afflicted empire.

It was the rigid attention of Aurelian even to the minutest articles of discipline which bestowed such uninterrupted success on his arms. His military regulations are contained in a very concise epistle to one of his inferior officers, who is commanded to enforce them, as he wishes to become a tribune, or as he is desirous to live. Gaming, drinking, and the arts of divination were severely prohibited. Aurelian expected that his soldiers should be modest, frugal, and laborious; that their armour should be constantly kept bright, their weapons sharp, their clothing and horses ready for immediate service; that they should live in their quarters with chastity and sobriety, without damaging the corn-fields, without stealing even a sheep, a fowl, or a bunch of grapes, without exacting from their landlords either salt, or oil, or wood. "The public allowance," continues the emperor, "is sufficient for their support; their wealth should be collected from the spoil of the enemy, not from the tears of the provincials." A single instance will serve to display the rigour, and even cruelty, of Aurelian. One of the soldiers had seduced the wife of his host. The guilty wretch was fastened to two trees forcibly drawn towards each other, and his limbs were torn asunder by their sudden separation. A few such examples impressed a salutary consternation. The punishments of Aurelian were terrible; but he had seldom occasion to punish more than once the same offence. His own conduct gave a sanction to his laws, and the seditious legions dreaded a chief who had learned to obey, and who was worthy to command.

The death of Claudius had revived the fainting spirit of the Goths. The troops which guarded the passes of Mount Hæmus and the banks of the Danube had been drawn away by the apprehension of a civil war; and it seems probable that the remaining body of the Gothic and Vandalic tribes embraced the favourable opportunity, abandoned their settlements of the Ukraine, traversed the rivers, and swelled with new multitudes the destroying host of their countrymen. Their united numbers were at length encountered by Aurelian, and the bloody and doubtful conflict ended only with the approach of night. Exhausted by so many calamities, which they had mutually endured and inflicted during a twenty years' war, the Goths and the Romans consented to a lasting and beneficial treaty. It was earnestly solicited by the barbarians, and cheerfully ratified by the legions, to whose suffrage the prudence of Aurelian referred the decision of that important question. The Gothic nation engaged to supply the armies of Rome with a body of two thousand auxiliaries, consisting entirely of cavalry, and stipulated in return an undisturbed retreat, with a regular market as far as the Danube, provided by the emperor's care, but at their own expense.

The treaty was observed with such religious fidelity that, when a party of five hundred men straggled from the camp in quest of plunder, the king or general of the barbarians commanded that the guilty leader should be apprehended and shot to death with darts, as a victim devoted to the sanctity of their engagements. It is, however, not unlikely that the precaution of Aurelian, who had exacted as hostages the sons and daughters of the Gothic chiefs, contributed something to this pacific temper. The youths he trained in the exercise of arms, and near his own person; to the damsels he gave a liberal and Roman education, and, by bestowing them in marriage on some of his principal officers, gradually introduced between the two nations the closest and most endearing connections.

But the most important condition of peace was understood rather than expressed in the treaty Aurelian withdrew the Roman forces from Dacia, and tacitly relinquished that great province to the Goths and Vandals. His manly judgment convinced him of the solid advantages, and taught him to despise the seeming disgrace, of thus contracting the frontiers of the monarchy. The Dacian subjects, removed from those distant possessions which they were unable to cultivate or defend, added strength and populousness to the southern side of the Danube. A fertile territory, which the repetition of barbarous inroads had changed into a desert, was yielded to their industry, and a new province of Dacia still preserved the memory of Trajan's conquests. The old country of that name detained, however, a considerable number of its inhabitants, who dreaded exile more than a Gothic master. These degenerate Romans continued to serve the empire, whose allegiance they had renounced, by introducing among their conquerors the first notions of agriculture, the useful arts, and the conveniences of civilised life. An intercourse of commerce and language was gradually established between the opposite banks of the Danube; and, after Dacia became an independent state, it often proved the firmest barrier of the empire against the invasions of the savages of the North. A sense of interest attached these more settled barbarians to the alliance of Rome, and a permanent interest very frequently ripens into sincere and useful friendship. This various colony, which filled the ancient province, and was insensibly blended into one great people, still acknowledged the superior renown and authority of the Gothic tribe, and claimed the fancied honour of a Scandinavian origin. At the same time the lucky, though accidental, resemblance of the

name of Getæ infused among the credulous Goths a vain persuasion that, in a remote age, their own ancestors, already seated in
the Dacian provinces, had received the instructions of Zamolxis,
and checked the victorious arms of Sesostris and Darius.

While the vigorous and moderate conduct of Aurelian restored
the Illyrian frontier, the nation of the Alemanni violated the conditions of peace which either Gallienus had purchased, or Claudius
had imposed, and, inflamed by their impatient youth, suddenly
flew to arms. Forty thousand horses appeared in the field, and the
numbers of the infantry doubled those of the cavalry. The first
objects of their avarice were a few cities of the Rhætian frontier;
but their hopes soon rising with success, the rapid march of the
Alemanni traced a line of devastation from the Danube to the Po.

As the light troops of the Alemanni had spread themselves from
the Alps to the Apennine, the incessant vigilance of Aurelian and
his officers was exercised in the discovery, the attack, and the pursuit of the numerous detachments. Notwithstanding this desultory
war, three considerable battles are mentioned, in which the principal force of both armies was obstinately engaged. The success was
various. In the first, fought near Placentia, the Romans received so
severe a blow that, according to the expression of a writer extremely
partial to Aurelian, the immediate dissolution of the empire was
apprehended. The crafty barbarians, who had lined the woods,
suddenly attacked the legions in the dusk of the evening, and, it is
most probable, after the fatigue and disorder of a long march. The
fury of their charge was irresistible; but at length, after a dreadful
slaughter, the patient firmness of the emperor rallied his troops,
and restored, in some degree, the honour of his arms. The second
battle was fought near Fano in Umbria; on the spot which, five
hundred years before, had been fatal to the brother of Hannibal.
Thus far the successful Germans had advanced along the Æmilian
and Flaminian way, with a design of sacking the defenceless
mistress of the world. But Aurelian, who, watchful for the safety of
Rome, still hung on their rear, found in this place the decisive
moment of giving them a total and irretrievable defeat. The flying remnant of their host was exterminated in a third and last
battle near Pavia; and Italy was delivered from the inroads of the
Alemanni.

The seven hills of Rome had been surrounded, by the successors
of Romulus, with an ancient wall of more than thirteen miles. The
vast enclosure may seem disproportioned to the strength and

numbers of the infant state. But it was necessary to secure an ample extent of pasture and arable land against the frequent and sudden incursions of the tribes of Latium, the perpetual enemies of the republic. With the progress of Roman greatness, the city and its inhabitants gradually increased, filled up the vacant space, pierced through the useless walls, covered the field of Mars, and, on every side, followed the public highways in long and beautiful suburbs. The extent of the new walls, erected by Aurelian, and finished in the reign of Probus, was magnified by popular estimation to near fifty, but is reduced by accurate measurement to about twenty-one miles. It was a great but a melancholy labour, since the defence of the capital betrayed the decline of the monarchy. The Romans of a more prosperous age, who trusted to the arms of the legions the safety of the frontier camps, were very far from entertaining a suspicion that it would ever become necessary to fortify the seal of empire against the inroads of the barbarians.

The victory of Claudius over the Goths, and the success of Aurelian against the Alemanni, had already restored to the arms of Rome their ancient superiority over the barbarous nations of the North. To chastise domestic tyrants, and to reunite the dismembered parts of the empire, was a task reserved for the second of those warlike emperors. Though he was acknowledged by the senate and people, the frontiers of Italy, Africa, Illyricum, and Thrace, confined the limits of his reign. Gaul, Spain, and Britain, Egypt, Syria, and Asia Minor, were still possessed by two rebels, who alone, out of so numerous a list, had hitherto escaped the dangers of their situation; and to complete the ignominy of Rome, these rival thrones had been usurped by women.

A rapid succession of monarchs had arisen and fallen in the provinces of Gaul. The rigid virtues of Posthumus served only to hasten his destruction. After suppressing a competitor who had assumed the purple at Mentz, he refused to gratify his troops with the plunder of the rebellious city; and, in the seventh year of his reign, became the victim of their disappointed avarice. The death of Victorinus, his friend and associate, was occasioned by a less worthy cause. The shining accomplishments of that prince were stained by a licentious passion, which he indulged in acts of violence, with too little regard to the laws of society, or even to those of love. He was slain at Cologne, by a conspiracy of jealous husbands, whose revenge would have appeared more justifiable had they spared the innocence of his son. After the murder of so many valiant princes, it is somewhat remarkable that a female for a long time controlled the fierce legions of Gaul, and still more singular that she was the mother of the unfortunate Victorinus. The arts and treasures of Victoria enabled her successively to place Marius and Tetricus on the throne, and to reign with a manly vigour under the name of those dependent emperors. Money of copper, of silver, and of gold, was coined in her name, she assumed the titles of Augusta and Mother of the Camps: her power ended only with her life; but her life was perhaps shortened by the ingratitude of Tetricus.

When, at the instigation of his ambitious patroness, Tetricus assumed the ensigns of royalty, he was governor of the peaceful province of Aquitaine, an employment suited to his character and education. He reigned four or five years over Gaul, Spain, and Britain, the slave and sovereign of a licentious army, whom he dreaded, and by whom he was despised. The valour and fortune of Aurelian at length opened the prospect of a deliverance. He ventured to disclose his melancholy situation, and conjured the emperor to hasten to the relief of his unhappy rival. Had this secret correspondence reached the ears of the soldiers, it would most probably have cost Tetricus his life; nor could he resign the sceptre of the West without committing an act of treason against himself. He affected the appearances of a civil war, led his forces into the field against Aurelian, posted them in the most disadvantageous manner, betrayed his own counsels to the enemy, and with a few chosen friends deserted in the beginning of the action. The rebel legions, though disordered and dismayed by the unexpected treachery of their chief, defended themselves with desperate valour, till they were cut in pieces almost to a man, in this bloody and memorable battle, which was fought near Châlons in Champagne. The retreat of the irregular auxiliaries, Franks and Batavians, whom the conqueror soon compelled or persuaded to repass the Rhine, restored the general tranquillity, and the power of Aurelian was acknowledged from the wall of Antoninus to the Columns of Hercules.

Aurelian had no sooner secured the person and provinces of Tetricus than he turned his arms against Zenobia, the celebrated queen of Palmyra and the East. Modern Europe has produced several illustrious women who have sustained with glory the weight of empire; nor is our own age destitute of such distinguished characters. But if we except the doubtful achievements of Semiramis,

Zenobia is perhaps the only female whose superior genius broke through the servile indolence imposed on her sex by the climate and manners of Asia. She claimed her descent from the Macedonian kings of Egypt, equalled in beauty her ancestor Cleopatra, and far surpassed that princess in chastity and valour. Zenobia was esteemed the most lovely as well as the most heroic of her sex. She was of a dark complexion (for in speaking of a lady these trifles become important). Her teeth were of a pearly whiteness, and her large black eyes sparkled with uncommon fire, tempered by the most attractive sweetness. Her voice was strong and harmonious. Her manly understanding was strengthened and adorned by study. She was not ignorant of the Latin tongue, but possesed in equal perfection the Greek, the Syriac, and the Egyptian languages. She had drawn up for her own use an epitome of oriental history, and familiarly compared the beauties of Homer and Plato under the tuition of the sublime Longinus.

This accomplished woman gave her hand to Odenathus, who, from a private station, raised himself to the dominion of the East. She soon became the friend and companion of a hero. In the intervals of war Odenathus passionately delighted in the exercise of hunting; he pursued with ardour the wild beasts of the desert, lions, panthers, and bears; and the ardour of Zenobia in that dangerous amusement was not inferior to his own. She had inured her constitution to fatigue, disdained the use of a covered carriage, generally appeared on horseback in a military habit, and sometimes marched several miles on foot at the head of the troops. The success of Odenathus was in a great measure ascribed to her incomparable prudence and fortitude. Their splendid victories over the Great King, whom they twice pursued as far as the gates of Ctesiphon, laid the foundations of their united fame and power. The armies which they commanded, and the provinces which they had saved, acknowledged not any other sovereigns than their invincible chiefs. The senate and people of Rome revered a stranger who had avenged their captive emperor, and even the insensible son of Valerian accepted Odenathus for his legitimate colleague.

After a successful expedition against the Gothic plunderers of Asia, the Palmyrenian prince returned to the city of Emesian Syria. Invincible in war, he was there cut off by domestic treason; and his favourite amusement of hunting was the cause, or at least the occasion, of his death. His nephew, Mæonius, presumed to dart his javelin before that of his uncle; and, though admonished of his error, repeated the same insolence. As a monarch, and as a sports-man, Odenathus was provoked, took away his horse, a mark of ignominy among the barbarians, and chastised the rash youth by a short confinement. The offence was soon forgot, but the punish-ment was remembered; and Mæonius, with a few daring associates, assassinated his uncle in the midst of a great entertainment. Herod, the son of Odenathus, though not of Zenobia, a young man of a soft and effeminate temper, was killed with his father. But Mæonius obtained only the pleasure of revenge by this bloody deed. He had scarcely time to assume the title of Augustus before he was sacri-ficed by Zenobia to the memory of her husband.

With the assistance of his most faithful friends, she immediately filled the vacant throne, and governed with manly counsels Palmyra, Syria, and the East, above five years. By the death of Odenathus, that authority was at an end which the senate had granted him only as a personal distinction; but his martial widow, disdaining both the senate and Gallienus, obliged one of the Roman generals who was sent against her to retreat into Europe, with the loss of his army and his reputation. Instead of the little passions which so frequently perplex a female reign, the steady administration of Zenobia was guided by the most judicious maxims of policy. If it was expedient to pardon, she could calm her resentment; if it was necessary to punish, she could impose silence on the voice of pity. Her strict economy was accused of avarice; yet on every proper occasion she appeared magnificent and liberal. The neighbouring states of Arabia, Armenia, and Persia, dreaded her enmity, and solicited her alliance. To the dominions of Odenathus, which extended from the Euphrates to the frontiers of Bithynia, his widow added the inheritance of her ancestors, the populous and fertile kingdom of Egypt. The emperor Claudius acknowledged her merit, and was content that, while *he* pursued the Gothic war, *she* should assert the dignity of the empire in the East. The conduct, however, of Zenobia was attended with some ambiguity; nor is it unlikely that she had conceived the design of erecting an independent and hostile monarchy. She blended with the popular manners of Roman princes the stately pomp of the courts of Asia, and exacted from her subjects the same adoration that was paid to the successors of Cyrus. She bestowed on her three sons a Latin education, and often showed them to the troops adorned with the Imperial purple. For herself she reserved the diadem, with the splendid but doubtful title of Queen of the East.

When Aurelian passed over into Asia, against an adversary whose sex alone could render her an object of contempt, his presence restored obedience to the province of Bithynia, already shaken by the arms and intrigues of Zenobia. Advancing at the head of his legions, he accepted the submission of Ancyra, and was admitted into Tyana, after an obstinate siege, by the help of a perfidious citizen. The generous though fierce temper of Aurelian abandoned the traitor to the rage of the soldiers: a superstitious reverence induced him to treat with lenity the countrymen of Apollonius the philosopher. Antioch was deserted on his approach, till the emperor, by his salutary edicts, recalled the fugitives, and granted a general pardon to all who, from necessity rather than choice, had been engaged in the service of the Palmyrenian queen. The unexpected mildness of such a conduct reconciled the minds of the Syrians, and, as far as the gates of Emesa, the wishes of the people seconded the terror of his arms.

Zenobia would have ill deserved her reputation had she indolently permitted the emperor of the West to approach within an hundred miles of her capital. The fate of the East was decided in two great battles; so similar in almost every circumstance, that we can scarcely distinguish them from each other, except by observing that the first was fought near Antioch, and the second near Emesa. In both the queen of Palmyra animated the armies by her presence, and devolved the execution of her orders on Zabdas, who had already signalised his military talents by the conquest of Egypt. The numerous forces of Zenobia consisted for the most part of light archers, and of heavy cavalry clothed in complete steel. The Moorish and Illyrian horse of Aurelian were unable to sustain the ponderous charge of their antagonists. They fled in real or affected disorder, engaged the Palmyrenians in a laborious pursuit, harassed them by a desultory combat, and at length discomfited this impenetrable but unwieldy body of cavalry. The light infantry, in the meantime, when they had exhausted their quivers, remaining without protection against a closer onset, exposed their naked sides to the swords of the legions. Aurelian had chosen these veteran troops who were usually stationed on the Upper Danube, and whose valour had been severely tried in the Alemannic war. After the defeat of Emesa, Zenobia found it impossible to collect a third army. As far as the frontier of Egypt, the nations subject to her empire had joined the standard of the conqueror, who detached Probus, the bravest of his generals, to possess himself of the

Egyptian provinces. Palmyra was the last resource of the widow of
Odenathus. She retired within the walls of her capital, made every
preparation for a vigorous resistance, and declared, with the
intrepidity of a heroine, that the last moment of her reign and of
her life should be the same.

Amid the barren deserts of Arabia a few cultivated spots rise
like islands out of the sandy ocean. Even the name of Tadmor, or
Palmyra, by its signification in the Syriac as well as in the Latin
language, denoted the multitude of palm-trees which afforded
shade and verdure to that temperate region. The air was pure, and
the soil, watered by some invaluable springs, was capable of
producing fruits as well as corn. A place possessed of such singular
advantages, and situated at a convenient distance between the Gulf
of Persia and the Mediterranean, was soon frequented by the
caravans which conveyed to the nations of Europe a considerable
part of the rich commodities of India. Palmyra insensibly increased
into an opulent and independent city, and, connecting the Roman
and the Parthian monarchies by the mutual benefits of commerce,
was suffered to observe an humble neutrality, till at length, after
the victories of Trajan, the little republic sunk into the bosom of
Rome, and flourished more than one hundred and fifty years in
the subordinate though honourable rank of a colony. It was during
that peaceful period, if we may judge from a few remaining
inscriptions, that the wealthy Palmyrenians constructed those
temples, palaces, and porticos of Grecian architecture, whose ruins,
scattered over an extent of several miles, have deserved the curiosity
of our travellers. The elevation of Odenathus and Zenobia appeared
to reflect new splendour on their country, and Palmyra, for a while,
stood forth the rival of Rome; but the competition was fatal, and
ages of prosperity were sacrificed to a moment of glory.

The firmness of Zenobia was supported by the hope that in a
very short time famine would compel the Roman army to repass
the desert; and by the reasonable expectation that the kings of the
East, and particularly the Persian monarch, would arm in the
defence of their most natural ally. But fortune and the perseverance
of Aurelian overcame every obstacle. The death of Sapor, which
happened about this time, distracted the councils of Persia, and the
inconsiderable succours that attempted to relieve Palmyra were
easily intercepted either by the arms or the liberality of the emperor.
From every part of Syria a regular succession of convoys safely
arrived in the camp, which was increased by the return of Probus

with his victorious troops from the conquest of Egypt. It was then that Zenobia resolved to fly. She mounted the fleetest of her drom-edaries, and had already reached the banks of the Euphrates, about sixty miles from Palmyra, when she was overtaken by the pursuit of Aurelian's light horse, seized and brought back a captive to the feet of the emperor.

Since the foundation of Rome no general had more nobly deserved a triumph than Aurelian; nor was a triumph ever celebrated with superior pride and magnificence. The pomp was opened by twenty elephants, four royal tigers, and above two hundred of the most curious animals from every climate of the North, the East, and the South. They were followed by sixteen hundred gladiators, devoted to the cruel amusement of the amphitheatre. The wealth of Asia, the arms and ensigns of so many conquered nations, and the magnificent plate and wardrobe of the Syrian queen, were disposed in exact symmetry or artful disorder. The ambassadors of the most remote parts of the earth, of Æthiopia, Arabia, Persia, Bactriana, India, and China, all remarkable by their rich or singular dresses, displayed the fame and power of the Roman emperor, who exposed likewise to the public view the presents that he had received, and particularly a great number of crowns of gold, the offerings of grateful cities. The victories of Aurelian were attested by the long train of captives who reluctantly attended his triumph–Goths, Vandals, Sarmatians, Alemanni, Franks, Gauls, Syrians, and Egyptians. Each people was distinguished by its peculiar inscription, and the title of Amazons was bestowed on ten martial heroines of the Gothic nation who had been taken in arms. But every eye, disregarding the crowd of captives, was fixed on the emperor Tetricus and the queen of the East. The former, as well as his son, whom he had created Augustus, was dressed in Gallic trousers, a saffron tunic, and a robe of purple. The beauteous figure of Zenobia was confined by fetters of gold; a slave supported the gold chain which encircled her neck, and she almost fainted under the intolerable weight of jewels. She preceded on foot the magnifi-cent chariot in which she once hoped to enter the gates of Rome. It was followed by two other chariots, still more sumptuous, of Odenathus and of the Persian monarch. The triumphal car of Aurelian (it had formerly been used by a Gothic king) was drawn, on this memorable occasion, either by four stags or by four elephants. The most illustrious of the senate, the people, and the army closed the solemn procession. Unfeigned joy, wonder, and gratitude swelled the acclamations of the multitude; but the satisfaction of the senate was clouded by the appearance of Tetricus; nor could they suppress a rising murmur that the haughty emperor should thus expose to public ignominy the person of a Roman and a magistrate.

But however, in the treatment of his unfortunate rivals Aurelian might indulge his pride, he behaved towards them with a generous clemency which was seldom exercised by the ancient conquerors. Princes who, without success, had defended their throne or freedom, were frequently strangled in prison as soon as the triumphal pomp ascended the Capitol. These usurpers, whom their defeat had convicted of the crime of treason, were permitted to spend their lives in affluence and honourable repose. The emperor presented Zenobia with an elegant villa at Tibur or Tivoli, about twenty miles from the capital; the Syrian queen insensibly sunk into a Roman matron, her daughters married into noble families, and her race was not yet extinct in the fifth century. Tetricus and his son were reinstated in their rank and fortunes. They erected on the Cælian hill a magnificent palace, and, as soon as it was finished, invited Aurelian to supper. On his entrance he was agreeably surprised with a picture which represented their singular history. They were delineated offering to the emperor a civic crown and the sceptre of Gaul, and again receiving at his hands the ornaments of the senatorial dignity. The father was afterwards invested with the government of Lucania, and Aurelian, who soon admitted the abdicated monarch to his friendship and conversation, familiarly asked him, Whether it were not more desirable to administer a province of Italy than to reign beyond the Alps? The son long continued a respectable member of the senate; nor was there any one of the Roman nobility more esteemed by Aurelian, as well as by his successors.

It was observed by one of the most sagacious of the Roman princes, that the talents of his predecessor Aurelian were better suited to the command of an army than to the government of an empire. Conscious of the character in which nature and experience had enabled him to excel, he again took the field a few months after his triumph. It was expedient to exercise the restless temper of the legions in some foreign war, and the Persian monarch, exulting in the shame of Valerian, still braved with impunity the offended majesty of Rome. At the head of an army, less formidable by its numbers than by its discipline and valour, the emperor advanced as far as the Straits which divide Europe from Asia. He there experienced that the most absolute power is a weak defence against the effects of despair. He had threatened one of his secretaries who was accused of extortion, and it was known that he seldom threatened in vain. The last hope which remained for the criminal was to involve some of the principal officers of the army in his danger, or at least in his fears. Artfully counterfeiting his master's hand, he showed them, in a long and bloody list, their own names devoted to death. Without suspecting or examining the fraud, they resolved to secure their lives by the murder of the emperor. On his march, between Byzantium and Heraclea, Aurelian was suddenly attacked by the conspirators, whose stations gave them a right to surround his person, and, after a short resistance, fell by the hand of Mucapor, a general whom he had always loved and trusted. He died regretted by the army, detested by the senate, but universally acknowledged as a warlike and fortunate prince, the useful though severe reformer of a degenerate state.

X

(275–285 A.D.) CONDUCT OF THE ARMY AND SENATE AFTER THE DEATH OF AURELIAN— REIGNS OF TACITUS, PROBUS, CARUS, AND HIS SONS

Such was the unhappy condition of the Roman emperors, that, whatever might be their conduct, their fate was commonly the same. A life of pleasure or virtue, of severity or mildness, of indolence or glory, alike led to an untimely grave; and almost every reign is closed by the same disgusting repetition of treason and murder. The death of Aurelian, however, is remarkable by its extraordinary consequences. The legions admired, lamented, and revenged their victorious chief. The artifice of his perfidious secretary was discovered and punished. The deluded conspirators attended the funeral of their injured sovereign with sincere or well-feigned contrition, and submitted to the unanimous resolution of the military order, which was signified by the following epistle: "The brave and fortunate armies to the senate and people of Rome.—The crime of one man, and the error of many, have deprived us of the late emperor Aurelian. May it please you, venerable lords and fathers! to place him in the number of the gods, and to appoint a successor whom your judgment shall declare worthy of the Imperial purple! None of those whose guilt or misfortune have contributed to our loss shall ever reign over us." The Roman senators heard, without surprise, that another emperor had been assassinated in his camp; they secretly rejoiced in the fall of Aurelian; but the modest and dutiful address of the legions, when it was communicated in full assembly by the consul, diffused the most pleasing astonishment. Such honours as fear and perhaps esteem could extort they liberally poured forth on the memory of their deceased sovereign. Such acknowledgments as gratitude could inspire they returned to the faithful armies of the republic, who entertained so just a sense of the legal authority of the senate in the choice of an emperor. Yet, notwithstanding this flattering appeal, the most prudent of the assembly declined exposing their safety and dignity to the caprice of an armed multitude. The strength of the legions was, indeed, a pledge of their sincerity, since those who may command are seldom reduced to the necessity of dissembling; but could it naturally be expected that a hasty repentance would correct the inveterate habits of fourscore years? Should the soldiers relapse into their accustomed seditions, their insolence might disgrace the majesty of the senate and prove fatal to the object of its choice. Motives like these dictated a decree by which the election of a new emperor was referred to the suffrage of the military order.

The contention that ensued is one of the best attested but most improbable events in the history of mankind. The troops, as if satiated with the exercise of power, again conjured the senate to invest one of its own body with the Imperial purple. The senate still persisted in its refusal; the army in its request. The reciprocal offer was pressed and rejected at least three times, and, whilst the obstinate modesty of either party was resolved to receive a master from the hands of the other, eight months insensibly elapsed; an amazing period of tranquil anarchy, during which the Roman world remained without a sovereign, without an usurper, and without a sedition. The generals and magistrates appointed by Aurelian continued to execute their ordinary functions; and it is observed that a proconsul of Asia was the only considerable person removed from his office in the whole course of the interregnum.

On the twenty-fifth of September, near eight months after the murder of Aurelian, the consul convoked an assembly of the senate, and reported the doubtful and dangerous situation of the empire. He slightly insinuated that the precarious loyalty of the soldiers depended on the chance of every hour and of every accident; but he represented, with the most convincing eloquence, the various dangers that might attend any further delay in the choice of an emperor. Intelligence, he said, was already received that the Germans had passed the Rhine and occupied some of the strongest and most opulent cities of Gaul. The ambition of the Persian king kept the East in perpetual alarms; Egypt, Africa, and Illyricum were exposed to foreign and domestic arms; and the levity of Syria would prefer even a female sceptre to the sanctity of the Roman laws. The consul then, addressing himself to Tacitus, the first of the senators, required his opinion on the important subject of a proper candidate for the vacant throne.

If we can prefer personal merit to accidental greatness, we shall esteem the birth of Tacitus more truly noble than that of kings. He claimed his descent from the philosophic historian whose writings will instruct the last generations of mankind. The senator Tacitus was then seventy-five years of age. The long period of his innocent life was adorned with wealth and honours. He had twice been invested with the consular dignity, and enjoyed with elegance and sobriety his ample patrimony of between two and three millions sterling. The experience of so many princes, whom he had esteemed or endured, from the vain follies of Elagabalus to the useful rigour of Aurelian, taught him to form a just estimate of the duties, the dangers, and the temptations of their sublime station. From the assiduous study of his immortal ancestor he derived the knowledge of the Roman constitution and of human nature. The voice of the people had already named Tacitus as the citizen the most worthy of empire. The ungrateful rumour reached his ears, and induced him to seek the retirement of one of his villas in Campania. He had passed two months in the delightful privacy of Baiæ, when he reluctantly obeyed the summons of the consul to resume his honourable place in the senate, and to assist the republic with his counsels on this important occasion.

He arose to speak, when, from every quarter of the house, he was saluted with the names of Augustus and Emperor. "Tacitus Augustus, the gods preserve thee! we choose thee for our sovereign, to thy care we intrust the republic and the world. Accept the empire from the authority of the senate. It is due to thy rank, to thy conduct, to thy manners." As soon as the tumult of acclamations subsided, Tacitus attempted to decline the dangerous honour, and to express his wonder that they should elect his age and infirmities to succeed the martial vigour of Aurelian. "Are these limbs, conscript fathers! fitted to sustain the weight of armour, or to practise the exercises of the camp? The variety of climates, and the hardships of a military life, would soon oppress a feeble constitution, which subsists only by the most tender management. My exhausted strength scarcely enables me to discharge the duty of a senator; how insufficient would it prove to the arduous labours of war and government! Can you hope that the legions will respect a weak old man, whose days have been spent in the shade of peace and retirement? Can you desire that I should ever find reason to regret the favourable opinion of the senate?"

The reluctance of Tacitus, and it might possibly be sincere, was encountered by the affectionate obstinacy of the senate. Five hundred voices repeated at once, in eloquent confusion, that the greatest of the Roman princes, Numa, Trajan, Hadrian, and the Antonines, had ascended the throne in a very advanced season of life; that the mind, not the body, a sovereign, not a soldier, was the object of their choice; and that they expected from him no more than to guide by his wisdom the valour of the legions. These pressing though tumultuary instances were seconded by a more regular oration of Metius Falconius, the next on the consular bench to Tacitus himself. He reminded the assembly of the evils which Rome had endured from the vices of headstrong and capricious youths, congratulated them on the election of a virtuous and experienced senator, and with a manly, though perhaps a selfish, freedom, exhorted Tacitus to remember the reasons of his elevation, and to seek a successor, not in his own family, but in the republic. The speech of Falconius was enforced by a general acclamation. The emperor elect submitted to the authority of his country, and received the voluntary homage of his equals. The judgment of the senate was confirmed by the consent of the Roman people and of the Prætorian guards.

Leaving the senators to enjoy their dream of freedom and ambition, Tacitus proceeded to the Thracian camp, and was there, by the Prætorian præfect, presented to the assembled troops as the prince whom they themselves had demanded, and whom the senate had bestowed. As soon as the præfect was silent the emperor addressed himself to the soldiers with eloquence and propriety. He gratified their avarice by a liberal distribution of treasure under the names of pay and donative. He engaged their esteem by a spirited declaration that, although his age might disable him from the performance of military exploits, his counsels should never be unworthy of a Roman general, the successor of the brave Aurelian.

But the glory and life of Tacitus were of short duration. Transported in the depth of winter from the soft retirement of Campania to the foot of Mount Caucasus, he sunk under the unaccustomed hardships of a military life. The fatigues of the body were aggravated by the cares of the mind. For a while the angry and selfish passions of the soldiers had been suspended by the enthusiasm of public virtue. They soon broke out with redoubled violence, and raged in the camp, and even in the tent of the aged emperor. His mild and amiable character served only to inspire contempt, and he was incessantly tormented with factions which he could not assuage, and by demands which it was impossible to satisfy. Whatever flattering expectations he had conceived of reconciling the public disorders, Tacitus soon was convinced that the licentiousness of the army disdained the feeble restraint of laws, and his last hour was hastened by anguish and disappointment. It may be doubtful whether the soldiers imbrued their hands in the blood of this innocent prince. It is certain that their insolence was the cause of his death. He expired at Tyana in Cappadocia, after a reign of only six months and about twenty days.

The peasants of Illyricum, who had already given Claudius and Aurelian to the sinking empire, had an equal right to glory in the elevation of Probus. Above twenty years before, the emperor Valerian, with his usual penetration, had discovered the rising merit of the young soldier, on whom he conferred the rank of tribune long before the age prescribed by the military regulations. The tribune soon justified his choice by a victory over a great body of Sarmatians, in which he saved the life of a near relation of Valerian; and deserved to receive from the emperor's hand the collars, bracelets, spears, and banners, the mural and the civic crown, and all the honourable rewards reserved by ancient Rome for successful valour. The third, and afterwards the tenth, legion were intrusted to the command of Probus, who, in every step of his promotion, showed himself superior to the station which he filled. Africa and Pontus, the Rhine, the Danube, the Euphrates, and the Nile, by turns afforded him the most splendid occasions of displaying his personal prowess and his conduct in war. Aurelian was indebted to him for the conquest of Egypt, and still more indebted for the honest courage with which he often checked the cruelty of his master. Tacitus, who desired by the abilities of his generals to supply his own deficiency of military talents, named him commander-in-chief of all the eastern provinces, with five times the usual salary, the promise of the consulship, and the hope of a triumph. When Probus ascended the Imperial throne he was about forty-four years of age; in the full possession of his fame, of the love of the army, and of a mature vigour of mind and body.

The strength of Aurelian had crushed on every side the enemies of Rome. After his death they seemed to revive with an increase of fury and of numbers. They were again vanquished by the active vigour of Probus, who, in a short reign of about six years, equalled the fame of ancient heroes, and restored peace and order

to every province of the Roman world. The dangerous frontier of
Rhætia he so firmly secured that he left it without the suspicion
of an enemy. He broke the wandering power of the Sarmatian
tribes, and by the terror of his arms compelled those barbarians to
relinquish their spoil. The Gothic nation courted the alliance of so
warlike an emperor. He attacked the Isaurians in their mountains,
besieged and took several of their strongest castles, and flattered
himself that he had for ever suppressed a domestic foe whose
independence so deeply wounded the majesty of the empire. The
troubles excited by the usurper Firmus in the Upper Egypt had never
been perfectly appeased, and the cities of Ptolemais and Coptos,
fortified by the alliance of the Blemmyes, still maintained an
obscure rebellion. The chastisement of those cities, and of their
auxiliaries the savages of the South, is said to have alarmed the
court of Persia, and the Great King sued in vain for the friendship
of Probus. Most of the exploits which distinguished his reign were
achieved by the personal valour and conduct of the emperor,
insomuch that the writer of his Life expresses some amazement
how, in so short a time, a single man could be present in so many
distant wars. The remaining actions he intrusted to the care of his
lieutenants, the judicious choice of whom forms no inconsiderable
part of his glory. Carus, Diocletian, Maximian, Constantius,
Galerius, Asclepiodatus, Annibalianus, and a crowd of other chiefs,
who afterwards ascended or supported the throne, were trained to
arms in the severe school of Aurelian and Probus.

But the most important service which Probus rendered to the
republic was the deliverance of Gaul, and the recovery of seventy
flourishing cities oppressed by the barbarians of Germany, who,
since the death of Aurelian, had ravaged that great province with
impunity. Among the various multitude of those fierce invaders, we
may distinguish, with some degree of clearness, three great armies,
or rather nations, successively vanquished by the valour of Probus.
Since the expedition of Maximin, the Roman generals had confined their ambition to a defensive war against the nations of
Germany, who perpetually pressed on the frontiers of the empire.
The more daring Probus pursued his Gallic victories, passed the
Rhine, and displayed his invincible eagles on the banks of the Elbe
and the Neckar. He was fully convinced that nothing could
reconcile the minds of the barbarians to peace, unless they
experienced in their own country the calamities of war. Germany,
exhausted by the ill success of the last emigration, was astonished

by his presence. Nine of the most considerable princes repaired to his camp, and fell prostrate at his feet. Such a treaty was humbly received by the Germans as it pleased the conqueror to dictate. He exacted a strict restitution of the effects and captives which they had carried away from the provinces; and obliged their own magistrates to punish the more obstinate robbers who presumed to detain any part of the spoil. A considerable tribute of corn, cattle, and horses, the only wealth of barbarians, was reserved for the use of the garrisons which Probus established on the limits of their territory. He even entertained some thoughts of compelling the Germans to relinquish the exercise of arms, and to trust their differences to the justice, their safety to the power, of Rome. To accomplish these salutary ends, the constant residence of an Imperial governor, supported by a numerous army, was indispensably requisite. Probus therefore judged it more expedient to defer the execution of so great a design; which was indeed rather of specious than solid utility. Had Germany been reduced into the state of a province, the Romans, with immense labour and expense, would have acquired only a more extensive boundary to defend against the fiercer and more active barbarians of Scythia.

Among the useful conditions of peace imposed by Probus on the vanquished nations of Germany was the obligation of supplying the Roman army with sixteen thousand recruits, the bravest and most robust of their youth. The emperor dispersed them through all the provinces, and distributed this dangerous reinforcement, in small bands of fifty or sixty each, among the national troops; judiciously observing that the aid which the republic derived from the barbarians should be felt but not seen. Their aid was now become necessary. The feeble elegance of Italy and the internal provinces could no longer support the weight of arms. The hardy frontier of the Rhine and Danube still produced minds and bodies equal to the labours of the camp; but a perpetual series of wars had gradually diminished their numbers. The infrequency of marriage, and the ruin of agriculture, affected the principles of population, and not only destroyed the strength of the present, but intercepted the hope of future generations. The wisdom of Probus embraced a great and beneficial plan of replenishing the exhausted frontiers by new colonies of captive or fugitive barbarians, on whom he bestowed lands, cattle, instruments of husbandry, and every encouragement that might engage them to educate a race of soldiers for the service of the republic. Into Britain, and most probably into Cambridgeshire, he transported a considerable body of Vandals. The impossibility of an escape reconciled them to their situation, and in the subsequent troubles of that island they approved themselves the most faithful servants of the state. Great numbers of Franks and Gepidæ were settled on the banks of the Danube and the Rhine. An hundred thousand Bastarnæ, expelled from their own country, cheerfully accepted an establishment in Thrace, and soon imbibed the manners and sentiments of Roman subjects. But the expectations of Probus were too often disappointed. The impatience and idleness of the barbarians could ill brook the slow labours of agriculture. Their unconquerable love of freedom, rising against despotism, provoked them into hasty rebellions, alike fatal to themselves and to the provinces, nor could these artificial supplies, however repeated by succeeding emperors, restore the important limit of Gaul and Illyricum to its ancient and native vigour.

The military discipline which reigned in the camps of Probus was less cruel than that of Aurelian, but it was equally rigid and exact. The latter had punished the irregularities of the soldiers with unrelenting severity, the former prevented them by employing the legions in constant and useful labours. When Probus commanded in Egypt, he executed many considerable works for the splendour and benefit of that rich country. The navigation of the Nile, so important to Rome itself, was improved; and temples, bridges, porticoes, and palaces, were constructed by the hands of the soldiers, who acted by turns as architects, as engineers, and as husbandmen. It was reported of Hannibal that, in order to preserve his troops from the dangerous temptations of idleness, he had obliged them to form large plantations of olive-trees along the coast of Africa. From a similar principle, Probus exercised his legions in covering with rich vineyards the hills of Gaul and Pannonia, and two considerable spots are described which were entirely dug and planted by military labour. One of these, known under the name of Mount Alma, was situated near Sirmium, the country where Probus was born, for which he ever retained a partial affection, and whose gratitude he endeavoured to secure, by converting into tillage a large and unhealthy tract of marshy ground. An army thus employed constituted perhaps the most useful as well as the bravest portion of Roman subjects.

But, in the prosecution of a favourite scheme, the best of men, satisfied with the rectitude of their intentions, are subject to forget the bounds of moderation; nor did Probus himself sufficiently consult the patience and disposition of his fierce legionaries. The dangers of the military profession seem only to be compensated by a life of pleasure and idleness; but if the duties of the soldier are incessantly aggravated by the labours of the peasant, he will at last sink under the intolerable burden or shake it off with indignation. The imprudence of Probus is said to have inflamed the discontent of his troops. More attentive to the interests of mankind than to those of the army, he expressed the vain hope that, by the establishment of universal peace, he should soon abolish the necessity of a standing and mercenary force. The unguarded expression proved fatal to him. In one of the hottest days of summer, as he severely urged the unwholesome labour of draining the marshes of Sirmium, the soldiers, impatient of fatigue, on a sudden threw down their tools, grasped their arms, and broke out into a furious mutiny. The emperor, conscious of his danger, took refuge in a lofty tower constructed for the purpose of surveying the progress of the work. The tower was instantly forced, and a thousand swords were plunged at once into the bosom of the unfortunate Probus. The rage of the troops subsided as soon as it had been gratified. They then lamented their fatal rashness, forgot the severity of the emperor whom they had massacred, and hastened to perpetuate, by an honourable monument, the memory of his virtues and victories.

When the legions had indulged their grief and repentance for the death of Probus, their unanimous consent declared Carus, his Prætorian præfect, the most deserving of the Imperial throne. The election of Carus was decided without expecting the approbation of the senate, and the new emperor contented himself with announcing, in a cold and stately epistle, that he had ascended the vacant throne. A behaviour so very opposite to that of his amiable predecessor afforded no favourable presage of the new reign: and the Romans, deprived of power and freedom, asserted their privilege of licentious murmurs. The voice of congratulation and flattery was not however silent; and we may still peruse, with pleasure and contempt, an eclogue which was composed on the accession of the emperor Carus. Two shepherds, avoiding the noontide heat, retire into the cave of Faunus. On a spreading beech they discover some recent characters. The rural deity had described, in prophetic verses, the felicity promised to the empire under the reign of so great a prince. Faunus hails the approach of that hero, who, receiving on his shoulders the sinking weight of the Roman world,

shall extinguish war and faction, and once again restore the innocence and security of the golden age.

It is more than probable that these elegant trifles never reached
the ears of a veteran general who, with the consent of the legions,
was preparing to execute the long-suspended design of the Persian
war. Before his departure for this distant expedition, Carus conferred on his two sons, Carinus and Numerian, the title of Cæsar,
and, investing the former with almost an equal share of the Imperial
power, directed the young prince first to suppress some troubles
which had arisen in Gaul, and afterwards to fix the seat of his
residence at Rome, and to assume the government of the Western
provinces. The safety of Illyricum was confirmed by a memorable
defeat of the Sarmatians; sixteen thousand of those barbarians
remained on the field of battle, and the number of captives
amounted to twenty thousand. The old emperor, animated with the
fame and prospect of victory, pursued his march, in the midst of
winter, through the countries of Thrace and Asia Minor, and at
length, with his younger son Numerian, arrived on the confines of
the Persian monarchy. There, encamping on the summit of a lofty
mountain, he pointed out to his troops the opulence and luxury of
the enemy whom they were about to invade.

The successor of Artaxerxes, Varanes, or Bahram, though he
had subdued the Segestans, one of the most warlike nations of
Upper Asia, was alarmed at the approach of the Romans, and
endeavoured to retard their progress by a negotiation of peace. His
ambassadors entered the camp about sunset, at the time when the
troops were satisfying their hunger with a frugal repast. The Persians
expressed their desire of being introduced to the presence of the
Roman emperor. They were at length conducted to a soldier who
was seated on the grass. A piece of stale bacon and a few hard peas
composed his supper. A coarse woollen garment of purple was the
only circumstance that announced his dignity. The conference was
conducted with the same disregard of courtly elegance. Carus,
taking off a cap which he wore to conceal his baldness, assured the
ambassadors that, unless their master acknowledged the superiority
of Rome, he would speedily render Persia as naked of trees as his
own head was destitute of hair. Notwithstanding some traces of art
and preparation, we may discover in this scene the manners of
Carus, and the severe simplicity which the martial princes who
succeeded Gallienus had already restored in the Roman camps.
The ministers of the Great King trembled and retired.

The threats of Carus were not without effect. He ravaged Mesopotamia, cut in pieces whatever opposed his passage, made himself master of the great cities of Seleucia and Ctesiphon (which seem to have surrendered without resistance), and carried his victorious arms beyond the Tigris. He had seized the favourable moment for an invasion. The Persian councils were distracted by domestic factions, and the greater part of their forces were detained on the frontiers of India. Rome and the East received with transport the news of such important advantages. Flattery and hope painted in the most lively colours the fall of Persia, the conquest of Arabia, the submission of Egypt, and a lasting deliverance from the inroads of the Scythian nations. But the reign of Carus was destined to expose the vanity of predictions. They were scarcely uttered before they were contradicted by his death; an event attended with such ambiguous circumstances that it may be related in a letter from his own secretary to the præfect of the city. "Carus," says he, "our dearest emperor, was confined by sickness to his bed, when a furious tempest arose in the camp. The darkness which overspread the sky was so thick that we could no longer distinguish each other; and the incessant flashes of lightning took from us the knowledge of all that passed in the general confusion. Immediately after the most violent clap of thunder we heard a sudden cry that the emperor was dead; and it soon appeared that his chamberlains, in a rage of grief, had set fire to the royal pavilion, a circumstance which gave rise to the report that Carus was killed by lightning. But, as far as we have been able to investigate the truth, his death was the natural effect of his disorder."

The vacancy of the throne was not productive of any disturbance. The ambition of the aspiring generals was checked by their mutual fears; and young Numerian, with his absent brother Carinus, were unanimously acknowledged as Roman emperors. The public expected that the successor of Carus would pursue his father's footsteps, and, without allowing the Persians to recover from their consternation, would advance sword in hand to the palaces of Susa and Ecbatana. But the legions, however strong in numbers and discipline, were dismayed by the most abject superstition. Notwithstanding all the arts that were practised to disguise the manner of the late emperor's death, it was found impossible to remove the opinion of the multitude, and the power of opinion is irresistible. Places or persons struck with lightning were considered by the ancients with pious horror, as singularly devoted to the wrath of Heaven. An oracle was remembered which marked the river Tigris as the fatal boundary of the Roman arms. The troops, terrified with the fate of Carus and with their own danger, called aloud on young Numerian to obey the will of the gods, and to lead them away from this inauspicious scene of war. The feeble emperor was unable to subdue their obstinate prejudice, and the Persians wondered at the unexpected retreat of a victorious enemy.

The only merit of the administration of Carinus that history could record, or poetry celebrate, was the uncommon splendour with which, in his own and his brother's name, he exhibited the Roman games of the theatre, the circus, and the amphitheatre. More than twenty years afterwards, when the courtiers of Diocletian represented to their frugal sovereign the fame and popularity of his munificent predecessor, he acknowledged that the reign of Carinus had indeed been a reign of pleasure. But this vain prodigality, which the prudence of Diocletian might justly despise, was enjoyed with surprise and transport by the Roman people. The oldest of the citizens, recollecting the spectacles of former days, the triumphal pomp of Probus or Aurelian, and the secular games of the emperor Philip, acknowledged that they were all surpassed by the superior magnificence of Carinus.

The talents of Numerian were rather of the contemplative than of the active kind. When his father's elevation reluctantly forced him from the shade of retirement, neither his temper nor his pursuits had qualified him for the command of armies. His constitution was destroyed by the hardships of the Persian war; and he had contracted, from the heat of the climate, such a weakness in his eyes, as obliged him, in the course of a long retreat, to confine himself to the solitude and darkness of a tent or litter. The administration of all affairs, civil as well as military, was devolved on Arrius Aper, the Prætorian præfect, who, to the power of his important office, added the honour of being father-in-law to Numerian. The Imperial pavilion was strictly guarded by his most trusty adherents, and during many days Aper delivered to the army the supposed mandates of their invisible sovereign.

It was not till eight months after the death of Carus that the Roman army, returning by slow marches from the banks of the Tigris, arrived on those of the Thracian Bosphorus. The legions halted at Chalcedon in Asia, while the court passed over to Heraclea, on the European side of the Propontis. But a report soon circulated through the camp, at first in secret whispers, and at length in loud clamours, of the emperor's death, and of the presumption of his ambitious minister, who still exercised the sovereign power in the name of a prince who was no more. The impatience of the soldiers could not long support a state of suspense. With rude curiosity they broke into the imperial tent, and discovered only the corpse of Numerian. The gradual decline of his health might have induced them to believe that his death was natural; but the concealment was interpreted as an evidence of guilt, and the measures which Aper had taken to secure his election became the immediate occasion of his ruin. Yet, even in the transport of their rage and grief, the troops observed a regular proceeding, which proves how firmly discipline had been reestablished by the martial successors of Gallienus. A general assembly of the army was appointed to be held at Chalcedon, whither Aper was transported in chains, as a prisoner and a criminal. A vacant tribunal was erected in the midst of the camp, and the generals and tribunes formed a great military council. They soon announced to the multitude that their choice had fallen on Diocletian, commander of the domestics or body-guards, as the person the most capable of revenging and succeeding their beloved emperor. The future fortunes of the candidate depended on the chance or conduct of the present hour. Conscious that the station which he had filled exposed him to some suspicions, Diocletian ascended the tribunal, and, raising his eyes towards the Sun, made a solemn profession of his own innocence, in the presence of that all-seeing Deity. Then, assuming the tone of a sovereign and a judge, he commanded that Aper should be brought in chains to the foot of the tribunal. "This man," said he, "is the murderer of Numerian"; and without giving him time to enter on a dangerous justification, drew his sword, and buried it in the breast of the unfortunate præfect. A charge supported by such decisive proof was admitted without contradiction, and the legions, with repeated acclamations, acknowledged the justice and authority of the emperor Diocletian.

Before we enter upon the memorable reign of that prince, it will be proper to punish and dismiss the unworthy brother of Numerian. Carinus possessed arms and treasures sufficient to support his legal title to the empire. But his personal vices overbalanced every advantage of birth and situation. The most faithful servants of the father despised the incapacity, and dreaded the cruel arrogance of the son. The hearts of the people were engaged in favour of his rival, and even the senate was inclined to prefer an usurper to a tyrant. The arts of Diocletian inflamed the general discontent; and the winter was employed in secret intrigues and open preparations for a civil war. In the spring the forces of the East and of the West encountered each other in the plains of Margus, a small city of Mæsia, in the neighbourhood of the Danube. The troops, so lately returned from the Persian war, had acquired their glory at the expense of health and numbers, nor were they in a condition to contend with the unexhausted strength of the legions of Europe. Their ranks were broken, and, for a moment, Diocletian despaired of the purple and of life. But the advantage which Carinus had obtained by the valour of his soldiers he quickly lost by the infidelity of his officers. A tribune, whose wife he had seduced, seized the opportunity of revenge, and by a single blow extinguished civil discord in the blood of the adulterer.

XI

(285–313 A.D.) THE REIGN OF DIOCLETIAN AND
HIS THREE ASSOCIATES, MAXIMIAN, GALERIUS,
AND CONSTANTIUS—GENERAL RE-ESTABLISH-
MENT OF ORDER AND TRANQUILITY—THE
NEW FORM OF ADMINISTRATION—ABDICA-
TION AND RETIREMENT OF DIOCLETIAN
AND MAXIMIAN

As the reign of Diocletian was more illustrious than that of any of
his predecessors, so was his birth more abject and obscure. The
strong claims of merit and of violence had frequently superseded
the ideal prerogatives of nobility; but a distinct line of separation
was hitherto preserved between the free and the servile part of
mankind. The parents of Diocletian had been slaves in the house
of Anulinus, a Roman senator; nor was he himself distinguished by
any other name than that which he derived from a small town in
Dalmatia, from whence his mother deduced her origin. It is, however, probable that his father obtained the freedom of the family,
and that he soon acquired an office of scribe, which was commonly
exercised by persons of his condition. Favourable oracles, or rather
the consciousness of superior merit, prompted his aspiring son to
pursue the profession of arms and the hopes of fortune; and it
would be extremely curious to observe the graduation of arts and
accidents which enabled him in the end to fulfil those oracles, and
to display that merit to the world. Diocletian was successively
promoted to the government of Mæsia, the honours of the consulship, and the important command of the guards of the palace.
He distinguished·his abilities in the Persian war; and after the death
of Numerian, the slave, by the confession and judgment of his
rivals, was declared the most worthy of the Imperial throne. The
malice of religious zeal, whilst it arraigns the savage fierceness of
his colleague Maximian, has affected to cast suspicion on the
personal courage of the emperor Diocletian. It would not be easy
to persuade us of the cowardice of a soldier of fortune who acquired

and preserved the esteem of the legions, as well as the favour of so many warlike princes. Yet even calumny is sagacious enough to discover and to attack the most vulnerable part. The valour of Diocletian was never found inadequate to his duty, or to the occasion; but he appears not to have possessed the daring and generous spirit of a hero, who courts danger and fame, disdains artifice, and boldly challenges the allegiance of his equals. His abilities were useful rather than splendid—a vigorous mind improved by the experience and study of mankind; dexterity and application in business; a judicious mixture of liberality and economy, of mildness and rigour; profound dissimulation under the disguise of military frankness; steadiness to pursue his ends; flexibility to vary his means; and, above all, the great art of submitting his own passions, as well as those of others, to the interest of his ambition, and of colouring his ambition with the most specious pretences of justice and public utility. Like Augustus, Diocletian may be considered as the founder of a new empire. Like the adopted son of Cæsar, he was distinguished as a statesman rather than as a warrior; nor did either of those princes employ force, whenever their purpose could be effected by policy.

The victory of Diocletian was remarkable for its singular mildness. A people accustomed to applaud the clemency of the conqueror, if the usual punishments of death, exile, and confiscation were inflicted with any degree of temper and equity, beheld, with the most pleasing astonishment, a civil war, the flames of which were extinguished in the field of battle. Diocletian received into his confidence Aristobulus, the principal minister of the house of Carus, respected the lives, the fortunes, and the dignity of his adversaries, and even continued in their respective stations the greater number of the servants of Carinus. It is not improbable that motives of prudence might assist the humanity of the artful Dalmatian: of these servants, many had purchased his favour by secret treachery; in others, he esteemed their grateful fidelity to an unfortunate master. The discerning judgment of Aurelian, of Probus, and of Carus, had filled the several departments of the state and army with officers of approved merit, whose removal would have injured the public service, without promoting the interest of the successor. Such a conduct, however, displayed to the Roman world the fairest prospect of the new reign, and the emperor affected to confirm this favourable prepossession by declaring that, among all the virtues of his predecessors, he was the most ambitious of imitating the humane philosophy of Marcus Antoninus.

The first considerable action of his reign seemed to evince his sincerity as well as his moderation. After the example of Marcus, he gave himself a colleague in the person of Maximian, on whom he bestowed at first the title of Cæsar, and afterwards that of Augustus. But the motives of his conduct, as well as the object of his choice, were of a very different nature from those of his admired predecessor. By investing a luxurious youth with the honours of the purple, Marcus had discharged a debt of private gratitude, at the expense, indeed, of the happiness of the state. By associating a friend and a fellow-soldier to the favours of government, Diocletian, in a time of public danger, provided for the defence both of the East and of the West. Maximian was born a peasant, and, like Aurelian, in the territory of Sirmium. Ignorant of letters, careless of laws, the rusticity of his appearance and manners still betrayed in the most elevated fortune the meanness of his extraction. War was the only art which he professed. In a long course of service he had distinguished himself on every frontier of the empire; and though his military talents were formed to obey rather than to command, though, perhaps, he never attained the skill of a consummate general, he was capable, by his valour, constancy, and experience, of executing the most arduous undertakings. Nor were the vices of Maximian less useful to his benefactor. Insensible to pity, and fearless of consequences, he was the ready instrument of every act of cruelty which the policy of that artful prince might at once suggest and disclaim. As soon as a bloody sacrifice had been offered to prudence or to revenge, Diocletian, by his seasonable intercession, saved the remaining few whom he had never designed to punish, gently censured the severity of his stern colleague, and enjoyed the comparison of a golden and an iron age, which was universally applied to their opposite maxims of government. Notwithstanding the difference of their characters, the two emperors maintained, on the throne, that friendship which they had contracted in a private station. The haughty, turbulent spirit of Maximian, so fatal afterwards to himself and to the public peace, was accustomed to respect the genius of Diocletian, and confessed the ascendant of reason over brutal violence. From a motive either of pride or superstition, the two emperors assumed the titles, the one of Jovius, the other of Herculius. Whilst the motion of the world (such was the language of their venal orators) was maintained by the all-seeing wisdom of Jupiter, the invincible arm of Hercules purged the earth from monsters and tyrants.

But even the omnipotence of Jovius and Herculius was insufficient to sustain the weight of the public administration. The prudence of Diocletian discovered that the empire, assailed on every side by the barbarians, required on every side the presence of a great army and of an emperor. With this view, he resolved once more to divide his unwieldy power, and, with the inferior title of *Cæsar*, to confer on two generals of approved merit an equal share of the sovereign authority. Galerius, surnamed Armentarius, from his original profession of a herdsman, and Constantius, who from his pale complexion had acquired the denomination of Chlorus, were the two persons invested with the second honours of the Imperial purple. In describing the country, extraction, and manners of Herculius, we have already delineated those of Galerius, who was often, and not improperly, styled the younger Maximian, though, in many instances both of virtue and ability, he appears to have possessed a manifest superiority over the elder. The birth of Constantius was less obscure than that of his colleagues. Eutropius, his father, was one of the most considerable nobles of Dardania, and his mother was the niece of the emperor Claudius. Although the youth of Constantius had been spent in arms, he was endowed with a mild and amiable disposition, and the popular voice had long since acknowledged him worthy of the rank which he at last attained. To strengthen the bonds of political, by those of domestic, union, each of the emperors assumed the character of a father to one of the Cæsars, Diocletian to Galerius, and Maximian to Constantius; and each, obliging them to repudiate their former wives, bestowed his daughter in marriage on his adopted son. These four princes distributed among themselves the wide extent of the Roman empire The defence of Gaul, Spain, and Britain was intrusted to Constantius: Galerius was stationed on the banks of the Danube, as the safeguard of the Illyrian provinces. Italy and Africa were considered as the department of Maximian; and for his peculiar portion Diocletian reserved Thrace, Egypt, and the rich countries of Asia. Every one was sovereign within his own jurisdiction; but their united authority extended over the whole monarchy, and each of them was prepared to assist his colleagues with his counsels or presence. The Cæsars, in their exalted rank, revered the majesty of the emperors, and the three younger princes invariably acknowledged, by their gratitude and obedience, the common parent of their fortunes. The suspicious jealousy of power found not any place among them; and the singular happiness of their union has been compared to a chorus of music, whose harmony was regulated and maintained by the skilful hand of the first artist.

Notwithstanding the policy of Diocletian, it was impossible to maintain an equal and undisturbed tranquillity during a reign of twenty years, and along a frontier of many hundred miles. Sometimes the barbarians suspended their domestic animosities, and the relaxed vigilance of the garrisons sometimes gave a passage to their strength or dexterity. Whenever the provinces were invaded, Diocletian conducted himself with that calm dignity which he always affected or possessed; reserved his presence for such occasions as were worthy of his interposition, never exposed his person or reputation to any unnecessary danger, ensured his success by every means that prudence could suggest, and displayed, with ostentation, the consequences of his victory. In wars of a more difficult nature, and more doubtful event, he employed the rough valour of Maximian; and that faithful soldier was content to ascribe his own victories to the wise counsels and auspicious influence of his benefactor. But after the adoption of the two Cæsars, the emperors, themselves retiring to a less laborious scene of action, devolved on their adopted sons the defence of the Danube and of the Rhine. The vigilant Galerius was never reduced to the necessity of vanquishing an army of barbarians on the Roman territory. The brave and active Constantius delivered Gaul from a very furious inroad of the Alemanni; and his victories of Langres and Vindonissa appear to have been actions of considerable danger and merit. As he traversed the open country with a feeble guard, he was encompassed on a sudden by the superior multitude of the enemy. He retreated with difficulty towards Langres; but, in the general consternation, the citizens refused to open their gates, and the wounded prince was drawn up the wall by the means of a rope. But, on the news of his distress, the Roman troops hastened from all sides to his relief, and before the evening he had satisfied his honour and revenge by the slaughter of six thousand Alemanni. From the monuments of those times the obscure traces of several other victories over the barbarians of Sarmatia and Germany might possibly be collected; but the tedious search would not be rewarded either with amusement or with instruction. The conduct which the emperor Probus had adopted in the disposal of the vanquished was imitated by Diocletian and his associates. The captive barbarians, exchanging death for slavery, were distributed among the provincials, and assigned to those districts (in Gaul, the territories of Amiens, Beauvais, Carnbray, Treves, Langres, and Troyes, are particularly specified) which had been depopulated by the calamities of war. They were usefully employed as shepherds and husbandmen, but were denied the exercise of arms, except when it was found expedient to enrol them in the military service. Nor did the emperors refuse the property of lands, with a less servile tenure, to such of the barbarians as solicited the protection of Rome. They granted a settlement to several colonies of the Carpi, the Bastarnæ, and the Sarmatians; and, by a dangerous indulgence, permitted them in some measure to retain their national manners and independence. Among the provincials it was a subject of flattering exultation that the barbarian, so lately an object of terror, now cultivated their lands, drove their cattle to the neighbouring fair, and contributed by his labour to the public plenty. They congratulated their masters on the powerful accession of subjects and soldiers; but they forgot to observe that multitudes of secret enemies, insolent from favour, or desperate from oppression, were introduced into the heart of the empire.

The arduous work of rescuing the distressed empire from tyrants and barbarians had now been completely achieved by a succession of Illyrian peasants. As soon as Diocletian entered into the twentieth year of his reign, he celebrated that memorable era, as well as the success of his arms, by the pomp of a Roman triumph. Maximian, the equal partner of his power, was his only companion in the glory of that day. The two Cæsars had fought and conquered, but the merit of their exploits was ascribed, according to the rigour of ancient maxims, to the auspicious influence of their fathers and emperors. The triumph of Diocletian and Maximian was less magnificent, perhaps, than those of Aurelian and Probus, but it was dignified by several circumstances of superior fame and good fortune. Africa and Britain, the Rhine, the Danube, and the Nile, furnished their respective trophies; but the most distinguished ornament was of a more singular nature, a Persian victory followed by an important conquest. The representations of rivers, mountains, and provinces were carried before the Imperial car. The images of the captive wives, the sisters, and the children of the Great King afforded a new and grateful spectacle to the vanity of the people. In the eyes of posterity this triumph is remarkable by a distinction of a less honourable kind. It was the last that Rome ever beheld. Soon after this period the emperors ceased to vanquish, and Rome ceased to be the capital of the empire.

Diocletian and Maximian were the first Roman princes who fixed, in time of peace, their ordinary residence in the provinces; and their conduct, however it might be suggested by private motives, was justified by very specious considerations of policy. The court of the emperor of the West was, for the most part, established at Milan, whose situation, at the foot of the Alps, appeared far more convenient than that of Rome, for the important purpose of watching the motions of the barbarians of Germany. Milan soon assumed the splendour of an Imperial city. The houses are described as numerous and well built; the manners of the people as polished and liberal. A circus, a theatre, a mint, a palace, baths, which bore the name of their founder Maximian; porticoes adorned with statues, and a double circumference of walls, contributed to the beauty of the new capital; nor did it seem oppressed even by the proximity of Rome. To rival the majesty of Rome was the ambition likewise of Diocletian, who employed his leisure and the wealth of the East in the embellishment of Nicomedia, a city placed on the verge of Europe and Asia, almost at an equal distance between the Danube and the Euphrates. By the taste of the monarch, and at the expense of the people, Nicomedia acquired, in the space of a few years, a degree of magnificence which might appear to have required the labour of ages, and became inferior only to Rome, Alexandria, and Antioch in extent or populousness. The life of Diocletian and Maximian was a life of action, and a considerable portion of it was spent in camps, or in their long and frequent marches; but whenever the public business allowed them any relaxation, they seemed to have retired with pleasure to their favourite residences of Nicomedia and Milan. Till Diocletian, in the twentieth year of his reign, celebrated his Roman triumph, it is extremely doubtful whether he ever visited the ancient capital of the empire. Even on that memorable occasion his stay did not exceed two months. Disgusted with the licentious familiarity of the people, he quitted Rome with precipitation thirteen days before it was expected that he should have appeared in the senate invested with the ensigns of the consular dignity.

The dislike expressed by Diocletian towards Rome and Roman freedom was not the effect of momentary caprice, but the result of the most artful policy. The crafty prince had framed a new system of Imperial government, which was afterwards completed by the family of Constantine; and as the image of the old constitution was religiously preserved in the senate, he resolved to deprive that order of its small remains of power and consideration. As long as the emperors resided at Rome, that assembly might be oppressed, but it could scarcely be neglected. The successors of Augustus exercised the power of dictating whatever laws their wisdom or caprice might suggest; but those laws were ratified by the sanction of the senate. The model of ancient freedom was preserved in its deliberations and decrees; and wise princes, who respected the prejudices of the Roman people, were in some measure obliged to assume the language and behaviour suitable to the general and first magistrate of the republic. In the armies and in the provinces they displayed the dignity of monarchs; and when they fixed their residence at a distance from the capital, they for ever laid aside the dissimulation which Augustus had recommended to his successors. In the exercise of the legislative as well as the executive power, the sovereign advised with his ministers, instead of consulting the great council of the nation. The name of the senate was mentioned with honour till the last period of the empire; the vanity of its members was still flattered with honorary distinctions; but the assembly which had so long been the source, and so long the instrument of power, was respectfully suffered to sink into oblivion. The senate of Rome, losing all connection with the Imperial court and the actual constitution, was left a venerable but useless monument of antiquity on the Capitoline hill.

When the Roman princes had lost sight of the senate and of their ancient capital, they easily forgot the origin and nature of their legal power. The civil offices of consul, of proconsul, of censor, and of tribune, by the union of which it had been formed, betrayed to the people its republican extraction. Those modest titles were laid aside; and if they still distinguished their high station by the appellation of Emperor, or IMPERATOR, that word was understood in a new and more dignified sense, and no longer denoted the general of the Roman armies, but the sovereign of the Roman world. The name of Emperor, which was at first of a military nature, was associated with another of a more servile kind. The epithet of DOMINUS, or Lord, in its primitive signification, was expressive not of the authority of a prince over his subjects, or of a commander over his soldiers, but of the despotic power of a master over his domestic slaves. Viewing it in that odious light, it had been rejected with abhorrence by the first Cæsars. Their resistance insensibly became more feeble, and the name less odious; till at length the style of *our Lord and Emperor* was not only bestowed by flattery, but was regularly admitted into the laws and public monuments. Such lofty epithets were sufficient to elate and satisfy the most excessive vanity; and if the successors of Diocletian still declined the title of King, it seems to have been the effect not so much of their moderation as of their delicacy. Wherever the Latin tongue was in use (and it was the language of government throughout the empire), the Imperial title, as it was peculiar to themselves, conveyed a more respectable idea than the name of king, which they must have shared with an hundred barbarian chieftains; or which, at the best, they could derive only from Romulus, or from Tarquin. But the sentiments of the East were very different from those of the West. From the earliest period of history, the sovereigns of Asia had been celebrated in the Greek language by the title of BASILEUS, or King; and since it was considered as the first distinction among men, it was soon employed by the servile provincials of the East in their humble addresses to the Roman throne. Even the attributes, or at least the titles, of the DIVINITY were usurped by Diocletian and Maximian, who transmitted them to a succession of Christian emperors. Such extravagant compliments, however, soon lose their impiety by losing their meaning; and when the ear is once accustomed to the sound, they are heard with indifference as vague though excessive professions of respect.

From the time of Augustus to that of Diocletian, the Roman princes, conversing in a familiar manner among their fellow-citizens, were saluted only with the same respect that was usually paid to senators and magistrates. Their principal distinction was the Imperial or military robe of purple; whilst the senatorial garment was marked by a broad, and the equestrian by a narrow, band or stripe of the same honourable colour. The pride, or rather the policy, of Diocletian, engaged that artful prince to introduce the stately magnificence of the court of Persia. He ventured to assume the diadem, an ornament detested by the Romans as the odious ensign of royalty, and the use of which had been considered as the most desperate act of the madness of Caligula. It was no more than a broad white fillet set with pearls, which encircled the emperor's head. The sumptuous robes of Diocletian and his successors were of silk and gold; and it is remarked with indignation that even their shoes were studded with the most precious gems. The access to their sacred person was every day rendered more difficult by the institution of new forms and ceremonies. The avenues of the palace were strictly guarded by the various *schools*, as they began to be called, of domestic officers. The interior apartments were intrusted to the jealous vigilance of the eunuchs; the increase of whose numbers and influence was the most infallible symptom of the progress of despotism. When a subject was at length admitted to the Imperial presence, he was obliged, whatever might be his rank, to fall prostrate on the ground, and to adore, according to the eastern fashion, the divinity of his lord and master. Diocletian was a man of sense, who, in the course of private as well as public life, had formed a just estimate both of himself and of mankind: nor is it easy to conceive that in substituting the manners of Persia to those of Rome he was seriously actuated by so mean a principle as that of vanity. He flattered himself that an ostentation of splendour and luxury would subdue the imagination of the multitude; that the monarch would be less exposed to the rude licence of the people and the soldiers, as his person was secluded from the public view; and that habits of submission would insensibly be productive of sentiments of veneration. Like the modesty affected by Augustus, the state maintained by Diocletian was a theatrical representation; but it must be confessed that, of the two comedies, the former was of a much more liberal and manly character than the latter. It was the aim of the one to disguise, and the object of the other to display, the unbounded power which the emperors possessed over the Roman world.

Ostentation was the first principle of the new system instituted by Diocletian. The second was division. He divided the empire, the provinces, and every branch of the civil as well as military administration. He multiplied the wheels of the machine of government, and rendered its operations less rapid but more secure. Whatever advantages and whatever defects might attend these innovations, they must be ascribed in a very great degree to the first inventor; but as the new frame of policy was gradually improved and completed by succeeding princes, it will be more satisfactory to delay the consideration of it till the season of its full maturity and perfection. Reserving, therefore, for the reign of Constantine a more exact picture of the new empire, we shall content ourselves with describing the principal and decisive outline, as it was traced by the hand of Diocletian. He had associated three colleagues in the exercise of the supreme power; and as he was convinced that the abilities of a single man were inadequate to the public defence, he considered the joint administration of four princes not as a temporary expedient, but as a fundamental law of the constitution. It was his intention that the two elder princes should be distinguished by the use of the diadem and the title of *Augusti*; that, as affection or esteem might direct their choice, they should regularly call to their assistance two subordinate colleagues; and that the *Cæsars*, rising in their turn to the first rank, should supply an uninterrupted succession of emperors. The empire was divided into four parts. The East and Italy were the most honourable, the Danube and the Rhine the most laborious stations. The former claimed the presence of the *Augusti*, the latter were intrusted to the administration of the Cæsars. The strength of the legions was in the hands of the four partners of sovereignty, and the despair of successively vanquishing four formidable rivals might intimidate the ambition of an aspiring general. In their civil government the emperors were supposed to exercise the undivided power of the monarch, and their edicts, inscribed with their joint names, were received in all the provinces as promulgated by their mutual councils and authority. Notwithstanding these precautions, the political union of the Roman world was gradually dissolved, and a principle of division was introduced, which, in the course of a few years, occasioned the perpetual separation of the eastern and western empires.

The system of Diocletian was accompanied with another very material disadvantage, which cannot even at present be totally overlooked; a more expensive establishment, and consequently an increase of taxes, and the oppression of the people. Instead of a modest family of slaves and freedmen, such as had contented the simple greatness of Augustus and Trajan, three or four magnificent courts were established in the various parts of the empire, and as many Roman *kings* contended with each other and with the Persian monarch for the vain superiority of pomp and luxury. The number of ministers, of magistrates, of officers, and of servants, who filled the different departments of the state, was multiplied beyond the example of former times; and (if we may borrow the warm expression of a contemporary), "when the proportion of those who received exceeded the proportion of those who contributed, the provinces were oppressed by the weight of tributes." From this period to the extinction of the empire, it would be easy to deduce an uninterrupted series of clamours and complaints. According to his religion and situation, each writer chooses either Diocletian, or Constantine, or Valens, or Theodosius, for the object of his invectives; but they unanimously agree in representing the burden of the public impositions, and particularly the land-tax and capitation, as the intolerable and increasing grievance of their own times. From such a concurrence, an impartial historian, who is obliged to extract truth from satire, as well as from panegyric, will be inclined to divide the blame among the princes whom they accuse, and to ascribe their exactions much less to their personal vices than to the uniform system of their administration. The emperor Diocletian was indeed the author of that system; but during his reign the growing evil was confined within the bounds of modesty and discretion, and he deserves the reproach of establishing pernicious precedents, rather than of exercising actual oppression. It may be added, that his revenues were managed with prudent economy; and that, after all the current expenses were discharged, there still remained in the Imperial treasury an ample provision either for judicious liberality or for any emergency of the state.

It was in the twenty-first year of his reign that Diocletian executed his memorable resolution of abdicating the empire; an action more naturally to have been expected from the elder or the younger Antoninus than from a prince who had never practised the lessons of philosophy either in the attainment or in the use of supreme power. Diocletian acquired the glory of giving to the world the first example of a resignation which has not been very frequently imitated by succeeding monarchs. He resolved to pass the remainder of his days in honourable repose, to place his glory beyond the reach of fortune, and to relinquish the theatre of the world to his younger and more active associates.

The ceremony of his abdication was performed in a spacious plain, about three miles from Nicomedia. The emperor ascended a lofty throne, and, in a speech full of reason and dignity, declared his intention, both to the people and to the soldiers who were assembled on this extraordinary occasion. As soon as he had divested himself of the purple, he withdrew from the gazing multitude, and, traversing the city in a covered chariot, proceeded without delay to the favourite retirement which he had chosen in his native country of Dalmatia. On the same day, which was the first of May, Maximian, as it had been previously concerted, made his resignation of the Imperial dignity at Milan. Even in the splendour of the Roman triumph, Diocletian had meditated his design of abdicating the government. As he wished to secure the obedience of Maximian, he exacted from him either a general assurance that he would submit his actions to the authority of his benefactor, or a particular promise that he would descend from the throne whenever he should receive the advice and the example. This engagement, though it was confirmed by the solemnity of an oath before the altar of the Capitoline Jupiter, would have proved a feeble restraint on the fierce temper of Maximian, whose passion was the love of power, and who neither desired present tranquillity nor future reputation. But he yielded, however reluctantly, to the ascendant which his wiser colleague had acquired over him, and retired immediately after his abdication to a villa in Lucania, where it was almost impossible that such an impatient spirit could find any lasting tranquillity.

Diocletian, who, from a servile origin, had raised himself to the throne, passed the nine last years of his life in a private condition. Reason had dictated, and content seems to have accompanied, his retreat, in which he enjoyed for a long time the respect of those princes to whom he had resigned the possession of the world. It is seldom that minds long exercised in business have formed any habits of conversing with themselves, and in the loss of power they principally regret the want of occupation. The amusements of letters and of devotion, which afford so many resources in solitude, were incapable of fixing the attention of Diocletian; but he had preserved, or at least he soon recovered, a taste for the most innocent as well as natural pleasures, and his leisure hours were sufficiently employed in building, planting, and gardening. His answer to Maximian is deservedly celebrated. He was solicited by that restless old man to reassume the reins of government and the Imperial purple. He rejected the temptation with a smile of pity, calmly observing that, if he could show Maximian the cabbages which he had planted with his own hands at Salona, he should no longer be urged to relinquish the enjoyment of happiness for the pursuit of power.

We are informed by a recent and very judicious traveller that the awful ruins of Spalatro are not less expressive of the decline of the arts than of the greatness of the Roman empire in the time of Diocletian. If such was indeed the state of architecture, we must naturally believe that painting and sculpture had experienced a still more sensible decay. The practice of architecture is directed by a few general and even mechanical rules. But sculpture, and, above all, painting, propose to themselves the imitation not only of the forms of nature, but of the characters and passions of the human soul. In those sublime arts the dexterity of the hand is of little avail unless it is animated by fancy and guided by the most correct taste and observation.

It is almost unnecessary to remark that the civil distractions of the empire, the licence of the soldiers, the inroads of the barbarians, and the progress of despotism, had proved very unfavourable to genius, and even to learning. The succession of Illyrian princes restored the empire without restoring the sciences. Their military education was not calculated to inspire them with the love of letters; and even the mind of Diocletian, however active and capacious in business, was totally uninformed by study or speculation. The professions of law and physic are of such common use and certain profit that they will always secure a sufficient number of practitioners endowed with a reasonable degree of abilities and knowledge; but it does not appear that the students in those two faculties appeal to any celebrated masters who have flourished within that period. The voice of poetry was silent. History was reduced to dry and confused abridgments, alike destitute of amusement and instruction. A languid and affected eloquence was still retained in the pay and service of the emperors, who encouraged not any arts except those which contributed to the gratification of their pride or the defence of their power.

XII

(305–324 A.D.) TROUBLES AFTER THE ABDICA-
TION OF DIOCLETIAN—DEATH OF CON-
STANTIUS—ELEVATION OF CONSTANTINE
AND MAXENTIUS—SIX EMPERORS AT THE
SAME TIME—DEATH OF MAXIMIAN AND
GALERIUS—VICTORIES OF CONSTANTINE
OVER MAXENTIUS AND LICINIUS—REUNION
OF THE EMPIRE UNDER THE AUTHORITY OF
CONSTANTINE

The balance of power established by Diocletian subsisted no longer
than while it was sustained by the firm and dexterous hand of the
founder. It required such a fortunate mixture of different tempers
and abilities as could scarcely be found, or even expected, a second
time; two emperors without jealousy, two Cæsars without ambition
and the same general interest invariably pursued by four independent princes. The abdication of Diocletian and Maximian was
succeeded by eighteen years of discord and confusion. The empire
was afflicted by five civil wars; and the remainder of the time was
not so much a state of tranquillity as a suspension of arms between
several hostile monarchs, who, viewing each other with an eye of
fear and hatred, strove to increase their respective forces at the
expense of their subjects.

After the elevation of Constantius and Galerius to the rank of
Augusti, two new *Cæsars* were required to supply their place, and
to complete the system of the Imperial government. Diocletian was
sincerely desirous of withdrawing himself from the world; he
considered Galerius, who had married his daughter, as the firmest
support of his family and of the empire; and he consented, without
reluctance, that his successor should assume the merit as well as
the envy of the important nomination. It was fixed without
consulting the interest or inclination of the princes of the West.
Each of them had a son who was arrived at the age of manhood,
and who might have been deemed the most natural candidates for

the vacant honour. But the impotent resentment of Maximian was no longer to be dreaded; and the moderate Constantius, though he might despise the dangers, was humanely apprehensive of the calamities, of civil war. The two persons whom Galerius promoted to the rank of Cæsar were much better suited to serve the views of his ambition; and their principal recommendation seems to have consisted in the want of merit or personal consequence. The first of these was Daza, or, as he was afterwards called, Maximin, whose mother was the sister of Galerius. The inexperienced youth still betrayed by his manners and language his rustic education, when, to his own astonishment, as well as that of the world, he was invested by Diocletian with the purple, exalted to the dignity of Cæsar, and intrusted with the sovereign command of Egypt and Syria. At the same time Severus, a faithful servant, addicted to pleasure but not incapable of business, was sent to Milan to receive from the reluctant hands of Maximian the Cæsarian ornaments and the possession of Italy and Africa. According to the forms of the constitution, Severus acknowledged the supremacy of the western emperor; but he was absolutely devoted to the commands of his benefactor Galerius, who, reserving to himself the intermediate countries from the confines of Italy to those of Syria, firmly established his power over three-fourths of the monarchy. In the full confidence that the approaching death of Constantius would leave him sole master of the Roman world, we are assured that he had arranged in his mind a long succession of future princes, and that he meditated his own retreat from public life after he should have accomplished a glorious reign of about twenty years.

But, within less than eighteen months, two unexpected revolutions overturned the ambitious schemes of Galerius. The hopes of uniting the western provinces to his empire were disappointed by the elevation of Constantine; whilst Italy and Africa were lost by the successful revolt of Maxentius.

The great Constantine was most probably born at Naissus, in Dacia; and it is not surprising that, in a family and province distinguished only by the profession of arms, the youth should discover very little inclination to improve his mind by the acquisition of knowledge. He was about eighteen years of age when his father was promoted to the rank of Cæsar; but that fortunate event was attended with his mother's divorce; and the splendour of an Imperial alliance reduced the son of Helena to a state of disgrace and humiliation. Instead of following Constantius in the West, he remained in the service of Diocletian, signalising his valour in the wars of Egypt and Persia, and gradually rose to the honourable station of a tribune of the first order. The figure of Constantine was tall and majestic; he was dexterous in all his exercises, intrepid in war, affable in peace; in his whole conduct the active spirit of youth was tempered by habitual prudence; and while his mind was engrossed by ambition, he appeared cold and insensible to the allurements of pleasure. The favour of the people and soldiers, who had named him as a worthy candidate for the rank of Cæsar, served only to exasperate the jealousy of Galerius; and though prudence might restrain him from exercising any open violence, an absolute monarch is seldom at a loss how to execute a sure and secret revenge. Every hour increased the danger of Constantine and the anxiety of his father, who, by repeated letters, expressed the warmest desire of embracing his son. For some time the policy of Galerius supplied him with delays and excuses, but it was impossible long to refuse so natural a request of his associate without maintaining his refusal by arms. The permission of the journey was reluctantly granted, and, whatever precautions the emperor might have taken to intercept a return, the consequences of which he with so much reason apprehended, they were effectually disappointed by the incredible diligence of Constantine. Leaving the palace of Nicomedia in the night, he travelled post through Bithynia, Thrace, Dacia, Pannonia, Italy, and, amidst the joyful acclamations of the people, reached the port of Boulogne in the very moment when his father was preparing to embark for Britain.

The British expedition, and an easy victory over the barbarians of Caledonia, were the last exploits of the reign of Constantius. He ended his life in the Imperial palace of York, fifteen months after he had received the title of Augustus, and almost fourteen years and a half after he had been promoted to the rank of Cæsar. His death was immediately succeeded by the elevation of Constantine. The ideas of inheritance and succession are so very familiar that the generality of mankind consider them as founded not only in reason but in nature itself. Our imagination readily transfers the same principles from private property to public dominion: and whenever a virtuous father leaves behind him a son whose merit seems to justify the esteem, or even the hopes, of the people, the joint influence of prejudice and of affection operates with irresistible weight. The flower of the western armies had followed

Constantius into Britain, and the national troops were reinforced by a numerous body of Alemanni, who obeyed the orders of Crocus, one of their hereditary chieftains. The opinion of their own importance, and the assurance that Britain, Gaul, and Spain would acquiesce in their nomination, were diligently inculcated to the legions by the adherents of Constantine. The soldiers were asked whether they could hesitate a moment between the honour of placing at their head the worthy son of their beloved emperor and the ignominy of tamely expecting the arrival of some obscure stranger, on whom it might please the sovereign of Asia to bestow the armies and provinces of the West? It was insinuated to them that gratitude and liberality held a distinguished place among the virtues of Constantine; nor did that artful prince show himself to the troops till they were prepared to salute him with the names of Augustus and Emperor. The throne was the object of his desires; and had he been less actuated by ambition, it was his only means of safety. He was well acquainted with the character and sentiments of Galerius, and sufficiently apprised that, if he wished to live, he must determine to reign. The decent, and even obstinate, resistance which he chose to affect was contrived to justify his usurpation; nor did he yield to the acclamations of the army till he had provided the proper materials for a letter, which he immediately despatched to the emperor of the East. Constantine informed him of the melancholy event of his father's death, modestly asserted his natural claim to the succession, and respectfully lamented that the affectionate violence of his troops had not permitted him to solicit the Imperial purple in the regular and constitutional manner. The first emotions of Galerius were those of surprise, disappointment, and rage; and, as he could seldom restrain his passions, he loudly threatened that he would commit to the flames both the letter and the messenger. But his resentment insensibly subsided, and when he recollected the doubtful chance of war, when he had weighed the character and strength of his adversary, he consented to embrace the honourable accommodation which the prudence of Constantine had left open to him. Without either condemning or ratifying the choice of the British army, Galerius accepted the son of his deceased colleague as the sovereign of the provinces beyond the Alps; but he gave him only the title of Cæsar, and the fourth rank among the Roman princes, whilst he conferred the vacant place of Augustus on his favourite Severus. The apparent harmony of the empire was still preserved, and Constantine, who already possessed the substance, expected, without impatience, an opportunity of obtaining the honours of supreme power.

About that time the avarice of Galerius, or perhaps the exigencies of the state, had induced him to make a very strict and rigorous inquisition into the property of his subjects for the purpose of a general taxation, both on their lands and on their persons. A very minute survey appears to have been taken of their real estates; and, wherever there was the slightest suspicion of concealment, torture was very freely employed to obtain a sincere declaration of their personal wealth. The privileges which had exalted Italy above the rank of the provinces were no longer regarded: and the officers of the revenue already began to number the Roman people, and to settle the proportion of the new taxes. Even when the spirit of freedom had been utterly extinguished, the tamest subjects have sometimes ventured to resist an unprecedented invasion of their property; but on this occasion the injury was aggravated by the insult, and the sense of private interest was quickened by that of national honour. The conquest of Macedonia, as we have already observed, had delivered the Roman people from the weight of personal taxes. Though they had experienced every form of despotism, they had now enjoyed that exemption near five hundred years; nor could they patiently brook the insolence of an Illyrian peasant, who, from his distant residence in Asia, presumed to number Rome among the tributary cities of his empire. The rising fury of the people was encouraged by the authority, or at least the connivance, of the senate; and the feeble remains of the Prætorian guards, who had reason to apprehend their own dissolution, embraced so honourable a pretence, and declared their readiness to draw their swords in the service of their oppressed country. It was the wish, and it soon became the hope, of every citizen that, after expelling from Italy their foreign tyrants, they should elect a prince who, by the place of his residence, and by his maxims of government, might once more deserve the title of Roman emperor. The name, as well as the situation of Maxentius, determined in his favour the popular enthusiasm.

Maxentius was the son of the emperor Maximian, and he had married the daughter of Galerius. His birth and alliance seemed to offer him the fairest promise of succeeding to the empire; but his vices and incapacity procured him the same exclusion from the dignity of Cæsar which Constantine had deserved by a dangerous superiority of merit. It is uncertain whether Maximian was previously acquainted with the conspiracy; but as soon as the standard of rebellion was erected at Rome, the old emperor broke from the retirement where the authority of Diocletian had condemned him to pass a life of melancholy solitude, and concealed his returning ambition under the disguise of paternal tenderness. At the request of his son and of the senate he condescended to reassume the purple. His ancient dignity, his experience, and his fame in arms added strength as well as reputation to the party of Maxentius.

According to the advice, or rather the orders, of his colleague, the emperor Severus immediately hastened to Rome, in the full confidence that, by his unexpected celerity, he should easily suppress the tumult of an unwarlike populace, commanded by a licentious youth. But he found on his arrival the gates of the city shut against him, the walls filled with men and arms, an experienced general at the head of the rebels, and his own troops without spirit or affection. A large body of Moors deserted to the enemy, allured by the promise of a large donative; and, if it be true that they had been levied by Maximian in his African war, preferring the natural feelings of gratitude to the artificial ties of allegiance. Anulinus, the Prætorian præfect, declared himself in favour of Maxentius, and drew after him the most considerable part of the troops accustomed to obey his commands. Rome, according to the expression of an orator, recalled her armies; and the unfortunate Severus, destitute of force and of counsel, retired, or rather fled, with precipitation to Ravenna. Here he might for some time have been safe. The fortifications of Ravenna were able to resist the attempts, and the morasses that surrounded the town were sufficient to prevent the approach, of the Italian army. The sea, which Severus commanded with a powerful fleet, secured him an inexhaustible supply of provisions, and gave a free entrance to the legions which, on the return of spring, would advance to his assistance from Illyricum and the East. Maximian, who conducted the siege in person, was soon convinced that he might waste his time and his army in the fruitless enterprise, and that he had nothing to hope either from force or famine. With an art more suitable to the character of Diocletian than to his own, he directed his attack not so much against the walls of Ravenna as against the mind of Severus. The treachery which he had experienced disposed that unhappy prince to distrust the most sincere of his friends and adherents. The emissaries of Maximian easily persuaded his credulity that a conspiracy was formed to betray the town, and prevailed upon his fears not to expose himself to the discretion of an irritated conqueror, but to accept the faith of an honourable capitulation. He was at first received with humanity and treated with respect. Maximian conducted the captive emperor to Rome, and gave him the most solemn assurances that he had secured his life by the resignation of the purple. But Severus could obtain only an easy death and an Imperial funeral. When the sentence was signified to him, the manner of executing it was left to his own choice; he preferred the favourite mode of the ancients, that of opening his veins; and, as soon as he expired, his body was carried to the sepulchre which had been constructed for the family of Gallienus.

The importance of the occasion called for the presence and abilities of Galerius. At the head of a powerful army collected from Illyricum and the East, he entered Italy, resolved to revenge the death of Severus and to chastise the rebellious Romans; or, as he expressed his intentions, in the furious language of a barbarian, to extirpate the senate, and to destroy the people by the sword. But the skill of Maximian had concerted a prudent system of defence. The invader found every place hostile, fortified, and inaccessible; and though he forced his way as far as Narni, within sixty miles of Rome, his dominion in Italy was confined to the narrow limits of his camp. Sensible of the increasing difficulties of his enterprise, the haughty Galerius made the first advances towards a reconciliation, and despatched two of his most considerable officers to tempt the Roman princes by the offer of a conference, and the declaration of his paternal regard for Maxentius, who might obtain much more from his liberality than he could hope from the doubtful chance of war. The offers of Galerius were rejected with firmness, his perfidious friendship refused with contempt, and it was not long before he discovered that unless he provided for his safety by a timely retreat, he had some reason to apprehend the fate of Severus.

The legions of Galerius exhibited a very melancholy proof of their disposition by the ravages which they committed in their retreat. They murdered, they ravished, they plundered, they drove away the flocks and herds of the Italians; they burnt the villages through which they passed, and they endeavoured to destroy the country which it had not been in their power to subdue. During the whole march Maxentius hung on their rear, but he very prudently declined a general engagement with those brave and desperate veterans. His father had undertaken a second journey into Gaul, with the hope of persuading Constantine, who had assembled an army on the frontier, to join the pursuit, and to complete the victory. But the actions of Constantine were guided by reason, and not by resentment. He persisted in the wise resolution of maintaining a balance of power in the divided empire, and he no longer hated Galerius when that aspiring prince had ceased to be an object of terror.

The mind of Galerius was the most susceptible of the sterner passions, but it was not, however, incapable of a sincere and lasting friendship. Licinius, whose manners as well as character were not unlike his own, seems to have engaged both his affection and esteem. Their intimacy had commenced in the happier period, perhaps, of their youth and obscurity. It had been cemented by the freedom and dangers of a military life; they had advanced almost by equal steps through the successive honours of the service; and as soon as Galerius was invested with the Imperial dignity, he seems to have conceived the design of raising his companion to the same rank with himself. During the short period of his prosperity, he considered the rank of Cæsar as unworthy of the age and merit of Licinius, and rather chose to reserve for him the place of Constantius, and the empire of the West. While the emperor was employed in the Italian war, he intrusted his friend with the defence of the Danube; and immediately after his return from that unfortunate expedition he invested Licinius with the vacant purple of Severus, resigning to his immediate command the provinces of Illyricum. The news of his promotion was no sooner carried into the East, than Maximin, who governed, or rather oppressed, the countries of Egypt and Syria, betrayed his envy and discontent, disdained the inferior name of Cæsar, and, notwithstanding the prayers as well as arguments of Galerius, exacted, almost by violence, the equal title of Augustus. For the first, and indeed for the last time, the Roman world was administered by six emperors. In the West, Constantine and Maxentius affected to reverence their father Maximian. In the East, Licinius and Maximin honoured with more real consideration their benefactor Galerius. The opposition of interest, and the memory of a recent war, divided the empire into two great hostile powers; but their mutual fears produced an apparent tranquillity, and even a feigned reconciliation, till the death of the elder princes, of Maximian, and more particularly of Galerius, gave a new direction to the views and passions of their surviving associates.

When Maximian had reluctantly abdicated the empire, the venal orators of the times applauded his philosophic moderation. When his ambition excited, or at least encouraged, a civil war, they returned thanks to his generous patriotism, and gently censured that love of ease and retirement which had withdrawn him from the public service. But it was impossible that minds like those of Maximian and his son could long possess in harmony an undivided power. Maxentius considered himself as the legal sovereign of Italy, elected by the Roman senate and people; nor would he endure the control of his father, who arrogantly declared that by *his* name and abilities the rash youth had been established on the throne. The cause was solemnly pleaded before the Prætorian guards; and those troops, who dreaded the severity of the old emperor, espoused the party of Maxentius. The life and freedom of Maximian were, however, respected, and he retired from Italy into Illyricum, affecting to lament his past conduct, and secretly contriving new mischiefs. But Galerius, who was well acquainted with his character, soon obliged him to leave his dominions, and the last refuge of the disappointed Maximian was the court of his son-in-law Constantine. He was received with respect by that artful prince, and with the appearance of filial tenderness by the empress Fausta. That he might remove every suspicion, he resigned the Imperial purple a second time, professing himself at length convinced of the vanity of greatness and ambition. Had he persevered in this resolution, he might have ended his life with less dignity, indeed, than in his first retirement, yet, however, with comfort and reputation. But the near prospect of a throne brought back to his remembrance the state from whence he was fallen, and he resolved, by a desperate effort, either to reign or to perish. An incursion of the Franks had summoned Constantine, with a part of his army, to the banks of the Rhine; the remainder of the troops were stationed in the southern provinces of Gaul, which lay exposed to the enterprises of the Italian emperor, and a considerable treasure was deposited in the city of Arles. Maximian either craftily invented, or hastily credited, a vain report of the death of Constantine. Without hesitation he ascended the throne, seized the treasure, and, scattering it with his accustomed profusion among the soldiers, endeavoured to awake in their minds the memory of his ancient dignity and exploits. Before he could establish his authority, or finish the negotiation which he appears to have entered into with his son Maxentius, the celerity of Constantine defeated all his hopes. A secret but irrevocable sentence of death was pronounced against the usurper; he obtained only the same favour which he had indulged to Severus, and it was published to the world that, oppressed by the remorse of his repeated crimes, he strangled himself with his own hands. After he had lost the assistance, and disdained the moderate counsels, of Diocletian, the second period of his active life was a series of public calamities and personal mortifications, which were terminated, in about three years, by an ignominious death. He deserved his fate; but we should find more reason to applaud the humanity of Constantine if he had spared an old man, the benefactor of his father and the father of his wife. During the whole of this melancholy transaction, it appears that Fausta sacrificed the sentiments of nature to her conjugal duties.

The last years of Galerius were less shameful and unfortunate; and though he had filled with more glory the subordinate station of Cæsar than the superior rank of Augustus, he preserved, till the moment of his death, the first place among the princes of the Roman world. He survived his retreat from Italy about four years; and, wisely relinquishing his views of universal empire, he devoted the remainder of his life to the enjoyment of pleasure and to the execution of some works of public utility, among which we may distinguish the discharging into the Danube the superfluous waters of the lake Pelso, and the cutting down the immense forests that encompassed it: an operation worthy of a monarch, since it gave an extensive country to the agriculture of his Pannonian subjects. His death was occasioned by a very painful and lingering disorder. His body, swelled by an intemperate course of life to an unwieldy corpulence, was covered with ulcers, and devoured by innumerable swarms of those insects who have given their name to a most loathsome disease; but as Galerius had offended a very zealous and powerful party among his subjects, his sufferings, instead of exciting their compassion, have been celebrated as the visible effects of divine justice. He had no sooner expired in his palace of Nicomedia than the two emperors, who were indebted for their purple to his favour, began to collect their forces, with the intention either of disputing or of dividing the dominions which he had left without a master. They were persuaded, however, to desist from the former design, and to agree in the latter. The provinces of Asia fell to the share of Maximin, and those of Europe augmented the portion of Licinius. The Hellespont and the Thracian Bosphorus formed their mutual boundary, and the banks of those narrow seas, which flowed in the midst of the Roman world, were covered with soldiers, with arms, and with fortifications. The deaths of Maximian and of Galerius reduced the number of emperors to four. The sense of their true interest soon connected Licinius and Constantine; a secret alliance was concluded between Maximin and Maxentius, and their unhappy subjects expected with terror the bloody consequences of their inevitable dissensions, which were no longer restrained by the fear or the respect which they had entertained for Galerius.

The virtues of Constantine were rendered more illustrious by the vices of Maxentius. Whilst the Gallic provinces enjoyed as much happiness as the condition of the times was capable of receiving, Italy and Africa groaned under the dominion of a tyrant as contemptible as he was odious. The zeal of flattery and faction has indeed too frequently sacrificed the reputation of the vanquished to the glory of their successful rivals; but even those writers who have revealed, with the most freedom and pleasure, the faults of Constantine, unanimously confess that Maxentius was cruel, rapacious, and profligate. He had the good fortune to suppress a slight rebellion in Africa. The governor and a few adherents had been guilty; the province suffered for their crime. The flourishing cities of Cirtha and Carthage, and the whole extent of that fertile country, were wasted by fire and sword. The abuse of victory was followed by the abuse of law and justice. A formidable army of sycophants and delators invaded Africa; the rich and the noble were easily convicted of a connection with the rebels; and those among them who experienced the emperor's clemency were only punished by the confiscation of their estates. So signal a victory was celebrated by a magnificent triumph, and Maxentius exposed to the eyes of the people the spoils and captives of a Roman province. The state of the capital was no less deserving of compassion than that of Africa. The wealth of Rome supplied an inexhaustible fund for his vain and prodigal expenses, and the ministers of his revenue were skilled in the arts of rapine. It was under his reign that the method of exacting a *free gift* from the senators was first invented; and as the sum was insensibly increased, the pretences of levying it, a victory, a birth, a marriage, or an Imperial consulship, were proportionately multiplied. Maxentius had imbibed the same implacable aversion to the senate which had characterised most of the former tyrants of Rome; nor was it possible for his ungrateful temper to forgive the generous fidelity which had raised him to the throne and supported him against all his enemies. The lives of the senators were exposed to his jealous suspicions, the dishonour of their wives and daughters heightened the gratification of his sensual passions. It may be presumed that an Imperial lover was seldom reduced to sigh in vain; but whenever persuasion proved ineffectual, he had recourse to violence; and there remains *one* memorable example of a noble matron who preserved her chastity by a voluntary death. The soldiers were the only order of men whom he appeared to respect, or studied to please. He filled Rome and Italy with armed troops, connived at their tumults, suffered them with impunity to plunder, and even to massacre, the defenceless people; and indulging them in the same licentiousness which their emperor enjoyed, Maxentius often bestowed on his military favourites the splendid villa, or the beautiful wife, of a senator. A prince, of such a character, alike incapable of governing either in peace or in war, might purchase the support, but he could never obtain the esteem, of the army. Yet his pride was equal to his other vices. Whilst he passed his indolent life, either within the walls of his palace or in the neighbouring gardens of Sallust, he was repeatedly heard to declare that *he alone* was emperor, and that the other princes were no more than his lieutenants, on whom he had devolved the defence of the frontier provinces, that he might enjoy without interruption the elegant luxury of the capital. Rome, which had so long regretted the absence, lamented, during the six years of his reign, the presence of her sovereign.

Though Constantine might view the conduct of Maxentius with abhorrence, and the situation of the Romans with compassion, we have no reason to presume that he would have taken up arms to punish the one or to relieve the other. But the tyrant of Italy rashly ventured to provoke a formidable enemy whose ambition had been hitherto restrained by considerations of prudence rather than by principles of justice. After the death of Maximian, his titles, according to the established custom, had been erased, and his statues thrown down with ignominy. His son, who had persecuted and deserted him when alive, affected to display the most pious regard for his memory, and gave orders that a similar treatment should be immediately inflicted on all the statues that had been erected in Italy and Africa to the honour of Constantine. That wise prince, who sincerely wished to decline a war, with the difficulty and importance of which he was sufficiently acquainted, at first dissembled the insult, and sought for redress by the milder expedients of negotiation, till he was convinced that the hostile and ambitious designs of the Italian emperor made it necessary for him to arm in his own defence. Maxentius, who openly avowed his pretensions to the whole monarchy of the West, had already prepared a very considerable force to invade the Gallic provinces on the side of Rhætia; and though he could not expect any assistance from Licinius, he was flattered with the hope that the legions of Illyricum, allured by his presents and promises, would desert the standard of that prince, and unanimously declare themselves his soldiers and subjects. Constantine no longer hesitated. He had deliberated with caution, he acted with vigour. He gave a private audience to the ambassadors who, in the name of the senate and people, conjured him to deliver Rome from a detested tyrant; and, without regarding the timid remonstrances of his council, he resolved to prevent the enemy, and to carry the war into the heart of Italy.

The enterprise was as full of danger as of glory; and the unsuccessful event of two former invasions was sufficient to inspire the most serious apprehensions. The veteran troops, who revered the name of Maximian, had embraced in both those wars the party of his son, and were now restrained by a sense of honour, as well as of interest, from entertaining an idea of a second desertion. Maxentius, who considered the Prætorian guards as the firmest defence of his throne, had increased them to their ancient establishment; and they composed, including the rest of the Italians who were enlisted into his service, a formidable body of fourscore thousand men. Forty thousand Moors and Carthaginians had been raised since the reduction of Africa. Even Sicily furnished its proportion of troops; and the armies of Maxentius amounted to one hundred and seventy thousand foot and eighteen thousand horse. The wealth of Italy supplied the expenses of the war; and the adjacent provinces were exhausted to form immense magazines of corn and every other kind of provisions.

The celerity of Constantine's march has been compared to the rapid conquest of Italy by the first of the Cæsars; nor is the flattering parallel repugnant to the truth of history, since no more than fifty-eight days elapsed between the surrender of Verona and the final decision of the war. Constantine had always apprehended that the tyrant would consult the dictates of fear, and perhaps of prudence; and that, instead of risking his last hopes in a general engagement, he would shut himself up within the walls of Rome.

His ample magazines secured him against the danger of famine; and as the situation of Constantine admitted not of delay, he might have been reduced to the sad necessity of destroying with fire and sword the Imperial city, the noblest reward of his victory, and the deliverance of which had been the motive, or rather indeed the pretence, of the civil war. It was with equal surprise and pleasure that, on his arrival at a place called Saxa Rubra, about nine miles from Rome, he discovered the army of Maxentius prepared to give him battle. Their long front filled a very spacious plain, and their deep array reached to the banks of the Tiber, which covered their rear, and forbade their retreat. We are informed, and we may believe, that Constantine disposed his troops with consummate skill, and that he chose for himself the post of honour and danger. Distinguished by the splendour of his arms, he charged in person the cavalry of his rival; and his irresistible attack determined the fortune of the day. The cavalry of Maxentius was principally composed either of unwieldy cuirassiers or of light Moors and Numidians. They yielded to the vigour of the Gallic horse, which possessed more activity than the one, more firmness than the other. The defeat of the two wings left the infantry without any protection on its flanks, and the undisciplined Italians fled without reluctance from the standard of a tyrant whom they had always hated, and whom they no longer feared. The Prætorians, conscious that their offences were beyond the reach of mercy, were animated by revenge and despair. Notwithstanding their repeated efforts, those brave veterans were unable to recover the victory; they obtained, however, an honourable death; and it was observed that their bodies covered the same ground which had been occupied by their ranks. The confusion then became general, and the dismayed troops of Maxentius, pursued by an implacable enemy, rushed by thousands into the deep and rapid stream of the Tiber. The emperor himself attempted to escape back into the city over the Milvian bridge, but the crowds which pressed together through that narrow passage forced him into the river, where he was immediately drowned by the weight of his armour. His body, which had sunk very deep into the mud, was found with some difficulty the next day. The sight of his head, when it was exposed to the eyes of the people, convinced them of their deliverance, and admonished them to receive with acclamations of loyalty and gratitude the fortunate Constantine, who thus achieved by his valour and ability the most splendid enterprise of his life.

In the use of victory Constantine neither deserved the praise of clemency nor incurred the censure of immoderate rigour. He inflicted the same treatment to which a defeat would have exposed his own person and family, put to death the two sons of the tyrant, and carefully extirpated his whole race. The most distinguished adherents of Maxentius must have expected to share his fate, as they had shared his prosperity and his crimes; but when the Roman people loudly demanded a greater number of victims, the conqueror resisted, with firmness and humanity, those servile clamours, which were dictated by flattery as well as by resentment. Informers were punished and discouraged; the innocent who had suffered under the late tyranny were recalled from exile, and restored to their estates. A general act of oblivion quieted the minds and settled the property of the people both in Italy and in Africa. The first time that Constantine honoured the senate with his presence he reca-pitulated his own services and exploits in a modest oration, assured that illustrious order of his sincere regard, and promised to re-establish its ancient dignity and privileges. The grateful senate repaid these unmeaning professions by the empty titles of honour which it was yet in their power to bestow; and, without presuming to ratify the authority of Constantine, they passed a decree to assign him the first rank among the three *Augusti* who governed the Roman world. Games and festivals were instituted to preserve the fame of his victory, and several edifices, raised at the expense of Maxentius, were dedicated to the honour of his successful rival. The triumphal arch of Constantine still remains a melancholy proof of the decline of the arts, and a singular testimony of the meanest vanity. As it was not possible to find in the capital of the empire a sculptor who was capable of adorning that public monument, the arch of Trajan, without any respect either for his memory or for the rules of propriety, was stripped of its most elegant figures. The difference of times and persons, of actions and characters, was totally disre-garded. The Parthian captives appear prostrate at the feet of a prince who never carried his arms beyond the Euphrates; and curious antiquarians can still discover the head of Trajan on the trophies of Constantine. The new ornaments which it was necessary to introduce between the vacancies of ancient sculpture are executed in the rudest and most unskilful manner.

Before Constantine marched into Italy he had secured the friendship, or at least the neutrality, of Licinius, the Illyrian emperor. He had promised his sister Constantia in marriage to that prince; but the celebration of the nuptials was deferred till after the conclusion of the war, and the interview of the two emperors at Milan, which was appointed for that purpose, appeared to cement the union of their families and interests. In the midst of the public festivity they were suddenly obliged to take leave of each other. An inroad of the Franks summoned Constantine to the Rhine, and the hostile approach of the sovereign of Asia demanded the immediate presence of Licinius. Maximin had been the secret ally of Maxentius, and, without being discouraged by his fate, he resolved to try the fortune of a civil war. He moved out of Syria, towards the frontiers of Bithynia, in the depth of winter. The season was severe and tempestuous; great numbers of men as well as horses perished in the snow; and as the roads were broken up by incessant rains, he was obliged to leave behind him a considerable part of the heavy baggage, which was unable to follow the rapidity of his forced marches. By this extraordinary effort of diligence, he arrived, with a harassed but formidable army, on the banks of the Thracian Bosphorus before the lieutenants of Licinius were apprised of his hostile intentions. Byzantium surrendered to the power of Maximin after a siege of eleven days. He was detained some days under the walls of Heraclea; and he had no sooner taken possession of that city than he was alarmed by the intelligence that Licinius had pitched his camp at the distance of only eighteen miles. After a fruitless negotiation, in which the two princes attempted to seduce the fidelity of each other's adherents, they had recourse to arms. The emperor of the East commanded a disciplined and veteran army of above seventy thousand men; and Licinius, who had collected about thirty thousand Illyrians, was at first oppressed by the superiority of numbers. His military skill and the firmness of his troops restored the day and obtained a decisive victory. The incredible speed which Maximin exerted in his flight is much more celebrated than his prowess in the battle. Twenty-four hours afterwards he was seen pale, trembling, and without his Imperial ornaments, at Nicomedia, one hundred and sixty miles from the place of his defeat. The wealth of Asia was yet unexhausted; and though the flower of his veterans had fallen in the late action, he had still power, if he could obtain time, to draw very numerous levies from Syria and Egypt. But he survived his misfortune only three or four months. His death, which happened at Tarsus, was variously ascribed to despair, to poison, and to the divine justice. As Maximin was alike destitute of abilities and of virtue, he was lamented neither by the people nor by the soldiers. The provinces of the East, delivered from the terrors of civil war cheerfully acknowledged the authority of Licinius.

The Roman world was now divided between Constantine and Licinius, the former of whom was master of the West, and the latter of the East. It might perhaps have been expected that the conquerors, fatigued with civil war, and connected by a private as well as public alliance, would have renounced, or at least would have suspended, any farther designs of ambition. And yet a year had scarcely elapsed after the death of Maximin, before the victorious emperors turned their arms against each other. The genius, the success, and the aspiring temper of Constantine, may seem to mark him out as the aggressor; but the perfidious character of Licinius justifies the most unfavourable suspicions, and by the faint light which history reflects on this transaction we may discover a conspiracy fomented by his arts against the authority of his colleague. The loss of two battles, and of his bravest veterans, reduced the fierce spirit of Licinius to sue for peace. His ambassador, Mistrianus, was admitted to the audience of Constantine: he expatiated on the common topics of moderation and humanity, which are so familiar to the eloquence of the vanquished; represented in the most insinuating language that the event of the war was still doubtful, whilst its inevitable calamities were alike pernicious to both the contending parties; and declared that he was authorised to propose a lasting and honourable peace. The successive defeats of Licinius had ruined his forces, but they had displayed his courage and abilities. His situation was almost desperate, but the efforts of despair are sometimes formidable, and the good sense of Constantine preferred a great and certain advantage to a third trial of the chance of arms. He consented to leave his rival, or, as he again styled Licinius, his friend and brother, in the possession of Thrace, Asia Minor, Syria, and Egypt; but the provinces of Pannonia, Dalmatia, Dacia, Macedonia, and Greece were yielded to the Western empire, and the dominions of Constantine now extended from the confines of Caledonia to the extremity of Peloponnesus. It was stipulated by the same treaty that three royal youths, the sons of the emperors, should be called to the hopes of the succession. Crispus and the young Constantine were soon afterwards declared Cæsars in the West, while the younger Licinius was invested with the same dignity in the East. In this double proportion of honours, the conqueror asserted the superiority of his arms and power.

In this exalted state of glory it was impossible that Constantine should any longer endure a partner in the empire. Confiding in the superiority of his genius and military power, he determined, without any previous injury, to exert them for the destruction of Licinius, whose advanced age and unpopular vices seemed to offer a very easy conquest. But the old emperor, awakened by the approaching danger, deceived the expectations of his friends as well as of his enemies. Calling forth that spirit and those abilities by which he had deserved the friendship of Galerius and the Imperial purple, he prepared himself for the contest, collected the forces of the East, and soon filled the plains of Hadrianople with his troops, and the Straits of the Hellespont with his fleet. The army consisted of one hundred and fifty thousand foot and fifteen thousand horse; and as the cavalry was drawn, for the most part, from Phrygia and Cappadocia, we may conceive a more favourable opinion of the beauty of the horses than of the courage and dexterity of their riders. The fleet was composed of three hundred and fifty galleys of three ranks of oars. An hundred and thirty of these were furnished by Egypt and the adjacent coast of Africa. An hundred and ten sailed from the ports of Phœnicia and the isle of Cyprus; and the maritime countries of Bithynia, Ionia, and Caria were likewise obliged to provide an hundred and ten galleys. The troops of Constantine were ordered to rendezvous at Thessalonica; they amounted to above an hundred and twenty thousand horse and foot. Their emperor was satisfied with their martial appearance, and his army contained more soldiers, though fewer men, than that of his eastern competitor. The legions of Constantine were levied in the warlike provinces of Europe; action had confirmed their discipline, victory had elevated their hopes, and there were among them a great number of veterans, who, after seventeen glorious campaigns under the same leader, prepared themselves to deserve an honourable dismission by a last effort of their valour. But the naval preparations of Constantine were in every respect much inferior to those of Licinius. The maritime cities of Greece sent their respective quotas of men and ships to the celebrated harbour of Piræus and their united forces consisted of no more than two hundred small vessels; a very feeble armament, if it is compared with those formidable fleets which were equipped and maintained by the republic of Athens during the Peloponnesian war. Since Italy was no longer the seat of government, the naval establishments of Misenum and Ravenna had been gradually neglected; and as the shipping and mariners of the empire were supported by commerce rather than by war, it was natural that they should the most abound in the industrious provinces of Egypt and Asia. It is only surprising that the eastern emperor, who possessed so great a superiority at sea, should have neglected the opportunity of carrying an offensive war into the centre of his rival's dominions.

The siege of Byzantium, which was immediately undertaken by Constantine, was attended with great labour and uncertainty. In the late civil wars, the fortifications of that place, so justly considered as the key of Europe and Asia, had been repaired and strengthened; and as long as Licinius remained master of the sea, the garrison was much less exposed to the danger of famine than the army of the besiegers. The naval commanders of Constantine were summoned to his camp, and received his positive orders to force the passage of the Hellespont, as the fleet of Licinius, instead of seeking and destroying their feeble enemy, continued inactive in those narrow straits, where its superiority of numbers was of little use or advantage. Crispus, the emperor's eldest son, was intrusted with the execution of this daring enterprise, which he performed with so much courage and success, that he deserved the esteem, and most probably excited the jealousy, of his father. The engagement lasted two days; and in the evening of the first, the contending fleets, after a considerable and mutual loss, retired into their respective harbours of Europe and Asia. The second day about noon a strong south wind sprang up, which carried the vessels of Crispus against the enemy; and as the casual advantage was improved by his skilful intrepidity, he soon obtained a complete victory. An hundred and thirty vessels were destroyed, five thousand men were slain, and Amandus, the admiral of the Asiatic fleet, escaped with the utmost difficulty to the shores of Chalcedon. As soon as the Hellespont was open, a plentiful convoy of provisions flowed into the camp of Constantine, who had already advanced the operations of the siege. He constructed artificial mounds of earth of an equal height with the ramparts of Byzantium. The lofty towers which were erected on that foundation galled the besieged with large stones and darts from the military engines, and the battering rams had shaken the walls in several places. If Licinius persisted much longer in the defence, he exposed himself to be involved in the ruin of the place. Before he was surrounded, he prudently removed his person and treasures to Chalcedon in Asia.

Such were still the resources, and such the abilities, of Licinius that, after so many successive defeats, he collected in Bithynia a new army of fifty or sixty thousand men, while the activity of Constantine was employed in the siege of Byzantium. The vigilant emperor did not, however, neglect the last struggles of his antagonist. A considerable part of his victorious army was transported over the Bosphorus in small vessels, and the decisive engagement was fought soon after their landing on the heights of Chrysopolis, or, as it is now called, of Scutari. The troops of Licinius, though they were lately raised, ill armed, and worse disciplined, made head against their conquerors with fruitless but desperate valour, till a total defeat, and the slaughter of five-and-twenty thousand men, irretrievably determined the fate of their leader. The memory of Licinius was branded with infamy, his statues were thrown down, and by a hasty edict, of such mischievous tendency that it was almost immediately corrected, all his laws and all the judicial proceedings of his reign were at once abolished. By this victory of Constantine the Roman world was again united under the authority of one emperor, thirty-seven years after Diocletian had divided his power and provinces with his associate Maximian.

XIII

THE PROGRESS OF THE CHRISTIAN RELIGION — SENTIMENTS, MANNERS, NUMBERS, AND CONDITIONS OF THE PRIMITIVE CHRISTIANS

A candid but rational inquiry into the progress and establishment of Christianity may be considered as a very essential part of the history of the Roman empire. While that great body was invaded by open violence, or undermined by slow decay, a pure and humble religion gently insinuated itself into the minds of men, grew up in silence and obscurity, derived new vigour from opposition, and finally erected the triumphant banner of the Cross on the ruins of the Capitol. Nor was the influence of Christianity confined to the period or to the limits of the Roman empire. After a revolution of thirteen or fourteen centuries, that religion is still professed by the nations of Europe, the most distinguished portion of human kind in arts and learning as well as in arms. By the industry and zeal of the Europeans it has been widely diffused to the most distant shores of Asia and Africa; and by the means of their colonies has been firmly established from Canada to Chili, in a world unknown to the ancients.

But this inquiry, however useful or entertaining, is attended with two peculiar difficulties. The scanty and suspicious materials of ecclesiastical history seldom enable us to dispel the dark cloud that hangs over the first age of the church. The great law of impartiality too often obliges us to reveal the imperfections of the uninspired teachers and believers of the Gospel; and, to a careless observer, *their* faults may seem to cast a shade on the faith which they professed. But the scandal of the pious Christian, and the fallacious triumph of the Infidel, should cease as soon as they recollect not only *by whom*, but likewise *to whom*, the Divine Revelation was given. The theologian may indulge the pleasing task of describing Religion as she descended from Heaven, arrayed in her native purity. A more melancholy duty is imposed on the historian. He must discover the inevitable mixture of error and corruption which she contracted in a long residence upon earth, among a weak and degenerate race of beings.

Our curiosity is naturally prompted to inquire by what means the Christian faith obtained so remarkable a victory over the established religions of the earth. To this inquiry an obvious but satisfactory answer may be returned; that it was owing to the convincing evidence of the doctrine itself, and to the ruling providence of its great Author. But as truth and reason seldom find so favourable a reception in the world, and as the wisdom of Providence frequently condescends to use the passions of the human heart, and the general circumstances of mankind, as instruments to execute its purpose, we may still be permitted, though with becoming submission, to ask, not indeed what were the first, but what were the secondary causes of the rapid growth of the Christian church? It will, perhaps, appear that it was most effectually favoured and assisted by the five following causes:—I. The inflexible, and, if we may use the expression, the intolerant zeal of the Christians, derived, it is true, from the Jewish religion, but purified from the narrow and unsocial spirit which, instead of inviting, had deterred the Gentiles from embracing the law of Moses. II. The doctrine of a future life, improved by every additional circumstance which could give weight and efficacy to that important truth. III. The miraculous powers ascribed to the primitive church. IV. The pure and austere morals of the Christians. V. The union and discipline of the Christian republic, which gradually formed an independent and increasing state in the heart of the Roman empire.

I. We have already described the religious harmony of the ancient world, and the facility with which the most different and even hostile nations embraced, or at least respected, each other's superstitions. A single people refused to join in the common intercourse of mankind. The Jews, who, under the Assyrian and Persian monarchies, had languished for many ages the most despised portion of their slaves, emerged from obscurity under the successors of Alexander; and as they multiplied to a surprising degree in the East, and afterwards in the West, they soon excited the curiosity and wonder of other nations. The sullen obstinacy with which they maintained their peculiar rites and unsocial manners seemed to mark them out a distinct species of men, who boldly professed, or who faintly disguised, their implacable hatred to the rest of human-kind. Neither the violence of Antiochus, nor the arts of Herod, nor the example of the circumjacent nations, could ever persuade the Jews to associate with the institutions of Moses the elegant mythology of the Greeks. According to the maxims of universal toleration, the Romans protected a superstition which they despised. The polite Augustus condescended to give orders that sacrifices should be offered for his prosperity in the temple of Jerusalem; while the meanest of the posterity of Abraham, who should have paid the same homage to the Jupiter of the Capitol, would have been an object of abhorrence to himself and to his brethren. But the moderation of the conquerors was insufficient to appease the jealous prejudices of their subjects, who were alarmed and scandalised at the ensigns of paganism, which necessarily introduced themselves into a Roman province. The mad attempt of Caligula to place his own statue in the temple of Jerusalem was defeated by the unanimous resolution of a people who dreaded death much less than such an idolatrous profanation. Their attachment to the law of Moses was equal to their detestation of foreign religions. The current of zeal and devotion, as it was contracted into a narrow channel, ran with the strength, and some-times with the fury, of a torrent.

This inflexible perseverance, which appeared so odious or so ridiculous to the ancient world, assumes a more awful character, since Providence has deigned to reveal to us the mysterious history of the chosen people. But the devout and even scrupulous attachment to the Mosaic religion, so conspicuous among the Jews who lived under the second temple, becomes still more surprising if it is compared with the stubborn incredulity of their forefathers. When the law was given in thunder from Mount Sinai; when the tides of the ocean and the course of the planets were suspended for the convenience of the Israelites; and when temporal rewards and punishments were the immediate consequences of their piety or disobedience, they perpetually relapsed into rebellion against the visible majesty of their Divine King, placed the idols of the nations in the sanctuary of Jehovah, and imitated every fantastic ceremony that was practised in the tents of the Arabs, or in the cities of Phœnicia. As the protection of Heaven was deservedly withdrawn from the ungrateful race, their faith acquired a proportionable degree of vigour and purity. The contemporaries of Moses and Joshua had beheld with careless indifference the most amazing miracles. Under the pressure of every calamity, the belief of those miracles has preserved the Jews of a later period from the universal contagion of idolatry; and in contradiction to every known principle of the human mind, that singular people seems to have yielded a stronger and more ready assent to the traditions of their remote ancestors than to the evidence of their own senses.

The Jewish religion was admirably fitted for defence, but it was never designed for conquest; and it seems probable that the number of proselytes was never much superior to that of apostates. The divine promises were originally made, and the distinguishing rite of circumcision was enjoined, to a single family. When the posterity of Abraham had multiplied like the sands of the sea, the Deity, from whose mouth they received a system of laws and ceremonies, declared himself the proper and as it were the national God of Israel; and with the most jealous care separated his favourite people from the rest of mankind. The conquest of the land of Canaan was accompanied with so many wonderful and with so many bloody circumstances, that the victorious Jews were left in a state of irreconcilable hostility with all their neighbours. They had been commanded to extirpate some of the most idolatrous tribes, and the execution of the Divine will had seldom been retarded by the weakness of humanity. With the other nations they were forbidden to contract any marriages or alliances; and the prohibition of receiving them into the congregation, which in some cases was perpetual, almost always extended to the third, to the seventh, or even to the tenth generation. The obligation of preaching to the Gentiles the faith of Moses had never been inculcated as a precept of the law, nor were the Jews inclined to impose it on themselves as a voluntary duty.

Under these circumstances, Christianity offered itself to the world, armed with the strength of the Mosaic law, and delivered from the weight of its fetters. An exclusive zeal for the truth of religion and the unity of God was as carefully inculcated in the new as in the ancient system: and whatever was now revealed to mankind concerning the nature and designs of the Supreme Being was fitted to increase their reverence for that mysterious doctrine. The divine authority of Moses and the prophets was admitted, and even established, as the firmest basis of Christianity. From the beginning of the world an uninterrupted series of predictions had announced and prepared the long-expected coming of the Messiah, who, in compliance with the gross apprehensions of the Jews, had been more frequently represented under the character of a King and Conqueror, than under that of a Prophet, a Martyr, and the

Son of God. By his expiatory sacrifice the imperfect sacrifices of the temple were at once consummated and abolished. The ceremonial law, which consisted only of types and figures, was succeeded by a pure and spiritual worship, equally adapted to all climates, as well as to every condition of mankind; and to the initiation of blood, was substituted a more harmless initiation of water. The promise of divine favour, instead of being partially confined to the posterity of Abraham, was universally proposed to the freeman and the slave, to the Greek and to the barbarian, to the Jew and to the Gentile. Every privilege that could raise the proselyte from earth to heaven, that could exalt his devotion, secure his happiness, or even gratify that secret pride which, under the semblance of devotion, insinuates itself into the human heart, was still reserved for the members of the Christian church; but at the same time all mankind was permitted, and even solicited, to accept the glorious distinction, which was not only proffered as a favour, but imposed as an obligation. It became the most sacred duty of a new convert to diffuse among his friends and relations the inestimable blessing which he had received, and to warn them against a refusal that would be severely punished as a criminal disobedience to the will of a benevolent but all-powerful Deity.

The enfranchisement of the church from the bonds of the synagogue was a work, however, of some time and of some difficulty. The Jewish converts, who acknowledged Jesus in the character of the Messiah foretold by their ancient oracles, respected him as a prophetic teacher of virtue and religion; but they obstinately adhered to the ceremonies of their ancestors, and were desirous of imposing them on the Gentiles, who continually augmented the number of believers. These Judaising Christians seem to have argued with some degree of plausibility from the Divine origin of the Mosaic law, and from the immutable perfections of its great Author. They affirmed, *that*, if the Being who is the same through all eternity had designed to abolish those sacred rites which had served to distinguish his chosen people, the repeal of them would have been no less clear and solemn than their first promulgation: *that*, instead of those frequent declarations which either suppose or assert the perpetuity of the Mosaic religion, it would have been represented as a provisionary scheme intended to last only till the coming of the Messiah, who should instruct mankind in a more perfect mode of faith and of worship: *that* the Messiah himself, and his disciples who conversed with him on earth, instead of authorising by their example the most minute observances of the Mosaic law, would have published to the world the abolition of those useless and obsolete ceremonies, without suffering Christianity to remain during so many years obscurely confounded among the sects of the Jewish church. Arguments like these appear to have been used in the defence of the expiring cause of the Mosaic law; but the industry of our learned divines has abundantly explained the ambiguous language of the Old Testament, and the ambiguous conduct of the apostolic teachers. It was proper gradually to unfold the system of the Gospel, and to pronounce with utmost caution and tenderness a sentence of condemnation so repugnant to the inclination and prejudices of the believing Jews.

The history of the church of Jerusalem affords a lively proof of the necessity of those precautions, and of the deep impression which the Jewish religion had made on the minds of its sectaries. The first fifteen bishops of Jerusalem were all circumcised Jews; and the congregation over which they presided united the law of Moses with the doctrine of Christ. It was natural that the primitive tradition of a church which was founded only forty days after the death of Christ, and was governed almost as many years under the immediate inspection of his apostle, should be received as the standard of orthodoxy. The distant churches very frequently appealed to the authority of their venerable Parent, and relieved her distresses by a liberal contribution of alms. But when numerous and opulent societies were established in the great cities of the empire, in Antioch, Alexandria, Ephesus, Corinth, and Rome, the reverence which Jerusalem had inspired to all the Christian colonies insensibly diminished. The Jewish converts, or, as they were afterwards called, the Nazarenes, who had laid the foundations of the church, soon found themselves overwhelmed by the increasing multitudes that from all the various religions of polytheism enlisted under the banner of Christ: and the Gentiles, who, with the approbation of their peculiar apostle, had rejected the intolerable weight of Mosaic ceremonies, at length refused to their more scrupulous brethren the same toleration which at first they had humbly solicited for their own practice. The ruin of the temple, of the city, and of the public religion of the Jews, was severely felt by the Nazarenes; as in their manners, though not in their faith, they maintained so intimate a connection with their impious countrymen, whose misfortunes were attributed by the Pagans to the contempt, and more justly ascribed by the Christians to the wrath, of the Supreme

Deity. The Nazarenes retired from the ruins of Jerusalem to the little town of Pella beyond the Jordan, where that ancient church languished above sixty years in solitude and obscurity. They still enjoyed the comfort of making frequent and devout visits to the *Holy City*, and the hope of being one day restored to those seats which both nature and religion taught them to love as well as to revere. But at length, under the reign of Hadrian, the desperate fanaticism of the Jews filled up the measure of their calamities; and the Romans, exasperated by their repeated rebellions, exercised the rights of victory with unusual rigour. The emperor founded, under the name of Ælia Capitolina, a new city on Mount Sion, to which he gave the privileges of a colony; and denouncing the severest penalties against any of the Jewish people who should dare to approach its precincts, he fixed a vigilant garrison of a Roman cohort to enforce the execution of his orders. The Nazarenes had only one way left to escape the common proscription, and the force of truth was on this occasion assisted by the influence of temporal advantages. They elected Marcus for their bishop, a prelate of the race of the Gentiles, and most probably a native either of Italy or of some of the Latin provinces. At his persuasion the most considerable part of the congregation renounced the Mosaic law, in the practice of which they had persevered above a century. By this sacrifice of their habits and prejudices they purchased a free admission into the colony of Hadrian, and more firmly cemented their union with the Catholic church.

When the name and honours of the church of Jerusalem had been restored to Mount Sion, the crimes of heresy and schism were imputed to the obscure remnant of the Nazarenes which refused to accompany their Latin bishop. They still preserved their former habitation of Pella, spread themselves into the villages adjacent to Damascus, and formed an inconsiderable church in the city of Berœa, or, as it is now called, of Aleppo, in Syria. The name of Nazarenes was deemed too honourable for those Christian Jews, and they soon received, from the supposed poverty of their understanding, as well as of their condition, the contemptuous epithet of Ebionites. In a few years after the return of the church of Jerusalem, it became a matter of doubt and controversy whether a man who sincerely acknowledged Jesus as the Messiah, but who still continued to observe the law of Moses, could possibly hope for salvation. The humane temper of Justin Martyr inclined him to answer this question in the affirmative; and though he expressed himself with the most guarded diffidence, he ventured to determine in favour of such an imperfect Christian, if he were content to practise the Mosaic ceremonies without pretending to assert their general use or necessity. But when Justin was pressed to declare the sentiment of the church, he confessed that there were very many among the orthodox Christians who not only excluded their Judaising brethren from the hope of salvation, but who declined any intercourse with them in the common offices of friendship, hospitality, and social life. The more rigorous opinion prevailed, as it was natural to expect, over the milder; and an eternal bar of separation was fixed between the disciples of Moses and those of Christ. The unfortunate Ebionites, rejected from one religion as apostates, and from the other as heretics, found themselves compelled to assume a more decided character; and although some traces of that obsolete sect may be discovered as late as the fourth century, they insensibly melted away either into the church or the synagogue.

It has been remarked with more ingenuity than truth that the virgin purity of the church was never violated by schism or heresy before the reign of Trajan or Hadrian, about one hundred years after the death of Christ. We may observe with much more propriety that, during that period, the disciples of the Messiah were indulged in a freer latitude both of faith and practice than has ever been allowed in succeeding ages. As the terms of communion were insensibly narrowed, and the spiritual authority of the prevailing party was exercised with increasing severity, many of its most respectable adherents, who were called upon to renounce, were provoked to assert their private opinions, to pursue the consequences of their mistaken principles, and openly to erect the standard of rebellion against the unity of the church. The Gnostics were distinguished as the most polite, the most learned, and the most wealthy of the Christian name; and that general appellation, which expressed a superiority of knowledge, was either assumed by their own pride, or ironically bestowed by the envy of their adversaries. They were almost without exception of the race of the Gentiles, and their principal founders seem to have been natives of Syria or Egypt, where the warmth of the climate disposes both the mind and the body to indolent and contemplative devotion. The Gnostics blended with the faith of Christ many sublime but obscure tenets, which they derived from oriental philosophy, and even from the religion of Zoroaster, concerning the eternity of matter, the existence of two principles, and the mysterious hierarchy of the invisible world. As soon as they launched out into that vast abyss, they delivered themselves to the guidance of a disordered imagination; and as the paths of error are various and infinite, the Gnostics were imperceptibly divided into more than fifty particular sects, of whom the most celebrated appear to have been the Basilidians, the Valentinians, the Marcionites, and, in a still later period, the Manichæans. Each of these sects could boast of its bishops and congregations, of its doctors and martyrs; and, instead of the Four Gospels adopted by the church, the heretics produced a multitude of histories, in which the actions and discourses of Christ and of his apostles were adapted to their respective tenets. The success of the Gnostics was rapid and extensive. They covered Asia and Egypt, established themselves in Rome, and sometimes penetrated into the provinces of the West. For the most part they arose in the second century, flourished during the third, and were suppressed in the fourth or fifth, by the prevalence of more fashionable controversies, and by the superior ascendant of the reigning power. Though they constantly disturbed the peace, and frequently disgraced the name of religion, they contributed to assist rather than to retard the progress of Christianity. The Gentile converts, whose strongest objections and prejudices were directed against the law of Moses, could find admission into many Christian societies, which required not from their untutored mind any belief of an antecedent revelation. Their faith was insensibly fortified and enlarged, and the church was ultimately benefited by the conquests of its most inveterate enemies.

But whatever difference of opinion might subsist between the Orthodox, the Ebionites, and the Gnostics, concerning the divinity or the obligation of the Mosaic law, they were all equally animated by the same exclusive zeal, and by the same abhorrence for idolatry, which had distinguished the Jews from the other nations of the ancient world. The philosopher, who considered the system of polytheism as a composition of human fraud and error, could disguise a smile of contempt under the mask of devotion, without apprehending that either the mockery or the compliance would expose him to the resentment of any invisible, or, as he conceived them, imaginary powers. But the established religions of Paganism were seen by the primitive Christians in a much more odious and formidable light. It was the universal sentiment both of the church and of heretics, that the dæmons were the authors, the patrons, and the objects of idolatry. Those rebellious spirits who had been degraded from the rank of angels, and cast down into the infernal pit, were still permitted to roam upon earth, to torment the bodies and to seduce the minds of sinful men. The dæmons soon discovered and abused the natural propensity of the human heart towards devotion, and, artfully withdrawing the adoration of mankind from their Creator, they usurped the place and honours of the Supreme Deity. By the success of their malicious contrivances, they at once gratified their own vanity and revenge, and obtained the only comfort of which they were yet susceptible, the hope of involving the human species in the participation of their guilt and misery. It was confessed, or at least it was imagined, that they had distributed among themselves the most important characters of polytheism, one dæmon assuming the name and attributes of Jupiter, another of Æsculapius, a third of Venus, and a fourth perhaps of Apollo; and that, by the advantage of their long experience and aërial nature, they were enabled to execute, with sufficient skill and dignity, the parts which they had undertaken. They lurked in the temples, instituted festivals and sacrifices, invented fables, pronounced oracles, and were frequently allowed to perform miracles. The Christians, who, by the interposition of evil spirits, could so readily explain every præternatural appearance, were disposed and even desirous to admit the most extravagant fictions of the Pagan mythology. But the belief of the Christian was accompanied with horror. The most trifling mark of respect to the national worship he considered as a direct homage yielded to the dæmon, and as an act of rebellion against the majesty of God.

The dangerous temptations which on every side lurked in ambush to surprise the unguarded believer assailed him with redoubled violence on the days of solemn festivals. So artfully were they framed and disposed throughout the year, that superstition always wore the appearance of pleasure, and often of virtue. Some of the most sacred festivals in the Roman ritual were destined to salute the new calends of January with vows of public and private felicity; to indulge the pious remembrance of the dead and living; to ascertain the inviolable bounds of property; to hail, on the return of spring, the genial powers of fecundity; to perpetuate the two memorable eras of Rome, the foundation of the city, and that of the republic; and to restore, during the humane licence of the Saturnalia, the primitive equality of mankind. Some idea may be conceived of the abhorrence of the Christians for such impious ceremonies, by the scrupulous delicacy which they displayed on a much less alarming occasion. On days of general festivity it was the custom of the ancients to adorn their doors with lamps and with branches of laurel, and to crown their heads with a garland of flowers. This innocent and elegant practice might perhaps have been tolerated as a mere civil institution. But it most unluckily happened that the doors were under the protection of the household gods, that the laurel was sacred to the lover of Daphne, and that garlands of flowers, though frequently worn as a symbol either of joy or mourning, had been dedicated in their first origin to the service of superstition. The trembling Christians, who were persuaded in this instance to comply with the fashion of their country and the commands of the magistrate, laboured under the most gloomy apprehensions, from the reproaches of their own conscience, the censures of the church, and the denunciations of divine vengeance.

Such was the anxious diligence which was required to guard the chastity of the Gospel from the infectious breath of idoltry. The superstitious observances of public or private rites were carelessly practised, from education and habit, by the followers of the established religion. But as often as they occurred, they afforded the Christians an opportunity of declaring and confirming their zealous opposition. By these frequent protestations their attachment to the faith was continually fortified; and in proportion to the increase of zeal, they combated with the more ardour and success in the holy war which they had undertaken against the empire of the dæmons.

II. The writings of Cicero represent in the most lively colours the ignorance, the errors, and the uncertainty of the ancient philosophers with regard to the immortality of the soul. When they are desirous of arming their disciples against the fear of death, they inculcate, as an obvious though melancholy position, that the fatal stroke of our dissolution releases us from the calamities of life; and that those can no longer suffer who no longer exist. Yet there were a few sages of Greece and Rome who had conceived a more exalted, and, in some respects, a juster idea of human nature, though it must be confessed that, in the sublime inquiry, their reason had been often guided by their imagination, and that their imagination had been prompted by their vanity. When they viewed with complacency the extent of their own mental powers, when they exercised the various faculties of memory, of fancy, and of judgment, in the most profound speculations or the most important labours, and when they reflected on the desire of fame, which transported them into future ages, far beyond the bounds of death and of the grave, they were unwilling to confound themselves with the beasts of the field, or to suppose that a being, for whose dignity they entertained the most sincere admiration, could be limited to a spot of earth, and to a few years of duration. With this favourable prepossession they summoned to their aid the science, or rather the language, of Metaphysics. They soon discovered that, as none of the properties of matter will apply to the operations of the mind, the human soul must consequently be a substance distinct from the body, pure, simple, and spiritual, incapable of dissolution, and susceptible of a much higher degree of virtue and happiness after the release from its corporeal prison. From these specious and noble principles the philosophers who trod in the footsteps of Plato deduced a very unjustifiable conclusion, since they asserted, not only the future immortality, but the past eternity of the human soul, which they were too apt to consider as a portion of the infinite and self-existing spirit which pervades and sustains the universe. A doctrine thus removed beyond the senses and the experience of mankind might serve to amuse the leisure of a philosophic mind; or, in the silence of solitude, it might sometimes impart a ray of comfort to desponding virtue; but the faint impression which had been received in the schools was soon obliterated by the commerce and business of active life. We are sufficiently acquainted with the eminent persons who flourished in the age of Cicero and of the first Cæsars, with their actions, their characters, and their motives, to be assured that their conduct in this life was never regulated by any serious conviction of the rewards or punishments of a future state. At the bar and in the senate of Rome the ablest orators were not apprehensive of giving offence to their hearers by exposing that doctrine as an idle and extravagant opinion, which was rejected with contempt by every man of a liberal education and understanding.

Since therefore the most sublime efforts of philosophy can extend no farther than feebly to point out the desire, the hope, or, at most, the probability of a future state, there is nothing, except a divine revelation that can ascertain the existence and describe the condition of the invisible country which is destined to receive the souls of men after their separation from the body. But we may perceive several defects inherent to the popular religions of Greece and Rome which rendered them very unequal to so arduous a task.

1. The general system of their mythology was unsupported by any solid proofs; and the wisest among the Pagans had already disclaimed its usurped authority. 2. The description of the infernal regions had been abandoned to the fancy of painters and of poets, who peopled them with so many phantoms and monsters who dispensed their rewards and punishments with so little equity, that a solemn truth, the most congenial to the human heart, was oppressed and disgraced by the absurd mixture of the wildest fictions. 3. The doctrine of a future state was scarcely considered among the devout poly-theists of Greece and Rome as a fundamental article of faith. The providence of the gods, as it related to public communities rather than to private individuals, was principally displayed on the visible theatre of the present world. The petitions which were offered on the altars of Jupiter or Apollo expressed the anxiety of their worshippers for temporal happiness, and their ignorance or indif-ference concerning a future life. The important truth of the immortality of the soul was inculcated with more diligence as well as success in India, in Assyria, in Egypt, and in Gaul; and since we cannot attribute such a difference to the superior knowledge of the barbarians, we must ascribe it to the influence of an established priesthood, which employed the motives of virtue as the instrument of ambition.

We might naturally expect that a principle so essential to religion would have been revealed in the clearest terms to the chosen people of Palestine, and that it might safely have been intrusted to the hereditary priesthood of Aaron. It is incumbent on us to adore the mysterious dispensations of Providence, when we discover that the doctrine of the immortality of the soul is omitted in the law of Moses; it is darkly insinuated by the prophets; and during the long period which elapsed between the Egyptian and the Babylonian servitudes, the hopes as well as fears of the Jews appear to have been confined within the narrow compass of the present life. After Cyrus had permitted the exiled nation to return into the promised land, and after Ezra had restored the ancient records of their religion, two celebrated sects, the Sadducees and the Pharisees, insensibly arose at Jerusalem. The former, selected from the more opulent and distinguished ranks of society, were strictly attached to the literal sense of the Mosaic law, and they piously rejected the immortality of the soul as an opinion that received no countenance from the divine book, which they revered as the only rule of their faith. To the authority of Scripture the Pharisees added that of tradition, and they accepted, under the name of traditions, several speculative tenets from the philosophy or religion of the eastern nations. The doctrines of fate or predestination, of angels and spirits, and of a future state of rewards and punishments, were in the number of these new articles of belief; and as the Pharisees, by the austerity of their manners, had drawn into their party the body of the Jewish people, the immortality of the soul became the prevailing sentiment of the synagogue under the reign of the Asmonæan princes and pontiffs. The temper of the Jews was incapable of contenting itself with such a cold and languid assent as might satisfy the mind of a Polytheist; and as soon as they admitted the idea of a future state, they embraced it with the zeal which has always formed the characteristic of the nation. Their zeal, however, added nothing to its evidence, or even probability; and it was still necessary that the doctrine of life and immortality, which had been dictated by nature, approved by reason, and received by superstition, should obtain the sanction of divine truth from the authority and example of Christ.

When the promise of eternal happiness was proposed to mankind on condition of adopting the faith, and of observing the precepts, of the Gospel, it is no wonder that so advantageous an offer should have been accepted by great numbers of every religion, of every rank, and of every province in the Roman empire. The ancient Christians were animated by a contempt for their present existence, and by a just confidence of immortality, of which the doubtful and imperfect faith of modern ages cannot give us any adequate notion. In the primitive church the influence of truth was very powerfully strengthened by an opinion which, however it may deserve respect for its usefulness and antiquity, has not been found agreeable to experience. It was universally believed that the end of the world, and the kingdom of heaven, were at hand. The near approach of this wonderful event had been predicted by the apostles; the tradition of it was preserved by their earliest disciples, and those who understood in their literal sense the discourses of Christ himself were obliged to expect the second and glorious coming of the Son of Man in the clouds, before that generation was totally extinguished which had beheld his humble condition upon earth, and which might still be witness of the calamities of the Jews under Vespasian or Hadrian. The revolution of seventeen centuries has instructed us not to press too closely the mysterious language of prophecy and revelation; but as long as, for wise purposes, this error was permitted to subsist in the church, it was productive of the most salutary effects on the faith and practice of Christians, who lived in the awful expectation of that moment when the globe itself, and all the various race of mankind, should tremble at the appearance of their divine Judge.

The ancient and popular doctrine of the Millennium was intimately connected with the second coming of Christ. As the works of the creation had been finished in six days, their duration in their present state, according to a tradition which was attributed to the prophet Elijah, was fixed to six thousand years. By the same analogy it was inferred that this long period of labour and contention, which was now almost elapsed, would be succeeded by a joyful Sabbath of a thousand years; and that Christ, with the triumphant band of the saints and the elect who had escaped death, or who had been miraculously revived, would reign upon earth till the time appointed for the last and general resurrection. So pleasing was this hope to the mind of believers, that the *new Jerusalem*, the seat of this blissful kingdom, was quickly adorned with all the gayest colours of the imagination. A felicity consisting only of pure and spiritual pleasure would have appeared too refined for its inhabitants, who were still supposed to possess their human nature and senses. A garden of Eden, with the amusements of the pastoral life, was no longer suited to the advanced state of society which prevailed under the Roman empire. A city was therefore erected of gold and precious stones, and a supernatural plenty of corn and wine was bestowed on the adjacent territory; in the free enjoyment of whose spontaneous productions the happy and benevolent people was never to be restrained by any jealous laws of exclusive property. The assurance of such a Millennium was carefully inculcated by a succession of fathers from Justin Martyr and Irenæus, who conversed with the immediate disciples of the apostles, down to Lactantius, who was preceptor to the son of Constantine. Though it might not be universally received, it appears to have been the reigning sentiment of the orthodox believers; and it seems so well adapted to the desires and apprehensions of mankind, that it must have contributed in a very considerable degree to the progress of the Christian faith. But when the edifice of the church was almost completed, the temporary support was laid aside. The doctrine of Christ's reign upon earth was at first treated as a profound allegory, was considered by degrees as a doubtful and useless opinion, and was at length rejected as the absurd invention of heresy and fanaticism. A mysterious prophecy, which still forms a part of the sacred canon, but which was thought to favour the exploded sentiment, has very narrowly escaped the proscription of the church.

Whilst the happiness and glory of a temporal reign were promised to the disciples of Christ, the most dreadful calamities were denounced against an unbelieving world. The edification of the new Jerusalem was to advance by equal steps with the destruction of the mystic Babylon; and as long as the emperors who reigned before Constantine persisted in the profession of idolatry, the epithet of Babylon was applied to the city and to the empire of Rome. A regular series was prepared of all the moral and physical evils which can afflict a flourishing nation; intestine discord, and the invasion of the fiercest barbarians from the unknown regions of the North; pestilence and famine, comets and eclipses, earthquakes and inundations. All these were only so many preparatory and alarming signs of the great catastrophe of Rome, when the country of the Scipios and Cæsars should be consumed by a flame from Heaven, and the city of the seven hills, with her palaces, her temples, and her triumphal arches, should be buried in a vast lake of fire and brimstone. It might, however, afford some consolation to Roman vanity, that the period of their empire would be that of the world itself; which, as it had once perished by the element of water, was destined to experience a second and a speedy destruction from the element of fire. In the opinion of a general conflagration the faith of the Christian very happily coincided with the tradition of the East, the philosophy of the Stoics, and the analogy of Nature; and even the country which, from religious motives, had been chosen for the origin and principal scene of the conflagration, was the best adapted for that purpose by natural and physical causes—by its deep caverns, beds of sulphur, and numerous volcanoes, of which those of Ætna, of Vesuvius, and of Lipari exhibit a very imperfect representation. The calmest and most intrepid sceptic could not refuse to acknowledge that the destruction of the present system of the world by fire was in itself extremely probable. The Christian, who founded his belief much less on the fallacious arguments of reason than on the authority of tradition and the interpretation of Scripture, expected it with terror and confidence as a certain and approaching event; and as his mind was perpetually filled with the solemn idea, he considered every disaster that happened to the empire as an infallible symptom of an expiring world.

The condemnation of the wisest and most virtuous of the Pagans, on account of their ignorance or disbelief of the divine truth, seems to offend the reason and the humanity of the present age. But the primitive church, whose faith was of a much firmer consistence, delivered over, without hesitation, to eternal torture the far greater part of the human species. A charitable hope might perhaps be indulged in favour of Socrates, or some other sages of antiquity, who had consulted the light of reason before that of the Gospel had arisen. But it was unanimously affirmed that those who, since the birth or the death of Christ, had obstinately persisted in the worship of the dæmons, neither deserved nor could expect a pardon from the irritated justice of the Deity. These rigid sentiments, which had been unknown to the ancient world, appear to have infused a spirit of bitterness into a system of love and harmony. The ties of blood and friendship were frequently torn asunder by the difference of religious faith; and the Christians, who, in this world, found themselves oppressed by the power of the Pagans, were sometimes seduced by resentment and spiritual pride to delight in the prospect of their future triumph. "You are fond of spectacles," exclaims the stern Tertullian, "except the greatest of all spectacles, the last and eternal judgment of the universe. How shall I admire, how laugh, how rejoice, how exult, when I behold so many proud monarchs, and fancied gods, groaning in the lowest abyss of darkness; so many magistrates, who persecuted the name of the Lord, liquefying in fiercer fires than they ever kindled against the Christians; so many sage philosophers blushing in red-hot flames with their deluded scholars; so many celebrated poets trembling before the tribunal, not of Minos, but of Christ; so many tragedians, more tuneful in the expression of their own sufferings; so many dancers—" But the humanity of the reader will permit me to draw a veil over the rest of this infernal description, which the zealous African pursues in a long variety of affected and unfeeling witticisms.

Doubtless there were many among the primitive Christians of a temper more suitable to the meekness and charity of their profession. There were many who felt a sincere compassion for the danger of their friends and countrymen, and who exerted the most benevolent zeal to save them from the impending destruction. The careless Polytheist, assailed by new and unexpected terrors, against which neither his priests nor his philosophers could afford him any certain protection, was very frequently terrified and subdued by the menace of eternal tortures. His fears might assist the progress of his faith and reason; and if he could once persuade himself to suspect that the Christian religion might possibly be true, it became an easy task to convince him that it was the safest and most prudent party that he could possibly embrace.

III. The supernatural gifts, which even in this life were ascribed to the Christians above the rest of mankind, must have conduced to their own comfort, and very frequently to the conviction of infidels. Besides the occasional prodigies, which might sometimes be effected by the immediate interposition of the Deity when he suspended the laws of Nature for the service of religion, the Christian church, from the time of the apostles and their first disciples, has claimed an uninterrupted succession of miraculous powers, the gift of tongues, of vision, and of prophecy, the power of expelling dæmons, of healing the sick, and of raising the dead. The knowledge of foreign languages was frequently communicated to the contemporaries of Irenæus, though Irenæus himself was left to struggle with the difficulties of a barbarous dialect whilst he preached the Gospel to the natives of Gaul. The divine inspiration, whether it was conveyed in the form of a waking or of a sleeping vision, is described as a favour very liberally bestowed on all ranks of the faithful, on women as on elders, on boys as well as upon bishops. When their devout minds were sufficiently prepared by a course of prayer, of fasting, and of vigils, to receive the extraordinary impulse, they were transported out of their senses, and delivered in ecstasy that was inspired, being mere organs of the Holy Spirit, just as a pipe or flute is of him who blows into it. We may add that the design of these visions was, for the most part, either to disclose the future history, or to guide the present administration, of the church. The expulsion of the dæmons from the bodies of those unhappy persons whom they had been permitted to torment was considered as a signal though ordinary triumph of religion, and is repeatedly alleged by the ancient apologists as the most convincing evidence of the truth of Christianity. The awful ceremony was usually performed in a public manner, and in the presence of a great number of spectators; the patient was relieved by the power or skill of the exorcist, and the vanquished dæmon was heard to confess that he was one of the fabled gods of antiquity, who had impiously usurped the adoration of mankind. But the miraculous cure of diseases of the most inveterate or even preternatural kind can no longer occasion any surprise, when we recollect that in the days of

Irenæus, about the end of the second century, the resurrection of the dead was very far from being esteemed an uncommon event; that the miracle was frequently performed on necessary occasions, by great fasting and the joint supplication of the church of the place, and that the persons thus restored to their prayers had lived afterwards among them many years. At such a period, when faith could boast of so many wonderful victories over death, it seems difficult to account for the scepticism of those philosophers who still rejected and derided the doctrine of the resurrection. A noble Grecian had rested on this important ground the whole controversy, and promised Theophilus, bishop of Antioch, that, if he could be gratified with the sight of a single person who had been actually raised from the dead, he would immediately embrace the Christian religion. It is somewhat remarkable that the prelate of the first eastern church, however anxious for the conversion of his friend, thought proper to decline this fair and reasonable challenge.

The miracles of the primitive church, after obtaining the sanction of ages, have been lately attacked in a very free and ingenious inquiry; which, though it has met with the most favourable reception from the public, appears to have excited a general scandal among the divines of our own as well as of the other Protestant churches of Europe. Our different sentiments on this subject will be much less influenced by any particular arguments than by our habits of study and reflection, and, above all, by the degree of the evidence which we have accustomed ourselves to require for the proof of a miraculous event. The duty of an historian does not call upon him to interpose his private judgment in this nice and important controversy; but he ought not to dissemble the difficulty of adopting such a theory as may reconcile the interest of religion with that of reason, of making a proper application of that theory, and of defining with precision the limits of that happy period, exempt from error and from deceit, to which we might be disposed to extend the gift of supernatural powers. From the first of the fathers to the last of the popes, a succession of bishops, of saints, of martyrs, and of miracles, is continued without interruption; and the progress of superstition was so gradual and almost imperceptible that we know not in what particular link we should break the chain of tradition. Every age bears testimony to the wonderful events by which it was distinguished, and its testimony appears no less weighty and respectable than that of the preceding generation, till we are insensibly led on to accuse our own inconsistency if, in the eighth or in the twelfth century, we deny to the venerable Bede, or to the holy Bernard, the same degree of confidence which, in the second century, we had so liberally granted to Justin or to Irenæus. If the truth of any of those miracles is appreciated by their apparent use and propriety, every age had unbelievers to convince, heretics to confute, and idolatrous nations to convert; and sufficient motives might always be produced to justify the interposition of Heaven. And yet, since every friend to revelation is persuaded of the reality, and every reasonable man is convinced of the cessation, of miraculous powers, it is evident that there must have been *some period* in which they were either suddenly or gradually withdrawn from the Christian church. Whatever era is chosen for that purpose, the death of the apostles, the conversion of the Roman empire, or the extinction of the Arian heresy, the insensibility of the Christians who lived at that time will equally afford a just matter of surprise. They still supported their pretensions after they had lost their power. Credulity performed the office of faith; fanaticism was permitted to assume the language of inspiration, and the effects of accident or contrivance were ascribed to supernatural causes. The recent experience of genuine miracles should have instructed the Christian world in the ways of Providence, and habituated their eye (if we may use a very inadequate expression) to the style of the Divine artist. Should the most skilful painter of modern Italy presume to decorate his feeble imitations with the name of Raphael or of Correggio, the insolent fraud would be soon discovered and indignantly rejected.

Whatever opinion may be entertained of the miracles of the primitive church since the time of the apostles, this unresisting softness of temper, so conspicuous among the believers of the second and third centuries, proved of some accidental benefit to the cause of truth and religion. In modern times, a latent and even involuntary scepticism adheres to the most pious dispositions. Their admission of supernatural truths is much less an active consent than a cold and passive acquiescence. Accustomed long since to observe and to respect the invariable order of Nature, our reason, or at least our imagination, is not sufficiently prepared to sustain the visible action of the Deity. But in the first ages of Christianity the situation of mankind was extremely different. The most curious, or the most credulous, among the Pagans were often persuaded to enter into a society which asserted an actual claim of miraculous powers. The primitive Christians perpetually trod on mystic ground, and their minds were exercised by the habits of believing the most extraordinary events. They felt, or they fancied, that on every side they were incessantly assaulted by dæmons, comforted by visions, instructed by prophecy, and surprisingly delivered from danger, sickness, and from death itself, by the supplications of the church. The real or imaginary prodigies, of which they so frequently conceived themselves to be the objects, the instruments, or the spectators, very happily disposed them to adopt with the same ease, but with far greater justice, the authentic wonders of the evangelic history; and thus miracles that exceeded not the measure of their own experience inspired them with the most lively assurance of mysteries which were acknowledged to surpass the limits of their understanding. It is this deep impression of supernatural truths which has been so much celebrated under the name of faith; a state of mind described as the surest pledge of the Divine favour and of future felicity, and recommended as the first or perhaps the only merit of a Christian. According to the more rigid doctors, the moral virtues, which may be equally practised by infidels, are destitute of any value or efficacy in the work of our justification.

IV. But the primitive Christian demonstrated his faith by his virtues; and it was very justly supposed that the Divine persuasion, which enlightened or subdued the understanding, must at the same time purify the heart and direct the actions of the believer. The first apologists of Christianity who justify the innocence of their brethren, and the writers of a later period who celebrate the sanctity of their ancestors, display, in the most lively colours, the reformation of manners which was introduced into the world by the preaching of the Gospel. As it is my intention to remark only such human causes as were permitted to second the influence of revelation, I shall slightly mention two motives which might naturally render the lives of the primitive Christians much purer and more austere than those of their Pagan contemporaries or their degenerate successors — repentance for their past sins, and the laudable desire of supporting the reputation of the society in which they were engaged.

When the new converts had been enrolled in the number of the faithful, and were admitted to the sacraments of the church, they found themselves restrained from relapsing into their past disorders by another consideration of a less spiritual but of a very innocent and respectable nature. Any particular society that has departed from the great body of the nation, or the religion to which it belonged, immediately becomes the object of universal as well as invidious observation. In proportion to the smallness of its numbers, the character of the society may be affected by the virtue and vices of the persons who compose it; and every member is engaged to watch with the most vigilant attention over his own behaviour, and over that of his brethren, since, as he must expect to incur a part of the common disgrace, he may hope to enjoy a share of the common reputation. When the Christians of Bithynia were brought before the tribunal of the younger Pliny, they assured the proconsul that, far from being engaged in any unlawful conspiracy, they were bound by a solemn obligation to abstain from the commission of those crimes which disturb the private or public peace of society, from theft, robbery, adultery, perjury, and fraud. Near a century afterwards, Tertullian with an honest pride could boast that very few Christians had suffered by the hand of the executioner, except on account of their religion. Their serious and sequestered life, averse to the gay luxury of the age, inured them to chastity, temperance, economy, and all the sober and domestic virtues. As the greater number were of some trade or profession, it was incumbent on them, by the strictest integrity and the fairest dealing, to remove the suspicions which the profane are too apt to conceive against the appearances of sanctity. The contempt of the world exercised them in the habits of humility, meekness, and patience. The more they were persecuted, the more closely they adhered to each other. Their mutual charity and unsuspecting confidence has been remarked by infidels, and was too often abused by perfidious friends.

It is a very honourable circumstance for the morals of the primitive Christians, that even their faults, or rather errors, were derived from an excess of virtue. The bishops and doctors of the church, whose evidence attests, and whose authority might influence, the professions, the principles, and even the practice of their contemporaries, had studied the Scriptures with less skill than devotion; and they often received in the most literal sense those rigid precepts of Christ and the apostles to which the prudence of succeeding commentators has applied a looser and more figurative mode of interpretation. Ambitious to exalt the perfection of the Gospel above the wisdom of philosophy, the zealous fathers have carried the duties of self-mortification, of purity, and of patience, to a height which it is scarcely possible to attain, and much less to preserve, in our present state of weakness and corruption. A doctrine so extraordinary and so sublime must inevitably command the veneration of the people; but it was ill calculated to obtain the suffrage of those worldly philosophers who, in the conduct of this transitory life, consult only the feelings of nature and the interest of society.

There are two very natural propensities which we may distinguish in the most virtuous and liberal dispositions, the love of pleasure and the love of action. If the former is refined by art and learning, improved by the charms of social intercourse, and corrected by a just regard to economy, to health, and to reputation, it is productive of the greatest part of the happiness of private life. The love of action is a principle of a much stronger and more doubtful nature. It often leads to anger, to ambition, and to revenge; but when it is guided by the sense of propriety and benevolence, it becomes the parent of every virtue, and, if those virtues are accompanied with equal abilities, a family, a state, or an empire may be indebted for their safety and prosperity to the undaunted courage of a single man. To the love of pleasure we may therefore ascribe most of the agreeable, to the love of action we may attribute most of the useful and respectable, qualifications. The character in which both the one and the other should be united and harmonised would seem to constitute the most perfect idea of human nature. The insensible and inactive disposition, which should be supposed alike destitute of both, would be rejected, by the common consent of mankind, as utterly incapable of procuring any happiness to the individual, or any public benefit to the world. But it was not in *this* world that the primitive Christians were desirous of making themselves either agreeable or useful.

The acquisition of knowledge, the exercise of our reason or fancy, and the cheerful flow of unguarded conversation, may employ the leisure of a liberal mind. Such amusements, however, were rejected with abhorrence, or admitted with the utmost caution, by the severity of the fathers, who despised all knowledge that was not useful to salvation, and who considered all levity of discourse as a criminal abuse of the gift of speech. In our present state of existence the body is so inseparably connected with the soul, that it seems to be our interest to taste, with innocence and moderation, the enjoyments of which that faithful companion is susceptible. Very different was the reasoning of our devout predecessors; vainly aspiring to imitate the perfection of angels, they disdained, or they affected to disdain, every earthly and corporeal delight. Some of our senses indeed are necessary for our preservation, others for our subsistence, and others again for our information; and thus far it was impossible to reject the use of them. The first sensation of pleasure was marked as the first moment of their abuse. The unfeeling candidate for heaven was instructed, not only to resist the grosser allurements of the taste or smell, but even to shut his ears against the profane harmony of sounds, and to view with indifference the most finished productions of human art. Gay apparel, magnificent houses, and elegant furniture were supposed to unite the double guilt of pride and of sensuality: a simple and mortified appearance was more suitable to the Christian who was certain of his sins and doubtful of his salvation. In their censures of luxury the fathers are extremely minute and circumstantial; and among the various articles which excite their pious indignation, we may enumerate false hair, garments of any colour except white, instruments of music, vases of gold or silver, downy pillows (as Jacob reposed his head on a stone), white bread, foreign wines, public salutations, the use of warm baths, and the practice of shaving the beard, which, according to the expression of Tertullian, is a lie against our own faces, and an impious attempt to improve the works of the Creator. When Christianity was introduced among the rich and the polite, the observation of these singular laws was left, as it would be at present, to the few who were ambitious of superior sanctity. But it is always easy, as well as agreeable, for the inferior ranks of mankind to claim a merit from the contempt of that pomp and pleasure which fortune has placed beyond their reach. The virtue of the primitive Christians, like that of the first Romans, was very frequently guarded by poverty and ignorance.

The chaste severity of the fathers in whatever related to the commerce of the two sexes flowed from the same principle—their abhorrence of every enjoyment which might gratify the sensual and degrade the spiritual nature of man. It was their favourite opinion, that if Adam had preserved his obedience to the Creator, he would have lived for ever in a state of virgin purity, and that some harmless mode of vegetation might have peopled paradise with a race of innocent and immortal beings. The use of marriage was permitted only to his fallen posterity, as a necessary expedient to continue the human species, and as a restraint, however imperfect, on the natural licentiousness of desire. The hesitation of the orthodox casuists on this interesting subject betrays the perplexity of men unwilling to approve an institution which they were compelled to tolerate. The enumeration of the very whimsical laws which they most circumstantially imposed on the marriage-bed would force a smile from the young and a blush from the fair. It was their unanimous sentiment that a first marriage was adequate to all the purposes of nature and of society. The sensual connection was refined into a resemblance of the mystic union of Christ with his church, and was pronounced to be indissoluble either by divorce or by death. The practice of second nuptials was branded with the name of a legal adultery; and the persons who were guilty of so scandalous an offence against Christian purity were soon excluded from the honours, and even from the arms, of the church. Since desire was imputed as a crime, and marriage was tolerated as a defect, it was consistent with the same principles to consider a state of celibacy as the nearest approach to the Divine perfection. It was with the utmost difficulty that ancient Rome could support the institution of six vestals; but the primitive church was filled with a great number of persons of either sex who had devoted themselves to the profession of perpetual chastity. A few of these, among whom we may reckon the learned Origen, judged it the most prudent to disarm the tempter. Some were insensible and some were invincible against the assaults of the flesh. Disdaining an ignominious flight, the virgins of the warm climate of Africa encountered the enemy in the closest engagement; they permitted priests and deacons to share their bed, and gloried amidst the flames in their unsullied purity. But insulted Nature sometimes vindicated her rights, and this new species of martyrdom served only to introduce a new scandal into the church. Among the Christian ascetics, however (a name which they soon acquired from their painful exercise), many, as they were less presumptuous, were probably more successful. The loss of sensual pleasure was supplied and compensated by spiritual pride. Even the multitude of Pagans were inclined to estimate the merit of the sacrifice by its apparent difficulty; and it was in the praise of these chaste spouses of Christ that the fathers have poured forth the troubled stream of their eloquence. Such are the early traces of monastic principles and institutions, which, in a subsequent age, have counterbalanced all the temporal advantages of Christianity.

The Christians were not less adverse to the business than to the pleasures of this world. The defence of our persons and property they knew not how to reconcile with the patient doctrine which enjoined an unlimited forgiveness of past injuries, and commanded them to invite the repetition of fresh insults. Their simplicity was offended by the use of oaths, by the pomp of magistracy, and by the active contention of public life; nor could their humane ignorance be convinced that it was lawful on any occasion to shed the blood of our fellow-creatures, either by the sword of justice or by that of war, even though their criminal or hostile attempts should threaten the peace and safety of the whole community. It was acknowledged that, under a less perfect law, the powers of the Jewish constitution had been exercised, with the approbation of Heaven, by inspired prophets and by anointed kings. The Christians felt and confessed that such institutions might be necessary for the present system of the world, and they cheerfully submitted to the authority of their Pagan governors. But while they inculcated the maxims of passive obedience, they refused to take any active part in the civil administration or the military defence of the empire. Some indulgence might perhaps be allowed to those persons who, before their conversion, were already engaged in such violent and sanguinary occupations; but it was impossible that the Christians, without renouncing a more sacred duty, could assume the character of soldiers, of magistrates, or of princes. This indolent, or even criminal disregard to the public welfare, exposed them to the contempt and reproaches of the Pagans, who very frequently asked, what must be the fate of the empire, attacked on every side by the barbarians, if all mankind should adopt the pusillanimous sentiments of the new sect? To this insulting question the Christian apologists returned obscure and ambiguous answers, as they were unwilling to reveal the secret cause of their security; the expectation that, before the conversion of mankind was accomplished, war, government, the Roman empire, and the world itself, would be no more. It may be observed that, in this instance likewise, the situation of the first Christians coincided very happily with their religious scruples, and that their aversion to an active life contributed rather to excuse them from the service than to exclude them from the honours of the state and army.

V. But the human character, however it may be exalted or depressed by a temporary enthusiasm, will return by degrees to its proper and natural level, and will resume those passions that seem the most adapted to its present condition. The primitive Christians were dead to the business and pleasures of the world; but their love of action, which could never be entirely extinguished, soon revived, and found a new occupation in the government of the church. A separate society, which attacked the established religion of the empire, was obliged to adopt some form of internal policy, and to appoint a sufficient number of ministers, intrusted not only with the spiritual functions, but even with the temporal direction of the Christian commonwealth. The safety of the society, its honour, its aggrandisement, were productive, even in the most pious minds, of a spirit of patriotism, such as the first of the Romans had felt for the republic, and sometimes of a similar indifference in the use of whatever means might probably conduce to so desirable an end. The ambition of raising themselves or their friends to the honours and offices of the church was disguised by the laudable intention of devoting to the public benefit the power and consideration which, for that purpose only, it became their duty to solicit. In the exercise of their functions they were frequently called upon to detect the errors of heresy or the arts of faction, to oppose the designs of perfidious brethren, to stigmatise their characters with deserved infamy, and to expel them from the bosom of a society whose peace and happiness they had attempted to disturb. The ecclesiastical governors of the Christians were taught to unite the wisdom of the serpent with the innocence of the dove; but as the former was refined, so the latter was insensibly corrupted, by the habits of government. In the church as well as in the world, the persons who were placed in any public station rendered themselves considerable by their eloquence and firmness, by their knowledge of mankind, and by their dexterity in business; and while they concealed from others, and perhaps from themselves, the secret motives of their conduct, they too frequently relapsed into all the turbulent passions of active life, which were tinctured with an additional degree of bitterness and obstinacy from the infusion of spiritual zeal.

The government of the church has often been the subject, as well as the prize, of religious contention. The hostile disputants of Rome, of Paris, of Oxford, and of Geneva, have alike struggled to reduce the primitive and apostolic model to the respective standards of their own policy. The few who have pursued this inquiry with more candour and impartiality are of opinion that the apostles declined the office of legislation, and rather chose to endure some partial scandals and divisions, than to exclude the Christians of a future age from the liberty of varying their forms of ecclesiastical government according to the changes of times and circumstances. The scheme of policy which, under their approbation, was adopted for the use of the first century, may be discovered from the practice of Jerusalem, of Ephesus, or of Corinth. The societies which were instituted in the cities of the Roman empire were united only by the ties of faith and charity. Independence and equality formed the basis of their internal constitution. The want of discipline and human learning was supplied by the occasional assistance of the *prophets*, who were called to that function without distinction of age, of sex, or of natural abilities, and who, as often as they felt the divine impulse, poured forth the effusions of the Spirit in the assembly of the faithful. But these extraordinary gifts were frequently abused or misapplied by the prophetic teachers. They displayed them at an improper season, presumptuously disturbed the service of the assembly, and by their pride or mistaken zeal they introduced, particularly into the apostolic church of Corinth, a long and melancholy train of disorders. As the institution of prophets became useless, and even pernicious, their powers were withdrawn, and their office abolished.

The public functions of religion were solely intrusted to the established ministers of the church, the *bishops* and the *presbyters*; two appellations which, in their first origin, appear to have distinguished the same office and the same order of persons. The name of Presbyter was expressive of their age, or rather of their gravity and wisdom. The title of Bishop denoted their inspection over the faith and manners of the Christians who were committed to their pastoral care. In proportion to the respective numbers of the faithful, a larger or smaller number of these *episcopal presbyters* guided each infant congregation with equal authority and with united counsels.

But the most perfect equality of freedom requires the directing hand of a superior magistrate: and the order of public deliberations soon introduces the office of a president, invested at least with the authority of collecting the sentiments, and of executing the resolutions, of the assembly. A regard for the public tranquillity, which would so frequently have been interrupted by annual or by occasional elections, induced the primitive Christians to constitute an honourable and perpetual magistracy, and to choose one of the wisest and most holy among their presbyters to execute, during his life, the duties of their ecclesiastical governor. It was under these circumstances that the lofty title of Bishop began to raise itself above the humble appellation of Presbyter; and while the latter remained the most natural distinction for the members of every Christian senate, the former was appropriated to the dignity of its new president. The advantages of this episcopal form of government, which appears to have been introduced before the end of the first century, were so obvious, and so important for the future greatness, as well as the present peace, of Christianity, that it was adopted without delay by all the societies which were already scattered over the empire, had acquired in a very early period the sanction of antiquity, and is still revered by the most powerful churches, both of the East and of the West, as a primitive and even as a divine establishment. It is needless to observe that the pious and humble presbyters who were first dignified with the episcopal title could not possess, and would probably have rejected, the power and pomp which now encircles the tiara of the Roman pontiff, or the mitre of a German prelate. But we may define in a few words the narrow limits of their original jurisdiction, which was chiefly of a spiritual, though in some instances of a temporal nature. It consisted in the administration of the sacraments and discipline of the church, the superintendency of religious ceremonies, which imperceptibly increased in number and variety, the consecration of ecclesiastical ministers, to whom the bishop assigned their respective functions, the management of the public fund, and the determination of all such differences as the faithful were unwilling to expose before the tribunal of an idolatrous judge. These powers, during a short period, were exercised according to the advice of the presbyteral college, and with the consent and approbation of the assembly of Christians. The primitive bishops were considered only as the first of their equals, and the honourable servants of a free people. Whenever the episcopal chair became vacant by death, a new president was chosen among the presbyters by the suffrage of the whole congregation, every member of which supposed himself invested with a sacred and sacerdotal character.

Such was the mild and equal constitution by which the Christians were governed more than an hundred years after the death of the apostles. Every society formed within itself a separate and independent republic; and although the most distant of these little states maintained a mutual as well as friendly intercourse of letters and deputations, the Christian world was not yet connected by any supreme authority or legislative assembly. As the numbers of the faithful were gradually multiplied, they discovered the advantages that might result from a closer union of their interest and designs. Towards the end of the second century, the churches of Greece and Asia adopted the useful institutions of provincial synods, and they may justly be supposed to have borrowed the model of a representative council from the celebrated examples of their own country, the Amphictyons, the Achæan league, or the assemblies of the Ionian cities. It was soon established as a custom and as a law, that the bishops of the independent churches should meet in the capital of the province at the stated periods of spring and autumn. Their deliberations were assisted by the advice of a few distinguished presbyters, and moderated by the presence of a listening multitude. Their decrees, which were styled Canons, regulated every important controversy of faith and discipline; and it was natural to believe that a liberal effusion of the Holy Spirit would be poured on the united assembly of the delegates of the Christian people. The institution of synods was so well suited to private ambition and to public interest, that in the space of a few years it was received throughout the whole empire. A regular correspondence was established between the provincial councils, which mutually communicated and approved their respective proceedings; and the catholic church soon assumed the form, and acquired the strength, of a great fœderative republic.

As the legislative authority of the particular churches was insensibly superseded by the use of councils, the bishops obtained by their alliance a much larger share of executive and arbitrary power; and as soon as they were connected by a sense of their common interest, they were enabled to attack, with united vigour, the original rights of their clergy and people. The prelates of the third century imperceptibly changed the language of exhortation into that of command, scattered the seeds of future usurpations, and supplied, by scripture allegories and declamatory rhetoric, their deficiency of force and of reason. They exalted the unity and power of the church, as it was represented in the EPISCOPAL OFFICE, of which every bishop enjoyed an equal and undivided portion. Princes and magistrates, it was often repeated, might boast an earthly claim to a transitory dominion: it was the episcopal authority alone which was derived from the Deity, and extended itself over this and over another world. The bishops were the vicegerents of Christ, the successors of the apostles, and the mystic substitutes of the high priest of the Mosaic law. Their exclusive privilege of conferring the sacerdotal character invaded the freedom both of clerical and of popular elections: and if, in the administration of the church, they still consulted the judgment of the presbyters or the inclination of the people, they most carefully inculcated the merit of such a voluntary condescension. The bishops acknowledged the supreme authority which resided in the assembly of their brethren; but in the government of his peculiar diocese each of them exacted from his *flock* the same implicit obedience as if that favourite metaphor had been literally just, and as if the shepherd had been of a more exalted nature than that of his sheep. This obedience, however, was not imposed without some efforts on one side, and some resistance on the other. The democratical part of the constitution was, in many places, very warmly supported by the zealous or interested opposition of the inferior clergy. But their patriotism received the ignominious epithets of faction and schism, and the episcopal cause was indebted for its rapid progress to the labours of many active prelates, who, like Cyprian of Carthage, could reconcile the arts of the most ambitious statesman with the Christian virtues which seem adapted to the character of a saint and martyr.

The same causes which at first had destroyed the equality of the presbyters introduced among the bishops a pre-eminence of rank, and from thence a superiority of jurisdiction. As often as in the spring and autumn they met in provincial synod, the difference of personal merit and reputation was very sensibly felt among the members of the assembly, and the multitude was governed by the wisdom and eloquence of the few. But the order of public proceedings required a more regular and less invidious distinction; the office of perpetual presidents in the councils of each province was conferred on the bishops of the principal city; and these aspiring prelates, who soon acquired the lofty titles of Metropolitans and Primates, secretly prepared themselves to usurp over their episcopal brethren the same authority which the bishops had so lately assumed above the college of presbyters. Nor was it long before an emulation of pre-eminence and power prevailed among the Metropolitans themselves, each of them affecting to display, in the most pompous terms, the temporal honours and advantages of the city over which he presided; the numbers and opulence of the Christians who were subject to their pastoral care; the saints and martyrs who had arisen among them; and the purity with which they preserved the tradition of the faith as it had been transmitted through a series of orthodox bishops from the apostle or the apostolic disciple to whom the foundation of their church was ascribed. From every cause, either of a civil or of an ecclesiastical nature, it was easy to foresee that Rome must enjoy the respect, and would soon claim the obedience, of the provinces. The society of the faithful bore a just proportion to the capital of the empire; and the

Roman church was the greatest, the most numerous, and, in regard to the West, the most ancient of all the Christian establishments, many of which had received their religion from the pious labours of her missionaries. Instead of *one* apostolic founder, the utmost boast of Antioch, of Ephesus, or of Corinth, the banks of the Tiber were supposed to have been honoured with the preaching and martyrdom of the *two* most eminent among the apostles; and the bishop of Rome very prudently claimed the inheritance of what-soever prerogatives were attributed either to the person or to the office of St. Peter. The bishops of Italy and of the provinces were disposed to allow them a primacy of order and association (such was their very accurate expression) in the Christian aristocracy. But the power of a monarch was rejected with abhorrence, and the aspiring genius of Rome experienced from the nations of Asia and Africa a more vigorous resistance to her spiritual than she had formerly done to her temporal dominion. The patriotic Cyprian, who ruled with the most absolute sway the church of Carthage and the provincial synods, opposed with resolution and success the ambition of the Roman pontiff, artfully connected his own cause with that of the eastern bishops, and, like Hannibal, sought out new allies in the heart of Asia. If this Punic war was carried on without any effusion of blood, it was owing much less to the moderation than to the weakness of the contending prelates. Invectives and excommunications were *their* only weapons; and these, during the progress of the whole controversy, they hurled against each other with equal fury and devotion. The hard necessity of censuring either a pope or a saint and martyr distresses the modern Catholics whenever they are obliged to relate the particulars of a dispute in which the champions of religion indulged such passions as seem much more adapted to the senate or to the camp.

The progress of the ecclesiastical authority gave birth to the memorable distinction of the laity and of the clergy, which had been unknown to the Greeks and Romans. The former of the appellations comprehended the body of the Christian people; the latter, according to the signification of the word, was appropriated to the chosen portion that had been set apart for the service of religion; a celebrated order of men which has furnished the most important, though not always the most edifying, subjects for modern history. Their mutual hostilities sometimes disturbed the peace of the infant church, but their zeal and activity were united in the common cause, and the love of power, which (under the most artful disguises) could insinuate itself into the breasts of bishops and martyrs, animated them to increase the number of their subjects, and to enlarge the limits of the Christian empire. They were destitute of any temporal force, and they were for a long time discouraged and oppressed, rather than assisted, by the civil magistrate; but they had acquired, and they employed within their own society, the two most efficacious instruments of government, rewards and punishments; the former derived from the pious liberality, the latter from the devout apprehensions, of the faithful.

I. The community of goods, which had so agreeably amused the imagination of Plato, and which subsisted in some degree among the austere sect of the Essenians, was adopted for a short time in the primitive church. The fervour of the first proselytes prompted them to sell those worldly possessions which they despised, to lay the price of them at the feet of the apostles, and to content themselves with receiving an equal share out of the general distribution. The progress of the Christian religion relaxed, and gradually abolished, this generous institution, which, in hands less pure than those of the apostles, would too soon have been corrupted and abused by the returning selfishness of human nature; and the converts who embraced the new religion were permitted to retain the possession of their patrimony, to receive legacies and inheritances, and to increase their separate property by all the lawful means of trade and industry. Instead of an absolute sacrifice, a moderate proportion was accepted by the ministers of the Gospel; and in their weekly or monthly assemblies every believer, according to the exigency of the occasion, and the measure of his wealth and piety, presented his voluntary offering for the use of the common fund. Nothing, however inconsiderable, was refused; but it was diligently inculcated that, in the article of tithes, the Mosaic law was still of divine obligation; and that, since the Jews, under a less perfect discipline, had been commanded to pay a tenth part of all that they possessed, it would become the disciples of Christ to distinguish themselves by a superior degree of liberality, and to acquire some merit by resigning a superfluous treasure, which must so soon be annihilated with the world itself. It is almost unnecessary to observe that the revenue of each particular church, which was of so uncertain and fluctuating a nature, must have varied with the poverty or the opulence of the faithful, as they were dispersed in obscure villages, or collected in the great cities of the empire. In the time of the emperor Decius it was the opinion of the magistrates that the Christians of Rome were possessed of very considerable wealth, that vessels of gold and silver were used in their religious worship, and that many among their proselytes had sold their lands and houses to increase the public riches of the sect, at the expense, indeed, of their unfortunate children, who found themselves beggars because their parents had been saints. We should listen with distrust to the suspicions of strangers and enemies; on this occasion, however, they receive a very specious and probable colour from the two following circumstances, the only ones that have reached our knowledge which define any precise sums or convey any distinct idea. Almost at the same period the bishop of Carthage, from a society less opulent than that of Rome, collected an hundred thousand sesterces (above eight hundred and fifty pounds sterling), on a sudden call of charity to redeem the brethren of Numidia, who had been carried away captives by the barbarians of the desert. About an hundred years before the reign of Decius the Roman church had received, in a single donation, the sum of two hundred thousand sesterces from a stranger of Pontus, who proposed to fix his residence in the capital. These oblations, for the most part, were made in money; nor was the society of Christians either desirous or capable of acquiring, to any considerable degree, the incumbrance of landed property. It had been provided by several laws, which were enacted with the same design as our statutes of mortmain, that no real estates should be given or bequeathed to any corporate body without either a special privilege or a particular dispensation from the emperor or from the senate; who were seldom disposed to grant them in favour of a sect, at first the object of their contempt, and at last of their fears and jealousy. A transaction, however, is related under the reign of Alexander Severus, which discovers that the restraint was sometimes eluded or suspended, and that the Christians were permitted to claim and to possess lands within the limits of Rome itself. The progress of Christianity, and the civil confusion of the empire, contributed to relax the severity of the laws; and, before the close of the third century, many considerable estates were bestowed on the opulent churches of Rome, Milan, Carthage, Antioch, Alexandria, and the other great cities of Italy and the provinces.

The bishop was the natural steward of the church; the public stock was intrusted to his care without account or control; the presbyters were confined to their spiritual functions, and the more dependent order of deacons was solely employed in the management and distribution of the ecclesiastical revenue. If we may give credit to the vehement declamations of Cyprian, there were too many among his African brethren who, in the execution of their charge, violated every precept, not only of evangelic perfection, but even of moral virtue. By some of these unfaithful stewards the riches of the church were lavished in sensual pleasures; by others they were perverted to the purposes of private gain, of fraudulent purchases, and of rapacious usury. But as long as the contributions of the Christian people were free and unconstrained, the abuse of their confidence could not be very frequent, and the general uses to which their liberality was applied reflected honour on the religious society. A decent portion was reserved for the maintenance of the bishop and his clergy; a sufficient sum was allotted for the expenses of the public worship, of which the feasts of love, the *agapæ*, as they were called, constituted a very pleasing part. The whole remainder was the sacred patrimony of the poor. According to the discretion of the bishop, it was distributed to support widows and orphans, the lame, the sick, and the aged of the community; to comfort strangers and pilgrims, and to alleviate the misfortunes of prisoners and captives, more especially when their sufferings had been occasioned by their firm attachment to the cause of religion. A generous intercourse of charity united the most distant provinces, and the smaller congregations were cheerfully assisted by the alms of their more opulent brethren. Such an institution, which paid less regard to the merit than to the distress of the object, very materially conduced to the progress of Christianity. The pagans, who were actuated by a sense of humanity, while they derided the doctrines, acknowledged the benevolence, of the new sect. The prospect of immediate relief and of future protection allured into its hospitable bosom many of those unhappy persons whom the neglect of the world would have abandoned to the miseries of want, of sickness, and of old age. There is some reason likewise to believe that great numbers of infants who, according to the inhuman practice of the times, had been exposed by their parents, were frequently rescued from death, baptised, educated, and maintained by the piety of the Christians, and at the expense of the public treasure.

II. It is the undoubted right of every society to exclude from its communion and benefits such among its members as reject or violate those regulations which have been established by general consent. In the exercise of this power the censures of the Christian church were chiefly directed against scandalous sinners, and particularly those who were guilty of murder, of fraud, or of incontinence; against the authors, or the followers, of any heretical opinions which had been condemned by the judgment of the episcopal order; and against those unhappy persons who, whether from choice or from compulsion, had polluted themselves after their baptism by any act of idolatrous worship. The consequences of excommunication were of temporal as well as a spiritual nature. The Christian against whom it was pronounced was deprived of any part in the oblations of the faithful. The ties both of religious and of private friendship were dissolved: he found himself a profane object of abhorrence to the persons whom he the most esteemed, or by whom he had been the most tenderly beloved; and as far as an expulsion from a respectable society could imprint on his character a mark of disgrace, he was shunned or suspected by the generality of mankind. The situation of these unfortunate exiles was in itself very painful and melancholy; but, as it usually happens, their apprehensions far exceeded their sufferings. The benefits of the Christian communion were those of eternal life; nor could they erase from their minds the awful opinion that to those ecclesiastical governors by whom they were condemned the Deity had committed the keys of Hell and of Paradise. The heretics, indeed, who might be supported by the consciousness of their intentions, and by the flattering hope that they alone had discovered the true path of salvation, endeavoured to regain, in their separate assemblies, those comforts, temporal as well as spiritual, which they no longer derived from the great society of Christians. But almost all those who had reluctantly yielded to the power of vice or idolatry were sensible of their fallen condition, and anxiously desirous of being restored to the benefits of the Christian communion.

With regard to the treatment of these penitents, two opposite opinions, the one of justice, the other of mercy, divided the primitive church. The more rigid and inflexible casuists refused them for ever, and without exception, the meanest place in the holy community which they had disgraced or deserted; and leaving them to the remorse of a guilty conscience, indulged them only with a faint ray of hope that the contrition of their life and death might possibly be accepted by the Supreme Being. A milder sentiment was embraced, in practice as well as in theory, by the purest and most respectable of the Christian churches. The gates of reconciliation and of heaven were seldom shut against the returning penitent; but a severe and solemn form of discipline was instituted, which, while it served to expiate his crime, might powerfully deter the spectators from the imitation of his example. Humbled by a public confession, emaciated by fasting, and clothed in sackcloth, the penitent lay prostrate at the door of the assembly, imploring with tears the pardon of his offences, and soliciting the prayers of the faithful. If the fault was of a very heinous nature, whole years of penance were esteemed an inadequate satisfaction to the Divine justice; and it was always by slow and painful gradations that the sinner, the heretic, or the apostate was readmitted into the bosom of the church. A sentence of perpetual excommunication was, however, reserved for some crimes of an extraordinary magnitude, and particularly for the inexcusable relapses of those penitents who had already experienced and abused the clemency of their ecclesiastical superiors. According to the circumstances or the number of the guilty, the exercise of the Christian discipline was varied by the discretion of the bishops. The councils of Ancyra and Illiberis were held about the same time, the one in Galatia, the other in Spain; but their respective canons, which are still extant, seem to breathe a very different spirit. The Galatian, who after his baptism had repeatedly sacrificed to idols, might obtain his pardon by a penance of seven years; and if he had seduced others to imitate his example, only three years more were added to the term of his exile. But the unhappy Spaniard who had committed the same offence was deprived of the hope of reconciliation even in the article of death; and his idolatry was placed at the head of a list of seventeen other crimes, against which a sentence no less terrible was pronounced. Among these we may distinguish the inexpiable guilt of calumniating a bishop, a presbyter, or even a deacon.

The well-tempered mixture of liberality and rigour, the judicious dispensation of rewards and punishments, according to the maxims of policy as well as justice, constituted the *human* strength of the church. The bishops, whose paternal care extended itself to the government of both worlds, were sensible of the importance of these prerogatives; and, covering their ambition with the fair pretence of the love of order, they were jealous of any rival in the exercise of a discipline so necessary to prevent the desertion of those troops which had enlisted themselves under the banner of the Cross, and whose numbers every day became more considerable. From the imperious declamations of Cyprian we should naturally conclude that the doctrines of excommunication and penance formed the most essential part of religion; and that it was much less dangerous for the disciples of Christ to neglect the observance of the moral duties than to despise the censures and authority of their bishops. Sometimes we might imagine that we were listening to the voice of Moses, when he commanded the earth to open, and to swallow up, in consuming flames, the rebellious race which refused obedience to the priesthood of Aaron; and we should sometimes suppose that we heard a Roman consul asserting the majesty of the republic, and declaring his inflexible resolution to enforce the rigour of the laws. "If such irregularities are suffered with impunity," (it is thus that the bishop of Carthage chides the lenity of his colleague), "if such irregularities are suffered, there is an end of EPISCOPAL VIGOUR, an end of the sublime and divine power of governing the Church; an end of Christianity itself." Cyprian had renounced those temporal honours which it is probable he would never have obtained; but the acquisition of such absolute command over the consciences and understanding of a congregation, however obscure or despised by the world, is more truly grateful to the pride of the human heart than the possession of the most despotic power imposed by arms and conquest on a reluctant people.

In the course of this important, though perhaps tedious, inquiry, I have attempted to display the secondary causes which so efficaciously assisted the truth of the Christian religion. If among these causes we have discovered any artificial ornaments, any accidental circumstances, or any mixture of error and passion, it cannot appear surprising that mankind should be the most sensibly affected by such motives as were suited to their imperfect nature. It was by the aid of these causes—exclusive zeal, the immediate expectation of another world, the claim of miracles, the practice of rigid virtue, and the constitution of the primitive church—that Christianity spread itself with so much success in the Roman empire. To the first of these the Christians were indebted for their invincible valour, which disdained to capitulate with the enemy whom they were resolved to vanquish. The three succeeding causes supplied their valour with the most formidable arms. The last of these causes united their courage, directed their arms, and gave their efforts that irresistible weight which even a small band of well-trained and intrepid volunteers has so often possessed over an undisciplined multitude, ignorant of the subject and careless of the event of the war. In the various religions of Polytheism, some wandering fanatics of Egypt and Syria, who addressed themselves to the credulous superstition of the populace, were perhaps the only order of priests that derived their whole support and credit from their sacerdotal profession, and were very deeply affected by a personal concern for the safety or prosperity of their tutelar deities. The ministers of Polytheism, both in Rome and in the provinces, were, for the most part, men of a noble birth and of an affluent fortune, who received, as an honourable distinction, the care of a celebrated temple or of a public sacrifice, exhibited, very frequently at their own expense, the sacred games, and with cold indifference performed the ancient rites, according to the laws and fashion of their country. As they were engaged in the ordinary occupations of life, their zeal and devotion were seldom animated by a sense of interest, or by the habits of an ecclesiastical character. Confined to their respective temples and cities, they remained without any connection of discipline or government; and whilst they acknowledged the supreme jurisdiction of the senate, of the college of pontiffs, and of the emperor, those civil magistrates contented themselves with the easy task of maintaining in peace and dignity the general worship of mankind. We have already seen how various, how loose, and how uncertain were the religious sentiments of Polytheists. They were abandoned, almost without control, to the natural workings of a superstitious fancy. The accidental circumstances of their life and situation determined the object as well as the degree of their devotion; and as long as their adoration was successively prostituted to a thousand deities, it was scarcely possible that their hearts could be susceptible of a very sincere or lively passion for any of them.

When Christianity appeared in the world, even these faint and imperfect impressions had lost much of their original power. Human reason, which by its unassisted strength is incapable of perceiving the mysteries of faith, had already obtained an easy triumph over the folly of Paganism, and when Tertullian or Lactantius employ their labours in exposing its falsehood and extravagance, they are obliged to transcribe the eloquence of Cicero or the wit of Lucian. The contagion of these sceptical writings had been diffused far beyond the number of their readers. The fashion of incredulity was communicated from the philosopher to the man of pleasure or business, from the noble to the plebeian, and from the master to the menial slave who waited at his table, and who eagerly listened to the freedom of his conversation. On public occasions the philosophic part of mankind affected to treat with respect and decency the religious institutions of their country, but their secret contempt penetrated through the thin and awkward disguise; and even the people, when they discovered that their deities were rejected and derided by those whose rank or understanding they were accustomed to reverence, were filled with doubts and apprehensions concerning the truth of those doctrines to which they had yielded the most implicit belief. The decline of ancient prejudice exposed a very numerous portion of human kind to the danger of a painful and comfortless situation. A state of scepticism and suspense may amuse a few inquisitive minds. But the practice of superstition is so congenial to the multitude that, if they are forcibly awakened, they still regret the loss of their pleasing vision. Their love of the marvellous and supernatural, their curiosity with regard to future events, and their strong propensity to extend their hopes and fears beyond the limits of the visible world, were the principal causes which favoured the establishment of Polytheism. So urgent on the vulgar is the necessity of believing, that the fall of any system of mythology will most probably be succeeded by the introduction of some other mode of superstition. Some deities of a more recent and fashionable cast might soon have occupied the deserted temples of Jupiter and Apollo, if, in the decisive moment, the wisdom of Providence had not interposed a genuine revelation fitted to inspire the most rational esteem and conviction, whilst, at the same time, it was adorned with all that could attract the curiosity, the wonder, and the veneration of the people. In their actual disposition, as many were almost disengaged from their artificial prejudices, but equally susceptible and desirous of a devout attachment, an object much less deserving would have been sufficient to fill the vacant place in their hearts, and to gratify the uncertain eagerness of their passions. Those who are inclined to pursue this reflection, instead of viewing with astonishment the rapid progress of Christianity, will perhaps be surprised that its success was not still more rapid and still more universal.

It has been observed, with truth as well as propriety, that the conquests of Rome prepared and facilitated those of Christianity. In the second chapter of this work we have attempted to explain in what manner the most civilised provinces of Europe, Asia, and Africa were united under the dominion of one sovereign, and gradually connected by the most intimate ties of laws, of manners, and of language. The Jews of Palestine, who had fondly expected a temporal deliverer, gave so cold a reception to the miracles of the divine prophet, that it was found unnecessary to publish, or at least to preserve, any Hebrew gospel. The authentic histories of the actions of Christ were composed in the Greek language, at a considerable distance from Jerusalem, and after the Gentile converts were grown extremely numerous. As soon as those histories were translated into the Latin tongue they were perfectly intelligible to all the subjects of Rome, excepting only to the peasants of Syria and Egypt, for whose benefit particular versions were afterwards made. The public highways, which had been constructed for the use of the legions, opened an easy passage for the Christian missionaries from Damascus to Corinth, and from Italy to the extremity of Spain or Britain; nor did those spiritual conquerors encounter any of the obstacles which usually retard or prevent the introduction of a foreign religion into a distant country. There is the strongest reason to believe that before the reigns of Diocletian and Constantine the faith of Christ had been preached in every province, and in all the great cities of the empire; but the foundation of the several congregations, the numbers of the faithful who composed them, and their proportion to the unbelieving multitude, are now buried in obscurity or disguised by fiction and declamation.

According to the irreproachable testimony of Origen, the proportion of the faithful was very inconsiderable, when compared with the multitude of an unbelieving world; but, as we are left without any distinct information, it is impossible to determine, and it is difficult even to conjecture, the real numbers of the primitive Christians. The most favourable calculation, however, that can be deduced from the examples of Antioch and of Rome will not permit us to imagine that more than a twentieth part of the subjects of the empire had enlisted themselves under the banner of the Cross before the important conversion of Constantine. But their habits of faith, of zeal, and of union, seemed to multiply their numbers; and the same causes which contributed to their future increase served to render their actual strength more apparent and more formidable.

Such is the constitution of civil society, that, whilst a few persons are distinguished by riches, by honours, and by knowledge, the body of the people is condemned to obscurity, ignorance, and poverty. The Christian religion, which addressed itself to the whole human race, must consequently collect a far greater number of proselytes from the lower than from the superior ranks of life. This innocent and natural circumstance has been improved into a very odious imputation, which seems to be less strenuously denied by the apologists than it is urged by the adversaries of the faith; that the new sect of Christians was almost entirely composed of the dregs of the populace, of peasants and mechanics, of boys and women, of beggars and slaves, the last of whom might sometimes introduce the missionaries into the rich and noble families to which they belonged. These obscure teachers (such was the charge of malice and infidelity) are as mute in public as they are loquacious and dogmatical in private. Whilst they cautiously avoid the dangerous encounter of philosophers, they mingle with the rude and illiterate crowd, and insinuate themselves into those minds whom their age, their sex, or their education has best disposed to receive the impression of superstitious terrors.

This unfavourable picture, though not devoid of a faint resemblance, betrays, by its dark colouring and distorted features, the pencil of an enemy. As the humble faith of Christ diffused itself through the world, it was embraced by several persons who derived some consequence from the advantages of nature or fortune. Aristides, who presented an eloquent apology to the emperor Hadrian, was an Athenian philosopher. Justin Martyr had sought divine knowledge in the schools of Zeno, of Aristotle, of Pythagoras, and of Plato, before he fortunately was accosted by the old man, or rather the angel, who turned his attention to the study of the Jewish prophets. Clemens of Alexandria had acquired much various reading in the Greek, and Tertullian in the Latin, language. Julius Africanus and Origen possessed a very considerable share of the learning of their times; and although the style of Cyprian is very different from that of Lactantius, we might almost discover that both those writers had been public teachers of rhetoric. Even the study of philosophy was at length introduced among the Christians, but it was not always productive of the most salutary effects; knowledge was as often the parent of heresy as of devotion, and the description which was designed for the followers of Artemon may, with equal propriety, be applied to the various sects that resisted the successors of the apostles. "They presume to alter the holy Scriptures, to abandon the ancient rule of faith, and to form their opinions according to the subtle precepts of logic. The science of the church is neglected for the study of geometry, and they lose sight of heaven while they are employed in measuring the earth. Euclid is perpetually in their hands. Aristotle and Theophrastus are the objects of their admiration; and they express an uncommon reverence for the works of Galen. Their errors are derived from the abuse of the arts and sciences of the infidels, and they corrupt the simplicity of the Gospel by the refinements of human reason." Nor can it be affirmed with truth that the advantages of birth and fortune were always separated from the profession of Christianity. Several Roman citizens were brought before the tribunal of Pliny, and he soon discovered that a great number of persons of *every order* of men in Bithynia had deserted the religion of their ancestors. His unsuspected testimony may, in this instance, obtain more credit than the bold challenge of Tertullian, when he addresses himself to the fears as well as to the humanity of the proconsul of Africa, by assuring him that if he persists in his cruel intentions he must decimate Carthage, and that he will find among the guilty many persons of his own rank, senators and matrons of noblest extraction, and the friends or relations of his most intimate friends. It appears, however, that about forty years afterwards the emperor Valerian was persuaded of the truth of this assertion, since in one of his rescripts he evidently supposes that senators, Roman knights, and ladies of quality, were engaged in the Christian sect. The church still continued to increase its outward splendour as it lost its internal purity; and, in the reign of Diocletian, the palace, the courts of justice, and even the army, concealed a multitude of Christians, who endeavoured to reconcile the interests of the present with those of a future life.

And yet these exceptions are either too few in number, or too recent in time, entirely to remove the imputation of ignorance and obscurity which has been so arrogantly cast on the first proselytes of Christianity. Instead of employing in our defence the fictions of later ages, it will be more prudent to convert the occasion of scandal into a subject of edification. Our serious thoughts will suggest to us that the apostles themselves were chosen by Providence among the fishermen of Galilee, and that, the lower we depress the temporal condition of the first Christians, the more reason we shall find to admire their merit and success. It is incumbent on us diligently to remember that the kingdom of heaven was promised to the poor in spirit, and that minds afflicted by calamity and the contempt of mankind cheerfully listen to the divine promise of future happiness; while, on the contrary, the fortunate are satisfied with the possession of this world; and the wise abuse in doubt and dispute their vain superiority of reason and knowledge.

We stand in need of such reflections to comfort us for the loss of some illustrious characters, which in our eyes might have seemed the most worthy of the heavenly present. The names of Seneca, of the elder and the younger Pliny, of Tacitus, of Plutarch, of Galen, of the slave Epictetus, and of the emperor Marcus Antoninus, adorn the age in which they flourished, and exalt the dignity of human nature. They filled with glory their respective stations, either in active or contemplative life; their excellent understandings were improved by study; philosophy had purified their minds from the prejudices of the popular superstition; and their days were spent in the pursuit of truth and the practice of virtue. Yet all these sages (it is no less an object of surprise than of concern) overlooked or rejected the perfection of the Christian system. Their language or their silence equally discover their contempt for the growing sect which in their time had diffused itself over the Roman empire. Those among them who condescend to mention the Christians consider them only as obstinate and perverse enthusiasts, who exacted an implicit submission to their mysterious doctrines, without being able to produce a single argument that could engage the attention of men of sense and learning.

It is at least doubtful whether any of these philosophers perused the apologies which the primitive Christians repeatedly published in behalf of themselves and of their religion; but it is much to be lamented that such a cause was not defended by abler advocates. They expose with superfluous wit and eloquence the extravagance of Polytheism. They interest our compassion by displaying the innocence and sufferings of their injured brethren. But when they would demonstrate the divine origin of Christianity, they insist much more strongly on the predictions which announced, than on the miracles which accompanied, the appearance of the Messiah. Their favourite argument might serve to edify a Christian or to convert a Jew, since both the one and the other acknowledge the authority of those prophecies, and both are obliged, with devout reverence, to search for their sense and their accomplishment. But this mode of persuasion loses much of its weight and influence when it is addressed to those who neither understand nor respect the Mosaic dispensation and the prophetic style. In the unskilful hands of Justin and of the succeeding apologists, the sublime meaning of the Hebrew oracles evaporates in distant types, affected conceits, and cold allegories; and even their authenticity was rendered suspicious to an unenlightened Gentile, by the mixture of pious forgeries which, under the names of Orpheus, Hermes, and the Sibyls, were obtruded on him as of equal value with the genuine inspirations of Heaven. The adoption of fraud and sophistry in the defence of revelation too often reminds us of the injudicious conduct of those poets who load their *invulnerable* heroes with a useless weight of cumbersome and brittle armour.

But how shall we excuse the supine inattention of the Pagan and philosophic world to those evidences which were presented by the hand of Omnipotence, not to their reason, but to their senses? During the age of Christ, of his apostles, and of their first disciples, the doctrine which they preached was confirmed by innumerable prodigies. The lame walked, the blind saw, the sick were healed, the dead were raised, dæmons were expelled, and the laws of Nature were frequently suspended for the benefit of the church. But the sages of Greece and Rome turned aside from the awful spectacle, and, pursuing the ordinary occupations of life and study, appeared unconscious of any alterations in the moral or physical government of the world. Under the reign of Tiberius, the whole earth, or at least a celebrated province of the Roman empire, was involved in a preternatural darkness of three hours. Even this miraculous event, which ought to have excited the wonder, the curiosity, and the devotion of mankind, passed without notice in an age of science and history. It happened during the lifetime of Seneca and the elder Pliny, who must have experienced the immediate effects, or received the earliest intelligence, of the prodigy. Each of these philosophers, in a laborious work, has recorded all the great phenomena of Nature, earthquakes, meteors, comets, and eclipses, which his indefatigable curiosity could collect. Both the one and the other have omitted to mention the greatest phenomenon to which the mortal eye has been witness since the creation of the globe. A distinct chapter of Pliny is designed for eclipses of an extraordinary nature and unusual duration; but he contents himself with describing the singular defect of light which followed the murder of Cæsar, when, during the greatest part of a year, the orb of the sun appeared pale and without splendour. This season of obscurity, which cannot surely be compared with the preternatural darkness of the Passion, had been already celebrated by most of the poets and historians of that memorable age.

XIV

(180–313 A.D.) THE CONDUCT OF THE ROMAN GOVERNMENT TOWARDS THE CHRISTIANS, FROM THE REIGN OF NERO TO THAT OF CONSTANTINE

If we seriously consider the purity of the Christian religion, the sanctity of its moral precepts, and the innocent as well as austere lives of the greater number of those who during the first ages embraced the faith of the Gospel, we should naturally suppose that so benevolent a doctrine would have been received with due reverence even by the unbelieving world; that the learned and the polite, however they might deride the miracles, would have esteemed the virtues of the new sect; and that the magistrates, instead of persecuting, would have protected an order of men who yielded the most passive obedience to the laws, though they declined the active cares of war and government. If, on the other hand, we recollect the universal toleration of Polytheism, as it was invariably maintained by the faith of the people, the incredulity of philosophers, and the policy of the Roman senate and emperors, we are at a loss to discover what new offence the Christians had committed, what new provocation could exasperate the mild indifference of antiquity, and what new motives could urge the Roman princes, who beheld without concern a thousand forms of religion subsisting in peace under their gentle sway, to inflict a severe punishment on any part of their subjects who had chosen for themselves a singular but an inoffensive mode of faith and worship.

The religious policy of the ancient world seems to have assumed a more stern and intolerant character to oppose the progress of Christianity. About fourscore years after the death of Christ, his innocent disciples were punished with death by the sentence of a proconsul of the most amiable and philosophic character, and according to the laws of an emperor distinguished by the wisdom and justice of his general administration. The apologies which were repeatedly addressed to the successors of Trajan are filled with the most pathetic complaints that the Christians, who obeyed the dictates and solicited the liberty of conscience, were alone, among all the subjects of the Roman empire, excluded from the common benefits of their auspicious government. The deaths of a few eminent martyrs have been recorded with care; and from the time that Christianity was invested with the supreme power, the governors of the church have been no less diligently employed in displaying the cruelty, than in imitating the conduct, of their Pagan adversaries. To separate (if it be possible) a few authentic as well as interesting facts from an undigested mass of fiction and error, and to relate, in a clear and rational manner, the causes, the extent, the duration, and the most important circumstances of the persecutions to which the first Christians were exposed, is the design of the present chapter.

The sectaries of a persecuted religion, depressed by fear, animated with resentment, and perhaps heated by enthusiasm, are seldom in a proper temper of mind calmly to investigate, or candidly to appreciate, the motives of their enemies, which often escape the impartial and discerning view even of those who are placed at a secure distance from the flames of persecution. A reason has been assigned for the conduct of the emperors towards the primitive Christians, which may appear the more specious and probable as it is drawn from the acknowledged genius of Polytheism. It has already been observed that the religious concord of the world was principally supported by the implicit assent and reverence which the nations of antiquity expressed for their respective traditions and ceremonies. It might therefore be expected that they would unite with indignation against any sect of people which should separate itself from the communion of mankind, and, claiming the exclusive pos- session of divine knowledge, should disdain every form of worship except its own as impious and idolatrous. The rights of toleration were held by mutual indulgence: they were justly forfeited by a refusal of the accustomed tribute. As the payment of this tribute was inflexibly refused by the Jews, and by them alone, the consideration of the treatment which they experienced from the Roman magistrates will serve to explain how far these speculations are justified by facts, and will lead us to discover the true causes of the persecution of Christianity.

Since the Jews, who rejected with abhorrence the deities adored by their sovereign and by their fellow-subjects, enjoyed, however, the free exercise of their unsocial religion, there must have existed some other cause which exposed the disciples of Christ to those severities from which the posterity of Abraham was exempt. The difference between them is simple and obvious, but, according to the sentiments of antiquity, it was of the highest importance. The Jews were a *nation*, the Christians were a *sect*: and if it was natural for every community to respect the sacred institutions of their neighbours, it was incumbent on them to persevere in those of their ancestors. The voice of oracles, the precepts of philosophers, and the authority of the laws, unanimously enforced this national obligation. By their lofty claim of superior sanctity the Jews might provoke the Polytheists to consider them as an odious and impure race. By disdaining the intercourse of other nations they might deserve their contempt. The laws of Moses might be for the most part frivolous or absurd; yet, since they had been received during many ages by a large society, his followers were justified by the example of mankind, and it was universally acknowledged that they had a right to practise what it would have been criminal in them to neglect. But this principle, which protected the Jewish synagogue, afforded not any favour or security to the primitive church. By embracing the faith of the Gospel the Christians incurred the supposed guilt of an unnatural and unpardonable offence. They dissolved the sacred ties of custom and education, violated the religious institutions of their country, and presumptuously despised whatever their fathers had believed as true or had reverenced as sacred. Nor was this apostasy (if we may use the expression) merely of a partial or local kind; since the pious deserter who withdrew himself from the temples of Egypt or Syria would equally disdain to seek an asylum in those of Athens or Carthage. Every Christian rejected with contempt the superstitions of his family, his city, and his province. The whole body of Christians unanimously refused to hold any communion with the gods of Rome, of the empire, and of mankind. It was in vain that the oppressed believer asserted the inalienable rights of conscience and private judgment. Though his situation might excite the pity, his arguments could never reach the understanding, either of the philosophic or of the believing part of the Pagan world. To their apprehensions it was no less a matter of surprise that any individuals should entertain scruples against complying with the established mode of worship than if they had conceived a sudden abhorrence to the manners, the dress, or the language of their native country.

The surprise of the Pagans was soon succeeded by resentment, and the most pious of men were exposed to the unjust but dangerous imputation of impiety. Malice and prejudice concurred in representing the Christians as a society of atheists, who, by the most daring attack on the religious constitution of the empire, had merited the severest animadversion of the civil magistrate. They had separated themselves (they gloried in the confession) from every mode of superstition which was received in any part of the globe by the various temper of Polytheism: but it was not altogether so evident what deity, or what form of worship, they had substituted to the gods and temples of antiquity. The pure and sublime idea which they entertained of the Supreme Being escaped the gross conception of the Pagan multitude, who were at a loss to discover a spiritual and solitary God, that was neither represented under any corporeal figure or visible symbol, nor was adored with the accustomed pomp of libations and festivals, of altars and sacrifices. The sages of Greece and Rome, who had elevated their minds to the contemplation of the existence and attributes of the First Cause, were induced by reason or by vanity to reserve for themselves and their chosen disciples the privilege of this philosophical devotion. They were far from admitting the prejudices of mankind as the standard of truth, but they considered them as flowing from the original disposition of human nature; and they supposed that any popular mode of faith and worship which presumed to disclaim the assistance of the senses would, in proportion as it receded from superstition, find itself incapable of restraining the wanderings of the fancy and the visions of fanaticism. The careless glance which men of wit and learning condescended to cast on the Christian revelation served only to confirm their hasty opinion, and to persuade them that the principle, which they might have revered, of the Divine Unity, was defaced by the wild enthusiasm, and annihilated by the airy speculations, of the new sectaries.

The personal guilt which every Christian had contracted, in thus preferring his private sentiment to the national religion, was aggravated in a very high degree by the number and union of the criminals. It is well known, and has been already observed, that Roman policy viewed with the utmost jealousy and distrust any association among its subjects; and that the privileges of private corporations, though formed for the most harmless or beneficial purposes, were bestowed with a very sparing hand. The religious assemblies of the Christians, who had separated themselves from the public worship, appeared of a much less innocent nature: they were illegal in their principle, and in their consequences might become dangerous; nor were the emperors conscious that they violated the laws of justice, when, for the peace of society, they prohibited those secret and sometimes nocturnal meetings. The pious disobedience of the Christians made their conduct, or perhaps their designs, appear in a much more serious and criminal light; and the Roman princes, who might perhaps have suffered themselves to be disarmed by a ready submission, deeming their honour concerned in the execution of their commands, sometimes attempted, by rigorous punishments, to subdue this independent spirit, which boldly acknowledged an authority superior to that of the magistrate. The extent and duration of this spiritual conspiracy seemed to render it every day more deserving of his animadversion. We have already seen that the active and successful zeal of the Christians had insensibly diffused them through every province and almost every city of the empire. The new converts seemed to renounce their family and country, that they might connect themselves in an indissoluble band of union with a peculiar society, which everywhere assumed a different character from the rest of mankind. Their gloomy and austere aspect, their abhorrence of the common business and pleasures of life, and their frequent predictions of impending calamities, inspired the Pagans with the apprehension of some danger which would arise from the new sect, the more alarming as it was the more obscure. " Whatever," says Pliny, "may be the principle of their conduct, their inflexible obstinacy appeared deserving of punishment."

The precautions with which the disciples of Christ performed the offices of religion were at first dictated by fear and necessity; but they were continued from choice. By imitating the awful secrecy which reigned in the Eleusinian mysteries, the Christians had flattered themselves that they should render their sacred institutions more respectable in the eyes of the Pagan World. But the event, as it often happens to the operations of subtile policy, deceived their wishes and their expectations. It was concluded that they only concealed what they would have blushed to disclose. Their mistaken prudence afforded an opportunity for malice to invent, and for suspicious credulity to believe, the horrid tales which described the Christians as the most wicked of human kind, who practised in their dark recesses every abomination that a depraved fancy could suggest, and who solicited the favour of their unknown God by the sacrifice of every moral virtue. There were many who pretended to confess or to relate the ceremonies of this abhorred society. It was asserted, "that a newborn infant, entirely covered over with flour, was presented, like some mystic symbol of initiation, to the knife of the proselyte, who unknowingly inflicted many a secret and mortal wound on the innocent victim of his error; that as soon as the cruel deed was perpetrated, the sectaries drank up the blood, greedily tore asunder the quivering members, and pledged themselves to eternal secrecy, by a mutual consciousness of guilt. It was as confidently affirmed that this inhuman sacrifice was succeeded by a suitable entertainment, in which intemperance served as a provocative to brutal lust; till, at the appointed moment, the lights were suddenly extinguished, shame was banished, nature was forgotten; and, as accident might direct, the darkness of the night was polluted by the incestuous commerce of sisters and brothers, of sons and of mothers."

But the perusal of the ancient apologies was sufficient to remove even the slightest suspicion from the mind of a candid adversary. The Christians, with the intrepid security of innocence, appeal from the voice of rumour to the equity of the magistrates. They acknowledge that, if any proof can be produced of the crimes which calumny has imputed to them, they are worthy of the most severe punishment. They provoke the punishment, and they challenge the proof. At the same time they urge, with equal truth and propriety, that the charge is not less devoid of probability than it is destitute of evidence; they ask whether any one can seriously believe that the pure and holy precepts of the Gospel, which so frequently restrain the use of the most lawful enjoyments, should inculcate the practice of the most abominable crimes; that a large society should resolve to dishonour itself in the eyes of its own members; and that a great number of persons, of either sex, and every age and character, insensible to the fear of death or infamy, should consent to violate those principles which nature and education had imprinted most deeply in their minds. Nothing, it should seem, could weaken the force or destroy the effect of so unanswerable a justification, unless it were the injudicious conduct of the apologists themselves, who betrayed the common cause of religion, to gratify their devout hatred to the domestic enemies of the church. It was sometimes faintly insinuated, and sometimes boldly asserted, that the same bloody sacrifices, and the same incestuous festivals, which were so falsely ascribed to the orthodox believers, were in reality celebrated by the Marcionites, by the Carpocratians, and by several other sects of the Gnostics, who, notwithstanding they might deviate into the paths of heresy, were still actuated by the sentiments of men, and still governed by the precepts of Christianity. Accusations of a similar kind were retorted upon the church by the schismatics who had departed from its communion, and it was confessed on all sides that the most scandalous licentiousness of manners prevailed among great numbers of those who affected the name of Christians. A Pagan magistrate, who possessed neither leisure nor abilities to discern the almost imperceptible line which divides the orthodox faith from heretical pravity, might easily have imagined that their mutual animosity had extorted the discovery of their common guilt. It was fortunate for the repose, or at least for the reputation, of the first Christians, that the magistrates sometimes proceeded with more temper and moderation than is usually consistent with religious zeal, and that they reported, as the impartial result of their judicial inquiry, that the sectaries who had deserted the established worship appeared to them sincere in their professions and blameless in their manners, however they might incur, by their absurd and excessive superstition, the censure of the laws.

History, which undertakes to record the transactions of the past, for the instruction of future ages, would ill deserve that honourable office if she condescended to plead the cause of tyrants, or to justify the maxims of persecution. It must, however, be acknowledged that the conduct of the emperors who appeared the least favourable to the primitive church is by no means so criminal as that of modern sovereigns who have employed the arm of violence and terror against the religious opinions of any part of their subjects. From their reflections, or even from their own feelings, a Charles V. or a Louis XIV. might have acquired a just knowledge of the rights of conscience, of the obligation of faith, and of the innocence of error. But the princes and magistrates of ancient Rome were strangers to those principles which inspired and authorised the inflexible obstinacy of the Christians in the cause of truth, nor could they themselves discover in their own breasts any motives which would have prompted them to refuse a legal, and as it were a natural, submission to the sacred institutions of their country. The same reason which contributes to alleviate the guilt, must have tended to abate the rigour, of their persecutions. As they were actuated, not by the furious zeal of bigots, but by the temperate policy of legislators, contempt must often have relaxed, and humanity must frequently have suspended, the execution of those laws which they enacted against the humble and obscure followers of Christ. From the general view of their character and motives we might naturally conclude: I. That a considerable time elapsed before they considered the new sectaries as an object deserving of the attention of government. II. That in the conviction of any of their subjects who were accused of so very singular a crime, they proceeded with caution and reluctance. III. That they were moderate in the use of punishments; and IV. That the afflicted church enjoyed many intervals of peace and tranquillity. Notwithstanding the careless indifference which the most copious and the most minute of the Pagan writers have shown to the affairs of the Christians, it may still be in our power to confirm each of these probable suppositions by the evidence of authentic facts.

I. By the wise dispensation of Providence a mysterious veil was cast over the infancy of the church, which, till the faith of the Christians was matured, and their numbers were multiplied, served to protect them not only from the malice but even from the knowledge of the Pagan world. The slow and gradual abolition of the Mosaic ceremonies afforded a safe and innocent disguise to the more early proselytes of the Gospel. As they were for the greater part of the race of Abraham, they were distinguished by the peculiar mark of circumcision, offered up their devotions in the Temple of Jerusalem till its final destruction, and received both the Law and the Prophets as the genuine inspirations of the Deity. The Gentile converts who by a spiritual adoption had been associated to the hope of Israel, were likewise confounded under the garb and appearance of Jews; and as the Polytheists paid less regard to articles of faith than to the external worship, the new sect, which carefully concealed, or faintly announced, its future greatness and ambition, was permitted to shelter itself under the general toleration which was granted to an ancient and celebrated people in the Roman empire. It was not long, perhaps, before the Jews themselves, animated with a fiercer zeal and a more jealous faith, perceived the gradual separation of their Nazarene brethren from the doctrine of the synagogue: and they would gladly have extinguished the dangerous heresy in the blood of its adherents. But the decrees of Heaven had already disarmed their malice; and though they might sometimes exert the licentious privilege of sedition, they no longer possessed the administration of criminal justice; nor did they find it easy to infuse into the calm breast of a Roman magistrate the rancour of their own zeal and prejudice. The provincial governors declared themselves ready to listen to any accusation that might affect the public safety; but as soon as they were informed that it was a question not of facts but of words, a dispute relating only to the interpretation of the Jewish laws and prophecies, they deemed it unworthy of the majesty of Rome seriously to discuss the obscure differences which might arise among a barbarous and superstitious people. The innocence of the first Christians was protected by ignorance and contempt; and the tribunal of the Pagan magistrate often proved their most assured refuge against the fury of the synagogue.

In the tenth year of the reign of Nero the capital of the empire was afflicted by a fire which raged beyond the memory or example of former ages. The monuments of Grecian art and of Roman virtue, the trophies of the Punic and Gallic wars, the most holy temples, and the most splendid palaces were involved in one common destruction. Of the fourteen regions or quarters into which Rome was divided, four only subsisted entire, three were levelled with the ground, and the remaining seven, which had experienced the fury of the flames, displayed a melancholy prospect of ruin and desolation. The vigilance of government appears not to have neglected any of the precautions which might alleviate the sense of so dreadful a calamity. The Imperial gardens were thrown open to the distressed multitude, temporary buildings were erected for their accommodation, and a plentiful supply of corn and provisions was distributed at a very moderate price. The most generous policy seemed to have dictated the edicts which regulated the disposition of the streets and the construction of private houses; and, as it usually happens in an age of prosperity, the conflagration of Rome, in the course of a few years, produced a new city, more regular and more beautiful than the former. But all the prudence and humanity affected by Nero on this occasion were insufficient to preserve him from the popular suspicion. Every crime might be imputed to the assassin of his wife and mother; nor could the prince who prostituted his person and dignity on the theatre be deemed incapable of the most extravagant folly. The voice of rumour accused the emperor as the incendiary of his own capital; and, as the most incredible stories are the best adapted to the genius of an enraged people, it was gravely reported, and firmly believed, that Nero, enjoying the calamity which he had occasioned,

amused himself with singing to his lyre the destruction of ancient
Troy. To divert a suspicion which the power of despotism was
unable to suppress, the emperor resolved to substitute in his own
place some fictitious criminals. "With this view (continues Tacitus)
he inflicted the most exquisite tortures on those men who, under
the vulgar appellation of Christians, were already branded with
deserved infamy. They derived their name and origin from Christ,
who, in the reign of Tiberius, had suffered death by the sentence
of the procurator Pontius Pilate. For a while this dire superstition
was checked, but it again burst forth; and not only spread itself over
Judæa, the first seat of this mischievous sect, but was even introduced into Rome, the common asylum which receives and protects
whatever is impure, whatever is atrocious. The confessions of those
who were seized discovered a great multitude of their accomplices,
and they were all convicted, not so much for the crime of setting
fire to the city as for their hatred of human kind. They died in
torments, and their torments were embittered by insult and derision.
Some were nailed on crosses; others sewn up in the skins of wild
beasts, and exposed to the fury of dogs; others again, smeared over
with combustible materials, were used as torches to illuminate the
darkness of the night. The gardens of Nero were destined for the
melancholy spectacle, which was accompanied with a horse-race,
and honoured with the presence of the emperor, who mingled with
the populace in the dress and attitude of a charioteer. The guilt of
the Christians deserved indeed the most exemplary punishment,
but the public abhorrence was changed into commiseration, from
the opinion that those unhappy wretches were sacrificed, not so
much to the public welfare as to the cruelty of a jealous tyrant."
Those who survey with a curious eye the revolutions of mankind
may observe that the gardens and circus of Nero on the Vatican,
which were polluted with the blood of the first Christians, have
been rendered still more famous by the triumph and by the abuse
of the persecuted religion. On the same spot a temple, which far
surpasses the ancient glories of the Capitol, has been since erected
by the Christian Pontiffs, who, deriving their claim of universal
dominion from an humble fisherman of Galilee, have succeeded
to the throne of the Cæsars, given laws to the barbarian conquerors
of Rome, and extended their spiritual jurisdiction from the coast of
the Baltic to the shores of the Pacific Ocean.

It is somewhat remarkable that the flames of war consumed
almost at the same time the Temple of Jerusalem and the Capitol

of Rome; and it appears no less singular that the tribute which devotion had destined to the former should have been converted by the power of an assaulting victor to restore and adorn the splendour of the latter. The emperors levied a general capitation tax on the Jewish people; and although the sum assessed on the head of each individual was inconsiderable, the use for which it was designed, and the severity with which it was exacted, were considered as an intolerable grievance. Since the officers of the revenue extended their unjust claim to many persons who were strangers to the blood or religion of the Jews, it was impossible that the Christians, who had so often sheltered themselves under the shade of the synagogue, should now escape this rapacious persecution. Anxious as they were to avoid the slightest infection of idolatry, their conscience forbade them to contribute to the honour of that dæmon who had assumed the character of the Capitoline Jupiter. As a very numerous though declining party among the Christians still adhered to the law of Moses, their efforts to dissemble their Jewish origin were detected by the decisive test of circumcision; nor were the Roman magistrates at leisure to inquire into the difference of their religious tenets. Among the Christians who were brought before the tribunal of the emperor, or, as it seems more probable, before that of the procurator of Judæa, two persons are said to have appeared, distinguished by their extraction, which was more truly noble than that of the greatest monarchs. These were the grandsons of St. Jude the apostle, who himself was the brother of Jesus Christ. Their natural pretensions to the throne of David might perhaps attract the respect of the people, and excite the jealousy of the governor; but the meanness of their garb and the simplicity of their answers soon convinced him that they were neither desirous nor capable of disturbing the peace of the Roman empire. They frankly confessed their royal origin, and their near relation to the Messiah, but they disclaimed any temporal views, and professed that his kingdom, which they devoutly expected, was purely of a spiritual and angelic nature. When they were examined concerning their fortune and occupation, they showed their hands hardened with daily labour, and declared that they derived their whole subsistence from the cultivation of a farm near the village of Cocaba, of the extent of about twenty-four English acres, and of the value of nine thousand drachms, or three hundred pounds sterling. The grandsons of St. Jude were dismissed with compassion and contempt.

But although the obscurity of the house of David might protect them from the suspicions of a tyrant, the present greatness of his own family alarmed the pusillanimous temper of Domitian, which could only be appeased by the blood of those Romans whom he either feared, or hated, or esteemed. Of the two sons of his uncle Flavius Sabinus, the elder was soon convicted of treasonable intentions, and the younger, who bore the name of Flavius Clemens, was indebted for his safety to his want of courage and ability. The emperor for a long time distinguished so harmless a kinsman by his favour and protection, bestowed on him his own niece Domitilla, adopted the children of that marriage to the hope of the succession, and invested their father with the honours of the consulship. But he had scarcely finished the term of his annual magistracy, when on a slight pretence he was condemned and executed; Domitilla was banished to a desolate island on the coast of Campania; and sentences either of death or of confiscation were pronounced against a great number of persons who were involved in the same accusation. The guilt imputed to their charge was that of *Atheism and Jewish manners*; a singular association of ideas, which cannot with any propriety be applied except to the Christians, as they were obscurely and imperfectly viewed by the magistrates and by the writers of that period. On the strength of so probable an interpretation, and too eagerly admitting the suspicions of a tyrant as an evidence of their honourable crime, the church has placed both Clemens and Domitilla among its first martyrs, and has branded the cruelty of Domitian with the name of the second persecution. But this persecution (if it deserves that epithet) was of no long duration. A few months after the death of Clemens and the banishment of Domitilla, Stephen, a freedman belonging to the latter, who had enjoyed the favour, but who had not surely embraced the faith, of his mistress, assassinated the emperor in his palace. The memory of Domitian was condemned by the senate; his acts were rescinded; his exiles recalled; and under the gentle administration of Nerva, while the innocent were restored to their rank and fortunes, even the most guilty either obtained pardon or escaped punishment.

II. About ten years afterwards, under the reign of Trajan, the younger Pliny was intrusted by his friend and master with the government of Bithynia and Pontus. He soon found himself at a loss to determine by what rule of justice or of law he should direct his conduct in the execution of an office the most repugnant to his humanity. Pliny had never assisted at any judicial proceedings against the Christians, with whose name alone he seems to be acquainted; and he was totally uninformed with regard to the nature of their guilt, the method of their conviction, and the degree of their punishment. In this perplexity he had recourse to his usual expedient, of submitting to the wisdom of Trajan an impartial, and, in some respects, a favourable account of the new superstition, requesting the emperor that he would condescend to resolve his doubts and to instruct his ignorance. The life of Pliny had been employed in the acquisition of learning, and in the business of the world. Since the age of nineteen he had pleaded with distinction in the tribunals of Rome, filled a place in the senate, had been invested with the honours of the consulship, and had formed very numerous connections with every order of men, both in Italy and in the provinces. From *his* ignorance therefore we may derive some useful information. We may assure ourselves that when he accepted the government of Bithynia there were no general laws or decrees of the senate in force against the Christians; that neither Trajan nor any of his virtuous predecessors, whose edicts were received into the civil and criminal jurisprudence, had publicly declared their intentions concerning the new sect; and that, whatever proceedings had been carried on against the Christians, there were none of sufficient weight and authority to establish a precedent for the conduct of a Roman magistrate.

The answer of Trajan, to which the Christians of the succeeding age have frequently appealed, discovers as much regard for justice and humanity as could be reconciled with his mistaken notions of religious policy. Instead of displaying the implacable zeal of an Inquisitor, anxious to discover the most minute particles of heresy, and exulting in the number of his victims, the emperor expresses much more solicitude to protect the security of the innocent than to prevent the escape of the guilty. He acknowledges the difficulty of fixing any general plan; but he lays down two salutary rules, which often afforded relief and support to the distressed Christians. Though he directs the magistrates to punish such persons as are legally convicted, he prohibits them, with a very humane inconsistency, from making any inquiries concerning the supposed criminals. Nor was the magistrate allowed to proceed on every kind of information. Anonymous charges the emperor rejects, as too repugnant to the equity of his government; and he strictly requires, for the conviction of those to whom the guilt of Christianity is imputed, the positive evidence of a fair and open accuser.

III. Punishment was not the inevitable consequence of conviction, and the Christians whose guilt was the most clearly proved by the testimony of witnesses, or even by their voluntary confession, still retained in their own power the alternative of life or death. It was not so much the past offence, as the actual resistance, which excited the indignation of the magistrate. He was persuaded that he offered them an easy pardon, since, if they consented to cast a few grains of incense upon the altar, they were dismissed from the tribunal in safety and with applause. It was esteemed the duty of a humane judge to endeavour to reclaim, rather than to punish, those deluded enthusiasts. Varying his tone according to the age, the sex, or the situation of the prisoners, he frequently condescended to set before their eyes every circumstance which could render life more pleasing, or death more terrible; and to solicit, nay to intreat them, that they would show some compassion to themselves, to their families, and to their friends. If threats and persuasions proved ineffectual, he had often recourse to violence; the scourge and the rack were called in to supply the deficiency of argument, and every art of cruelty was employed to subdue such inflexible, and, as it appeared to the Pagans, such criminal obstinacy. The ancient apologists of Christianity have censured, with equal truth and severity, the irregular conduct of their persecutors, who, contrary to every principle of judicial proceeding, admitted the use of torture, in order to obtain, not a confession, but a denial, of the crime which was the object of their inquiry. The monks of succeeding ages, who, in their peaceful solitudes, entertained themselves with diversifying the deaths and sufferings of the primitive martyrs, have frequently invented torments of a much more refined and ingenious nature. In particular, it has pleased them to suppose that the zeal of the Roman magistrates, disdaining every consideration of moral virtue or public decency, endeavoured to seduce those whom they were unable to vanquish, and that by their orders the most brutal violence was offered to those whom they found it impossible to seduce. It is related that pious females, who were prepared to despise death, were sometimes condemned to a more severe trial, and called upon to determine whether they set a higher value on their religion or on their chastity. The youths to whose licentious embraces they were abandoned received a solemn exhortation from the judge to exert their most strenuous efforts to maintain the honour of Venus against the impious virgin who refused to burn incense on her altars. Their violence, however, was commonly disappointed, and the seasonable interposition of some miraculous power preserved the chaste spouses of Christ from the dishonour even of an involuntary defeat. We should not indeed neglect to remark that the more ancient as well as authentic memorials of the church are seldom polluted with these extravagant and indecent fictions. The total disregard of truth and probability in the representation of these primitive martyrdoms was occasioned by a very natural mistake. The ecclesiastical writers of the fourth or fifth centuries ascribed to the magistrates of Rome the same degree of implacable and unrelenting zeal which filled their own breasts against the heretics or the idolaters of their own times.

The sober discretion of the present age will more readily censure than admire, but can more easily admire than imitate, the fervour of the first Christians, who, according to the lively expression of Sulpicius Severus, desired martyrdom with more eagerness than his own contemporaries solicited a bishopric. The epistles which Ignatius composed as he was carried in chains through the cities of Asia breathe sentiments the most repugnant to the ordinary feelings of human nature. He earnestly beseeches the Romans that, when he should be exposed in the amphitheatre, they would not, by their kind but unseasonable intercession, deprive him of the crown of glory; and he declares his resolution to provoke and irritate the wild beasts which might be employed as the instruments of his death. Some stories are related of the courage of martyrs who actually performed what Ignatius had intended, who exasperated the fury of the lions, pressed the executioner to hasten his office, cheerfully leaped into the fires which were kindled to consume them, and discovered a sensation of joy and pleasure in the midst of the most exquisite tortures. Several examples have been preserved of a zeal impatient of those restraints which the emperors had provided for the security of the church. The Christians some-times supplied by their voluntary declaration the want of an accuser, rudely disturbed the public service of paganism, and, rushing in crowds round the tribunal of the magistrates, called upon them to pronounce and to inflict the sentence of the law. The behaviour of the Christians was too remarkable to escape the notice of the ancient philosophers, but they seem to have considered it with much less admiration than astonishment. Incapable of conceiving the motives which sometimes transported the fortitude of believers beyond the bounds of prudence or reason, they treated such an eagerness to die as the strange result of obstinate despair,

of stupid insensibility, or of superstitious frenzy. "Unhappy men!"
exclaimed the proconsul Antoninus to the Christians of Asia,
"unhappy men! if you are thus weary of your lives, is it so difficult
for you to find ropes and precipices?" He was extremely cautious
(as it is observed by a learned and pious historian) of punishing
men who had found no accusers but themselves, the imperial laws
not having made any provisions for so unexpected a case; condemning therefore a few as a warning to their brethren, he dismissed
the multitude with indignation and contempt.

As the lives of the faithful became less mortified and austere,
they were every day less ambitious of the honours of martyrdom;
and the soldiers of Christ, instead of distinguishing themselves by
voluntary deeds of heroism, frequently deserted their post, and fled
in confusion before the enemy whom it was their duty to resist.
There were three methods, however, of escaping the flames of
persecution, which were not attended with an equal degree of guilt:
the first indeed was generally allowed to be innocent; the second
was of a doubtful or at least of a venial, nature; but the third
implied a direct and criminal apostasy from the Christian faith.

I. A modern Inquisitor would hear with surprise, that, whenever
an information was given to a Roman magistrate of any person
within his jurisdiction who had embraced the sect of the Christians,
the charge was communicated to the party accused, and that a
convenient time was allowed him to settle his domestic concerns,
and to prepare an answer to the crime which was imputed to him.
If he entertained any doubt of his own constancy, such a delay
afforded him the opportunity of preserving his life and honour by
flight, of withdrawing himself into some obscure retirement or
some distant province, and of patiently expecting the return of
peace and security. A measure so consonant to reason was soon
authorised by the advice and example of the most holy prelates;
and seems to have been censured by few, except by the Montanists,
who deviated into heresy by their strict and obstinate adherence to
the rigour of ancient discipline. II. The provincial governors, whose
zeal was less prevalent than their avarice, had countenanced the
practice of selling certificates (or libels as they were called), which
attested that the persons therein mentioned had complied with the
laws, and sacrificed to the Roman deities. By producing these false
declarations, the opulent and timid Christians were enabled to
silence the malice of an informer, and to reconcile in some measure
their safety with their religion. A slight penance atoned for this

profane dissimulation. III. In every persecution there were great numbers of unworthy Christians who publicly disowned or renounced the faith which they had professed; and who confirmed the sincerity of their abjuration by the legal acts of burning incense or of offering sacrifices. Some of these apostates had yielded on the first menace or exhortation of the magistrate; whilst the patience of others had been subdued by the length and repetition of tortures. The affrighted countenances of some betrayed their inward remorse, while others advanced with confidence and alacrity to the altars of the gods. But the disguise which fear had imposed subsisted no longer than the present danger. As soon as the severity of the persecution was abated, the doors of the churches were assailed by the returning multitude of penitents, who detested their idolatrous submission, and who solicited with equal ardour, but with various success, their readmission into the society of Christians.

IV. Notwithstanding the general rules established for the conviction and punishment of the Christians, the fate of those sectaries, in an extensive and arbitrary government, must still, in a great measure, have depended on their own behaviour, the circumstances of the times, and the temper of their supreme as well as subordinate rulers. Zeal might sometimes provoke, and prudence might sometimes avert or assuage, the superstitious fury of the Pagans. A variety of motives might dispose the provincial governors either to enforce or to relax the execution of the laws; and of these motives the most forcible was their regard not only for the public edicts, but for the secret intentions of the emperor, a glance from whose eye was sufficient to kindle or to extinguish the flames of persecution. As often as any occasional severities were exercised in the different parts of the empire, the primitive Christians lamented and perhaps magnified their own sufferings; but the celebrated number of *ten* persecutions has been determined by the ecclesiastical writers of the fifth century, who possessed a more distinct view of the prosperous or adverse fortunes of the church from the age of Nero to that of Diocletian. The ingenious parallels of the *ten* plagues of Egypt, and of the *ten* horns of the Apocalypse, first suggested this calculation to their minds; and in their application of the faith of prophecy to the truth of history they were careful to select those reigns which were indeed the most hostile to the Christian cause. But these transient persecutions served only to revive the zeal and to restore the discipline of the faithful; and the moments of extraordinary rigour were compensated by much longer intervals of peace and security. The indifference of some princes and the indulgence of others permitted the Christians to enjoy, though not perhaps a legal, yet an actual and public toleration of their religion.

During the whole course of his reign Marcus despised the Christians as a philosopher, and punished them as a sovereign. By a singular fatality, the hardships which they had endured under the government of a virtuous prince immediately ceased on the accession of a tyrant; and as none except themselves had experienced the injustice of Marcus, so they alone were protected by the lenity of Commodus. The celebrated Marcia, the most favoured of his concubines, and who at length contrived the murder of her Imperial lover, entertained a singular affection for the oppressed church; and though it was impossible that she could reconcile the practice of vice with the precepts of the Gospel, she might hope to atone for the frailties of her sex and profession by declaring herself the patroness of the Christians. Under the gracious protection of Marcia they passed in safety the thirteen years of a cruel tyranny; and when the empire was established in the house of Severus, they formed a domestic but more honourable connection with the new court. The emperor was persuaded that, in a dangerous sickness, he had derived some benefit, either spiritual or physical, from the holy oil with which one of his slaves had anointed him. He always treated with peculiar distinction several persons of both sexes who had embraced the new religion. The nurse as well as the preceptor of Caracalla were Christians; and if that young prince ever betrayed a sentiment of humanity, it was occasioned by an incident which, however trifling, bore some relation to the cause of Christianity. Under the reign of Severus the fury of the populace was checked; the rigour of ancient laws was for some time suspended; and the provincial governors were satisfied with receiving an annual present from the churches within their jurisdiction, as the price, or as the reward, of their moderation. The controversy concerning the precise time of the celebration of Easter armed the bishops of Asia and Italy against each other, and was considered as the most important business of this period of leisure and tranquillity. Nor was the peace of the church interrupted till the increasing numbers of proselytes seem at length to have attracted the attention, and to have alienated the mind, of Severus. With the design of restraining the progress of Christianity, he published an edict, which, though it was designed to affect only the new converts, could not be carried into strict execution without exposing to danger and punishment the most zealous of their teachers and missionaries. In this mitigated persecution we may still discover the indulgent spirit of Rome and of the Polytheism, which so readily admitted every excuse in favour of those who practised the religious ceremonies of their fathers.

But the laws which Severus had enacted soon expired with the authority of that emperor; and the Christians, after this accidental tempest, enjoyed a calm of thirty-eight years. Till this period they had usually held their assemblies in private houses and sequestered places. They were now permitted to erect and consecrate convenient edifices for the purpose of religious worship; to purchase lands, even at Rome itself, for the use of the community; and to conduct the elections of their ecclesiastical ministers in so public, but at the same time in so exemplary a manner, as to deserve the respectful attention of the Gentiles. This long repose of the church was accompanied with dignity. The reigns of those princes who derived their extraction from the Asiatic provinces proved the most favourable to the Christians; the eminent persons of the sect, instead of being reduced to implore the protection of a slave or concubine, were admitted into the palace in the honourable characters of priests and philosophers; and their mysterious doctrines, which were already diffused among the people, insensibly attracted the curiosity of their sovereign. When the empress Mamæa passed through Antioch, she expressed a desire of conversing with the celebrated Origen, the fame of whose piety and learning was spread over the East. Origen obeyed so flattering an invitation, and, though he could not expect to succeed in the conversion of an artful and ambitious woman, she listened with pleasure to his eloquent exhortations, and honourably dismissed him to his retirement in Palestine. The sentiments of Mamæa were adopted by her son Alexander, and the philosophic devotion of that emperor was marked by a singular but injudicious regard for the Christian religion. In his domestic chapel he placed the statues of Abraham, of Orpheus, of Apollonius, and of Christ, as an honour justly due to those respectable sages who had instructed mankind in the various modes of addressing their homage to the supreme and universal Deity. A purer faith, as well as worship, was openly professed and practised among his household. Bishops, perhaps for the first time, were seen at court; and, after the death of Alexander, when the inhuman Maximin discharged his fury on the favourites and servants of his unfortunate benefactor, a great number of Christians, of every rank, and of both sexes, were involved in the promiscuous massacre, which, on their account, has improperly received the name of Persecution.

Notwithstanding the cruel disposition of Maximin, the effects of his resentment against the Christians were of a very local and temporary nature, and the pious Origen, who had been proscribed as a devoted victim, was still reserved to convey the truths of the Gospel to the ear of monarchs. He addressed several edifying letters to the emperor Philip, to his wife, and to his mother, and as soon as that prince, who was born in the neighbourhood of Palestine, had usurped the Imperial sceptre, the Christians acquired a friend and a protector. The public and even partial favour of Philip towards the sectaries of the new religion, and his constant reverence for the ministers of the church, gave some colour to the suspicion, which prevailed in his own times, that the emperor himself was become a convert to the faith; and afforded some grounds for a fable which was afterwards invented, that he had been purified by confession and penance from the guilt contracted by the murder of his innocent predecessor. The fall of Philip introduced, with the change of masters, a new system of government, so oppressive to the Christians, that their former condition, ever since the time of Domitian, was represented as a state of perfect freedom and security, if compared with the rigorous treatment which they experienced under the short reign of Decius. The virtues of that prince will scarcely allow us to suspect that he was actuated by a mean resentment against the favourites of his predecessor; and it is more reasonable to believe that, in the prosecution of his general design to restore the purity of Roman manners, he was desirous of delivering the empire from what he condemned as a recent and criminal superstition. The bishops of the most considerable cities were removed by exile or death: the vigilance of the magistrates prevented the clergy of Rome during sixteen months from pro-ceeding to a new election; and it was the opinion of the Christians that the emperor would more patiently endure a competitor for the purple than a bishop in the capital. Were it possible to suppose that the penetration of Decius had discovered pride under the disguise of humility, or that he could foresee the temporal dominion which might insensibly arise from the claims of spiritual authority, we might be less surprised that he should consider the successors of St. Peter as the most formidable rivals to those of Augustus.

The administration of Valerian was distinguished by a levity and inconstancy ill suited to the gravity of the *Roman Censor*. In the first part of his reign he surpassed in clemency those princes who had been suspected of an attachment to the Christian faith. In the last three years and a half, listening to the insinuations of a minister addicted to the superstitions of Egypt, he adopted the maxims, and imitated the severity, of his predecessor Decius. The accession of Gallienus, which increased the calamities of the empire, restored peace to the church; and the Christians obtained the free exercise of their religion by an edict addressed to the bishops, and conceived in such terms as seemed to acknowledge their office and public character. The ancient laws, without being formally repealed, were suffered to sink into oblivion; and (excepting only some hostile intentions which are attributed to the emperor Aurelian) the disciples of Christ passed above forty years in a state of prosperity, far more dangerous to their virtue than the severest trials of persecution.

Notwithstanding a celebrated era of martyrs has been deduced from the accession of Diocletian, the new system of policy, introduced and maintained by the wisdom of that prince, continued, during more than eighteen years, to breathe the mildest and most liberal spirit of religious toleration. The mind of Diocletian himself was less adapted indeed to speculative inquiries than to the active labours of war and government. His prudence rendered him averse to any great innovation, and, though his temper was not very susceptible of zeal or enthusiasm, he always maintained an habitual regard for the ancient deities of the empire. But the leisure of the two empresses, of his wife Prisca, and of Valeria his daughter, permitted them to listen with more attention and respect to the truths of Christianity, which in every age has acknowledged its important obligations to female devotion. The principal eunuchs, Lucian and Dorotheus, Gorgonius and Andrew, who attended the person, possessed the favour, and governed the household of Diocletian, protected by their powerful influence the faith which they had embraced. Their example was imitated by many of the most considerable officers of the palace, who, in their respective stations, had the care of the Imperial ornaments, of the robes, of the furniture, of the jewels, and even of the private treasury; and, though it might sometimes be incumbent on them to accompany the emperor when he sacrificed in the temple, they enjoyed, with their wives, their children, and their slaves, the free exercise of the Christian religion. Diocletian and his colleagues frequently conferred the most important offices on those persons who avowed their abhorrence for the worship of the gods, but who had displayed abilities proper for the service of the state.

The bishops held an honourable rank in their respective provinces, and were treated with distinction and respect, not only by the people, but by the magistrates themselves. Almost in every city the ancient churches were found insufficient to contain the increasing multitude of proselytes; and in their place more stately and capacious edifices were erected for the public worship of the faithful. The corruption of manners and principles, so forcibly lamented by Eusebius, may be considered, not only as a consequence, but as a proof, of the liberty which the Christians enjoyed and abused under the reign of Diocletian. Prosperity had relaxed the nerves of discipline. Fraud, envy, and malice prevailed in every congregation. The presbyters aspired to the episcopal office, which every day became an object more worthy of their ambition. The bishops, who contended with each other for ecclesiastical pre-eminence, appeared by their conduct to claim a secular and tyrannical power in the church; and the lively faith which still distinguished the Christians from the Gentiles was shown much less in their lives than in their controversial writings.

Although the policy of Diocletian and humanity of Constantius inclined them to preserve inviolate the maxims of toleration, it was soon discovered that their two associates, Maximian and Galerius, entertained the most implacable aversion for the name and religion of the Christians. After the success of the Persian war had raised the hopes and the reputation of Galerius, he passed a winter with Diocletian in the palace of Nicomedia; and the fate of Christianity became the object of their secret consultations. The experienced emperor was still inclined to pursue measures of lenity; and though he readily consented to exclude the Christians from holding any employments in the household or the army, he urged in the strongest terms the danger as well as cruelty of shedding the blood of those deluded fanatics. Galerius at length extorted from him the permission of summoning a council, composed of a few persons the most distinguished in the civil and military departments of the state. The important question was agitated in their presence, and those ambitious courtiers easily discerned that it was incumbent on them to second, by their own eloquence, the importunate violence of the Cæsar. It may be presumed that they insisted on every topic which might interest the pride, the piety, or the fears, of their sovereign in the destruction of Christianity. Perhaps they represented that the glorious work of the deliverance of the empire was left imperfect, as long as an independent people was permitted to subsist and multiply in the heart of the provinces. The Christians (it might speciously be alleged), renouncing the gods and the institutions of Rome, had constituted a distinct republic, which might yet be suppressed before it had acquired any military force; but which was already governed by its own laws and magistrates, was possessed of a public treasure, and was intimately connected in all its parts by the frequent assemblies of the bishops, to whose decrees their numerous and opulent congregations yielded an implicit obedience. Arguments like these may seem to have determined the reluctant mind of Diocletian to embrace a new system of persecution: but though we may suspect, it is not in our power to relate, the secret intrigues of the palace, the private views and resentments, the jealousy of women or eunuchs, and all those trifling but decisive causes which so often influence the fate of empires and the councils of the wisest monarchs.

The pleasure of the emperors was at length signified to the Christians, who, during the course of this melancholy winter, had expected, with anxiety, the result of so many secret consultations. The twenty-third of February, which coincided with the Roman festival of the Terminalia, was appointed (whether from accident or design) to set bounds to the progress of Christianity. At the earliest dawn of day the Prætorian præfect, accompanied by several generals, tribunes, and officers of the revenue, repaired to the principal church of Nicomedia, which was situated on an eminence in the most populous and beautiful part of the city. The doors were instantly broken open; they rushed into the sanctuary; and as they searched in vain for some visible object of worship, they were obliged to content themselves with committing to the flames the volumes of Holy Scripture. The ministers of Diocletian were followed by a numerous body of guards and pioneers, who marched in order of battle, and were provided with all the instruments used in the destruction of fortified cities. By their incessant labour, a sacred edifice, which towered above the Imperial palace, and had long excited the indignation and envy of the Gentiles, was in a few hours levelled with the ground.

The next day the general edict of persecution was published; and though Diocletian, still averse to the effusion of blood, had moderated the fury of Galerius, who proposed that every one refusing to offer sacrifice should immediately be burnt alive, the penalties inflicted on the obstinacy of the Christians might be deemed sufficiently rigorous and effectual. It was enacted that their churches, in all the provinces of the empire, should be demolished to their foundations; and the punishment of death was denounced against all who should presume to hold any secret assemblies for the purpose of religious worship. The philosophers, who now assumed the unworthy office of directing the blind zeal of persecution, had diligently studied the nature and genius of the Christian religion; and as they were not ignorant that the speculative doctrines of the faith were supposed to be contained in the writings of the prophets, of the evangelists, and of the apostles, they most probably suggested the order that the bishops and presbyters should deliver all their sacred books into the hands of the magistrates; who were commanded, under the severest penalties, to burn them in a public and solemn manner. By the same edict, the property of the church was at once confiscated; and the several parts of which it might consist were either sold to the highest bidder, united to the Imperial domain, bestowed on the cities and corporations, or granted to the solicitations of rapacious courtiers. After taking such effectual measures to abolish the worship and to dissolve the government of the Christians, it was thought necessary to subject to the most intolerable hardships the condition of those perverse individuals who should still reject the religion of nature, of Rome, and of their ancestors. Persons of a liberal birth were declared incapable of holding any honours or employments; slaves were for ever deprived of the hopes of freedom; and the whole body of the people were put out of the protection of the law. The judges were authorised to hear and to determine every action that was brought against Christian. But the Christians were not permitted to complain of any injury which they themselves had suffered; and thus those unfortunate sectaries were exposed to the severity, while they were excluded from the benefits, of public justice. This new species of martyrdom, so painful and lingering, so obscure and ignominious, was, perhaps, the most proper to weary the constancy of the faithful: nor can it be doubted that the passions and interest of mankind were disposed on this occasion to second the designs of the emperors. But the policy of a well-ordered government must some-times have interposed in behalf of the oppressed Christians; nor was it possible for the Roman princes entirely to remove the apprehension of punishment, or to connive at every act of fraud and violence, without exposing their own authority and the rest of their subjects to the most alarming dangers.

This edict was scarcely exhibited to the public view, in the most conspicuous place of Nicomedia, before it was torn down by the hands of a Christian, who expressed at the same time, by the bitterest invectives, his contempt as well as abhorrence for such impious and tyrannical governors. His offence, according to the mildest laws, amounted to treason, and deserved death. And if it be true that he was a person of rank and education, those circumstances could serve only to aggravate his guilt. He was burnt, or rather roasted, by a slow fire; and his executioners, zealous to revenge the personal insult which had been offered to the emperors, exhausted every refinement of cruelty, without being able to subdue his patience, or to alter the steady and insulting smile which, in his dying agonies, he still preserved in his countenance. The Christians, though they confessed that his conduct had not been strictly conformable to the laws of prudence, admired the divine fervour of his zeal; and the excessive commendations which they lavished on the memory of their hero and martyr contributed to fix a deep impression of terror and hatred in the mind of Diocletian.

His fears were soon alarmed by the view of a danger from which he very narrowly escaped. Within fifteen days the palace of Nicomedia, and even the bedchamber of Diocletian, were twice in flames; and though both times they were extinguished without any material damage, the singular repetition of the fire was justly considered as an evident proof that it had not been the effect of chance or negligence. The suspicion naturally fell on the Christians; and it was suggested, with some degree of probability, that those desperate fanatics, provoked by their present sufferings, and apprehensive of impending calamities, had entered into a conspiracy with their faithful brethren, the eunuchs of the palace, against the lives of two emperors whom they detested as the irreconcilable enemies of the church of God. Jealousy and resentment prevailed in every breast, but especially in that of Diocletian. A great number of persons, distinguished either by the offices which they had filled or by the favour which they had enjoyed, were thrown into prison. Every mode of torture was put in practice, and the court, as well as city, was polluted with many bloody executions. But as it was found impossible to extort any discovery of this mysterious transaction, it seems incumbent on us either to presume the innocence, or to admire the resolution, of the sufferers. A few days afterwards Galerius hastily withdrew himself from Nicomedia, declaring that, if he delayed his departure from that devoted palace, he should fall a sacrifice to the rage of the Christians. The ecclesiastical historians, from whom alone we derive a partial and imperfect knowledge of this persecution, are at a loss how to account for the fears and danger of the emperors. Two of these writers, a prince and a rhetorician, were eye-witnesses of the fire of Nicomedia. The one ascribes it to lightning and the divine wrath, the other affirms that it was kindled by the malice of Galerius himself.

Diocletian had no sooner published his edicts against the Christians than, as if he had been desirous of committing to other hands the work of persecution, he divested himself of the Imperial purple. The character and situation of his colleagues and successors sometimes urged them to enforce, and sometimes inclined them to suspend, the execution of these rigorous laws; nor can we acquire a just and distinct idea of this important period of ecclesiastical history unless we separately consider the state of Christianity, in the different parts of the empire, during the space of ten years which elapsed between the first edicts of Diocletian and the final peace of the church.

The mild and humane temper of Constantius was averse to the oppression of any part of his subjects. The principal offices of his palace were exercised by Christians. He loved their persons, esteemed their fidelity, and entertained not any dislike to their religious principles. But as long as Constantius remained in the subordinate station of Cæsar, it was not in his power openly to reject the edicts of Diocletian, or to disobey the commands of Maximian. His authority contributed, however, to alleviate the sufferings which he pitied and abhorred. He consented with reluctance to the ruin of the churches, but he ventured to protect the Christians themselves from the fury of the populace and from the rigour of the laws. The provinces of Gaul (under which we may probably include those of Britain) were indebted for the singular tranquillity which they enjoyed to the gentle interposition of their sovereign. But Datianus, the president or governor of Spain, actuated either by zeal or policy, chose rather to execute the public edicts of the emperors than to understand the secret intentions of Constantius; and it can scarcely be doubted that his provincial administration was stained with the blood of a few martyrs.

The elevation of Constantius to the supreme and independent dignity of Augustus gave a free scope to the exercise of his virtues, and the shortness of his reign did not prevent him from establishing a system of toleration of which he left the precept and the example to his son Constantine. His fortunate son, from the first moment of his accession declaring himself the protector of the church, at length deserved the appellation of the first emperor who publicly professed and established the Christian religion. The motives of his conversion, as they may variously be deduced from benevolence, from policy, from conviction, or from remorse, and the progress of the revolution, which, under his powerful influence and that of his sons, rendered Christianity the reigning religion of the Roman empire, will form a very interesting and important chapter in the second volume of this history. At present it may be sufficient to observe that every victory of Constantine was productive of some relief or benefit to the church.

The provinces of Italy and Africa experienced a short but violent persecution. The rigorous edicts of Diocletian were strictly and cheerfully executed by his associate Maximian, who had long hated the Christians, and who delighted in acts of blood and violence. In the autumn of the first year of the persecution the two emperors met at Rome to celebrate their triumph; several oppressive laws appear to have issued from their secret consultations, and the diligence of the magistrates was animated by the presence of their sovereigns. After Diocletian had divested himself of the purple, Italy and Africa were administered under the name of Severus, and were exposed, without defence, to the implacable resentment of his master Galerius. Among the martyrs of Rome, Adauctus deserves the notice of posterity. He was of a noble family in Italy, and had raised himself, through the successive honours of the palace, to the important office of treasurer of the private demesnes. Adauctus is the more remarkable for being the only person of rank and distinction who appears to have suffered death during the whole course of this general persecution.

The revolt of Maxentius immediately restored peace to the churches of Italy and Africa, and the same tyrant who oppressed every other class of his subjects showed himself just, humane, and even partial, towards the afflicted Christians. He depended on their gratitude and affection, and very naturally presumed that the injuries which they had suffered, and the dangers which they still apprehended, from his most inveterate enemy, would secure the fidelity of a party already considerable by their numbers and opulence.

The sanguinary temper of Galerius, the first and principal author of the persecution, was formidable to those Christians whom their misfortunes had placed within the limits of his dominions; and it may fairly be presumed that many persons of a middle rank, who were not confined by the chains either of wealth or of poverty, very frequently deserted their native country, and sought a refuge in the milder climate of the West. As long as he commanded only the armies and provinces of Illyricum, he could with difficulty either find or make a considerable number of martyrs in a warlike country which had entertained the missionaries of the Gospel with more coldness and reluctance than any other part of the empire. But when Galerius had obtained the supreme power and the government of the East, he indulged in their fullest extent his zeal and cruelty, not only in the provinces of Thrace and Asia, which acknowledged his immediate jurisdiction, but in those of Syria, Palestine, and Egypt, where Maximin gratified his own inclination by yielding a rigorous obedience to the stern commands of his benefactor.

The frequent disappointments of his ambitious views, the experience of six years of persecution, and the salutary reflections which a lingering and painful distemper suggested to the mind of Galerius, at length convinced him that the most violent efforts of despotism are insufficient to extirpate a whole people, or to subdue their religious prejudices. Desirous of repairing the mischief that he had occasioned, he published in his own name, and in those of Licinius and Constantine, a general edict, which, after a pompous recital of the Imperial titles, proceeded in the following manner:

"Among the important cares which have occupied our mind for the utility and preservation of the empire, it was our intention to correct and re-establish all things according to the ancient laws and public discipline of the Romans. We were particularly desirous of reclaiming into the way of reason and nature the deluded Christians who had renounced the religion and ceremonies instituted by their fathers, and, presumptuously despising the practice of antiquity, had invented extravagant laws and opinions according to the dictates of their fancy, and had collected a various society from the different provinces of our empire. The edicts which we have published to enforce the worship of the gods having exposed many of the Christians to danger and distress, many having suffered death, and many more, who still persist in their impious folly, being left destitute of *any* public exercise of religion, we are disposed to extend to those unhappy men the effects of our wonted clemency. We permit them, therefore, freely to profess their private opinions, and to assemble in their conventicles without fear or molestation, provided always that they preserve a due respect to the established laws and government. By another rescript we shall signify our intentions to the judges and magistrates, and we hope that our indulgence will engage the Christians to offer up their prayers to the Deity whom they adore for our safety and prosperity, for their own, and for that of the republic." It is not usually in the language of edicts and manifestos that we should search for the real character of the secret motives of princes; but as these were the words of a dying emperor, his situation, perhaps, may be admitted as a pledge of his sincerity.

When Galerius subscribed this edict of toleration, he was well assured that Licinius would readily comply with the inclinations of his friend and benefactor, and that any measures in favour of the Christians would obtain the approbation of Constantine. But the emperor would not venture to insert in the preamble the name of Maximin, whose consent was of the greatest importance, and who succeeded a few days afterwards to the provinces of Asia. In the first six months, however, of his new reign, Maximin affected to adopt the prudent counsels of his predecessor; and though he never condescended to secure the tranquillity of the church by a public edict, Sabinus, his Prætorian præfect, addressed a circular letter to all the governors and magistrates of the provinces, expatiating on the Imperial clemency, acknowledging the invincible obstinacy of the Christians, and directing the officers of justice to cease their ineffectual prosecutions, and to connive at the secret assemblies of those enthusiasts.

The vague descriptions of exile and imprisonment, of pain and torture, are so easily exaggerated or softened by the pencil of an artful orator, that we are naturally induced to inquire into a fact of a more distinct and stubborn kind; the number of persons who suffered death in consequence of the edicts published by Diocletian, his associates, and his successors. The recent legendaries record whole armies and cities which were at once swept away by the undistinguishing rage of persecution. The more ancient writers content themselves with pouring out a liberal effusion of loose and tragical invectives, without condescending to ascertain the precise number of those persons who were permitted to seal with their blood their belief of the Gospel. From the history of Eusebius it may however be collected that only nine bishops were punished with death; and we are assured, by his particular enumeration of the martyrs of Palestine, that no more than ninety-two Christians were entitled to that honourable appellation. As we are unacquainted with the degree of episcopal zeal and courage which prevailed at that time, it is not in our power to draw any useful inferences from the former of these facts: but the latter may serve to justify a very important and probable conclusion. According to the distribution of Roman provinces, Palestine may be considered as the sixteenth part of the Eastern empire: and since there were some governors who, from a real or affected clemency, had preserved their hands unstained with the blood of the faithful, it is reasonable to believe that the country which had given birth to Christianity produced at least the sixteenth part of the martyrs who suffered death within the dominions of Galerius and Maximin; the whole might consequently amount to about fifteen hundred, a number which, if it is equally divided between the ten years of the persecution, will allow an annual consumption of one hundred and fifty martyrs. Allotting the same proportion to the provinces of Italy, Africa, and perhaps Spain, where, at the end of two or three years, the rigour of the penal laws was either suspended or abolished, the multitude of Christians in the Roman empire, on whom a capital punishment was inflicted by a judicial sentence, will be reduced to somewhat less than two thousand persons. Since it cannot be doubted that the Christians were more numerous, and their enemies more exasperated, in the time of Diocletian than they had ever been in any former persecution, this probable and moderate computation may teach us to estimate the number of primitive saints and martyrs who sacrificed their lives for the important purpose of introducing Christianity into the world.

We shall conclude this chapter by a melancholy truth which obtrudes itself on the reluctant mind; that, even admitting, without hesitation or inquiry, all that history has recorded, or devotion has feigned, on the subject of martyrdoms, it must still be acknowledged that the Christians, in the course of their intestine dissensions, have inflicted far greater severities on each other than they had experienced from the zeal of infidels. During the ages of ignorance which followed the subversion of the Roman empire in the West, the bishops of the Imperial city extended their dominion over the laity as well as clergy of the Latin church. The fabric of superstition which they had erected, and which might long have defied the feeble efforts of reason, was at length assaulted by a crowd of daring fanatics, who, from the twelfth to the sixteenth century, assumed the popular character of reformers. The church of Rome defended by violence the empire which she had acquired by fraud; a system of peace and benevolence was soon disgraced by the proscriptions, wars, massacres, and the institution of the holy office. And as the reformers were animated by the love of civil as well as of religious freedom, the Catholic princes connected their own interest with that of the clergy, and enforced by fire and the sword the terrors of spiritual censures. In the Netherlands alone more than one hundred thousand of the subjects of Charles V. are said to have suffered by the hand of the executioner; and this extraordinary number is attested by Grotius, a man of genius and learning, who preserved his moderation amidst the fury of contending sects, and who composed the annals of his own age and country at a time when the invention of printing had facilitated the means of intelligence and increased the danger of detection. If we are obliged to submit our belief to the authority of Grotius, it must be allowed that the number of Protestants who were executed in a single province and a single reign, far exceeded that of the primitive martyrs in the space of three centuries and of the Roman empire. But if the improbability of the fact itself should prevail over the weight of evidence; if Grotius should be convicted of exaggerating the merit and sufferings of the reformers; we shall be naturally led to inquire what confidence can be placed in the doubtful and imperfect monuments of ancient credulity; what degree of credit can be assigned to a courtly bishop and a passionate declaimer, who, under the protection of Constantine, enjoyed the exclusive privilege of recording the persecutions inflicted on the Christians by the vanquished rivals or disregarded predecessors of their gracious sovereign.

XV

(300–500 A.D.) FOUNDATION OF CONSTAN-
TINOPLE—POLITICAL SYSTEM OF CON-
STANTINE AND HIS SUCCESSORS—MILITARY
DISCIPLINE—THE PALACE—THE FINANCES

The unfortunate Licinius was the last rival who opposed the greatness,
and the last captive who adorned the triumph, of Constantine.
After a tranquil and prosperous reign the conqueror bequeathed to
his family the inheritance of the Roman empire; a new capital, a
new policy, and a new religion; and the innovations which he
established have been embraced and consecrated by succeeding
generations. The age of the great Constantine and his sons is filled
with important events; but the historian must be oppressed by their
number and variety, unless he diligently separates from each other
the scenes which are connected only by the order of time. He will
describe the political institutions that gave strength and stability to
the empire before he proceeds to relate the wars and revolutions
which hastened its decline. He will adopt the division unknown to
the ancients of civil and ecclesiastical affairs: the victory of the
Christians, and their intestine discord, will supply copious and
distinct materials both for edification and for scandal.

After the defeat and abdication of Licinius his victorious rival
proceeded to lay the foundations of a city destined to reign in
future times the mistress of the East, and to survive the empire and
religion of Constantine. The motives, whether of pride or of policy,
which first induced Diocletian to withdraw himself from the
ancient seat of government, had acquired additional weight by the
example of his successors and the habits of forty years. Rome was
insensibly confounded with the dependent kingdoms which had
once acknowledged her supremacy; and the country of the Cæsars
was viewed with cold indifference by a martial prince, born in the
neighbourhood of the Danube, educated in the courts and armies
of Asia, and invested with the purple by the legions of Britain. The
Italians, who had received Constantine as their deliverer, submissively

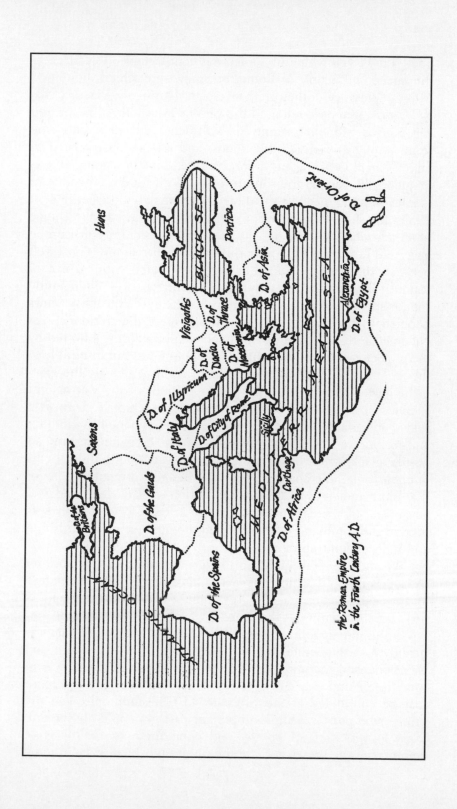

the Roman Empire
in the Fourth Century A.D.

obeyed the edicts which he sometimes condescended to address to the senate and people of Rome; but they were seldom honoured with the presence of their new sovereign. During the vigour of his age Constantine, according to the various exigencies of peace and war, moved with slow dignity or with active diligence along the frontiers of his extensive dominions; and was always prepared to take the field either against a foreign or a domestic enemy. But as he gradually reached the summit of prosperity and the decline of life, he began to meditate the design of fixing in a more permanent station the strength as well as majesty of the throne. In the choice of an advantageous situation he preferred the confines of Europe and Asia; to curb with a powerful arm the barbarians who dwelt between the Danube and the Tanais; to watch with an eye of jealousy the conduct of the Persian monarch, who indignantly supported the yoke of an ignominious treaty. With these views Diocletian had selected and embellished the residence of Nicomedia: but the memory of Diocletian was justly abhorred by the protector of the church; and Constantine was not insensible to the ambition of founding a city which might perpetuate the glory of his own name. During the late operations of the war against Licinius he had sufficient opportunity to contemplate, both as a soldier and as a statesman, the incomparable position of Byzantium; and to observe how strongly it was guarded by nature against an hostile attack, whilst it was accessible on every side to the benefits of commercial intercourse. Many ages before Constantine, one of the most judicious historians of antiquity had described the advantages of a situation from whence a feeble colony of Greeks derived the command of the sea, and the honours of a flourishing and independent republic.

We are at present qualified to view the advantageous position of Constantinople, which appears to have been formed by nature for the centre and capital of a great monarchy. Situated in the forty-first degree of latitude, the Imperial city commanded, from her seven hills, the opposite shores of Europe and Asia; the climate was healthy and temperate, the soil fertile, the harbour secure and capacious, and the approach on the side of the continent was of small extent and easy defence. The Bosphorus and the Hellespont may be considered as the two gates of Constantinople, and the prince who possessed those important passages could always shut them against a naval enemy and open them to the fleets of commerce. The preservation of the eastern provinces may, in some degree, be ascribed to the policy of Constantine, as the barbarians of the Euxine, who in the preceding age had poured their armaments into the heart of the Mediterranean, soon desisted from the exercise of piracy, and despaired of forcing this insurmountable barrier. When the gates of the Hellespont and Bosphorus were shut, the capital still enjoyed within their spacious enclosure every production which could supply the wants or gratify the luxury of its numerous inhabitants. The seacoasts of Thrace and Bithynia, which languish under the weight of Turkish oppression, still exhibit a rich prospect of vineyards, of gardens, and of plentiful harvests; and the Propontis has ever been renowned for an inexhaustible store of the most exquisite fish, that are taken in their stated seasons, without skill, and almost without labour. But when the passages of the straits were thrown open for trade, they alternately admitted the natural and artificial riches of the north and south, of the Euxine and of the Mediterranean. Whatever rude commodities were collected in the forests of Germany and Scythia, as far as the sources of the Tanais and the Borysthenes; whatsoever was manufactured by the skill of Europe or Asia; the corn of Egypt, and the gems and spices of the farthest India, were brought by the varying winds into the port of Constantinople, which, for many ages, attracted the commerce of the ancient world.

The master of the Roman world, who aspired to erect an eternal monument of the glories of his reign, could employ in the prosecution of that great work the wealth, the labour, and all that yet remained of the genius, of obedient millions. Some estimate may be formed of the expense bestowed with Imperial liberality on the foundation of Constantinople by the allowance of about two millions five hundred thousand pounds for the construction of the walls, the porticoes, and the aqueducts. The forests that overshadowed the shores of the Euxine, and the celebrated quarries of white marble in the little island of Proconnesus, supplied an inexhaustible stock of materials, ready to be conveyed, by the convenience of a short water-carriage, to the harbour of Byzantium. A multitude of labourers and artificers urged the conclusion of the work with incessant toil; but the impatience of Constantine soon discovered that, in the decline of the arts, the skill as well as numbers of his architects bore a very unequal proportion to the greatness of his designs. The magistrates of the most distant provinces were therefore directed to institute schools, to appoint professors, and, by the hopes of rewards and privileges, to engage in the study and practice of architecture a sufficient number of ingenious youths who had received a liberal education. The buildings of the new city were executed by such artificers as the reign of Constantine could afford; but they were decorated by the hands of the most celebrated masters of the age of Pericles and Alexander. To revive the genius of Phidias and Lysippus surpassed indeed the power of a Roman emperor; but the immortal productions which they had bequeathed to posterity were exposed without defence to the rapacious vanity of a despot. By his commands the cities of Greece and Asia were despoiled of their most valuable ornaments. The trophies of memorable wars, the objects of religious veneration, the most finished statues of the gods and heroes, of the sages and poets of ancient times, contributed to the splendid triumph of Constantinople; and gave occasion to the remark of the historian Cedrenus, who observes, with some enthusiasm, that nothing seemed wanting except the souls of the illustrious men whom these admirable monuments were intended to represent. But it is not in the city of Constantine, nor in the declining period of an empire, when the human mind was depressed by civil and religious slavery, that we should seek for the souls of Homer and of Demosthenes.

We should deviate from the design of this history if we attempted minutely to describe the different buildings or quarters of the city. It may be sufficient to observe that whatever could adorn the dignity of a great capital, or contribute to the benefit or pleasure of its numerous inhabitants, was contained within the walls of Constantinople. A particular description, composed about a century after its foundation, enumerates a capitol or school of learning, a circus, two theatres, eight public and one hundred and fifty-three private baths, fifty-two porticoes, five granaries, eight aqueducts or reservoirs of water, four spacious halls for the meetings of the senate or courts of justice, fourteen churches, fourteen palaces, and four thousand three hundred and eighty-eight houses which, for their size or beauty, deserved to be distinguished from the multitude of plebeian habitations.

The populousness of his favoured city was the next and most serious object of the attention of its founder. In the dark ages which succeeded the translation of the empire, the remote and the immediate consequences of that memorable event were strangely confounded by the vanity of the Greeks and the credulity of the Latins. It was asserted and believed that all the noble families of Rome, the senate, and the equestrian order, with their innumerable attendants, had followed their emperor to the banks of the Propontis; that a spurious race of strangers and plebeians was left to possess the solitude of the ancient capital; and that the lands of Italy, long since converted into gardens, were at once deprived of cultivation and inhabitants. In the course of this history such exaggerations will be reduced to their just value; yet, since the growth of Constantinople cannot be ascribed to the general increase of mankind and of industry, it must be admitted that this artificial colony was raised at the expense of the ancient cities of the empire. Many opulent senators of Rome and of the eastern provinces were probably invited by Constantine to adopt for their country the fortunate spot which he had chosen for his own residence. The invitations of a master are scarcely to be distinguished from commands, and the liberality of the emperor obtained a ready and cheerful obedience. In less than a century Constantinople disputed with Rome itself the pre-eminence of riches and numbers. New piles of buildings, crowded together with too little regard to health or convenience, scarcely allowed the intervals of narrow streets for the perpetual throng of men, of horses, and of carriages. The allotted space of ground was insufficient to contain the increasing people, and the additional foundations, which on either side were advanced into the sea, might alone have composed a very considerable city.

The frequent and regular distributions of wine and oil, of corn or bread, of money or provisions, had almost exempted the poorer citizens of Rome from the necessity of labour. The magnificence of the first Cæsars was in some measure imitated by the founder of Constantinople: but his liberality, however it might excite the applause of the people, has incurred the censure of posterity. A nation of legislators and conquerors might assert their claim to the harvests of Africa, which had been purchased with their blood; and it was artfully contrived by Augustus, that, in the enjoyment of plenty, the Romans should lose the memory of freedom. But the prodigality of Constantine could not be excused by any consideration either of public or private interest; and the annual tribute of corn imposed upon Egypt for the benefit of his new capital was applied to feed a lazy and insolent populace, at the expense of the husbandmen of an industrious province. Some other regulations of this emperor are less liable to blame, but they are less deserving of notice. He divided Constantinople into fourteen regions or quarters, dignified the public council with the appellation of senate, communicated to the citizens the privileges of Italy, and bestowed on the rising city the title of Colony, the first and most favoured daughter of ancient Rome. The venerable parent still maintained the legal and acknowledged supremacy, which was due to her age, to her dignity, and to the remembrance of her former greatness.

The foundation of a new capital is naturally connected with the establishment of a new form of civil and military administration. The distinct view of the complicated system of policy introduced by Diocletian, improved by Constantine, and completed by his immediate successors, may not only amuse the fancy by the singular picture of a great empire, but will tend to illustrate the secret and internal causes of its rapid decay. In the pursuit of any remarkable institution, we may be frequently led into the more early or the more recent times of the Roman history; but the proper limits of this inquiry will be included within a period of about one hundred and thirty years, from the accession of Constantine to the publication of the Theodosian code; from which, as well as from the *Notitia* of the East and West, we derive the most copious and authentic information of the state of the empire. This variety of objects will suspend, for some time, the course of the narrative; but the interruption will be censured only by those readers who are insensible to the importance of laws and manners, while they peruse with eager curiosity, the transient intrigues of a court, or the accidental event of a battle.

The principal officers of the empire were saluted, even by the sovereign himself, with the deceitful titles of your *Sincerity*, your *Gravity*, your *Excellency*, your *Eminence*, your *sublime and wonderful Magnitude*, your *illustrious and magnificent Highness*. By a philosophic observer the system of the Roman government might have been mistaken for a splendid theatre, filled with players of every character and degree, who repeated the language, and imitated the passions, of their original model. All the magistrates of sufficient importance to find a place in the general state of the empire were accurately divided into three classes—1, The *Illustrious*; 2, The *Spectabiles*, or *Respectable*; and, 3, The *Clarissimi*, whom we may translate by the word *Honourable*. In the times of Roman simplicity, the last-mentioned epithet was used only as a vague expression of deference, till it became at length the peculiar and appropriated title of all who were members of the senate, and consequently of all who, from that venerable body, were selected to govern the provinces. The vanity of those who, from their rank and office, might claim a superior distinction above the rest of the senatorial order, was long afterwards indulged with the new appellation of *Respectable*: but the title of *Illustrious* was always reserved to some eminent personages who were obeyed or reverenced by the two subordinate classes. It was communicated only, I. To the consuls and patricians; II. To the Prætorian præfects, with the præfects of Rome and Constantinople; III. To the masters general of the cavalry and the infantry; and, IV. To the seven ministers of the palace, who exercised their *sacred* functions about the person of the emperor.

I. As long as the Roman consuls were the first magistrates of a free state, they derived their right to power from the choice of the people. As long as the emperors condescended to disguise the servitude which they imposed, the consuls were still elected by the real or apparent suffrage of the senate. From the reign of Diocletian even these vestiges of liberty were abolished, and the successful candidates, who were invested with the annual honours of the consulship, affected to deplore the humiliating condition of their predecessors. The Scipios and the Catos had been reduced to solicit the votes of plebeians, to pass through the tedious and expensive forms of a popular election, and to expose their dignity to the shame of a public refusal; while their own happier fate had reserved them for an age and government in which the rewards of virtue were assigned by the unerring wisdom of a gracious sovereign. Their abilities (unless they were employed in more effective offices) were of little moment; and their names served only as the legal date of the year in which they had filled the chair of Marius and of Cicero. Yet it was still felt and acknowledged, in the last period of Roman servitude, that this empty name might be compared, and even preferred, to the possession of substantial power. The title of consul was still the most splendid object of ambition, the noblest reward of virtue and loyalty. The emperors themselves, who disdained the faint shadow of the republic, were conscious that they acquired an additional splendour and majesty as often as they assumed the annual honours of the consular dignity.

The proudest and most perfect separation which can be found in any age or country between the nobles and the people is perhaps that of the Patricians and the Plebeians, as it was established in the first age of the Roman republic. Wealth and honours, the offices of the state, and the ceremonies of religion, were almost exclusively possessed by the former; who, preserving the purity of their blood with the most insulting jealousy, held their clients in a condition of specious vassalage. But these distinctions, so incompatible with the spirit of a free people, were removed, after a long struggle, by the persevering efforts of the Tribunes. The most active and successful of the Plebeians accumulated wealth, aspired to honours, deserved triumphs, contracted alliances, and, after some generations, assumed the pride of ancient nobility. The Patrician families, on the other hand, whose original number was never recruited till the end of the commonwealth, either failed in the ordinary course of nature, or were extinguished in so many foreign and domestic wars, or, through a want of merit or fortune, insensibly mingled with the mass of the people. Very few remained who could derive their pure and genuine origin from the infancy of the city, or even from that of the republic, when Cæsar and Augustus, Claudius and Vespasian, created from the body of the senate a competent number of new Patrician families, in the hope of perpetuating an order which was still considered as honourable and sacred. But these artificial supplies (in which the reigning house was always included) were rapidly swept away by the rage of tyrants, by frequent revolutions, by the change of manners, and by the intermixture of nations. Little more was left when Constantine ascended the throne than a vague and imperfect tradition that the Patricians had once been the first of the Romans. To form a body of nobles, whose influence may restrain while it secures the authority of the monarch, would have been very inconsistent with the character and policy of Constantine; but, had he seriously entertained such a design, it might have exceeded the measure of his power to ratify by an arbitrary edict an institution which must expect the sanction of time and of opinion. He revived, indeed, the title of PATRICIANS, but he revived it as a personal, not as an hereditary distinction. They yielded only to the transient superiority of the annual consuls; but they enjoyed the pre-eminence over all the great officers of state, with the most familiar access to the person of the prince. This honourable rank was bestowed on them for life; and, as they were usually favourites and ministers who had grown old in the Imperial court, the true etymology of the word was perverted by ignorance and flattery; and the Patricians of Constantine were reverenced as the adopted *Fathers* of the emperor and the republic.

II. The fortunes of the Prætorian præfects were essentially different from those of the consuls and Patricians. The latter saw their ancient greatness evaporate in a vain title. The former, rising by degrees from the most humble condition, were invested with the civil and military administration of the Roman world. From the reign of Severus to that of Diocletian, the guards and the palace, the laws and the finances, the armies and the provinces, were intrusted to their superintending care; and, like the vizirs of the East, they held with one hand the seal, and with the other the standard, of the empire. The ambition of the præfects, always formidable, and sometimes fatal to the masters whom they served, was supported by the strength of the Prætorian bands; but, after those haughty troops had been weakened by Diocletian and finally suppressed by Constantine, the præfects, who survived their fall, were reduced without difficulty to the station of useful and obedient ministers. When they were no longer responsible for the safety of the emperor's person, they resigned the jurisdiction which they had hitherto claimed and exercised over all the departments of the palace. They were deprived by Constantine of all military command as soon as they had ceased to lead into the field, under their immediate orders, the flower of the Roman troops; and, at length, by a singular revolution, the captains of the guards were transformed into the civil magistrates of the provinces. According to the plan of government instituted by Diocletian, the four princes had each their Prætorian præfect; and after the monarchy was once more united in the person of Constantine, he still continued to create the same number of FOUR PRAEFECTS, and intrusted to their care the same provinces which they already administered. To their wisdom was committed the supreme administration of justice and of the finances, the two objects which, in a state of peace, comprehend almost all the respective duties of the sovereign and of the people; of the former, to protect the citizens who are obedient to the laws; of the latter, to contribute the share of their property which is required for the expenses of the state. The coin, the highways, the posts, the granaries, the manufactures, whatever could interest the public prosperity, was moderated by the authority of the Prætorian præfects. As the immediate representatives of the Imperial majesty, they were empowered to explain, to enforce, and on some occasions to modify, the general edicts by their discretionary proclamations. They watched over the conduct of the provincial governors, removed the negligent, and inflicted punishments on the guilty. From all the inferior jurisdictions an appeal in every matter of importance, either civil or criminal, might be brought before the tribunal of the præfect: but *his* sentence was final and absolute; and the emperors themselves refused to admit any complaints against the judgment or the integrity of a magistrate whom they honoured with such unbounded confidence. His appointments were suitable to his dignity; and, if avarice was his ruling passion, he enjoyed frequent opportunities of collecting a rich harvest of fees, of presents, and of perquisites. Though the emperors no longer dreaded the ambition of their præfects, they were attentive to counterbalance the power of this great office by the uncertainty and shortness of its duration.

Those who in the Imperial hierarchy were distinguished by the title of *Respectable* formed an intermediate class between the *illustrious* præfects and the *honourable* magistrates of the provinces. In this class the proconsuls of Asia, Achaia, and Africa claimed a pre-eminence, which was yielded to the remembrance of their ancient dignity; and the appeal from their tribunal to that of the præfects was almost the only mark of their dependence. But the civil government of the empire was distributed into thirteen great DIOCESES, each of which equalled the just measure of a powerful kingdom. The first of these dioceses was subject to the jurisdiction of the count of the East; and we may convey some idea of the importance and variety of his functions by observing that six hundred apparitors, who would be styled at present either secretaries, or clerks, or ushers, or messengers, were employed in his immediate office. The place of *Augustal præfect* of Egypt was no longer filled by a Roman knight, but the name was retained; and the extraordinary powers which the situation of the country and the temper of the inhabitants had once made indispensable were still continued to the governor. The eleven remaining dioceses—of Asiana, Pontica, and Thrace; of Macedonia, Dacia, and Pannonia, or Western Illyricum; of Italy and Africa; of Gaul, Spain, and Britain—were governed by twelve *vicars* or *vice-præfects*, whose name sufficiently explains the nature and dependence of their office. It may be added that the lieutenant-generals of the Roman armies, the military counts and dukes, who will be hereafter mentioned, were allowed the rank and title of *Respectable*.

As the spirit of jealousy and ostentation prevailed in the councils of the emperors, they proceeded with anxious diligence to divide the substance and to multiply the titles of power. The vast countries which the Roman conquerors had united under the same simple form of administration were imperceptibly crumbled into minute fragments, till at length the whole empire was distributed into one hundred and sixteen provinces, each of which supported an expensive and splendid establishment. Of these, three were governed by *proconsuls*, thirty-seven by *consulars*, five by *correctors*, and seventy-one by *presidents*. The appellations of these magistrates were different; they ranked in successive order, the ensigns of their dignity were curiously varied, and their situation, from accidental circumstances, might be more or less agreeable or advantageous. But they were all (excepting only the proconsuls) alike included in the class of *honourable* persons; and they were alike intrusted, during the pleasure of the prince, and under the authority of the præfects or their deputies, with the administration of justice and the finances in their respective districts.

III. In the system of policy introduced by Augustus, the governors, those at least of the Imperial provinces, were invested with the full powers of the sovereign himself. Ministers of peace and war, the distribution of rewards and punishments depended on them alone, and they successively appeared on their tribunal in the robes of civil magistracy, and in complete armour at the head of the Roman legions. The influence of the revenue, the authority of law, and the command of a military force, concurred to render their power supreme and absolute; and whenever they were tempted to violate their allegiance, the loyal province which they involved in their rebellion was scarcely sensible of any change in its political state. From the time of Commodus to the reign of Constantine near one hundred governors might be enumerated, who, with various success, erected the standard of revolt; and though the innocent were too often sacrificed, the guilty might be sometimes prevented, by the suspicious cruelty of their master. To secure his throne and the public tranquillity from these formidable servants, Constantine resolved to divide the military from the civil administration, and to establish, as a permanent and professional distinction, a practice which had been adopted only as an occasional expedient The supreme jurisdiction exercised by the Prætorian præfects over the armies of the empire was transferred to the two *masters general* whom he instituted, the one for the *cavalry*, the other for the *infantry*; and though each of these *illustrious* officers was more peculiarly responsible for the discipline of those troops which were under his immediate inspection, they both indifferently commanded in the field the several bodies, whether of horse or foot, which were united in the same army. Their number was soon doubled by the division of the East and West; and as separate generals of the same rank and title were appointed on the four important frontiers of the

Rhine, of the Upper and the Lower Danube, and of the Euphrates, the defence of the Roman empire was at length committed to eight masters general of the cavalry and infantry. Under their orders, thirty-five military commanders were stationed in the provinces: three in Britain, six in Gaul, one in Spain, one in Italy, five on the Upper and four on the Lower Danube, in Asia eight, three in Egypt, and four in Africa. The titles of *counts* and *dukes*, by which they were properly distinguished, have obtained in modern languages so very different a sense that the use of them may occasion some surprise. But it should be recollected that the second of those appellations is only a corruption of the Latin word which was indiscriminately applied to any military chief. All these provincial generals were therefore *dukes*; but no more than ten among them were dignified with the rank of *counts* or companions, a title of honour, or rather of favour, which had been recently invented in the court of Constantine. A gold belt was the ensign which distinguished the office of the counts and dukes; and, besides their pay, they received a liberal allowance sufficient to maintain one hundred and ninety servants and one hundred and fifty-eight horses. They were strictly prohibited from interfering in any matter which related to the administration of justice or the revenue; but the command which they exercised over the troops of their department was independent of the authority of the magistrates. About the same time that Constantine gave a legal sanction to the ecclesiastical order, he instituted in the Roman empire the nice balance of the civil and the military powers. The emulation, and sometimes the discord, which reigned between two professions of opposite interests and incompatible manners, was productive of beneficial and of pernicious consequences. It was seldom to be expected that the general and the civil governor of a province should either conspire for the disturbance, or should unite for the service, of their country. While the one delayed to offer the assistance which the other disdained to solicit, the troops very frequently remained without orders or without supplies, the public safety was betrayed, and the defenceless subjects were left exposed to the fury of the barbarians. The divided administration, which had been formed by Constantine, relaxed the vigour of the state, while it secured the tranquillity of the monarch.

The memory of Constantine has been deservedly censured for another innovation which corrupted military discipline, and prepared the ruin of the empire. The nineteen years which preceded his final victory over Licinius had been a period of licence and intestine war. The rivals who contended for the possession of the Roman world had withdrawn the greatest part of their forces from the guard of the general frontier; and the principal cities which formed the boundary of their respective dominions were filled with soldiers, who considered their countrymen as their most implacable enemies. After the use of these internal garrisons had ceased with the civil war, the conqueror wanted either wisdom or firmness to revive the severe discipline of Diocletian, and to suppress a fatal indulgence which habit had endeared and almost confirmed to the military order. From the reign of Constantine a popular and even legal distinction was admitted between the *Palatines* and the *Borderers*; the troops of the court, as they were improperly styled, and the troops of the frontier. The former, elevated by the superiority of their pay and privileges, were permitted, except in the extraordinary emergencies of war, to occupy their tranquil stations in the heart of the provinces. The most flourishing cities were oppressed by the intolerable weight of quarters.

The soldiers insensibly forgot the virtues of their profession, and contracted only the vices of civil life. They were either degraded by the industry of mechanic trades, or enervated by the luxury of baths and theatres. They soon became careless of their martial exercises, curious in their diet and apparel, and, while they inspired terror to the subjects of the empire, they trembled at the hostile approach of the barbarians. The chain of fortifications which Diocletian and his colleagues had extended along the banks of the great rivers was no longer maintained with the same care, or defended with the same vigilance. The numbers which still remained under the name of the troops of the frontier might be sufficient for the ordinary defence. But their spirit was degraded by the humiliating reflection that *they*, who were exposed to the hardships and dangers of a perpetual warfare, were rewarded only with about two-thirds of the pay and emoluments which were lavished on the troops of the court. Even the bands or legions that were raised the nearest to the level of those unworthy favourites were in some measure disgraced by the title of honour which they were allowed to assume. It was in vain that Constantine repeated the most dreadful menaces of fire and sword against the Borderers who should dare to desert their colours, to connive at the inroads of the barbarians, or to participate in the spoil. The mischiefs which flow from injudicious counsels are seldom removed by the application of partial severities:

and though succeeding princes laboured to restore the strength and numbers of the frontier garrisons, the empire, till the last moment of its dissolution, continued to languish under the mortal wound which had been so rashly or so weakly inflicted by the hand of Constantine.

In the various states of society armies are recruited from very different motives. Barbarians are urged by their love of war; the citizens of a free republic may be prompted by a principle of duty; the subjects, or at least the nobles, of a monarchy are animated by a sentiment of honour; but the timid and luxurious inhabitants of a declining empire must be allured into the service by the hopes of profit, or compelled by the dread of punishment. The resources of the Roman treasury were exhausted by the increase of pay, by the repetition of donatives, and by the invention of new emoluments and indulgences, which, in the opinion of the provincial youth, might compensate the hardships and dangers of a military life. Yet, although the stature was lowered, although slaves, at least by a tacit connivance, were indiscriminately received into the ranks, the insurmountable difficulty of procuring a regular and adequate supply of volunteers obliged the emperors to adopt more effectual and coercive methods. The lands bestowed on the veterans, as the free reward of their valour, were henceforward granted under a condition which contains the first rudiments of the feudal tenures—that their sons, who succeeded to the inheritance, should devote themselves to the profession of arms as soon as they attained the age of manhood; and their cowardly refusal was punished by the loss of honour, of fortune, or even of life. But as the annual growth of the sons of the veterans bore a very small proportion to the demands of the service, levies of men were frequently required from the provinces, and every proprietor was obliged either to take up arms, or to procure a substitute, or to purchase his exemption by the payment of a heavy fine. The sum of forty-two pieces of gold, to which it was *reduced*, ascertains the exorbitant price of volunteers, and the reluctance with which the government admitted of this alternative. Such was the horror for the profession of a soldier which had affected the minds of the degenerate Romans that many of the youth of Italy and the provinces chose to cut off the fingers of their right hand to escape from being pressed into the service; and this strange expedient was so commonly practised as to deserve the severe animadversion of the laws, and a peculiar name in the Latin language.

The introduction of barbarians into the Roman armies became every day more universal, more necessary, and more fatal. The most daring of the Scythians, of the Goths, and of the Germans, who delighted in war, and who found it more profitable to defend than to ravage the provinces, were enrolled not only in the auxiliaries of their respective nations, but in the legions themselves, and among the most distinguished of the Palatine troops. As they freely mingled with the subjects of the empire, they gradually learned to despise their manners and to imitate their arts. They abjured the implicit reverence which the pride of Rome had exacted from their ignorance, while they acquired the knowledge and possession of those advantages by which alone she supported her declining greatness. The barbarian soldiers who displayed any military talents were advanced, without exception, to the most important commands; and the names of the tribunes, of the counts and dukes, and of the generals themselves, betray a foreign origin, which they no longer condescended to disguise. They were often intrusted with the conduct of a war against their countrymen; and though most of them preferred the ties of allegiance to those of blood, they did not always avoid the guilt, or at least the suspicion, of holding a treasonable correspondence with the enemy, of inviting his invasion, or of sparing his retreat. The camps and the palace of the son of Constantine were governed by the powerful faction of the Franks, who preserved the strictest connection with each other and with their country, and who resented every personal affront as a national indignity. When the tyrant Caligula was suspected of an intention to invest a very extraordinary candidate with the consular robes, the sacrilegious profanation would have scarcely excited less astonishment if, instead of a horse, the noblest chieftain of Germany or Britain had been the object of his choice. The revolution of three centuries had produced so remarkable a change in the prejudices of the people, that, with the public approbation, Constantine showed his successors the example of bestowing the honours of the consulship on the barbarians who, by their merit and services, had deserved to be ranked among the first of the Romans. But as these hardy veterans, who had been educated in the ignorance or contempt of the laws were incapable of exercising any civil offices, the powers of the human mind were contracted by the irreconcilable separation of talents as well as of professions. The accomplished citizens of the Greek and Roman republics, whose characters could adapt themselves to the bar, the senate, the camp, or the schools, had learned to write, to speak, and to act with the same spirit, and with equal abilities.

IV. Besides the magistrates and generals, who at a distance from the court diffused their delegated authority over the provinces and armies, the emperor conferred the rank of *Illustrious* on seven of his more immediate servants, to whose fidelity he intrusted his safety, or his counsels, or his treasures. 1. The private apartments of the palace were governed by a favourite eunuch, who, in the language of that age, was styled the *præpositus*, or præfect of the sacred bedchamber. His duty was to attend the emperor in his hours of state or in those of amusement, and to perform about his person all those menial services which can only derive their splendour from the influence of royalty. 2. The principal administration of public affairs was committed to the diligence and abilities of the *master of the offices*. He was the supreme magistrate of the palace, inspected the discipline of the civil and military *schools*, and received appeals from all parts of the empire, in the causes which related to that numerous army of privileged persons who, as the servants of the court, had obtained for themselves and families a right to decline the authority of the ordinary judges. The correspondence between the prince and his subjects was managed by the four *scrinia*, or offices of this minister of state. The first was appropriated to memorials, the second to epistles, the third to petitions, and the fourth to papers and orders of a miscellaneous kind. Each of these was directed by an inferior *master* of *respectable* dignity, and the whole business was despatched by an hundred and forty-eight secretaries, chosen for the most part from the profession of the law, on account of the variety of abstracts of reports and references which frequently occurred in the exercise of their several functions. 3. In the course of nine centuries the office of *quæstor* had experienced a very singular revolution. In the infancy of Rome, two inferior magistrates were annually elected by the people, to relieve the consuls from the invidious management of the public treasure. Whilst Augustus affected to maintain the freedom of election, he consented to accept the annual privilege of recommending, or rather indeed of nominating, a certain proportion of candidates; and it was his custom to select one of these distinguished youths to read his orations or epistles in the assemblies of the senate. The practice of Augustus was imitated by succeeding princes; the occasional commission was established as a permanent office; and the favoured quæstor, assuming a new and more illustrious character, alone survived the suppression of his ancient and useless colleagues. As the orations which he composed in the name of the emperor acquired the force, and at length the form, of absolute edicts, he was considered as the representative of the legislative power, the oracle of the council, and the original source of the civil jurisprudence. He was sometimes invited to take his seat in the supreme judicature of the Imperial consistory, with the Prætorian præfects and the master of the offices; and he was frequently requested to resolve the doubts of inferior judges: but as he was not oppressed with a variety of subordinate business, his leisure and talents were employed to cultivate that dignified style of eloquence which, in the corruption of taste and language, still preserves the majesty of the Roman laws. In some respects the office of the Imperial quæstor may be compared with that of a modern chancellor; but the use of a great seal, which seems to have been adopted by the illiterate barbarians, was never introduced to attest the public acts of the emperors. 4. The extraordinary title of *count of the sacred largesses* was bestowed on the treasurer-general of the revenue, with the intention perhaps of inculcating that every payment flowed from the voluntary bounty of the monarch. To conceive the almost infinite detail of the annual and daily expense of the civil and military administration in every part of a great empire would exceed the powers of the most vigorous imagination. The actual account employed several hundred persons, distributed into eleven different offices, which were artfully contrived to examine and control their respective operations. The multitude of these agents had a natural tendency to increase; and it was more than once thought expedient to dismiss to their native homes the useless supernumeraries, who, deserting their honest labours, had pressed with too much eagerness into the lucrative profession of the finances. 5. Besides the public revenue, which an absolute monarch might levy and expend according to his pleasure, the emperors, in the capacity of opulent citizens, possessed a very extensive property, which was administered by the *count* or treasurer of *the private estate.* Some part had perhaps been the ancient demesnes of kings and republics; some accessions might be derived from the families which were successively invested with the purple; but the most considerable portion flowed from the impure source of confiscations and forfeitures. The Imperial estates were scattered through the provinces from Mauritania to Britain; but the rich and fertile soil of Cappadocia tempted the monarch to acquire in that country his fairest possessions, and either Constantine or his successors embraced the occasion of justifying avarice by religious zeal. They suppressed the rich temple of Comana, where the high-priest of the goddess of war supported the dignity of a sovereign prince; and they applied to their private use the consecrated lands, which were inhabited by six thousand subjects or slaves of the deity and her ministers. 6, 7. The chosen bands of cavalry and infantry, which guarded the person of the emperor, were under the immediate command of the *two counts of the domestics*. The whole number consisted of three thousand and five hundred men, divided into seven *schools*, or troops, of five hundred each; and in the East this honourable service was almost entirely appropriated to the Armenians. Whenever, on public ceremonies, they were drawn up in the courts and porticos of the palace, their lofty stature, silent order, and splendid arms of silver and gold, displayed a martial pomp not unworthy of the Roman majesty. From the seven schools two companies of horse and foot were selected, of the *protectors*, whose advantageous station was the hope and reward of the most deserving soldiers. They mounted guard in the interior apartments, and were occasionally despatched into the provinces, to execute with celerity and vigour the orders of their master. The counts of the domestics had succeeded to the office of the Prætorian præfects; like the præfects, they aspired from the service of the palace to the command of armies.

The perpetual intercourse between the court and the provinces was facilitated by the construction of roads and the institution of posts. But these beneficial establishments were accidentally connected with a pernicious and intolerable abuse. Two or three hundred *agents* or messengers were employed, under the jurisdiction of the master of the offices, to announce the names of the annual consuls, and the edicts or victories of the emperors. They insensibly assumed the licence of reporting whatever they could observe of the conduct either of magistrates or of private citizens; and were soon considered as the eyes of the monarch and the scourge of the people. Under the warm influence of a feeble reign they multiplied to the incredible number of ten thousand, disdained the mild though frequent admonitions of the laws, and exercised in the profitable management of the posts a rapacious and insolent oppression. These official spies, who regularly corresponded with the palace, were encouraged, by favour and reward, anxiously to watch the progress of every treasonable design, from the faint and latent symptoms of disaffection, to the actual preparation of an open revolt.

Their careless or criminal violation of truth and justice was covered by the consecrated mask of zeal; and they might securely aim their poisoned arrows at the breast either of the guilty or the innocent, who had provoked their resentment, or refused to purchase their silence. A faithful subject, of Syria perhaps, or of Britain, was exposed to the danger, or at least to the dread, of being dragged in chains to the court of Milan or Constantinople, to defend his life and fortune against the malicious charge of these privileged informers. The ordinary administration was conducted by those methods which extreme necessity can alone palliate; and the defects of evidence were diligently supplied by the use of torture.

These evils, however terrible they may appear, were confined to the smaller number of Roman subjects whose dangerous situation was in some degree compensated by the enjoyment of those advantages, either of nature or of fortune, which exposed them to the jealousy of the monarch. The obscure millions of a great empire have much less to dread from the cruelty than from the avarice of their masters; and *their* humble happiness is principally affected by the grievance of excessive taxes, which, gently pressing on the wealthy, descend with accelerated weight on the meaner and more indigent classes of society. An ingenious philosopher has calculated the universal measure of the public impositions by the degrees of freedom and servitude; and ventures to assert that, according to an invariable law of nature, it must always increase with the former, and diminish in a just proportion to the latter. But this reflection, which would tend to alleviate the miseries of despotism, is contradicted at least by the history of the Roman empire; which accuses the same princes of despoiling the senate of its authority, and the provinces of their wealth. Without abolishing all the various customs and duties on merchandises, which are imperceptibly discharged by the apparent choice of the purchaser, the policy of Constantine and his successors preferred a simple and direct mode of taxation, more congenial to the spirit of an arbitrary government.

The name and use of the *indictions*, which serve to ascertain the chronology of the middle ages, was derived from the regular practice of the Roman tributes. The emperor subscribed with his own hand, and in purple ink, the solemn edict, or indiction, which was fixed up in the principal city of each diocese during two months previous to the first day of September. And, by a very easy connection of ideas, the word *indiction* was transferred to the measure of tribute which it prescribed, and to the annual term which it allowed for the payment. This general estimate of the supplies was proportioned to the real and imaginary wants of the state; but as often as the expense exceeded the revenue, or the revenue fell short of the computation, an additional tax, under the name of *superindiction*, was imposed on the people, and the most valuable attribute of sovereignty was communicated to the Prætorian præfects, who, on some occasions, were permitted to provide for the unforeseen and extraordinary exigencies of the public service. The execution of these laws (which it would be tedious to pursue in their minute and intricate detail) consisted of two distinct operations: the resolving the general imposition into its constituent parts, which were assessed on the provinces, the cities, and the individuals of the Roman world; and the collecting the separate contributions of the individuals, the cities, and the provinces, till the aocumulated sums were poured into the Imperial treasuries. But as the account between the monarch and the subject was perpetually open, and as the renewal of the demand anticipated the perfect discharge of the preceding obligation, the weighty machine of the finances was moved by the same hands round the circle of its yearly revolution. Whatever was honourable or important in the administration of the revenue was committed to the wisdom of the præfects and their provincial representatives; the lucrative functions were claimed by a crowd of subordinate officers, some of whom depended on the treasurer, others on the governor of the province; and who, in the inevitable conflicts of a perplexed jurisdiction, had frequent opportunities of disputing with each other the spoils of the people. The laborious offices, which could be productive only of envy and reproach, of expense and danger, were imposed on the *Decurions*, who formed the corporations of the cities, and whom the severity of the Imperial laws had condemned to sustain the burthens of civil society. The whole landed property of the empire (without excepting the patrimonial estates of the monarch) was the object of ordinary taxation; and every new purchaser contracted the obligations of the former proprietor. An accurate *census*, or survey, was the only equitable mode of ascertaining the proportion which every citizen should be obliged to contribute for the public service; and from the well-known period of the indictions, there is reason to believe that this difficult and expensive operation was repeated at the regular distance of fifteen years. The lands were measured by surveyors, who were sent into the provinces; their nature, whether arable or pasture, or vineyards or woods, was distinctly reported;

and an estimate was made of their common value from the average produce of five years. The numbers of slaves and of cattle consti- tuted an essential part of the report; an oath was administered to the proprietors which bound them to disclose the true state of the affairs; and their attempts to prevaricate, or elude the intention of the legislator, were severely watched, and punished as a capital crime, which included the double guilt of treason and sacrilege. A large portion of the tribute was paid in money; and of the current coin of the empire, gold alone could be legally accepted. The remainder of the taxes, according to the proportions determined by the annual indiction, was furnished in a manner still more direct, and still more oppressive. According to the different nature of lands, their real produce in the various articles of wine or oil, corn or barley, wood or iron, was transported by the labour or at the expense of the provincials to the Imperial magazines, from whence they were occasionally distributed, for the use of the court, of the army, and of the two capitals, Rome and Constantinople. The commissioners of the revenue were so frequently obliged to make considerable purchases, that they were strictly prohibited from allowing any compensation, or from receiving in money the value of those supplies which were exacted in kind. In the primitive simplicity of small communities this method may be well adapted to collect the almost voluntary offerings of the people; but it is at once susceptible of the utmost latitude and of the utmost strictness, which in a corrupt and absolute monarchy must introduce a perpetual contest between the power of oppression and the arts of fraud. The agriculture of the Roman provinces was insensibly ruined, and, in the progress of despotism, which tends to disap- point its own purpose, the emperors were obliged to derive some merit from the forgiveness of debts, or the remission of tributes, which their subjects were utterly incapable of paying. According to the new division of Italy, the fertile and happy province of Campania, the scene of the early victories and of the delicious retirements of the citizens of Rome, extended between the sea and the Apennine from the Tiber to the Silarus. Within sixty years after the death of Constantine, and on the evidence of an actual survey, an exemption was granted in favour of three hundred and thirty thousand English acres of desert and uncul- tivated land, which amounted to one-eighth of the whole surface of the province. As the footsteps of the barbarians had not yet been seen in Italy, the cause of this amazing desolation, which is recorded in the laws, can be ascribed only to the administration of the Roman emperors.

But this tax or capitation on the proprietors of land would have suffered a rich and numerous class of free citizens to escape. With the view of sharing that species of wealth which is derived from art or labour, and which exists in money or in merchandise, the emperors imposed a distinct and personal tribute on the trading part of their subjects. Some exemptions, very strictly confined both in time and place, were allowed to the proprietors who disposed of the produce of their own estates. Some indulgence was granted to the profession of the liberal arts; but every other branch of commercial industry was affected by the severity of the law. The honourable merchant of Alexandria, who imported the gems and spices of India for the use of the western world; the usurer, who derived from the interest of money a silent and ignominious profit; the ingenious manufacturer, the diligent mechanic, and even the most obscure retailer of a sequestered village, were obliged to admit the officers of the revenue into the partnership of their gain; and the sovereign of the Roman empire, who tolerated the profession, consented to share the infamous salary of public prostitutes. As this general tax upon industry was collected every fourth year, it was styled the *Lustral Contribution*: and the historian Zosimus laments that the approach of the fatal period was announced by the tears and terrors of the citizens, who were often compelled by the impending scourge to embrace the most abhorred and unnatural methods of procuring the sum at which their poverty had been assessed. The testimony of Zosimus cannot indeed be justified from the charge of passion and prejudice; but, from the nature of this tribute, it seems reasonable to conclude that it was arbitrary in the distribution, and extremely rigorous in the mode of collecting. The secret wealth of commerce, and the precarious profits of art or labour, are susceptible only of a discretionary valuation, which is seldom disadvantageous to the interest of the treasury; and as the person of the trader supplies the want of a visible and permanent security, the payment of the imposition, which, in the case of a land-tax, may be obtained by the seizure of property, can rarely be extorted by any other means than those of corporal punishments. The cruel treatment of the insolvent debtors of the state is attested, and was perhaps mitigated, by a very humane edict of Constantine, who, disclaiming the use of racks and of scourges, allots a spacious and airy prison for the place of their confinement.

These general taxes were imposed and levied by the absolute authority of the monarch; but the occasional offerings of the *coronary gold* still retained the name and semblance of popular consent. It was an ancient custom that the allies of the republic, who ascribed their safety or deliverance to the success of the Roman arms, and even the cities of Italy, who admired the virtues of their victorious general, adorned the pomp of his triumph by their voluntary gifts of crowns of gold, which, after the ceremony, were consecrated in the temple of Jupiter, to remain a lasting monument of his glory to future ages. The progress of zeal and flattery soon multiplied the number, and increased the size, of these popular donations; and the triumph of Cæsar was enriched with two thousand eight hundred and twenty-two massy crowns, whose weight amounted to twenty thousand four hundred and fourteen pounds of gold. This treasure was immediately melted down by the prudent dictator, who was satisfied that it would be more serviceable to his soldiers than to the gods: his example was imitated by his successors; and the custom was introduced of exchanging these splendid ornaments for the more acceptable present of the current gold coin of the empire. The spontaneous offering was at length exacted as the debt of duty; and, instead of being confined to the occasion of a triumph, it was supposed to be granted by the several cities and provinces of the monarchy as often as the emperor condescended to announce his accession, his consulship, the birth of a son, the creation of a Cæsar, a victory over the barbarians, or any other real or imaginary event which graced the annals of his reign. The peculiar free gift of the senate of Rome was fixed by custom at sixteen hundred pounds of gold, or about sixty-four thousand pounds sterling. The oppressed subjects celebrated their own felicity that their sovereign should graciously consent to accept this feeble but voluntary testimony of their loyalty and gratitude.

A people elated by pride, or soured by discontent, is seldom qualified to form a just estimate of their actual situation. The subjects of Constantine were incapable of discerning the decline of genius and manly virtue, which so far degraded them below the dignity of their ancestors; but they could feel and lament the rage of tyranny, the relaxation of discipline, and the increase of taxes. The impartial historian, who acknowledges the justice of their complaints, will observe some favourable circumstances which tended to alleviate the misery of their condition. The threatening tempest of barbarians, which so soon subverted the foundations of Roman greatness, was still repelled, or suspended, on the frontiers. The arts of luxury and literature were cultivated, and the elegant pleasures of society were enjoyed, by the inhabitants of a considerable portion of the globe. The forms, the pomp, and the expense of the civil administration contributed to restrain the irregular licence of the soldiers; and although the laws were violated by power, or perverted by subtlety, the sage principles of the Roman jurisprudence preserved a sense of order and equity unknown to the despotic governments of the East. The rights of mankind might derive some protection from religion and philosophy; and the name of freedom, which could no longer alarm, might sometimes admonish, the successors of Augustus, that they did not reign over a nation of Slaves or Barbarians.

XVI

(324–353 A.D.) CHARACTER OF CONSTANTINE
—GOTHIC WAR—DEATH OF CONSTANTINE—
DIVISION OF THE EMPIRE AMONG HIS
THREE SONS—PERSIAN WAR—TRAGIC DEATHS
OF CONSTANTINE THE YOUNGER AND
CONSTANS—USURPATION OF MAGNENTIUS—
CIVIL WAR—VICTORY OF CONSTANTIUS

The character of the prince who removed the seat of empire, and introduced such important changes into the civil and religious constitution of his country, has fixed the attention, and divided the opinions, of mankind. By the grateful zeal of the Christians the deliverer of the church has been decorated with every attribute of a hero, and even of a saint; while the discontent of the vanquished party has compared Constantine to the most abhorred of those tyrants who, by their vice and weakness, dishonoured the Imperial purple. The same passions have, in some degree, been perpetuated to succeeding generations, and the character of Constantine is considered, even in the present age, as an object either of satire or of panegyric. By the impartial union of those defects which are confessed by his warmest admirers, and of those virtues which are acknowledged by his most implacable enemies, we might hope to delineate a just portrait of that extraordinary man, which the truth and candour of history should adopt without a blush. But it would soon appear that the vain attempt to blend such discordant colours, and to reconcile such inconsistent qualities, must produce a figure monstrous rather than human, unless it is viewed in its proper and distinct lights by a careful separation of the different periods of the reign of Constantine.

The person, as well as the mind, of Constantine had been enriched by nature with her choicest endowments. His stature was lofty, his countenance majestic, his deportment graceful; his strength and activity were displayed in every manly exercise, and, from his earliest youth to a very advanced season of life, he preserved the vigour of his constitution by a strict adherence to the domestic virtues of chastity and of temperance. He delighted in the social intercourse of familiar conversation; and though he might sometimes indulge his disposition to raillery with less reserve than was required by the severe dignity of his station, the courtesy and liberality of his manners gained the hearts of all who approached him. The sincerity of his friendship has been suspected; yet he showed, on some occasions, that he was not incapable of a warm and lasting attachment. The disadvantage of an illiterate education had not prevented him from forming a just estimate of the value of learning; and the arts and sciences derived some encouragement from the munificent protection of Constantine. In the despatch of business his diligence was indefatigable; and the active powers of his mind were almost continually exercised in reading, writing, or meditating, in giving audience to ambassadors, and in examining the complaints of his subjects. Even those who censured the propriety of his measures were compelled to acknowledge that he possessed magnanimity to conceive, and patience to execute, the most arduous designs, without being checked either by the prejudices of education or by the clamours of the multitude. In the field he infused his own intrepid spirit into the troops, whom he conducted with the talents of a consummate general; and to his abilities, rather than to his fortune, we may ascribe the signal victories which he obtained over the foreign and domestic foes of the republic. He loved glory as the reward, perhaps as the motive, of his labours. The boundless ambition which, from the moment of his accepting the purple at York, appears as the ruling passion of his soul, may be justified by the dangers of his own situation, by the character of his rivals, by the consciousness of superior merit, and by the prospect that his success would enable him to restore peace and order to the distracted empire. In his civil wars against Maxentius and Licinius he had engaged on his side the inclinations of the people, who compared the undissembled vices of those tyrants with the spirit of wisdom and justice which seemed to direct the general tenor of the administration of Constantine.

Had Constantine fallen on the banks of the Tiber, or even in the plains of Hadrianople, such is the character which, with a few exceptions, he might have transmitted to posterity. But the conclusion of his reign (according to the moderate and indeed tender sentence of a writer of the same age) degraded him from the rank which he had acquired among the most deserving of the Roman princes. In the life of Augustus we behold the tyrant of the republic converted almost by imperceptible degrees into the father of his country and of human kind. In that of Constantine we may contemplate a hero, who had so long inspired his subjects with love and his enemies with terror, degenerating into a cruel and dissolute monarch, corrupted by his fortune, or raised by conquest above the necessity of dissimulation. The general peace which he maintained during the last fourteen years of his reign was a period of apparent splendour rather than of real prosperity; and the old age of Constantine was disgraced by the opposite yet reconcilable vices of rapaciousness and prodigality. The accumulated treasures found in the palaces of Maxentius and Licinius were lavishly consumed; the various innovations introduced by the conqueror were attended with an increasing expense; the cost of his buildings, his court, and his festivals required an immediate and plentiful supply; and the oppression of the people was the only fund which could support the magnificence of the sovereign. His unworthy favourites, enriched by the boundless liberality of their master, usurped with impunity the privilege of rapine and corruption. A secret but universal decay was felt in every part of the public administration, and the emperor himself, though he still retained the obedience, gradually lost the esteem, of his subjects. The dress and manners which, towards the decline of life, he chose to effect, served only to degrade him in the eyes of mankind. The Asiatic pomp which had been adopted by the pride of Diocletian assumed an air of softness and effeminacy in the person of Constantine. He is represented with false hair of various colours, laboriously arranged by the skilful artists of the times; a diadem of a new and more expensive fashion; a profusion of gems and pearls, of collars and bracelets; and a variegated flowing robe of silk, most curiously embroidered with flowers of gold. In such apparel, scarcely to be excused by the youth and folly of Elagabalus, we are at a loss to discover the wisdom of an aged monarch and the simplicity of a Roman veteran. A mind thus relaxed by prosperity and indulgence was incapable of rising to that magnanimity which disdains suspicion and dares to forgive. The deaths of Maximian and Licinius may perhaps be justified by the maxims of policy as they are taught in the schools of tyrants; but an impartial narrative of the executions, or rather murders, which sullied the declining age of Constantine, will suggest to our most candid thoughts the idea of a prince who could sacrifice, without reluctance, the laws of justice and the feelings of nature to the dictates either of his passions or of his interest.

The same fortune which so invariably followed the standard of Constantine seemed to secure the hopes and comforts of his domestic life. Those among his predecessors who had enjoyed the longest and most prosperous reigns, Augustus, Trajan, and Diocletian, had been disappointed of posterity; and the frequent revolutions had never allowed sufficient time for any imperial family to grow up and multiply under the shade of the purple. But the royalty of the Flavian line, which had been first ennobled by the Gothic Claudius, descended through several generations; and Constantine himself derived from his royal father the hereditary honours which he transmitted to his children. The emperor had been twice married. Minervina, the obscure but lawful object of his youthful attachment, had left him only one son, who was called Crispus. By Fausta, the daughter of Maximian, he had three daughters, and three sons known by the kindred names of Constantine, Constantius, and Constans. The unambitious brothers of the Great Constantine, Julius Constantius, Dalmatius, and Hannibalianus, were permitted to enjoy the most honourable rank and the most affluent fortune that could be consistent with a private station. The youngest of the three lived without a name and died without posterity. His two elder brothers obtained in marriage the daughters of wealthy senators, and propagated new branches of the Imperial race. Gallus and Julian afterwards became the most illustrious of the children of Julius Constantius, the *Patrician*. The two sons of Dalmatius, who had been decorated with the vain title of *Censor*, were named Dalmatius and Hannibalianus. The two sisters of the great Constantine, Anastasia and Eutropia, were bestowed on Optatus and Nepotianus, two senators of noble birth and of consular dignity. His third sister, Constantia, was distinguished by her pre-eminence of greatness and of misery. She remained the widow of the vanquished Licinius; and it was by her entreaties that an innocent boy, the offspring of their marriage, preserved, for some time, his life, the title of Cæsar, and a precarious hope of the succession. Besides the females and the allies of the Flavian house, ten or twelve males, to whom the language of modern courts would apply the title of princes of the blood, seemed, according to the order of their birth, to be destined either to inherit or to support the throne of Constantine. But in less than thirty years this numerous and increasing family was reduced to the persons of

Constantius and Julian, who alone had survived a series of crimes and calamities such as the tragic poets have deplored in the devoted lines of Pelops and of Cadmus.

Crispus, the eldest son of Constantine, and the presumptive heir of the empire, is represented by impartial historians as an amiable and accomplished youth. The care of his education, or at least of his studies, was intrusted to Lactantius, the most eloquent of the Christians; a preceptor admirably qualified to form the taste and to excite the virtues of his illustrious disciple. At the age of seventeen Crispus was invested with the title of Cæsar, and the administration of the Gallic provinces, where the inroads of the Germans gave him an early occasion of signalising his military prowess. In the civil war which broke out soon afterwards, the father and son divided their powers; and this history has already celebrated the valour as well as conduct displayed by the latter in forcing the straits of the Hellespont, so obstinately defended by the superior fleet of Licinius. This naval victory contributed to determine the event of the war, and the names of Constantine and of Crispus were united in the joyful acclamations of their eastern subjects, who loudly proclaimed that the world had been subdued, and was now governed, by an emperor endowed with every virtue, and by his illustrious son, a prince beloved of Heaven, and the lively image of his father's perfections.

This dangerous popularity soon excited the attention of Constantine, who, both as a father and as a king, was impatient of an equal. Instead of attempting to secure the allegiance of his son by the generous ties of confidence and gratitude, he resolved to prevent the mischiefs which might be apprehended from dissatisfied ambition. The policy of Constantine maintained, however, the same appearances of regard and confidence towards a son whom he began to consider as his most irreconcilable enemy. Medals were struck with the customary vows for the long and auspicious reign of the young Cæsar; and as the people, who was not admitted into the secrets of the palace, still loved his virtues and respected his dignity, a poet, who solicits his recall from exile, adores with equal devotion the majesty of the father and that of the son. The time was now arrived for celebrating the august ceremony of the twentieth year of the reign of Constantine, and the emperor, for that purpose, removed his court from Nicomedia to Rome, where the most splendid preparations had been made for his reception. Every eye and every tongue affected to express their sense of the general happiness, and the veil of ceremony and dissimulation was drawn for a while over the darkest designs of revenge and murder. In the midst of the festival the unfortunate Crispus was apprehended by order of the emperor, who laid aside the tenderness of a father without assuming the equity of a judge. The examination was short and private; and as it was thought decent to conceal the fate of the young prince from the eyes of the Roman people, he was sent under a strong guard to Pola, in Istria, where, soon afterwards, he was put to death, either by the hand of the executioner or by the more gentle operation of poison. The Cæsar Licinius, a youth of amiable manners, was involved in the ruin of Crispus, and the stern jealousy of Constantine was unmoved by the prayers and tears of his favourite sister, pleading for the life of a son whose rank was his only crime, and whose loss she did not long survive. The story of these unhappy princes, the nature and evidence of their guilt, the forms of their trial, and the circumstances of their death, were buried in mysterious obscurity, and the courtly bishop, who has celebrated in an elaborate work the virtues and piety of his hero, observes a prudent silence on the subject of these tragic events.

By the death of Crispus the inheritance of the empire seemed to devolve on the three sons of Fausta, who have been already mentioned under the names of Constantine, Constantius, and of Constans. These young princes were successively invested with the title of Cæsar, and the dates of their promotion may be referred to the tenth, the twentieth, and the thirtieth years of the reign of their father. This conduct, though it tended to multiply the future masters of the Roman world, might be excused by the partiality of paternal affection; but it is not so easy to understand the motives of the emperor, when he endangered the safety both of his family and of his people by the unnecessary elevation of his two nephews, Dalmatius and Hannibalianus. The former was raised, by the title of Cæsar, to an equality with his cousins. In favour of the latter, Constantine invented the new and singular appellation of *Nobilissimus*, to which he annexed the flattering distinction of a robe of purple and gold. But of the whole series of Roman princes in any age of the empire Hannibalianus alone was distinguished by the title of KING, a name which the subjects of Tiberius would have detested as the profane and cruel insult of capricious tyranny.

The genius of Constantine himself had been formed by adversity and experience. In the free intercourse of private life, and amidst the dangers of the court of Galerius, he had learned to command his own passions, to encounter those of his equals, and to depend for his present safety and future greatness on the prudence and firmness of his personal conduct. His destined successors had the misfortune of being born and educated in the Imperial purple. Incessantly surrounded with a train of flatterers, they passed their youth in the enjoyment of luxury and the expectation of a throne; nor would the dignity of their rank permit them to descend from that elevated station from whence the various characters of human nature appear to wear a smooth and uniform aspect. The indulgence of Constantine admitted them, at a very tender age, to share the administration of the empire; and they studied the art of reigning, at the expense of the people intrusted to their care. The younger Constantine was appointed to hold his court in Gaul; and his brother Constantius exchanged that department, the ancient patrimony of their father, for the more opulent, but less martial, countries of the East. Italy, the Western Illyricum, and Africa, were accustomed to revere Constans, the third of his sons, as the representative of the great Constantine. He fixed Dalmatius on the Gothic frontier, to which he annexed the government of Thrace, Macedonia, and Greece. The city of Cæsarea was chosen for the residence of Hannibalianus; and the provinces of Pontus, Cappadocia, and the Lesser Armenia, were designed to form the extent of his new kingdom. For each of these princes a suitable establishment was provided. A just proportion of guards, of legions, and of auxiliaries, was allotted for their respective dignity and defence. The ministers and generals who were placed about their persons were such as Constantine could trust to assist, and even to control, these youthful sovereigns in the exercise of their delegated power. As they advanced in years and experience, the limits of their authority were insensibly enlarged: but the emperor always reserved for himself the title of Augustus; and while he showed the *Cæsars* to the armies and provinces, he maintained every part of the empire in equal obedience to its supreme head. The tranquillity of the last fourteen years of his reign was scarcely interrupted by the contemptible insurrection of a camel-driver in the island of Cyprus, or by the active part which the policy of Constantine engaged him to assume in the wars of the Goths and Sarmatians.

Although the Sarmatians did not illustrate their name by any memorable exploits, they occasionally assisted their eastern and western neighbours, the Goths and the Germans, with a formidable body of cavalry. They lived under the irregular aristocracy of their chieftains; but after they had received into their bosom the fugitive Vandals, who yielded to the pressure of the Gothic power, they seem to have chosen a king from that nation, and from the illustrious race of the Astingi, who had formerly dwelt on the shores of the northern ocean. This motive of enmity must have inflamed the subjects of contention which perpetually arise on the confines of warlike and independent nations. The Vandal princes were stimulated by fear and revenge; the Gothic kings aspired to extend their dominion from the Euxine to the frontiers of Germany; and the waters of the Maros, a small river which falls into the Theiss, were stained with the blood of the contending barbarians. After some experience of the superior strength and numbers of their adversaries, the Sarmatians implored the protection of the Roman monarch, who beheld with pleasure the discord of the nations, but who was justly alarmed by the progress of the Gothic arms. As soon as Constantine had declared himself in favour of the weaker party, the haughty Araric, king of the Goths, instead of expecting the attack of the legions, boldly passed the Danube, and spread terror and devastation through the province of Mæsia. To oppose the inroad of this destroying host the aged emperor took the field in person; but on this occasion either his conduct or his fortune betrayed the glory which he had acquired in so many foreign and domestic wars. He had the mortification of seeing his troops fly before an inconsiderable detachment of the barbarians, who pursued them to the edge of their fortified camp, and obliged him to consult his safety by a precipitate and ignominious retreat. The event of a second and more successful action retrieved the honour of the Roman name; and the powers of art and discipline prevailed, after an obstinate contest, over the efforts of irregular valour. The broken army of the Goths abandoned the field of battle, the wasted province, and the passage of the Danube: and although the eldest of the sons of Constantine was permitted to supply the place of his father, the merit of the victory, which diffused universal joy, was ascribed to the auspicious counsels of the emperor himself.

The Sarmatians soon forgot, with the levity of barbarians, the services which they had so lately received, and the dangers which still threatened their safety. Their inroads on the territory of the empire provoked the indignation of Constantine to leave them to their fate; and he no longer opposed the ambition of Geberic, a renowned warrior, who had recently ascended the Gothic throne.

Wisumar, the Vandal king, whilst, alone and unassisted, he defended his dominions with undaunted courage, was vanquished and slain in a decisive battle which swept away the flower of the Sarmatian youth. The remainder of the nation embraced the desperate expedient of arming their slaves, a hardy race of hunters and herdsmen, by whose tumultuary aid they revenged their defeat, and expelled the invader from their confines. But they soon discovered that they had exchanged a foreign for a domestic enemy, more dangerous and more implacable. Enraged by their former servitude, elated by their present glory, the slaves, under the name of Limigantes, claimed and usurped the possession of the country which they had saved. Their masters, unable to withstand the ungoverned fury of the populace, preferred the hardships of exile to the tyranny of their servants. Some of the fugitive Sarmatians solicited a less ignominious dependence under the hostile standard of the Goths. A more numerous band retired beyond the Carpathian mountains, among the Quadi, their German allies, and were easily admitted to share a superfluous waste of uncultivated land. But the far greater part of the distressed nation turned their eyes towards the fruitful provinces of Rome. Imploring the protection and forgiveness of the emperor, they solemnly promised, as subjects in peace, and as soldiers in war, the most inviolable fidelity to the empire which should graciously receive them into its bosom. According to the maxims adopted by Probus and his successors, the offers of this barbarian colony were eagerly accepted; and a competent portion of lands in the provinces of Pannonia, Thrace, Macedonia, and Italy, were immediately assigned for the habitation and subsistence of three hundred thousand Sarmatians.

By chastising the pride of the Goths, and by accepting the homage of a suppliant nation, Constantine asserted the majesty of the Roman empire; and the ambassadors of Æthiopia, Persia, and the most remote countries of India, congratulated the peace and prosperity of his government. If he reckoned among the favours of fortune the death of his eldest son, of his nephew, and perhaps of his wife, he enjoyed an uninterrupted flow of private as well as public felicity till the thirtieth year of his reign; a period which none of his predecessors, since Augustus, had been permitted to celebrate. Constantine survived that solemn festival about ten months; and, at the mature age of sixty-four, after a short illness, he ended his memorable life at the palace of Aquyrion, in the suburbs of Nicomedia, whither he had retired for the benefit of the air, and with the hope of recruiting his exhausted strength by the use of the warm baths. The excessive demonstrations of grief, or at least of mourning, surpassed whatever had been practised on any former occasion.

It was soon discovered that the will of the most absolute monarch is seldom obeyed when his subjects have no longer anything to hope from his favour, or to dread from is resentment. The same ministers and generals who bowed with such reverential awe before the inanimate corpse of their deceased sovereign were engaged in secret consultations to exclude his two nephews, Dalmatius and Hannibalianus, from the share which he had assigned them in the succession of the empire. We are too imperfectly acquainted with the court of Constantine to form any judgment of the real motives which influenced the leaders of the conspiracy; unless we should suppose that they were actuated by a spirit of jealousy and revenge against the præfect Ablavius, a proud favourite, who had long directed the counsels and abused the confidence of the late emperor. The arguments by which they solicited the concurrence of the soldiers and people are of a more obvious nature: and they might with decency, as well as truth, insist on the superior rank of the children of Constantine, the danger of multiplying the number of sovereigns, and the impending mischiefs which threatened the republic, from the discord of so many rival princes who were not connected by the tender sympathy of fraternal affection. The intrigue was conducted with zeal and secrecy, till a loud and unanimous declaration was procured from the troops that they would suffer none except the sons of their lamented monarch to reign over the Roman empire. The younger Dalmatius, who was united with his collateral relations by the ties of friendship and interest, is allowed to have inherited a considerable share of the abilities of the great Constantine; but, on this occasion, he does not appear to have concerted any measures for supporting by arms the just claims which himself and his royal brother derived from the liberality of their uncle. Astonished and overwhelmed by the tide of popular fury, they seem to have remained, without the power of flight or of resistance, in the hands of their implacable enemies. Their fate was suspended till the arrival of Constantius, the second, and perhaps the most favoured, of the sons of Constantine.

The voice of the dying emperor had recommended the care of his funeral to the piety of Constantius; and that prince, by the vicinity of his eastern station, could easily prevent the diligence of his brothers, who resided in their distant governments of Italy and Gaul. As soon as he had taken possession of the palace of Constantinople, his first care was to remove the apprehensions of his kinsmen, by a solemn oath which he pledged for their security. His next employment was to find some specious pretence which might release his conscience from the obligation of an imprudent promise. The arts of fraud were made subservient to the designs of cruelty; and a manifest forgery was attested by a person of the most sacred character. From the hands of the bishop of Nicomedia, Constantius received a fatal scroll, affirmed to be the genuine testament of his father; in which the emperor expressed his suspicions that he had been poisoned by his brothers; and conjured his sons to revenge his death, and to consult their own safety, by the punishment of the guilty. Whatever reasons might have been alleged by these unfortunate princes to defend their life and honour against so incredible an accusation, they were silenced by the furious clamours of the soldiers, who declared themselves, at once, their enemies, their judges, and their executioners. The spirit, and even the forms, of legal proceedings were repeatedly violated in a promiscuous massacre; which involved the two uncles of Constantius, seven of his cousins, of whom Dalmatius and Hannibalianus were the most illustrious, the Patrician Optatus, who had married a sister of the late emperor, and the præfect Ablavius, whose power and riches had inspired him with some hopes of obtaining the purple. If it were necessary to aggravate the horrors of this bloody scene, we might add that Constantius himself had espoused the daughter of his uncle Julius, and that he had bestowed his sister in marriage on his cousin Hannibalianus. These alliances, which the policy of Constantine, regardless of the public prejudice, had formed between the several branches of the Imperial house, served only to convince mankind that these princes were as cold to the endearments of conjugal affection, as they were insensible to the ties of consanguinity and the moving entreaties of youth and innocence. Of so numerous a family, Gallus and Julian alone, the two youngest children of Julius Constantius, were saved from the hands of the assassins, till their rage, satiated with slaughter, had in some measure subsided. The emperor Constantius, who, in the absence of his brothers, was the most obnoxious to guilt and reproach, discovered, on some future occasions, a faint and transient remorse for those cruelties which the perfidious counsels of his ministers and the irresistible violence of the troops, had extorted from his inexperienced youth.

The massacre of the Flavian race was succeeded by a new division of the provinces, which was ratified in a personal interview of the three brothers. Constantine, the eldest of the Cæsars, obtained, with a certain pre-eminence of rank, the possession of the new capital, which bore his own name and that of his father. Thrace and the countries of the East were allotted for the patrimony of Constantius; and Constans was acknowledged as the lawful sovereign of Italy, Africa, and the western Illyricum. The armies submitted to their hereditary right, and they condescended, after some delay, to accept from the Roman senate the title of *Augustus*. When they first assumed the reins of government, the eldest of these princes was twenty-one, the second twenty, and the third only seventeen, years of age.

During the long period of the reign of Constantius the provinces of the East were afflicted by the calamities of the Persian war. The irregular incursions of the light troops alternately spread terror and devastation beyond the Tigris and beyond the Euphrates, from the gates of Ctesiphon to those of Antioch; and this active service was performed by the Arabs of the desert, who were divided in their interest and affections, some of their independent chiefs being enlisted in the party of Sapor, whilst others had engaged their doubtful fidelity to the emperor. The more grave and important operations of the war were conducted with equal vigour; and the armies of Rome and Persia encountered each other in nine bloody fields, in two of which Constantius himself commanded in person. The event of the day was most commonly adverse to the Romans.

Whatever advantages might attend the arms of Sapor in the field, though nine repeated victories diffused among the nations the fame of his valour and conduct, he could not hope to succeed in the execution of his designs while the fortified towns of Mesopotamia, and, above all, the strong and ancient city of Nisibis, remained in the possession of the Romans. In the space of twelve years Nisibis, which, since the time of Lucullus, had been deservedly esteemed the bulwark of the East, sustained three memorable sieges against the power of Sapor; and the disappointed monarch, after urging his attacks above sixty, eighty, and an hundred days, was thrice repulsed with loss and ignominy. This large and populous city was situated about two days' journey from the Tigris, in the midst of a pleasant and fertile plain at the foot of

Mount Masius. A treble enclosure of brick walls was defended by a deep ditch; and the intrepid resistance of Count Lucilianus and his garrison was seconded by the desperate courage of the people. The citizens of Nisibis were animated by the exhortations of their bishop, inured to arms by the presence of danger, and convinced of the intentions of Sapor to plant a Persian colony in their room, and to lead them away into distant and barbarous captivity. The event of the two former sieges elated their confidence and exasperated the haughty spirit of the Great King, who advanced a third time towards Nisibis, at the head of the united forces of Persia and India. The ordinary machines, invented to batter or undermine the walls, were rendered ineffectual by the superior skill of the Romans, and many days had vainly elapsed when Sapor embraced a resolution worthy of an eastern monarch who believed that the elements themselves were subject to his power. At the stated season of the melting of the snows in Armenia, the river Mygdonius, which divides the plain and the city of Nisibis, forms, like the Nile, an inundation over the adjacent country. By the labour of the Persians the course of the river was stopped below the town, and the waters were confined on every side by solid mounds of earth. On this artificial lake a fleet of armed vessels, filled with soldiers, and with engines which discharged stones of five hundred pounds weight, advanced in order of battle, and engaged, almost upon a level, the troops which defended the ramparts. The irresistible force of the waters was alternately fatal to the contending parties, till at length a portion of the walls, unable to sustain the accumulated pressure, gave way at once, and exposed an ample breach of one hundred and fifty feet. The Persians were instantly driven to the assault, and the fate of Nisibis depended on the event of the day. The heavy-armed cavalry, who led the van of a deep column, were embarrassed in the mud, and great numbers were drowned in the unseen holes which had been filled by the rushing waters. The elephants, made furious by their wounds, increased the disorder, and trampled down thousands of the Persian archers. The Great King, who, from an exalted throne, beheld the misfortunes of his arms, sounded, with reluctant indignation, the signal of the retreat, and suspended for some hours the prosecution of the attack. But the vigilant citizens improved the opportunity of the night, and the return of day discovered a new wall of six feet in height rising every moment to fill up the interval of the breach. Notwithstanding the disappointment of his hopes and the loss of more than twenty thousand men, Sapor still pressed the reduction of Nisibis with an obstinate firmness which could have yielded only to the necessity of defending the eastern provinces of Persia against a formidable invasion of the Massagetæ. Alarmed by this intelligence, he hastily relinquished the siege, and marched with rapid diligence from the banks of the Tigris to those of the Oxus. The danger and difficulties of the Scythian war engaged him soon afterwards to conclude, or at least to observe, a truce with the Roman emperor, which was equally grateful to both princes, as Constantius himself, after the deaths of his two brothers, was involved, by the revolutions of the West, in a civil contest which required and seemed to exceed the most vigorous exertion of his undivided strength.

After the partition of the empire three years had scarcely elapsed before the sons of Constantine seemed impatient to convince mankind that they were incapable of contenting themselves with the dominions which they were unqualified to govern. The eldest of those princes soon complained that he was defrauded of his just proportion of the spoils of their murdered kinsmen; and though he might yield to the superior guilt and merit of Constantius, he exacted from Constans the cession of the African provinces, as an equivalent for the rich countries of Macedonia and Greece which his brother had acquired by the death of Dalmatius. The want of sincerity which Constantine experienced in a tedious and fruitless negotiation exasperated the fierceness of his temper, and he eagerly listened to those favourites who suggested to him that his honour, as well as his interest, was concerned in the prosecution of the quarrel. At the head of a tumultuary band, suited for rapine rather than for conquest, he suddenly broke into the dominions of Constans, by the way of the Julian Alps, and the country round Aquileia felt the first effects of his resentment. The measures of Constans, who then resided in Dacia, were directed with more prudence and ability. On the news of his brother's invasion he detached a select and disciplined body of his Illyrian troops, proposing to follow them in person with the remainder of his forces. But the conduct of his lieutenants soon terminated the unnatural contest. By the artful appearances of flight, Constantine was betrayed into an ambuscade, which had been concealed in a wood, where the rash youth, with a few attendants, was surprised, surrounded, and slain. His body, after it had been found in the obscure stream of the Alsa, obtained the honours of an Imperial sepulchre, but his provinces transferred their allegiance to the conqueror, who, refusing to admit his elder brother Constantius to any share in these new acquisitions, maintained the undisputed possession of more than two-thirds of the Roman empire.

The fate of Constans himself was delayed about ten years longer, and the revenge of his brother's death was reserved for the more ignoble hand of a domestic traitor. The pernicious tendency of the system introduced by Constantine was displayed in the feeble administration of his sons, who, by their vices and weakness, soon lost the esteem and affections of their people. The pride assumed by Constans from the unmerited success of his arms was rendered more contemptible by his want of abilities and application. His fond partiality towards some German captives, distinguished only by the charms of youth, was an object of scandal to the people; and Magnentius, an ambitious soldier, who was himself of barbarian extraction, was encouraged by the public discontent to assert the honour of the Roman name. By his secrecy and diligence he entertained some hopes of surprising the person of Constans, who was pursuing in the adjacent forest his favourite amusement of hunting, or perhaps some pleasures of a more private and criminal nature. The rapid progress of fame allowed him, however, an instant for flight, though the desertion of his soldiers and subjects deprived him of the power of resistance. Before he could reach a seaport in Spain, where he intended to embark, he was overtaken near Helena, at the foot of the Pyrenees, by a party of light cavalry, whose chief, regardless of the sanctity of a temple, executed his commission by the murder of the son of Constantine.

As soon as the death of Constans had decided this easy but important revolution, the example of the court of Autun was imitated by the provinces of the West. The authority of Magnentius was acknowledged through the whole extent of the two great præfectures of Gaul and Italy; and the usurper prepared, by every act of oppression, to collect a treasure which might discharge the obligation of an immense donative and supply the expenses of a civil war. Constantius had declared his intention of deciding the quarrel in the fields of Cibalis, a name that would animate his troops by the remembrance of the victory which, on the same auspicious ground, had been obtained by the arms of his father Constantine. Yet, by the impregnable fortifications with which the emperor encompassed his camp, he appeared to decline rather than to invite a general engagement. It was the object of Magnentius to tempt or to compel his adversary to relinquish this advantageous position; and he employed with that view the various marches, evolutions, and stratagems which the knowledge of the art of war could suggest to an experienced officer. He carried by assault the important town of Siscia; made an attack on the city of Sirmium, which lay in the rear of the Imperial camp; attempted to force a passage over the Save into the eastern provinces of Illyricum; and cut in pieces a numerous detachment which he had allured into the narrow passes of Adarne.

The city of Mursa, or Essek, celebrated in modern times for a bridge of boats, five miles in length, over the river Drave, and the adjacent morasses, has been always considered as a place of importance in the wars of Hungary. Magnentius, directing his march towards Mursa, set fire to the gates, and, by a sudden assault, had almost scaled the walls of the town. The vigilance of the garrison extinguished the flames; the approach of Constantius left him no time to continue the operations of the siege; and the emperor soon removed the only obstacle that could embarrass his motions, by forcing a body of troops which had taken post in an adjoining amphitheatre. The field of battle round Mursa was a naked and level plain: on this ground the army of Constantius formed, with the Drave on their right; while their left, either from the nature of their disposition, or from the superiority of their cavalry, extended far beyond the right flank of Magnentius. The troops on both sides remained under arms in anxious expectation during the greatest part of the morning; and the son of Constantine, after animating his soldiers by an eloquent speech, retired into a church at some distance from the field of battle, and committed to his generals the conduct of this decisive day. They deserved his confidence by the valour and military skill which they exerted. They wisely began the action upon the left; and advancing their whole wing of cavalry in an oblique line, they suddenly wheeled it on the right flank of the enemy, which was unprepared to resist the impetuosity of their charge. But the Romans of the West soon rallied by the habits of discipline; and the barbarians of Germany supported the renown of their national bravery. The engagement soon became general; was maintained with various and singular turns of fortune; and scarcely ended with the darkness of the night. The signal victory which Constantius obtained is attributed to the arms of his cavalry. His cuirassiers are described as so many massy statues of steel, glittering with their scaly armour, and breaking with their ponderous lances the firm array of the Gallic legions. As soon as the legions gave way, the lighter and more active squadrons of the second line rode sword in hand into the intervals and completed the disorder. In the meanwhile, the huge bodies of the Germans were exposed almost naked to the dexterity of the Oriental archers; and whole troops of those barbarians were urged by anguish and despair to precipitate themselves into the broad and rapid stream of the Drave. The number of the slain was computed at fifty-four thousand men, and the slaughter of the conquerors was more considerable than that of the vanquished; a circumstance which proves the obstinacy of the contest, and justifies the observation of an ancient writer, that the forces of the empire were consumed in the fatal battle of Mursa, by the loss of a veteran army, sufficient to defend the frontiers, or to add new triumphs to the glory of Rome. Notwithstanding the invectives of a servile orator, there is not the least reason to believe that the tyrant deserted his own standard in the beginning of the engagement. He seems to have displayed the virtues of a general and of a soldier till the day was irrecoverably lost, and his camp in the possession of the enemy. Magnentius then consulted his safety, and, throwing away the Imperial ornaments, escaped with some difficulty from the pursuit of the light horse, who incessantly followed his rapid flight from the banks of the Drave to the foot of the Julian Alps.

XVII

(351–360 A.D.) CONSTANTIUS SOLE EMPEROR— ELEVATION AND DEATH OF GALLUS—DANGER AND ELEVATION OF JULIAN—SARMATIAN AND PERSIAN WARS—VICTORIES OF JULIAN IN GAUL

The divided provinces of the empire were again united by the victory of Constantius; but as that feeble prince was destitute of personal merit either in peace or war; as he feared his generals, and distrusted his ministers; the triumph of his arms served only to establish the reign of the *eunuchs* over the Roman world. Those unhappy beings, the ancient production of Oriental jealousy and despotism, were introduced into Greece and Rome by the contagion of Asiatic luxury. Their progress was rapid; and the eunuchs, who, in the time of Augustus, had been abhorred, as the monstrous retinue of an Egyptian queen, were gradually admitted into the families of matrons, of senators, and of the emperors themselves. Restrained by the severe edicts of Domitian and Nerva, cherished by the pride of Diocletian, reduced to an humble station by the prudence of Constantine, they multiplied in the palaces of his degenerate sons, and insensibly acquired the knowledge, and at length the direction, of the secret councils of Constantius. The aversion and contempt which mankind has so uniformly entertained for that imperfect species appears to have degraded their character, and to have rendered them almost as incapable as they were supposed to be of conceiving any generous sentiment, or of performing any worthy action. But the eunuchs were skilled in the arts of flattery and intrigue; and they alternately governed the mind of Constantius by his fears, his indolence, and his vanity. Whilst he viewed in a deceitful mirror the fair appearance of public prosperity, he supinely permitted them to intercept the complaints of the injured provinces; to accumulate immense treasures by the sale of justice and of honours; to disgrace the most important dignities by the promotion of those who had purchased at their hands the powers of oppression; and to gratify their resentment against the few independent spirits who arrogantly refused to solicit the protection of slaves. Of these slaves the most distinguished was the chamberlain Eusebius, who ruled the monarch and the palace with such absolute sway, that Constantius, according to the sarcasm of an impartial historian, possessed some credit with this haughty favourite. By his artful suggestions, the emperor was persuaded to subscribe the condemnation of the unfortunate Gallus, and to add a new crime to the long list of unnatural murders which pollute the honour of the house of Constantine.

When the two nephews of Constantine, Gallus and Julian, were saved from the fury of the soldiers, the former was about twelve, and the latter about six, years of age; and, as the eldest was thought to be of a sickly constitution, they obtained with the less difficulty a precarious and dependent life from the affected pity of Constantius, who was sensible that the execution of these helpless orphans would have been esteemed, by all mankind, an act of the most deliberate cruelty. Different cities of Ionia and Bithynia were assigned for the places of their exile and education; but as soon as their growing years excited the jealousy of the emperor, he judged it more prudent to secure those unhappy youths in the strong castle of Macellum, near Cæsarea. The treatment which they experienced during a six years' confinement was partly such as they could hope from a careful guardian, and partly such as they might dread from a suspicious tyrant. At length, however, the emergencies of the state compelled the emperor, or rather his eunuchs, to invest Gallus, in the twenty-fifth year of his age, with the title of Cæsar, and to cement this political connection by his marriage with the princess Constantina. After a formal interview, in which the two princes mutually engaged their faith never to undertake anything to the prejudice of each other, they repaired without delay to their respective stations. Constantius continued his march towards the West, and Gallus fixed his residence at Antioch; from whence, with a delegated authority, he administered the five great dioceses of the eastern præfecture. In this fortunate change, the new Cæsar was not unmindful of his brother Julian, who obtained the honours of his rank, the appearances of liberty, and the restitution of an ample patrimony.

The writers the most indulgent to the memory of Gallus, and even Julian himself, though he wished to cast a veil over the frailities of his brother, are obliged to confess that the Cæsar was incapable of reigning. Transported from a prison to a throne, he possessed neither genius nor application, nor docility to compensate for the want of knowledge and experience. A temper naturally morose and violent, instead of being corrected, was soured by solitude and adversity; the remembrance of what he had endured disposed him to retaliation rather than to sympathy; and the ungoverned sallies of his rage were often fatal to those who approached his person, or were subject to his power. Constantina, his wife, is described, not as a woman, but as one of the infernal furies tormented with an insatiate thirst of human blood. Instead of employing her influence to insinuate the mild counsels of prudence and humanity, she exasperated the fierce passions of her husband; and as she retained the vanity, though she had renounced the gentleness of her sex, a pearl necklace was esteemed an equivalent price for the murder of an innocent and virtuous nobleman. The cruelty of Gallus was sometimes displayed in the undissembled violence of popular or military executions: and was sometimes disguised by the abuse of law and the forms of judicial proceedings. The private houses of Antioch, and the palaces of public resort, were besieged by spies and informers; and the Cæsar himself, concealed in a plebeian habit, very frequently conde-scended to assume that odious character. Every apartment of the palace was adorned with the instruments of death and torture, and a general consternation was diffused through the capital of Syria. The prince of the East, as if he had been conscious how much he had to fear, and how little he deserved to reign, selected for the objects of his resentment the provincials accused of some imaginary treason, and his own courtiers, whom with more reason he suspected of incensing, by their secret correspondence, the timid and suspicious mind of Constantius. But he forgot that he was depriving himself of his only support, the affection of the people; whilst he furnished the malice of his enemies with the arms of truth, and afforded the emperor the fairest pretence of exacting the forfeit of his purple and of his life.

As long as the civil war suspended the fate of the Roman world, Constantius dissembled his knowledge of the weak and cruel administration to which his choice had subjected the East; and the discovery of some assassins, secretly despatched to Antioch by the tyrant of Gaul, was employed to convince the public that the emperor and the Cæsar were united by the same interest, and pursued by the same enemies. But when the victory was decided in favour of Constantius, his dependent colleague became less useful and less formidable. Every circumstance of his conduct was severely and suspiciously examined, and it was privately resolved either to deprive Gallus of the purple, or at least to remove him from the indolent luxury of Asia to the hardships and dangers of a German war. But as it still appeared dangerous to arrest Gallus in his capital, the slow and safer arts of dissimulation were practised with success. The frequent and pressing epistles of Constantius were filled with professions of confidence and friendship, exhorting the Cæsar to discharge the duties of his high station, to relieve his colleague from a part of the public cares, and to assist the West by his presence, his counsels, and his arms. After so many reciprocal injuries, Gallus had reason to fear and to distrust. But he had neglected the opportunities of flight and of resistance; he was seduced by the flattering assurances of the tribune Scudilo, who, under the semblance of a rough soldier, disguised the most artful insinuation; and he depended on the credit of his wife Constantina till the unseasonable death of that princess completed the ruin in which he had been involved by her impetuous passions.

After a long delay the reluctant Cæsar set forwards on his journey to the Imperial court. The dissimulation which had hitherto been preserved was laid aside at Petovio in Pannonia. He was conducted to a palace in the suburbs, where the general Barbatio, with a select band of soldiers, who could neither be moved by pity nor corrupted by rewards, expected the arrival of his illustrious victim. In the close of the evening he was arrested, ignominiously stripped of the ensigns of Cæsar, and hurried away to Pola, in Istria, a sequestered prison, which had been so recently polluted with royal blood. The horror which he felt was soon increased by the appearance of his implacable enemy the eunuch Eusebius, who, with the assistance of a notary and a tribune, proceeded to interrogate him concerning the administration of the East. The Cæsar sunk under the weight of shame and guilt, confessed all the criminal actions and all the treasonable designs with which he was charged; and, by imputing them to the advice of his wife, exasperated the indignation of Constantius, who reviewed with partial prejudice the minutes of the examination. The emperor was easily convinced that his own safety was incompatible with the life of his cousin: the sentence of death was signed, despatched, and executed; and the nephew of Constantine, with his hands tied behind his back, was beheaded in prison, like the vilest malefactor.

Besides the reigning emperor, Julian alone survived of all the numerous posterity of Constantius Chlorus. The misfortune of his royal birth involved him in the disgrace of Gallus. From his retirement in the happy country of Ionia he was conveyed, under a strong guard, to the court of Milan, where he languished above seven months in the continual apprehension of suffering the same ignominious death which was daily inflicted, almost before his eyes, on the friends and adherents of his persecuted family. His looks, his gestures, his silence, were scrutinised with malignant curiosity, and he was perpetually assaulted by enemies whom he had never offended, and by arts to which he was a stranger. But in the school of adversity Julian insensibly acquired the virtues of firmness and discretion. He defended his honour, as well as his life, against the ensnaring subtleties of the eunuchs, who endeavoured to extort some declaration of his sentiments; and whilst he cautiously suppressed his grief and resentment, he nobly disdained to flatter the tyrant by any seeming approbation of his brother's murder. Julian most devoutly ascribes his miraculous deliverance to the protection of the gods, who had exempted his innocence from the sentence of destruction pronounced by their justice against the impious house of Constantine. As the most effectual instrument of their providence, he gratefully acknowledges the steady and generous friendship of the empress Eusebia, a woman of beauty and merit, who, by the ascendant which she had gained over the mind of her husband, counterbalanced in some measure the powerful conspiracy of the eunuchs. By the intercession of his patroness Julian was admitted into the Imperial presence: he pleaded his cause with a decent freedom; he was heard with favour; and, notwithstanding the efforts of his enemies, who urged the danger of sparing an avenger of the blood of Gallus, the milder sentiment of Eusebia prevailed in the council. But the effects of a second interview were dreaded by the eunuchs; and Julian was advised to withdraw for a while into the neighbourhood of Milan, till the emperor thought proper to assign the city of Athens for the place of his honourable exile.

Whilst his hours were passed in studious retirement, the empress, resolute to achieve the generous design which she had undertaken, was not unmindful of the care of his fortune. The death of the late Cæsar had left Constantius invested with the sole command, and oppressed by the accumulated weight, of a mighty empire. Before the wounds of civil discord could be healed, the provinces of Gaul were overwhelmed by a deluge of barbarians. The Sarmatians no longer respected the barrier of the Danube. The impunity of rapine had increased the boldness and numbers of the wild Isaurians; those robbers descended from their craggy mountains to ravage the adjacent country, and had even presumed, though without success, to besiege the important city of Seleucia, which was defended by a garrison of three Roman legions. Above all, the Persian monarch, elated by victory, again threatened the peace of Asia; and the presence of the emperor was indispensably required both in the West and in the East. For the first time Constantius sincerely acknowledged that his single strength was unequal to such an extent of care and of dominion. Insensible to the voice of flattery, which assured him that his allpowerful virtue and celestial fortune would still continue to triumph over every obstacle, he listened with complacency to the advice of Eusebia, which gratified his indolence, without offending his suspicious pride. As she perceived that the remembrance of Gallus dwelt on the emperor's mind, she artfully turned his attention to the opposite characters of the two brothers, which from their infancy had been compared to those of Domitian and of Titus. She accustomed her husband to consider Julian as a youth of a mild, unambitious disposition, whose allegiance and gratitude might be secured by the gift of the purple, and who was qualified to fill with honour a subordinate station, without aspiring to dispute the commands or to shade the glories of his sovereign and benefactor. After an obstinate though secret struggle, the opposition of the favourite eunuchs submitted to the ascendancy of the empress; and it was resolved that Julian, after celebrating his nuptials with Helena, sister of Constantius, should be appointed, with the title of Cæsar, to reign over the countries beyond the Alps.

Although the order which recalled him to court was probably accompanied by some intimation of his approaching greatness he appeals to the people of Athens to witness his tears of undissembled sorrow, when he was reluctantly torn away from his beloved retirement. He trembled for his life, for his fame, and even for his virtue; and his sole confidence was derived from the persuasion that Minerva inspired all his actions, and that he was protected by an invisible guard of angels, whom for that purpose she had borrowed from the Sun and Moon. He approached with honor the palace of Milan; nor could the ingenuous youth conceal his indignation when he found himself accosted with false and servile respect by the assassins of his family. Eusebia, rejoicing in the success of her benevolent schemes, embraced him with the tenderness of a sister, and endeavoured, by the most soothing caresses, to dispel his terrors and reconcile him to his fortune. But the ceremony of shaving his beard, and his awkward demeanour when he first exchanged the cloak of a Greek philosopher for the military habit of a Roman prince, amused during a few days the levity of the Imperial court.

While the Roman emperor and the Persian monarch, at the distance of three thousand miles, defended their extreme limits against the barbarians of the Danube and of the Oxus, their intermediate frontier experienced the vicissitudes of a languid war and a precarious truce. Two of the eastern ministers of Constantius, the Præitorian præfect Musonian, whose abilities were disgraced by the want of truth and integrity, and Cassian duke of Mesopotamia, a hardy and veteran soldier, opened a secret negotiation with the satrap Tamsapor. These overtures of peace, translated into the servile and flattering language of Asia, were transmitted to the camp of the Great King, who resolved to signify, by an ambassador, the terms which he was inclined to grant to the suppliant Romans. Narses, whom he invested with that character, was honourably received in his passage through Antioch and Constantinople: he reached Sirmium after a long journey, and, at his first audience, respectfully unfolded the silken veil which covered the haughty epistle of his sovereign. Sapor, King of Kings, and Brother of the Sun and Moon (such were the lofty titles affected by oriental vanity), expressed his satisfaction that his brother, Constantius Cæsar, had been taught wisdom by adversity. As the lawful successor of Darius Hystaspes, Sapor asserted that the river Strymon, in Macedonia, was the true and ancient boundary of his empire; declaring, however, that, as an evidence of his moderation, he would content himself with the provinces of Armenia and Mesopotamia, which had been fraudulently extorted from his ancestors. He alleged that, without the restitution of these disputed countries, it was impossible to establish any treaty on a solid and permanent basis; and he arrogantly threatened that, if his ambassador returned in vain, he was prepared to take the field in the spring, and to support the justice of his cause by the strength of his invincible arms. Narses, who was endowed with the most polite and amiable manners, endeavoured, as far as was consistent with his duty, to soften the harshness of the message. Both the style and substance were maturely weighed in the Imperial council, and he was dismissed with the following answer: "Constantius had a right to disclaim the officiousness of his ministers, who had acted without any specific orders from the throne: he was not, however, averse to an equal and honourable treaty; but it was highly indecent, as well as absurd, to propose to the sole and victorious emperor of the Roman world the same conditions of peace which he had indignantly rejected at the time when his power was contracted within the narrow limits of the East: the chance of arms was uncertain; and Sapor should recollect that, if the Romans had sometimes been vanquished in battle, they had almost always been successful in the event of the war." A few days after the departure of Narses, three ambassadors were sent to the court of Sapor, who was already returned from the Scythian expedition to his ordinary residence of Ctesiphon. A count, a notary, and a sophist, had been selected for this important commission; and Constantius, who was secretly anxious for the conclusion of the peace, entertained some hopes that the dignity of the first of these ministers, the dexterity of the second, and the rhetoric of the third, would persuade the Persian monarch to abate the rigour of his demands. But the progress of their negotiation was opposed and defeated by the hostile arts of Antoninus, a Roman subject of Syria, who had fled from oppression, and was admitted into the councils of Sapor, and even to the royal table, where, according to the custom of the Persians, the most important business was frequently discussed. The dexterous fugitive promoted his interest by the same conduct which gratified his revenge. He incessantly urged the ambition of his new master to embrace the favourable opportunity when the bravest of the Palatine troops were employed with the emperor in a distant war on the Danube. He pressed Sapor to invade the exhausted and defenceless provinces of the East, with the numerous armies of Persia, now fortified by the alliance and accession of the fiercest barbarians. The ambassadors of Rome retired without success, and a second embassy, of a still more honourable rank, was detained in strict confinement, and threatened either with death or exile.

The ancient city of Amid or Amida, which sometimes assumes the provincial appellation of Diarbekir, is advantageously situate in a fertile plain, watered by the natural and artificial channels of the Tigris, of which the least inconsiderable stream bends in a semi-circular form round the eastern part of the city. The emperor Constantius had recently conferred on Amida the honour of his own name, and the additional fortifications of strong walls and lofty towers. It was provided with an arsenal of military engines, and the ordinary garrison had been reinforced to the amount of seven legions, when the place was invested by the arms of Sapor. His first and most sanguine hopes depended on the success of a general assault. After Sapor had tried, without success, the efficacy of force and of stratagem, he had recourse to the slower but more certain operations of a regular siege, in the conduct of which he was instructed by the skill of the Roman deserters. The trenches were opened at a convenient distance, and the troops destined for that service advanced, under the portable cover of strong hurdles, to fill up the ditch, and undermine the foundations of the walls. Wooden towers were at the same time constructed, and moved forwards on wheels, till the soldiers, who were provided with every species of missile weapons, could engage almost on level ground with the troops who defended the rampart. Every mode of resistance which art could suggest, or courage could execute, was employed in the defence of Amida, and the works of Sapor were more than once destroyed by the fire of the Romans. But the resources of a besieged city may be exhausted. The Persians repaired their losses and pushed their approaches; a large breach was made by the battering-ram, and the strength of the garrison, wasted by the sword and by disease, yielded to the fury of the assault. The soldiers, the citizens, their wives, their children, all who had not time to escape through the opposite gate, were involved by the conquerors in a promiscuous massacre.

But the ruin of Amida was the safety of the Roman provinces. As soon as the first transports of victory had subsided, Sapor was at leisure to reflect that to chastise a disobedient city he had lost the flower of his troops and the most favourable season for conquest. Thirty thousand of his veterans had fallen under the walls of Amida during the continuance of a siege which lasted seventy-three days; and the disappointed monarch returned to his capital with affected triumph and secret mortification.

The defence of the East against the arms of Sapor required, and would have exercised, the abilities of the most consummate general; and it seemed fortunate for the state that it was the actual province of the brave Ursicinus, who alone deserved the confidence of the soldiers and people. In the hour of danger Ursicinus was removed from his station by the intrigues of the eunuchs; and the military command of the East was bestowed, by the same influence, on Sabinian, a wealthy and subtle veteran, who had attained the infirmities, without acquiring the experience, of age. By a second order, which issued from the same jealous and inconstant counsels, Ursicinus was again despatched to the frontier of Mesopotamia, and condemned to sustain the labours of a war, the honours of which had been transferred to his unworthy rival. Sabinian fixed his indolent station under the walls of Edessa; and while he amused himself with the idle parade of military exercise, and moved to the sound of flutes in the Pyrrhic dance, the public defence was abandoned to the boldness and diligence of the former general of the East. But whenever Ursicinus recommended any vigorous plan of operations; when he proposed, at the head of a light and active army, to wheel round the foot of the mountains, to intercept the convoys of the enemy, to harass the wide extent of the Persian lines and to relieve the distress of Amida; the timid and envious commander alleged that he was restrained by his positive orders from endangering the safety of the troops. Amida was at length taken; its bravest defenders, who had escaped the sword of the barbarians, died in the Roman camp by the hand of the executioner; and Ursicinus himself, after supporting the disgrace of a partial inquiry, was punished for the misconduct of Sabinian by the loss of his military rank. But Constantius soon experienced the truth of the prediction which honest indignation had extorted from his injured lieutenant, that, as long as such maxims of government were suffered to prevail, the emperor himself would find it no easy task to defend his eastern dominions from the invasion of a foreign enemy. When he had subdued or pacified the barbarians of the Danube, Constantius proceeded by slow marches into the East; and after he had wept over the smoking ruins of Amida, he formed, with a powerful army, the siege of Bezabde. The walls were shaken by the reiterated efforts of the most enormous of the battering-rams; the town was reduced to the last extremity; but it was still defended by the patient and intrepid valour of the garrison, till the approach of the rainy season obliged the emperor to raise the siege, and ingloriously to retreat into his winter-quarters at Antioch. The pride of Constantius, and the ingenuity of his courtiers, were at a loss to discover any materials for panegyric in the events of the Persian war; while the glory of his cousin Julian, to whose military command he had intrusted the provinces of Gaul, was proclaimed to the world in the simple and concise narrative of his exploits.

In the blind fury of civil discord, Constantius had abandoned to the barbarians of Germany the countries of Gaul, which still acknowledged the authority of his rival. A numerous swarm of Franks and Alemanni were invited to cross the Rhine by presents and promises, by the hopes of spoil, and by a perpetual grant of all the territories which they should be able to subdue. But the emperor, who for a temporary service had thus imprudently provoked the rapacious spirit of the barbarians, soon discovered and lamented the difficulty of dismissing these formidable allies, after they had tasted the richness of the Roman soil. Regardless of the nice distinction of loyalty and rebellion, these undisciplined robbers treated as their natural enemies all the subjects of the empire who possessed any property which they were desirous of acquiring. Forty-five flourishing cities, Tongres, Cologne, Treves, Worms, Spires, Strasburg, etc., besides a far greater number of towns and villages, were pillaged, and for the most part reduced to ashes. The barbarians of Germany, still faithful to the maxims of their ancestors, abhorred the confinement of walls, to which they applied the odious names of prisons and sepulchres; and, fixing their independent habitations on the banks of rivers, the Rhine, the Moselle, and the Meuse, they secured themselves against the danger of a surprise, by a rude and hasty fortification of large trees, which were felled and thrown across the roads. The Alemanni were established in the modern countries of Alsace and Lorraine; the Franks occupied the island of the Batavians, together with an extensive district of Brabant, which was then known by the appellation of Toxandria, and may deserve to be considered as the original seat of their Gallic monarchy. From the sources to the mouth of the Rhine, the conquests of the Germans extended above forty miles to the west of that river, over a country peopled by colonies of their own name and nation; and the scene of their devastations was three times more extensive than that of their conquests. At a still greater distance the open towns of Gaul were deserted, and the inhabitants of the fortified cities, who trusted to their strength and vigilance, were obliged to content themselves with such supplies of corn as they could raise on the vacant land within the enclosure of their walls. The diminished legions, destitute of pay and provisions, of arms and discipline, trembled at the approach, and even at the name, of the barbarians.

Under these melancholy circumstances, an inexperienced youth was appointed to save and to govern the provinces of Gaul, or rather, as he expresses it himself, to exhibit the vain image of Imperial greatness. The retired scholastic education of Julian, in which he had been more conversant with books than with arms, with the dead than with the living, left him in profound ignorance of the practical arts of war and government; and when he awkwardly repeated some military exercise which it was necessary for him to learn, he exclaimed with a sigh, "O Plato, Plato, what a task for a philosopher!" Immediately after Julian had received the purple at Milan he was sent into Gaul with a feeble retinue of three hundred and sixty soldiers. At Vienna, where he passed a painful and anxious winter, in the hands of those ministers to whom Constantius had intrusted the direction of his conduct, the Cæsar was informed of the siege and deliverance of Autun. That large and ancient city, protected only by a ruined wall and pusillanimous garrison, was saved by the generous resolution of a few veterans, who resumed their arms for the defence of their country. In his march from Autun, through the heart of the Gallic provinces, Julian embraced with ardour the earliest opportunity of signalising his courage. At the head of a small body of archers and heavy cavalry, he preferred the shorter but the more dangerous of two roads; and sometimes eluding and sometimes resisting the attacks of the barbarians, who were masters of the field, he arrived with honour and safety at the camp near Rheims, where the Roman troops had been ordered to assemble. The aspect of their young prince revived the drooping spirit of the soldiers, and they marched from Rheims in search of the enemy with a confidence which had almost proved fatal to them. The Alemanni, familiarised to the knowledge of the country, secretly collected their scattered forces, and, seizing the opportunity of a dark and rainy day, poured with unexpected fury on the rear-guard of the Romans. Before the inevitable disorder could be reme-died, two legions were destroyed; and Julian was taught by experience that caution and vigilance are the most important lessons of the art of war. In a second and more successful action he recovered and established his military fame; but as the agility of the barbarians saved them from the pursuit, his victory was neither bloody nor decisive.

A very judicious plan of operations was adopted for the approaching campaign. Julian himself, at the head of the remains of the veteran bands, and of some new levies which he had been permitted to form, boldly penetrated into the centre of the German cantonments, and carefully re-established the fortifications of

Saverne, in an advantageous post which would either check the incursions or intercept the retreat of the enemy. At the same time Barbatio, general of the infantry, advanced from Milan with an army of thirty thousand men, and, passing the mountains, prepared to throw a bridge over the Rhine, in the neighbourhood of Basil. It was reasonable to expect that the Alemanni, pressed on either side by the Roman arms, would soon be forced to evacuate the provinces of Gaul, and to hasten to the defence of their native country. But the hopes of the campaign were defeated by the incapacity, or the envy, or the secret instructions of Barbatio, who acted as if he had been the enemy of the Cæsar, and the secret ally of the barbarians. The negligence with which he permitted a troop of pillagers freely to pass, and to return, almost before the gates of his camp, may be imputed to his want of abilities; but the treasonable act of burning a number of boats, and a superfluous stock of provisions, which would have been of the most essential service to the army of Gaul, was an evidence of his hostile and criminal intentions. The Germans despised an enemy who appeared destitute either of power or of inclination to offend them; and the ignominious retreat of Barbatio deprived Julian of the expected support, and left him to extricate himself from a hazardous situation, where he could neither remain with safety, nor retire with honour.

As soon as they were delivered from the fears of invasion, the Alemanni prepared to chastise the Roman youth who presumed to dispute the possession of that country which they claimed as their own by the right of conquest and of treaties. They employed three days, and as many nights, in transporting over the Rhine their military powers. The fierce Chnodomar, shaking the ponderous javelin which he had victoriously wielded against the brother of Magnentius, led the van of the barbarians, and moderated by his experience the martial ardour which his example inspired. He was followed by six other kings, by ten princes of regal extraction, by a long train of high-spirited nobles, and by thirty-five thousand of the bravest warriors of the tribes of Germany. The confidence derived from the view of their own strength was increased by the intelligence which they received from a deserter, that the Cæsar, with a feeble army of thirteen thousand men, occupied a post about one-and-twenty miles from their camp of Strasburg. With this inadequate force Julian resolved to seek and to encounter the barbarian host; and the chance of a general action was preferred to the tedious and uncertain operation of separately engaging the dispersed parties of the Alemanni. The Romans marched in close order, and in two columns; the cavalry on the right, the infantry on the left; and the day was so far spent when they appeared in sight of the enemy, that Julian was desirous of deferring the battle till the next morning, and of allowing his troops to recruit their exhausted strength by the necessary refreshments of sleep and food. Yielding, however, with some reluctance, to the clamours of the soldiers, and even to the opinion of his council, he exhorted them to justify by their valour the eager impatience which, in case of a defeat, would be universally branded with the epithets of rashness and presumption. The trumpets sounded, the military shout was heard through the field, and the two armies rushed with equal fury to the charge. The Cæsar, who conducted in person his right wing, depended on the dexterity of his archers and the weight of his cuirassiers. But his ranks were instantly broken by an irregular mixture of light-horse and of light-infantry, and he had the mortification of beholding the flight of six hundred of his most renowned cuirassiers. The fugitives were stopped and rallied by the presence and authority of Julian, who, careless of his own safety, threw himself before them, and, urging every motive of shame and honour, led them back against the victorious enemy. The conflict between the two lines of infantry was obstinate and bloody. The Germans possessed the superiority of strength and stature, the Romans that of discipline and temper; and as the barbarians who served under the standard of the empire united the respective advantages of both parties, their strenuous efforts, guided by a skilful leader, at length determined the event of the day. The Romans lost four tribunes, and two hundred and forty-three soldiers, in this memorable battle of Strasburg, so glorious to the Cæsar, and so salutary to the afflicted provinces of Gaul. Six thousand of the Alemanni were slain in the field, without including those who were drowned in the Rhine, or transfixed with darts whilst they attempted to swim across the river. Chnodomar himself was surrounded and taken prisoner, with three of his brave companions, who had devoted themselves to follow in life or death the fate of their chieftain. Julian received him with military pomp in the council of his officers; and expressing a generous pity for the fallen state, dissembled his inward contempt for the abject humiliation of his captive. Instead of exhibiting the vanquished king of the Alemanni as a grateful spectacle to the cities of Gaul, he respectfully laid at the feet of the emperor this splendid trophy of his victory.

Chnodomar experienced an honourable treatment: but the impatient barbarian could not long survive his defeat, his confinement, and his exile.

As soon as the valour and conduct of Julian had secured an interval of peace, he applied himself to a work more congenial to his humane and philosophic temper. The cities of Gaul, which had suffered from the inroads of the barbarians, he diligently repaired; and seven important posts, between Mentz and the mouth of the Rhine, are particularly mentioned as having been rebuilt and fortified by the order of Julian. The vanquished Germans had submitted to the just but humiliating condition of preparing and conveying the necessary materials. The active zeal of Julian urged the prosecution of the work; and such was the spirit which he had diffused among the troops, that the auxiliaries themselves, waiving their exemption from any duties of fatigue, contended in the most servile labours with the diligence of the Roman soldiers. It was incumbent on the Cæsar to provide for the subsistence as well as for the safety of the inhabitants and of the garrisons. The desertion of the former, and the mutiny of the latter, must have been the fatal and inevitable consequences of famine. The tillage of the provinces of Gaul had been interrupted by the calamities of war; but the scanty harvests of the continent were supplied, by his paternal care, from the plenty of the adjacent island. Six hundred large barques, framed in the forest of the Ardennes, made several voyages to the coast of Britain; and returning from thence, laden with corn, sailed up the Rhine, and distributed their cargoes to the several towns and fortresses along the banks of the river. The arms of Julian had restored a free and secure navigation, which Constantius had offered to purchase at the expense of his dignity, and of a tributary present of two thousand pounds of silver. The emperor parsimoniously refused to his soldiers the sums which he granted with a lavish and trembling hand to the barbarians. The dexterity, as well as the firmness of Julian, was put to a severe trial, when he took the field with a discontented army, which had already served two campaigns without receiving any regular pay or any extraordinary donative.

The precarious and dependent situation of Julian displayed his virtues and concealed his defects. The young hero who supported, in Gaul, the throne of Constantius, was not permitted to reform the vices of the government; but he had courage to alleviate or to pity the distress of the people. Unless he had been able to revive the martial spirit of the Romans, or to introduce the arts of industry and refinement among their savage enemies, he could not entertain any rational hopes of securing the public tranquillity, either by the peace or conquest of Germany. Yet the victories of Julian suspended for a short time the inroads of the barbarians, and delayed the ruin of the Western Empire. His salutary influence restored the cities of Gaul, which had been so long exposed to the evils of civil discord, barbarian war, and domestic tyranny; and the spirit of industry was revived with the hopes of enjoyment. Agriculture, manufactures, and commerce again flourished under the protection of the laws; and the *curiæ*, or civil corporations, were again filled with useful and respectable members: the youth were no longer apprehensive of marriage; and married persons were no longer apprehensive of posterity: the public and private festivals were celebrated with customary pomp; and the frequent and secure intercourse of the provinces displayed the image of national prosperity.

XVIII

(306–438 A.D.) THE PROGRESS AND EFFECTS OF THE CONVERSION OF CONSTANTINE — LEGAL ESTABLISHMENT AND CONSTITUTION OF THE CHRISTIAN OR CATHOLIC CHURCH

The public establishment of Christianity may be considered as one of the most important and domestic revolutions which excite the most lively curiosity, and afford the most valuable instruction. The victories and the civil policy of Constantine no longer influence the state of Europe; but a considerable portion of the globe still retains the impression which it received from the conversion of that monarch; and the ecclesiastical institutions of his reign are still connected, by an indissoluble chain, with the opinions, the passions, and the interests of the present generation.

The gratitude of the church has exalted the virtues and excused the failings of a generous patron, who seated Christianity on the throne of the Roman world; and the Greeks, who celebrate the festival of the Imperial saint, seldom mention the name of Constantine without adding the title of *equal to the Apostles.* Such a comparison, if it alludes to the character of those divine missionaries, must be imputed to the extravagance of impious flattery. But if the parallel is confined to the extent and number of their evangelic victories, the success of Constantine might perhaps equal that of the Apostles themselves. By the edicts of toleration he removed the temporal disadvantages which had hitherto retarded the progress of Christianity; and its active and numerous ministers received a free permission, a liberal encouragement, to recommend the salutary truths of revelation by every argument which could affect the reason or piety of mankind. The exact balance of the two religions continued but a moment; and the piercing eye of ambition and avarice soon discovered that the profession of Christianity might contribute to the interest of the present, as well as of a future life. The hopes of wealth and honours, the example of an emperor, his exhortations, his irresistible smiles, diffused conviction among the venal and obsequious crowds which usually fill the apartments of a palace. The cities which signalised a forward zeal by the voluntary destruction of their temples were distinguished by municipal privileges and rewarded with popular donatives; and the new capital of the East gloried in the singular advantage that Constantinople was never profaned by the worship of idols. As the lower ranks of society are governed by imitation, the conversion of those who possessed any eminence of birth, of power, or of riches, was soon followed by dependent multitudes. The salvation of the common people was purchased at an easy rate, if it be true that, in one year, twelve thousand men were baptised at Rome, besides a proportionable number of women and children, and that a white garment, with twenty pieces of gold, had been promised by the emperor to every convert. The powerful influence of Constantine was not circumscribed by the narrow limits of his life or of his dominions. The education which he bestowed on his sons and nephews secured to the empire a race of princes whose faith was still more lively and sincere, as they imbibed, in their earliest infancy, the spirit, or at least the doctrine, of Christianity. War and commerce had spread the knowledge of the Gospel beyond the confines of the Roman provinces; and the barbarians, who had disdained an humble and proscribed sect, soon learned to esteem a religion which had been so lately embraced by the greatest monarch and the most civilised nation of the globe. The Goths and Germans, who enlisted under the standard of Rome, revered the cross which glittered at the head of the legions, and their fierce countrymen received at the same time the lessons of faith and of humanity. The kings of Iberia and Armenia worshipped the God of their protector; and their subjects, who have invariably preserved the name of Christians, soon formed a sacred and perpetual connection with their Roman brethren. The Christians of Persia were suspected, in time of war, of preferring their religion to their country; but as long as peace subsisted between the two empires, the persecuting spirit of the Magi was effectually restrained by the interposition of Constantine. The rays of the Gospel illuminated the coast of India. The colonies of Jews who had penetrated into Arabia and Æthiopia opposed the progress of Christianity; but the labour of the missionaries was in some measure facilitated by a previous knowledge of the Mosaic revelation; and Abyssinia still reveres the memory of Frumentius, who, in the time of Constantine, devoted his life to the conversion of those sequestered regions.

The catholic church was administered by the spiritual and legal jurisdiction of eighteen hundred bishops; of whom one thousand were seated in the Greek, and eight hundred in the Latin, provinces of the empire. The extent and boundaries of their respective dioceses had been variously and accidentally decided by the zeal and success of the first missionaries, by the wishes of the people, and by the propagation of the Gospel. Episcopal churches were closely planted along the banks of the Nile, on the sea-coast of Africa, in the proconsular Asia, and through the southern provinces of Italy. The bishops of Gaul and Spain, of Thrace and Pontus, reigned over an ample territory, and delegated their rural suffragans to execute the subordinate duties of the pastoral office. A Christian diocese might be spread over a province, or reduced to a village; but all the bishops possessed an equal and indelible character; they all derived the same powers and privileges from the apostles, from the people, and from the laws. While the *civil* and *military* professions were separated by the policy of Constantine, a new and perpetual order of *ecclesiastical* ministers, always respectable, sometimes dangerous, was established in the church and state. The important review of their station and attributes may be distributed under the following heads: I. Popular election. II. Ordination of the clergy. III. Property. IV. Civil jurisdiction. V. Spiritual censures. VI. Exercise of public oratory. VII. Privilege of legislative assemblies.

I. The freedom of elections subsisted long after the legal establishment of Christianity, and the subjects of Rome enjoyed in the church the privilege which they had lost in the republic, of choosing the magistrates whom they were bound to obey. As soon as a bishop had closed his eyes, the metropolitan issued a commission to one of his suffragans to administer the vacant see, and prepare, within a limited time, the future election. The right of voting was vested in the inferior clergy, who were best qualified to judge of the merit of the candidates; in the senators or nobles of the city, all those who were distinguished by their rank or property; and finally in the whole body of the people, who on the appointed day flocked in multitudes from the most remote parts of the diocese, and sometimes silenced, by their tumultuous acclamations, the voice of reason and the laws of discipline. These acclamations might accidentally fix on the head of the most deserving competitor, of some ancient presbyter, some holy monk, or some layman conspicuous for his zeal and piety. But the episcopal chair was solicited, especially in the great and opulent cities of the empire, as a temporal rather than as a spiritual dignity. The interested views, the selfish and angry passions, the arts of perfidy and dissimulation, the secret corruption, the open and even bloody violence which had formerly disgraced the freedom of election in the commonwealths of Greece and Rome, too often influenced the choice of the successors of the apostles. While one of the candidates boasted the honours of his family, a second allured his judges by the delicacies of a plentiful table, and a third, more guilty than his rivals, offered to share the plunder of the church among the accomplices of his sacrilegious hopes. The civil as well as ecclesiastical laws attempted to exclude the populace from this solemn and important transaction. The canons of ancient discipline, by requiring several episcopal qualifications of age, station, etc., restrained in some measure the indiscriminate caprice of the electors. The authority of the provincial bishops, who were assembled in the vacant church to consecrate the choice of the people, was interposed to moderate their passions and to correct their mistakes. The bishops could refuse to ordain an unworthy candidate, and the rage of contending factions sometimes accepted their impartial mediation.

II. The bishops alone possessed the faculty of *spiritual* generation, and this extraordinary privilege might compensate, in some degree, for the painful celibacy which was imposed as a virtue, as a duty, and at length as a positive obligation. The religions of antiquity, which established a separate order of priests, dedicated a holy race, a tribe or family, to the perpetual service of the gods. Such institutions were founded for possession rather than conquest. The children of the priests enjoyed, with proud and indolent security, their sacred inheritance; and the fiery spirit of enthusiasm was abated by the cares, the pleasures, and the endearments of domestic life. But the Christian sanctuary was open to every ambitious candidate who aspired to its heavenly promises or temporal possessions. The office of priests, like that of soldiers or magistrates, was strenuously exercised by those men whose temper and abilities had prompted them to embrace the ecclesiastical profession, or who had been selected by a discerning bishop as the best qualified to promote the glory and interest of the church. The bishops (till the abuse was restrained by the prudence of the laws) might constrain the reluctant and protect the distressed, and the imposition of hands for ever bestowed some of the most valuable privileges of civil society. The whole body of the catholic clergy, more numerous, perhaps, than the legions, was exempted by the emperors from all service, private or public, all municipal offices, and all personal taxes and contributions, which pressed on their fellow-citizens with intolerable weight; and the duties of their holy profession were accepted as a full discharge of their obligations to the republic. Each bishop acquired an absolute and indefeasible right to the perpetual obedience of the clerk whom he ordained; the clergy of each episcopal church, with its dependent parishes, formed a regular and permanent society; and the cathedrals of Constantinople and Carthage maintained their peculiar establishment of five hundred ecclesiastical ministers. Their ranks and numbers were insensibly multiplied by the superstition of the times, which introduced into the church the splendid ceremonies of a Jewish or Pagan temple; and a long train of priests, deacons, subdeacons, acolytes, exorcists, readers, singers, and doorkeepers contributed, in their respective stations, to swell the pomp and harmony of religious worship. The clerical name and privilege were extended to many pious fraternities, who devoutly supported the ecclesiastical throne. Six hundred *parabolani*, or adventurers, visited the sick at Alexandria; eleven hundred *copiatæ*, or gravediggers, buried the dead at Constantinople; and the swarms of monks, who arose from the Nile, overspread and darkened the face of the Christian world.

III. The edict of Milan secured the revenue as well as the peace of the church. The Christians not only recovered the lands and houses of which they had been stripped by the persecuting laws of Diocletian, but they acquired a perfect title to all the possessions which they had hitherto enjoyed by the connivance of the magistrate. As soon as Christianity became the religion of the emperor and the empire, the national clergy might claim a decent and honourable maintenance: and the payment of an annual tax might have delivered the people from the more oppressive tribute which superstition imposes on her votaries. But as the wants and expenses of the church increased with her prosperity, the ecclesiastical order was still supported and enriched by the voluntary oblations of the faithful. Eight years after the edict of Milan, Constantine granted to all his subjects the free and universal permission of bequeathing their fortunes to the holy catholic church; and their devout liberality, which during their lives was checked by luxury or avarice, flowed with a profuse stream at the hour of their death.

The wealthy Christians were encouraged by the example of their sovereign. In the space of two centuries, from the reign of Constantine to that of Justinian, the eighteen hundred churches of the empire were enriched by the frequent and unalienable gifts of the prince and people. An annual income of six hundred pounds sterling may be reasonably assigned to the bishops, who were placed at an equal distance between riches and poverty, but the standard of their wealth insensibly rose with the dignity and opulence of the cities which they governed. An authentic but imperfect rent-roll specifies some houses, shops, gardens, and farms, which belonged to the three *Basilica* of Rome—St. Peter, St. Paul, and St. John Lateran—in the provinces of Italy, Africa, and the East. They produce, besides a reserved rent of oil, linen, paper, aromatics, etc., a clear annual revenue of twenty-two thousand pieces of gold, or twelve thousand pounds sterling. In the age of Constantine and Justinian the bishops no longer possessed, perhaps they no longer deserved, the unsuspecting confidence of their clergy and people. The ecclesiastical revenues of each diocese were divided into four parts, for the respective uses of the bishop himself, of his inferior clergy, of the poor, and of the public worship; and the abuse of this sacred trust was strictly and repeatedly checked. The patrimony of the church was still subject to all the public impositions of the state. The clergy of Rome, Alexandria, Thessalonica, etc., might solicit and obtain some partial exemptions; but the premature attempt of the great council of Rimini, which aspired to universal freedom, was successfully resisted by the son of Constantine.

IV. The Latin clergy, who erected their tribunal on the ruins of the civil and common law, have modestly accepted, as the gift of Constantine, the independent jurisdiction which was the fruit of time, of accident, and of their own industry. But the liberality of the Christian emperors had actually endowed them with some legal prerogatives which secured and dignified the sacerdotal character. 1. Under a despotic government, the bishops alone enjoyed and asserted the inestimable privilege of being tried only by their *peers*; and even in a capital accusation, a synod of their brethren were the sole judges of their guilt or innocence. Such a tribunal, unless it was inflamed by personal resentment or religious discord, might be favourable, or even partial, to the sacerdotal order: but Constantine was satisfied that secret impunity would be less pernicious than public scandal, and the Nicene council was edified by his public declaration, that, if he surprised a bishop in the act of adultery, he should cast his Imperial mantle over the episcopal sinner. 2. The domestic jurisdiction of the bishops was at once a privilege and a restraint of the ecclesiastical order, whose civil causes were decently withdrawn from the cognisance of a secular judge. Their venial offences were not exposed to the shame of a public trial or punishment; and the gentle correction which the tenderness of youth may endure from its parents or instructors was inflicted by the temperate severity of the bishops. But if the clergy were guilty of any crime which could not be sufficiently expiated by their degradation from an honourable and beneficial profession, the Roman magistrate drew the sword of justice, without any regard to ecclesiastical immunities. 3. The arbitration of the bishops was ratified by a positive law; and the judges were instructed to execute, without appeal or delay, the episcopal decrees, whose validity had hitherto depended on the consent of the parties. The conversion of the magistrates themselves, and of the whole empire, might gradually remove the fears and scruples of the Christians. But they still resorted to the tribunal of the bishops, whose abilities and integrity they esteemed; and the venerable Austin enjoyed the satisfaction of complaining that his spiritual functions were perpetually interrupted by the invidious labour of deciding the claim or the possession of silver and gold, of lands and cattle. 4. The ancient privilege of sanctuary was transferred to the Christian temples, and extended, by the liberal piety of the younger Theodosius, to the precincts of consecrated ground. The fugitive, and even guilty, suppliants were permitted to implore either the justice or the mercy of the Deity and his ministers. The rash violence of despotism was suspended by the mild interposition of the church, and the lives or fortunes of the most eminent subjects might be protected by the mediation of the bishop.

V. The bishop was the perpetual censor of the morals of his people. The discipline of penance was digested into a system of canonical jurisprudence, which accurately defined the duty of private or public confession, the rules of evidence, the degrees of guilt, and the measure of punishment. It was impossible to execute this spiritual censure, if the Christian pontiff who punished the obscure sins of the multitude, respected the conspicuous vices and destructive crimes of the magistrate: but it was impossible to arraign the conduct of the magistrate without controlling the administration of civil government. Some considerations of religion, or loyalty, or fear, protected the sacred persons of the emperors from the zeal or resentment of the bishops; but they boldly censured and excommunicated the subordinate tyrants who were not invested with the majesty of the purple.

VI. Every popular government has experienced the effects of rude or artificial eloquence. The coldest nature is animated, the firmest reason is moved, by the rapid communication of the prevailing impulse; and each hearer is affected by his own passions and by those of the surrounding multitude. The ruin of civil liberty had silenced the demagogues of Athens and the tribunes of Rome; the custom of preaching, which seems to constitute a considerable part of Christian devotion, had not been introduced into the temples of antiquity; and the ears of monarchs were never invaded by the harsh sound of popular eloquence till the pulpits of the empire were filled with sacred orators, who possessed some advantages unknown to their profane predecessors. The arguments and rhetoric of the tribune were instantly opposed, with equal arms, by skilful and resolute antagonists; and the cause of truth and reason might derive an accidental support from the conflict of hostile passions. The bishop, or some distinguished presbyter to whom he cautiously delegated the powers of preaching, harangued, without the danger of interruption or reply, a submissive multitude, whose minds had been prepared and subdued by the awful ceremonies of religion. Such was the strict subordination of the catholic church, that the same concerted sounds might issue at once from an hundred pulpits of Italy or Egypt, if they were *tuned* by the master-hand of the Roman or Alexandrian primate. The design of this institution was laudable, but the fruits were not always salutary. The preachers recommended the practice of the social duties; but they exalted the perfection of monastic virtue, which is painful to the individual, and useless to mankind. Their charitable exhortations betrayed a secret wish that the clergy might be permitted to manage the wealth of the faithful for the benefit of the poor. The most sublime representations of the attributes and laws of the Deity were sullied by an idle mixture of metaphysical subtleties, puerile rites, and fictitious miracles: and they expatiated, with the most fervent zeal, on the religious merit of hating the adversaries and obeying the ministers of the church. When the public peace was distracted by heresy and schism, the sacred orators sounded the trumpet of discord, and perhaps of sedition. The understandings of their congregations were perplexed by mystery, their passions were inflamed by invectives; and they rushed from the Christian temples of Antioch or Alexandria, prepared either to suffer or to inflict martyrdom. The corruption of taste and language is strongly marked in the vehement declamations of the Latin bishops; but the compositions of Gregory and Chrysostom have been compared with the most splendid models of Attic, or at least of Asiatic, eloquence.

VII. The representatives of the Christian republic were regularly assembled in the spring and autumn of each year; and these synods diffused the spirit of ecclesiastical discipline and legislation through the hundred and twenty provinces of the Roman world. The archbishop or metropolitan was empowered by the laws to summon the suffragan bishops of his province; to revise their conduct, to vindicate their rights, to declare their faith, and to examine the merit of the candidates who were elected by the clergy and people to supply the vacancies of the episcopal college. The primates of Rome, Alexandria, Antioch, Carthage, and afterwards Constantinople, who exercised a more ample jurisdiction, convened the numerous assembly of their dependent bishops. But the convocation of great and extraordinary synods was the prerogative of the emperor alone. Whenever the emergencies of the church required this decisive measure, he despatched a peremptory summons to the bishops or the deputies of each province, with an order for the use of post-horses and a competent allowance for the expenses of their journey. At an early period, when Constantine was the protector rather than the proselyte of Christianity, he referred the African controversy to the council of Arles; in which the bishops of York, of Treves, of Milan, and of Carthage, met as friends and brethren, to debate in their native tongue on the common interest of the Latin or Western church. Eleven years afterwards, a more numerous and celebrated assembly was convened at Nice in Bithynia, to extinguish, by their final sentence, the subtle disputes which had arisen in Egypt on the subject of the Trinity. Three hundred and eighteen bishops obeyed the summons of their indulgent master; the ecclesiastics of every rank and sect and denomination have been computed at two thousand and forty-eight persons; the Greeks appeared in person; and the consent of the Latins was expressed by the legates of the Roman pontiff. The session, which lasted about two months, was frequently honoured by the presence of the emperor. Leaving his guards at the door, he seated himself (with the permission of the council) on a low stool in the midst of the hall. Constantine listened with patience and spoke with modesty; and while he influenced the debates, he humbly professed that he was the minister, not the judge, of the successors of the apostles, who had been established as priests and as gods upon earth. Such profound reverence of an absolute monarch towards a feeble and unarmed assembly of his own subjects can only be compared to the respect with which the senate had been treated by the Roman princes who adopted the policy of Augustus. Within the space of fifty years, a philosophic spectator of the vicissitudes of human affairs might have contemplated Tacitus in the senate of Rome, and Constantine in the council of Nice. The fathers of the Capitol and those of the church had alike degenerated from the virtues of their founders; but as the bishops were more deeply rooted in the public opinion, they sustained their dignity with more decent pride, and sometimes opposed with a manly spirit the wishes of their sovereign. The progress of time and superstition erased the memory of the weakness, the passion, the ignorance, which disgraced these ecclesiastical synods; and the catholic world has unanimously submitted to the *infallible* decrees of the general councils.

XIX

(312–362 A.D.) PERSECUTION OF HERESY—THE
SCHISM OF THE DONATISTS—THE ARIAN
CONTROVERSY—ATHANASIUS—DISTRACTED
STATE OF THE CHURCH AND EMPIRE UNDER
CONSTANTINE AND HIS SONS—TOLERATION
OF PAGANISM

The grateful applause of the clergy has consecrated the memory of
a prince, who indulged their passions and promoted their interest.
Constantine gave them security, wealth, honours, and revenge; and
the support of the orthodox faith was considered as the most sacred
and important duty of the civil magistrate. The edict of Milan, the
great charter of toleration, had confirmed to each individual of the
Roman world the privilege of choosing and professing his own
religion. But this inestimable privilege was soon violated: with the
knowledge of truth the emperor imbibed the maxims of persecution;
and the sects which dissented from the catholic church were
afflicted and oppressed by the triumph of Christianity. Constantine
easily believed that the heretics, who presumed to dispute *his*
opinions or to oppose *his* commands, were guilty of the most
absurd and criminal obstinacy; and that a seasonable application
of moderate severities might save those unhappy men from the
danger of an everlasting condemnation. Not a moment was lost in
excluding the ministers and teachers of the separated congregations
from any share of the rewards and immunities which the emperor
had so liberally bestowed on the orthodox clergy. But as the sectaries
might still exist under the cloud of royal disgrace, the conquest of
the East was immediately followed by an edict which announced
their total destruction. After a preamble filled with passion and
reproach, Constantine absolutely prohibits the assemblies of the
heretics, and confiscates their public property to the use either of
the revenue or of the catholic church. The sects against whom the
Imperial severity was directed appear to have been the adherents
of Paul of Samosata; the Montanists of Phrygia, who maintained

an enthusiastic succession of prophecy; the Novatians, who sternly rejected the temporal efficacy of repentance; the Marcionites and Valentinians, under whose leading banners the various Gnostics of Asia and Egypt had insensibly rallied; and perhaps the Manichæans, who had recently imported from Persia a more artful composition of Oriental and Christian theology. The design of extirpating the name, or at least of restraining the progress, of these odious heretics, was prosecuted with vigour and effect. Some of the penal regulations were copied from the edicts of Diocletian; and this method of conversion was applauded by the same bishops who had felt the hand of oppression, and had pleaded for the rights of humanity.

The complaints and mutual accusations which assailed the throne of Constantine, as soon as the death of Maxentius had submitted Africa to his victorious arms, were ill adapted to edify an imperfect proselyte. He learned with surprise that the provinces of that great country, from the confines of Cyrene to the Columns of Hercules, were distracted with religious discord. The source of the division was derived from a double election in the church of Carthage, the second in rank and opulence of the ecclesiastical thrones of the West. Cæcilian and Majorinus were the two rival primates of Africa; and the death of the latter soon made room for Donatus, who, by his superior abilities and apparent virtues, was the firmest support of his party. The advantage which Cæcilian might claim from the priority of his ordination was destroyed by the illegal, or at least indecent, haste with which it had been performed, without expecting the arrival of the bishops of Numidia. The authority of these bishops, who, to the number of seventy, condemned Cæcilian, and consecrated Majorinus, is again weakened by the infamy of some of their personal characters; and by the female intrigues, sacrilegious bargains, and tumultuous proceedings, which are imputed to this Numidian council. The bishops of the contending factions maintained, with equal ardour and obstinacy, that their adversaries were degraded, or at least dishonoured, by the odious crime of delivering the Holy Scriptures to the officers of Diocletian. From their mutual reproaches, as well as from the story of this dark transaction, it may justly be inferred that the late persecution had embittered the zeal, without reforming the manners, of the African Christians. That divided church was incapable of affording an impartial judicature; the controversy was solemnly tried in five successive tribunals, which were appointed by the emperor; and the whole proceeding, from the first appeal to the final sentence, lasted above three years. A severe inquisition, which was taken by the prætorian vicar and the proconsul of Africa, the report of two episcopal visitors who had been sent to Carthage, the decrees of the councils of Rome and of Arles, and the supreme judgment of Constantine himself in his sacred consistory, were all favourable to the cause of Cæcilian; and he was unanimously acknowledged by the civil and ecclesiastical powers as the true and lawful primate of Africa. The honours and estates of the church were attributed to *his* suffragan bishops, and it was not without difficulty that Constantine was satisfied with inflicting the punishment of exile on the principal leaders of the Donatist faction. As their cause was examined with attention, perhaps it was determined with justice. Perhaps their complaint was not without foundation, that the credulity of the emperor had been abused by the insidious arts of his favourite Osius. The influence of falsehood and corruption might procure the condemnation of the innocent, or aggravate the sentence of the guilty. Such an act, however, of injustice, if it concluded an importunate dispute, might be numbered among the transient evils of a despotic administration, which are neither felt nor remembered by posterity.

But this incident, so inconsiderable that it scarcely deserves a place in history, was productive of a memorable schism, which afflicted the provinces of Africa above three hundred years, and was extinguished only with Christianity itself. The inflexible zeal of freedom and fanaticism animated the Donatists to refuse obedience to the usurpers, whose election they disputed, and whose spiritual powers they denied. Excluded from the civil and religious communion of mankind, they boldly excommunicated the rest of mankind who had embraced the impious party of Cæcilian, and of the Traditors, from whom he derived his pretended ordination. They asserted with confidence, and almost with exultation, that the Apostolical succession was interrupted; that *all* the bishops of Europe and Asia were infected by the contagion of guilt and schism; and that the prerogatives of the catholic church were confined to the chosen portion of the African believers, who alone had preserved inviolate the integrity of their faith and discipline.

The schism of the Donatists was confined to Africa; the more diffusive mischief of the Trinitarian controversy successively penetrated into every part of the Christian world. The former was an accidental quarrel, occasioned by the abuse of freedom; the latter was a high and mysterious argument, derived from the abuse of philosophy. From the age of Constantine to that of Clovis and Theodoric, the temporal interests both of the Romans and barbarians were deeply involved in the theological disputes of Arianism. The historian may therefore be permitted respectfully to withdraw the veil of the sanctuary, and to deduce the progress of reason and faith, of error and passion, from the school of Plato to the decline and fall of the empire.

The genius of Plato, informed by his own meditation or by the traditional knowledge of the priests of Egypt, had ventured to explore the mysterious nature of the Deity. When he had elevated his mind to the sublime contemplation of the first self-existent, necessary cause of the universe, the Athenian sage was incapable of conceiving *how* the simple unity of his essence could admit the infinite variety of distinct and successive ideas which compose the model of the intellectual world; *how* a Being purely incorporeal could execute that perfect model, and mould with a plastic hand the rude and independent chaos. The vain hope of extricating himself from these difficulties, which must ever oppress the feeble powers of the human mind, might induce Plato to consider the divine nature under the threefold modification—of the first cause, the reason, or *Logos*, and the soul or spirit of the universe. His poetical imagination sometimes fixed and animated these metaphysical abstractions; the three *archical* or original principles were represented in the Platonic system as three Gods, united with each other by a mysterious and ineffable generation; and the Logos was particularly considered under the more accessible character of the Son of an Eternal Father, and the Creator and Governor of the world. Such appear to have been the secret doctrines which were cautiously whispered in the gardens of the Academy; and which, according to the more recent disciples of Plato, could not be perfectly understood till after an assiduous study of thirty years.

A prophet, or apostle, inspired by the Deity, can alone exercise a lawful dominion over the faith of mankind: and the theology of Plato might have been for ever confounded with the philosophical visions of the Academy, the Porch, and the Lyceum, if the name and divine attributes of the *Logos* had not been confirmed by the celestial pen of the last and most sublime of the Evangelists. The Christian Revelation, which was consummated under the reign of Nerva, disclosed to the world the amazing secret, that the Logos, who was with God from the beginning, and was God, who had made all things, and for whom all things had been made, was incarnate in the person of Jesus of Nazareth; who had been born of a virgin, and suffered death on the cross.

A chosen society of philosophers, men of a liberal education and curious disposition, might silently meditate, and temperately discuss in the gardens of Athens or the library of Alexandria, the abstruse questions of metaphysical science. The lofty speculations, which neither convinced the understanding nor agitated the passions of the Platonists themselves, were carelessly overlooked by the idle, the busy, and even the studious part of mankind. But after the *Logos* had been revealed as the sacred object of the faith, the hope, and the religious worship of the Christians, the mysterious system was embraced by a numerous and increasing multitude in every province of the Roman world. Those persons who, from their age, or sex, or occupations, were the least qualified to judge, who were the least exercised in the habits of abstract reasoning, aspired to contemplate the economy of the Divine Nature: and it is the boast of Tertullian that a Christian mechanic could readily answer such questions as had perplexed the wisest of the Grecian sages. Where the subject lies so far beyond our reach, the difference between the highest and the lowest of human understandings may indeed be calculated as infinitely small; yet the degree of weakness may perhaps be measured by the degree of obstinacy and dogmatic confidence. These speculations, instead of being treated as the amusement of a vacant hour, became the most serious business of the present, and the most useful preparation for a future, life. A theology which it was incumbent to believe, which it was impious to doubt, and which it might be dangerous, and even fatal, to mistake, became the familiar topic of private meditation and popular discourse.

After the edict of toleration had restored peace and leisure to the Christians, the Trinitarian controversy was revived in the ancient seat of Platonism, the learned, the opulent, the tumultuous city of Alexandria; and the flame of religious discord was rapidly communicated from the schools to the clergy, the people, the provinces, and the East. The abstruse question of the eternity of the *Logos* was agitated in ecclesiastic conferences and popular sermons; and the heterodox opinions of Arius were soon made public by his own zeal and by that of his adversaries. His most implacable adversaries have acknowledged the learning and blameless life of the eminent presbyter, who, in a former election, had declined, and perhaps generously declined, his pretensions to the episcopal throne. His competitor Alexander assumed the office of his judge. The important cause was argued before him; and if at first he seemed to hesitate, he at length pronounced his final sentence as an absolute rule of faith. The undaunted presbyter, who presumed to resist the authority of his angry bishop, was separated from the communion of the church. But the pride of Arius was supported by the applause of a numerous party. He reckoned among his immediate followers two bishops of Egypt, seven presbyters, twelve deacons, and (what may appear almost incredible) seven hundred virgins. A large majority of the bishops of Asia appeared to support or favour his cause; and their measures were conducted by Eusebius of Cæsarea, the most learned of the Christian prelates; and by Eusebius of Nicomedia, who had acquired the reputation of a statesman without forfeiting that of a saint. Synods in Palestine and Bithynia were opposed to the synods of Egypt. The attention of the prince and people was attracted by this theological dispute; and the decision, at the end of six years, was referred to the supreme authority of the general council of Nice.

When the mysteries of the Christian faith were dangerously exposed to public debate, it might be observed that the human understanding was capable of forming three distinct, though imperfect, systems concerning the nature of the Divine Trinity, and it was pronounced that none of these systems, in a pure and absolute sense, were exempt from heresy and error. I. According to the first hypothesis, which was maintained by Arius and his disciples, the *Logos* was a dependent and spontaneous production, created from nothing by the will of the Father. The Son, by whom all things were made, had been begotten before all worlds, and the longest of the astronomical periods could be compared only as a fleeting moment to the extent of his duration; yet this duration was not infinite, and there *had* been a time which preceded the ineffable generation of the *Logos*. On this only-begotten Son the Almighty Father had transfused his ample spirit, and impressed the effulgence of his glory. Visible image of invisible perfection, he saw, at an immeasurable distance beneath his feet, the thrones of the brightest archangels; yet he shone only with a reflected light, and, like the sons of the Roman emperors, who were invested with the titles of Cæsar or Augustus, he governed the universe in obedience to the will of his Father and Monarch. II. In the second hypothesis, the *Logos* possessed all the inherent, incommunicable perfections which religion and philosophy appropriate to the Supreme God.

Three distinct and infinite minds or substances, three co-equal and co-eternal beings, composed the Divine Essence; and it would have implied contradiction that any of them should not have existed, or that they should ever cease to exist. The advocates of a system which seemed to establish three independent Deities attempted to preserve the unity of the First Cause, so conspicuous in the design and order of the world, by the perpetual concord of their administration and the essential agreement of their will. A faint resemblance of this unity of action may be discovered in the societies of men, and even of animals. The causes which disturb their harmony proceed only from the imperfection and inequality of their faculties; but the omnipotence which is guided by infinite wisdom and goodness cannot fail of choosing the same means for the accomplishment of the same ends. III. Three beings, who, by the selfderived necessity of their existence, possess all the divine attributes in the most perfect degree, who are eternal in duration, infinite in space, and intimately present to each other and to the whole universe, irresistibly force themselves on the astonished mind as one and the same Being, who, in the economy of grace, as well as in that of nature, may manifest himself under different forms, and be considered under different aspects. By this hypothesis a real substantial trinity is refined into a trinity of names and abstract modifications that subsist only in the mind which conceives them. The *Logos* is no longer a person, but an attribute; and it is only in a figurative sense that the epithet of Son can be applied to the eternal reason which was with God from the beginning, and by *which*, not by *whom*, all things were made. The incarnation of the *Logos* is reduced to a mere inspiration of the Divine Wisdom, which filled the soul and directed all the actions of the man Jesus. Thus, after revolving round the theological circle, we are surprised to find that the Sabellian ends where the Ebionite had begun, and that the incomprehensible mystery which excites our adoration eludes our inquiry.

If the bishops of the council of Nice had been permitted to follow the unbiassed dictates of their conscience, Arius and his associates could scarcely have flattered themselves with the hopes of obtaining a majority of votes in favour of an hypothesis so directly adverse to the two most popular opinions of the catholic world. The Arians soon perceived the danger of their situation, and prudently assumed those modest virtues which, in the fury of civil and religious dissensions, are seldom practised, or even praised, except by the weaker party. They recommended the exercise of Christian charity and moderation, urged the incomprehensible nature of the controversy, disclaimed the use of any terms or definitions which could not be found in the Scriptures, and offered, by very liberal concessions, to satisfy their adversaries without renouncing the integrity of their own principles. The victorious faction received all their proposals with haughty suspicion, and anxiously sought for some irreconcilable mark of distinction, the rejection of which might involve the Arians in the guilt and consequences of heresy. A letter was publicly read and ignominiously torn, in which their patron, Eusebius of Nicomedia, ingenuously confessed that the admission of the HOMOOUSION, or Consubstantial, a word already familiar to the Platonists, was incompatible with the principles of their theological system. The more fashionable saints of the Arian times, the intrepid Athanasius, the learned Gregory Nazianzen, and the other pillars of the church, who supported with ability and success the Nicene doctrine, appeared to consider the expression of *substance* as if it had been synonymous with that of *nature*; and they ventured to illustrate their meaning by affirming that three men, as they belong to the same common species, are consubstantial or homoousian to each other. This pure and distinct equality was tempered, on the one hand, by the internal connection and spiritual penetration which indissolubly unites the divine persons; and, on the other, by the pre-eminence of the Father, which was acknowledged as far as it is compatible with the independence of the Son. Within these limits the almost invisible and tremulous ball of orthodoxy was allowed securely to vibrate. On either side, beyond this consecrated ground, the heretics and the dæmons lurked in ambush to surprise and devour the unhappy wanderer. But as the degrees of theological hatred depend on the spirit of the war rather than on the importance of the controversy, the heretics who degraded were treated with more severity than those who annihilated the person of the Son. The life of Athanasius was consumed in irreconcilable opposition to the impious *madness* of the Arians, but he defended above twenty years the Sabellianism of Marcellus of Ancyra; and when at last he was compelled to withdraw himself from his communion, he continued to mention with an ambiguous smile the venial errors of his respectable friend.

The authority of a general council, to which the Arians themselves had been compelled to submit, inscribed on the banners of the orthodox party the mysterious characters of the word Homoousion,

which essentially contributed, notwithstanding some obscure disputes, some nocturnal combats, to maintain and perpetuate the
uniformity of faith, or at least of language. The Consubstantialists,
who by their success have deserved and obtained the title of
Catholics, gloried in the simplicity and steadiness of their own
creed, and insulted the repeated variations of their adversaries, who
were destitute of any certain rule of faith. The sincerity or the cunning of the Arian chiefs, the fear of the laws or of the people, their
reverence for Christ, their hatred of Athanasius, all the causes,
human and divine, that influence and disturb the counsels of a
theological faction, introduced among the sectaries a spirit of
discord and inconstancy, which in the course of a few years erected
eighteen different models of religion, and avenged the violated
dignity of the church. These Arians were powerfully supported by
the weight and abilities of their leaders, who had succeeded to the
management of the Eusebian interest, and who occupied the principal
thrones of the East. They professed to believe, either without
reserve or according to the Scriptures, that the Son was different
from all *other* creatures, and similar only to the Father. But they
denied that he was either of the same or of a similar substance;
sometimes boldly justifying their dissent, and sometimes objecting
to the use of the word substance, which seems to imply an adequate,
or at least a distinct, notion of the nature of the Deity. The sect
which asserted the doctrine of a similar substance was the most
numerous, at least in the provinces of Asia; and when the leaders
of both parties were assembled in the council of Seleucia, *their*
opinion would have prevailed by a majority of one hundred and
five to forty-three bishops. The Greek word which was chosen to
express this mysterious resemblance bears so close an affinity to the
orthodox symbol, that the profane of every age have derided the
furious contests which the difference of a single diphthong excited
between the Homoousians and the Homoiousians. As it frequently
happens that the sounds and characters which approach the nearest
to each other accidentally represent the most opposite ideas, the
observation would be itself ridiculous, if it were possible to mark
any real and sensible distinction between the doctrine of the Semi-
Arians, as they were improperly styled, and that of the Catholics
themselves. The bishop of Poitiers, who in his Phrygian exile very
wisely aimed at a coalition of parties, endeavours to prove that, by
a pious and faithful interpretation, the *Homoiousion* may be
reduced to a consubstantial sense. Yet he confesses that the word

has a dark and suspicious aspect; and, as if darkness were congenial to theological disputes, the Semi-Arians, who advanced to the doors of the church, assailed them with the most unrelenting fury.

The provinces of Egypt and Asia, which cultivated the language and manners of the Greeks, had deeply imbibed the venom of the Arian controversy. The familiar study of the Platonic system, a vain and argumentative disposition, a copious and flexible idiom, supplied the clergy and people of the East with an inexhaustible flow of words and distinctions; and, in the midst of their fierce contentions, they easily forgot the doubt which is recommended by philosophy, and the submission which is enjoined by religion. The inhabitants of the West were of a less inquisitive spirit; their passions were not so forcibly moved by invisible objects, their minds were less frequently exercised by the habits of dispute; and such was the happy ignorance of the Gallican church, that Hilary himself, above thirty years after the first general council, was still a stranger to the Nicene creed.

The unhappy spirit of discord which pervaded the provinces of the East interrupted the triumph of Constantine; but the emperor continued for some time to view with cool and careless indifference the object of the dispute. As he was yet ignorant of the difficulty of appeasing the quarrels of theologians, he addressed to the contending parties, to Alexander and to Arius, a moderating epistle; which may be ascribed with far greater reason to the untutored sense of a soldier and statesman than to the dictates of any of his episcopal counsellors. He attributes the origin of the whole controversy to a trifling and subtle question concerning an incomprehensible point of the law, which was foolishly asked by the bishop, and imprudently resolved by the presbyter. He laments that the Christian people, who had the same God, the same religion, and the same worship, should be divided by such inconsiderable distinctions; and he seriously recommends to the clergy of Alexandria the example of the Greek philosophers, who could maintain their arguments without losing their temper, and assert their freedom without violating their friendship. The indifference and contempt of the sovereign would have been, perhaps, the most effectual method of silencing the dispute, if the popular current had been less rapid and impetuous, and if Constantine himself, in the midst of faction and fanaticism, could have preserved the calm possession of his own mind. But his ecclesiastical ministers soon contrived to seduce the impartiality of the magistrate, and to awaken the zeal of the proselyte. He was provoked by the insults which had been offered to his statues; he was alarmed by the real as well as the imaginary magnitude of the spreading mischief; and he extinguished the hope of peace and toleration, from the moment that he assembled three hundred bishops within the walls of the same palace. The presence of the monarch swelled the importance of the debate; his attention multiplied the arguments; and he exposed his person with a patient intrepidity which animated the valour of the combatants. Notwithstanding the applause which has been bestowed on the eloquence and sagacity of Constantine, a Roman general, whose religion might be still a subject of doubt, and whose mind had not been enlightened either by study or by inspiration, was indifferently qualified to discuss, in the Greek language, a metaphysical question, or an article of faith. But the credit of his favourite Osius, who appears to have presided in the council of Nice, might dispose the emperor in favour of the orthodox party; and a well-timed insinuation, that the same Eusebius of Nicomedia, who now protected the heretic, had lately assisted the tyrant, might exasperate him against their adversaries. The Nicene creed was ratified by Constantine; and his firm declaration, that those who resisted the divine judgment of the synod must prepare themselves for an immediate exile, annihilated the murmurs of a feeble opposition; which, from seventeen, was almost instantly reduced to two, protesting bishops. Eusebius of Cæsarea yielded a reluctant and ambiguous consent to the homoousion; and the wavering conduct of the Nicomedian Eusebius served only to delay about three months his disgrace and exile. The impious Arius was banished into one of the remote provinces of Illyricum; his person and disciples were branded, by law, with the odious name of Porphyrians; his writings were condemned to the flames, and a capital punishment was denounced against those in whose possession they should be found. The emperor had now imbibed the spirit of controversy, and the angry sarcastic style of his edicts was designed to inspire his subjects with the hatred which he had conceived against the enemies of Christ.

But, as if the conduct of the emperor had been guided by passion instead of principle, three years from the council of Nice were scarcely elapsed before he discovered some symptoms of mercy, and even of indulgence, towards the proscribed sect, which was secretly protected by his favourite sister. The exiles were recalled; and Eusebius, who gradually resumed his influence over the mind of Constantine, was restored to the episcopal throne, from which he had been ignominiously degraded. Arius himself was treated by the whole court with the respect which would have been due to an innocent and oppressed man. His faith was approved by the synod of Jerusalem; and the emperor seemed impatient to repair his injustice, by issuing an absolute command that he should be solemnly admitted to the communion in the cathedral of Constantinople. On the same day which had been fixed for the triumph of Arius, he expired; and the strange and horrid circumstances of his death might excite a suspicion that the orthodox saints had contributed more efficaciously than by their prayers to deliver the church from the most formidable of her enemies. The three principal leaders of the catholics, Athanasius of Alexandria, Eustathius of Antioch, and Paul of Constantinople, were deposed on various accusations, by the sentence of numerous councils; and were afterwards banished into distant provinces by the first of the Christian emperors, who, in the last moments of his life received the rites of baptism from the Arian bishop of Nicomedia.

We have seldom an opportunity of observing, either in active or speculative life, what effect may be produced, or what obstacles may be surmounted, by the force of a single mind, when it is inflexibly applied to the pursuit of a single object. The immortal name of Athanasius will never be separated from the catholic doctrine of the Trinity, to whose defence he consecrated every moment and every faculty of his being. Educated in the family of Alexander, he had vigorously opposed the early progress of the Arian heresy: he exercised the important functions of secretary under the aged prelate; and the fathers of the Nicene council beheld with surprise and respect the rising virtues of the young deacon. In a time of public danger the dull claims of age and of rank are sometimes superseded; and within five months after his return from Nice the deacon Athanasius was seated on the archiepiscopal throne of Egypt. He filled that eminent station above forty-six years, and his long administration was spent in a perpetual combat against the powers of Arianism. Five times was Athanasius expelled from his throne; twenty years he passed as an exile or a fugitive; and almost every province of the Roman empire was successively witness to his merit, and his sufferings in the cause of the Homoousion, which he considered as the sole pleasure and business, as the duty and as the glory of his life. Amidst the storms of persecution, the archbishop of Alexandria was patient of labour,

jealous of fame, careless of safety; and although his mind was tainted
by the contagion of fanaticism, Athanasius displayed a superiority
of character and abilities which would have qualified him, far better
than the degenerate sons of Constantine, for the government of a
great monarchy. His learning was much less profound and extensive than that of Eusebius of Cæsarea, and his rude eloquence
could not be compared with the polished oratory of Gregory or
Basil; but whenever the primate of Egypt was called upon to justify
his sentiments or his conduct, his unpremeditated style, either of
speaking or writing, was clear, forcible, and persuasive. He has
always been revered in the orthodox school as one of the most
accurate masters of the Christian theology; and he was supposed
to possess two profane sciences, less adapted to the episcopal
character—the knowledge of jurisprudence, and that of divination.
Some fortunate conjectures of future events, which impartial reasoners might ascribe to the experience and judgment of Athanasius,
were attributed by his friends to heavenly inspiration, and imputed
by his enemies to infernal magic.

But as Athanasius was continually engaged with the prejudices
and passions of every order of men, from the monk to the emperor,
the knowledge of human nature was his first and most important
science. He preserved a distinct and unbroken view of a scene
which was incessantly shifting; and never failed to improve those
decisive moments which are irrecoverably past before they are
perceived by a common eye. The archbishop of Alexandria was
capable of distinguishing how far he might boldly command, and
where he must dexterously insinuate; how long he might contend
with power, and when he must withdraw from persecution; and while
he directed the thunders of the church against heresy and rebellion,
he could assume, in the bosom of his own party, the flexible and
indulgent temper of a prudent leader. The election of Athanasius
has not escaped the reproach of irregularity and precipitation; but
the propriety of his behaviour conciliated the affections both of the
clergy and of the people. The Alexandrians were impatient to rise
in arms for the defence of an eloquent and liberal pastor. In his
distress he always derived support, or at least consolation, from the
faithful attachment of his parochial clergy; and the hundred bishops
of Egypt adhered, with unshaken zeal, to the cause of Athanasius.
In the modest equipage which pride and policy would affect, he
frequently performed the episcopal visitation of his provinces, from
the mouth of the Nile to the confines of Æthiopia; familiarly

conversing with the meanest of the populace, and humbly saluting the saints and hermits of the desert. Nor was it only in ecclesiastical assemblies, among men whose education and manners were similar to his own, that Athanasius displayed the ascendancy of his genius. He appeared with easy and respectful firmness in the courts of princes; and in the various turns of his prosperous and adverse fortune he never lost the confidence of his friends, or the esteem of his enemies.

The persecution of Athanasius and of so many respectable bishops, who suffered for the truth of their opinions, or at least for the integrity of their conscience, was a just subject of indignation and discontent to all Christians, except those who were blindly devoted to the Arian faction. The people regretted the loss of their faithful pastors, whose banishment was usually followed by the intrusion of a stranger into the episcopal chair, and loudly complained that the right of election was violated, and that they were condemned to obey a mercenary usurper, whose person was unknown and whose principles were suspected. The catholics might prove to the world that they were not involved in the guilt and heresy of their ecclesiastical governor, by publicly testifying their dissent, or by totally separating themselves from his communion. The first of these methods was invented at Antioch, and practised with such success that it was soon diffused over the Christian world. The doxology, or sacred hymn, which celebrates the *glory* of the Trinity, is susceptible of very nice, but material, inflections; and the substance of an orthodox or an heretical creed may be expressed by the difference of a disjunctive or a copulative particle. Alternate responses and a more regular psalmody were introduced into the public service by Flavianus and Diodorus, two devout and active laymen, who were attached to the Nicene faith. Under their conduct a swarm of monks issued from the adjacent desert, bands of well-disciplined singers were stationed in the cathedral of Antioch, the Glory to the Father, AND the Son AND the Holy Ghost was triumphantly chanted by a full chorus of voices, and the catholics insulted, by the purity of their doctrine, the Arian prelate who had usurped the throne of the venerable Eustathius. The same zeal which inspired their songs prompted the more scrupulous members of the orthodox party to form separate assemblies, which were governed by the presbyters, till the death of their exiled bishop allowed the election and consecration of a new episcopal pastor. The revolutions of the court multiplied the number of pretenders, and the same city was often disputed, under the reign of Constantius, by two, or three, or even four bishops, who exercised their spiritual jurisdiction over their respective followers, and alternately lost and regained the temporal possessions of the church. The abuse of Christianity introduced into the Roman government new causes of tyranny and sedition; the bands of civil society were torn asunder by the fury of religious factions; and the obscure citizen, who might calmly have surveyed the elevation and fall of successive emperors, imagined and experienced that his own life and fortune were connected with the interests of a popular ecclesiastic.

Notwithstanding the rapid increase of Christians under the reign of the Flavian family, Rome, Alexandria, and the other great cities of the empire, still contained a strong and powerful faction of Infidels, who envied the prosperity, and who ridiculed, even in their theatres, the theological disputes of the church. Constantinople alone enjoyed the advantage of being born and educated in the bosom of the faith. The capital of the East had never been polluted by the worship of idols, and the whole body of the people had deeply imbibed the opinions, the virtues, and the passions which distinguished the Christians of that age from the rest of mankind. After the death of Alexander the episcopal throne was disputed by Paul and Macedonius. By their zeal and abilities they both deserved the eminent station to which they aspired; and if the moral character of Macedonius was less exceptionable, his competitor had the advantage of a prior election and a more orthodox doctrine. His firm attachment to the Nicene creed, which has given Paul a place in the calendar among saints and martyrs, exposed him to the resentment of the Arians. In the space of fourteen years he was five times driven from his throne, to which he was more frequently restored by the violence of the people than by the permission of the prince, and the power of Macedonius could be secured only by the death of his rival. The unfortunate Paul was dragged in chains from the sandy deserts of Mesopotamia to the most desolate places of Mount Taurus, confined in a dark and narrow dungeon, left six days without food, and at length strangled, by the order of Philip, one of the principal ministers of the emperor Constantius. The first blood which stained the new capital was spilt in this ecclesiastical contest, and many persons were slain on both sides in the furious and obstinate seditions of the people. The commission of enforcing a sentence of banishment against Paul had been intrusted to Hermogenes, the master-general of the cavalry, but the execution of it was fatal to himself. The catholics rose in the defence of their bishop; the palace of Hermogenes was consumed; the first military officer of the empire was dragged by the heels through the streets of Constantinople, and, after he expired, his lifeless corpse was exposed to their wanton insults. The fate of Hermogenes instructed Philip, the Prætorian præfect, to act with more precaution on a similar occasion. In the most gentle and honourable terms he required the attendance of Paul in the baths of Zeuxippus, which had a private communication with the palace and the sea. A vessel, which lay ready at the garden stairs, immediately hoisted sail, and, while the people were still ignorant of the meditated sacrilege, their bishop was already embarked on his voyage to Thessalonica. They soon beheld, with surprise and indignation, the gates of the palace thrown open, and the usurper Macedonius seated by the side of the præfect on a lofty chariot, which was surrounded by troops of guards with drawn swords. The military procession advanced towards the cathedral; and the Arians and the catholics eagerly rushed to occupy that important post, and three thousand one hundred and fifty persons lost their lives in the confusion of the tumult. Macedonius, who was supported by a regular force, obtained a decisive victory, but his reign was disturbed by clamour and sedition, and the causes which appeared the least connected with the subject of dispute were sufficient to nourish and to kindle the flame of civil discord. As the chapel in which the body of the great Constantine had been deposited was in a ruinous condition, the bishop transported those venerable remains into the church of St. Acacius. This prudent and even pious measure was represented as a wicked profanation by the whole party which adhered to the Homoousian doctrine. The factions immediately flew to arms, the consecrated ground was used as their field of battle, and one of the ecclesiastical historians has observed, as a real fact, not as a figure of rhetoric, that the well before the church overflowed with a stream of blood which filled the porticoes and the adjacent courts. The writer who should impute these tumults solely to a religious principle would betray a very imperfect knowledge of human nature; yet it must be confessed that the motive which misled the sincerity of zeal, and the pretence which disguised the licentiousness of passion, suppressed the remorse which, in another cause, would have succeeded to the rage of the Christians of Constantinople.

The cruel and arbitrary disposition of Constantius, which did not always require the provocations of guilt and resistance, was justly exasperated by the tumults of his capital and the criminal behaviour of a faction which opposed the authority and religion of their sovereign. The ordinary punishments of death, exile, and confiscation were inflicted with partial rigour, and the Greeks still revere the holy memory of two clerks, a reader and a subdeacon, who were accused of the murder of Hermogenes, and beheaded at the gates of Constantinople. By an edict of Constantius against the catholics, which has not been judged worthy of a place in the Theodosian code, those who refused to communicate with the Arian bishops, and particularly with Macedonius, were deprived of the immunities of ecclesiastics and of the rights of Christians; they were compelled to relinquish the possession of the churches, and were strictly prohibited from holding their assemblies within the walls of the city. The execution of this unjust law in the provinces of Thrace and Asia Minor was committed to the zeal of Macedonius; the civil and military powers were directed to obey his commands; and the cruelties exercised by this Semi-Arian tyrant in the support of the *Homoiousion* exceeded the commission and disgraced the reign of Constantius. The sacraments of the church were administered to the reluctant victims, who denied the vocation and abhorred the principles of Macedonius. The rites of baptism were conferred on women and children who, for that purpose, had been torn from the arms of their friends and parents; the mouths of the communicants were held open by a wooden engine while the consecrated bread was forced down their throat; the breasts of tender virgins were either burnt with red-hot egg-shells, or inhumanly compressed between sharp and heavy boards. The Novatians of Constantinople and the adjacent country, by their firm attachment to the Homoousian standard, deserved to be confounded with the catholics themselves. Macedonius was informed that a large district of Paphlagonia was almost entirely inhabited by those sectaries. He resolved either to convert or to extirpate them, and, as he distrusted on this occasion the efficacy of an ecclesiastical mission, he commanded a body of four thousand legionaries to march against the rebels, and to reduce the territory of Mantinium under his spiritual dominion. The Novatian peasants, animated by despair and religious fury, boldly encountered the invaders of their country, and, though many of the Paphlagonians were slain, the Roman legions were vanquished by an irregular multitude, armed only with scythes and axes, and, except a few who escaped by an ignominious flight, four thousand soldiers were left dead on the field of battle.

The successor of Constantius has expressed, in a concise but lively manner, some of the theological calamities which afflicted the empire, and more especially the East, in the reign of a prince who was the slave of his own passions and of those of his eunuchs. "Many were imprisoned, and persecuted, and driven into exile. Whole troops of those who are styled heretics were massacred, particularly at Cyzicus and at Samosata. In Paphlagonia, Bithynia, Galatia, and in many other provinces, towns and villages were laid waste and utterly destroyed."

While the flames of the Arian controversy consumed the vitals of the empire, the African provinces were infested by their peculiar enemies, the savage fanatics who, under the name of *Circumcellions*, formed the strength and scandal of the Donatist party. The severe execution of the laws of Constantine had excited a spirit of discontent and resistance; the strenuous efforts of his son Constans to restore the unity of the church exasperated the sentiments of mutual hatred which had first occasioned the separation; and the methods of force and corruption employed by the two Imperial commissioners, Paul and Macarius, furnished the schismatics with a specious contrast between the maxims of the apostles and the conduct of their pretended successors. The peasants who inhabited the villages of Numidia and Mauritania were a ferocious race, who had been imperfectly reduced under the authority of the Roman laws, who were imperfectly converted to the Christian faith, but who were actuated by a blind and furious enthusiasm in the cause of their Donatist teachers. They indignantly supported the exile of their bishops, the demolition of their churches, and the interruption of their secret assemblies. The violence of the officers of justice, who were usually sustained by a military guard, was sometimes repelled with equal violence, and the blood of some popular ecclesiastics, which had been shed in the quarrel, inflamed their rude followers with an eager desire of revenging the death of these holy martyrs. By their own cruelty and rashness the ministers of persecution sometimes provoked their fate, and the guilt of an accidental tumult precipitated the criminals into despair and rebellion. Driven from their native villages, the Donatist peasants assembled in formidable gangs on the edge of the Gætulian desert, and readily exchanged the habits of labour for a life of idleness and rapine, which was consecrated by the name of religion, and faintly condemned by the doctors of the sect. The leaders of the Circumcellions assumed the title of captains of the saints; their principal weapon, as they were indifferently provided with swords and spears, was a huge and weighty club, which they termed an *Israelite*, and the well-known sound of "Praise be to God!" which they used as their cry of war, diffused consternation over the unarmed provinces of Africa. At first their depredations were coloured by the plea of necessity, but they soon exceeded the measure of subsistence, indulged without control their intemperance and avarice, burnt the villages which they had pillaged, and reigned the licentious tyrants of the open country. The occupations of husbandry and the administration of justice were interrupted; and, as the Circumcellions pretended to restore the primitive equality of mankind, and to reform the abuses of civil society, they opened a secure asylum for the slaves and debtors who flocked in crowds to their holy standard. When they were not resisted they usually contented themselves with plunder, but the slightest opposition provoked them to acts of violence and murder; and some catholic priests, who had imprudently signalised their zeal, were tortured by the fanatics with the most refined and wanton barbarity. The spirit of the Circumcellions was not always exerted against their defenceless enemies; they engaged, and sometimes defeated, the troops of the province, and in the bloody action of Bagai they attacked in the open field, but with unsuccessful valour, an advanced guard of the Imperial cavalry. The Donatists who were taken in arms received, and they soon deserved, the same treatment which might have been shown to the wild beasts of the desert. The captives died, without a murmur, either by the sword, the axe, or the fire; and the measures of retaliation were multiplied in a rapid proportion, which aggravated the horrors of rebellion and excluded the hope of mutual forgiveness.

Such disorders are the natural effects of religious tyranny; but the rage of the Donatists was inflamed by a frenzy of a very extraordinary kind; and which, if it really prevailed among them in so extravagant a degree, cannot surely be paralleled in any country or in any age. Many of these fanatics were possessed with the horror of life, and the desire of martyrdom; and they deemed it of little moment by what means, or by what hands, they perished, if their conduct was sanctified by the intention of devoting themselves to the glory of the true faith, and the hope of eternal happiness. Sometimes they rudely disturbed the festivals, and profaned the temples of Paganism, with the design of exciting the most zealous of the idolaters to revenge the insulted honour of their gods. They sometimes forced their way into the courts of justice, and compelled the affrighted judge to give orders for their immediate execution. They frequently stopped travellers on the public highways, and obliged them to inflict the stroke of martyrdom, by the promise of a reward if they consented, and by the threat of instant death if they refused to grant so very singular a favour. When they were disappointed of every other resource, they announced the day on which, in the presence of their friends and brethren, they should cast themselves headlong from some lofty rock; and many precipices were shown which had acquired fame by the number of religious suicides. In the actions of these desperate enthusiasts, who were admired by one party as the martyrs of God, and abhorred by the other as the victims of Satan, an impartial philosopher may discover the influence and the last abuse of that inflexible spirit which was originally derived from the character and principals of the Jewish nation.

The simple narrative of the intestine divisions which distracted the peace and dishonoured the triumph of the church, will confirm the remark of a Pagan historian, and justify the complaint of a venerable bishop. The experience of Ammianus had convinced him that the enmity of the Christians towards each other surpassed the fury of savage beasts against man; and Gregory Nazianzen most pathetically laments that the kingdom of heaven was converted by discord into the image of chaos, of a nocturnal tempest, and of hell itself. The fierce and partial writers of the times, ascribing *all* virtue to themselves, and imputing *all* guilt to their adversaries, have painted the battle of the angels and dæmons. Our calmer reason will reject such pure and perfect monsters of vice or sanctity, and will impute an equal, or at least an indiscriminate, measure of good and evil to the hostile sectaries, who assumed and bestowed the appellations of orthodox and heretics. They had been educated in the same religion and the same civil society. Their hopes and fears in the present, or in a future life, were balanced in the same proportion. On either side the error might be innocent, the faith sincere, the practice meritorious or corrupt. Their passions were excited by similar objects; and they might alternately abuse the favour of the court, or of the people. The metaphysical opinions of the Athanasians and the Arians could not influence their moral character; and they were alike actuated by the intolerant spirit which has been extracted from the pure and simple maxims of the Gospel.

The divisions of Christianity suspended the ruin of Paganism; and the holy war against the infidels was less vigorously prosecuted by princes and bishops who were more immediately alarmed by the guilt and danger of domestic rebellion. The extirpation of idolatry might have been justified by the established principles of intolerance: but the hostile sects, which alternately reigned in the Imperial court, were mutually apprehensive of alienating, and perhaps exasperating, the minds of a powerful, though declining faction. Every motive of authority and fashion, of interest and reason, now militated on the side of Christianity; but two or three generations elapsed before their victorious influence was universally felt. The religion which had so long and so lately been established in the Roman empire was still revered by a numerous people, less attached indeed to speculative opinion than to ancient custom. The honours of the state and army were indifferently bestowed on all the subjects of Constantine and Constantius; and a considerable portion of knowledge and wealth and valours was still engaged in the service of polytheism. The superstition of the senator and of the peasant, of the poet and the philosopher, was derived from very different causes, but they met with equal devotion in the temples of the gods. Their zeal was insensibly provoked by the insulting triumph of a proscribed sect; and their hopes were revived by the well-grounded confidence that the presumptive heir of the empire, a young and valiant hero, who had delivered Gaul from the arms of the barbarians, had secretly embraced the religion of his ancestors.

XX

(360–361 A.D.) JULIAN IS DECLARED EMPEROR BY THE LEGIONS OF GAUL—HIS MARCH AND SUCCESS—THE DEATH OF CONSTANTIUS—CIVIL ADMINISTRATION OF JULIAN

While the Romans languished under the ignominious tyranny of eunuchs and bishops, the praises of Julian were repeated with transport in every part of the empire, except in the palace of Constantius. The barbarians of Germany had felt, and still dreaded, the arms of the young Cæsar; his soldiers were the companions of his victory; the grateful provincials enjoyed the blessings of his reign; but the favourites, who had opposed his elevation, were offended by his virtues; and they justly considered the friend of the people as the enemy of the court. As long as the fame of Julian was doubtful, the buffoons of the palace, who were skilled in the language of satire, tried the efficacy of those arts which they had so often practised with success. They easily discovered that his simplicity was not exempt from affectation: the ridiculous epithets of an hairy savage, of an ape invested with the purple, were applied to the dress and person of the philosophic warrior; and his modest despatches were stigmatised as the vain and elaborate fictions of a loquacious Greek, a speculative soldier, who had studied the art of war amidst the groves of the Academy. The voice of malicious folly was at length silenced by the shouts of victory; the conqueror of the Franks and Alemanni could no longer be painted as an object of contempt; and the monarch himself was meanly ambitious of stealing from his lieutenant the honourable reward of his labours. In the letters crowned with laurel, which, according to ancient custom, were addressed to the provinces, the name of Julian was omitted. "Constantius had made his dispositions in person; *he* had signalised his valour in the foremost ranks; *his* military conduct had secured the victory; and the captive king of the barbarians was presented to *him* on the field of battle," from which he was at that time distant above forty days' journey. So extravagant a fable was incapable, however, of deceiving the public credulity, or even of satisfying the pride of the emperor himself. Secretly conscious that the applause and favour of the Romans accompanied the rising fortunes of Julian, his discontented mind was prepared to receive the subtle poison of those artful sycophants who coloured their mischievous designs with the fairest appearances of truth and candour. Instead of depreciating the merits of Julian, they acknowledged, and even exaggerated, his popular fame, superior talents, and important services. But they darkly insinuated that the virtues of the Cæsar might instantly be converted into the most dangerous crimes, if the inconstant multitude should prefer their inclinations to their duty; or if the general of a victorious army should be tempted from his allegiance by the hopes of revenge and independent greatness. The personal fears of Constantius were interpreted by his council as a laudable anxiety for the public safety; whilst in private, and perhaps in his own breast, he disguised, under the less odious appellation of fear, the sentiments of hatred and envy which he had secretly conceived for the inimitable virtues of Julian.

The apparent tranquillity of Gaul, and the imminent danger of the eastern provinces, offered a specious pretence for the design which was artfully concerted by the Imperial ministers. They resolved to disarm the Cæsar; to recall those faithful troops who guarded his person and dignity; and to employ, in a distant war against the Persian monarch, the hardy veterans who had vanquished, on the banks of the Rhine, the fiercest nations of Germany. While Julian used the laborious hours of his winter quarters at Paris in the administration of power, which, in his hands, was the exercise of virtue, he was surprised by the hasty arrival of a tribune and a notary, with positive orders from the emperor, which *they* were directed to execute, and *he* was commanded not to oppose. Constantius signified his pleasure that four entire legions—the Celtæ and Petulants, the Heruli and the Batavians—should be separated from the standard of Julian, under which they had acquired their fame and discipline; that in each of the remaining bands three hundred of the bravest youths should be selected; and that this numerous detachment, the strength of the Gallic army, should instantly begin their march, and exert their utmost diligence to arrive, before the opening of the campaign, on the frontiers of Persia. The Cæsar foresaw and lamented the consequences of this fatal mandate. Most of the auxiliaries, who engaged their voluntary service, had stipulated that they should never be obliged to pass the Alps. The public faith of Rome, and the personal honour of Julian, had been pledged for the observance of this condition. Such an act of treachery and oppression would destroy the confidence, and excite the resentment of the independent warriors of Germany, who considered truth as the noblest of their virtues, and freedom as the most valuable of their possessions. The legionaries, who enjoyed the title and privileges of Romans, were enlisted for the general defence of the republic; but those mercenary troops heard with cold indifference the antiquated names of the republic and of Rome. Attached, either from birth or long habit, to the climate and manners of Gaul, they loved and admired Julian; they despised, and perhaps hated, the emperor; they dreaded the laborious march, the Persian arrows, and the burning deserts of Asia. They claimed as their own the country which they had saved; and excused their want of spirit by pleading the sacred and more immediate duty of protecting their families and friends. The apprehensions of the Gauls were derived from the knowledge of the impending and inevitable danger. As soon as the provinces were exhausted of their military strength, the Germans would violate a treaty which had been imposed on their fears; and notwithstanding the abilities and valour of Julian, the general of a nominal army, to whom the public calamities would be imputed, must find himself, after a vain resistance, either a prisoner in the camp of the barbarians, or a criminal in the palace of Constantius. If Julian complied with the orders which he had received he subscribed his own destruction, and that of a people who deserved his affection. But a positive refusal was an act of rebellion and a declaration of war. The inexorable jealousy of the emperor, the peremptory, and perhaps insidious, nature of his commands, left not any room for a fair apology or candid interpretation; and the dependent station of the Cæsar scarcely allowed him to pause or to deliberate. Solitude increased the perplexity of Julian; he could no longer apply to the faithful counsels of Sallust, who had been removed from his office by the judicious malice of the eunuchs; he could not even enforce his representations by the concurrence of the ministers, who would have been afraid or ashamed to approve the ruin of Gaul. The moment had been chosen when Lupicinus, the general of the cavalry, was despatched into Britain, to repulse the inroads of the Scots and Picts; and Florentius was occupied at Vienne by the assessment of the tribute.

The latter, a crafty and corrupt statesman, declining to assume a responsible part of this dangerous occasion, eluded the pressing and repeated invitations of Julian, who represented to him that in every important measure the presence of the præfect was indispensable in the council of the prince. In the meanwhile the Cæsar was oppressed by the rude and importunate solicitations of the Imperial messengers, who presumed to suggest that, if he expected the return of his ministers, he could charge himself with the guilt of the delay, and reserve for them the merit of the execution. Unable to resist, unwilling to comply, Julian expressed in the most serious terms his wish, and even his intention, of resigning the purple, which he could not preserve with honour, but which he could not abdicate with safety.

After a painful conflict, Julian was compelled to acknowledge that obedience was the virtue of the most eminent subject, and that the sovereign alone was entitled to judge of the public welfare. He issued the necessary orders for carrying into execution the commands of Constantius; a part of the troops began their march for the Alps; and the detachments from the several garrisons moved towards their respective places of assembly. They advanced with difficulty through the trembling and affrighted crowds of provincials, who attempted to excite their pity by silent despair or loud lamentations; while the wives of the soldiers, holding their infants in their arms, accused the desertion of their husbands in the mixed language of grief, of tenderness, and of indignation. This scene of general distress afflicted the humanity of the Cæsar; he granted a sufficient number of post-waggons to transport the wives and families of the soldiers, endeavoured to alleviate the hardships which he was constrained to inflict, and increased by the most laudable arts his own popularity and the discontent of the exiled troops. The grief of an armed multitude is soon converted into rage; their licentious murmurs, which every hour were communicated from tent to tent with more boldness and effect, prepared their minds for the most daring acts of sedition; and by the connivance of their tribunes a seasonable libel was secretly dispersed, which painted in lively colours the disgrace of the Cæsar, the oppression of the Gallic army, and the feeble vices of the tyrant of Asia. The servants of Constantius were astonished and alarmed by the progress of this dangerous spirit. They pressed the Cæsar to hasten the departure of the troops; but they imprudently rejected the honest and judicious advice of Julian, who proposed that they should not march through Paris, and suggested the danger and temptation of a last interview.

As soon as the approach of the troops was announced, the Cæsar went out to meet them, and ascended his tribunal, which had been erected in a plain before the gates of the city. After distinguishing the officers and soldiers who by their rank or merit deserved a peculiar attention; Julian addressed himself in a studied oration to the surrounding multitude: he celebrated their exploits with grateful applause; encouraged them to accept, with alacrity, the honour of serving under the eyes of a powerful and liberal monarch; and admonished them that the commands of Augustus required an instant and cheerful obedience. The soldiers, who were apprehensive of offending their general by an indecent clamour, or of belying their sentiments by false and venal acclamations, maintained an obstinate silence; and, after a short pause, were dismissed to their quarters. The principal officers were entertained by the Cæsar, who professed, in the warmest language of friendship, his desire and his inability to reward, according to their deserts, the brave companions of his victories. They retired from the feast full of grief and perplexity; and lamented the hardship of their fate, which tore them from their beloved general and their native country. The only expedient which could prevent their separation was boldly agitated and approved; the popular resentment was insensibly moulded into a regular conspiracy; their just reasons of complaint were heightened by passion, and their passions were inflamed by wine, as on the eve of their departure the troops were indulged in licentious festivity. At the hour of midnight the impetuous multi-tude, with swords, and bows, and torches in their hands, rushed into the suburbs; encompassed the palace; and, careless of future dangers, pronounced the fatal and irrevocable words, JULIAN AUGUSTUS! The prince, whose anxious suspense was interrupted by their disorderly acclamations, secured the doors against their intrusion; and, as long as it was in his power, secluded his person and dignity from the accidents of a nocturnal tumult. At the dawn of the day the soldiers, whose zeal was irritated by opposition, forcibly entered the palace, seized, with respectful violence, the object of their choice, guarded Julian with drawn swords through the streets of Paris, placed him on the tribunal, and with repeated shouts saluted him as their emperor. Prudence as well as loyalty inculcated the propriety of resisting their treasonable designs, and of preparing for his oppressed virtue the excuse of violence.

Addressing himself by turns to the multitude and to individuals, he sometimes implored their mercy, and sometimes expressed his indignation; conjured them not to sully the fame of their immortal victories; ventured to promise that, if they would immediately return to their allegiance, he would undertake to obtain from the emperor not only a free and gracious pardon, but even the revocation of the orders which had excited their resentment. But the soldiers, who were conscious of their guilt, chose rather to depend on the gratitude of Julian than on the clemency of the emperor. Their zeal was insensibly turned into impatience, and their impatience into rage. The inflexible Cæsar sustained, till the third hour of the day, their prayers, their reproaches, and their menaces; nor did he yield till he had been repeatedly assured that, if he wished to live, he must consent to reign. He was exalted on a shield in the presence and amidst the unanimous acclamations of the troops; a rich military collar, which was offered by chance, supplied the want of a diadem; the ceremony was concluded by the promise of a moderate donative; and the new emperor, overwhelmed with real or affected grief, retired into the most secret recesses of his apartment.

The hopes of Julian depended much less on the number of his troops than on the celerity of his motions. In the execution of a daring enterprise he availed himself of every precaution, as far as prudence could suggest; and where prudence could no longer accompany his steps, he trusted the event to valour and to fortune. In the neighbourhood of Basel he assembled and divided his army. One body, which consisted of ten thousand men, was directed, under the command of Nevitta, general of the cavalry, to advance through the midland parts of Rhætia and Noricum. A similar division of troops, under the orders of Jovius and Jovinus, prepared to follow the oblique course of the highways through the Alps and the northern confines of Italy. The instructions to the generals were conceived with energy and precision: to hasten their march in close and compact columns, which, according to the disposition of the ground, might readily be changed into any order of battle; to secure themselves against the surprises of the night by strong posts and vigilant guards; to prevent resistance by their unexpected arrival; to elude examination by their sudden departure; to spread the opinion of their strength, and the terror of his name; and to join their sovereign under the walls of Sirmium. For himself Julian had reserved a more difficult and extraordinary part. He selected three

thousand brave and active volunteers, resolved, like their leader, to
cast behind them every hope of a retreat; at the head of this faithful
band he fearlessly plunged into the recesses of the Marcian, or
Black Forest, which conceals the sources of the Danube; and, for
many days, the fate of Julian was unknown to the world. The
secrecy of his march, his diligence, and vigour, surmounted every
obstacle; he forced his way over mountains and morasses, occupied
the bridges or swam the rivers, pursued his direct course without
reflecting whether he traversed the territory of the Romans or of
the barbarians, and at length emerged, between Ratisbon and
Vienna, at the place where he designed to embark his troops on
the Danube. By a well-concerted stratagem he seized a fleet of light
brigantines as it lay at anchor; secured a supply of coarse provisions
sufficient to satisfy the indelicate, but voracious, appetite of a Gallic
army; and boldly committed himself to the stream of the Danube.
The labours of his mariners, who plied their oars with incessant
diligence, and the steady continuance of a favourable wind, carried
his fleet above seven hundred miles in eleven days; and he had
already disembarked his troops at Bononia, only nineteen miles
from Sirmium, before his enemies could receive any certain
intelligence that he had left the banks of the Rhine. In the course
of this long and rapid navigation, the mind of Julian was fixed on
the object of his enterprise; and though he accepted the deputation of some cities, which hastened to claim the merit of an early
submission, he passed before the hostile stations, which were
placed along the river, without indulging the temptation of
signalising a useless and ill-timed valour. The banks of the Danube
were crowded on either side with spectators, who gazed on the
military pomp, anticipated the importance of the event, and
diffused through the adjacent country the fame of a young hero,
who advanced with more than mortal speed at the head of the
innumerable forces of the West. Lucilian, who, with the rank of
general of the cavalry commanded the military powers of Illyricum,
was alarmed and perplexed by the doubtful reports, which he could
neither reject nor believe. He had taken some slow and irresolute
measures for the purpose of collecting his troops, when he was
surprised by Dagalaiphus, an active officer, whom Julian, as soon
as he landed at Bononia, had pushed forward with some light
infantry. The captive general, uncertain of his life or death, was
hastily thrown upon a horse, and conducted to the presence of
Julian, who kindly raised him from the ground, and dispelled the

terror and amazement which seemed to stupefy his faculties. But Lucilian had no sooner recovered his spirits than he betrayed his want of discretion, by presuming to admonish his conqueror that he had rashly ventured, with a handful of men, to expose his person in the midst of his enemies. "Reserve for your master Constantius these timid remonstrances," replied Julian, with a smile of contempt; "when I gave you my purple to kiss, I received you not as a counsellor, but as a suppliant." Conscious that success alone could justify his attempt, and that boldness only could command success, he instantly advanced, at the head of three thousand soldiers, to attack the strongest and most populous city of the Illyrian provinces. As he entered the long suburb of Sirmium, he was received by the joyful acclamations of the army and people, who, crowned with flowers, and holding lighted tapers in their hands, conducted their acknowledged sovereign to the imperial residence. Two days were devoted to the public joy, which was celebrated by the games of the Circus; but, early on the morning of the third day, Julian marched to occupy the narrow pass of Succi, in the defiles of Mount Hæmus; which, almost in the midway between Sirmium and Constantinople, separates the provinces of Thrace and Dacia, by an abrupt descent towards the former, and a gentle declivity on the side of the latter. The defence of this important post was intrusted to the brave Nevitta, who, as well as the generals of the Italian division, successfully executed the plan of the march and junction which their master had so ably conceived.

But the humanity of Julian was preserved from the cruel alternative which he pathetically laments of destroying or of being himself destroyed: and the seasonable death of Constantius delivered the Roman empire from the calamities of civil war. The approach of winter could not detain the monarch at Antioch; and his favourites durst not oppose his impatient desire of revenge. A slight fever, which was perhaps occasioned by the agitation of his spirits, was increased by the fatigues of the journey, and Constantius was obliged to halt at the little town of Mopsucrene, twelve miles beyond Tarsus, where he expired, after a short illness, in the forty-fifth year of his age, and the twenty-fourth of his reign. His genuine character, which was composed of pride and weakness, of superstition and cruelty, has been fully displayed in the preceding narrative of civil and ecclesiastical events. The long abuse of power rendered him a considerable object in the eyes of his contemporaries; but, as personal merit can alone deserve the notice of posterity, the last of the sons of Constantine may be dismissed from the world with the remark that he inherited the defects, without the abilities, of his father. Before Constantius expired, he is said to have named Julian for his successor; nor does it seem improbable that his anxious concern for the fate of a young and tender wife, whom he left with child, may have prevailed in his last moments over the harsher passions of hatred and revenge. Eusebius and his guilty associates made a faint attempt to prolong the reign of the eunuchs by the election of another emperor; but their intrigues were rejected with disdain by an army which now abhorred the thought of civil discord; and two officers of rank were instantly despatched to assure Julian that every sword in the empire would be drawn for his service. The military designs of that prince, who had formed three different attacks against Thrace, were prevented by this fortunate event. Without shedding the blood of his fellow-citizens, he escaped the dangers of a doubtful conflict, and acquired the advantages of a complete victory. Impatient to visit the place of his birth and the new capital of the empire, he advanced from Naissus through the mountains of Hæmus and the cities of Thrace. When he reached Heraclea, at the distance of sixty miles, all Constantinople was poured forth to receive him; and he made his triumphal entry amidst the dutiful acclamations of the soldiers, the people, and the senate. An innumerable multitude pressed around him with eager respect, and were perhaps disappointed when they beheld the small stature and simple garb of a hero, whose inexperienced youth had vanquished the barbarians of Germany, and who had now traversed, in a successful career, the whole continent of Europe from the shores of the Atlantic to those of the Bosphorus. A few days afterwards, when the remains of the deceased emperor were landed in the harbour, the subjects of Julian applauded the real or affected humanity of their sovereign. On foot, without his diadem, and clothed in a mourning habit, he accompanied the funeral as far as the church of the Holy Apostles, where the body was deposited: and if these marks of respect may be interpreted as a selfish tribute to the birth and dignity of his Imperial kinsman, the tears of Julian professed to the world that he had forgot the injuries, and remembered only the obligations, which he had received from Constantius. As soon as the legions of Aquileia were assured of the death of the emperor, they opened the gates of the city, and, by the sacrifice of their guilty leaders, obtained an easy pardon from the prudence or lenity of Julian; who, in the thirty-second year of his age, acquired the undisputed possession of the Roman empire.

Philosophy had instructed Julian to compare the advantages of action and retirement; but the elevation of his birth and the accidents of his life never allowed him the freedom of choice. He might perhaps sincerely have preferred the groves of the Academy and the society of Athens; but he was constrained, at first by the will, and afterwards by the injustice of Constantius, to expose his person and fame to the dangers of Imperial greatness; and to make himself accountable to the world and to posterity for the happiness of millions. Julian recollected with terror the observation of his master Plato, that the government of our flocks and herds is always committed to beings of a superior species; and that the conduct of nations requires and deserves the celestial powers of the Gods or of the Genii. From this principle he justly concluded that the man who presumes to reign should aspire to the perfection of the divine nature; that he should purify his soul from her mortal and terrestrial part; that he should extinguish his appetites, enlighten his under-standing, regulate his passions, and subdue the wild beast which, according to the lively metaphor of Aristotle, seldom fails to ascend the throne of a despot. The throne of Julian, which the death of Constantius fixed on an independent basis, was the seat of reason, of virtue, and perhaps of vanity. He despised the honours, renounced the pleasures, and discharged with incessant diligence the duties of his exalted station: and there were few among his subjects who would have consented to relieve him from the weight of the diadem, had they been obliged to submit their time and their actions to the rigorous laws which their philosophic emperor imposed on himself. One of his most intimate friends, who had often shared the frugal simplicity of his table, has remarked that his light and sparing diet (which was usually of the vegetable kind) left his mind and body always free and active for the various and important business of an author, a pontiff, a magistrate, a general, and a prince. In one and the same day he gave audience to several ambassadors, and wrote or dictated a great number of letters to his generals, his civil magistrates, his private friends, and the different cities of his dominions. He listened to the memorials which had been received, considered the subject of the petitions, and signified his intentions more rapidly than they could be taken in shorthand by the diligence of his secretaries. He possessed such flexibility of thought, and such firmness of attention, that he could employ his hand to write, his ear to listen, and his voice to dictate; and pursue at once three several trains of ideas without hesitation, and without error. While his ministers reposed, the prince flew with agility from one labour to another; and, after a hasty dinner, retired into his library till the public business which he had appointed for the evening summoned him to interrupt the prosecution of his studies. The supper of the emperor was still less substantial than the former meal; his sleep was never clouded by the fumes of indigestion; and, except in the short interval of a marriage which was the effect of policy rather than love, the chaste Julian never shared his bed with a female companion. He was soon awakened by the entrance of fresh secretaries, who had slept the preceding day; and his servants were obliged to wait alternately, while their indefatigable master allowed himself scarcely any other refreshment than the change of occupations. The predecessors of Julian, his uncle, his brother, and his cousin, indulged their puerile taste for the games of the Circus, under the specious pretence of complying with the inclinations of the people; and they frequently remained the greatest part of the day as idle spectators, and as a part of the splendid spectacle, till the ordinary round of twenty-four races was completely finished. On solemn festivals, Julian, who felt and professed an unfashionable dislike to these frivolous amusements, condescended to appear in the Circus; and, after bestowing a careless glance on five or six of the races, he hastily withdrew with the impatience of a philosopher, who considered every moment as lost that was not devoted to the advantage of the public or the improvement of his own mind. By this avarice of time he seemed to protract the short duration of his reign; and, if the dates were less securely ascertained, we should refuse to believe that only sixteen months elapsed between the death of Constantius and the departure of his successor for the Persian war. The actions of Julian can only be preserved by the care of the historian; but the portion of his voluminous writings which is still extant remains as a monument of the application, as well as of the genius, of the emperor. The Misopogon, the Cæsars, several of his orations, and his elaborate work against the Christian religion, were composed in the long nights of the two winters, the former of which he passed at Constantinople, and the latter at Antioch.

The luxury of the palace excited the contempt and indignation of Julian, who usually slept on the ground, who yielded with reluctance to the indispensable calls of nature, and who placed his vanity not in emulating, but in despising the pomp of royalty. By the total extirpation of a mischief which was magnified even beyond its real extent, he was impatient to relieve the distress and to appease the murmurs of the people, who support with less uneasiness the weight of taxes if they are convinced that the fruits of their industry are appropriated to the service of the state. But in the execution of this salutary work Julian is accused of proceeding with too much haste and inconsiderate severity. By a single edict he reduced the palace of Constantinople to an immense desert, and dismissed with ignominy the whole train of slaves and dependents, without providing any just, or at least benevolent, exceptions for the age, the services, or the poverty of the faithful domestics of the Imperial family. Such indeed was the temper of Julian, who seldom recollected the fundamental maxim of Aristotle, that true virtue is placed at an equal distance between the opposite vices. The splendid and effeminate dress of the Asiatics, the curls and paint, the collars and bracelets, which had appeared so ridiculous in the person of Constantine, were consistently rejected by his philosophic successor. But with the fopperies, Julian affected to renounce the decencies of dress; and seemed to value himself for his neglect of the laws of cleanliness. In a satirical performance, which was designed for the public eye, the emperor descants with pleasure, and even with pride, on the length of his nails and the inky blackness of his hands; protests that, although the greatest part of his body was covered with hair, the use of the razor was confined to his head alone; and celebrates with visible complacency the shaggy and *populous* beard which he fondly cherished, after the example of the philosophers of Greece. Had Julian consulted the simple dictates of reason, the first magistrate of the Romans would have scorned the affection of Diogenes, as well as that of Darius.

The numerous army of spies, of agents, and informers, enlisted by Constantius to secure the repose of one man, and to interrupt that of millions, was immediately disbanded by this generous successor. Julian was slow in his suspicions, and gentle in his punishments; and his contempt of treason was the result of judgment, of vanity, and of courage. Conscious of superior merit, he was persuaded that few among his subjects would dare to meet him in the field, to attempt his life, or even to seat themselves on his vacant throne. The philosopher could excuse the hasty sallies of discontent, and the hero could despise the ambitious projects which surpassed the fortune or the abilities of the rash conspirators. A citizen of Ancyra had prepared for his own use a purple garment, and this indiscreet action, which, under the reign of Constantius, would have been considered as a capital offence, was reported to Julian by the officious importunity of a private enemy. The monarch, after making some inquiry into the rank and character of his rival, despatched the informer with a present of a pair of purple slippers, to complete the magnificence of his Imperial habit. A more dangerous conspiracy was formed by ten of the domestic guards, who had resolved to assassinate Julian in the field of exercise near Antioch. Their intemperance revealed their guilt, and they were conducted in chains to the presence of their injured sovereign, who, after a lively representation of the wickedness and folly of their enterprise, instead of a death of torture, which they deserved and expected, pronounced a sentence of exile against the two principal offenders. The only instance in which Julian seemed to depart from his accustomed clemency was the execution of a rash youth, who, with a feeble hand, had aspired to seize the reins of empire. But that youth was the son of Marcellus, the general of cavalry, who, in the first campaign of the Gallic war, had deserted the standard of the Cæsar and the republic. Without appearing to indulge his personal resentment, Julian might easily confound the crime of the son and of the father; but he was reconciled by the distress of Marcellus, and the liberality of the emperor endeavoured to heal the wound which had been inflicted by the hand of justice.

Julian was not insensible of the advantages of freedom. From his studies he had imbibed the spirit of ancient sages and heroes; his life and fortunes had depended on the caprice of a tyrant; and, when he ascended the throne, his pride was sometimes mortified by the reflection that the slaves who would not dare to censure his defects were not worthy to applaud his virtues. He sincerely abhorred the system of oriental despotism which Diocletian, Constantine, and the patient habits of fourscore years, had established in the empire. A motive of superstition prevented the execution of the design which Julian had frequently meditated, of relieving his head from the weight of a costly diadem; but he absolutely refused the title of *Dominus* or *Lord*, a word which was grown so familiar to the ears of the Romans, that they no longer remembered its servile and humiliating origin. The office, or rather the name, of consul was cherished by a prince who contemplated with reverence the ruins of the republic; and the same behaviour which had been assumed by the prudence of Augustus was adopted by Julian from choice and inclination. On the calends of January, at break of day, the new consuls, Mamertinus and Nevitta, hastened to the palace to salute the emperor. As soon as he was informed of their approach, he leaped from his throne, eagerly advanced to meet them, and compelled the blushing magistrates to receive the demonstrations of his affected humility. From the palace they proceeded to the senate. The emperor, on foot, marched before their litters, and the gazing multitude admired the image of ancient times, or secretly blamed a conduct which, in their eyes, degraded the majesty of the purple. But the behaviour of Julian was uniformly supported. During the games of the Circus, he had, imprudently or designedly, performed the manumission of a slave in the presence of the consul. The moment he was reminded that he had trespassed on the jurisdiction of *another* magistrate, he condemned himself to pay a fine of ten pounds of gold, and embraced this public occasion of declaring to the world that he was subject, like the rest of his fellow-citizens, to the laws, and even to the forms, of the republic. The spirit of his administration, and his regard for the place of his nativity, induced Julian to confer on the senate of Constantinople the same honours, privileges, and authority which were still enjoyed by the senate of ancient Rome. A legal fiction was introduced and gradually established, that one half of the national council had migrated into the East, and the despotic successors of Julian, accepting the title of Senators, acknowledged themselves the members of a respectable body which was permitted to represent the majesty of the Roman name. From Constantinople the attention of the monarch was extended to the municipal senates of the provinces. He abolished, by repeated edicts, the unjust and pernicious exemptions which had withdrawn so many idle citizens from the service of their country; and by imposing an equal distribution of public duties, he restored the strength, the splendour, or, according to the glowing expression of Libanius, the soul of the expiring cities of his empire.

The generality of princes, if they were stripped of their purple and cast naked into the world, would immediately sink to the lowest rank of society, without a hope of emerging from their obscurity. But the personal merit of Julian was, in some measure, independent of his fortune. Whatever had been his choice of life, by the force of intrepid courage, lively wit, and intense application, he would have obtained, or at least he would have deserved, the highest honours of his profession, and Julian might have raised himself to the rank of minister or general of the state in which he was born a private citizen. If the jealous caprice of power had disappointed his expectations; if he had prudently declined the paths of greatness, the employment of the same talents in studious solitude would have placed beyond the reach of kings his present happiness and his immortal fame. When we inspect with minute, or perhaps malevolent, attention the portrait of Julian, something seems wanting to the grace and perfection of the whole figure. His genius was less powerful and sublime than that of Cæsar, nor did he possess the consummate prudence of Augustus. The virtues of Trajan appear more steady and natural, and the philosophy of Marcus is more simple and consistent. Yet Julian sustained adversity with firmness, and prosperity with moderation. After an interval of one hundred and twenty years from the death of Alexander Severus, the Romans beheld an emperor who made no distinction between his duties and his pleasures, who laboured to relieve the distress and to revive the spirit of his subjects, and who endeavoured always to connect authority with merit, and happiness with virtue. Even faction, and religious faction, was constrained to acknowledge the superiority of his genius in peace as well as in war, and to confess, with a sigh, that the apostate Julian was a lover of his country, and that he deserved the empire of the world.

XXI

(351–363 A.D.) THE RELIGION OF JULIAN—
UNIVERSAL TOLERATION—HE ATTEMPTS
TO RESTORE AND REFORM THE PAGAN
WORSHIP—HIS ARTFUL PERSECUTION OF
THE CHRISTIANS—MUTUAL ZEAL AND IN-
JUSTICE

The character of Apostate has injured the reputation of Julian;
and the enthusiasm which clouded his virtues has exaggerated the
real and apparent magnitude of his faults. Our partial ignorance
may represent him as a philosophic monarch, who studied to
protect, with an equal hand, the religious factions of the empire,
and to allay the theological fever which had inflamed the minds
of the people from the edicts of Diocletian to the exile of Athanasius.
A more accurate view of the character and conduct of Julian will
remove this favourable prepossession for a prince who did not
escape the general contagion of the times. We enjoy the singular
advantage of comparing the pictures which have been delineated
by his fondest admirers and his implacable enemies. The actions
of Julian are faithfully related by a judicious and candid historian,
the impartial spectator of his life and death. The unanimous
evidence of his contemporaries is confirmed by the public and
private declarations of the emperor himself; and his various
writings express the uniform tenor of his religious sentiments,
which policy would have prompted him to dissemble rather than
to affect. A devout and sincere attachment for the gods of Athens
and Rome constituted the ruling passion of Julian; the powers of
an enlightened understanding were betrayed and corrupted by
the influence of superstitious prejudice; and the phantoms which
existed only in the mind of the emperor had a real and pernicious effect on the government of the empire. The vehement zeal
of the Christians, who despised the worship, and overturned the
altars, of those fabulous deities, engaged their votary in a state of
irreconcilable hostility with a very numerous party of his subjects;

and he was sometimes tempted, by the desire of victory or the shame of a repulse, to violate the laws of prudence, and even of justice. The triumph of the party which he deserted and opposed has fixed a stain of infamy on the name of Julian; and the unsuccessful apostate has been overwhelmed with a torrent of pious invectives, of which the signal was given by the sonorous trumpet of Gregory Nazianzen. The interesting nature of the events which were crowded into the short reign of this active emperor deserves a just and circumstantial narrative. His motive, his counsels, and his actions, as far as they are connected with the history of religion, will be the subject of the present chapter.

The cause of his strange and fatal apostasy may be derived from the early period of his life when he was left an orphan in the hands of the murderers of his family. The names of Christ and of Constantius, the ideas of slavery and of religion, were soon associated in a youthful imagination, which was susceptible of the most lively impressions. The care of his infancy was intrusted to Eusebius, bishop of Nicomedia, who was related to him on the side of his mother; and till Julian reached the twentieth year of his age, he received from his Christian preceptors the education not of a hero but of a saint. The emperor, less jealous of a heavenly than of an earthly crown, contented himself with the imperfect character of a catechumen, while he bestowed the advantages of baptism on the nephews of Constantine. They were even admitted to the inferior offices of the ecclesiastical order; and Julian publicly read the Holy Scriptures in the church of Nicomedia. The study of religion, which they assiduously cultivated, appeared to produce the fairest fruits of faith and devotion. They prayed, they fasted, they distributed alms to the poor, gifts to the clergy, and oblations to the tombs of the martyrs; and the splendid monument of St. Mamas, at Cæsarea, was erected, or at least was undertaken, by the joint labour of Gallus and Julian. They respectfully conversed with the bishops who were eminent for superior sanctity, and solicited the benediction of the monks and hermits who had introduced into Cappadocia the voluntary hardships of the ascetic life. As the two princes advanced towards the years of manhood, they discovered, in their religious sentiments, the difference of their characters. The dull and obstinate understanding of Gallus embraced, with implicit zeal, the doctrines of Christianity, which never influenced his conduct, or moderated his passions. The mild disposition of the younger brother was less repugnant to the precepts of the Gospel; and his active curiosity might have been gratified by a theological system which explains the mysterious essence of the Deity, and opens the boundless prospect of invisible and future worlds. But the independent spirit of Julian refused to yield the passive and unresisting obedience which was required, in the name of religion, by the haughty ministers of the church. Their speculative opinions were imposed as positive laws, and guarded by the terrors of eternal punishments; but while they prescribed the rigid formulary of the thoughts, the words, and the actions of the young prince; whilst they silenced his objections, and severely checked the freedom of his inquiries, they secretly provoked his impatient genius to disclaim the authority of his ecclesiastical guides. He was educated in the lesser Asia, amidst the scandals of the Arian controversy. The fierce contests of the Eastern bishops, the incessant alterations of their creeds, and the profane motives which appeared to actuate their conduct, insensibly strengthened the prejudice of Julian that they neither understood nor believed the religion for which they so fiercely contended. Instead of listening to the proofs of Christianity with that favourable attention which adds weight to the most respectable evidence, he heard with suspicion, and disputed with obstinacy and acuteness, the doctrines for which he already entertained an invincible aversion. Whenever the young princes were directed to compose declamations on the subject of the prevailing controversies, Julian always declared himself the advocate of Paganism, under the specious excuse that, in the defence of the weaker cause, his learning and ingenuity might be more advantageously exercised and displayed.

The theological system of Julian appears to have contained the sublime and important principles of natural religion. But as the faith which is not founded on revelation must remain destitute of any firm assurance, the disciple of Plato imprudently relapsed into the habits of vulgar superstition; and the popular and philosophic notion of the Deity seems to have been confounded in the practice, the writings, and even in the mind of Julian. The pious emperor acknowledged and adored the Eternal Cause of the universe, to whom he ascribed all the perfections of an infinite nature, invisible to the eyes and inaccessible to the understanding of feeble mortals. The Supreme God had created, or rather, in the Platonic language, had generated, the gradual succession of dependent spirits, of gods, of dæmons, of heroes, and of men; and every being which derived its existence immediately from the First Cause received the inherent gift of immortality. That so precious an advantage might not be lavished upon unworthy objects, the Creator had intrusted to the skill and power of the inferior gods the office of forming the human body, and of arranging the beautiful harmony of the animal, the vegetable, and the mineral kingdoms. To the conduct of these divine ministers he delegated the temporal government of this lower world; but their imperfect administration is not exempt from discord or error. The earth and its inhabitants are divided among them, and the characters of Mars or Minerva, of Mercury or Venus, may be distinctly traced in the laws and manners of their peculiar votaries. As long as our immortal souls are confined in a mortal prison, it is our interest, as well as our duty, to solicit the favour, and to deprecate the wrath, of the powers of heaven; whose pride is gratified by the devotion of mankind, and whose grosser parts may be supposed to derive some nourishment from the fumes of sacrifice. The inferior gods might sometimes condescend to animate the statues, and to inhabit the temples, which were dedicated to their honour. They might occasionally visit the earth, but the heavens were the proper throne and symbol of their glory. The invariable order of the sun, moon, and stars was hastily admitted by Julian as a proof of their *eternal* duration; and their eternity was a sufficient evidence that they were the workmanship, not of an inferior deity, but of the Omnipotent King. In the system of the Platonists the visible was a type of the invisible world. The celestial bodies, as they were informed by a divine spirit, might be considered as the objects the most worthy of religious worships. The SUN, whose genial influence pervades and sustains the universe, justly claimed the adoration of mankind, as the bright representative of the LOGOS, the lively, the rational, the beneficent image of the intellectual Father.

The Christians, who beheld with horror and indignation the apostasy of Julian, had much more to fear from his power than from his arguments. The Pagans, who were conscious of his fervent zeal, expected, perhaps with impatience, that the flames of persecution should be immediately kindled against the enemies of the gods; and that the ingenious malice of Julian would invent some cruel refinements of death and torture which had been unknown to the rude and inexperienced fury of his predecessors. But the hopes, as well as the fears, of the religious factions were apparently disappointed by the prudent humanity of a prince who was careful of his own fame, of the public peace, and of the rights of mankind. Instructed by history and reflection, Julian was persuaded that, if the diseases of the body may sometimes be cured by salutary violence, neither steel nor fire can eradicate the erroneous opinions of the mind. The reluctant victim may be dragged to the foot of the altar; but the heart still abhors and disclaims the sacrilegious act of the hand. Religious obstinacy is hardened and exasperated by oppression; and, as soon as the persecution subsides, those who have yielded are restored as penitents, and those who have resisted are honoured as saints and martyrs. If Julian adopted the unsuccessful cruelty of Diocletian and his colleagues, he was sensible that he should stain his memory with the name of tyrant, and add new glories to the catholic church, which had derived strength and increase from the severity of the Pagan magistrates. Actuated by these motives, and apprehensive of disturbing the repose of an unsettled reign, Julian surprised the world by an edict which was not unworthy of a statesman or a philosopher. He extended to all the inhabitants of the Roman world the benefits of a free and equal toleration; and the only hardship which he inflicted on the Christians was to deprive them of the power of tormenting their fellow-subjects, whom they stigmatised with the odious titles of idolaters and heretics. The Pagans received a gracious permission, or rather an express order, to open ALL their temples; and they were at once delivered from the oppressive laws and arbitrary vexations which they had sustained under the reign of Constanine and of his sons. At the same time, the bishops and clergy who had been banished by the Arian monarch were recalled from exile, and restored to their respective churches; the Donatists, the Novatians, the Macedonians, the Eunomians, and those who, with a more prosperous fortune, adhered to the doctrine of the council of Nice. Julian, who understood and derided their theological disputes, invited to the palace the leaders of the hostile sects, that he might enjoy the agreeable spectacle of their furious encounters. The clamour of controversy sometimes provoked the emperor to exclaim, "Hear me! the Franks have heard me, and the Alemanni"; but he soon discovered that he was now engaged with more obstinate and implacable enemies; and though he exerted the powers of oratory to persuade them to live in concord, or at least in peace, he was perfectly satisfied, before he dismissed them from his presence, that he had nothing to dread from the union of the Christians. The impartial Ammianus has ascribed this affected clemency to the desire of fomenting the intestine divisions of the church; and the insidious design of undermining the foundations of Christianity was inseparably connected with the zeal which Julian professed to restore the ancient religion of the empire.

Julian still continued to maintain the freedom of religious worship, without distinguishing whether this universal toleration proceeded from his justice or his clemency. He affected to pity the unhappy Christians, who were mistaken in the most important object of their lives; but his pity was degraded by contempt, his contempt was embittered by hatred; and the sentiments of Julian were expressed in a style of sarcastic wit, which inflicts a deep and deadly wound whenever it issues from the mouth of a sovereign. As he was sensible that the Christians gloried in the name of their Redeemer, he countenanced, and perhaps enjoined, the use of the less honourable appellation of GALILÆANS. He declared that, by the folly of the Galilæans, whom he describes as a sect of fanatics, contemptible to men and odious to the gods, the empire had been reduced to the brink of destruction; and he insinuates in a public edict that a frantic patient might sometimes be cured by salutary violence. An ungenerous distinction was admitted into the mind and counsels of Julian, that, according to the difference of their religious sentiments, one part of his subjects deserved his favour and friendship, while the other was entitled only to the common benefits that his justice could not refuse to an obedient people. According to a principle pregnant with mischief and oppression, the emperor transferred to the pontiffs of his own religion the management of the liberal allowances from the public revenue which had been granted to the church by the piety of Constantine and his sons. The proud system of clerical honours and immunities, which had been constructed with so much art and labour, was levelled to the ground; the hopes of testamentary donations were intercepted by the rigour of the laws; and the priests of the Christian sect were confounded with the last and most ignominious class of the people. Such of these regulations as appeared necessary to check the ambition and avarice of the ecclesiastics were soon afterwards imitated by the wisdom of an orthodox prince. The peculiar distinctions which policy has bestowed, or superstition has lavished, on the sacerdotal order, *must* be confined to those priests who profess the religion of the state. But the will of the legislator was not exempt from prejudice and passion; and it was the object of the insidious policy of Julian to deprive the Christians of all the temporal honours and advantages which rendered them respectable in the eyes of the world.

A just and severe censure has been inflicted on the law which prohibited the Christians from teaching the arts of grammar and rhetoric. The motives alleged by the emperor to justify this partial and oppressive measure might command, during his lifetime, the silence of slaves and the applause of flatterers. Julian abuses the ambiguous meaning of a word which might be indifferently applied to the language and the religion of the GREEKS: he contemptuously observes that the men who exalt the merit of implicit faith are unfit to claim or to enjoy the advantages of science; and he vainly contends that, if they refuse to adore the gods of Homer and Demosthenes, they ought to content themselves with expounding Luke and Matthew in the churches of the Galilæans. In all the cities of the Roman world the education of the youth was intrusted to masters of grammar and rhetoric, who were elected by the magistrates, maintained at the public expense, and distinguished by many lucrative and honourable privileges. The edict of Julian appears to have included the physicians, and professors of all the liberal arts; and the emperor, who reserved to himself the approbation of the candidates, was authorised by the laws to corrupt, or to punish, the religious constancy of the most learned of the Christians. As soon as the resignation of the more obstinate teachers had established the unrivalled dominion of the Pagan sophists, Julian invited the rising generation to resort with freedom to the public schools, in a just confidence that their tender minds would receive the impressions of literature and idolatry. If the greatest part of the Christian youth should be deterred by their own scruples, or by those of their parents, from accepting this dangerous mode of instruction, they must, at the same time, relinquish the benefits of a liberal education. Julian had reason to expect that, in the space of a few years, the church would relapse into its primæval simplicity, and that the theologians, who possessed an adequate share of the learning and eloquence of the age, would be succeeded by a generation of blind and ignorant fanatics, incapable of defending the truth of their own principles, or of exposing the various follies of Polytheism.

The most effectual instrument of oppression was the law that obliged the Christians to make full and ample satisfaction for the temples which they had destroyed under the preceding reign. The zeal of the triumphant church had not always expected the sanction of the public authority; and the bishops, who were secure of impunity, had often marched at the head of their congregations to attack and demolish the fortresses of the prince of darkness. The consecrated lands, which had increased the patrimony of the sovereign or of the clergy, were clearly defined, and easily restored. But on these lands, and on the ruins of Pagan superstition, the Christians had frequently erected their own religious edifices: and as it was necessary to remove the church before the temple could be rebuilt, the justice and piety of the emperor were applauded by one party, while the other deplored and execrated his sacrilegious violence. After the ground was cleared, the restitution of those stately structures which had been levelled with the dust, and of the precious ornaments which had been converted to Christian uses, swelled into a very large account of damages and debt. The authors of the injury had neither the ability nor the inclination to discharge this accumulated demand: and the impartial wisdom of a legislator would have been displayed in balancing the adverse claims and complaints by an equitable and temperate arbitration. But the whole empire, and particularly the East, was thrown into confusion by the rash edicts of Julian; and the Pagan magistrates, inflamed by zeal and revenge, abused the rigorous privilege of the Roman law, which substitutes, in the place of his inadequate property, the person of the insolvent debtor.

I have endeavoured faithfully to represent the artful system by which Julian proposed to obtain the effects, without incurring the guilt of reproach, of persecution. But if the deadly spirit of fanaticism perverted the heart and understanding of a virtuous prince, it must, at the same time, be confessed, that the *real* sufferings of the Christians were inflamed and magnified by human passions and religious enthusiasm. The meekness and resignation which had distinguished the primitive disciples of the Gospel was the object of the applause, rather than of the imitation, of their successors. The Christians, who had now possessed above forty years the civil and ecclesiastical government of the empire, had contracted the insolent vices of prosperity, and the habit of believing that the saints alone were entitled to reign over the earth. As soon as the enmity of Julian deprived the clergy of the privileges which had been conferred by the favour of Constantine, they complained of the most cruel oppression; and the free toleration of idolaters and heretics was a subject of grief and scandal to the orthodox party. The acts of violence, which were no longer countenanced by the magistrates, were still committed by the zeal of the people. At Pessinus the altar of Cybele was overturned almost in the presence of the emperor; and in the city of Cæsarea, in Cappadocia, the temple of Fortune, the sole place of worship which had been left to the Pagans, was destroyed by the rage of a popular tumult. On these occasions, a Prince who felt for the honour of the gods was not disposed to interrupt the course of justice; and his mind was still more deeply exasperated when he found that the fanatics, who had deserved and suffered the punishment of incendiaries, were rewarded with the honours of martyrdom. The Christian subjects of Julian were assured of the hostile designs of their sovereign; and, to their jealous apprehension, every circumstance of his government might afford some ground of discontent and suspicion. In the ordinary administration of the laws, the Christians, who formed so large a part of the people, must frequently be condemned; but their indulgent brethren, without examining the merits of the cause, presumed their innocence, allowed their claims, and imputed the severity of their judge to the partial malice of religious persecution. These present hardships, intolerable as they might appear, were represented as a slight prelude of the impending calamities. The Christians considered Julian as a cruel and crafty tyrant, who suspended the execution of his revenge till he should return victorious from the Persian war. They expected that, as soon as he had triumphed over the foreign enemies of Rome, he would lay aside the irksome mask of dissimulation; that the amphitheatres would stream with the blood of hermits and bishops; and that the Christians who still persevered in the profession of the faith would be deprived of the common benefits of nature and society. Every calumny that could wound the reputation of the Apostate was credulously embraced by the fears and hatred of his adversaries; and their indiscreet clamours provoked the temper of a sovereign whom it was their duty to respect, and their interest to flatter. They still protested that prayers and tears were their only weapons against the impious tyrant, whose head they devoted to the justice of offended Heaven. But they insinuated, with sullen resolution, that their submission was no longer the effect of weakness; and that, in the imperfect state of human virtue, the patience which is founded on principle may be exhausted by persecution. It is impossible to determine how far the zeal of Julian would have prevailed over his good sense and humanity; but, if we seriously reflect on the strength and spirit of the church, we shall be convinced that, before the emperor could have extinguished the religion of Christ, he must have involved his country in the horrors of a civil war.

XXII

(314–390 A.D.) RESIDENCE OF JULIAN AT ANTIOCH—HIS SUCCESSFUL EXPEDITION AGAINST THE PERSIANS—PASSAGE OF THE TIGRIS—THE RETREAT AND DEATH OF JULIAN —ELECTION OF JOVIAN—HE SAVES THE ROMAN ARMY BY A DISGRACEFUL TREATY

In the cool moments of reflection, Julian preferred the useful and benevolent virtues of Antoninus; but his ambitious spirit was inflamed by the glory of Alexander, and he solicited, with equal ardour, the esteem of the wise and the applause of the multitude. In the season of life when the powers of the mind and body enjoy the most active vigour, the emperor, who was instructed by the experience and animated by the success of the German war, resolved to signalise his reign by some more splendid and memorable achievement. The ambassadors of the East, from the continent of India and the isle of Ceylon, had respectfully saluted the Roman purple. The nations of the West esteemed and dreaded the personal virtues of Julian both in peace and war. He despised the trophies of a Gothic victory, and was satisfied that the rapacious barbarians of the Danube would be restrained from any future violation of the faith of treaties by the terror of his name and the additional fortifications with which he strengthened the Thracian and Illyrian frontiers. The successor of Cyrus and Artaxerxes was the only rival whom he deemed worthy of his arms, and he resolved, by the final conquest of Persia, to chastise the haughty nation which had so long resisted and insulted the majesty of Rome. As soon as the Persian monarch was informed that the throne of Constantius was filled by a prince of a very different character, he condescended to make some artful or perhaps sincere overtures towards a negotiation of peace. But the pride of Sapor was astonished by the firmness of Julian, who sternly declared that he would never consent to hold a peaceful conference among the flames and ruins of the cities of Mesopotamia, and who added, with a smile of contempt, that it was needless to treat by ambassadors, as he himself had determined to visit speedily the court of Persia. The impatience of the emperor urged the diligence of the military preparations. The generals were named, a formidable army was destined for this important service, and Julian, marching from Constantinople through the provinces of Asia Minor, arrived at Antioch about eight months after the death of his predecessor. His ardent desire to march into the heart of Persia was checked by the indispensable duty of regulating the state of the empire, by his zeal to revive the worship of the gods, and by the advice of his wisest friends, who represented the necessity of allowing the salutary interval of winter quarters to restore the exhausted strength of the legions of Gaul and the discipline and spirit of the Eastern troops. Julian was persuaded to fix, till the ensuing spring, his residence at Antioch, among a people maliciously disposed to deride the haste and to censure the delays of their sovereign.

The army of Julian, the most numerous that any of the Cæsars had ever led against Persia, consisted of sixty-five thousand effective and well-disciplined soldiers. The veteran bands of cavalry and infantry, of Romans and barbarians, had been selected from the different provinces, and a just pre-eminence of loyalty and valour was claimed by the hardy Gauls, who guarded the throne and person of their beloved prince. A formidable body of Scythian auxiliaries had been transported from another climate, and almost from another world, to invade a distant country of whose name and situation they were ignorant. The love of rapine and war allured to the Imperial standard several tribes of Saracens, or roving Arabs, whose service Julian had commanded, while he sternly refused the payment of the accustomed subsidies. The broad channel of the Euphrates was crowded by a fleet of eleven hundred ships, destined to attend the motions and to satisfy the wants of the Roman army. The military strength of the fleet was composed of fifty armed galleys, and these were accompanied by an equal number of flat-bottomed boats, which might occasionally be connected into the form of temporary bridges. The rest of the ships, partly constructed of timber and partly covered with raw hides, were laden with an almost inexhaustible supply of arms and engines, of utensils and provisions. The vigilant humanity of Julian had embarked a very large magazine of vinegar and biscuit for the use of the soldiers, but he prohibited the indulgence of wine, and rigorously stopped a long string of superfluous camels that attempted to follow the rear of the army. The river Chaboras falls into the Euphrates at Circesium, and, as soon as the trumpet gave the signal of march, the Romans passed the little stream which separated two mighty and hostile empires.

The fields of Assyria were devoted by Julian to the calamities of war; and the philosopher retaliated on a guiltless people the acts of rapine and cruelty which had been committed by their haughty master in the Roman provinces. The trembling Assyrians summoned the rivers to their assistance; and completed with their own hands the ruin of their country. The roads were rendered impracticable; a flood of waters was poured into the camp; and, during several days, the troops of Julian were obliged to contend with the most discouraging hardships. But every obstacle was surmounted by the perseverance of the legionaries, who were inured to toil as well as to danger, and who felt themselves animated by the spirit of their leader. The damage was gradually repaired; the waters were restored to their proper channels; while groves of palm-trees were cut down and placed along the broken parts of the road; and the army passed over the broad and deeper canals on bridges of floating rafts, which were supported by the help of bladders.

The neighbourhood of the capital of Persia was adorned with three stately palaces, laboriously enriched with every production that could gratify the luxury and pride of an Eastern monarch. The pleasant situation of the gardens along the banks of the Tigris was improved, according to the Persian taste, by the symmetry of flowers, fountains, and shady walks: and spacious parks were enclosed by the reception of the bears, lions, and wild boars, which were maintained at a considerable expense for the pleasure of the royal chase. The park-walls were broken down, the savage game was abandoned to the darts of the soldiers, and the palaces of Sapor were reduced to ashes, by the command of the Roman emperor. Julian, on this occasion, showed himself ignorant or careless of the laws of civility, which the prudence and refinement of polished ages have established between hostile princes. Yet these wanton ravages need not excite in our breasts any vehement emotions of pity or resentment. A simple, naked statue, finished by the hand of a Grecian artist, is of more genuine value than all these rude and costly monuments of barbaric labour; and, if we are more deeply affected by the ruin of a palace than by the conflagration of a cottage, our humanity must have formed a very erroneous estimate of the miseries of human life.

Julian was an object of terror and hatred to the Persians; and the painters of that nation represented the invader of their country under the emblem of a furious lion, who vomited from his mouth a consuming fire. To his friends and soldiers the philosophic hero appeared in a more amiable light; and his virtues were never more conspicuously displayed than in the last and most active period of his life. He practised, without effort, and almost without merit, the habitual qualities of temperance and sobriety. According to the dictates of that artificial wisdom which assumes an absolute dominion over the mind and body, he sternly refused himself the indulgence of the most natural appetites. In the warm climate of Assyria, which solicited a luxurious people to the gratification of every sensual desire, a youthful conqueror preserved his chastity pure and inviolate: nor was Julian ever tempted, even by a motive of curiosity, to visit his female captives of exquisite beauty, who, instead of resisting his power, would have disputed with each other the honour of his embraces. With the same firmness that he resisted the allurements of love, he sustained the hardships of war. When the Romans marched through the flat and flooded country, their sovereign, on foot, at the head of his legions, shared their fatigues and animated their diligence. In every useful labour the hand of Julian was prompt and strenuous; and the Imperial purple was wet and dirty, as the coarse garment of the meanest soldier. Two sieges allowed him some remarkable opportunities of signalising his personal valour, which, in the improved state of the military art, can seldom be exerted by a prudent general. The emperor stood before the citadel of Perisabor, insensible of his extreme danger, and encouraged his troops to burst open the gates of iron, till he was almost overwhelmed under a cloud of missile weapons and huge stones that were directed against his person. As he examined the exterior fortifications of Maogamalcha, two Persians, devoting themselves for their country, suddenly rushed upon him with drawn scimitars: the emperor dexterously received their blows on his uplifted shield; and, with a steady and well-aimed thrust, laid one of his adversaries dead at his feet. The esteem of a prince who possesses the virtues which he approves is the noblest recompense of a deserving subject; and the authority which Julian derived from his personal merit enabled him to revive and enforce the rigour of ancient discipline. He punished with death, or ignominy, the misbehaviour of three troops of horse, who, in a skirmish with the Surenas, had lost their honour and one of their standards: and he distinguished with *obsidional* crowns the valour of the foremost soldiers who had ascended into the city of Maogamalcha.

While the Persians beheld from the walls of Ctesiphon the desolation of the adjacent country, Julian cast many an anxious look towards the North, in full expectation that, as he himself had victoriously penetrated to the capital of Sapor, the march and junction of his lieutenants, Sebastian and Procopius, would be executed with the same courage and diligence. His expectations were disappointed by the treachery of the Armenian king, who permitted, and most probably directed, the desertion of his auxiliary troops from the camp of the Romans; and by the dissensions of the two generals, who were incapable of forming or executing any plan for the public service. When the emperor had relinquished the hope of this important reinforcement, he condescended to hold a council of war, and approved, after a full debate, the sentiment of those generals who dissuaded the siege of Ctesiphon, as a fruitless and pernicious undertaking. It is not easy for us to conceive by what arts of fortification a city thrice besieged and taken by the predecessors of Julian could be rendered impregnable against an army of sixty thousand Romans, commanded by a brave and experienced general, and abundantly supplied with ships, provisions, battering engines, and military stores. But we may rest assured, from the love of glory, and contempt of danger, which formed the character of Julian, that he was not discouraged by any trivial or imaginary obstacles. At the very time when he declined the siege of Ctesiphon, he rejected, with obstinacy and disdain, the most flattering offers of a negotiation of peace. Sapor, who had been so long accustomed to the tardy ostentation of Constantius, was surprised by the intrepid diligence of his successor. As far as the confines of India and Scythia, the satraps of the distant provinces were ordered to assemble their troops, and to march, without delay, to the assistance of their monarch. But their preparations were dilatory, their motions slow; and before Sapor could lead an army into the field, he received the melancholy intelligence of the devastation of Assyria, the ruin of his palaces, and the slaughter of his bravest troops, who defended the passage of the Tigris. The pride of royalty was humbled in the dust; he took his repasts on the ground; and the disorder of his hair expressed the grief and anxiety of his mind. Perhaps he would not have refused to purchase, with one half of his kingdom, the safety of the remainder; and he would have gladly subscribed himself, in a treaty of peace, the faithful and dependent ally of the Roman conqueror. Under the pretence of private business, a minister of rank and confidence was secretly despatched to embrace the knees of Hormisdas, and to request, in the language of a suppliant, that he might be introduced into the presence of the emperor. The Sassanian prince, whether he listened to the voice of pride or humanity, whether he consulted the sentiments of his birth or the duties of his situation, was equally inclined to promote a salutary measure which would terminate the calamities of Persia, and secure the triumph of Rome. He was astonished by the inflexible firmness of a hero who remembered, most unfortunately for himself and for his country, that Alexander had uniformly rejected the propositions of Darius. But as Julian was sensible that the hope of a safe and honourable peace might cool the ardour of his troops, he earnestly requested that Hormisdas would privately dismiss the minister of Sapor, and conceal this dangerous temptation from the knowledge of the camp.

The honour, as well as interest, of Julian, forbade him to consume his time under the impregnable walls of Ctesiphon; and as often as he defied the barbarians, who defended the city, to meet him on the open plain, they prudently replied that, if he desired to exercise his valour, he might seek the army of the Great King. He felt the insult, and he accepted the advice. Instead of confining his servile march to the banks of the Euphrates and Tigris, he resolved to imitate the adventurous spirit of Alexander, and boldly to advance into the inland provinces, till he forced his rival to contend with him, perhaps in the plains of Arbela, for the empire of Asia. The magnanimity of Julian was applauded and betrayed by the arts of a noble Persian, who, in the cause of his country, had generously submitted to act a part full of danger, of falsehood, and of shame. With a train of faithful followers he deserted to the Imperial camp; exposed, in a specious tale, the injuries which he had sustained; exaggerated the cruelty of Sapor, the discontent of the people, and the weakness of the monarchy; and confidently offered himself as the hostage and guide of the Roman march. The most rational grounds of suspicion were urged, without effect, by the wisdom and experience of Hormisdas; and the credulous Julian, receiving the traitor into his bosom, was persuaded to issue an hasty order, which, in the opinion of mankind, appeared to arraign his prudence and to endanger his safety. He destroyed in a single hour the whole navy, which had been transported above five hundred miles, at so great an expense of toil, of treasure, and of blood. Twelve, or, at the most, twenty-two, small vessels were saved, to accompany, on carriages, the march of the army, and to form occasional bridges for the passage of the rivers. A supply of twenty days' provisions was reserved for the use of the soldiers; and the rest of the magazines, with a fleet of eleven hundred vessels, which rode at anchor in the Tigris, were abandoned to the flames by the absolute command of the emperor. The Christian bishops, Gregory and Augustin, insult the madness of the apostate, who executed, with his own hands, the sentence of divine justice. Their authority, of less weight, perhaps, in a military question, is confirmed by the cool judgment of an experienced soldier, who was himself spectator of the conflagration, and who could not disapprove the reluctant murmurs of the troops. Yet there are not wanting some specious, and perhaps solid, reasons, which might justify the resolution of Julian. The navigation of the Euphrates never ascended above Babylon, nor that of the Tigris above Opis. The distance of the last-mentioned city from the Roman camp was not very considerable; and Julian must soon have renounced the vain and impracticable attempt of forcing upwards a great fleet against the stream of a rapid river, which in several places was embarrassed by natural or artificial cataracts. The power of sails and oars was insufficient, it became necessary to tow the ships against the current of the river; the strength of twenty thousand soldiers was exhausted in this tedious and servile labour; and if the Romans continued to march along the banks of the Tigris, they could only expect to return home without achieving any enterprise worthy of the genius or fortune of their leader. If, on the contrary, it was advisable to advance into the inland country, the destruction of the fleet and magazines was the only measure which could save that valuable prize from the hands of the numerous and active troops which might suddenly be poured from the gates of Ctesiphon. Had the arms of Julian been victorious, we should now admire the conduct as well as the courage of a hero who, by depriving his soldiers of the hopes of a retreat, left them only the alternative of death or conquest.

The cumbersome train of artillery and waggons, which retards the operations of a modern army, was in a great measure unknown in the camps of the Romans. Yet, in every age, the subsistence of sixty thousand men must have been one of the most important cares of a prudent general; and that subsistence could only be drawn from his own or from the enemy's country. Had it been possible for Julian to maintain a bridge of communication on the

Tigris, and to preserve the conquered places of Assyria, a desolated province could not afford any large or regular supplies in a season of the year when the lands were covered by the inundation of the Euphrates, and the unwholesome air was darkened with swarms of innumerable insects. The appearance of the hostile country was far more inviting. The extensive region that lies between the river Tigris and the mountains of Media was filled with villages and towns; and the fertile soil, for the most part, was in a very improved state of cultivation. Julian might expect that a conqueror who possessed the two forcible instruments of persuasion, steel and gold, would easily procure a plentiful subsistence from the fears or avarice of the natives. But on the approach of the Romans this rich and smiling prospect was instantly blasted. Wherever they moved, the inhabitants deserted the open villages and took shelter in the fortified towns; the cattle was driven away; the grass and ripe corn were consumed with fire; and, as soon as the flames had subsided which interrupted the march of Julian, he beheld the melancholy face of a smoking and naked desert. This desperate but effectual method of defence can only be executed by the enthusiasm of a people who prefer their independence to their property; or by the rigour of an arbitrary government, which consults the public safety without submitting to their inclinations the liberty of choice. On the present occasion the zeal and obedience of the Persians seconded the commands of Sapor; and the emperor was soon reduced to the scanty stock of provisions which continually wasted in his hands. Before they were entirely consumed he might still have reached the wealthy and unwarlike cities of Ecbatana or Susa by the effort of a rapid and well-directed march; but he was deprived of this last resource by his ignorance of the roads and by the perfidy of his guides. The Romans wandered several days in the country to the eastward of Bagdad; the Persian deserter, who had artfully led them into the snare, escaped from their resentment; and his followers, as soon as they were put to the torture, confessed the secret of the conspiracy. The visionary conquests of Hyrcania and India, which had so long amused, now tormented, the mind of Julian. Conscious that his own imprudence was the cause of the public distress, he anxiously balanced the hopes of safety or success without obtaining a satisfactory answer either from gods or men. At length, as the only practicable measure, he embraced the resolution of directing his steps towards the banks of the Tigris, with the design of saving the army by a hasty march to the confines of Corduene, a fertile and friendly province, which acknowledged the sovereignty of Rome. The desponding troops obeyed the signal of the retreat, only seventy days after they had passed the Chaboras with the sanguine expectation of subverting the throne of Persia.

While Julian struggled with the almost insuperable difficulties of his situation, the silent hours of the night were still devoted to study and contemplation. Whenever he closed his eyes in short and interrupted slumbers, his mind was agitated with painful anxiety: nor can it be thought surprising that the Genius of the empire should once more appear before him, covering with a funeral veil his head and his horn of abundance, and slowly retiring from the Imperial tent. The monarch started from his couch, and, stepping forth to refresh his wearied spirits with the coolness of the midnight air, he beheld a fiery meteor, which shot athwart the sky, and suddenly vanished. Julian was convinced that he had seen the menacing countenance of the god of war; the council which he summoned, of Tuscan Haruspices, unanimously pronounced that he should abstain from action; but, on this occasion, necessity and reason were more prevalent than superstition; and the trumpets sounded at the break of day. The army marched through a hilly country; and the hills had been secretly occupied by the Persians. Julian led the van with the skill and attention of a consummate general; he was alarmed by the intelligence that his rear was suddenly attacked. The heat of the weather had tempted him to lay aside his cuirass; but he snatched a shield from one of his attendants, and hastened, with a sufficient reinforcement, to the relief of the rear guard. A similar danger recalled the intrepid prince to the defence of the front; and, as he galloped between the columns, the centre of the left was attacked, and almost overpowered, by a furious charge of the Persian cavalry and elephants. This huge body was soon defeated by the well-timed evolution of the light infantry, who aimed their weapons, with dexterity and effect, against the backs of the horsemen, and the legs of the elephants. The barbarians fled; and Julian, who was foremost in every danger, animated the pursuit with his voice and gestures. His trembling guards, scattered and oppressed by the disorderly throng of friends and enemies, reminded their fearless sovereign that he was without armour; and conjured him to decline the fall of the impending ruin. As they exclaimed, a cloud of darts and arrows was discharged from the flying squadrons; and a javelin, after razing the skin of his arm, transpierced the ribs, and fixed in the inferior part of the liver.

Julian attempted to draw the deadly weapon from his side; but his fingers were cut by the sharpness of the steel, and he fell senseless from his horse. His guards flew to his relief; and the wounded emperor was gently raised from the ground, and conveyed out of the tumult of the battle into an adjacent tent. The report of the melancholy event passed from rank to rank; but the grief of the Romans inspired them with invincible valour, and the desire of revenge. The bloody and obstinate conflict was maintained by the two armies till they were separated by the total darkness of the night. The Persians derived some honour from the advantage which they obtained against the left wing, where Anatolius, master of the offices, was slain, and the præfect Sallust very narrowly escaped. But the event of the day was adverse to the barbarians. They abandoned the field; their two generals, Meranes and Nohordates, fifty nobles or satraps, and a multitude of their bravest soldiers [were slain]: and the success of the Romans, if Julian had survived, might have been improved into a decisive and useful victory.

The first words that Julian uttered, after his recovery from the fainting fit into which he had been thrown by loss of blood, were expressive of his martial spirit. He called for his horse and arms, and was impatient to rush into the battle. His remaining strength was exhausted by the painful effort; and the surgeons, who examined his wound, discovered the symptoms of approaching death. He employed the awful moments with the firm temper of a hero and a sage; the philosophers who had accompanied him in this fatal expedition compared the tent of Julian with the prison of Socrates; and the spectators, whom duty, or friendship, or curiosity, had assembled round his couch, listened with respectful grief to the funeral oration of their dying emperor. "Friends and fellow-soldiers, the seasonable period of my departure is now arrived, and I discharge, with the cheerfulness of a ready debtor, the demands of nature. I have learned from philosophy how much the soul is more excellent than the body; and that the separation of the nobler substance should be the subject of joy, rather than of affliction. I have learned from religion that an early death has often been the reward of piety; and I accept, as a favour of the gods, the mortal stroke that secures me from the danger of disgracing a character which has hitherto been supported by virtue and fortitude. I die without remorse, as I have lived without guilt. I am pleased to reflect on the innocence of my private life; and I can affirm with confidence that the supreme authority, that emanation of the

Divine Power, has been preserved in my hands pure and immaculate. Detesting the corrupt and destructive maxims of despotism, I have considered the happiness of the people as the end of government. Submitting my actions to the laws of prudence, of justice, and of moderation, I have trusted the event to the care of Providence. Peace was the object of my counsels, as long as peace was consistent with the public welfare; but when the imperious voice of my country summoned me to arms, I exposed my person to the dangers of war, with the clear foreknowledge (which I had acquired from the art of divination) that I was destined to fall by the sword. I now offer my tribute of gratitude to the Eternal Being, who has not suffered me to perish by the cruelty of a tyrant, by the secret dagger of conspiracy, or by the slow tortures of lingering disease. He has given me, in the midst of an honourable career, a splendid and glorious departure from this world; and I hold it equally absurd, equally base, to solicit, or to decline, the stroke of fate.—Thus much I have attempted to say; but my strength fails me, and I feel the approach of death.—I shall cautiously refrain from any word that may tend to influence your suffrages in the election of an emperor. My choice might be imprudent or injudicious; and if it should not be ratified by the consent of the army, it might be fatal to the person whom I should recommend. I shall only, as a good citizen, express my hopes that the Romans may be blessed with the government of a virtuous sovereign." After this discourse, which Julian pronounced in a firm and gentle tone of voice, he distributed, by a military testament, the remains of his private fortune; and making some inquiry why Anatolius was not present, he understood, from the answer of Sallust, that Anatolius was killed; and bewailed, with amiable inconsistency, the loss of his friend. At the same time he reproved the immoderate grief of the spectators; and conjured them not to disgrace, by unmanly tears, the fate of a prince who in a few moments would be united with heaven and with the stars. The spectators were silent; and Julian entered into a metaphysical argument with the philosophers Priscus and Maximus on the nature of the soul. The efforts which he made, of mind as well as body, most probably hastened his death. His wound began to bleed with fresh violence: his respiration was embarrassed by the swelling of the veins: he called for a draught of cold water, and, as soon as he had drunk it, expired without pain, about the hour of midnight. Such was the end of that extraordinary man, in the thirty-second year of his age, after a reign of one year and about eight months from the death of Constantius. In his last moments he displayed, perhaps with some ostentation, the love of virtue and of fame, which had been the ruling passions of his life.

The triumph of Christianity, and the calamities of the empire, may, in some measure, be ascribed to Julian himself, who had neglected to secure the future execution of his designs by the timely and judicious nomination of an associate and successor. But the royal race of Constantius Chlorus was reduced to his own person; and if he entertained any serious thoughts of investing with the purple the most worthy among the Romans, he was diverted from his resolution by the difficulty of the choice, the jealousy of power, the fear of ingratitude, and the natural presumption of health, of youth, and of prosperity. His unexpected death left the empire without a master, and without an heir, in a state of perplexity and danger which, in the space of fourscore years, had never been experienced, since the election of Diocletian. In a government which had almost forgotten the distinction of pure and noble blood, the superiority of birth was of little moment; the claims of official rank were accidental and precarious; and the candidates who might aspire to ascend the vacant throne could be supported only by the consciousness of personal merit, or by the hopes of popular favour. But the situation of a famished army, encompassed on all sides by an host of barbarians, shortened the moments of grief and deliberation. In this scene of terror and distress, the body of the deceased prince, according to his own directions, was decently embalmed; and, at the dawn of day, the generals convened a military senate, at which the commanders of the legions, and the officers both of cavalry and infantry, were invited to assist. Three or four hours of the night had not passed away without some secret cabals; and when the election of an emperor was proposed, the spirit of faction began to agitate the assembly. Victor and Arinthæus collected the remains of the court of Constantius; the friends of Julian attached themselves to the Gallic chiefs Dagalaiphus and Nevitta; and the most fatal consequences might be apprehended from the discord of two factions, so opposite in their character and interest, in their maxims of government, and perhaps in their religious principles. The superior virtues of Sallust could alone reconcile their divisions and unite their suffrages; and the venerable præfect would immediately have been declared the successor of Julian, if he himself, with sincere and modest firmness, had not alleged his age and infirmities, so unequal to the weight of the diadem. The generals, who were surprised and perplexed by his refusal, showed some disposition to adopt the salutary advice of an inferior officer, that they should act as they would have acted in the absence of the emperor; that they should exert their abilities to extricate the army from the present distress; and, if they were fortunate enough to reach the confines of Mesopotamia, they should proceed with united and deliberate counsels in the election of a lawful sovereign. While they debated, a few voices saluted Jovian, who was no more than *first* of the domestics, with the names of Emperor and Augustus. The tumultuary acclamation was instantly repeated by the guards who surrounded the tent, and passed, in a few minutes, to the extremities of the line. The new prince, astonished with his own fortune, was hastily invested with the Imperial ornaments, and received an oath of fidelity from the generals, whose favour and protection he so lately solicited. The strongest recommendation of Jovian was the merit of his father, Count Varronian, who enjoyed, in honourable retirement, the fruit of his long services. In the obscure freedom of a private station, the son indulged his taste for wine and women; yet he supported, with credit, the character of a Christian and a soldier. Without being conspicuous for any of the ambitious qualifications which excite the admiration and envy of mankind, the comely person of Jovian, his cheerful temper, and familiar wit, had gained the affection of his fellow-soldiers; and the generals of both parties acquiesced in a popular election which had not been conducted by the arts of their enemies. The pride of this unexpected elevation was moderated by the just apprehension that the same day might terminate the life and reign of the new emperor. The pressing voice of necessity was obeyed without delay; and the first orders issued by Jovian, a few hours after his predecessor had expired, were to prosecute a march which could alone extricate the Romans from their actual distress.

In this hopeless situation, the fainting spirits of the Romans were revived by the sound of peace. The transient presumption of Sapor had vanished: he observed, with serious concern, that, in the repetition of doubtful combats, he had lost his most faithful and intrepid nobles, his bravest troops, and the greatest part of his train of elephants: and the experienced monarch feared to provoke the resistance of despair, the vicissitudes of fortune, and the unexhausted powers of the Roman empire, which might soon advance to relieve, or to revenge, the successor of Julian. The Surenas himself, accompanied by another satrap, appeared in the camp of Jovian, and declared that the clemency of his sovereign was not averse to signify the conditions on which he would consent to spare and to dismiss the Cæsar with the relics of his captive army. The hopes of safety subdued the firmness of the Romans; the emperor was compelled, by the advice of his council and the cries of the soldiers, to embrace the offer of peace; and the præfect Sallust was immediately sent, with the general Arinthæus, to understand the pleasure of the Great King. The crafty Persian delayed, under various pretences, the conclusion of the agreement; started difficulties, required explanations, suggested expedients, receded from his concessions, increased his demands, and wasted four days in the arts of negotiation, till he had consumed the stock of provisions which yet remained in the camp of the Romans. Had Jovian been capable of executing a bold and prudent measure, he would have continued his march with unremitting diligence; the progress of the treaty would have suspended the attacks of the barbarians; and, before the expiration of the fourth day, he might have safely reached the fruitful province of Corduene, at the distance only of one hundred miles. The irresolute emperor, instead of breaking through the toils of the enemy, expected his fate with patient resignation; and accepted the humiliating conditions of peace which it was no longer in his power to refuse. The five provinces beyond the Tigris, which had been ceded by the grandfather of Sapor, were restored to the Persian monarchy. He acquired, by a single article, the impregnable city of Nisibis, which had sustained, in three successive sieges, the effort of his arms. Singara and the castle of the Moors, one of the strongest places of Mesopotamia, were likewise dismembered from the empire. It was considered as an indulgence that the inhabitants of those fortresses were permitted to retire with their effects; but the conqueror rigorously insisted that the Romans should for ever abandon the king and kingdom of Armenia. A peace, or rather a long truce, of thirty years, was stipulated between the hostile nations; the faith of the treaty was ratified by solemn oaths and religious ceremonies; and hostages of distinguished rank were reciprocally delivered to secure the performance of the condition.

The loss which the army sustained in the passage of the Tigris was not inferior to the carnage of a day of battle. As soon as the Romans had landed on the western bank, they were delivered from the hostile pursuit of the barbarians; but in a laborious march of two hundred miles over the plains of Mesopotamia they endured the last extremities of thirst and hunger. They were obliged to traverse a sandy desert, which, in the extent of seventy miles, did not afford a single blade of sweet grass nor a single spring of fresh water, and the rest of the inhospitable waste was untrod by the footsteps either of friend or enemies. Whenever a small measure of flour could be discovered in the camp, twenty pounds weight were greedily purchased with ten pieces of gold, the beasts of burden were slaughtered and devoured, and the desert was strewed with the arms and baggage of the Roman soldiers, whose tattered garments and meagre countenances displayed their past sufferings and actual misery. A small convoy of provisions advanced to meet the army as far as the castle of Ur; and the supply was the more grateful, since it declared the fidelity of Sebastian and Procopius. At Thilsaphata the emperor most graciously received the generals of Mesopotamia, and the remains of a once flourishing army at length reposed themselves under the walls of Nisibis. The messengers of Jovian had already proclaimed, in the language of flattery, his election, his treaty, and his return, and the new prince had taken the most effectual measures to secure the allegiance of the armies and provinces of Europe by placing the military command in the hands of those officers who, from motives of interest or inclination, would firmly support the cause of their benefactor.

The friends of Julian had confidently announced the success of his expedition. They entertained a fond persuasion that the temples of the gods would be enriched with the spoils of the East; that Persia would be reduced to the humble state of a tributary province, governed by the laws and magistrates of Rome; that the barbarians would adopt the dress, and manners, and language of their conquerors; and that the youth of Ecbatana and Susa would study the art of rhetoric under Grecian masters. The progress of the arms of Julian interrupted his communication with the empire, and, from the moment that he passed the Tigris, his affectionate subjects were ignorant of the fate and fortunes of their prince. Their contemplation of fancied triumphs was disturbed by the melancholy rumour of his death, and they persisted to doubt, after they could no longer deny, the truth of that fatal event. The messengers of Jovian promulgated the specious tale of a prudent and necessary peace; the voice of fame, louder and more sincere, revealed the disgrace of the emperor and the conditions of the ignominious treaty. The minds of the people were filled with astonishment and grief, with indignation and terror, when they were informed that the unworthy successor of Julian relinquished the five provinces which had been acquired by the victory of Galerius, and that he shamefully surrendered to the barbarians the important city of Nisibis, the firmest bulwark of the provinces of the East. The deep and dangerous question, how far the public faith should be observed when it becomes incompatible with the public safety, was freely agitated in popular conversation, and some hopes were entertained that the emperor would redeem his pusil-lanimous behaviour by a splendid act of patriotic perfidy. The inflexible spirit of the Roman senate had always disclaimed the unequal conditions which were extorted from the distress of her captive armies; and, if it were necessary to satisfy the national honour by delivering the guilty general into the hands of the barbarians, the greatest part of the subjects of Jovian would have cheerfully acquiesced in the precedent of ancient times.

But the emperor, whatever might be the limits of his constitu-tional authority, was the absolute master of the laws and arms of the state; and the same motives which had forced him to subscribe, now pressed him to execute the treaty of peace. He was impatient to secure an empire at the expense of a few provinces, and the respectable names of religion and honour concealed the personal fears and the ambition of Jovian. Sapor enjoyed the glory and the fruits of his victory; and this ignominious peace has justly been con-sidered as a memorable era in the decline and fall of the Roman empire. The predecessors of Jovian had sometimes relinquished the dominion of distant and unprofitable provinces; but, since the foundation of the city, the genius of Rome, the god Terminus, who guarded the boundaries of the republic, had never retired before the sword of a victorious enemy.

After Jovian had performed those engagements which the voice of his people might have tempted him to violate, he hastened away from the scene of his disgrace, and proceeded with his whole court to enjoy the luxury of Antioch. Without consulting the dictates of religious zeal, he was prompted, by humanity and gratitude, to bestow the last honours on the remains of his deceased sovereign; and Procopius, who sincerely bewailed the loss of his kinsman, was removed from the command of the army, under the decent pretence of conducting the funeral. The corpse of Julian was trans-ported from Nisibis to Tarsus, in a slow march of fifteen days, and, as it passed through the cities of the East, was saluted by the hostile factions with mournful lamentations and clamorous insults. The

Pagans already placed their beloved hero in the rank of those gods whose worship he had restored, while the invectives of the Christians pursued the soul of the apostate to hell, and his body to the grave. One party lamented the approaching ruin of their altars, the other celebrated the marvellous deliverance of the church. The Christians applauded, in lofty and ambiguous strains, the stroke of divine vengeance which had been so long suspended over the guilty head of Julian. They acknowledged that the death of the tyrant, at the instant he expired beyond the Tigris, was *revealed* to the saints of Egypt, Syria, and Cappadocia; and instead of suffering him to fall by the Persian darts, their indiscretion ascribed the heroic deed to the obscure hand of some mortal or immortal champion of the faith. Such imprudent declarations were eagerly adopted by the malice or credulity of their adversaries, who darkly insinuated or confidently asserted that the governors of the church had instigated and directed the fanaticism of a domestic assassin. Above sixteen years after the death of Julian, the charge was solemnly and vehemently urged in a public oration addressed by Libanius to the emperor Theodosius. His suspicions are unsupported by fact or argument, and we can only esteem the generous zeal of the sophist of Antioch for the cold and neglected ashes of his friend.

It was an ancient custom in the funerals, as well as in the triumphs of the Romans that the voice of praise should be corrected by that of satire and ridicule, and that, in the midst of the splendid pageants which displayed the glory of the living or of the dead, their imperfections should not be concealed from the eyes of the world. This custom was practised in the funeral of Julian. The comedians, who resented his contempt and aversion for the theatre, exhibited, with the applause of a Christian audience, the lively and exaggerated representation of the faults and follies of the deceased emperor. His various character and singular manners afforded an ample scope for pleasantry and ridicule. In the exercise of his uncommon talents he often descended below the majesty of his rank. Alexander was transformed into Diogenes –the philosopher was degraded into a priest. The purity of his virtue was sullied by excessive vanity; his superstition disturbed the peace and endangered the safety of a mighty empire; and his irregular sallies were the less entitled to indulgence, as they appeared to be the laborious efforts of art, or even of affectation. The remains of Julian were interred at Tarsus in Cilicia; but his stately tomb, which arose in that city on the banks of the cold and limpid Cydnus, was displeasing to the faithful friends who loved and revered the memory of that extraordinary man. The philosopher expressed a very reasonable wish that the disciple of Plato might have reposed amidst the groves of the Academy, while the soldier exclaimed, in bolder accents, that the ashes of Julian should have been mingled with those of Cæsar, in the field of Mars, and among the ancient monuments of Roman virtue. The history of princes does not very frequently renew the example of a similar competition.

XXIII

(343–384 A.D.) THE GOVERNMENT AND DEATH OF JOVIAN—ELECTION OF VALENTINIAN, WHO ASSOCIATES HIS BROTHER VALENS, AND MAKES THE FINAL DIVISION OF THE EASTERN AND WESTERN EMPIRES—CIVIL AND ECCLESIASTICAL ADMINISTRATION— BRITAIN—THE EAST—THE DANUBE—DEATH OF VALENTINIAN—HIS TWO SONS, GRATIAN AND VALENTINIAN II, SUCCEED TO THE WESTERN EMPIRE

The death of Julian had left the public affairs of the empire in a very doubtful and dangerous situation. The Roman army was saved by an inglorious, perhaps a necessary, treaty; and the first moments of peace were consecrated by the pious Jovian to restore the domestic tranquillity of the church and state. The indiscretion of his predecessor, instead of reconciling, had artfully fomented the religious war; and the balance which he affected to preserve between the hostile factions served only to perpetuate the contest by the vicissitudes of hope and fear, by the rival claims of ancient possession and actual favour. The Christians had forgotten the spirit of the Gospel, and the Pagans had imbibed the spirit of the church. In private families the sentiments of nature were extinguished by the blind fury of zeal and revenge; the majesty of the laws was violated or abused, the cities of the East were stained with blood; and the most implacable enemies of the Romans were in the bosom of their country. Jovian was educated in the profession of Christianity; and as he marched from Nisibis to Antioch, the banner of the Cross, the LABARUM of Constantine, which was again displayed at the head of the legions, announced to the people the faith of their new emperor. As soon as he ascended the throne he transmitted a circular epistle to all the governors of provinces, in which he confessed the divine truth and secured the legal establishment of the Christian religion. The insidious edicts of Julian were abolished, the ecclesiastical immunities were restored and enlarged, and Jovian condescended to lament that the distress of the times obliged him to diminish the measure of charitable distributions. The Christians were unanimous in the loud and sincere applause which they bestowed on the pious successor of Julian; but they were still ignorant what creed or what synod he would choose for the standard of orthodoxy, and the peace of the church immediately revived those eager disputes which had been suspended during the season of persecution. The episcopal leaders of the contending sects, convinced from experience how much their fate would depend on the earliest impressions that were made on the mind of an untutored soldier, hastened to the court of Edessa, or Antioch. The highways of the East were crowded with Homoousian, and Arian, and Semi-Arian, and Eunomian bishops, who struggled to outstrip each other in the holy race; the apartments of the palace resounded with their clamours, and the ears of the prince were assaulted, and perhaps astonished, by the singular mixture of metaphysical argument and passionate invective. The moderation of Jovian, who recommended concord and charity, and referred the disputants to the sentence of a future council, was interpreted as a symptom of indifference; but his attachment to the Nicene Creed was at length discovered and declared by the reverence which he expressed for the *celestial* virtues of the great Athanasius.

In the space of seven months the Roman troops, who were now returned to Antioch, had performed a march of fifteen hundred miles, in which they had endured all the hardships of war, of famine, and of climate. Notwithstanding their services, their fatigues, and the approach of winter, the timid and impatient Jovian allowed only to the men and horses a respite of six weeks. The emperor could not sustain the indiscreet and malicious raillery of the people of Antioch. He was impatient to possess the palace of Constantinople, and to prevent the ambition of some competitor who might occupy the vacant allegiance of Europe; but he soon received the grateful intelligence that his authority was acknowledged from the Thracian Bosphorus to the Atlantic ocean. By the first letters which he despatched from the camp of Mesopotamia, he had delegated the military command of Gaul and Illyricum to Malarich, a brave and faithful officer of the nation of the Franks, and to his father-in-law, Count Lucillian, who had formerly distinguished his courage and conduct in the defence of Nisibis. Malarich had declined an office to which he thought himself unequal, and Lucillian was massacred at Rheims, in an accidental mutiny of the Batavian cohorts. But the moderation of Jovinus, master-general of the cavalry, who forgave the intention of his disgrace, soon appeased the tumult and confirmed the uncertain minds of the soldiers. The oath of fidelity was administered and taken with loyal acclamations, and the deputies of the Western armies saluted their new sovereign as he descended from Mount Taurus to the city of Tyana, in Cappadocia. From Tyana he continued his hasty march to Ancyra, capital of the province of Galatia, where Jovian assumed, with his infant son, the name and ensigns of the consulship. Dadastana, an obscure town, almost at an equal distance between Ancyra and Nice, was marked for the fatal term of his journey and his life. After indulging himself with a plentiful, perhaps an intemperate supper, he retired to rest, and the next morning the emperor Jovian was found dead in his bed. The cause of this sudden death was variously understood. By some it was ascribed to the consequences of an indigestion, occasioned either by the quantity of the wine or the quality of the mushrooms which he had swallowed in the evening. According to others, he was suffocated in his sleep by the vapour of charcoal, which extracted from the walls of the apartment the unwholesome moisture of the fresh plaster.

After the death of Jovian the throne of the Roman world remained ten days without a master. The ministers and generals still continued to meet in council, to exercise their respective functions, to maintain the public order, and peaceably to conduct the army to the city of Nice in Bithynia, which was chosen for the place of the election. In a solemn assembly of the civil and military powers of the empire, the diadem was again unanimously offered to the præfect Sallust. He enjoyed the glory of a second refusal; and, when the virtues of the father were alleged in favour of the son, the præfect, with the firmness of a disinterested patriot, declared to the electors that the feeble age of the one, and the inexperienced youth of the other, were equally incapable of the laborious duties of government. Several candidates were proposed, and, after weighing the objections of character or situation, they were successively rejected: but as soon as the name of Valentinian was pronounced, the merit of that officer united the suffrages of the whole assembly, and obtained the sincere approbation of

Sallust himself. Valentinian was the son of Count Gratian, a native of Cibalis, in Pannonia, who from an obscure condition had raised himself, by matchless strength and dexterity, to the military commands of Africa and Britain, from which he retired with an ample fortune and suspicious integrity. The rank and services of Gratian contributed, however, to smooth the first steps of the promotion of his son, and afforded him an early opportunity of displaying those solid and useful qualifications which raised his character above the ordinary level of his fellow-soldiers. The person of Valentinian was tall, graceful, and majestic. His manly countenance, deeply marked with the impression of sense and spirit, inspired his friends with awe, and his enemies with fear; and, to second the efforts of his undaunted courage, the son of Gratian had inherited the advantages of a strong and healthy constitution. By the habits of chastity and temperance, which restrain the appetites and invigorate the faculties, Valentinian preserved his own and the public esteem. The avocations of a military life had diverted his youth from the elegant pursuits of literature; he was ignorant of the Greek language and the arts of rhetoric; but, as the mind of the orator was never disconcerted by timid perplexity, he was able, as often as the occasion prompted him, to deliver his decided sentiments with bold and ready elocution. The laws of martial discipline were the only laws that he had studied, and he was soon distinguished by the laborious diligence and inflexible severity with which he discharged and enforced the duties of the camp. In the time of Julian he provoked the danger of disgrace by the contempt which he publicly expressed for the reigning religion; and it should seem, from his subsequent conduct, that the indiscreet and unseasonable freedom of Valentinian was the effect of military spirit rather than of Christian zeal. He was pardoned, however, and still employed by a prince who esteemed his merit, and in the various events of the Persian war he improved the reputation which he had already acquired on the banks of the Rhine. The celerity and success with which he executed an important commission recommended him to the favour of Jovian, and to the honourable command of the second *school*, or company, of Targeteers of the domestic guards. In the march from Antioch he had reached his quarters at Ancyra, when he was unexpectedly summoned, without guilt and without intrigue, to assume, in the forty-third year of his age, the absolute government of the Roman empire. In one of the suburbs of that capital, thirty days after his own elevation, he bestowed the title of Augustus on his brother Valens: and as the boldest patriots were convinced that their opposition, without being serviceable to their country, would be fatal to themselves, the declaration of his absolute will was received with silent submission. Valens was now in the thirty-sixth year of his age, but his abilities had never been exercised in any employment, military or civil, and his character had not inspired the world with any sanguine expectations. He possessed, however, one quality which recommended him to Valentinian, and preserved the domestic peace of the empire: a devout and grateful attachment to his benefactor, whose superiority of genius, as well as of authority, Valens humbly and cheerfully acknowledged in every action of his life.

Before Valentinian divided the provinces, he reformed the administration of the empire. All ranks of subjects who had been injured or oppressed under the reign of Julian were invited to support their public accusations. The silence of mankind attested the spotless integrity of the præfect Sallust, and his own pressing solicitations that he might be permitted to retire from the business of the state were rejected by Valentinian with the most honourable expressions of friendship and esteem. But among the favourites of the late emperor there were many who had abused his credulity or superstition, and who could no longer hope to be protected either by favour or justice. The greater part of the ministers of the palace and the governors of the provinces were removed from their respective stations, yet the eminent merit of some officers was distinguished from the obnoxious crowd, and, notwithstanding the opposite clamours of zeal and resentment, the whole proceedings of this delicate inquiry appear to have been conducted with a reasonable share of wisdom and moderation. The festivity of a new reign received a short and suspicious interruption from the sudden illness of the two princes, but as soon as their health was restored they left Constantinople in the beginning of the spring. In the castle or palace of Mediana, only three miles from Naissus, they executed the solemn and final division of the Roman empire. Valentinian bestowed on his brother the rich præfecture of the *East*, from the Lower Danube to the confines of Persia; whilst he reserved for his immediate government the warlike præfectures of *Illyricum*, *Italy*, and *Gaul*, from the extremity of Greece to the Caledonian rampart and from the rampart of Caledonia to the foot of Mount Atlas. The provincial administration remained on its former basis, but a double supply of generals and magistrates was required for two councils and two courts; the division was made with a just regard to their peculiar merit and situation, and seven master-generals were soon created either of the cavalry or infantry. When this important business had been amicably transacted, Valentinian and Valens embraced for the last time. The emperor of the West established his temporary residence at Milan, and the emperor of the East returned to Constantinople to assume the dominion of fifty provinces, of whose language he was totally ignorant.

When Tacitus describes the deaths of the innocent and illustrious Romans who were sacrificed to the cruelty of the first Cæsars, the art of the historian, or the merit of the sufferers, excites in our breasts the most lively sensations of terror, of admiration, and of pity. The coarse and undistinguishing pencil of Ammianus has delineated his bloody figures with tedious and disgusting accuracy. But as our attention is no longer engaged by the contrast of freedom and servitude, of recent greatness and of actual misery, we should turn with horror from the frequent executions which disgraced, both at Rome and Antioch, the reign of the two brothers. Valens was of a timid, and Valentinian of a choleric, disposition. An anxious regard to his personal safety was the ruling principle of the administration of Valens. In the condition of a subject, he had kissed, with trembling awe, the hand of the oppressor; and when he ascended the throne, he reasonably expected that the same fears which had subdued his own mind would secure the patient submission of his people. The favourites of Valens obtained, by the privilege of rapine and confiscation, the wealth which his economy would have refused. They urged, with persuasive eloquence, *that*, in all cases of treason, suspicion is equivalent to proof; *that* the power supposes the intention of mischief; *that* the intention is not less criminal than the act; and *that* a subject no longer deserves to live, if his life may threaten the safety, or disturb the repose, of his sovereign. The judgment of Valentinian was sometimes deceived, and his confidence abused; but he would have silenced the informers with a contemptuous smile, had they presumed to alarm his fortitude by the sound of danger. They praised his inflexible love of justice; and, in the pursuit of justice, the emperor was easily tempted to consider clemency as a weakness, and passion as a virtue. As long as he wrestled with his equals in the bold competition of an active and ambitious life, Valentinian was seldom injured, and never insulted, with impunity: if his prudence was arraigned, his spirit was applauded; and the proudest and most powerful generals were apprehensive of provoking the resentment of a fearless soldier. After he became master of the world, he unfortunately forgot that, where no resistance can be made, no courage can be exerted; and instead of consulting the dictates of reason and magnanimity, he indulged the furious emotions of his temper, at a time when they were disgraceful to himself, and fatal to the defenceless objects of his displeasure. In the government of his household, or of his empire, slight, or even imaginary offences—a hasty word, a casual omission, an involuntary delay—were chastised by a sentence of immediate death. The expressions which issued the most readily from the mouth of the emperor of the West were, "Strike off his head";—"Burn him alive";—"Let him be beaten with clubs till he expires"; and his most favoured ministers soon understood that, by a rash attempt to dispute or suspend the execution of his sanguinary commands, they might involve themselves in the guilt and punishment of disobedience. The repeated gratification of this savage justice hardened the mind of Valentinian against pity and remorse; and the sallies of passion were confirmed by the habits of cruelty. He could behold with calm satisfaction the convulsive agonies of torture and death: he reserved his friendship for those faithful servants whose temper was the most congenial to his own. The merit of Maximin, who had slaughtered the noblest families of Rome, was rewarded with the royal approbation, and the præfecture of Gaul. Two fierce and enormous bears, distinguished by the appellations of *Innocence* and *Mica Aurea*, could alone deserve to share the favour of Maximin. The cages of those trusty guards were always placed near the bedchamber of Valentinian, who frequently amused his eyes with the grateful spectacle of seeing them tear and devour the bleeding limbs of the malefactors who were abandoned to their rage. Their diet and exercises were carefully inspected by the Roman emperor; and when *Innocence* had earned her discharge, by a long course of meritorious service, the faithful animal was again restored to the freedom of her native woods.

But in the calmer moments of reflection, when the mind of Valens was not agitated by fear, or that of Valentinian by rage, the tyrant resumed the sentiments, or at least the conduct, of the father of his country. The dispassionate judgment of the Western emperor could clearly perceive, and accurately pursue, his own and the public interest; and the sovereign of the East, who imitated with equal docility the various examples which he received from his elder brother, was sometimes guided by the wisdom and virtue of the præfect Sallust. Both princes invariably retained, in the purple, the chaste and temperate simplicity which had adorned their private life; and, under their reign, the pleasures of the court never cost the people a blush or a sigh. They gradually reformed many of the abuses of the times of Constantius; judiciously adopted and improved the designs of Julian and his successor; and displayed a style and spirit of legislation which might inspire posterity with the most favourable opinion of their character and government. It is not from the master of *Innocence* that we should expect the tender regard for the welfare of his subjects which prompted Valentinian to condemn the exposition of new-born infants, and to establish fourteen skilful physicians, with stipends and privileges, in the fourteen quarters of Rome. The good sense of an illiterate soldier founded an useful and liberal institution for the education of youth, and the support of declining science. It was his intention that the arts of rhetoric and grammar should be taught, in the Greek and Latin languages, in the metropolis of every province; and as the size and dignity of the school was usually proportioned to the importance of the city, the academies of Rome and Constantinople claimed a just and singular preëminence. The fragments of the literary edicts of Valentinian imperfectly represent the school of Constantinople, which was gradually improved by subsequent regulations. That school consisted of thirty-one professors in different branches of learning. One philosopher and two lawyers; five sophists and ten grammarians for the Greek, and three orators and ten grammarians for the Latin tongue; besides seven scribes, or, as they were then styled, antiquarians, whose laborious pens supplied the public library with fair and correct copies of the classic writers. The rule of conduct which was prescribed to the students is the more curious, as it affords the first outlines of the form and discipline of a modern university. It was required that they should bring proper certificates from the magistrates of their native province. Their names, professions, and places of abode, were regularly entered in a public register. The studious youth were severely prohibited from wasting their time in feasts or in the theatre; and the term of their education was limited to the age of twenty. The præfect of the city was empowered to chastise the idle and refractory by stripes or expulsion; and he was directed to make an annual report to the master of the offices, that the knowledge and abilities of the

scholars might be usefully applied to the public service. The institutions of Valentinian contributed to secure the benefits of peace
and plenty; and the cities were guarded by the establishment of
the *Defensors*; freely elected as the tribunes and advocates of the
people, to support their rights, and to expose their grievances,
before the tribunals of the civil magistrates, or even at the foot of
the Imperial throne. The finances were diligently administered
by two princes who had been so long accustomed to the rigid
economy of a private fortune; but in the receipt and application of
the revenue, a discerning eye might observe some difference
between the government of the East and of the West. Valens was
persuaded that royal liberality can be supplied only by public
oppression, and his ambition never aspired to secure, by their
actual distress, the future strength and prosperity of his people.
Instead of increasing the weight of taxes, which in the space of forty
years had been gradually doubled, he reduced, in the first years of
his reign, one-fourth of the tribute of the East. Valentinian appears
to have been less attentive and less anxious to relieve the burthens
of his people. He might reform the abuses of the fiscal administration; but he exacted, without scruple, a very large share of the
private property; as he was convinced that the revenues which
supported the luxury of individuals would be much more advantageously employed for the defence and improvement of the state.
The subjects of the East, who enjoyed the present benefit,
applauded the indulgence of their prince. The solid, but less
splendid merit of Valentinian was felt and acknowledged by the
subsequent generation.

But the most honourable circumstance of the character of
Valentinian is the firm and temperate impartiality which he
uniformly preserved in an age of religious contention. His strong
sense, unenlightened, but uncorrupted, by study, declined, with
respectful indifference, the subtle questions of theological debate.
The government of the *Earth* claimed his vigilance, and satisfied
his ambition; and while he remembered that he was the disciple
of the church, he never forgot that he was the sovereign of the
clergy. Under the reign of an apostate, he had signalised his zeal
for the honour of Christianity: he allowed to his subjects the
privilege which he had assumed for himself; and they might accept
with gratitude and confidence the general toleration which was
granted by a prince addicted to passion, but incapable of fear or of
disguise. The Pagans, the Jews, and all the various sects which

acknowledged the divine authority of Christ, were protected by the laws from arbitrary power or popular insult; nor was any mode of worship prohibited by Valentinian, except those secret and criminal practices which abused the name of religion for the dark purposes of vice and disorder. The art of magic, as it was more cruelly punished, was more strictly proscribed: but the emperor admitted a formal distinction to protect the ancient methods of divination, which were approved by the senate and exercised by the Tuscan haruspices. He had condemned, with the consent of the most rational Pagans, the licence of nocturnal sacrifices; but he immediately admitted the petition of Prætextatus, proconsul of Achaia, who represented that the life of the Greeks would become dreary and comfortless if they were deprived of the invaluable blessing of the Eleusinian mysteries. Philosophy alone can boast (and perhaps it is no more than the boast of philosophy) that her gentle hand is able to eradicate from the human mind the latent and deadly principle of fanaticism. But this truce of twelve years, which was inforced by the wise and vigorous government of Valentinian, by suspending the repetition of mutual injuries, contributed to soften the manners, and abate the prejudices, of the religious factions.

The strict regulations which have been framed by the wisdom of modern legislators to restrain the wealth and avarice of the clergy may be originally deduced from the example of the emperor Valentinian. His edict, addressed to Damasus, bishop of Rome, was publicly read in the churches of the city. He admonished the ecclesiastics and monks not to frequent the houses of widows and virgins; and menaced their disobedience with the animadversion of the civil judge. The director was no longer permitted to receive any gift, or legacy, or inheritance, from the liberality of his spiritual daughter: every testament contrary to his edict was declared null and void: and the illegal donation was confiscated for the use of the treasury. By a subsequent regulation it should seem that the same provisions were extended to nuns and bishops; and that all persons of the ecclesiastical order were rendered incapable of receiving any testamentary gifts, and strictly confined to the natural and legal rights of inheritance. As the guardian of domestic happiness and virtue, Valentinian applied this severe remedy to the growing evil. In the capital of the empire the females of noble and opulent houses possessed a very ample share of independent property; and many of those devout females had embraced the doctrines of Christianity, not only with the cold assent of the understanding, but with the warmth of affection, and perhaps with the eagerness of fashion. They sacrificed the pleasures of dress and luxury; and renounced, for the praise of chastity, the soft endearments of conjugal society. Some ecclesiastic, of real or apparent sanctity, was chosen to direct their timorous conscience, and to amuse the vacant tenderness of their heart: and the unbounded confidence which they hastily bestowed was often abused by knaves and enthusiasts, who hastened from the extremities of the East, to enjoy, on a splendid theatre, the privileges of the monastic profession. By their contempt of the world, they insensibly acquired its most desirable advantages; the lively attachment, perhaps, of a young and beautiful woman, the delicate plenty of an opulent household, and the respectful homage of the slaves, the freedmen, and the clients of a senatorial family. The immense fortunes of the Roman ladies were gradually consumed in lavish alms and expensive pilgrimages; and the artful monk, who had assigned himself the first, or possibly the sole place, in the testament of his spiritual daughter, still presumed to declare, with the smooth face of hypocrisy, that *he* was only the instrument of charity, and the steward of the poor. The lucrative, but disgraceful, trade, which was exercised by the clergy to defraud the expectations of the natural heirs, had provoked the indignation of a superstitious age: and two of the most respectable of the Latin fathers very honestly confess that the ignominious edict of Valentinian was just and necessary; and that the Christian priests had deserved to lose a privilege which was still enjoyed by comedians, charioteers, and the ministers of idols. But the wisdom and authority of the legislator are seldom victorious in a contest with the vigilant dexterity of private interest: and Jerom, or Ambrose, might patiently acquiesce in the justice of an ineffectual or salutary law. If the ecclesiastics were checked in the pursuit of personal emolument, they would exert a more laudable industry to increase the wealth of the church; and dignify their covetousness with the specious names of piety and patriotism.

Damasus, bishop of Rome, who was constrained to stigmatise the avarice of his clergy by the publication of the law of Valentinian, had the good sense, or the good fortune, to engage in his service the zeal and abilities of the learned Jerom; and the grateful saint has celebrated the merit and purity of a very ambiguous character. But the splendid vices of the church of Rome, under the reign of Valentinian and Damasus, have been curiously observed by the historian Ammianus, who delivers his impartial sense in these expressive words:–"The præfecture of Juventius was accompanied with peace and plenty, but the tranquillity of his government was soon disturbed by a bloody sedition of the distracted people. The ardour of Damasus and Ursinus to seize the episcopal seat surpassed the ordinary measure of human ambition. They contended with the rage of party; the quarrel was maintained by the wounds and death of their followers; and the præfect, unable to resist or to appease the tumult, was constrained by superior violence to retire into the suburbs. Damasus prevailed: the well-disputed victory remained on the side of his faction; one hundred and thirty-seven dead bodies were found in the *Basilica* of Sicininus, where the Christians hold their religious assemblies; and it was long before the angry minds of the people resumed their accustomed tranquillity. When I consider the splendour of the capital, I am not astonished that so valuable a prize should inflame the desires of ambitious men, and produce the fiercest and most obstinate contests. The successful candidate is secure that he will be enriched by the offerings of matrons; that, as soon as his dress is composed with becoming care and elegance, he may proceed in his chariot through the streets of Rome; and that the sumptuousness of the Imperial table will not equal the profuse and delicate entertainments provided by the taste and at the expense of the Roman pontiffs. How much more rationally (continues the honest Pagan) would those pontiffs consult their true happiness, if, instead of alleging the greatness of the city as an excuse for their manners, they would imitate the exemplary life of some provincial bishops, whose temperance and sobriety, whose mean apparel and downcast looks, recommend their pure and modest virtue to the Deity and his true worshippers!" The schism of Damasus and Ursinus was extinguished by the exile of the latter; and the wisdom of the præfect Prætextatus restored the tranquillity of the city. Prætextatus was a philosophic Pagan, a man of learning, of taste, and politeness; who disguised a reproach in the form of a jest, when he assured Damasus that if he could obtain the bishopric of Rome, he himself would immediately embrace the Christian religion. This lively picture of the wealth and luxury of the popes in the fourth century becomes the more curious as it represents the intermediate degree between the humble poverty of the apostolic fisherman and the royal state of a temporal prince whose dominions extend from the confines of Naples to the banks of the Po.

The land was covered by the fortifications of Valentinian; but the sea-coast of Gaul and Britain was exposed to the depredations of the Saxons. That celebrated name, in which we have a clear and domestic interest, escaped the notice of Tacitus; and in the maps of Ptolemy it faintly marks the narrow neck of the Cimbric peninsula, and three small islands towards the mouth of the Elbe. This contracted territory, the present duchy of Schleswig, or perhaps of Holstein, was incapable of pouring forth the inexhaustible swarms of Saxons who reigned over the ocean, who filled the British island with their language, their laws, and their colonies, and who so long defended the liberty of the North against the arms of Charlemagne. The solution of this difficulty is easily derived from the similar manners and loose constitution of the tribes of Germany, which were blended with each other by the slightest accidents of war or friendship. The situation of the native Saxons disposed them to embrace the hazardous professions of fishermen and pirates; and the success of their first adventures would naturally excite the emulation of their bravest countrymen, who were impatient of the gloomy solitude of their woods and mountains. Every tide might float down the Elbe whole fleets of canoes, filled with hardy and intrepid associates, who aspired to behold the unbounded prospect of the ocean, and to taste the wealth and luxury of unknown worlds. It should seem probable, however, that the most numerous auxiliaries of the Saxons were furnished by the nations who dwelt along the shores of the Baltic. They possessed arms and ships, the art of navigation, and the habits of naval war; but the difficulty of issuing through the northern Columns of Hercules (which during several months of the year are obstructed with ice) confined their skill and courage within the limits of a spacious lake. The rumour of the successful armaments which sailed from the mouth of the Elbe would soon provoke them to cross the narrow isthmus of Schleswig, and to launch their vessels on the great sea. The various troops of pirates and adventurers who fought under the same standard were insensibly united in a permanent society, at first of rapine, and afterwards of government. A military confederation was gradually moulded into a national body by the gentle operation of marriage and consanguinity; and the adjacent tribes, who solicited the alliance, accepted the name and laws of the Saxons. If the fact were not established by the most unquestionable evidence, we should appear to abuse the credulity of our readers by the description of the vessels in which the Saxon pirates

ventured to sport in the waves of the German Ocean, the British
Channel, and the Bay of Biscay. The keel of their large flat-bottomed
boats was framed of light timber, but the sides and upper works
consisted only of wicker, with a covering of strong hides. In the
course of their slow and distant navigations they must always have
been exposed to the danger, and very frequently to the misfortune,
of shipwreck; and the naval annals of the Saxons were undoubtedly
filled with the accounts of the losses which they sustained on the
coasts of Britain and Gaul. But the daring spirit of the pirates
braved the perils both of the sea and of the shore: their skill was
confirmed by the habits of enterprise; the meanest of their mariners
was alike capable of handling an oar, of rearing a sail, or of conducting a vessel; and the Saxons rejoiced in the appearance of a
tempest, which concealed their design, and dispersed the fleets of
the enemy. After they had acquired an accurate knowledge of the
maritime provinces of the West they extended the scene of their
depredations, and the most sequestered places had no reason to
presume on their security. The Saxon boats drew so little water that
they could easily proceed fourscore or an hundred miles up the
great rivers; their weight was so inconsiderable that they were transported on waggons from one river to another; and the pirates who
had entered the mouth of the Seine or of the Rhine might descend,
with the rapid stream of the Rhone, into the Mediterranean. Under
the reign of Valentinian the maritime provinces of Gaul were
afflicted by the Saxons: a military count was stationed for the
defence of the sea-coast, or Armorican limit; and that officer, who
found his strength or his abilities unequal to the task, implored the
assistance of Severus, master-general of the infantry. The Saxons,
surrounded and outnumbered, were forced to relinquish their spoil,
and to yield a select band of their tall and robust youth to serve in
the Imperial armies. They stipulated only a safe and honourable
retreat; and the condition was readily granted by the Roman
general, who meditated an act of perfidy, imprudent as it was
inhuman, while a Saxon remained alive and in arms to revenge
the fate of his countrymen. The premature eagerness of the
infantry, who were secretly posted in a deep valley, betrayed the
ambuscade; and they would perhaps have fallen the victims of their
own treachery, if a large body of cuirassiers, alarmed by the noise
of the combat, had not hastily advanced to extricate their
companions, and to overwhelm the undaunted valour of the Saxons.
Some of the prisoners were saved from the edge of the sword to

shed their blood in the amphitheatre; and the orator Symmachus complains that twenty-nine of those desperate savages, by strangling themselves with their own hands, had disappointed the amusement of the public. Yet the polite and philosophic citizens of Rome were impressed with the deepest horror when they were informed that the Saxons consecrated to the gods the tithe of their *human* spoil; and that they ascertained by lot the objects of the barbarous sacrifice.

Six years after the death of Constantine the destructive inroads of the Scots and Picts required the presence of his youngest son, who reigned in the Western empire. Constans visited his British dominions: but we may form some estimate of the importance of his achievements by the language of panegyric, which celebrates only his triumph over the elements, or, in other words, the good fortune of a safe and easy passage from the port of Boulogne to the harbour of Sandwich. The calamities which the afflicted provincials continued to experience from foreign war and domestic tyranny were aggravated by the feeble and corrupt administration of the eunuchs of Constantius; and the transient relief which they might obtain from the virtues of Julian was soon lost by the absence and death of their benefactor. The sums of gold and silver which had been painfully collected, or liberally transmitted, for the payment of the troops, were intercepted by the avarice of the commanders; discharges, or, at least, exemptions, from the military service, were publicly sold; the distress of the soldiers, who were injuriously deprived of their legal and scanty subsistence, provoked them to frequent desertion; the nerves of discipline were relaxed, and the highways were infested with robbers. The oppression of the good and the impunity of the wicked equally contributed to diffuse through the island a spirit of discontent and revolt; and every ambitious subject, every desperate exile, might entertain a reasonable hope of subverting the weak and distracted government of Britain. The hostile tribes of the North, who detested the pride and power of the King of the World, suspended their domestic feuds; and the barbarians of the land and sea, the Scots, the Picts, and the Saxons, spread themselves, with rapid and irresistible fury, from the wall of Antonius to the shores of Kent. Every production of art and nature, every object of convenience or luxury, which they were incapable of creating by labour or procuring by trade, was accumulated in the rich and fruitful province of Britain. A philosopher may deplore the eternal discord of the human race, but he will confess that the desire of spoil is a more rational provocation than the vanity of conquest. From the age of Constantine to that of the Plantagenets this rapacious spirit continued to instigate the poor and hardy Caledonians: but the same people whose generous humanity seems to inspire the songs of Ossian was disgraced by a savage ignorance of the virtues of peace and of the laws of war. Their southern neighbours have felt, and perhaps exaggerated, the cruel depredations of the Scots and Picts; and a valiant tribe of Caledonia, the Attacotti, the enemies, and afterwards the soldiers, of Valentinian, are accused by an eye-witness of delighting in the taste of human flesh. When they hunted the woods for prey, it is said that they attacked the shepherd rather than his flock; and that they curiously selected the most delicate and brawny parts both of males and females, which they prepared for their horrid repasts. If in the neighbourhood of the commercial and literary town of Glasgow a race of cannibals has really existed, we may contemplate in the period of the Scottish history the opposite extremes of savage and civilised life. Such reflections tend to enlarge the circle of our ideas, and to encourage the pleasing hope that New Zealand may produce in some future age the Hume of the Southern Hemisphere.

Every messenger who escaped across the British channel conveyed the most melancholy and alarming tidings to the ears of Valentinian, and the emperor was soon informed that the two military commanders of the province had been surprised and cut off by the barbarians. Severus, count of the domestics, was hastily despatched, and as suddenly recalled, by the court of Trèves. The representations of Jovinus served only to indicate the greatness of the evil, and, after a long and serious consultation, the defence, or rather the recovery, of Britain was intrusted to the abilities of the brave Theodosius. The exploits of that general, the father of a line of emperors, have been celebrated, with peculiar complacency, by the writers of the age; but his real merit deserved their applause, and his nomination was received, by the army and province, as a sure presage of approaching victory. He seized the favourable moment of navigation, and securely landed the numerous and veteran bands of the Heruli and Batavians, the Jovians and the Victors. In his march from Sandwich to London, Theodosius defeated several parties of the barbarians, released a multitude of captives, and, after distributing to his soldiers a small portion of the spoil, established the fame of disinterested justice by the restitution of the remainder to the rightful proprietors. The citizens of London, who had almost despaired of their safety, threw open their gates, and, as soon as Theodosius had obtained from the court of Trèves the important aid of a military lieutenant and a civil governor, he executed with wisdom and vigour the laborious task of the deliverance of Britain. The vagrant soldiers were recalled to their standard, an edict of amnesty dispelled the public apprehensions, and his cheerful example alleviated the rigour of martial discipline. The scattered and desultory warfare of the barbarians, who infested the land and sea, deprived him of the glory of a signal victory; but the prudent spirit and consummate art of the Roman general were displayed in the operations of two campaigns, which successively rescued every part of the province from the hands of a cruel and rapacious enemy. The splendour of the cities and the security of the fortifications were diligently restored by the paternal care of Theodosius, who with a strong hand confined the trembling Caledonians to the northern angle of the island, and perpetuated, by the name and settlement of the new province of *Valentia*, the glories of the reign of Valentinian.

The ignominious treaty which saved the army of Jovian had been faithfully executed on the side of the Romans; and as they had solemnly renounced the sovereignty and alliance of Armenia and Iberia, those tributary Kingdoms were exposed, without protection, to the arms of the Persian monarch. Sapor entered the Armenian territories at the head of a formidable host of cuirassiers, of archers, and of mercenary foot; but it was the invariable practice of Sapor to mix war and negotiation, and to consider falsehood and perjury as the most powerful instruments of regal policy. He affected to praise the prudent and moderate conduct of the king of Armenia; and the unsuspicious Tiranus was persuaded, by the repeated assurances of insidious friendship, to deliver his person into the hands of a faithless and cruel enemy. In the midst of a splendid entertainment, he was bound in chains of silver, as an honour due to the blood of the Arsacides; and, after a short confinement in the Tower of Oblivion at Ecbatana, he was released from the miseries of life, either by his own dagger or by that of an assassin. The kingdom of Armenia was reduced to the state of a Persian province; the administration was shared between a distinguished satrap and a favourite eunuch; and Sapor marched, without delay, to subdue the martial spirit of the Iberians. Sauromaces, who reigned in that country by the permission of the emperors, was expelled by a superior force, and, as an insult on the majesty of Rome, the king of kings placed a diadem on the head of his abject vassal Aspacuras.

The emperor of the West, who had resigned to his brother the command of the Lower Danube, reserved for his immediate care the defence of the Rhætian and Illyrian provinces, which spread so many hundred miles along the greatest of the European rivers. The active policy of Valentinian was continually employed in adding new fortifications to the security of the frontier: but the abuse of this policy provoked the just resentment of the barbarians. The Quadi complained that the ground for an intended fortress had been marked out on their territories, and their complaints were urged with so much reason and moderation, that Equitius, master-general of Illyricum, consented to suspend the prosecution of the work till he should be more clearly informed of the will of his sovereign. This fair occasion of injuring a rival, and of advancing the fortune of his son, was eagerly embraced by the inhuman Maximin, the præfect, or rather tyrant, of Gaul. The passions of Valentinian were impatient of control, and he credulously listened to the assurances of his favourite, that, if the government of Valeria, and the direction of the work, were intrusted to the zeal of his son Marcellinus, the emperor should no longer be importuned with the audacious remonstrances of the barbarians. The subjects of Rome, and the natives of Germany, were insulted by the arrogance of a young and worthless minister, who considered his rapid elevation as the proof and reward of his superior merit. He affected, however, to receive the modest application of Gabinius, king of the Quadi, with some attention and regard; but this artful civility concealed a dark and bloody design, and the credulous prince was persuaded to accept the pressing invitation of Marcellinus. I am at a loss how to vary the narrative of similar crimes; or how to relate that, in the course of the same year, but in remote parts of the empire, the inhospitable table of two Imperial generals was stained with the royal blood of two guests and allies, inhumanly murdered by their order, and in their presence. The fate of Gabinius, and of Para, was the same: but the cruel death of their sovereign was resented in a very different manner by the servile temper of the Armenians and the free and daring spirit of the Germans. The Quadi were much declined from that formidable power which, in the time of Marcus Antoninus, had spread terror to the gates of Rome. But they still possessed arms and courage; their courage was animated by despair, and they obtained the usual reinforcement of the cavalry of their Sarmatian allies. So improvident was the assassin Marcellinus, that he chose the moment when the bravest veterans had been drawn away to suppress the revolt of Firmus, and the whole province was exposed, with a very feeble defence, to the rage of the exasperated barbarians. They invaded Pannonia in the season of harvest, unmercifully destroyed every object of plunder which they could not easily transport, and either disregarded or demolished the empty fortifications. The princess Constantia, the daughter of the emperor Constantius, and the granddaughter of the great Constantine, very narrowly escaped. That royal maid was now the destined wife of the heir of the Western empire. She traversed the peaceful province with a splendid and unarmed train. Her person was saved from danger, and the republic from disgrace, by the active zeal of Messalla, governor of the provinces. As soon as he was informed that the village where she stopped only to dine was almost encompassed by the barbarians, he hastily placed her in his own chariot, and drove full speed till he reached the gates of Sirmium, which were at the distance of six-and-twenty miles. Even Sirmium might not have been secure if the Quadi and Sarmatians had diligently advanced during the general consterna- tion of the magistrates and people. Their delay allowed Probus, the Prætorian præfect, sufficient time to recover his own spirits and to revive the courage of the citizens. He skilfully directed their stren- uous efforts to repair and strengthen the decayed fortifications, and procured the seasonable and effectual assistance of a company of archers to protect the capital of the Illyrian provinces. Disappointed in their attempts against the walls of Sirmium, the indignant barbarians turned their arms against the master-general of the frontier, to whom they unjustly attributed the murder of their king. Equitius could bring into the field no more than two legions, but they contained the veteran strength of the Mæsian and Pannonian bands. The obstinacy with which they disputed the vain honours of rank and precedency was the cause of their destruction, and, while they acted with separate forces and divided councils, they were surprised and slaughtered by the active vigour of the Sarmatian horse. The success of this invasion provoked the emulation of the bordering tribes, and the province of Mæsia would infallibly have been lost if young Theodosius, the duke or military commander of the frontier, had not signalised, in the defeat of the public enemy, an intrepid genius worthy of his illustrious father and of his future greatness.

The mind of Valentinian, who then resided at Trèves, was deeply affected by the calamities of Illyricum, but the lateness of the season suspended the execution of his designs till the ensuing spring. He marched in person, with a considerable part of the forces of Gaul, from the banks of the Moselle; and to the suppliant ambassadors of the Sarmatians, who met him on the way, he returned a doubtful answer, that as soon as he reached the scene of action he should examine and pronounce. When he arrived at Sirmium he gave audience to the deputies of the Illyrian provinces, who loudly congratulated their own felicity under the auspicious government of Probus, his Prætorian præfect. Valentinian, who was flattered by these demonstrations of their loyalty and gratitude, imprudently asked the deputy of Epirus, a Cynic philosopher of intrepid sincerity, whether he was freely sent by the wishes of the province? "With tears and groans am I sent (replied Iphicles) by a reluctant people." The emperor paused, but the impunity of his ministers established the pernicious maxim that they might oppress his subjects without injuring his service. A strict inquiry into their conduct would have relieved the public discontent. The severe condemnation of the murder of Gabinius was the only measure which could restore the confidence of the Germans, and vindicate the honour of the Roman name. But the haughty monarch was incapable of the magnanimity which dares to acknowledge a fault. He forgot the provocation, remembered only the injury, and advanced into the country of the Quadi with an insatiate thirst of blood and revenge. The extreme devastation and promiscuous massacre of a savage war were justified in the eyes of the emperor, and perhaps in those of the world, by the cruel equity of retaliation; and such was the discipline of the Romans, and the consternation of the enemy, that Valentinian repassed the Danube without the loss of a single man. As he had resolved to complete the destruction of the Quadi by a second campaign, he fixed his winterquarters at Bregetio, on the Danube, near the Hungarian city of Presburg. While the operations of war were suspended by the severity of the weather, the Quadi made an humble attempt to deprecate the wrath of their conqueror, and, at the earnest persuasion of Equitius, their ambassadors were introduced into the Imperial council. They approached the throne with bended bodies and dejected countenances, and, without daring to complain of the murder of their king, they affirmed, with solemn oaths, that the late invasion was the crime of some irregular robbers, which the public council of the nation condemned and abhorred. The answer of the emperor left them but little hope from his clemency or compassion. He reviled, in the most intemperate language, their baseness, their ingratitude, their insolence. His eyes, his voice, his colour, his gestures, expressed the violence of his ungoverned fury; and while his whole frame was agitated with convulsive passion a large blood-vessel suddenly burst in his body, and Valentinian fell speechless into the arms of his attendants. Their pious care immediately concealed his situation from the crowd, but in a few minutes the emperor of the West expired in an agony of pain, retaining his senses till the last, and struggling, without success, to declare his intentions to the generals and ministers who surrounded the royal couch. Valentinian was about fifty-four years of age, and he wanted only one hundred days to accomplish the twelve years of his reign.

The polygamy of Valentinian is seriously attested by an ecclesiastical historian. "The empress Severa (I relate the fable) admitted into her familiar society the lovely Justina, the daughter of an Italian governor; her admiration of those naked charms, which she had often seen in the bath, was expressed with such lavish and imprudent praise that the emperor was tempted to introduce a second wife into his bed; and his public edict extended to all the subjects of the empire the same domestic privilege which he had assumed for himself." But we may be assured, from the evidence of reason as well as history, that the two marriages of Valentinian with Severa and with Justina were *successively* contracted, and that he used the ancient permission of divorce, which was still allowed by the laws, though it was condemned by the church. Severa was the mother of Gratian, who seemed to unite every claim which could entitle him to the undoubted succession of the Western empire. He was the eldest son of a monarch whose glorious reign had confirmed the free and honourable choice of his fellow-soldiers. Before he had attained the ninth year of his age the royal youth received from the hands of his indulgent father the purple robe and diadem, with the title of Augustus; the election was solemnly ratified by the consent and applause of the armies of Gaul, and the name of Gratian was added to the names of Valentinian and Valens in all the legal transactions of the Roman government. By his marriage with the grand-daughter of Constantine, the son of Valentinian acquired all the hereditary rights of the Flavian family, which, in a series of three Imperial generations, were sanctified by time, religion, and the reverence of the people. At the death of his father the royal youth was in the seventeenth year of his age, and his virtues already justified the favourable opinion of the army and people. But Gratian resided, without apprehension, in the palace of Trèves, whilst at the distance of many hundred miles Valentinian suddenly expired in the camp of Bregetio. The passions which had been so long suppressed by the presence of a master immediately revived in the Imperial council, and the ambitious design of reigning in the name of an infant was artfully executed by Mellobaudes and Equitius, who commanded the attachment of the Illyrian and Italian bands. They contrived the most honourable pretences to remove the popular leaders and the troops of Gaul, who might have asserted the claims of the lawful successor; they suggested the necessity of extinguishing the hopes of foreign and domestic enemies by a bold and decisive measure. The empress Justina, who had been left in a palace about one hundred miles from Bregetio, was respectfully invited to appear in the camp with the son of the deceased emperor. On the sixth day after the death of Valentinian, the infant prince of the same name, who was only four years old, was shown, in the arms of his mother, to the legions, and solemnly invested, by military acclamation, with the titles and ensigns of supreme power. The impending dangers of a civil war were seasonably prevented by the wise and moderate conduct of the emperor Gratian. He cheerfully accepted the choice of the army, declared that he should always consider the son of Justina as a brother, not as a rival, and advised the empress, with her son Valentinian, to fix their residence at Milan, in the fair and peaceful province of Italy, while he assumed the more arduous command of the countries beyond the Alps. Gratian dissembled his resentment till he could safely punish or disgrace the authors of the conspiracy; and though he uniformly behaved with tenderness and regard to his infant colleague, he gradually confounded, in the administration of the Western empire, the office of a guardian with the authority of a sovereign. The government of the Roman world was exercised in the united names of Valens and his two nephews; but the feeble emperor of the East, who succeeded to the rank of his elder brother, never obtained any weight or influence in the councils of the West.

XXIV

(365–395 A.D.) PROGRESS OF THE HUNS FROM
CHINA TO EUROPE—FLIGHT OF THE GOTHS—
DEFEAT AND DEATH OF VALENS—GRATIAN
INVESTS THEODOSIUS WITH THE EASTERN
EMPIRE—PEACE AND SETTLEMENT OF THE
GOTHS

In the second year of the reign of Valentinian and Valens, on the morning of the twenty-first day of July, the greatest part of the Roman world was shaken by a violent and destructive earthquake. The impression was communicated to the waters; the shores of the Mediterranean were left dry by the sudden retreat of the sea; great quantities of fish were caught with the hand; large vessels were stranded on the mud; and a curious spectator amused his eye, or rather his fancy, by contemplating the various appearance of valleys and mountains which had never, since the formation of the globe, been exposed to the sun. But the tide soon returned with the weight of an immense and irresistible deluge, which was severely felt on the coasts of Sicily, of Dalmatia, of Greece, and of Egypt; large boats were transported and lodged on the roofs of houses, or at the distance of two miles from the shore; the people, with their habitations, were swept away by the waters; and the city of Alexandria annually commemorated the fatal day on which fifty thousand persons had lost their lives in the inundation. This calamity, the report of which was magnified from one province to another, astonished and terrified the subjects of Rome, and their affrighted imagination enlarged the real extent of a momentary evil. They recollected the preceding earthquakes, which had subverted the cities of Palestine and Bithynia; they considered these alarming strokes as the prelude only of still more dreadful calamities; and their fearful vanity was disposed to confound the symptoms of a declining empire and a sinking world. It was the fashion of the times to attribute every remarkable event to the particular will of the Deity; the alterations of nature were connected, by an invisible chain, with the moral and metaphysical opinions of the human mind; and the most sagacious divines could distinguish, according to the colour of their respective prejudices, that the establishment of heresy tended to produce an earthquake, or that a deluge was the inevitable consequence of the progress of sin and error. Without presuming to discuss the truth or propriety of these lofty speculations, the historian may content himself with an observation, which seems to be justified by experience, that man has much more to fear from the passions of his fellow-creatures than from the convulsions of the elements. The mischievous effects of an earthquake or deluge, a hurricane or the eruption of a volcano, bear a very inconsiderable proportion to the ordinary calamities of war, as they are now moderated by the prudence or humanity of the princes of Europe, who amuse their own leisure and exercise the courage of their subjects in the practice of the military art. But the laws and manners of modern nations protect the safety and freedom of the vanquished soldier; and the peaceful citizen has seldom reason to complain that his life or even his fortune is exposed to the rage of war. In the disastrous period of the fall of the Roman empire, which may justly be dated from the reign of Valens, the happiness and security of each individual were personally attacked, and the arts and labours of ages were rudely defaced by the barbarians of Scythia and Germany. The invasion of the Huns precipitated on the provinces of the West the Gothic nation, which advanced, in less than forty years, from the Danube to the Atlantic, and opened a way, by the success of their arms, to the inroads of so many hostile tribes more savage than themselves.

The Huns, who under the reign of Valens threatened the empire of Rome, had been formidable, in a much earlier period, to the empire of China. Their ancient, perhaps their original, seat was an extensive, though dry and barren, tract of country immediately on the north side of the great wall. Their place is at present occupied by the forty-nine Hordes or Banners of the Mongous, a pastoral nation, which consists of about two hundred thousand families. But the valour of the Huns had extended the narrow limits of their dominions; and their rustic chiefs, who assumed the appellation of *Tanjou*, gradually became the conquerors and the sovereigns of a formidable empire. Towards the east their victorious arms were stopped only by the ocean; and the tribes, which are thinly scattered between the Amoor and the extreme peninsula of Corea, adhered with reluctance to the standard of the Huns. On the west, near the head of the Irtish, and in the valleys of Imaus, they found a more ample space, and more numerous enemies. One of the lieutenants of the Tanjou subdued, in a single expedition, twenty-six nations; the Igours, distinguished above the Tartar race by the use of letters, were in the number of his vassals; and, by the strange connection of human events, the flight of one of those vagrant tribes recalled the victorious Parthians from the invasion of Syria. On the side of the north, the ocean was assigned as the limit of the power of the Huns. Without enemies to resist their progress, or witnesses to contradict their vanity, they might securely achieve a real, or imaginary, conquest of the frozen regions of Siberia. The *Northern Sea* was fixed as the remote boundary of their empire. But the name of that sea, on whose shores the patriot Sovou embraced the life of a shepherd and an exile, may be transferred, with much more probability, to the Baikal, a capacious basin, above three hundred miles in length, which disdains the modest appellation of a lake, and which actually communicates with the seas of the North, by the long course of the Angara, the Tonguska, and the Yenesei. The submission of so many distant nations might flatter the pride of the Tanjou; but the valour of the Huns could be rewarded only by the enjoyment of the wealth and luxury of the empire of the South. In the third century before the Christian era, a wall of fifteen hundred miles in length was constructed, to defend the frontiers of China against the inroads of the Huns; but this stupendous work, which holds a conspicuous place in the map of the world, has never contributed to the safety of an unwarlike people. The cavalry of the Tanjou frequently consisted of two or three hundred thousand men, formidable by the matchless dexterity with which they managed their bows and their horses; by their hardy patience in supporting the inclemency of the weather; and by the incredible speed of their march, which was seldom checked by torrents or precipices, by the deepest rivers, or by the most lofty mountains.

They spread themselves at once over the face of the country; and their rapid impetuosity surprised, astonished, and disconcerted the grave and elaborate tactics of a Chinese army. The emperor Kaoti, a soldier of fortune, whose personal merit had raised him to the throne, marched against the Huns with those veteran troops which had been trained in the civil wars of China. But he was soon surrounded by the barbarians; and, after a siege of seven days, the monarch, hopeless of relief, was reduced to purchase his deliverance by an ignominious capitulation. The successors of Kaoti, whose lives were dedicated to the arts of peace, or the luxury of the palace, submitted to a more permanent disgrace. They too hastily confessed the insufficiency of arms and fortifications. They were too easily convinced that, while the blazing signals announced on every side the approach of the Huns, the Chinese troops, who slept with the helmet on their head, and the cuirass on their back, were destroyed by the incessant labour of ineffectual marches. A regular payment of money and silk was stipulated as the condition of a temporary and precarious peace; and the wretched expedient of disguising a real tribute under the names of a gift or subsidy was practised by the emperors of China as well as by those of Rome. But there still remained a more disgraceful article of tribute, which violated the sacred feelings of humanity and nature. The hardships of the savage life, which destroy in their infancy the children who are born with a less healthy and robust constitution, introduce a remarkable disproportion between the numbers of the two sexes. The Tartars are an ugly and even deformed race; and while they consider their own women as the instruments of domestic labour, their desires, or rather their appetites, are directed to the enjoyment of more elegant beauty. A select band of the fairest maidens of China was annually devoted to the rude embraces of the Huns; and the alliance of the haughty Tanjous was secured by their marriage with the genuine, or adopted, daughters of the Imperial family, which vainly attempted to escape the sacrilegious pollution. The situation of these unhappy victims is described in the verses of a Chinese princess, who laments that she had been condemned by her parents to a distant exile, under a barbarian husband; who complains that sour milk was her only drink, raw flesh her only food, a tent her only palace; and who expresses, in a strain of pathetic simplicity, the natural wish that she were transformed into a bird, to fly back to her dear country, the object of her tender and perpetual regret.

The Huns, with their flocks and herds, their wives and children, their dependents and allies, were transported to the West of the Volga, and they boldly advanced to invade the country of the Alani, a pastoral people, who occupied, or wasted, an extensive tract of the deserts of Scythia. The plains between the Volga and the Tanais were covered with the tents of the Alani, but their name and manners were diffused over the wide extent of their conquests; and the painted tribes of the Agathyrsi and Geloni were confounded among their vassals. Towards the north they penetrated into the frozen regions of Siberia, among the savages who were accustomed, in their rage or hunger, to the taste of human flesh; and their southern inroads were pushed as far as the confines of Persia and India. The mixture of Sarmatic and German blood had contributed to improve the features of the Alani, to whiten their swarthy complexions, and to tinge their hair with a yellowish cast, which is seldom found in the Tartar race. They were less deformed in their persons, less brutish in their manners, than the Huns; but they did not yield to those formidable barbarians in their martial and independent spirit; in the love of freedom, which rejected even the use of domestic slaves; and in the love of arms, which considered war and rapine as the pleasure and the glory of mankind. A naked scimitar, fixed in the ground, was the only object of their religious worship; the scalps of their enemies formed the costly trappings of their horses; and they viewed with pity and contempt the pusillanimous warriors who patiently expected the infirmities of age and the tortures of lingering disease. On the banks of the Tanais the military power of the Huns and the Alani encountered each other with equal valour, but with unequal success. The Huns prevailed in the bloody contest; the king of the Alani was slain; and the remains of the vanquished nation were dispersed by the ordinary alternative of flight or submission. A colony of exiles found a secure refuge in the mountains of Caucasus, between the Euxine and the Caspian, where they still preserve their name and their independence. Another colony advanced, with more intrepid courage, towards the shores of the Baltic; associated themselves with the northern tribes of Germany; and shared the spoil of the Roman provinces of Gaul and Spain. But the greatest part of the nation of the Alani embraced the offers of an honourable and advantageous union; and the Huns, who esteemed the valour of their less fortunate enemies, proceeded, with an increase of numbers and confidence, to invade the limits of the Gothic empire.

The great Hermanric, whose dominions extended from the Baltic to the Euxine, enjoyed, in the full maturity of age and reputation, the fruit of his victories, when he was alarmed by the formidable approach of an host of unknown enemies, on whom his barbarous subjects might, without injustice, bestow the epithet of barbarians. The numbers, the strength, the rapid motions, and the implacable cruelty of the Huns were felt, and dreaded, and magnified by the astonished Goths, who beheld their fields and villages consumed with flames and deluged with indiscriminate slaughter. To these real terrors they added the surprise and abhorrence which were excited by the shrill voice, the uncouth gestures, and the strange deformity of the Huns. These savages of Scythia were compared (and the picture had some resemblance) to the animals who walk very awkwardly on two legs, and to the misshapen figures, the *Termini*, which were often placed on the bridges of antiquity. They were distinguished from the rest of the human species by their broad shoulders, flat noses, and small black eyes, deeply buried in the head; and as they were almost destitute of beards, they never enjoyed either the manly graces of youth or the venerable aspect of age. A fabulous origin was assigned worthy of their form and manners—that the witches of Scythia, who, for their foul and deadly practices, had been driven from society, had copulated in the desert with infernal spirits, and that the Huns were the offspring of this execrable conjunction. The tale, so full of horror and absurdity, was greedily embraced by the credulous hatred of the Goths; but while it gratified their hatred it increased their fear, since the posterity of dæmons and witches might be supposed to inherit some share of the preternatural powers as well as of the malignant temper of their parents. The ordinary speed of the Huns was checked by the weight of baggage and the encumbrance of captives; but their military skill deceived and almost destroyed the army of Athanaric. While the Judge of the Visigoths defended the banks of the Dniester he was encompassed and attacked by a numerous detachment of cavalry, who, by the light of the moon, had passed the river in a fordable place; and it was not without the utmost efforts of courage and conduct that he was able to effect his retreat towards the hilly country. The undaunted general had already formed a new and judicious plan of defensive war; and the strong lines which he was preparing to construct between the mountains, the Pruth, and the Danube, would have secured the extensive and fertile territory that bears the modern name of Wallachia from the destructive inroads of the Huns. But the hopes and measures of the Judge of the Visigoths were soon disappointed by the trembling impatience of his dismayed countrymen, who were persuaded by their fears that the interposition of the Danube was the only barrier that could save them from the rapid pursuit and invincible valour of the barbarians of Scythia. Under the command of Fritigern and Alavivus, the body of the nation hastily advanced to the banks of the great river and implored the protection of the Roman emperor of the East. He was informed that the North was agitated by a furious tempest; that the irruption of the Huns, an unknown and monstrous race of savages, had subverted the power of the Goths; and that the suppliant multitudes of that warlike nation, whose pride was now humbled in the dust, covered a space many miles along the banks of the river. With outstretched arms and pathetic lamentations they loudly deplored their past misfortunes and their present danger; acknowledged that their only hope of safety was in the clemency of the Roman government; and most solemnly protested that, if the gracious liberality of the emperor would permit them to cultivate the waste lands of Thrace, they should ever hold themselves bound, by the strongest obligations of duty and gratitude, to obey the laws and to guard the limits of the republic. These assurances were confirmed by the ambassadors of the Goths, who impatiently expected from the mouth of Valens an answer that must finally determine the fate of their unhappy countrymen. The emperor of the East was no longer guided by the wisdom and authority of his elder brother, whose death happened towards the end of the preceding year; and as the distressful situation of the Goths required an instant and peremptory decision, he was deprived of the favourite resource of feeble and timid minds, who consider the use of the dilatory and ambiguous measures as the most admirable efforts of consummate prudence. As long as the same passions and interests subsist among mankind, the questions of war and peace, of justice and policy, which were debated in the councils of antiquity, will frequently present themselves as the subject of modern deliberation. But the most experienced statesman of Europe has never been summoned to consider the propriety or the danger of admitting or rejecting an innumerable multitude of barbarians, who are driven by despair and hunger to solicit a settlement on the territories of a civilised nation. When that important proposition, so essentially connected with the public safety, was referred to the ministers of Valens, they were perplexed and divided; but they soon acquiesced in the flattering sentiment which seemed the most favourable to the pride, the indolence, and the avarice of their sovereign. The slaves, who were decorated with the titles of præfects and generals, dissembled or disregarded the terrors of this national emigration—so extremely different from the partial and accidental colonies which had been received on the extreme limits of the empire. But they applauded the liberality of fortune which had conducted, from the most distant countries of the globe, a numerous and invincible army of strangers to defend the throne of Valens, who might now add to the royal treasures the immense sums of gold supplied by the provincials to compensate their annual proportion of recruits. The prayers of the Goths were granted, and their service was accepted by the Imperial court; and orders were immediately despatched by the civil and military governors of the Thracian diocese to make the necessary preparations for the passage and subsistence of a great people, till a proper and sufficient territory could be allotted for their future residence. The liberality of the emperor was accompanied, however, with two harsh and rigorous conditions, which prudence might justify on the side of the Romans, but which distress alone could extort from the indignant Goths. Before they passed the Danube they were required to deliver their arms, and it was insisted that their children should be taken from them and dispersed through the provinces of Asia, where they might be civilised by the arts of education, and serve as hostages to secure the fidelity of their parents.

During this suspense of a doubtful and distant negotiation, the impatient Goths made some rash attempts to pass the Danube without the permission of the government whose protection they had implored. Their motions were strictly observed by the vigilance of the troops which were stationed along the river, and their foremost detachments were defeated with considerable slaughter; yet such were the timid councils of the reign of Valens, that the brave officers who had served their country in the execution of their duty were punished by the loss of their employments, and narrowly escaped the loss of their heads. The Imperial mandate was at length received for transportation over the Danube the whole body of the Gothic nation; but the execution of this order was a task of labour and difficulty. The stream of the Danube, which in those parts is above a mile broad, had been swelled by incessant rains, and in this tumultuous passage many were swept away and drowned by the rapid violence of the current. A large fleet of vessels, of boats, and of canoes, was provided; many days and nights they passed and repassed with indefatigable toil; and the most strenuous diligence was exerted by the officers of Valens that not a single barbarian, of those who were reserved to subvert the foundations of Rome, should be left on the opposite shore. It was thought expedient that an accurate account should be taken of their numbers; but the persons who were employed soon desisted, with amazement and dismay, from the prosecution of the endless and impracticable task; and the principal historian of the age most seriously affirms that the prodigious armies of Darius and Xerxes, which had so long been considered as the fables of vain and credulous antiquity, were now justified, in the eyes of mankind, by the evidence of fact and experience. A probable testimony has fixed the number of the Gothic warriors at two hundred thousand men; and if we can venture to add the just proportion of women, of children, and of slaves, the whole mass of people which composed this formidable emigration must have amounted to near a million of persons, of both sexes and of all ages. The children of the Goths, those at least of a distinguished rank, were separated from the multitude. They were conducted without delay to the distant seats assigned for their residence and education; and as the numerous train of hostages or captives passed through the cities, their gay and splendid apparel, their robust and martial figure, excited the surprise and envy of the provincials. But the stipulation, the most offensive to the Goths and the most important to the Romans, was shamefully eluded. The barbarians, who considered their arms as the ensigns of honour and the pledges of safety, were disposed to offer a price which the lust or avarice of the Imperial officers was easily tempted to accept. To preserve their arms, the haughty warriors consented, with some reluctance, to prostitute their wives or their daughters; the charms of a beauteous maid, or a comely boy, secured the connivance of the inspectors, who sometimes cast an eye of covetousness on the fringed carpets and linen garments of their new allies, or who sacrificed their duty to the mean consideration of filling their farms with cattle and their houses with slaves. The Goths, with arms in their hands, were permitted to enter the boats; and when their strength was collected on the other side of the river, the immense camp which was spread over the plains and the hills of the Lower Mæsia assumed a threatening and even hostile aspect. The leaders of the Ostrogoths, Alatheus and Saphrax, the guardians of their infant king, appeared soon afterwards on the northern banks of the Danube, and immediately despatched their ambassadors to the court of Antioch to solicit, with the same professions of allegiance and gratitude, the same favour which had been granted to the suppliant Visigoths. The absolute refusal of Valens suspended their progress, and discovered the repentance, the suspicions, and the fears of the Imperial council.

An undisciplined and unsettled nation of barbarians required the firmest temper and the most dexterous management. The daily subsistence of near a million of extraordinary subjects could be supplied only by constant and skilful diligence, and might continually be interrupted by mistake or accident. The insolence or the indignation of the Goths, if they conceived themselves to be the objects either of fear or of contempt, might urge them to the most desperate extremities, and the fortune of the state seemed to depend on the prudence, as well as the integrity, of the generals of Valens. At this important crisis the military government of Thrace was exercised by Lupicinus and Maximus, in whose venal minds the slightest hope of private emolument outweighed every consideration of public advantage, and whose guilt was only alleviated by their incapacity of discerning the pernicious effects of their rash and criminal administration. Instead of obeying the orders of their sovereign, and satisfying, with decent liberality, the demands of the Goths, they levied an ungenerous and oppressive tax on the wants of the hungry barbarians. The vilest food was sold at an extravagant price, and, in the room of wholesome and substantial provisions, the markets were filled with the flesh of dogs and of unclean animals who had died of disease. To obtain the valuable acquisition of a pound of bread, the Goths resigned the possession of an expensive though serviceable slave, and a small quantity of meat was greedily purchased with ten pounds of a precious but useless metal. When their property was exhausted, they continued this necessary traffic by the sale of their sons and daughters; and notwithstanding the love of freedom which animated every Gothic breast, they submitted to the humiliating maxim that it was better for their children to be maintained in a servile condition than to perish in a state of wretched and helpless independence. The most lively resentment is excited by the tyranny of pretended benefactors, who sternly exact the debt of gratitude which they have cancelled by subsequent injuries; a spirit of discontent insensibly arose in the camp of the barbarians, who pleaded, without success, the merit of their patient and dutiful behaviour, and loudly complained of the inhospitable treatment which they had received from their new allies. They beheld around them the wealth and plenty of a fertile province, in the midst of which they suffered the intolerable hardships of artificial famine. But the means of relief, and even of revenge, were in their hands, since the rapaciousness of their tyrants had left to an injured people the possession and the use of arms. The clamours of a multitude, untaught to disguise their sentiments, announced the first symptoms of resistance, and alarmed the timid and guilty minds of Lupicinus and Maximus. Those crafty ministers, who substituted the cunning of temporary expedients to the wise and salutary counsels of general policy, attempted to remove the Goths from their dangerous station on the frontiers of the empire, and to disperse them, in separate quarters of cantonment, through the interior provinces. As they were conscious how ill they had deserved the respect or confidence of the barbarians, they diligently collected from every side a military force that might urge the tardy and reluctant march of a people who had not yet renounced the title or the duties of Roman subjects. But the generals of Valens, while their attention was solely directed to the discontented Visigoths, imprudently disarmed the ships and the fortifications which constituted the defence of the Danube. The fatal oversight was observed and improved by Alatheus and Saphrax, who anxiously watched the favourable moment of escaping from the pursuit of the Huns. By the help of such rafts and vessels as could be hastily procured, the leaders of the Ostrogoths transported, without opposition, their king and their army, and boldly fixed an hostile and independent camp on the territories of the empire.

Under the name of Judges, Alavivus and Fritigern were the leaders of the Visigoths in peace and war; and the authority which they derived from their birth was ratified by the free consent of the nation. In a season of tranquillity their power might have been equal as well as their rank; but, as soon as their countrymen were exasperated by hunger and oppression, the superior abilities of Fritigern assumed the military command, which he was qualified to exercise for the public welfare. He restrained the impatient spirit of the Visigoths till the injuries and the insults of their tyrants should justify their resistance in the opinion of mankind: but he was not disposed to sacrifice any solid advantages for the empty praise of justice and moderation. Sensible of the benefits which would result from the union of the Gothic powers under the same standard, he secretly cultivated the friendship of the Ostrogoths; and while he professed an implicit obedience to the orders of the Roman generals, he proceeded by slow marches towards Marcianopolis, the capital of the Lower Mæsia, about seventy miles from the banks of the Danube. On that fatal spot the flames of discord and mutual hatred burst forth into a dreadful conflagration. Lupicinus had invited the Gothic chiefs to a splendid entertainment; and their martial train remained under arms at the entrance of the palace. But the gates of the city were strictly guarded, and the barbarians were sternly excluded from the use of a plentiful market, to which they asserted their equal claim of subjects and allies. Their humble prayers were rejected with insolence and derision; and as their patience was now exhausted, the townsmen, the soldiers, and the Goths were soon involved in a conflict of passionate altercation and angry reproaches. A blow was imprudently given; a sword was hastily drawn; and the first blood that was spilt in this accidental quarrel became the signal of a long and destructive war. In the midst of noise and brutal intemperance Lupicinus was informed by a secret messenger that many of his soldiers were slain and despoiled of their arms; and as he was already inflamed by wine and oppressed by sleep, he issued a rash command, that their death should be revenged by the massacre of the guards of Fritigern and Alavivus. The clamorous shouts and dying groans apprised Fritigern of his extreme danger; and, as he possessed the calm and intrepid spirit of a hero, he saw that he was lost if he allowed a moment of deliberation to the man who had so deeply injured him. "A trifling dispute," said the Gothic leader, with a firm but gentle tone of voice, "appears to have arisen between the two nations; but it may be productive of the most dangerous consequences, unless the tumult is immediately pacified by the assurance of our safety and the authority of our presence." At these words Fritigern and his companions drew their swords, opened their passage through the unresisting crowd, which filled the palace, the streets, and the gates of Marcianopolis, and, mounting their horses, hastily vanished from the eyes of the astonished Romans. The generals of the Goths were saluted by the fierce and joyful acclamations of the camp; war was instantly resolved, and the resolution was executed without delay: the banners of the nation were displayed according to the custom of their ancestors; and the air resounded with the harsh and mournful music of the barbarian trumpet. The weak and guilty Lupicinus, who had dared to provoke, who had neglected to destroy, and who still presumed to despise his formidable enemy, marched against the Goths, at the head of such a military force as could be collected on this sudden emergency. The barbarians expected his approach about nine miles from Marcianopolis; and on this occasion the talents of the general were found to be of more prevailing efficacy than the weapons and discipline of the troops. The valour of the Goths was so ably directed by the genius of Fritigern, that they broke, by a close and vigorous attack, the ranks of the Roman legions. Lupicinus left his arms and standards, his tribunes and his bravest soldiers, on the field of battle; and their useless courage served only to protect the ignominious flight of their leader. "That successful day put an end to the distress of the barbarians and the security of the Romans: from that day the Goths, renouncing the precarious condition of strangers and exiles, assumed the character of citizens and masters, claimed an absolute dominion over the possessors of land, and held, in their own right, the northern provinces of the empire, which are bounded by the Danube." Such are the words of the Gothic historian, who celebrates, with rude eloquence, the glory of his countrymen. But the dominion of the barbarians was exercised only for the purposes of rapine and destruction. As they had been deprived by the ministers of the emperor of the common benefits of nature and the fair intercourse of social life, they retaliated the injustice on the subjects of the empire; and the crimes of Lupicinus were expiated by the ruin of the peaceful husbandmen of Thrace, the conflagration of their villages, and the massacre or captivity of their innocent families. The report of the Gothic victory was soon diffused over the adjacent country; and while it filled the minds of the Romans with terror and dismay, their own hasty imprudence contributed to increase the forces of Fritigern and the calamities of the province. Some time before the great emigration a numerous body of Goths, under the command of Suerid and Colias, had been received into the protection and service of the empire. They were encamped under the walls of Hadrianople: but the ministers of Valens were anxious to remove them beyond the Hellespont, at a distance from the dangerous temptation which might so easily be communicated by the neighbourhood and the success of their countrymen. The respectful submission with which they yielded to the order of their march might be considered as a proof of their fidelity; and their moderate request of a sufficient allowance of provisions and of a delay of only two days was expressed in the most dutiful terms. But the first magistrate of Hadrianople, incensed by some disorders which had been committed at his country-house, refused this indulgence; and arming against them the inhabitants and manufacturers of a populous city, he urged, with hostile threats, their instant departure. The barbarians stood silent and amazed, till they were exasperated by the insulting clamours and missile weapons of the populace: but when patience or contempt was fatigued, they crushed the undisciplined multitude, inflicted many a shameful wound on the backs of their flying enemies, and despoiled them of the splendid armour which they were unworthy to bear. The resemblance of their sufferings and their actions soon united this victorious detachment to the nation of the Visigoths; the troops of Colias and Suerid expected the approach of the great Fritigern, ranged themselves under his standard, and signalised their ardour in the siege of Hadrianople. But the resistance of the garrison informed the barbarians that in the attack of regular fortifications the efforts of unskilful courage are seldom effectual. Their general acknowledged his error, raised the siege, declared that "he was at peace with stone walls," and revenged his disappointment on the adjacent country. He accepted with pleasure the useful reinforcement of hardy workmen who laboured in the gold-mines of Thrace for the emolument and under the lash of an unfeeling master: and these new associates conducted the barbarians through the secret paths to the most sequestered places, which had been chosen to secure the inhabitants, the cattle, and the magazines of corn. With the assistance of such guides nothing could remain impervious or inaccessible: resistance was fatal; flight was impracticable; and the patient submission of helpless innocence seldom found mercy from the barbarian conqueror. In the course of these depredations a great number of the children of the Goths, who had been sold into captivity, were restored to the embraces of their afflicted parents; but these tender interviews, which might have revived and cherished in their minds some sentiments of humanity, tended only to stimulate their native fierceness by the desire of revenge. They listened with eager attention to the complaints of their captive children, who had suffered the most cruel indignities from the lustful or angry passions of their masters, and the same cruelties, the same indignities, were severely retaliated on the sons and daughters of the Romans.

The imprudence of Valens and his ministers had introduced into the heart of the empire a nation of enemies; but the Visigoths might even yet have been reconciled by the manly confession of past errors and the sincere performance of former engagements. These healing and temperate measures seemed to concur with the timorous disposition of the sovereign of the East: but on this occasion alone Valens was brave; and his unseasonable bravery was fatal to himself and to his subjects. He declared his intention of marching from Antioch to Constantinople, to subdue this dangerous rebellion; and, as he was not ignorant of the difficulties of the enterprise, he solicited the assistance of his nephew, the emperor Gratian, who commanded all the forces of the West. While Gratian deserved and enjoyed the applause of his subjects, the emperor Valens, who at length had removed his court and army from Antioch, was received by the people of Constantinople as the author of the public calamity. Before he had reposed himself ten days in the capital he was urged by the licentious clamours of the Hippodrome to march against the barbarians whom he had invited into his dominions: and the citizens, who are always brave at a distance from any real danger, declared, with confidence, that if they were supplied with arms, *they* alone would undertake to deliver the province from the ravages of an insulting foe. The vain reproaches of an ignorant multitude hastened the downfall of the Roman empire; they provoked the desperate rashness of Valens, who did not find, either in his reputation or in his mind, any motives to support with firmness the public contempt. He was soon persuaded by the successful achievements of his lieutenants to despise the power of the Goths, who, by the diligence of Fritigern, were now collected in the neighbourhood of Hadrianople. The march of the Taifalæ had been intercepted by the valiant Frigerid; the king of those licentious barbarians was slain in battle; and the suppliant captives were sent into distant exile to cultivate the lands of Italy, which were assigned for their settlement in the vacant territories of Modena and Parma. The exploits of Sebastian, who was recently engaged in the service of Valens, and promoted to the rank of master-general of the infantry, were still more honourable to himself, and useful to the republic. He obtained the permission of selecting three hundred soldiers from each of the legions, and this separate detachment soon acquired the spirit of discipline and the exercise of arms, which were almost forgotten under the reign of Valens. By the vigour and conduct of Sebastian, a large body of the Goths was surprised in their camp; and the immense spoil which was recovered from their hands filled the city of Hadrianople and the adjacent plain. The splendid narratives which the general transmitted of his own exploits alarmed the Imperial court by the appearance of superior merit; and though he cautiously insisted on the difficulties of the Gothic war, his valour was praised, his advice was rejected; and Valens, who listened with pride and pleasure to the flattering suggestions of the eunuchs of the palace, was impatient to seize the glory of an easy and assured conquest. His army was strengthened by a numerous reinforcement of veterans; and his march from Constantinople to Hadrianople was conducted with so much military skill that he prevented the activity of the barbarians, who designed to occupy the intermediate defiles, and to intercept either the troops themselves or their convoys of provisions. The camp of

Valens, which he pitched under the walls of Hadrianople, was fortified according to the practice of the Romans, with a ditch and rampart; and a most important council was summoned to decide the fate of the emperor and of the empire. The party of reason and of delay was strenuously maintained by Victor, who had corrected, by the lessons of experience, the native fierceness of the Sarmatian character; while Sebastian, with the flexible and obsequious eloquence of a courtier, represented every precaution and every measure that implied a doubt of immediate victory as unworthy of the courage and majesty of their invincible monarch. The ruin of Valens was precipitated by the deceitful arts of Fritigern and the prudent admonitions of the emperor of the West. The advantages of negotiating in the midst of war were perfectly understood by the general of the barbarians; and a Christian ecclesiastic was despatched, as the holy minister of peace, to penetrate and to perplex the councils of the enemy. The misfortunes, as well as the provocations, of the Gothic nation were forcibly and truly described by their ambassador, who protested, in the name of Fritigern, that he was still disposed to lay down his arms, or to employ them only in the defence of the empire, if he could secure for his wandering countrymen a tranquil settlement on the waste lands of Thrace, and a sufficient allowance of corn and cattle. But he added, in a whisper of confidential friendship, that the exasperated barbarians were averse to these reasonable conditions; and that Fritigern was doubtful whether he could accomplish the conclusion of the treaty unless he found himself supported by the presence and terrors of an Imperial army. About the same time, Count Richomer returned from the West to announce the defeat and submission of the Alemanni; to inform Valens that his nephew advanced by rapid marches at the head of the veteran and victorious legions of Gaul; and to request, in the name of Gratian and of the republic, that every dangerous and decisive measure might be suspended till the junction of the two emperors should ensure the success of the Gothic war. But the feeble sovereign of the East was actuated only by the fatal illusions of pride and jealousy. He disdained the importunate advice; he rejected the humiliating aid; he secretly compared the ignominious, at least the inglorious, period of his own reign with the fame of a beardless youth; and Valens rushed into the field to erect his imaginary trophy before the diligence of his colleague could usurp any share of the triumphs of the day.

On the 9th of August, a day which has deserved to be marked among the most inauspicious of the Roman calendar, the emperor Valens, leaving, under a strong guard, his baggage and military treasure, marched from Hadrianople to attack the Goths, who were encamped about twelve miles from the city. By some mistake of the orders, or some ignorance of the ground, the right wing or column of cavalry arrived in sight of the enemy whilst the left was still at a considerable distance; the soldiers were compelled, in the sultry heat of summer, to precipitate their pace; and the line of battle was formed with tedious confusion and irregular delay. The Gothic cavalry had been detached to forage in the adjacent country; and Fritigern still continued to practise his customary arts. He despatched messengers of peace, made proposals, required hostages, and wasted the hours, till the Romans, exposed without shelter to the burning rays of the sun, were exhausted by thirst, hunger, and intolerable fatigue. The emperor was persuaded to send an ambassador to the Gothic camp; the zeal of Richomer, who alone had courage to accept the dangerous commission, was applauded; and the count of the domestics, adorned with the splendid ensigns of his dignity, had proceeded some way in the space between the two armies when he was suddenly recalled by the alarm of battle. The hasty and imprudent attack was made by Bacurius the Iberian, who commanded a body of archers and targeteers: and, as they advanced with rashness, they retreated with loss and disgrace. In the same moment the flying squadrons of Alatheus and Saphrax, whose return was anxiously expected by the general of the Goths, descended like a whirlwind from the hills, swept across the plain, and added new terrors to the tumultuous but irresistible charge of the barbarian host. The event of the battle of Hadrianople, so fatal to Valens and to the empire, may be described in a few words: the Roman cavalry fled; the infantry was abandoned, surrounded, and cut in pieces. The most skilful evolutions, the firmest courage, are scarcely sufficient to extricate a body of foot encompassed on an open plain by superior numbers of horse; but the troops of Valens, oppressed by the weight of the enemy and their own fears, were crowded into a narrow space, where it was impossible for them to extend their ranks, or even to use, with effect, their swords and javelins. In the midst of tumult, of slaughter, and of dismay, the emperor, deserted by his guards, and wounded, as it was supposed, with an arrow, sought protection among the Lancearii and the Mattiarii, who still maintained their ground with some appearance of order and firmness. His faithful generals, Trajan and Victor, who perceived his danger, loudly exclaimed that all was lost unless the person of the emperor could be saved. Some troops, animated by their exhortation, advanced to his relief: they found only a bloody spot, covered with a heap of broken arms and mangled bodies, without being able to discover their unfortunate prince either among the living or the dead. Their search could not indeed be successful, if there is any truth in the circumstances with which some historians have related the death of the emperor. By the care of his attendants, Valens was removed from the field of battle to a neighbouring cottage, where they attempted to dress his wound and to provide for his future safety. But this humble retreat was instantly surrounded by the enemy; they tried to force the door; they were provoked by a discharge of arrows from the roof; till at length, impatient of delay, they set fire to a pile of dry faggots, and consumed the cottage with the Roman emperor and his train. Valens perished in the flames; and a youth, who dropped from the window, alone escaped, to attest the melancholy tale and to inform the Goths of the inestimable prize which they had lost by their own rashness. A great number of brave and distinguished officers perished in the battle of Hadrianople, which equalled in the actual loss, and far surpassed in the fatal consequences, the misfortune which Rome had formerly sustained in the fields of Cannæ. Two master-generals of the cavalry and infantry, two great officers of the palace, and thirty-five tribunes, were found among the slain; and the death of Sebastian might satisfy the world that he was the victim as well as the author of the public calamity. Above two-thirds of the Roman army were destroyed: and the darkness of the night was esteemed a very favourable circumstance, as it served to conceal the flight of the multitude, and to protect the more orderly retreat of Victor and Richomer, who alone, amidst the general consternation, maintained the advantage of calm courage and regular discipline.

The Romans, who so coolly and so concisely mention the acts of *justice* which were exercised by the legions, reserved their compassion and their eloquence for their own sufferings when the provinces were invaded and desolated by the arms of the successful barbarians. The simple circumstantial narrative (did such a narrative exist) of the ruin of a single town, of the misfortunes of a single family, might exhibit an interesting and instructive picture of human manners; but the tedious repetition of vague and declamatory complaints would fatigue the attention of the most patient reader.

The same censure may be applied, though not perhaps in an equal degree, to the profane and the ecclesiastical writers of this unhappy period; that their minds were inflamed by popular and religious animosity, and that the true size and colour of every object is falsified by the exaggerations of their corrupt eloquence. The vehement Jerom might justly deplore the calamities inflicted by the Goths and their barbarous allies on his native country of Pannonia, and the wide extent of the provinces from the walls of Constantinople, to the foot of the Julian Alps; the rapes, the massacres, the conflagrations, and, above all, the profanation of the churches that were turned into stables, and the contemptuous treatment of the relics of holy martyrs. But the saint is surely transported beyond the limits of nature and history when he affirms, "that in those desert countries nothing was left except the sky and the earth; that, after the destruction of the cities and the extirpation of the human race, the land was overgrown with thick forests and inextricable brambles; and that the universal desolation, announced by the prophet Zephaniah, was accomplished in the scarcity of the beasts, the birds, and even of the fish." These complaints were pronounced about twenty years after the death of Valens; and the Illyrian provinces, which were constantly exposed to the invasion and passage of the barbarians, still continued, after a calamitous period of ten centuries, to supply new materials for rapine and destruction. Could it even be supposed that a large tract of country had been left without cultivation and without inhabitants, the consequences might not have been so fatal to the inferior productions of animated nature. The useful and feeble animals, which are nourished by the hand of man, might suffer and perish if they were deprived of his protection; but the beasts of the forest, his enemies or his victims, would multiply in the free and undisturbed possession of their solitary domain. The various tribes that peopled the air or the waters are still less connected with the fate of the human species; and it is highly probable that the fish of the Danube would have felt more terror and distress from the approach of a voracious pike than from the hostile inroad of a Gothic army.

Whatever may have been the just measure of the calamities of Europe, there was reason to fear that the same calamities would soon extend to the peaceful countries of Asia. The sons of the Goths had been judiciously distributed through the cities of the East, and the arts of education were employed to polish and subdue the native fierceness of their temper. In the space of about twelve years their numbers had continually increased; and the children who in the first emigration were sent over the Hellespont had attained with rapid growth the strength and spirit of perfect manhood. It was impossible to conceal from their knowledge the events of the Gothic war; and, as those daring youths had not studied the language of dissimulation, they betrayed their wish, their desire, perhaps their intention, to emulate the glorious example of their fathers. The danger of the times seemed to justify the jealous suspicions of the provincials; and these suspicions were admitted as unquestionable evidence that the Goths of Asia had formed a secret and dangerous conspiracy against the public safety. The death of Valens had left the East without a sovereign; and Julius, who filled the important station of master-general of the troops, with a high reputation of diligence and ability, thought it his duty to consult the senate of Constantinople, which he considered, during the vacancy of the throne, as the representative council of the nation. As soon as he had obtained the discretionary power of acting as he should judge most expedient for the good of the republic, he assembled the principal officers and privately concerted effectual measures for the execution of his bloody design. An order was immediately promulgated that, on a stated day, the Gothic youth should assemble in the capital cities of their respective provinces; and, as a report was industriously circulated that they were summoned to receive a liberal gift of lands and money, the pleasing hope allayed the fury of their resentment, and perhaps suspended the motions of the conspiracy. On the appointed day the unarmed crowd of the Gothic youth was carefully collected in the square or forum; the streets and avenues were occupied by the Roman troops, and the roofs of the houses were covered with archers and slingers. At the same hour, in all the cities of the East, the signal was given of indiscriminate slaughter; and the provinces of Asia were delivered, by the cruel prudence of Julius, from a domestic enemy, who in a few months might have carried fire and sword from the Hellespont to the Euphrates. The urgent consideration of the public safety may undoubtedly authorise the violation of every positive law. How far that or any other consideration may operate to dissolve the natural obligations of humanity and justice, is a doctrine of which I still desire to remain ignorant.

The emperor Gratian was far advanced on his march towards the plains of Hadrianople when he was informed, at first by the confused voice of fame, and afterwards by the more accurate reports of Victor and Richomer, that his impatient colleague had been slain in battle, and that two-thirds of the Roman army were exterminated by the sword of the victorious Goths. Whatever resentment the rash and jealous vanity of his uncle might deserve, the resentment of a generous mind is easily subdued by the softer emotions of grief and compassion; and even the sense of pity was soon lost in the serious and alarming consideration of the state of the republic. Gratian was too late to assist, he was too weak to revenge, his unfortunate colleague; and the valiant and modest youth felt himself unequal to the support of a sinking world. A formidable tempest of the barbarians of Germany seemed ready to burst over the provinces of Gaul, and the mind of Gratian was oppressed and distracted by the administration of the Western empire. In this important crisis the government of the East and the conduct of the Gothic war required the undivided attention of a hero and a statesman. A subject invested with such ample command would not long have preserved his fidelity to a distant benefactor; and the Imperial council embraced the wise and manly resolution of conferring an obligation rather than of yielding to an insult. It was the wish of Gratian to bestow the purple as the reward of virtue; but at the age of nineteen it is not easy for a prince, educated in the supreme rank, to understand the true characters of his ministers and generals. He attempted to weigh, with an impartial hand, their various merits and defects; and whilst he checked the rash confidence of ambition, he distrusted the cautious wisdom which despaired of the republic. As each moment of delay diminished something of the power and resources of the future sovereign of the East, the situation of the times would not allow a tedious debate. The choice of Gratian was soon declared in favour of an exile, whose father, only three years before, had suffered, under the sanction of *his* authority, an unjust and ignominious death. The great Theodosius, a name celebrated in history and dear to the catholic church, was summoned to the Imperial court, which had gradually retreated from the confines of Thrace to the more secure station of Sirmium. Five months after the death of Valens the emperor Gratian produced before the assembled troops *his* colleague and *their* master, who, after a modest, perhaps a sincere resistance, was compelled to accept, amidst the general acclamations, the diadem, the purple, and the equal title of Augustus. The provinces of Thrace, Asia, and Egypt, over which Valens had reigned, were resigned to the administration of the new emperor; but as he was specially intrusted with the conduct of the Gothic war, the Illyrian præfecture was dismembered, and the two great dioceses of Dacia and Macedonia were added to the dominions of the Eastern empire.

The fabric of a mighty state, which has been reared by the labours of successive ages, could not be overturned by the misfortune of a single day, if the fatal power of the imagination did not exaggerate the real measure of the calamity. The loss of forty thousand Romans, who fell in the plains of Hadrianople, might have been soon recruited in the populous provinces of the East, which contained so many millions of inhabitants. The courage of a soldier is found to be the cheapest and most common quality of human nature; and sufficient skill to encounter an undisciplined foe might have been speedily taught by the care of the surviving centurions. If the barbarians were mounted on the horses, and equipped with the armour, of their vanquished enemies, the numerous studs of Cappadocia and Spain would have supplied new squadrons of cavalry; the thirty-four arsenals of the empire were plentifully stored with magazines of offensive and defensive arms; and the wealth of Asia might still have yielded an ample fund for the expenses of the war. But the effects which were produced by the battle of Hadrianople on the minds of the barbarians and of the Romans, extended the victory of the former, and the defeat of the latter, far beyond the limits of a single day. A Gothic chief was heard to declare, with insolent moderation, that, for his own part, he was fatigued with slaughter; but that he was astonished how a people who fled before him like a flock of sheep could still presume to dispute the possession of their treasures and provinces. The same terrors which the name of the Huns had spread among the Gothic tribes were inspired, by the formidable name of the Goths, among the subjects and soldiers of the Roman empire. If Theodosius, hastily collecting his scattered forces, had led them into the field to encounter a victorious enemy, his army would have been vanquished by their own fears; and his rashness could not have been excused by the chance of success. But the *great* Theodosius, an epithet which he honourably deserved on this momentous occasion, conducted himself as the firm and faithful guardian of the republic. He fixed his headquarters at Thessalonica, the capital of the Macedonian diocese; from whence he could watch the irregular motions of the barbarians, and direct the operations of his lieutenants, from the gates of Constantinople to the shores of the Hadriatic. The fortifications and garrisons of the cities were strengthened; and the troops, among whom a sense of order and discipline was revived, were insensibly emboldened by the confidence of their own safety. From these secure stations they were encouraged to make frequent sallies on the barbarians, who infested the adjacent country; and, as they were seldom allowed to engage, without some decisive superiority, either of ground or of numbers, their enterprises were, for the most part, successful; and they were soon convinced, by their own experience, of the possibility of vanquishing their *invincible* enemies. The detachments of these separate garrisons were gradually united into small armies; the same cautious measures were pursued, according to an extensive and well-concerted plan of operations; the events of each day added strength and spirit to the Roman arms; and the artful diligence of the emperor who circulated the most favourable reports of the success of the war, contributed to subdue the pride of the barbarians, and to animate the hopes and courage of his subjects.

The deliverance and peace of the Roman provinces was the work of prudence, rather than of valour: the prudence of Theodosius was seconded by fortune; and the emperor never failed to seize, and to improve, every favourable circumstance. As long as the superior genius of Fritigern preserved the union and directed the motions of the barbarians, their power was not inadequate to the conquest of a great empire. The death of that hero, the predecessor and master of the renowned Alaric, relieved an impatient multitude from the intolerable yoke of discipline and discretion. The barbarians, who had been restrained by his authority, abandoned themselves to the dictates of their passions; and their passions were seldom uniform or consistent. An army of conquerors was broken into many disorderly bands of savage robbers; and their blind and irregular fury was not less pernicious to themselves than to their enemies. Their mischievous disposition was shown in the destruction of every object which they wanted strength to remove, or taste to enjoy; and they often consumed, with improvident rage, the harvests, or the granaries, which soon afterwards became necessary for their own subsistence. A spirit of discord arose among the independent tribes and nations, which had been united only by the bands of a loose and voluntary alliance. The troops of the Huns and the Alani would naturally upbraid the flight of the Goths, who were not disposed to use with moderation the advantages of their fortune: the ancient jealousy of the Ostrogoths and the Visigoths could not long be suspended; and the haughty chiefs still remembered the insults and injuries which they had reciprocally offered or sustained while the nation was seated in the countries beyond the Danube. The progress of domestic faction abated the more diffusive sentiment of national animosity; and the officers of Theodosius were instructed to purchase, with liberal gifts and promises, the retreat or service of the discontented party. The acquisition of Modar, a prince of the royal blood of the Amali, gave a bold and faithful champion to the cause of Rome. The illustrious deserter soon obtained the rank of master-general, with an important command; surprised an army of his countrymen, who were immersed in wine and sleep; and, after a cruel slaughter of the astonished Goths, returned with an immense spoil, and four thousand waggons, to the Imperial camp. In the hands of a skilful politician the most different means may be successfully applied to the same ends; and the peace of the empire, which had been forwarded by the divisions, was accomplished by the re-union of the Gothic nation. Athanaric, who had been a patient spectator of these extraordinary events, was at length driven, by the chance of arms, from the dark recesses of the woods of Caucaland. He no longer hesitated to pass the Danube; and a very considerable part of the subjects of Fritigern, who already felt the inconveniences of anarchy, were easily persuaded to acknowledge for their king a Gothic Judge, whose birth they respected, and whose abilities they had frequently experienced. But age had chilled the daring spirit of Athanaric; and instead of leading his people to the field of battle and victory, he wisely listened to the fair proposal of an honourable and advantageous treaty. Theodosius, who was acquainted with the merit and power of his new ally, condescended to meet him at the distance of several miles from Constantinople; and entertained him in the Imperial city, with the confidence of a friend, and the magnificence of a monarch. "The barbarian prince observed, with curious attention, the variety of objects which attracted his notice, and at last broke out into a sincere and passionate exclamation of wonder. I now behold (said he) what I never could believe, the glories of this stupendous capital! And as he cast his eyes around, he viewed and he admired the commanding situation of the city, the strength and beauty of the walls and public edifices, the capacious harbour crowded with innumerable vessels, the perpetual concourse of distant nations, and the arms and discipline of the troops. Indeed (continued Athanaric), the emperor of the Romans is a god upon earth; and the presumptuous man who dares to lift his hand against him is guilty of his own blood." The Gothic king did not long enjoy this splendid and honourable reception; and, as temperance was not the virtue of his nation, it may justly be suspected that his mortal disease was contracted amidst the pleasures of the Imperial banquets. But the policy of Theodosius derived more solid benefit from the death than he could have expected from the most faithful services of his ally. The funeral of Athanaric was performed with solemn rites in the capital of the East; a stately monument was erected to his memory; and his whole army, won by the liberal courtesy and decent grief of Theodosius, enlisted under the standard of the Roman empire. The submission of so great a body of the Visigoths was productive of the most salutary consequences; and the mixed influence of force, of reason, and of corruption, became every day more powerful and more extensive. Each independent chieftain hastened to obtain a separate treaty, from the apprehension that an obstinate delay might expose *him*, alone and unprotected, to the revenge or justice of the conqueror. The general, or rather the final, capitulation of the Goths, may be dated four years, one month, and twenty-five days, after the defeat and death of the emperor Valens.

The original treaty, which fixed the settlement of the Goths, ascertained their privileges, and stipulated their obligations, would illustrate the history of Theodosius and his successors. The series of their history has imperfectly preserved the spirit and substance of this singular agreement. The ravages of war and tyranny had provided many large tracts of fertile but uncultivated land for the use of those barbarians who might not disdain the practice of agriculture. A numerous colony of the Visigoths was seated in Thrace; the remains of the Ostrogoths were planted in Phrygia and Lydia; their immediate wants were supplied by a distribution of corn and cattle; and their future industry was encouraged by an exemption from tribute during a certain term of years. The barbarians would have deserved to feel the cruel and perfidious policy of the Imperial court if they had suffered themselves to be dispersed through the provinces. They required and they obtained the sole possession of the villages and districts assigned for their residence; they still cherished and propagated their native manners and language; asserted, in the bosom of despotism, the freedom of their domestic government; and acknowledged the sovereignty of the emperor, without submitting to the inferior jurisdiction of the laws and magistrates of Rome. The hereditary chiefs of the tribes and families were still permitted to command their followers in peace and war: but the royal dignity was abolished; and the generals of the Goths were appointed and removed at the pleasure of the emperor. An army of forty thousand Goths was maintained for the perpetual service of the empire of the East; and those haughty troops, who assumed the title of *Fœderati*, or allies, were distinguished by their gold collars, liberal pay, and licentious privileges. Their native courage was improved by the use of arms and the knowledge of discipline; and, while the republic was guarded or threatened by the doubtful sword of the barbarians, the last sparks of the military flame were finally extinguished in the minds of the Romans. Theodosius had the address to persuade his allies that the conditions of peace, which had been extorted from him by prudence and necessity, were the voluntary expressions of his sincere friendship for the Gothic nation. A different mode of vindication or apology was opposed to the complaints of the people, who loudly censured these shameful and dangerous concessions. The calamities of the war were painted in the most lively colours; and the first symptoms of the return of order, of plenty, and security were diligently exaggerated. The advocates of Theodosius could affirm, with some appearance of truth and reason, that it was impossible to extirpate so many warlike tribes, who were rendered desperate by the loss of their native country; and that the exhausted provinces would be revived by a fresh supply of soldiers and husbandmen. The barbarians still wore an angry and hostile aspect; but the experience of past times might encourage the hope that they would acquire the habits of industry and obedience; that their manners would be polished by time, education, and the influence of Christianity; and that their posterity would insensibly blend with the great body of the Roman people.

Notwithstanding these specious arguments and these sanguine expectations, it was apparent to every discerning eye that the Goths would long remain the enemies, and might soon become the conquerors, of the Roman empire. Their rude and insolent behaviour expressed their contempt of the citizens and provincials, whom they insulted with impunity. To the zeal and valour of the barbarians Theodosius was indebted for the success of his arms: but their assistance was precarious; and they were sometimes seduced, by a treacherous and inconstant disposition, to abandon his standard at the moment when their service was the most essential. During the civil war against Maximus a great number of Gothic deserters retired into the morasses of Macedonia, wasted the adjacent provinces, and obliged the intrepid monarch to expose his person and exert his power to suppress the rising flame of rebellion. The public apprehensions were fortified by the strong suspicion that these tumults were not the effect of accidental passion, but the result of deep and premeditated design. It was generally believed that the Goths had signed the treaty of peace with an hostile and insidious spirit; and that their chiefs had previously bound themselves by a solemn and secret oath never to keep faith with the Romans, to maintain the fairest show of loyalty and friendship, and to watch the favourable moment of rapine, of conquest, and of revenge. But as the minds of the barbarians were not insensible to the power of gratitude, several of the Gothic leaders sincerely devoted themselves to the service of the empire, or, at least, of the emperor: the whole nation was insensibly divided into two opposite factions, and much sophistry was employed in conversation and dispute to compare the obligations of their first and second engagements. The Goths who considered themselves as the friends of peace, of justice, and of Rome, were directed by the authority of Fravitta, a valiant and honourable youth, distinguished above the rest of his countrymen by the politeness of his manners, the liberality of his sentiments, and the mild virtues of social life. But the more numerous faction adhered to the fierce and faithless Priulf, who inflamed the passions and asserted the independence of his warlike followers. On one of the solemn festivals, when the chiefs of both parties were invited to the Imperial table, they were insensibly heated by wine, till they forgot the usual restraints of discretion and respect, and betrayed in the presence of Theodosius the fatal secret of their domestic disputes. The emperor, who had been the reluctant witness of this extraordinary controversy, dissembled his fears and resentment, and soon dismissed the tumultuous assembly. Fravitta, alarmed and exasperated by the insolence of his rival, whose departure from the palace might have been the signal of a civil war, boldly followed him, and, drawing his sword, laid Priulf dead at his feet. Their companions flew to arms; and the faithful champion of Rome would have been oppressed by superior numbers if he had not been protected by the seasonable interposition of the Imperial guards. Such were the scenes of barbaric rage which disgraced the palace and table of the Roman emperor; and, as the impatient Goths could only be restrained by the firm and temperate character of Theodosius, the public safety seemed to depend on the life and abilities of a single man.

XXV

(340–397 A.D.) CHARACTER, ADMINISTRATION, AND PENANCE, OF THEODOSIUS—DEATH OF THEODOSIUS

In his Chapter XXVII Gibbon related how Gratian alienated his troops by adopting the dress and manners of the Alani and because of his addiction to hunting, and how Maximus successfully overthrew him. Gratian was avenged by Theodosius, who put Gratian's half-brother Valentinian on the throne, but he in turn was betrayed by his Frankish minister, Arbogastes, who put Eugenius on the throne. Once more Theodosius overthrew the usurpers, but he died within four months, leaving the western half of the empire to his son Honorius, and the eastern half to his son Arcadius.

Three passages only of this chapter are given here, but they are important in delineating the genius of Theodosius, the power of the church, and the temper of the times.

The orator, who may be silent without danger, may praise without difficulty and without reluctance; and posterity will confess that the character of Theodosius might furnish the subject of a sincere and ample panegyric. The wisdom of his laws and the success of his arms rendered his administration respectable in the eyes both of his subjects and of his enemies. He loved and practised the virtues of domestic life, which seldom hold their residence in the palaces of kings. Theodosius was chaste and temperate; he enjoyed, without excess, the sensual and social pleasures of the table, and the warmth of his amorous passions was never diverted from their lawful objects. The proud titles of Imperial greatness were adorned by the tender names of a faithful husband, an indulgent father; his uncle was raised, by his affectionate esteem, to the rank of a second parent; Theodosius embraced, as his own, the children of his brother and sister, and the expressions of his regard were extended to the most distant and obscure branches of his numerous kindred. His familiar friends were judiciously selected from among those persons who, in the equal intercourse of private life, had appeared before his eyes without a mask; the consciousness of personal and superior merit enabled him to despise the accidental distinction of the purple, and he proved by his conduct that he had forgotten all the injuries, while he most gratefully remembered all the favours and services which he had received before he ascended the throne of the Roman empire. The serious or lively tone of his conversation was adapted to the age, the rank, or the character of his subjects whom he admitted into his society; and the affability of his manners displayed the image of his mind. Theodosius respected the simplicity of the good and virtuous: every art, every talent, of an useful or even of an innocent nature, was rewarded by his judicious liberality; and, except the heretics, whom he persecuted with implacable hatred, the diffusive circle of his benevolence was circumscribed only by the limits of the human race. The government of a mighty empire may assuredly suffice to occupy the time and the abilities of a mortal; yet the diligent prince, without aspiring to the unsuitable reputation of profound learning, always reserved some moments of his leisure for the instructive amusement of reading. History, which enlarged his experience, was his favourite study. The annals of Rome, in the long period of eleven hundred years, presented him with a various and splendid picture of human life; and it has been particularly observed that, whenever he perused the cruel acts of Cinna, of Marius, or of Sylla, he warmly expressed his generous detestation of those enemies of humanity and freedom. His disinterested opinion of past events was usefully applied as the rule of his own actions, and Theodosius has deserved the singular commendation that his virtues always seemed to expand with his fortune; the season of his prosperity was that of his moderation, and his clemency appeared the most conspicuous after the danger and success of the civil war. The Moorish guards of the tyrant had been massacred in the first heat of the victory, and a small number of the most obnoxious criminals suffered the punishment of the law. But the emperor showed himself much more attentive to relieve the innocent than to chastise the guilty. The oppressed subjects of the West, who would have deemed themselves happy in the restoration of their lands, were astonished to receive a sum of money equivalent to their losses; and the liberality of the conqueror supported the aged mother and educated the orphan daughters of Maximus. A character thus accomplished might almost excuse the extravagant supposition of the orator Pacatus that, if the elder Brutus could be permitted to revisit the earth, the stern republican would abjure, at the feet of Theodosius, his hatred of kings; and ingenuously confess that such a monarch was the most faithful guardian of the happiness and dignity of the Roman people.

Yet the piercing eye of the founder of the republic must have discerned two essential imperfections, which might, perhaps, have abated his recent love of despotism. The virtuous mind of Theodosius was often relaxed by indolence, and it was sometimes inflamed by passion. In the pursuit of an important object his active courage was capable of the most vigorous exertions; but as soon as the design was accomplished, or the danger was surmounted, the hero sunk into inglorious repose, and, forgetful that the time of a prince is the property of his people, resigned himself to the enjoyment of the innocent but trifling pleasures of a luxurious court. The natural disposition of Theodosius was hasty and choleric; and, in a station where none could resist and few would dissuade the fatal consequence of his resentment, the humane monarch was justly alarmed by the consciousness of his infirmity and of his power. It was the constant study of his life to suppress or regulate the intemperate sallies of passion; and the success of his efforts enhanced the merit of his clemency. But the painful virtue which claims the merit of victory is exposed to the danger of defeat; and the reign of a wise and merciful prince was polluted by an act of cruelty which would stain the annals of Nero or Domitian.

The sedition of Thessalonica is ascribed to a shameful cause and was productive of dreadful consequences. That great city, the metropolis of all the Illyrian provinces, had been protected from the dangers of the Gothic war by strong fortifications and a numerous garrison. Botheric, the general of those troops, and, as it should seem from his name, a barbarian, had among his slaves a beautiful boy, who excited the impure desires of one of the charioteers of the circus. The insolent and brutal lover was thrown into prison by the order of Botheric; and he sternly rejected the importunate clamours of the multitude, who, on the day of the public games, lamented the absence of their favourite, and considered the skill of a charioteer as an object of more importance than his virtue. The resentment of the people was embittered by some previous disputes; and, as the strength of the garrison had been drawn away for the service of the Italian war, the feeble remnant, whose numbers were reduced by desertion, could not save the unhappy general from their licentious fury. Botheric and several of his principal officers were inhumanly murdered; their mangled bodies were dragged about the streets; and the emperor, who then resided at Milan, was surprised by the intelligence of the audacious and wanton cruelty of the people of Thessalonica. The sentence of a dispassionate judge would have inflicted a severe punishment on the authors of the crime; and the merit of Botheric might contribute to exasperate the grief and indignation of his master. The fiery and choleric temper of Theodosius was impatient of the dilatory forms of a judicial inquiry; and he hastily resolved that the blood of his lieutenant should be expiated by the blood of the guilty people. Yet his mind still fluctuated between the counsels of clemency and of revenge; the zeal of the bishops had almost extorted from the reluctant emperor the promise of a general pardon; his passion was again inflamed by the flattering suggestions of his minister Rufinus; and, after Theodosius had despatched the messengers of death, he attempted, when it was too late, to prevent the execution of his orders. The punishment of a Roman city was blindly committed to the undistinguishing sword of the barbarians; and the hostile preparations were concerted with the dark and perfidious artifice of an illegal conspiracy. The people of Thessalonica were treacherously invited, in the name of their sovereign, to the games of the circus; and such was their insatiate avidity for those amusements that every consideration of fear or suspicion was disregarded by the numerous spectators. As soon as the assembly was complete, the soldiers, who had secretly been posted round the circus, received the signal, not of the races, but of a general massacre. The promiscuous carnage continued three hours, without discrimination of strangers or natives, of age or sex, of innocence or guilt; the most moderate accounts state the number of the slain at seven thousand; and it is affirmed by some writers that more than fifteen thousand victims were sacrificed to the manes of Botheric. A foreign merchant, who had probably no concern in his murder, offered his own life and all his wealth to supply the place of *one* of his two sons; but while the father hesitated with equal tenderness, while he was doubtful to choose, and unwilling to condemn, the soldiers determined his suspense by plunging their daggers at the same moment into the breasts of the defenceless youths. The apology of the assassins, that they were obliged to produce the prescribed number of heads, serves only to increase, by an appearance of order and design, the horrors of the massacre, which was executed by the commands of Theodosius. The guilt of the emperor is aggravated by his long and frequent residence at Thessalonica. The situation of the unfortunate city, the aspect of the streets and buildings, the dress and faces of the inhabitants, were familiar, and even present, to his imagination; and Theodosius possessed a quick and lively sense of the existence of the people whom he destroyed.

The respectful attachment of the emperor for the orthodox clergy had disposed him to love and admire the character of Ambrose, who united all the episcopal virtues in the most eminent degree. The friends and ministers of Theodosius imitated the example of their sovereign; and he observed, with more surprise than displeasure, that all his secret counsels were immediately communicated to the archbishop, who acted from the laudable persuasion that every measure of civil government may have some connection with the glory of God and the interest of the true religion. The monks and populace of Callinicum, an obscure town on the frontier of Persia, excited by their own fanaticism, and by that of their bishop, had tumultuously burnt a conventicle of the Valentinians and a synagogue of the Jews. The seditious prelate was condemned by the magistrate of the provinces either to rebuild the synagogue or to repay the damage; and this moderate sentence was confirmed by the emperor. But it was not confirmed by the archbishop of Milan. He dictated an epistle of censure and reproach, more suitable perhaps if the emperor had received the mark of circumcision and renounced the faith of his baptism. Ambrose considers the toleration of the Jewish as the persecution of the Christian religion; boldly declares that he himself and every true believer would eagerly dispute with the bishop of Callinicum the merit of the deed and the crown of martyrdom; and laments, in the most pathetic terms, that the execution of the sentence would be fatal to the fame and salvation of Theodosius. As this private admonition did not produce an immediate effect, the archbishop from his pulpit publicly addressed the emperor on his throne; nor would he consent to offer the oblation of the altar till he had obtained from Theodosius a solemn and positive declaration which secured the impunity of the bishop and monks of Callinicum. The recantation of Theodosius was sincere; and, during the term of his residence at Milan, his affection for Ambrose was continually increased by the habits of pious and familiar conversation.

When Ambrose was informed of the massacre of Thessalonica, his mind was filled with horror and anguish. He retired into the country to indulge his grief and to avoid the presence of Theodosius. But as the archbishop was satisfied that a timid silence would render him the accomplice of his guilt, he represented in a private letter the enormity of the crime, which could only be effaced by the tears of penitence. The episcopal vigour of Ambrose was tempered by prudence; and he contented himself with signifying an indirect sort of excommunication, by the assurance that he had been warned in a vision not to offer the oblation in the name or in the presence of Theodosius, and by the advice that he would confine himself to the use of prayer, without presuming to approach the altar of Christ, or to receive the holy eucharist with those hands that were still polluted with the blood of an innocent people. The emperor was deeply affected by his own reproaches and by those of his spiritual father; and after he had bewailed the mischievous and irreparable consequences of his rash fury, he proceeded in the accustomed manner to perform his devotions in the great church of Milan. He was stopped in the porch by the archbishop, who, in the tone and language of an ambassador of Heaven, declared to his sovereign that private contrition was not sufficient to atone for a public fault or to appease the justice of the offended Deity. Theodosius humbly represented that, if he had contracted the guilt of homicide, David, the man after God's own heart, had been guilty not only of murder but of adultery. "You have imitated David in his crime, imitate then his repentance," was the reply of the undaunted Ambrose. The rigorous conditions of peace and pardon were accepted; and the public penance of the emperor Theodosius has been recorded as one of the most honourable events in the annals of the church. According to the mildest rules of ecclesiastical discipline which were established in the fourth century, the crime of homicide was expiated by the penitence of twenty years: and as it was impossible in the period of human life to purge the accumulated guilt of the massacre of Thessalonica, the murderer should have been excluded from the holy communion till the hour of his death. But the archbishop, consulting the maxims of religious policy, granted some indulgence to the rank of his illustrious penitent, who humbled in the dust the pride of the diadem; and the public edification might be admitted as a weighty reason to abridge the duration of his punishment. It was sufficient that the emperor of the Romans, stripped of the ensigns of royalty, should appear in a mournful and suppliant posture; and that, in the midst of the church of Milan, he should humbly solicit, with sighs and tears, the pardon of his sins. In this spiritual cure Ambrose employed the various methods of mildness and severity. After a delay of about eight months Theodosius was restored to the communion of the faithful;

and the edict, which interposes a salutary interval of thirty days between the sentence and the execution, may be accepted as the worthy fruits of his repentance. Posterity has applauded the virtuous firmness of the archbishop: and the example of Theodosius may prove the beneficial influence of those principles which could force a monarch, exalted above the apprehension of human punishment, to respect the laws and ministers of an invisible Judge. "The prince," says Montesquieu, "who is actuated by the hopes and fears of religion, may be compared to a lion, docile only to the voice, and tractable to the hand, of his keeper." The motions of the royal animal will therefore depend on the inclination and interest of the man who has acquired such dangerous authority over him; and the priest who holds in his hand the conscience of a king may inflame or moderate his sanguinary passions. The cause of humanity and that of persecution have been asserted by the same Ambrose with equal energy and with equal success.

After the defeat of Eugenius, the merit, as well as the authority, of Theodosius was cheerfully acknowledged by all the inhabitants of the Roman world. The experience of his past conduct encouraged the most pleasing expectations of his future reign; and the age of the emperor, which did not exceed fifty years, seemed to extend the prospect of the public felicity. His death, only four months after his victory, was considered by the people as an unforeseen and fatal event, which destroyed in a moment the hopes of the rising generation. But the indulgence of ease and luxury had secretly nourished the principles of disease. The strength of Theodosius was unable to support the sudden and violent transition from the palace to the camp; and the increasing symptoms of a dropsy announced the speedy dissolution of the emperor. The opinion, and perhaps the interest, of the public had confirmed the division of the Eastern and Western empires; and the two royal youths, Arcadius and Honorius, who had already obtained, from the tenderness of their father, the title of Augustus, were destined to fill the thrones of Constantinople and of Rome. Those princes were not permitted to share the danger and glory of the civil war; but as soon as Theodosius had triumphed over his unworthy rivals, he called his younger son, Honorius, to enjoy the fruits of the victory, and to receive the sceptre of the West from the hands of his dying father. The arrival of Honorius at Milan was welcomed by a splendid exhibition of the games of the circus; and the emperor, though he was oppressed by the weight of his disorder, contributed by his presence to the public joy. But the remains of his strength were exhausted by the painful effort which he made to assist at the spectacles of the morning. Honorius supplied, during the rest of the day, the place of his father; and the great Theodosius expired in the ensuing night. Notwithstanding the recent animosities of a civil war, his death was universally lamented. The barbarians, whom he had vanquished, and the churchmen, by whom he had been subdued, celebrated with loud and sincere applause the qualities of the deceased emperor which appeared the most valuable in their eyes. The Romans were terrified by the impending dangers of a feeble and divided administration; and every disgraceful moment of the unfortunate reigns of Arcadius and Honorius revived the memory of their irreparable loss.

In the faithful picture of the virtues of Theodosius, his imperfections have not been dissembled; the act of cruelty, and the habits of indolence, which tarnished the glory of one of the greatest of the Roman princes. An historian perpetually adverse to the fame of Theodosius has exaggerated his vices and their pernicious effects; he boldly asserts that every rank of subjects imitated the effeminate manners of their sovereign; that every species of corruption polluted the course of public and private life; and that the feeble restraints of order and decency were insufficient to resist the progress of that degenerate spirit which sacrifices, without a blush, the consideration of duty and interest to the base indulgence of sloth and appetite. The complaints of contemporary writers, who deplore the increase of luxury and depravation of manners, are commonly expressive of their peculiar temper and situation. There are few observers who possess a clear and comprehensive view of the revolutions of society, and who are capable of discovering the nice and secret springs of action which impel, in the same uniform direction, the blind and capricious passions of a multitude of individuals. If it can be affirmed, with any degree of truth, that the luxury of the Romans was more shameless and dissolute in the reign of Theodosius than in the age of Constantine, perhaps, or of Augustus, the alteration cannot be ascribed to any beneficial improvements which had gradually increased the stock of national riches. A long period of calamity or decay must have checked the industry and diminished the wealth of the people; and their profuse luxury must have been the result of that indolent despair which enjoys the present hour and declines the thoughts of futurity. The uncertain condition of their property discouraged the subjects of

Theodosius from engaging in those useful and laborious under-takings which require an immediate expense, and promise a slow and distant advantage. The frequent examples of ruin and desolation tempted them not to spare the remains of a patrimony which might, every hour, become the prey of the rapacious Goth. And the mad prodigality which prevails in the confusion of a shipwreck or a siege may serve to explain the progress of luxury amidst the misfortunes and terrors of a sinking nation.

The effeminate luxury, which infected the manners of courts and cities, had instilled a secret and destructive poison into the camps of the legions; and their degeneracy has been marked by the pen of a military writer, who had accurately studied the genuine and ancient principles of Roman discipline. It is the just and important observation of Vegetius, that the infantry was invariably covered with defensive armour from the foundation of the city to the reign of the emperor Gratian. The relaxation of discipline and the disuse of exercise rendered the soldiers less able and less willing to support the fatigues of the service; they complained of the weight of the armour, which they seldom wore; and they successively obtained the permission of laying aside both their cuirasses and their helmets. The heavy weapons of their ancestors, the short sword and the formidable *pilum*, which had subdued the world, insensibly dropped from their feeble hands. As the use of the shield is incompatible with that of the bow, they reluctantly marched into the field, condemned to suffer either the pain of wounds or the ignominy of flight, and always disposed to prefer the more shameful alternative. The cavalry of the Goths, the Huns, and the Alani, had felt the benefits and adopted the use of defensive armour; and, as they excelled in the management of missile weapons, they easily overwhelmed the naked and trembling legions, whose heads and breasts were exposed, without defence, to the arrows of the barbarians. The loss of armies, the destruction of cities, and the dishonour of the Roman name, ineffectually solicited the successors of Gratian to restore the helmets and cuirasses of the infantry. The enervated soldiers abandoned their own and the public defence; and their pusillanimous indolence may be considered as the immediate cause of the downfall of the empire.

XXVI

(378–420 A.D.) FINAL DESTRUCTION OF PAGANISM—INTRODUCTION OF THE WORSHIP OF SAINTS AND RELICS AMONG THE CHRISTIANS

The ruin of Paganism, in the age of Theodosius, is perhaps the only example of the total extirpation of any ancient and popular superstition, and may therefore deserve to be considered as a singular event in the history of the human mind. The Christians, more especially the clergy, had impatiently supported the prudent delays of Constantine and the equal toleration of the elder Valentinian; nor could they deem their conquest perfect or secure as long as their adversaries were permitted to exist. The influence which Ambrose and his brethren had acquired over the youth of Gratian and the piety of Theodosius was employed to infuse the maxims of persecution into the breasts of their Imperial proselytes. Two specious principles of religious jurisprudence were established, from whence they deduced a direct and rigorous conclusion against the subjects of the empire who still adhered to the ceremonies of their ancestors: *that* the magistrate is, in some measure, guilty of the crimes which he neglects to prohibit or to punish; and *that* the idolatrous worship of fabulous deities and real dæmons is the most abominable crime against the supreme majesty of the Creator. The laws of Moses and the examples of Jewish history were hastily, perhaps erroneously, applied by the clergy to the mild and universal reign of Christianity. The zeal of the emperors was excited to vindicate their own honour and that of the Deity; and the temples of the Roman world were subverted about sixty years after the conversion of Constantine.

The filial piety of the emperors themselves engaged them to proceed with some caution and tenderness in the reformation of the eternal city. Those absolute monarchs acted with less regard to the prejudices of the provincials. The pious labour, which had been suspended near twenty years since the death of Constantius, was vigorously resumed, and finally accomplished, by the zeal of Theodosius. Whilst that warlike prince yet struggled with the Goths, not for the glory, but for the safety of the republic, he ventured to offend a considerable party of his subjects, by some acts which might perhaps secure the protection of Heaven, but which must seem rash and unseasonable in the eye of human prudence. The success of his first experiments against the Pagans encouraged the pious emperor to reiterate and enforce his edicts of pro- scription: the same laws which had been originally published in the provinces of the East, were applied, after the defeat of Maximus, to the whole extent of the Western empire; and every victory of the orthodox Theodosius contributed to the triumph of the Christian and catholic faith. He attacked superstition in her most vital part, by prohibiting the use of sacrifices, which he declared to be criminal as well as infamous; and if the terms of his edicts more strictly condemned the impious curiosity which examined the entrails of the victims, every subsequent explanation tended to involve in the same guilt the general practice of *immolation*, which essentially constituted the religion of the Pagans. As the temples had been erected for the purpose of sacrifice, it was the duty of a benevolent prince to remove from his subjects the dangerous temptation of offending against the laws which he had enacted. A special commission was granted to Cynegius, the Prætorian præfect of the East, and afterwards to the counts Jovius and Gaudentius, two officers of distinguished rank in the West, by which they were directed to shut the temples, to seize or destroy the instruments of idolatry, to abolish the privileges of the priests, and to confiscate the consecrated property for the benefit of the emperor, of the church, or of the army. Here the desolation might have stopped: and the naked edifices, which were no longer employed in the service of idolatry, might have been protected from the destructive rage of fanaticism. Many of those temples were the most splendid and beautiful monuments of Grecian architecture: and the emperor himself was interested not to deface the splendour of his own cities, or to diminish the value of his own possessions. Those stately edifices might be suffered to remain, as so many lasting trophies of the victory of Christ. In the decline of the arts, they might be usefully converted into magazines, manufactures, or places of public assembly: and perhaps, when the walls of the temple had been sufficiently purified by holy rites, the worship of the true Deity might be allowed to expiate the ancient guilt of idolatry. But as long as they subsisted, the Pagans fondly cherished the secret hope that an auspicious revolution, a second Julian, might again restore the altars of the gods: and the earnestness with which they addressed their unavailing prayers to the throne increased the zeal of the Christian reformers to extirpate, without mercy, the root of superstition. The laws of the emperors exhibit some symptoms of a milder disposition: but their cold and languid efforts were insufficient to stem the torrent of enthusiasm and rapine, which was conducted, or rather impelled, by the spiritual rulers of the church. In Gaul, the holy Martin, bishop of Tours, marched at the head of his faithful monks to destroy the idols, the temples, and the consecrated trees of his extensive diocese; and, in the execution of this arduous task, the prudent reader will judge whether Martin was supported by the aid of miraculous powers or of carnal weapons.

The temples of the Roman empire were deserted or destroyed; but the ingenious superstition of the Pagans still attempted to elude the laws of Theodosius, by which all sacrifices had been severely prohibited. The inhabitants of the country, whose conduct was less exposed to the eye of malicious curiosity, disguised their *religious* under the appearance of *convivial* meetings. On the days of solemn festivals they assembled in great numbers under the spreading shade of some consecrated trees; sheep and oxen were slaughtered and roasted; and this rural entertainment was sanctified by the use of incense and by the hymns which were sung in honour of the gods. But it was alleged that, as no part of the animal was made a burnt-offering, as no altar was provided to receive the blood, and as the previous oblation of salt cakes and the concluding ceremony of libations were carefully omitted, these festal meetings did not involve the guests in the guilt or penalty of an illegal sacrifice. Whatever might be the truth of the facts or the merit of the distinction, these vain pretences were swept away by the last edict of Theodosius, which inflicted a deadly wound on the superstition of the Pagans. This prohibitory law is expressed in the most absolute and comprehensive terms. "It is our will and pleasure," says the emperor, "that none of our subjects, whether magistrates or private citizens, however exalted or however humble may be their rank and condition, shall presume in any city or in any place to worship an inanimate idol by the sacrifice of a guiltless victim." The act of sacrificing and the practice of divination by the entrails of the victim are declared (without any regard to the object of the inquiry) a crime of high treason against the state, which can be expiated only by the death of the guilty. The rites of Pagan superstition which might seem less bloody and atrocious are abolished as highly injurious to the truth and honour of religion; luminaries, garlands, frankincense, and libations of wine are specially enumerated and condemned; and the harmless claims of the domestic genius, of the household gods, are included in this rigorous proscription. The use of any of these profane and illegal ceremonies subjects the offender to the forfeiture of the house or estate where they have been performed; and if he has artfully chosen the property of another for the scene of his impiety, he is compelled to discharge, without delay, a heavy fine of twenty-five pounds of gold, or more than one thousand pounds sterling. A fine not less considerable is imposed on the connivance of the secret enemies of religion who shall neglect the duty of their respective stations, either to reveal or to punish the guilt of idolatry. Such was the persecuting spirit of the laws of Theodosius, which were repeatedly enforced by his sons and grandsons, with the loud and unamimous applause of the Christian world.

In the cruel reigns of Decius and Diocletian Christianity had been proscribed, as a revolt from the ancient and hereditary religion of the empire; and the unjust suspicions which were entertained of a dark and dangerous faction were in some measure countenanced by the inseparable union and rapid conquests of the catholic church. But the same excuses of fear and ignorance cannot be applied to the Christian emperors, who violated the precepts of humanity and of the Gospel. The experience of ages had betrayed the weakness as well as folly of Paganism; the light of reason and of faith had already exposed to the greatest part of mankind the vanity of idols; and the declining sect, which still adhered to their worship, might have been permitted to enjoy in peace and obscurity the religious customs of their ancestors. Had the Pagans been animated by the undaunted zeal which possessed the minds of the primitive believers, the triumph of the church must have been stained with blood; and the martyrs of Jupiter and Apollo might have embraced the glorious opportunity of devoting their lives and fortunes at the foot of their altars. But such obstinate zeal was not congenial to the loose and careless temper of Polytheism. The violent and repeated strokes of the orthodox princes were broken by the soft and yielding substance against which they were directed; and the ready obedience of the Pagans protected them from the pains and penalties of the Theodosian Code. Instead of asserting that the authority of the gods was superior to that of the emperor, they desisted, with a plaintive murmur, from the use of those scared rites which their sovereign had condemned. If they were sometimes tempted by a sally of passion, or by the hopes of concealment, to indulge their favourite superstition, their humble repentance disarmed the severity of the Christian magistrate, and they seldom refused to atone for their rashness by submitting, with some secret reluctance, to the yoke of the Gospel. The churches were filled with the increasing multitude of these unworthy proselytes, who had conformed, from temporal motives, to the reigning religion; and whilst they devoutly imitated the postures and recited the prayers of the faithful, they satisfied their conscience by the silent and sincere invocation of the gods of antiquity. If the Pagans wanted patience to suffer, they wanted spirit to resist; and the scattered myriads, who deplored the ruin of the temples, yielded, without a contest, to the fortune of their adversaries. The disorderly opposition of the peasants of Syria and the populace of Alexandria to the rage of private fanaticism was silenced by the name and authority of the emperor.

The devotion of the poet or the philosopher may be secretly nourished by prayer, meditation, and study; but the exercise of public worship appears to be the only solid foundation of the religious sentiments of the people, which derive their force from imitation and habit. The interruption of that public exercise may consummate, in the period of a few years, the important work of a national revolution. The memory of theological opinions cannot long be preserved without the artificial helps of priests, of temples, and of books. The ignorant vulgar, whose minds are still agitated by the blind hopes and terrors of superstition, will be soon persuaded by their superiors to direct their vows to the reigning deities of the age; and will insensibly imbibe an ardent zeal for the support and propagation of the new doctrine, which spiritual hunger at first compelled them to accept. The generation that arose in the world after the promulgation of the Imperial laws was attracted within the pale of the catholic church: and so rapid, yet so gentle, was the fall of Paganism, that only twenty-eight years after the death of Theodosius the faint and minute vestiges were no longer visible to the eye of the legislator.

The honours of the saints and martyrs, after a feeble and ineffectual murmur of profane reason, were universally established;

and in the age of Ambrose and Jerom something was still deemed wanting to the sanctity of a Christian church, till it had been consecrated by some portion of holy relics, which fixed and inflamed the devotion of the faithful. In the long period of twelve hundred years, which elapsed between the reign of Constantine and the reformation of Luther, the worship of saints and relics corrupted the pure and perfect simplicity of the Christian model; and some symptoms of degeneracy may be observed even in the first generations which adopted and cherished this pernicious innovation. The satisfactory experience that the relics of saints were more valuable than gold or precious stones stimulated the clergy to multiply the treasures of the church. Without much regard for truth or probability, they invented names for skeletons, and actions for names. The fame of the apostles, and of the holy men who had imitated their virtues, was darkened by religious fiction. To the invincible band of genuine and primitive martyrs they added myriads of imaginary heroes, who had never existed, except in the fancy of crafty or credulous legendaries; and there is reason to suspect that Tours might not be the only diocese in which the bones of a malefactor were adored instead of those of a saint. A superstitious practice, which tended to increase the temptations of fraud and credulity, insensibly extinguished the light of history and of reason in the Christian world.

The innumerable miracles, of which the tombs of the martyrs were the perpetual theatre, revealed to the pious believer the actual state and constitution of the invisible world; and his religious speculations appeared to be founded on the firm basis of fact and experience. Whatever might be the condition of vulgar souls in the long interval between the dissolution and the resurrection of their bodies, it was evident that the superior spirits of the saints and martyrs did not consume that portion of their existence in silent and inglorious sleep. It was evident (without presuming to determine the place of their habitation, or the nature of their felicity) that they enjoyed the lively and active consciousness of their happiness, their virtue, and their powers; and that they had already secured the possession of their eternal reward. The enlargement of their intellectual faculties surpassed the measure of the human imagination; since it was proved by *experience* that they were capable of hearing and understanding the various petitions of their numerous votaries, who, in the same moment of time, but in the most distant parts of the world, invoked the name and assistance of Stephen or of Martin. The confidence of their petitioners was founded on the persuasion that the saints, who reigned with Christ, cast an eye of pity upon earth; that they were warmly interested in the prosperity of the catholic church; and that the individuals who imitated the example of their faith and piety were the peculiar and favourite objects of their most tender regard. Sometimes, indeed, their friendship might be influenced by considerations of a less exalted kind: they viewed with partial affection the places which had been consecrated by their birth, their residence, their death, their burial, or the possession of their relics. The meaner passions of pride, avarice, and revenge, may be deemed unworthy of a celestial breast; yet the saints themselves condescended to testify their grateful approbation of the liberality of their votaries; and the sharpest bolts of punishment were hurled against those impious wretches who violated their magnificent shrines, or disbelieved their supernatural power. Atrocious, indeed, must have been the guilt, and strange would have been the scepticism, of those men, if they had obstinately resisted the proofs of a divine agency, which the elements, the whole range of the animal creation, and even the subtle and invisible operations of the human mind, were compelled to obey. The immediate, and almost instantaneous, effects, that were supposed to follow the prayer, or the offence, satisfied the Christians of the ample measure of favour and authority which the saints enjoyed in the presence of the Supreme God; and it seemed almost superfluous to inquire whether they were continually obliged to intercede before the throne of grace, or whether they might not be permitted to exercise, according to the dictates of their benevolence and justice, the delegated powers of their subordinate ministry. The imagination, which had been raised by a painful effort to the contemplation and worship of the Universal Cause, eagerly embraced such inferior objects of adoration as were more proportioned to its gross conceptions and imperfect faculties The sublime and simple theology of the primitive Christians was gradually corrupted: and the MONARCHY of heaven, already clouded by metaphysical subtleties, was degraded by the introduction of a popular mythology which tended to restore the reign of polytheism.

As the objects of religion were gradually reduced to the standard of the imagination, the rites and ceremonies were introduced that seemed most powerfully to affect the senses of the vulgar. If, in the beginning of the fifth century, Tertullian, or

Lactantius, had been suddenly raised from the dead, to assist at the festival of some popular saint or martyr, they would have gazed with astonishment and indignation on the profane spectacle which had succeeded to the pure and spiritual worship of a Christian congregation. As soon as the doors of the church were thrown open, they must have been offended by the smoke of incense, the perfume of flowers, and the glare of lamps and tapers, which diffused, at noon-day, a gaudy, superfluous, and, in their opinion, a sacrilegious light. If they approached the balustrade of the altar, they made their way through the prostrate crowd, consisting, for the most part, of strangers and pilgrims, who resorted to the city on the vigil of the feast; and who already felt the strong intoxication of fanaticism, and, perhaps, of wine. Their devout kisses were imprinted on the walls and pavement of the sacred edifice; and their fervent prayers were directed, whatever might be the language of their church, to the bones, the blood, or the ashes of the saint, which were usually concealed, by a linen or silken veil, from the eyes of the vulgar. The Christians frequented the tombs of the martyrs, in the hope of obtaining, from their powerful intercession, every sort of spiritual, but more especially of temporal, blessings. They implored the preservation of their health, or the cure of their infirmities; the fruitfulness of their barren wives, or the safety and happiness of their children. Whenever they undertook any distant or dangerous journey, they requested that the holy martyrs would be their guides and protectors on the road; and if they returned without having experienced any misfortune, they again hastened to the tombs of the martyrs, to celebrate, with grateful thanksgivings, their obligations to the memory and relics of those heavenly patrons. The walls were hung round with symbols of the favours which they had received; eyes, and hands, and feet, of gold and silver: and edifying pictures, which could not long escape the abuse of indiscreet or idolatrous devotion, represented the image, the attributes, and the miracles of the tutelar saint. The same uniform original spirit of superstition might suggest, in the most distant ages and countries, the same methods of deceiving the credulity, and of affecting the senses of mankind: but it must ingenuously be confessed that the ministers of the catholic church imitated the profane model which they were impatient to destroy. The most respectable bishops had persuaded themselves that the ignorant rustics would more cheerfully renounce the superstitions of Paganism, if they found some resemblance, some compensation, in the bosom of Christianity. The religion of Constantine achieved, in less than a century, the final conquest of the Roman empire: but the victors themselves were insensibly subdued by the arts of their vanquished rivals.

Gibbon's Chapter XXIX is chiefly concerned with the intrigues of the Eastern and Western courts: in the East with the ascendancy of the venal favourites Rufinus and Eutropius over Arcadius, in the West of the general Stilicho over Honorius. Of the latter Gibbon concludes by saying, "The son of Theodosius passed the slumber of his life a captive in his palace, a stranger in his country, and the patient, almost the indifferent, spectator of the ruin of the Western Empire, which was repeatedly attacked and finally subverted, by the arms of the barbarians. In the eventful history of a reign of twenty-eight years, it will seldom be necessary to mention the name of the emperor Honorius."

XXVII

(395–408 A.D.) REVOLT OF THE GOTHS—THEY PLUNDER GREECE—TWO GREAT INVASIONS OF ITALY BY ALARIC AND RADAGAISUS—THEY ARE REPULSED BY STILICHO—THE GERMANS OVERRUN GAUL—USURPATION OF CONSTANTINE IN THE WEST—DISGRACE AND DEATH OF STILICHO

If the subjects of Rome could be ignorant of their obligations to the great Theodosius, they were too soon convinced how painfully the spirit and abilities of their deceased emperor had supported the frail and mouldering edifice of the republic. He died in the month of January; and before the end of the winter of the same year, the Gothic nation was in arms. The barbarian auxiliaries erected their independent standard, and boldly avowed the hostile designs which they had long cherished in their ferocious minds. Their countrymen, who had been condemned by the conditions of the last treaty to a life of tranquillity and labour, deserted their farms at the first sound of the trumpet, and eagerly resumed the weapons which they had reluctantly laid down. The barriers of the Danube were thrown open; the savage warriors of Scythia issued from their forests; and the uncommon severity of the winter allowed the poet to remark "that they rolled their ponderous waggons over the broad and icy back of the indignant river." The unhappy natives of the provinces to the south of the Danube submitted to the calamities which, in the course of twenty years, were almost grown familiar to their imagination; and the various troops of barbarians who gloried in the Gothic name were irregularly spread from the woody shores of Dalmatia to the walls of Constantinople. The interruption, or at least the diminution, of the subsidy which the Goths had received from the prudent liberality of Theodosius, was the specious pretence of their revolt: the affront was embittered by their contempt for the unwarlike sons of Theodosius; and their resentment was inflamed by the weakness or treachery of the minister of Arcadius.

The frequent visits of Rufinus to the camp of the barbarians, whose arms and apparel he affected to imitate, were considered as a sufficient evidence of his guilty correspondence; and the public enemy, from a motive either of gratitude or of policy, was attentive, amidst the general devastation, to spare the private estates of the unpopular præfect. The Goths, instead of being impelled by the blind and headstrong passions of their chiefs, were now directed by the bold and artful genius of Alaric. That renowned leader was descended from the noble race of the Balti, which yielded only to the royal dignity of the Amali: he had solicited the command of the Roman armies; and the Imperial court provoked him to demonstrate the folly of their refusal, and the importance of their loss. Whatever hopes might be entertained of the conquest of Constantinople, the judicious general soon abandoned an impracticable enterprise. In the midst of a divided court and a discontented people, the emperor Arcadius was terrified by the aspect of the Gothic arms: but the want of wisdom and valour was supplied by the strength of the city; and the fortifications, both of the sea and land, might securely brave the impotent and random darts of the barbarians. Alaric disdained to trample any longer on the prostrate and ruined countries of Thrace and Dacia, and he resolved to seek a plentiful harvest of fame and riches in a province which had hitherto escaped the ravages of war.

The character of the civil and military officers on whom Rufinus had devolved the government of Greece confirmed the public suspicion that he had betrayed the ancient seat of freedom and learning to the Gothic invader. The proconsul Antiochus was the unworthy son of a respectable father; and Gerontius; who commanded the provincial troops, was much better qualified to execute the oppressive orders of a tyrant than to defend, with courage and ability, a country most remarkably fortified by the hand of nature. Alaric had traversed, without resistance, the plains of Macedonia and Thessaly, as far as the foot of Mount Oeta, a steep and woody range of hills, almost impervious to his cavalry. They stretched from east to west, to the edge of the sea-shore; and left, between the precipice and the Malian Gulf, an interval of three hundred feet, which in some places was contracted to a road capable of admitting only a single carriage. In this narrow pass of Thermopylæ, where Leonidas and the three hundred Spartans had gloriously devoted their lives, the Goths might have been stopped, or destroyed, by a skilful general; and perhaps the view of that sacred spot might have kindled some sparks of military ardour in the breasts of the degenerate Greeks. The troops which had been posted to defend the straits of Thermopylæ retired, as they were directed, without attempting to disturb the secure and rapid passage of Alaric; and the fertile fields of Phocis and Bœotia were instantly covered by a deluge of barbarians, who massacred the males of an age to bear arms, and drove away the beautiful females, with the spoil and cattle of the flaming villages. The travellers who visited Greece several years afterwards could easily discover the deep and bloody traces of the march of the Goths; and Thebes was less indebted for her preservation to the strength of her seven gates than to the eager haste of Alaric, who advanced to occupy the city of Athens and the important harbour of the Piræus.

A Grecian philosopher, who visited Constantinople soon after the death of Theodosius, published his liberal opinions concerning the duties of kings and the state of the Roman republic. Synesius observes and deplores the fatal abuse which the imprudent bounty of the late emperor had introduced into the military service. The citizens and subjects had purchased an exemption from the indispensable duty of defending their country, which was supported by the arms of barbarian mercenaries. He exhorts the emperor to revive the courage of his subjects by the example of manly virtue; to banish luxury from the court and from the camp; to substitute, in the place of the barbarian mercenaries, an army of men interested in the defence of their laws and of their property; to force, in such a moment of public danger, the mechanic from his shop and the philosopher from his school; to rouse the indolent citizen from his dream of pleasure; and to arm, for the protection of agriculture, the hands of the laborious husbandman. At the head of such troops, who might deserve the name and would display the spirit of Romans, he animates the son of Theodosius to encounter a race of barbarians who were destitute of any real courage; and never to lay down his arms till he had chased them far away into the solitudes of Scythia, or had reduced them to the state of ignominious servitude which the Lacedæmonians formerly imposed on the captive Helots. The court of Arcadius indulged the zeal, applauded the eloquence, and neglected the advice of Synesius. While the oration of Synesius and the downfall of the barbarians were the topics of popular conversation, an edict was published at Constantinople which declared the promotion of Alaric to the rank of master-general of the Eastern Illyricum. The Roman provincials, and the allies who had respected the faith of treaties, were justly indignant that the ruin of Greece and Epirus should be so liberally rewarded. The Gothic conqueror was received as a lawful magistrate in the cities which he had so lately besieged. The fathers whose sons he had massacred, the husbands whose wives he had violated, were subject to his authority; and the success of his rebellion encouraged the ambition of every leader of the foreign mercenaries. The use to which Alaric applied his new command distinguishes the firm and judicious character of his policy. He issued his orders to the four magazines and manufactures of offensive and defensive arms, Margus, Ratiaria, Naissus, and Thessalonica, to provide his troops with an extraordinary supply of shields, helmets, swords, and spears; the unhappy provincials were compelled to forge the instruments of their own destruction; and the barbarians removed the only defect which had sometimes disappointed the efforts of their courage. The birth of Alaric, the glory of his past exploits, and the confidence in his future designs, insensibly united the body of the nation under his victorious standards; and, with the unanimous consent of the barbarian chieftains, the master-general of Illyricum was elevated, according to ancient custom, on a shield, and solemnly proclaimed king of the Visigoths. Armed with this double power, seated on the verge of the two empires, he alternately sold his deceitful promises to the courts of Arcadius and Honorius, till he declared and executed his resolution of invading the dominions of the West. The provinces of Europe which belonged to the Eastern emperor were already exhausted, those of Asia were inaccessible, and the strength of Constantinople had resisted his attack. But he was tempted by the fame, the beauty, the wealth of Italy, which he had twice visited; and he secretly aspired to plant the Gothic standard on the walls of Rome, and to enrich his army with the accumulated spoils of three hundred triumphs.

The scarcity of facts, and the uncertainty of dates, oppose our attempts to describe the circumstances of the first invasion of Italy by the arms of Alaric. His march, perhaps from Thessalonica, through the warlike and hostile country of Pannonia, as far as the foot of the Julian Alps; his passage of those mountains, which were strongly guarded by troops and entrenchments; the siege of Aquileia, and the conquest of the provinces of Istria and Venetia, appear to have employed a considerable time. Unless his operations were extremely cautious and slow, the length of the interval would suggest a probable suspicion that the Gothic king retreated towards the banks of the Danube, and reinforced his army with fresh swarms of barbarians, before he again attempted to penetrate into the heart of Italy.

The emperor Honorius was distinguished, above his subjects, by the pre-eminence of fear as well as of rank. The pride and luxury in which he was educated had not allowed him to suspect that there existed on the earth any power presumptuous enough to invade the repose of the successor of Augustus. The arts of flattery concealed the impending danger till Alaric approached the palace of Milan. But when the sound of war had awakened the young emperor, instead of flying to arms with the spirit, or even the rashness, of his age, he eagerly listened to those timid counsellors who proposed to convey his sacred person and his faithful attendants to some secure and distant station in the provinces of Gaul. Stilicho alone had courage and authority to resist this disgraceful measure, which would have abandoned Rome and Italy to the barbarians; but as the troops of the palace had been lately detached to the Rhætian frontier, and as the resource of new levies was slow and precarious, the general of the West could only promise that, if the court of Milan would maintain their ground during his absence, he would soon return with an army equal to the encounter of the Gothic king. Without losing a moment (while each moment was so important to the public safety), Stilicho hastily embarked on the Larian lake, ascended the mountains of ice and snow amidst the severity of an Alpine winter, and suddenly repressed, by his unexpected presence, the enemy, who had disturbed the tranquillity of Rhætia. The barbarians, perhaps some tribes of the Alemanni, respected the firmness of a chief who still assumed the language of command; and the choice which he condescended to make of a select number of their bravest youth was considered as a mark of his esteem and favour. The cohorts, who were delivered from the neighbouring foe, diligently repaired to the Imperial standard; and Stilicho issued his orders to the most remote troops of the West, to advance, by rapid marches, to the defence of Honorius and of Italy. The fortresses of the Rhine were abandoned; and the safety of Gaul was protected only by the faith of the Germans, and the ancient terror of the Roman name. Even the legion which had been stationed to guard the wall of Britain against the Caledonians of the North was hastily recalled; and a numerous body of the cavalry of the Alani was persuaded to engage in the service of the emperor, who anxiously expected the return of his general. The prudence and vigour of Stilicho were conspicuous on this occasion, which revealed, at the same time, the weakness of the falling empire. The legions of Rome, which had long since languished in the gradual decay of discipline and courage, were exterminated by the Gothic and civil wars; and it was found impossible without exhausting and exposing the provinces, to assemble an army for the defence of Italy.

When Stilicho seemed to abandon his sovereign in the unguarded palace of Milan, he had probably calculated the term of his absence, the distance of the enemy, and the obstacles that might retard their march. He principally depended on the rivers of Italy, the Adige, the Mincius, the Oglio, and the Addua, which, in the winter or spring, by the fall of rains, or by the melting of the snows, are commonly swelled into broad and impetuous torrents. But the season happened to be remarkably dry; and the Goths could traverse, without impediment, the wide and stony beds, whose centre was faintly marked by the course of a shallow stream. The bridge and passage of the Addua was secured by a strong detachment of the Gothic army; and as Alaric approached the walls, or rather the suburbs, of Milan, he enjoyed the proud satisfaction of seeing the emperor of the Romans fly before him. Honorius, accompanied by a feeble train of statesmen and eunuchs, hastily retreated towards the Alps, with a design of securing his person in the city of Arles, which had often been the royal residence of his predecessors. But Honorius had scarcely passed the Po before he was overtaken by the speed of the Gothic cavalry; since the urgency of the danger compelled him to seek a temporary shelter within the fortification of Asta, a town of Liguria or Piemont, situate on the banks of the Tanarus. The siege of an obscure place, which contained so rich a prize, and seemed incapable of a long resistance, was instantly formed, and indefatigably pressed, by the king of the Goths; and the bold declaration, which the emperor might afterwards make, that his breast had never been susceptible of fear, did not probably obtain much credit even in his own court. In the last and almost hopeless extremity, after the barbarians had already proposed the indignity of a capitulation, the Imperial captive was suddenly relieved by the fame, the approach, and at length the presence, of the hero whom he had so long expected. At the head of a chosen and intrepid vanguard, Stilicho swam the stream of the Addua, to gain the time which he must have lost in the attack of the bridge; the passage of the Po was an enterprise of much less hazard and difficulty; and the successful action, in which he cut his way through the Gothic camp under the walls of Asta, revived the hopes and vindicated the honour of Rome. Instead of grasping the fruit of his victory, the barbarian was gradually invested, on every side, by the troops of the West, who successively issued through all the passes of the Alps; his quarters were straitened; his convoys were intercepted; and the vigilance of the Romans prepared to form a chain of fortifications, and to besiege the lines of the besiegers. A military council was assembled of the long-haired chiefs of the Gothic nation; of aged warriors, whose bodies were wrapped in furs, and whose stern countenances were marked with honourable wounds. They weighed the glory of persisting in their attempt against the advantage of securing their plunder; and they recommended the prudent measure of a seasonable retreat. In this important debate, Alaric displayed the spirit of the conqueror of Rome; and after he had reminded his countrymen of their achievements and of their designs, he concluded his animating speech by the solemn and positive assurance that he was resolved to find in Italy either a kingdom or a grave.

The capital was saved by the active and incessant diligence of Stilicho; but he respected the despair of his enemy; and, instead of committing the fate of the republic to the chance of another battle, he proposed to purchase the absence of the barbarians. The spirit of Alaric would have rejected such terms, the permission of a retreat, and the offer of a pension, with contempt and indignation; but he exercised a limited and precarious authority over the independent chieftains who had raised him, for *their* service, above the rank of his equals; they were still less disposed to follow an unsuccessful general, and many of them were tempted to consult their interest by a private negotiation with the minister of Honorius. The king submitted to the voice of his people, ratified the treaty with the empire of the West, and repassed the Po with the remains of the flourishing army which he had led into Italy. A considerable part of the Roman forces still continued to attend his motions: and Stilicho, who maintained a secret correspondence with some of the barbarian chiefs, was punctually appraised of the designs that were formed in the camp and council of Alaric. The king of the Goths, ambitious to signalise his retreat by some splendid achievement, had resolved to occupy the important city of Verona, which commands the principal passage of the Rhætian Alps; and, directing his march through the territories of those

German tribes whose alliance would restore his exhausted strength, to invade, on the side of the Rhine, the wealthy and unsuspecting provinces of Gaul. Ignorant of the treason which had already betrayed his bold and judicious enterprise, he advanced towards the passes of the mountains, already possessed by the Imperial troops; where he was exposed, almost at the same instant, to a general attack in the front, on his flanks, and in the rear. In this bloody action, at a small distance from the walls of Verona, the loss of the Goths was not less heavy than that which they had sustained in the defeat of Pollentia; and their valiant king, who escaped by the swiftness of his horse, must either have been slain or made prisoner, if the hasty rashness of the Alani had not disappointed the measures of the Roman general. Alaric secured the remains of his army on the adjacent rocks; and prepared himself, with undaunted resolution, to maintain a siege against the superior numbers of the enemy, who invested him on all sides. But he could not oppose the destructive progress of hunger and disease; nor was it possible for him to check the continual desertion of his impatient and capricious barbarians. In this extremity he still found resources in his own courage, or in the moderation of his adversary; and the retreat of the Gothic king was considered as the deliverance of Italy. Yet the people, and even the clergy, incapable of forming any rational judgment of the business of peace and war, presumed to arraign the policy of Stilicho, who so often vanquished, so often surrounded, and so often dismissed the implacable enemy of the republic. The first moment of the public safety is devoted to gratitude and joy; but the second is diligently occupied by envy and calumny.

The recent danger to which the person of the emperor had been exposed in the defenceless palace of Milan urged him to seek a retreat in some inaccessible fortress of Italy, where he might securely remain, while the open country was covered by a deluge of barbarians. On the coast of the Hadriatic, about ten or twelve miles from the most southern of the seven mouths of the Po, the Thessalians had founded the ancient colony of RAVENNA, which they afterwards resigned to the natives of Umbria. Augustus, who had observed the opportunity of the place, prepared, at the distance of three miles from the old town, a capacious harbour for the reception of two hundred and fifty ships of war. This naval establishment, which included the arsenals and magazines, the barracks of the troops, and the houses of the artificers, derived its origin and

name from the permanent station of the Roman fleet; the intermediate space was soon filled with buildings and inhabitants, and
the three extensive and populous quarters of Ravenna gradually
contributed to form one of the most important cities of Italy. The
principal canal of Augustus poured a copious stream of the waters
of the Po through the midst of the city, to the entrance of the
harbour; the same waters were introduced into the profound
ditches that encompassed the walls; they were distributed by a
thousand subordinate canals into every part of the city, which they
divided into a variety of small islands; the communication was
maintained only by the use of boats and bridges; and the houses
of Ravenna, whose appearance may be compared to that of Venice,
were raised on the foundation of wooden piles. The adjacent country,
to the distance of many miles, was a deep and impassable morass;
and the artificial causeway which connected Ravenna with the continent might be easily guarded or destroyed on the approach of an
hostile army. These morasses were interspersed, however, with
vineyards; and though the soil was exhausted by four or five crops,
the town enjoyed a more plentiful supply of wine than of fresh
water. The air, instead of receiving the sickly and almost pestilential
exhalations of low and marshy grounds, was distinguished, like the
neighbourhood of Alexandria, as uncommonly pure and salubrious;
and this singular advantage was ascribed to the regular tides of
the Hadriatic, which swept the canals, interrupted the unwholesome stagnation of the waters, and floated, every day, the vessels of
the adjacent country into the heart of Ravenna. The gradual retreat
of the sea has left the modern city at the distance of four miles
from the Hadriatic, and as early as the fifth or sixth century of the
Christian era the port of Augustus was converted into pleasant
orchards, and a lonely grove of pines covered the ground where
the Roman fleet once rode at anchor. Even this alteration contributed
to increase the natural strength of the place, and the shallowness
of the water was a sufficient barrier against the large ships of the
enemy. This advantageous situation was fortified by art and labour;
and in the twentieth year of his age the emperor of the West, anxious
only for his personal safety, retired to the perpetual confinement of
the walls and morasses of Ravenna. The example of Honorius was
imitated by his feeble successors, the Gothic kings, and afterwards
the Exarchs, who occupied the throne and palace of the emperors;
and till the middle of the eighth century Ravenna was considered
as the seat of government and the capital of Italy.

The fears of Honorius were not without foundation, nor were his precautions without effect. While Italy rejoiced in her deliverance from the Goths, a furious tempest was excited among the nations of Germany, who yielded to the irresistible impulse that appears to have been gradually communicated from the eastern extremity of the continent of Asia. The North must again have been alarmed and agitated by the invasion of the Huns; and the nations who retreated before them must have pressed with incumbent weight on the confines of Germany. The inhabitants of those regions which the ancients have assigned to the Suevi, the Vandals, and the Burgundians, might embrace the resolution of abandoning to the fugitives of Sarmatia their woods and morasses, or at least discharging their superfluous numbers on the provinces of the Roman empire. About four years after the victorious Toulun had assumed the title of Khan of the Geougen, another barbarian, the haughty Rhodogast, or Radagaisus, marched from the northern extremities of Germany almost to the gates of Rome, and left the remains of his army to achieve the destruction of the West. The Vandals, the Suevi, and the Burgundians, formed the strength of this mighty host; but the Alani, who had found an hospitable reception in their new seats, added their active cavalry to the heavy infantry of the Germans; and the Gothic adventurers crowded so eagerly to the standard of Radagaisus, that, by some historians, he has been styled the King of the Goths. Twelve thousand warriors, distinguished above the vulgar by their noble birth or their valiant deeds, glittered in the van; and the whole multitude, which was not less than two hundred thousand fighting men, might be increased, by the accession of women, of children, and of slaves, to the amount of four hundred thousand persons. This formidable emigration issued from the same coast of the Baltic which had poured forth the myriads of the Cimbri and Teutones to assault Rome and Italy in the vigour of the republic. After the departure of those barbarians, their native country, which was marked by the vestiges of their greatness, long ramparts and gigantic moles, remained, during some ages, a vast and dreary solitude; till the human species was renewed by the powers of generation, and the vacancy was filled by the influx of new inhabitants. The nations who now usurp an extent of land which they are unable to cultivate would soon be assisted by the industrious poverty of their neighbours, if the government of Europe did not protect the claims of dominion and property.

The correspondence of nations was in that age so imperfect and precarious, that the revolutions of the North might escape the knowledge of the court of Ravenna, till the dark cloud, which was collected along the coast of the Baltic, burst in thunder upon the banks of the Upper Danube. The emperor of the West, if his ministers disturbed his amusements by the news of the impending danger, was satisfied with being the occasion and the spectator of the war. The safety of Rome was intrusted to the counsels and the sword of Stilicho; but such was the feeble and exhausted state of the empire, that it was impossible to restore the fortifications of the Danube, or to prevent by a vigorous effort the invasion of the Germans. The hopes of the vigilant minister of Honorius were confined to the defence of Italy. He once more abandoned the provinces, recalled the troops, pressed the new levies, which, were rigorously exacted and pusillanimously eluded; employed the most efficacious means to arrest or allure the deserters; and offered the gift of freedom and of two pieces of gold to all the slaves who would enlist. By these efforts he painfully collected from the subjects of a great empire an army of thirty or forty thousand men, which, in the days of Scipio or Camillus, would have been instantly furnished by the free citizens of the territory of Rome. The thirty legions of Stilicho were reinforced by a large body of barbarian auxiliaries; the faithful Alani were personally attached to his service; and the troops of Huns and of Goths, who marched under the banners of their native princes Huldin and Sarus, were animated by interest and resentment to oppose the ambition of Radagaisus. The king of the confederate Germans passed without resistance the Alps, the Po, and the Apennine; leaving on one hand the inaccessible palace of Honorius securely buried among the marshes of Ravenna, and, on the other, the camp of Stilicho, who had fixed his head-quarters at Ticinum, or Pavia, but who seems to have avoided a decisive battle till he had assembled his distant forces. Many cities of Italy were pillaged or destroyed; and the siege of Florence by Radagaisus is one of the earliest events in the history of that celebrated republic, whose firmness checked and delayed the unskilful fury of the barbarians.

Florence was reduced to the last extremity; and the fainting courage of the citizens was supported only by the authority of St. Ambrose, who had communicated in a dream the promise of a speedy deliverance. On a sudden they beheld from their walls the banners of Stilicho, who advanced with his united force to the relief of the faithful city, and who soon marked that fatal spot for the grave of the barbarian host. The apparent contradictions of those writers who variously relate the defeat of Radagaisus, may be reconciled without offering much violence to their respective testimonies. Orosius and Augustin, who were intimately connected by friendship and religion, ascribe this miraculous victory to the providence of God rather than to the valour of man. They strictly exclude every idea of chance, or even of bloodshed, and positively affirm that the Romans, whose camp was the scene of plenty and idleness, enjoyed the distress of the barbarians slowly expiring on the sharp and barren ridge of the hills of Fæsulæ, which rise above the city of Florence. Their extravagant assertion that not a single soldier of the Christian army was killed, or even wounded, may be dismissed with silent contempt; but the rest of the narrative of Augustin and Orosius is consistent with the state of the war and the character of Stilicho. Conscious that he commanded the *last* army of the republic, his prudence would not expose it in the open field to the headstrong fury of the Germans. The method of surrounding the enemy with strong lines of circumvallation, which he had twice employed against the Gothic king, was repeated on a larger scale and with more considerable effect. The examples of Cæsar must have been familiar to the most illiterate of the Roman warriors; and the fortifications of Dyrrachium, which connected twenty-four castles by a perpetual ditch and rampart of fifteen miles, afforded the model of an entrenchment which might confine and starve the most numerous host of barbarians. The Roman troops had less degenerated from the industry than from the valour of their ancestors; and if the servile and laborious work offended the pride of the soldiers, Tuscany could supply many thousand peasants who would labour, though perhaps they would not fight, for the salvation of their native country. The imprisoned multitude of horses and men was gradually destroyed by famine rather than by the sword; but the Romans were exposed during the progress of such an extensive work to the frequent attacks of an impatient enemy. The despair of the hungry barbarians would precipitate them against the fortifications of Stilicho; the general might sometimes indulge the ardour of his brave auxiliaries, who eagerly pressed to assault the camp of the Germans; and these various incidents might produce the sharp and bloody conflict which dignify the narrative of Zosimus and the Chronicles of Prosper and Marcellinus. A seasonable supply of men and provisions had been introduced into the walls of Florence, and the famished host of Radagaisus was in its turn besieged. The proud monarch of so many warlike nations, after the loss of his bravest warriors, was reduced to confide either in the faith of a capitulation, or in the clemency of Stilicho. But the death of the royal captive, who was ignominiously beheaded, disgraced the triumph of Rome and of Christianity; and the short delay of his execution was sufficient to brand the conqueror with the guilt of cool and deliberate cruelty. The famished Germans who escaped the fury of the auxiliaries were sold as slaves, at the contemptible price of as many single pieces of gold; but the difference of food and climate swept away great numbers of those unhappy strangers; and it was observed that the inhuman purchasers, instead of reaping the fruits of their labour, were soon obliged to provide the expense of their interment. Stilicho informed the emperor and the senate of his success, and deserved a second time the glorious title of Deliverer of Italy.

After the defeat of Radagaisus, two parts of the German host, which must have exceeded the number of one hundred thousand men, still remained in arms between the Apennine and the Alps, or between the Alps and the Danube. It is uncertain whether they attempted to revenge the death of their general; but their irregular fury was soon diverted by the prudence and firmness of Stilicho, who opposed their march and facilitated their retreat, who considered the safety of Rome and Italy as the great object of his care, and who sacrificed with too much indifference the wealth and tranquillity of the distant provinces. The barbarians acquired, from the junction of some Pannonian deserters, the knowledge of the country and of the roads, and the invasion of Gaul, which Alaric had designed, was executed by the remains of the great army of Radagaisus.

Yet if they expected to derive any assistance from the tribes of Germany who inhabited the banks of the Rhine, their hopes were disappointed. The Alemanni preserved a state of inactive neutrality, and the Franks distinguish their zeal and courage in the defence of the empire. When the limits of Gaul and Germany were shaken by the northern emigration, the Franks bravely encountered the single force of the Vandals, who, regardless of the lessons of adversity, had again separated their troops from the standard of their barbarian allies. They paid the penalty of their rashness; and twenty thousand Vandals, with their king Godigisclus, were slain in the field of battle. The whole people must have been extirpated if the squadrons of the Alani, advancing to their relief, had not trampled down the infantry of the Franks, who, after an honourable resistance, were compelled to relinquish the unequal contest. The victorious confederates pursued their march, and on the last day of the year, in a season when the waters of the Rhine were most probably frozen, they entered without opposition the defenceless provinces of Gaul. This memorable passage of the Suevi, the Vandals, the Alani, and the Burgundians, who never afterwards retreated, may be considered as the fall of the Roman empire in the countries beyond the Alps; and the barriers, which had so long separated the savage and the civilised nations of the earth, were from that fatal moment levelled with the ground.

While the peace of Germany was secured by the attachment of the Franks and the neutrality of the Alemanni, the subjects of Rome, unconscious of their approaching calamities, enjoyed the state of quiet and prosperity which had seldom blessed the frontiers of Gaul. Their flocks and herds were permitted to graze in the pastures of the barbarians; their huntsmen penetrated, without fear or danger, into the darkest recesses of the Hercynian wood. The banks of the Rhine were crowned, like those of the Tiber, with elegant houses and well-cultivated farms; and if a poet descended the river, he might express his doubt on which side was situated the territory of the Romans. This scene of peace and plenty was suddenly changed into a desert; and the prospect of the smoking ruins could alone distinguish the solitude of nature from the desolation of man. The flourishing city of Mentz was surprised and destroyed, and many thousand Christians were inhumanly massacred in the church. Worms perished after a long and obstinate siege; Strasburg, Spires, Rheims, Tournay, Arras, Amiens, experienced the cruel oppression of the German yoke; and the consuming flames of war spread from the banks of the Rhine over the greatest part of the seventeen provinces of Gaul. That rich and extensive country, as far as the ocean, the Alps, and the Pyrenees, was delivered to the barbarians, who drove before them in a promiscuous crowd the bishop, the senator, and the virgin, laden with the spoils of their houses and altars. The ecclesiastics, to whom we are indebted for this vague description of the public calamities, embraced the opportunity of exhorting the Christians to repent of the sins which had provoked the Divine Justice, and to renounce the perishable goods of a wretched and deceitful world. But as the Pelagian controversy, which attempts to sound the abyss of grace and predestination, soon became the serious employment of the Latin clergy, the Providence which had decreed, or foreseen, or permitted, such a train of moral and natural evils, was rashly weighed in the imperfect and fallacious balance of reason.

The spirit of revolt, which had formerly disturbed the age of Gallienus, was revived by the capricious violence of the soldiers; and the unfortunate, perhaps the ambitious, candidates, who were the objects of their choice, were the instruments, and at length the victims, of their passion. Marcus was the first whom they placed on the throne, as the lawful emperor of Britain and of the West. They violated, by the hasty murder of Marcus, the oath of fidelity which they had imposed on themselves; and *their* disapprobation of his manners may seem to inscribe an honourable epitaph on his tomb. Gratian was the next whom they adorned with the diadem and the purple; and, at the end of four months, Gratian experienced the fate of his predecessor. The memory of the great Constantine, whom the British legions had given to the church and to the empire, suggested the singular motive of their third choice. They discovered in the ranks a private soldier of the name of Constantine, and their impetuous levity had already seated him on the throne, before they perceived his incapacity to sustain the weight of that glorious appellation. Yet the authority of Constantine was less precarious, and his government was more successful, than the transient reigns of Marcus and of Gratian. The danger of leaving his inactive troops in those camps which had been twice polluted with blood and sedition urged him to attempt the reduction of the Western provinces. He landed at Boulogne with an inconsiderable force; and after he had reposed himself some days, he summoned the cities of Gaul, which had escaped the yoke of the barbarians, to acknowledge their lawful sovereign. They obeyed the summons without reluctance. The neglect of the court of Ravenna had absolved a deserted people from the duty of allegiance; their actual distress encouraged them to accept any circumstances of change, without apprehension, and, perhaps, with some degree of hope; and they might flatter themselves that the troops, the authority, and even the name of a Roman emperor, who fixed his residence in Gaul, would protect the unhappy country from the rage of the barbarians. The first successes of Constantine against the detached parties of the Germans were magnified by the voice of adulation into splendid and decisive victories, which the reunion and insolence of the enemy soon reduced to their just value. His negotiations procured a short and precarious truce; and if some tribes of the barbarians were engaged, by the liberality of his gifts and promises, to undertake the defence of the Rhine, these expensive and uncertain treaties, instead of restoring the pristine vigour of the Gallic frontier, served only to disgrace the majesty of the prince, and to exhaust what yet remained of the treasures of the republic.

Adversity had exercised and displayed the genius of Alaric; and the fame of his valour invited to the Gothic standard the bravest of the barbarian warriors, who, from the Euxine to the Rhine, were agitated by the desire of rapine and conquest. He had deserved the esteem, and he soon accepted the friendship, of Stilicho himself. Renouncing the service of the emperor of the East, Alaric concluded, with the court of Ravenna, a treaty of peace and alliance, by which he was declared master-general of the Roman armies throughout the præfecture of Illyricum; as it was claimed, according to the true and ancient limits, by the minister of Honorius. The execution of the ambitious design, which was either stipulated or implied in the articles of the treaty, appears to have been suspended by the formidable irruption of Radagaisus; and the neutrality of the Gothic king may perhaps be compared to the indifference of Cæsar, who, in the conspiracy of Catiline, refused either to assist or to oppose the enemy of the republic. After the defeat of the Vandals, Stilicho resumed his pretensions to the provinces of the East; appointed civil magistrates for the administration of justice and of the finances; and declared his impatience to lead to the gates of Constantinople the united armies of the Romans and of the Goths. The prudence, however, of Stilicho, his aversion to civil war, and his perfect knowledge of the weakness of the state, may countenance the suspicion that domestic peace, rather than foreign conquest, was the object of his policy; and that his principal care was to employ the forces of Alaric at a distance from Italy. This design could not long escape the penetration of the Gothic king, who continued to hold a doubtful, and perhaps a treacherous, correspondence with the rival courts; who protracted, like a dissatisfied mercenary, his languid operations of Thessaly and Epirus; and who soon returned to claim the extravagant reward of his ineffectual services. From his camp near Æmona, on the confines of Italy, he transmitted to the emperor of the West a long account of promises, of expenses, and of demands; called for immediate satisfaction, and clearly intimated the consequences of a refusal. Yet, if his conduct was hostile, his language was decent and dutiful. He humbly professed himself the friend of Stilicho, and the soldier of Honorius; offered his person and his troops to march, without delay, against the usurper of Gaul; and solicited, as a permanent retreat for the Gothic nation, the possession of some vacant province of the Western empire.

The political and secret transactions of two statesmen who laboured to deceive each other and the world must for ever have been concealed in the impenetrable darkness of the cabinet, if the debates of a popular assembly had not thrown some rays of light on the correspondence of Alaric and Stilicho. The necessity of finding some artificial support for a government which, from a principle, not of moderation, but of weakness, was reduced to negotiate with its own subjects, had insensibly revived the authority of the Roman senate: and the minister of Honorius respectfully consulted the legislative council of the republic. Stilicho assembled the senate in the palace of the Cæsars; represented, in a studied oration, the actual state of affairs; proposed the demands of the Gothic king; and submitted to their consideration the choice of peace or war. "The payment of a subsidy, which had excited the indignation of the Romans, ought not (such was the language of Stilicho) to be considered in the odious light either of a tribute or of a ransom, extorted by the menaces of a barbarian enemy. Alaric had faithfully asserted the just pretensions of the republic to the provinces which were usurped by the Greeks of Constantinople: he modestly required the fair and stipulated recompense of his services; and if he had desisted from the prosecution of his enterprise, he had obeyed, in his retreat, the peremptory, though private, letters of the emperor himself." These ostensible reasons, which faintly disguise the obscure intrigues of the palace of Ravenna, were supported by the authority of Stilicho; and obtained, after a warm debate, the reluctant approbation of the senate.

But the reign of Stilicho drew towards its end; and the proud minister might perceive the symptoms of his approaching disgrace. The troops, who still assumed the name and prerogatives of the Roman legions, were exasperated by the partial affection of Stilicho for the barbarians: and the people imputed to the mischievous policy of the minister the public misfortunes, which were the natural consequence of their own degeneracy. Yet Stilicho might have continued to brave the clamours of the people, and even of the soldiers, if he could have maintained his dominion over the feeble mind of his pupil. But the respectful attachment of Honorius was converted into fear, suspicion, and hatred. The crafty Olympius, who concealed his vices under the mask of Christian piety, had secretly undermined the benefactor by whose favour he was promoted to the honourable offices of the Imperial palace. Olympius revealed to the unsuspecting emperor, who had attained the twenty-fifth year of his age, that he was without weight or authority in his own government; and artfully alarmed his timid and indolent disposition by a lively picture of the designs of Stilicho, who already meditated the death of his sovereign, with the ambitious hope of placing the diadem on the head of his son Eucherius. The emperor was instigated by his new favourite to assume the tone of independent dignity; and the minister was astonished to find that secret resolutions were formed in the court and council, which were repugnant to his interest, or to his intentions. Instead of residing in the palace of Rome, Honorius declared that it was his pleasure to return to the secure fortress of Ravenna. On the first intelligence of the death of his brother Arcadius, he prepared to visit Constantinople, and to regulate, with the authority of a guardian, the provinces of the infant Theodosius. The representation of the difficulty and expense of such a distant expedition checked this strange and sudden sally of active diligence; but the dangerous project of showing the emperor to the camp of Pavia, which was composed of the Roman troops, the enemies of Stilicho and his barbarian auxiliaries, remained fixed and unalterable. The minister was pressed, by the advice of his confidant, Justinian, a Roman advocate, of a lively and penetrating genius, to oppose a journey so prejudicial to his reputation and safety. His strenuous, but ineffectual, efforts confirmed the triumph of Olympius; and the prudent lawyer withdrew himself from the impending ruin of his patron.

In the passage of the emperor through Bologna a mutiny of the guards was excited and appeased by the secret policy of Stilicho, who announced his instructions to decimate the guilty, and ascribed to his own intercession the merit of their pardon. After this tumult, Honorius embraced, for the last time, the minister whom he now considered as a tyrant, and proceeded on his way to the camp of Pavia, where he was received by the loyal acclamations of the troops who were assembled for the service of the Gallic war. On the morning of the fourth day he pronounced, as he had been taught, a military oration in the presence of the soldiers, whom the charitable visits and artful discourses of Olympius had prepared to execute a dark and bloody conspiracy. At the first signal they massacred the friends of Stilicho, the most illustrious officers of the empire; two Prætorian præfects, of Gaul and of Italy; two masters-general of the cavalry and infantry; the master of the offices, the quaestor, the treasurer, and the count of the domestics. Many lives were lost, many houses were plundered; the furious sedition continued to rage till the close of the evening; and the trembling emperor, who was seen in the streets of Pavia without his robes or diadem, yielded to the persuasions of his favourite, condemned the memory of the slain, and solemnly approved the innocence and fidelity of their assassins. The intelligence of the massacre of Pavia filled the mind of Stilicho with just and gloomy apprehensions, and he instantly summoned, in the camp of Bologna, a council of the confederate leaders who were attached to his service, and would be involved in his ruin. The impetuous voice of the assembly called aloud for arms and for revenge; to march, without a moment's delay, under the banners of a hero whom they had so often followed to victory; to surprise, to oppress, to extirpate the guilty Olympius and his degenerate Romans, and perhaps to fix the diadem on the head of their injured general. Instead of executing a resolution which might have been justified by success, Stilicho hesitated till he was irrecoverably lost. He was still ignorant of the fate of the emperor; he distrusted the fidelity of his own party; and he viewed with horror the fatal consequences of arming a crowd of licentious barbarians against the soldiers and people of Italy. The confederates, impatient of his timorous and doubtful delay, hastily retired with fear and indignation. At the hour of midnight Sarus, a Gothic warrior, renowned among the barbarians themselves for his strength and valour, suddenly invaded the camp of his benefactor, plundered the baggage, cut in pieces the faithful Huns who guarded his person, and penetrated to the tent, where the minister, pensive and sleepless, meditated on the dangers of his situation. Stilicho escaped with difficulty from the sword of the Goths, and after issuing a last and generous admonition to the cities of Italy to shut their gates against the barbarians, his confidence or his despair urged him to throw himself into Ravenna, which was already in the absolute possession of his enemies. Olympius, who had assumed the dominion of Honorius, was speedily informed that his rival had embraced, as a suppliant, the altar of the Christian church. The base and cruel disposition of the hypocrite was incapable of pity or remorse; but he piously affected to elude, rather than to violate, the privilege of the sanctuary. Count Heraclian, with a troop of soldiers, appeared at the dawn of day before the gates of the church of Ravenna. The bishop was satisfied by a solemn oath that the Imperial mandate only directed them to secure the person of Stilicho: but as soon as the unfortunate minister had been tempted beyond the holy threshold, he produced the warrant for his instant execution. Stilicho supported with calm resignation the injurious names of traitor and parricide; repressed the unseasonable zeal of his followers, who were ready to attempt an ineffectual rescue; and, with a firmness not unworthy of the last of the Roman generals, submitted his neck to the sword of Heraclian.

The servile crowd of the palace, who had so long adored the fortune of Stilicho, affected to insult his fall; and the most distant connection with the master-general of the West, which had so lately been a title to wealth and honours, was studiously denied, and rigorously punished. His family, united by a triple alliance with the family of Theodosius, might envy the condition of the meanest peasant. The flight of his son Eucherius was intercepted; and the death of that innocent youth soon followed the divorce of Thermantia, who filled the place of her sister Maria, and who, like Maria, had remained a virgin in the Imperial bed. The friends of Stilicho who had escaped the massacre of Pavia were persecuted by the implacable revenge of Olympius, and the most exquisite cruelty was employed to extort the confession of a treasonable and sacrilegious conspiracy. They died in silence; their firmness justified the choice, and perhaps absolved the innocence, of their patron; and the despotic power which could take his life without a trial, and stigmatise his memory without a proof, has no jurisdiction over the impartial suffrage of posterity. The services of Stilicho are great and manifest; his crimes, as they are vaguely stated in the language of flattery and hatred, are obscure, at least, and improbable. About four months after his death an edict was published, in the name of Honorius, to restore the free communication of the two empires, which had been so long interrupted by the *public enemy*. The minister, whose fame and fortune depended on the prosperity of the state, was accused of betraying Italy to the barbarians, whom he repeatedly vanquished at Pollentia, at Verona, and before the walls of Florence. His pretended design of placing the diadem on the head of his son Eucherius could not have been conducted without preparations or accomplices; and the ambitious father would not surely have left the future emperor, till the twentieth year of his age, in the humble station of tribune of the notaries. Even the religion of Stilicho was arraigned by the malice of his rival. The seasonable, and almost miraculous, deliverance was devoutly celebrated by the applause of the clergy, who asserted that the restoration of idols and the persecution of the church would have been the first measure of the reign of Eucherius. The son of Stilicho, however, was educated in the bosom of Christianity, which his father had uniformly professed and zealously supported. Serena had borrowed her magnificent necklace from the statue of Vesta; and the Pagans execrated the memory of the sacrilegious minister, by whose order the Sibylline books, the oracles of Rome, had been committed to the flames. The pride and power of Stilicho constituted his real guilt. An honourable reluctance to shed the blood of his countrymen appears to have contributed to the success of his unworthy rival; and it is the last humiliation of the character of Honorius, that posterity has not condescended to reproach him with his base ingratitude to the guardian of his youth and the support of his empire.

XXVIII

(408–449 A.D.) INVASION OF ITALY BY ALARIC—
ROME IS THRICE BESIEGED, AND AT LENGTH
PILLAGED, BY THE GOTHS—DEATH OF
ALARIC—THE GOTHS EVACUATE ITALY—
FALL OF CONSTANTINE—GAUL AND SPAIN
ARE OCCUPIED BY THE BARBARIANS—
INDEPENDENCE OF BRITAIN

In the arts of negotiation, as well as in those of war, the Gothic king maintained his superior ascendant over an enemy whose seeming changes proceeded from the total want of counsel and design. From his camp, on the confines of Italy, Alaric attentively observed the revolutions of the palace, watched the progress of faction and discontent, disguised the hostile aspect of a barbarian invader, and assumed the more popular appearance of the friend and ally of the great Stilicho; to whose virtues, when they were no longer formidable, he could pay a just tribute of sincere praise and regret. The pressing invitation of the malcontents, who urged the king of the Goths to invade Italy, was enforced by a lively sense of his personal injuries; and he might speciously complain that the Imperial ministers still delayed and eluded the payment of the four thousand pounds of gold which had been granted by the Roman senate either to reward his services or to appease his fury. His decent firmness was supported by an artful moderation, which contributed to the success of his designs. He required a fair and reasonable satisfaction; but he gave the strongest assurances that, as soon as he had obtained it, he would immediately retire. He refused to trust the faith of the Romans, unless Aëtius and Jason, the sons of two great officers of state, were sent as hostages to his camp: but he offered to deliver in exchange several of the noblest youths of the Gothic nation. The modesty of Alaric was interpreted by the ministers of Ravenna as a sure evidence of his weakness and fear. They disdained either to negotiate a treaty or to assemble an army; and with a rash confidence, derived only from their ignorance of the extreme danger, irretrievably wasted the decisive moments of peace and war. While they expected, in sullen silence, that the barbarians should evacuate the confines of Italy, Alaric, with bold and rapid marches, passed the Alps and the Po; hastily pillaged the cities of Aquileia, Altinum, Concordia, and Cremona, which yielded to his arms; increased his forces by the accession of thirty thousand auxiliaries; and, without meeting a single enemy in the field, advanced as far as the edge of the morass which protected the impregnable residence of the emperor of the West. Instead of attempting the hopeless siege of Ravenna, the prudent leader of the Goths proceeded to Rimini, stretched his ravages along the sea-coast of the Hadriatic, and meditated the conquest of the ancient mistress of the world. An Italian hermit, whose zeal and sanctity were respected by the barbarians themselves, encountered the victorious monarch, and boldly denounced the indignation of Heaven against the oppressors of the earth: but the saint himself was confounded by the solemn asseveration of Alaric that he felt a secret and præternatural impulse, which directed, and even compelled, his march to the gates of Rome. He felt that his genius and his fortune were equal to the most arduous enterprises; and the enthusiasm which he communicated to the Goths insensibly removed the popular and almost superstitious reverence of the nations for the majesty of the Roman name. His troops, animated by the hopes of spoil, followed the course of the Flaminian way, occupied the unguarded passes of the Apennine, descended into the rich plains of Umbria; and, as they lay encamped on the banks of the Clitumnus, might wantonly slaughter and devour the milk-white oxen which had been so long reserved for the use of Roman triumphs. A lofty situation and a seasonable tempest of thunder and lightning preserved the little city of Narni: but the king of the Goths, despising the ignoble prey, still advanced with unabated vigour; and after he had passed through the stately arches, adorned with the spoils of barbaric victories, he pitched his camp under the walls of Rome.

By a skilful disposition of his numerous forces, who impatiently watched the moment of an assault, Alaric encompassed the walls, commanded the twelve principal gates, intercepted all communication with the adjacent country, and vigilantly guarded the navigation of the Tiber, from which the Romans derived the surest and most plentiful supply of provisions. The first emotions of the nobles and of the people were those of surprise and indignation, that a vile barbarian should dare to insult the capital of the world; but their arrogance was soon humbled by misfortune; and their unmanly rage, instead of being directed against an enemy in arms, was meanly exercised on a defenceless and innocent victim. Perhaps in the person of Serena the Romans might have respected the niece of Theodosius, the aunt, nay even the adoptive mother, of the reigning emperor; they abhorred the widow of Stilicho; and they listened with credulous passion to the tale of calumny which accused her of maintaining a secret and criminal correspondence with the Gothic invader. Actuated, or overawed, by the same popular frenzy, the senate, without requiring any evidence of her guilt, pronounced the sentence of her death. Serena was ignominiously strangled; and the infatuated multitude were astonished to find that this cruel act of injustice did not immediately produce the retreat of the barbarians and the deliverance of the city. That unfortunate city gradually experienced the distress of scarcity, and at length the horrid calamities of famine. The daily allowance of three pounds of bread was reduced to one-half, to one-third, to nothing; and the price of corn still continued to rise in a rapid and extravagant proportion. The poorer citizens, who were unable to purchase the necessaries of life, solicited the precarious charity of the rich; and for a while the public misery was alleviated by the humanity of Læta, the widow of the emperor Gratian, who had fixed her residence at Rome, and consecrated, to the use of the indigent, the princely revenue which she annually received from the grateful successors of her husband. But these private and temporary donatives were insufficient to appease the hunger of a numerous people; and the progress of famine invaded the marble palaces of the senators themselves. The persons of both sexes, who had been educated in the enjoyment of ease and luxury, discovered how little is requisite to supply the demands of nature; and lavished their unavailing treasures of gold and silver to obtain the coarse and scanty sustenance which they would formerly have rejected with disdain. The food the most repugnant to sense or imagination, the aliments the most unwholesome and pernicious to the constitution, were eagerly devoured, and fiercely disputed, by the rage of hunger. A dark suspicion was entertained that some desperate wretches fed on the bodies of their fellow-creatures whom they had secretly murdered; and even mothers (such was the horrid conflict of the two most powerful instincts implanted by nature in the human breast), even mothers are said to have tasted the flesh of their slaughtered infants! Many thousands of the inhabitants of Rome expired in their houses, or in the streets, for want of sustenance; and as the public sepulchres without the walls were in the power of the enemy, the stench which arose from so many putrid and unburied carcasses infected the air; and the miseries of famine were succeeded and aggravated by the contagion of a pestilential disease. The assurances of speedy and effectual relief, which were repeatedly transmitted from the court of Ravenna, supported, for some time, the fainting resolution of the Romans, till at length the despair of any human aid tempted them to accept the offers of a præternatural deliverance. Pompeianus, præfect of the city, had been persuaded, by the art or fanaticism of some Tuscan diviners, that, by the mysterious force of spells and sacrifices, they could extract the lightning from the clouds, and point those celestial fires against the camp of the barbarians. The important secret was communicated to Innocent, the bishop of Rome; and the successor of St. Peter is accused, perhaps without foundation, of preferring the safety of the republic to the rigid severity of the Christian worship. But when the question was agitated in the senate; when it was proposed, as an essential condition, that those sacrifices should be performed in the Capitol, by the authority and in the presence of the magistrates; the majority of that respectable assembly, apprehensive either of the Divine or of the Imperial displeasure, refused to join in an act which appeared almost equivalent to the public restoration of Paganism.

The last resource of the Romans was in the clemency, or at least in the moderation, of the king of the Goths. The senate, who in this emergency assumed the supreme powers of government, appointed two ambassadors to negotiate with the enemy. This important trust was delegated to Basilius, a senator of Spanish extraction, and already conspicuous in the administration of provinces; and to John, the first tribune of the notaries, who was peculiarly qualified, by his dexterity in business, as well as by his former intimacy with the Gothic prince. When they were introduced into his presence, they declared, perhaps in a more lofty style than became their abject condition, that the Romans were resolved to maintain their dignity, either in peace or war; and that, if Alaric refused them a fair and honourable capitulation, he might sound his trumpets, and prepare to give battle to an innumerable people, exercised in arms and animated by despair. "The thicker the hay, the easier it is mowed," was the concise reply of the barbarian; and this rustic metaphor was accompanied by a loud and insulting laugh, expressive of his contempt for the menaces of an unwarlike populace, enervated by luxury before they were emaciated by famine. He then condescended to fix the ransom which he would accept as the price of his retreat from the walls of Rome: *all* the gold and silver in the city, whether it were the property of the state, or of individuals; *all* the rich and precious movables; and *all* the slaves who could prove their title to the name of *barbarians*. The ministers of the senate presumed to ask, in a modest and suppliant tone, "If such, O king! are your demands, what do you intend to leave us?" "YOUR LIVES," replied the haughty conqueror: they trembled and retired. Yet before they retired, a short suspension of arms was granted, which allowed some time for a more temperate negotiation. The stern features of Alaric were insensibly relaxed; he abated much of the rigour of his terms; and at length consented to raise the siege, on the immediate payment of five thousand pounds of gold, of thirty thousand pounds of silver, of four thousand robes of silk, of three thousand pieces of fine scarlet cloth, and of three thousand pounds weight of pepper. But the public treasury was exhausted; the annual rents of the great estates in Italy and the provinces were intercepted by the calamities of war; the gold and gems had been exchanged, during the famine, for the vilest sustenance; the hoards of secret wealth were still concealed by the obstinacy of avarice; and some remains of consecrated spoils afforded the only resource that could avert the impending ruin of the city. As soon as the Romans had satisfied the rapacious demands of Alaric, they were restored, in some measure, to the enjoyment of peace and plenty. Several of the gates were cautiously opened; the importation of provisions from the river and the adjacent country was no longer obstructed by the Goths; the citizens resorted in crowds to the free market which was held during three days in the suburbs; and while the merchants who undertook this gainful trade made a considerable profit, the future subsistence of the city was secured by the ample magazines which were deposited in the public and private granaries. A more regular discipline than could have been expected was maintained in the camp of Alaric; and the wise barbarian justified his regard for the faith of treaties, by the just severity with which he chastised a party of licentious Goths who had insulted some Roman citizens on the road to Ostia. His army, enriched by the contributions of the capital, slowly advanced into the fair and fruitful province of

Tuscany, where he proposed to establish his winter-quarters; and the Gothic standard became the refuge of forty thousand barbarian slaves, who had broke their chains, and aspired, under the command of their great deliverer, to revenge the injuries and the disgrace of their cruel servitude. About the same time he received a more honourable reinforcement of Goths and Huns, whom Adolphus, the brother of his wife, had conducted, at his pressing invitation, from the banks of the Danube to those of the Tiber, and who had cut their way, with some difficulty and loss, through the superior numbers of the Imperial troops. A victorious leader, who united the daring spirit of a barbarian with the art and discipline of a Roman general, was at the head of an hundred thousand fighting men; and Italy pronounced with terror and respect the formidable name of Alaric.

At the distance of fourteen centuries we may be satisfied with relating the military exploits of the conquerors of Rome, without presuming to investigate the motives of their political conduct. In the midst of his apparent prosperity, Alaric was conscious, perhaps, of some secret weakness, some internal defect; or perhaps the moderation which he displayed was intended only to deceive and disarm the easy credulity of the ministers of Honorius. The king of the Goths repeatedly declared that it was his desire to be considered as the friend of peace and of the Romans. Three senators, at his earnest request, were sent ambassadors to the court of Ravenna, to solicit the exchange of hostages and the conclusion of the treaty; and the proposals which he more clearly expressed during the course of the negotiations could only inspire a doubt of his sincerity, as they might seem inadequate to the state of his fortune. The barbarian still aspired to the rank of master-general of the armies of the West; he stipulated an annual subsidy of corn and money; and he chose the provinces of Dalmatia, Noricum, and Venetia for the seat of his new kingdom, which would have commanded the important communication between Italy and the Danube. If these modest terms should be rejected, Alaric showed a disposition to relinquish his pecuniary demands, and even to content himself with the possession of Noricum; an exhausted and impoverished country, perpetually exposed to the inroads of the barbarians of Germany. But the emperor was persuaded to assume a lofty tone of inflexible dignity, such as neither his situation nor his character could enable him to support; and a letter, signed with the name of Honorius, was immediately despatched to the Prætorian præfect, granting him a free permission to dispose of the public money, but sternly refusing to prostitute the military honours of Rome to the proud demands of a barbarian. This letter was imprudently communicated to Alaric himself; and the Goth, who in the whole transaction had behaved with temper and decency, expressed in the most outrageous language his lively sense of the insult so wantonly offered to his person and to his nation. The conference of Rimini was hastily interrupted; and the præfect Jovius, on his return to Ravenna, was compelled to adopt, and even to encourage, the fashionable opinions of the court. By his advice and example the principal officers of the state and army were obliged to swear that, without listening in *any* circumstances to *any* conditions of peace, they would still persevere in perpetual and implacable war against the enemy of the republic. This rash engagement opposed an insuperable bar to all future negotiation. The ministers of Honorius were heard to declare that, if they had only invoked the name of the Deity, they would consult the public safety, and trust their souls to the mercy of Heaven: but they had sworn by the sacred head of the emperor himself; they had touched in solemn ceremony that august seat of majesty and wisdom; and the violation of their oath would expose them to the temporal penalties of sacrilege and rebellion.

While the emperor and his court enjoyed with sullen pride the security of the marshes and fortifications of Ravenna, they abandoned Rome, almost without defence, to the resentment of Alaric. Yet such was the moderation which he still preserved, or affected, that as he moved with his army along the Flaminian way he successively despatched the bishops of the towns of Italy to reiterate his offers of peace, and to conjure the emperor that he would save the city and its inhabitants from hostile fire and the sword of the barbarians. These impending calamities were however averted, not indeed by the wisdom of Honorius, but by the prudence or humanity of the Gothic king, who employed a milder, though not less effectual, method of conquest. Instead of assaulting the capital he successfully directed his efforts against the *Port* of Ostia, one of the boldest and most stupendous works of Roman magnificence. The accidents to which the precarious subsistence of the city was continually exposed in a winter navigation and an open road had suggested to the genius of the first Cæsar the useful design which was executed under the reign of Claudius. The artifical moles which formed the narrow entrance advanced far into the sea, and firmly repelled the fury of the waves, while the largest vessels securely rode at anchor within three deep and capacious basins which received the northern branch of the Tiber about two miles from the ancient colony of Ostia. The Roman *Port* insensibly swelled to the size of an episcopal city, where the corn of Africa was deposited in spacious granaries for the use of the capital. As soon as Alaric was in possession of that important place he summoned the city to surrender at discretion; and his demands were enforced by the positive declaration that a refusal, or even a delay, should be instantly followed by the destruction of the magazines on which the life of the Roman people depended. The clamours of that people and the terror of famine subdued the pride of the senate; they listened without reluctance to the proposal of placing a new emperor on the throne of the unworthy Honorius; and the suffrage of the Gothic conqueror bestowed the purple on Attalus, præfect of the city. The grateful monarch immediately acknowledged his protector as master-general of the armies of the West; Adolphus, with the rank of count of the domestics, obtained the custody of the person of Attalus; and the two hostile nations seemed to be united in the closest bands of friendship and alliance.

The gates of the city were thrown open, and the new emperor of the Romans, encompassed on every side by the Gothic arms, was conducted in tumultuous procession to the palace of Augustus and Trajan. After he had distributed the civil and military dignities among his favourites and followers, Attalus convened an assembly of the senate, before whom, in a formal and florid speech, he asserted his resolution of restoring the majesty of the republic, and of uniting to the empire the provinces of Egypt and the East which had once acknowledged the sovereignty of Rome. Such extravagant promises inspired every reasonable citizen with a just contempt for the character of an unwarlike usurper, whose elevation was the deepest and most ignominious wound which the republic had yet sustained from the insolence of the barbarians. But the populace, with their usual levity, applauded the change of masters. The public discontent was favourable to the rival of Honorius; and the sectaries, oppressed by his persecuting edicts, expected some degree of countenance, or at least of toleration, from a prince who, in his native country of Ionia, had been educated in the Pagan superstition, and who had since received the sacrament of baptism from the hands of an Arian bishop. The first days of the reign of Attalus were fair and prosperous. An officer of confidence was sent with an inconsiderable body of troops to secure the obedience of Africa; the greatest part of Italy submitted to the terror of the Gothic powers; and though the city of Bologna made a vigorous and effectual resistance, the people of Milan, dissatisfied perhaps with the absence of Honorius, accepted with loud acclamations the choice of the Roman senate. At the head of a formidable army, Alaric conducted his royal captive almost to the gates of Ravenna; and a solemn embassy of the principal ministers—of Jovius the Prætorian præfect, of Valens, master of the cavalry and infantry, of the quæstor Potamius, and of Julian, the first of the notaries—was introduced with martial pomp into the Gothic camp. In the name of their sovereign they consented to acknowledge the lawful election of his competitor, and to divide the provinces of Italy and the West between the two emperors. Their proposals were rejected with disdain; and the refusal was aggravated by the insulting clemency of Attalus, who condescended to promise that if Honorius would instantly resign the purple he should be permitted to pass the remainder of his life in the peaceful exile of some remote island. So desperate indeed did the situation of the son of Theodosius appear to those who were the best acquainted with his strength and resources, that Jovius and Valens, his minister and his general, betrayed their trust, infamously deserted the sinking cause of their benefactor, and devoted their treacherous allegiance to the service of his more fortunate rival. Astonished by such examples of domestic treason, Honorius trembled at the approach of every servant, at the arrival of every messenger. He dreaded the secret enemies who might lurk in his capital, his palace, his bed-chamber; and some ships lay ready in the harbour of Ravenna to transport the abdicated monarch to the dominions of his infant nephew, the emperor of the East.

But there *is* a Providence (such at least was the opinion of the historian Procopius) that watches over innocence and folly, and the pretensions of Honorius to its peculiar care cannot reasonably be disputed. At the moment when his despair, incapable of any wise or manly resolution, meditated a shameful flight, a seasonable reinforcement of four thousand veterans unexpectedly landed in the port of Ravenna. To these valiant strangers, whose fidelity had not been corrupted by the factions of the court, he committed the walls and gates of the city, and the slumbers of the emperor were no longer disturbed by the apprehension of imminent and internal danger. The favourable intelligence which was received from Africa suddenly changed the opinions of men and the state of public affairs. The troops and officers whom Attalus had sent into that province were defeated and slain, and the active zeal of Heraclian maintained his own allegiance and that of his people. The faithful count of Africa transmitted a large sum of money, which fixed the attachment of the Imperial guards; and his vigilance in preventing the exportation of corn and oil introduced famine, tumult and discontent into the walls of Rome. The failure of the African expedition was the source of mutual complaint and recrimination in the party of Attalus, and the mind of his protector was insensibly alienated from the interest of a prince who wanted spirit to command or docility to obey. The most imprudent measures were adopted, without the knowledge or against the advice of Alaric, and the obstinate refusal of the senate to allow in the embarkation the mixture even of five hundred Goths, betrayed a suspicious and distrustful temper which in their situation was neither generous nor prudent. The resentment of the Gothic king was exasperated by the malicious arts of Jovius, who had been raised to the rank of patrician, and who afterwards excused his double perfidy by declaring without a blush that he had only *seemed* to abandon the service of Honorius more effectually to ruin the cause of the usurper. In a large plain near Rimini, and in the presence of an innumerable multitude of Romans and barbarians, the wretched Attalus was publicly despoiled of the diadem and purple; and those ensigns of royalty were sent by Alaric as the pledge of peace and friendship to the son of Theodosius. The officers who returned to their duty were reinstated in their employments, and even the merit of a tardy repentance was graciously allowed; but the degraded emperor of the Romans, desirous of life and insensible of disgrace, implored the permission of following the Gothic camp in the train of a haughty and capricious barbarian.

The degradation of Attalus removed the only real obstacle to the conclusion of the peace, and Alaric advanced within three miles of Ravenna to press the irresolution of the Imperial ministers, whose insolence soon returned with the return of fortune. His indignation was kindled by the report that a rival chieftain, that Sarus, the personal enemy of Adolphus, and the hereditary foe of the house of Balti, had been received into the palace. At the head of three hundred followers that fearless barbarian immediately sallied from the gates of Ravenna, surprised and cut in pieces a considerable body of Goths, re-entered the city in triumph, and was permitted to insult his adversary by the voice of a herald, who publicly declared that the guilt of Alaric had for ever excluded him from the friendship and alliance of the emperor. The crime and folly of the court of Ravenna was expiated a third time by the calamities of Rome. The king of the Goths, who no longer dissembled his appetite for plunder and revenge, appeared in arms under the walls of the capital; and the trembling senate, without any hopes of relief, prepared by a desperate resistance to delay the ruin of their country. But they were unable to guard against the secret conspiracy of their slaves and domestics, who either from birth or interest were attached to the cause of the enemy. At the hour of midnight the Salarian gate was silently opened, and the inhabitants were awakened by the tremendous sound of the Gothic trumpet. Eleven hundred and sixty-three years after the foundation of Rome, the Imperial city, which had subdued and civilised so considerable a part of mankind, was delivered to the licentious fury of the tribes of Germany and Scythia.

The proclamation of Alaric, when he forced his entrance into a vanquished city, discovered, however, some regard for the laws of humanity and religion. He encouraged his troops boldly to seize the rewards of valour, and to enrich themselves with the spoils of a wealthy and effeminate people; but he exhorted them at the same time to spare the lives of the unresisting citizens, and to respect the churches of the apostles St. Peter and St. Paul as holy and inviolable sanctuaries. Amidst the horrors of a nocturnal tumult several of the Christian Goths displayed the fervour of a recent conversion; and some instances of their uncommon piety and moderation are related, and perhaps adorned, by the zeal of ecclesiastical writers. While the barbarians roamed through the city in quest of prey, the humble dwelling of an aged virgin, who had devoted her life to the service of the altar, was forced open by one of the powerful Goths. He immediately demanded, though in civil language, all the gold and silver in her possession, and was astonished at the readiness with which she conducted him to a splendid hoard of massy plate of the richest materials and the most curious workmanship. The barbarian viewed with wonder and delight this valuable acquisition, till he was interrupted by a serious admonition, addressed to him in the following words: "These," said she, "are the consecrated vessels belonging to St. Peter: if you presume to touch them, the sacrilegious deed will remain on your conscience. For my part, I dare not keep what I am unable to defend."

The Gothic captain, struck with reverential awe, despatched a messenger to inform the king of the treasure which he had discovered, and received a peremptory order from Alaric, that all the consecrated plate and ornaments should be transported, without damage or delay, to the church of the apostle. From the extremity, perhaps, of the Quirinal hill to the distant quarter of the Vatican, a numerous detachment of Goths, marching in order of battle through the principal streets, protected with glittering arms the long train of their devout companions who bore aloft on their heads the sacred vessels of gold and silver, and the martial shouts of the barbarians were mingled with the sound of religious psalmody. From all the adjacent houses a crowd of Christians hastened to join this edifying procession, and a multitude of fugitives, without distinction of age or rank, or even of sect, had the good fortune to escape to the secure and hospitable sanctuary of the Vatican. The learned work concerning the *City of God* was professedly composed by St. Augustin, to justify the ways of Providence in the destruction of the Roman greatness. He celebrates with peculiar satisfaction this memorable triumph of Christ, and insults his adversaries by challenging them to produce some similar example of a town taken by storm, in which the fabulous gods of antiquity had been able to protect either themselves or their deluded votaries.

The retreat of the victorious Goths, who evacuated Rome on the sixth day, might be the result of prudence, but it was not surely the effect of fear. At the head of an army encumbered with rich and weighty spoils, their intrepid leader advanced along the Appian Way into the southern provinces of Italy, destroying whatever dared to oppose his passage, and contenting himself with the plunder of the unresisting country. Above four years elapsed from the successful invasion of Italy by the arms of Alaric, to the voluntary retreat of the Goths under the conduct of his successor Adolphus; and, during the whole time, they reigned without control over a country which, in the opinion of the ancients, had united all the various excellences of nature and art. The prosperity, indeed, which Italy had attained in the auspicious age of the Antonines, had gradually declined with the decline of the empire. The fruits of a long peace perished under the rude grasp of the barbarians; and they themselves were incapable of tasting the more elegant refinements of luxury which had been prepared for the use of the soft and polished Italians. Each soldier, however, claimed an ample portion of the substantial plenty, the corn and cattle, oil and wine, that was daily collected and consumed, in the Gothic camp; and the principal warriors insulted the villas and gardens, once inhabited by Lucullus and Cicero, along the beauteous coast of Campania. Their trembling captives, the sons and daughters of Roman senators, presented, in goblets of gold and gems, large draughts of Falernian wine to the haughty victors, who stretched their huge limbs under the shade of plane-trees, artificially disposed to exclude the scorching rays, and to admit the genial warmth, of the sun. These delights were enhanced by the memory of past hardships: the comparison of their native soil, the bleak and barren hills of Scythia, and the frozen banks of the Elbe and Danube, added new charms to the felicity of the Italian climate.

Whether fame, or conquest, or riches were the object of Alaric, he pursued that object with an indefatigable ardour which could neither be quelled by adversity nor satiated by success. No sooner had he reached the extreme land of Italy than he was attracted by the neighbouring prospect of a fertile and peaceful island. Yet even the possession of Sicily he considered only an intermediate step to the important expedition which he already meditated against the continent of Africa. The straits of Rhegium and Messina are twelve miles in length, and in the narrowest passage about one mile and a half broad; and the fabulous monsters of the deep, the rocks of Scylla and the whirlpool of Charybdis, could terrify none but the most timid and unskilled mariners. Yet as soon as the first division of the Goths had embarked, a sudden tempest arose, which sunk or scattered many of the transports; their courage was daunted by the terrors of a new element; and the whole design was defeated by the premature death of Alaric, which fixed, after a short illness, the fatal term of his conquests. The ferocious character of the barbarians was displayed in the funeral of a hero whose valour and fortune they celebrated with mournful applause. By the labour of a captive multitude they forcibly diverted the course of the Busentinus, a small river that washes the walls of Consentia. The royal sepulchre, adorned with the splendid spoils and trophies of Rome, was constructed in the vacant bed; the waters were then restored to their natural channel; and the secret spot where the remains of Alaric had been deposited was for ever concealed by the inhuman massacre of the prisoners who had been employed to execute the work.

The personal animosities and hereditary feuds of the barbarians were suspended by the strong necessity of their affairs; and the brave Adolphus, the brother-in-law of the deceased monarch, was unanimously elected to succeed to his throne. The character and political system of the new king of the Goths may be best understood from his own conversation with an illustrious citizen of Narbonne, who afterwards, in a pilgrimage to the Holy Land, related it to St. Jerom, in the presence of the historian Orosius. "In the full confidence of valour and victory, I once aspired (said Adolphus) to change the face of the universe; to obliterate the name of Rome; to erect on its ruins the dominion of the Goths; and to acquire, like Augustus, the immortal fame of the founder of a new empire. By repeated experiments I was gradually convinced that laws are essentially necessary to maintain and regulate a well-constituted state; and that the fierce untractable humour of the Goths was incapable of bearing the salutary yoke of laws and civil government. From that moment I proposed to myself a different object of glory and ambition; and it is now my sincere wish that the gratitude of future ages should acknowledge the merit of a stranger, who employed the sword of the Goths, not to subvert, but to restore and maintain, the prosperity of the Roman empire." With these pacific views the successor of Alaric suspended the operations of war, and seriously negotiated with the Imperial court a treaty of friendship and alliance. It was the interest of the ministers of Honorius, who were now released from the obligation of their extravagant oath, to deliver Italy from the intolerable weight of the Gothic powers, and they readily accepted their service against the tyrants and barbarians who infested the provinces beyond the Alps. Adolphus, assuming the character of a Roman General, directed his march from the extremity of Campania to the southern provinces of Gaul. His troops, either by force or agreement, immediately occupied the cities of Narbonne, Toulouse, and Bordeaux; and though they were repulsed by Count Boniface from the walls of Marseilles, they soon extended their quarters from the Mediterranean to the ocean. The oppressed provincials might exclaim that the miserable remnant which the enemy had spared was cruelly ravished by their pretended allies; yet some specious colours were not wanting to palliate or justify the violence of the Goths. The cities of Gaul which they attacked might perhaps be considered as in a state of rebellion against the government of Honorius: the articles of the treaty or the secret instructions of the court might sometimes be alleged in favour of the seeming usurpations of Adolphus; and the guilt of any irregular unsuccessful act of hostility might always be imputed, with an appearance of truth, to the ungovernable spirit of a barbarian host impatient of peace or discipline. The luxury of Italy had been less effectual to soften the temper than to relax the courage of the Goths; and they had imbibed the vices, without imitating the arts and institutions, of civilised society.

The victorious barbarians detained, either as a hostage or a captive, the sister of Honorius; but while she was exposed to the disgrace of following round Italy the motions of a Gothic camp, she experienced, however, a decent and respectful treatment. The authority of Jornandes, who praises the beauty of Placidia, may perhaps be counterbalanced by the silence, the expressive silence, of her flatterers: yet the splendour of her birth, the bloom of youth, the elegance of manners, and the dexterous insinuations which she condescended to employ, made a deep impression on the mind of Adolphus; and the Gothic king aspired to call himself the brother of the emperor. The ministers of Honorius rejected with disdain the proposal of an alliance so injurious to every sentiment of Roman pride; and repeatedly urged the restitution of Placidia as an indispensable condition of the treaty of peace. But the daughter of Theodosius submitted without reluctance to the desires of the conqueror, a young and valiant prince, who yielded to Alaric in loftiness of stature, but who excelled in the more attractive qualities of grace and beauty. The marriage of Adolphus and Placidia was consummated before the Goths retired from Italy; and the solemn, perhaps the anniversary, day of their nuptials was afterwards celebrated in the house of Ingenuus, one of the most illustrious citizens of Narbonne in Gaul. The bride, attired and adorned like a Roman empress, was placed on a throne of state; and the king of the Goths, who assumed on this occasion the Roman habit, contented himself with a less honourable seat by her side.

At a time when it was universally confessed that almost every man in the empire was superior in personal merit to the princes whom the accident of their birth had seated on the throne, a rapid succession of usurpers, regardless of the fate of their predecessors, still continued to arise. This mischief was peculiarly felt in the provinces of Spain and Gaul, where the principles of order and obedience had been extinguished by war and rebellion. Before Constantine resigned the purple, and in the fourth month of the siege of Arles, intelligence was received in the Imperial camp that Jovinus had assumed the diadem at Mentz, in the Upper Germany,

at the instigation of Goar, king of the Alani, and of Guntiarius, king
of the Burgundians; and that the candidate on whom they had
bestowed the empire advanced with a formidable host of barbarians from the banks of the Rhine to those of the Rhone. Every
circumstance is dark and extraordinary in the short history of the
reign of Jovinus. It was natural to expect that a brave and skilful
general, at the head of a victorius army, would have asserted, in a
field of battle, the justice of the cause of Honorius. The hasty
retreat of Constantius might be justified by weighty reasons; but he
resigned without a struggle the possession of Gaul; and Dardanus,
the Prætorian præfect, is recorded as the only magistrate who
refused to yield obedience to the usurper. When the Goths, two
years after the siege of Rome, established their quarters in Gaul, it
was natural to suppose that their inclinations could be divided only
between the emperor Honorius, with whom they had formed a
recent alliance, and the degraded Attalus, whom they reserved in
their camp for the occasional purpose of acting the part of a
musician or a monarch. Yet in a moment of disgust (for which it
is not easy to assign a cause or a date) Adolphus connected himself
with the usurper of Gaul; and imposed on Attalus the ignominious
task of negotiating the treaty which ratified his own disgrace. We
are again surprised to read, that, instead of considering the Gothic
alliance as the firmest support of his throne, Jovinus upbraided, in
dark and ambiguous language, the officious importunity of Attalus;
that, scorning the advice of his great ally, he invested with the
purple his brother Sebastian; and that he most imprudently
accepted the service of Sarus, when that gallant chief, the soldier
of Honorius, was provoked to desert the court of a prince who knew
not how to reward or punish. Adolphus, educated among a race of
warriors, who esteemed the duty of revenge as the most precious
and sacred portion of their inheritance, advanced with a body of
ten thousand Goths to encounter the hereditary enemy of the
house of Balti. He attacked Sarus at an unguarded moment, when
he was accompanied only by eighteen or twenty of his valiant
followers. United by friendship, animated by despair, but at length
oppressed by multitudes, this band of heroes deserved the esteem,
without exciting the compassion, of their enemies; and the lion was
no sooner taken in the toils than he was instantly despatched. The
death of Sarus dissolved the loose alliance which Adolphus still
maintained with the usurpers of Gaul. He again listened to the
dictates of love and prudence; and soon satisfied the brother of

Placidia, by the assurance that he would immediately transmit to the palace of Ravenna the heads of the two tyrants, Jovinus and Sebastian. The king of the Goths executed his promise without difficulty or delay: the helpless brothers, unsupported by any personal merit, were abandoned by their barbarian auxiliaries; and the short opposition of Valentia was expiated by the ruin of one of the oldest cities of Gaul. The emperor chosen by the Roman senate, who had been promoted, degraded, insulted, restored, again degraded, and again insulted, was finally abandoned to his fate; but when the Gothic king withdrew his protection, he was restrained, by pity or contempt, from offering any violence to the person of Attalus. The unfortunate Attalus, who was left without subjects or allies, embarked in one of the ports of Spain, in search of some secure and solitary retreat; but he was intercepted at sea, conducted to the presence of Honorius, led in triumph through the streets of Rome or Ravenna, and publicly exposed to the gazing multitude, on the second step of the throne of his *invincible* conqueror. The same measure of punishment with which, in the days of his prosperity, he was accused of menacing his rival, was inflicted on Attalus himself: he was condemned, after the amputation of two fingers, to a perpetual exile in the isle of Lipari, where he was supplied with the decent necessaries of life. The remainder of the reign of Honorius was undisturbed by rebellion; and it may be observed that in the space of five years seven usurpers had yielded to the fortune of a prince who was himself incapable either of counsel or of action.

The situation of Spain, separated on all sides from the enemies of Rome, by the sea, by the mountains, and by intermediate provinces, had secured the long tranquillity of that remote and sequestered country; and we may observe, as a sure symptom of domestic happiness, that, in a period of four hundred years, Spain furnished very few materials to the history of the Roman empire. The footsteps of the barbarians, who, in the reign of Gallienus, had penetrated beyond the Pyrenees, were soon obliterated by the return of peace; and in the fourth century of the Christian era, the cities of Emerita or Merida, of Corduba, Seville, Bracara, and Tarragona, were numbered with the most illustrious of the Roman world. The various plenty of the animal, the vegetable, and the mineral kingdoms, was improved and manufactured by the skill of an industrious people; and the peculiar advantages of naval stores contributed to support an extensive and profitable trade. The arts and sciences flourished under the protection of the emperors; and if the character of the Spaniards was enfeebled by peace and servitude, the hostile approach of the Germans, who had spread terror and desolation from the Rhine to the Pyrenees, seemed to rekindle some sparks of military ardour. As long as the defence of the mountains was intrusted to the hardy and faithful militia of the country, they successfully repelled the frequent attempts of the barbarians. But no sooner had the national troops been compelled to resign their post of the Honorian bands in the service of Constantine, than the gates of Spain were treacherously betrayed to the public enemy, about ten months before the sack of Rome by the Goths. The consciousness of guilt, and the thirst of rapine, prompted the mercenary guards of the Pyrenees to desert their station; to invite the arms of the Suevi, the Vandals, and the Alani; and to swell the torrent which was poured with irresistible violence from the frontiers of Gaul to the sea of Africa. The misfortunes of Spain may be described in the language of its most eloquent historian, who has concisely expressed the passionate, and perhaps exaggerated, declamations of contemporary writers. "The irruption of these nations was followed by the most dreadful calamities: as the barbarians exercised their indiscriminate cruelty on the fortunes of the Romans and the Spaniards, and ravaged with equal fury the cities and the open country. The progress of famine reduced the miserable inhabitants to feed on the flesh of their fellow-creatures; and even the wild beasts, who multiplied, without control, in the desert, were exasperated by the taste of blood and the impatience of hunger boldly to attack and devour their human prey. Pestilence soon appeared, the inseparable companion of famine; a large proportion of the people was swept away; and the groans of the dying excited only the envy of their surviving friends. At length the barbarians, satiated with carnage and rapine, and afflicted by the contagious evils which they themselves had introduced, fixed their permanent seats in the depopulated country. The ancient Gallicia, whose limits included the kingdom of Old Castille, was divided between the Suevi and the Vandals; the Alani were scattered over the provinces of Carthagena and Lusitania, from the Mediterranean to the Atlantic Ocean; and the fruitful territory of Bætica was allotted to the Silingi, another branch of the Vandalic nation. After regulating this partition, the conquerors contracted with their new subjects some reciprocal engagements of protection and obedience; the lands were again cultivated; and the towns and villages were again occupied by a captive people. The greatest part of the Spaniards was even disposed to prefer this new condition of poverty and barbarism to the severe oppressions of the Roman government; yet there were many who still asserted their native freedom, and who refused, more especially in the mountains of Gallicia, to submit to the barbarian yoke.

The important present of the heads of Jovinus and Sebastian had approved the friendship of Adolphus, and restored Gaul to the obedience of his brother Honorius. Peace was incompatible with the situation and temper of the king of the Goths. He readily accepted the proposal of turning his victorious arms against the barbarians of Spain; the troops of Constantius intercepted his communication with the seaports of Gaul, and gently pressed his march towards the Pyrenees: he passed the mountains, and surprised, in the name of the emperor, the city of Barcelona. The fondness of Adolphus for his Roman bride was not abated by time or possession; and the birth of a son, surnamed, from his illustrious grandsire, Theodosius, appeared to fix him for ever in the interest of the public. The loss of that infant, whose remains were deposited in a silver coffin in one of the churches near Barcelona, afflicted his parents; but the grief of the Gothic king was suspended by the labours of the field; and the course of his victories was soon interrupted by domestic treason. He had imprudently received into his service one of the followers of Sarus, a barbarian of a daring spirit, but of a diminutive stature, whose secret desire of revenging the death of his beloved patron was continually irritated by the sarcasms of his insolent master. Adolphus was assassinated in the palace of Barcelona; the laws of the succession were violated by a tumultuous faction; and a stranger to the royal race, Singeric, the brother of Sarus himself, was seated on the Gothic throne. The first act of his reign was the inhuman murder of the six children of Adolphus, the issue of a former marriage, whom he tore, without pity, from the feeble arms of a venerable bishop. The unfortunate Placidia, instead of the respectful compassion which she might have excited in the most savage breasts, was treated with cruel and wanton insult The daughter of the emperor Theodosius, confounded among a crowd of vulgar captives, was compelled to march on foot above twelve miles, before the horse of a barbarian, the assassin of an husband whom Placidia loved and lamented.

But Placidia soon obtained the pleasure of revenge; and the view of her ignominious sufferings might rouse an indignant people against the tyrant, who was assassinated on the seventh day of his usurpation. After the death of Singeric, the free choice of the nation bestowed the Gothic sceptre on Wallia, whose warlike and ambitious temper appeared, in the beginning of his reign, extremely hostile to the republic. He marched in arms from Barcelona to the shores of the Atlantic Ocean, which the ancients revered and dreaded as the boundary of the world. But when he reached the southern promontory of Spain, and, from the rock now covered by the fortress of Gibraltar, contemplated the neighbouring and fertile coast of Africa, Wallia resumed the designs of conquest which had been interrupted by the death of Alaric. The winds and waves again disappointed the enterprise of the Goths; and the minds of a superstitious people were deeply affected by the repeated disasters of storms and shipwrecks. In this disposition, the successor of Adolphus no longer refused to listen to a Roman ambassador, whose proposals were enforced by the real, or supposed, approach of a numerous army, under the conduct of the brave Constantius. A solemn treaty was stipulated and observed: Placidia was honourably restored to her brother; six hundred thousand measures of wheat were delivered to the hungry Goths; and Wallia engaged to draw his sword in the service of the empire. A bloody war was instantly excited among the barbarians of Spain; and the contending princes are said to have addressed their letters, their ambassadors, and their hostages, to the throne of the Western emperor, exhorting him to remain a tranquil spectator of their contest, the events of which must be favourable to the Romans by the mutual slaughter of their common enemies. The Spanish war was obstinately supported, during three campaigns, with desperate valour and various success; and the martial achievements of Wallia diffused through the empire the superior renown of the Gothic hero. He exterminated the Silingi, who had irretrievably ruined the elegant plenty of the province of Bætica. He slew, in battle, the king of the Alani; and the remains of those Scythian wanderers who escaped from the field, instead of choosing a new leader, humbly sought a refuge under the standard of the Vandals, with whom they were ever afterwards confounded. The Vandals themselves, and the Suevi, yielded to the efforts of the invincible Goths. The promiscuous multitude of barbarians, whose retreat had been intercepted, were driven into the mountains of Gallicia; where they still continued, in a narrow compass and on a barren soil, to exercise their domestic and implacable hostilities. In the pride of victory, Wallia was faithful to his engagements: he restored his Spanish conquests to the obedience of Honorius; and the tyranny of the

Imperial officers soon reduced an oppressed people to regret the time of their barbarian servitude. While the event of the war was still doubtful, the first advantages obtained by the arms of Wallia had encouraged the court of Ravenna to decree the honours of a triumph to their feeble sovereign. He entered Rome like the ancient conquerors of nations; and if the monuments of servile corruption had not long since met with the fate which they deserved, we should probably find that a crowd of poets and orators, of magistrates and bishops, applauded the fortune, the wisdom, and the invincible courage of the emperor Honorius.

Such a triumph might have been justly claimed by the ally of Rome, if Wallia, before he repassed the Pyrenees, had extirpated the seeds of the Spanish war. His victorious Goths, forty-three years after they had passed the Danube, were established, according to the faith of treaties, in the possession of the second Aquitain, a maritime province between the Garonne and the Loire, under the civil and ecclesiastical jurisdiction of Bordeaux. That metropolis, advantageously situated for the trade of the ocean, was built in a regular and elegant form; and its numerous inhabitants were distinguished among the Gauls by their wealth, their learning, and the politeness of their manners. The adjacent province, which has been fondly compared to the garden of Eden, is blessed with a fruitful soil and a temperate climate; the face of the country displayed the arts and the rewards of industry; and the Goths, after their martial toils, luxuriously exhausted the rich vineyards of Aquitain. The Gothic limits were enlarged by the additional gift of some neighbouring dioceses; and the successors of Alaric fixed their royal residence at Toulouse, which included five populous quarters, or cities, within the spacious circuit of its walls. About the same time, in the last years of the reign of Honorius, the GOTHS, the BURGUNDIANS, and the FRANKS, obtained a permanent seat and dominion in the provinces of Gaul. The liberal grant of the usurper Jovinus to his Burgundian allies was confirmed by the lawful emperor; the lands of the First, or Upper, Germany were ceded to those formidable barbarians; and they gradually occupied, either by conquest or treaty, the two provinces which still retain, with the titles of *Duchy* and of *County*, the national appellation of Burgundy. The Franks, the valiant and faithful allies of the Roman republic, were soon tempted to imitate the invaders whom they had so bravely resisted. Trèves, the capital of Gaul, was pillaged by their lawless bands; and the humble colony which they so long maintained in the district of Toxandria, in Brabant, insensibly multiplied along the banks of the Meuse and Scheld, till their independent power filled the whole extent of the Second, or Lower, Germany.

The odious name of conquerors was softened into the mild and friendly appellation of the *guests* of the Romans; and the barbarians of Gaul, more especially the Goths, repeatedly declared that they were bound to the people by the ties of hospitality, and to the emperor by the duty of allegiance and military service. The title of Honorius and his successors, their laws and their civil magistrates, were still respected in the provinces of Gaul, of which they had resigned the possession to the barbarian allies; and the kings, who exercised a supreme and independent authority over their native subjects, ambitiously solicited the more honourable rank of master-generals of the Imperial armies. Such was the involuntary reverence which the Roman name still impressed on the minds of those warriors who had borne away in triumph the spoils of the Capitol.

Whilst Italy was ravaged by the Goths, and a succession of feeble tyrants oppressed the provinces beyond the Alps, the British island separated itself from the body of the Roman empire. The regular forces which guarded that remote province had been gradually withdrawn; all Britain was abandoned, without defence, to the Saxon pirates and the savages of Ireland and Caledonia. The Britons, reduced to this extremity, no longer relied on the tardy and doubtful aid of a declining monarchy. They assembled in arms, repelled the invaders, and rejoiced in the important discovery of their own strength. Afflicted by similar calamities, and actuated by the same spirit, the Armorican provinces (a name which compre-hended the maritime countries of Gaul between the Seine and the Loire) resolved to imitate the example of the neighbouring island. They expelled the Roman magistrate, who acted under the authority of the usurper Constantine; and a free government was established among a people who had so long been subject to the arbitrary will of a master. The independence of Britain and Armorica was soon confirmed by Honorius himself, the lawful emperor of the West; and the letters by which he committed to the new states the care of their own safety might be interpreted as an absolute and perpetual abdication of the exercise and rights of sovereignty. This interpretation was, in some measure, justified by the event. After the usurpers of Gaul had successively fallen, the maritime provinces were restored to the empire. Yet their obedience was imperfect, and precarious: the vain, the inconstant, rebellious disposition of the people, was incompatible either with freedom or servitude; and Armorica, though it could not long maintain the form of a republic, was agitated by frequent and destructive revolts. Britain was irrecoverably lost. But as the emperors wisely acquiesced in the independence of a remote province, the separation was not embittered by the reproach of tyranny or rebellion; and the claims of allegiance and protection were succeeded by the mutual and voluntary offices of national friendship.

XXIX

(423–455 A.D.) DEATH OF HONORIUS—
VALENTINIAN III EMPEROR OF THE WEST—
ADMINISTRATION OF HIS MOTHER PLACIDIA—
AËTIUS AND BONIFACE—CONQUEST OF
AFRICA BY THE VANDALS

During a long and disgraceful reign of twenty-eight years, Honorius, emperor of the West, was separated from the friendship of his brother, and afterwards of his nephew, who reigned over the East; and Constantinople beheld, with apparent indifference and secret joy, the calamities of Rome. The strange adventures of Placidia gradually renewed and cemented the alliance of the two empires. The daughter of the great Theodosius had been the captive and the queen of the Goths; she lost an affectionate husband; she was dragged in chains by his insulting assassin; she tasted the pleasure of revenge, and was exchanged, in the treaty of peace, for six hundred thousand measures of wheat. After her return from Spain to Italy, Placidia experienced a new persecution in the bosom of her family. She was averse to a marriage which had been stipulated without her consent; and the brave Constantius, as a noble reward for the tyrants whom he had vanquished, received, from the hand of Honorius himself, the struggling and reluctant hand of the widow of Adolphus. But her resistance ended with the ceremony of the nuptials; nor did Placidia refuse to become the mother of Honoria and Valentinian the Third, or to assume and exercise an absolute dominion over the mind of her grateful husband. The generous soldier, whose time had hitherto been divided between social pleasure and military service, was taught new lessons of avarice and ambition: he extorted the title of Augustus; and the servant of Honorius was associated to the empire of the West. The death of Constantius, in the seventh month of his reign, instead of diminishing, seemed to increase, the power of Placidia; and the indecent familiarity of her brother, which might be no more than the symptoms of a childish affection, were universally attributed to incestuous love.

On a sudden, by some base intrigues of a steward and a nurse, this excessive fondness was converted into an irreconcilable quarrel: the debates of the emperor and his sister were not long confined within the walls of the palace; and as the Gothic soldiers adhered to their queen, the city of Ravenna was agitated with bloody and dangerous tumults, which could only be appeased by the forced or voluntary retreat of Placidia and her children. The royal exiles landed at Constantinople, soon after the marriage of Theodosius, during the festival of the Persian victories. They were treated with kindness and magnificence; but as the statues of the emperor Constantius had been rejected by the Eastern court, the title of Augusta could not decently be allowed to his widow. Within a few months after the arrival of Placidia a swift messenger announced the death of Honorius, the consequence of a dropsy; but the important secret was not divulged till the necessary orders had been despatched for the march of a large body of troops to the sea-coast of Dalmatia. The shops and the gates of Constantinople remained shut during seven days; and the loss of a foreign prince, who could neither be esteemed nor regretted, was celebrated with loud and affected demonstrations of the public grief.

In a monarchy which, according to various precedents, might be considered as elective, or hereditary, or patrimonial, it was impossible that the intricate claims of female and collateral succession should be clearly defined; and Theodosius, by the right of consanguinity or conquest, might have reigned the sole legitimate emperor of the Romans. For a moment, perhaps, his eyes were dazzled by the prospect of unbounded sway; but his indolent temper gradually acquiesced in the dictates of sound policy. He contented himself with the possession of the East; and wisely relinquished the laborious task of waging a distant and doubtful war against the barbarians beyond the Alps, or of securing the obedience of the Italians and Africans, whose minds were alienated by the irreconcilable difference of language and interest. Instead of listening to the voice of ambition, Theodosius resolved to imitate the moderation of his grandfather, and to seat his cousin Valentinian on the throne of the West. The royal infant was distinguished at Constantinople by the title of *Nobilissimus*: he was promoted, before his departure from Thessalonica, to the rank and dignity of *Cæsar*: and, after the conquest of Italy, the patrician Helion, by the authority of Theodosius, and in the presence of the senate, saluted Valentinian the Third by the name of Augustus, and solemnly invested him with the diadem and the Imperial purple. By the agreement of the three females who governed the Roman world, the son of Placidia was betrothed to Eudoxia, the daughter of Theodosius and Athenais; and, as soon as the lover and his bride had attained the age of puberty, this honourable alliance was faithfully accomplished. At the same time, as a compensation, perhaps, for the expenses of the war, the Western Illyricum was detached from the Italian dominions, and yielded to the throne of Constantinople. The emperor of the East acquired the useful dominion of the rich and maritime province of Dalmatia, and the dangerous sovereignty of Pannonia and Noricum, which had been filled and ravaged above twenty years by a promiscuous crowd of Huns, Ostrogoths, Vandals, and *Bavarians*. Theodosius and Valentinian continued to respect the obligations of their public and domestic alliance; but the unity of the Roman government was finally dissolved. By a positive declaration, the validity of all future laws was limited to the dominions of their peculiar author; unless he should think proper to communicate them, subscribed with his own hand, for the approbation of his independent colleague.

Valentinian, when he received the title of Augustus, was no more than six years of age; and his long minority was intrusted to the guardian care of a mother who might assert a female claim to the succession of the Western empire. Placidia envied, but she could not equal, the reputation and virtues of the wife and sister of Theodosius; the elegant genius of Eudocia, the wise and successful policy of Pulcheria. The mother of Valentinian was jealous of the power which she was incapable of exercising: she reigned twenty-five years, in the name of her son; and the character of that unworthy emperor gradually countenanced the suspicion that Placidia had enervated his youth by a dissolute education, and studiously diverted his attention from every manly and honourable pursuit. Amidst the decay of military spirit, her armies were commanded by two generals, Aëtius and Boniface, who may be deservedly named as the last of the Romans. Their union might have supported a sinking empire; their discord was the fatal and immediate cause of the loss of Africa. The invasion and defeat of Attila has immortalised the fame of Aëtius; and though time has thrown a shade over the exploits of his rival, the defence of Marseilles, and the deliverance of Africa, attest the military talents of Count Boniface. In the field of battle, in partial encounters, in single combats, he was still the terror of the barbarians: the clergy, and particularly his friend Augustin, were edified by the Christian piety which had once tempted him to retire from the world; the people applauded his spotless integrity; the army dreaded his equal and inexorable justice, which may be displayed in a very singular example. A peasant, who complained of the criminal intimacy between his wife and a Gothic soldier, was directed to attend his tribunal the following day: in the evening the count, who had diligently informed himself of the time and place of the assignation, mounted his horse, rode ten miles into the country, surprised the guilty couple, punished the soldier with instant death, and silenced the complaints of the husband, by presenting him, the next morning, with the head of the adulterer. The abilities of Aëtius and Boniface might have been usefully employed against the public enemies in separate and important commands; but the experience of their past conduct should have decided the real favour and confidence of the empress Placidia. In the melancholy season of her exile and distress, Boniface alone had maintained her cause with unshaken fidelity. But Aëtius possessed an advantage of singular moment in a female reign: he was present: he besieged with artful and assiduous flattery the palace of Ravenna; disguised his dark designs with the mask of loyalty and friendship; and at length deceived both his mistress and his absent rival, by a subtle conspiracy which a weak woman and a brave man could not easily suspect. He secretly persuaded Placidia to recall Boniface from the government of Africa; he secretly advised Boniface to disobey the Imperial summons: to the one, he represented the order as a sentence of death; to the other, he stated the refusal as a signal of revolt; and when the credulous and unsuspectful count had armed the province in his defence, Aëtius applauded his sagacity in foreseeing the rebellion which his own perfidy had excited. A temperate inquiry into the real motives of Boniface would have restored a faithful servant to his duty and to the republic; but the arts of Aëtius still continued to betray and to inflame, and the count was urged by persecution to embrace the most desperate counsels The success with which he eluded or repelled the first attacks could not inspire a vain confidence that, at the head of some loose disorderly Africans, he should be able to withstand the regular forces of the West, commanded by a rival whose military character it was impossible for him to despise. After some hesitation, the last struggles of prudence and loyalty, Boniface despatched a trusty friend to the court, or rather to the camp, of Gonderic, king of the Vandals, with the proposal of a strict alliance, and the offer of an advantageous and perpetual settlement.

After the retreat of the Goths the authority of Honorius had obtained a precarious establishment in Spain, except only in the province of Gallicia, where the Suevi and the Vandals had fortified their camps in mutual discord and hostile independence. The Vandals prevailed, and their adversaries were besieged in the Nervasian hills, between Leon and Oviedo, till the approach of Count Asterius compelled, or rather provoked, the victorious barbarians to remove the scene of the war to the plains of Bætica. The rapid progress of the Vandals soon required a more effectual opposition, and the master-general Castinus marched against them with a numerous army of Romans and Goths. Vanquished in battle by an inferior enemy, Castinus fled with dishonour to Tarragona; and this memorable defeat, which has been represented as the punishment, was most probably the effect, of his rash presumption. Seville and Carthagena became the reward, or rather the prey, of the ferocious conquerors; and the vessels which they found in the harbour of Carthagena might easily transport them to the isles of Majorca and Minorca, where the Spanish fugitives, as in a secure recess, had vainly concealed their families and their fortunes. The experience of navigation, and perhaps the prospect of Africa, encouraged the Vandals to accept the invitation which they received from Count Boniface, and the death of Gonderic served only to forward and animate the bold enterprise. In the room of a prince not conspicuous for any superior powers of the mind or body, they acquired his bastard brother, the terrible Genseric; a name which in the destruction of the Roman empire has reserved an equal rank with the names of Alaric and Attila. The king of the Vandals is described to have been of a middle stature, with a lameness in one leg, which he had contracted by an accidental fall from his horse. His slow and cautious speech seldom declared the deep purposes of his soul: he disdained to imitate the luxury of the vanquished, but he indulged the sterner passions of anger and revenge. The ambition of Genseric was without bounds and without scruples, and the warrior could dexterously employ the dark engines of policy to solicit the allies who might be useful to his success, or to scatter among his enemies the seeds of hatred and contention. Almost in the moment of his departure he was informed that Hermanric, king of the Suevi, had presumed to ravage the Spanish territories which he was resolved to abandon.

Impatient of the insult, Genseric pursued the hasty retreat of the Suevi as far as Merida, precipitated the king and his army into the river Anas, and calmly returned to the sea-shore to embark his victorious troops. The vessels which transported the Vandals over the modern Straits of Gibraltar, a channel only twelve miles in breadth, were furnished by the Spaniards, who anxiously wished their departure, and by the African general, who had implored their formidable assistance.

Our fancy, so long accustomed to exaggerate and multiply the martial swarms of barbarians that seemed to issue from the North, will perhaps be surprised by the account of the army which Genseric mustered on the coast of Mauritania. The Vandals, who in twenty years had penetrated from the Elbe to Mount Atlas, were united under the command of their warlike king; and he reigned with equal authority over the Alani, who had passed within the term of human life from the cold of Scythia to the excessive heat of an African climate. The hopes of the bold enterprise had excited many brave adventurers of the Gothic nation, and many desperate provincials were tempted to repair their fortunes by the same means which had occasioned their ruin. Yet this various multitude amounted only to fifty thousand effective men; and though Genseric artfully magnified his apparent strength by appointing eighty *chiliarchs*, or commanders of thousands, the fallacious increase of old men, of children, and of slaves, would scarcely have swelled his army to the number of fourscore thousand persons. But his own dexterity and the discontents of Africa soon fortified the Vandal powers by the accession of numerous and active allies. The parts of Mauritania which border on the great desert and the Atlantic ocean were filled with a fierce and untractable race of men, whose savage temper had been exasperated rather than reclaimed by their dread of the Roman arms. The wandering Moors, as they gradually ventured to approach the sea-shore and the camp of the Vandals, must have viewed with terror and astonishment the dress, the armour, the martial pride and discipline of the unknown strangers who had landed on their coast; and the fair complexions of the blue-eyed warriors of Germany formed a very singular contrast with the swarthy or olive hue which is derived from the neighbourhood of the torrid zone. After the first difficulties had in some measure been removed, which arose from the mutual ignorance of their respective language, the Moors, regardless of any future consequence, embraced the alliance of the enemies of Rome, and a crowd of naked savages rushed from the woods and valleys of Mount Atlas, to satiate their revenge on the polished tyrants who had injuriously expelled them from the native sovereignty of the land.

The persecution of the Donatists was an event not less favourable to the designs of Genseric. Seventeen years before he landed in Africa, a public conference was held at Carthage by the order of the magistrate. The catholics were satisfied that, after the invincible reasons which they had alleged, the obstinacy of the schismatics must be inexcusable and voluntary, and the emperor Honorius was persuaded to inflict the most rigorous penalties on a faction which had so long abused his patience and clemency. Under these circumstances Genseric, a Christian, but an enemy of the orthodox communion, showed himself to the Donatists as a powerful deliverer, from whom they might reasonably expect the repeal of the odious and oppressive edicts of the Roman emperors. The conquest of Africa was facilitated by the active zeal or the secret favour of a domestic faction; the wanton outrages against the churches and the clergy, of which the Vandals are accused, may be fairly imputed to the fanaticism of their allies; and the intolerant spirit which disgraced the triumph of Christianity contributed to the loss of the most important province of the West.

The court and the people were astonished by the strange intelligence that a virtuous hero, after so many favours and so many services, had renounced his allegiance and invited the barbarians to destroy the province intrusted to his command. The friends of Boniface, who still believed that his criminal behaviour might be excused by some honourable motive, solicited, during the absence of Aëtius, a free conference with the Count of Africa; and Darius, an officer of high distinction, was named for the important embassy. In their first interview at Carthage the imaginary provocations were mutually explained, the opposite letters of Aëtius were produced and compared, and the fraud was easily detected. Placidia and Boniface lamented their fatal error, and the count had sufficient magnanimity to confide in the forgiveness of his sovereign, or to expose his head to her future resentment. His repentance was fervent and sincere; but he soon discovered that it was no longer in his power to restore the edifice which he had shaken to its foundations. Carthage and the Roman garrisons returned with their general to the allegiance of Valentinian, but the rest of Africa was still distracted with war and faction; and the inexorable king of the Vandals, disdaining all terms of accommodation, sternly refused to relinquish the possession of his prey. The band of veterans who marched under the standard of Boniface, and his hasty levies of provincial troops, were defeated with considerable loss; the victorious barbarians insulted the open country; and Carthage, Cirta, and Hippo Regius, were the only cities that appeared to rise above the general inundation.

The convulsions of Africa, which had favoured *Genseric's* attack, opposed the firm establishment of his power; and the various seditions of the Moors and Germans, the Donatists and catholics, continually disturbed or threatened the unsettled reign of the conqueror. As he advanced towards Carthage he was forced to withdraw his troops from the Western provinces; the sea-coast was exposed to the naval enterprises of the Romans of Spain and Italy; and, in the heart of Numidia, the strong inland city of Cirta still persisted in obstinate independence. These difficulties were gradually subdued by the spirit, the perseverance, and the cruelty of Genseric, who alternately applied the arts of peace and war to the establishment of his African kingdom. He subscribed a solemn treaty, with the hope of deriving some advantage from the term of its continuance and the moment of its violation. The vigilance of his enemies was relaxed by the protestations of friendship which concealed his hostile approach; and Carthage was at length surprised by the Vandals, five hundred and eighty-five years after the destruction of the city and republic by the younger Scipio.

A new city had arisen from its ruins, with the title of a colony; and though Carthage might yield to the royal prerogatives of Constantinople, and perhaps to the trade of Alexandria, or the splendour of Antioch, she still maintained the second rank in the West; as the *Rome* (if we may use the style of contemporaries) of the African world. That wealthy and opulent metropolis displayed, in a dependent condition, the image of a flourishing republic. Carthage contained the manufactures, the arms, and the treasures of the six provinces. A regular subordination of civil honours gradually ascended from the procurators of the streets and quarters of the city to the tribunal of the supreme magistrate, who, with the title of proconsul, represented the state and dignity of a consul of ancient Rome. Schools and *gymnasia* were instituted for the education of the African youth; and the liberal arts and manners, grammar, rhetoric, and philosophy, were publicly taught in the Greek and Latin languages. The buildings of Carthage were uniform and magnificent; a shady grove was planted in the midst of the capital; the *new* port, a secure and capacious harbour, was subservient to the commercial industry of citizens and strangers; and the splendid games of the circus and theatre were exhibited almost in the presence of the barbarians. The reputation of the Carthaginians was not equal to that of their country, and the reproach of Punic faith still adhered to their subtle and faithless character. The habits of trade and the abuse of luxury had corrupted their manners; but their impious contempt of monks and the shameless practice of unnatural lusts are the two abominations which excite the pious vehemence of Salvian, the preacher of the age. The king of the Vandals severely reformed the vices of a voluptuous people; and the ancient, noble, ingenuous freedom of Carthage (these expressions of Victor are not without energy) was reduced by Genseric into a state of ignominious servitude. After he had permitted his licentious troops to satiate their rage and avarice, he instituted a more regular system of rapine and oppression. An edict was promulgated, which enjoined all persons, without fraud or delay, to deliver their gold, silver, jewels, and valuable furniture or apparel to the royal officers; and the attempt to secrete any part of their patrimony was inexorably punished with death and torture as an act of treason against the state. The lands of the proconsular province, which formed the immediate district of Carthage, were accurately measured and divided among the barbarians; and the conqueror reserved for his peculiar domain the fertile territory of Byzacium and the adjacent parts of Numidia and Gætulia. It was natural enough that Genseric should hate those whom he had injured: the nobility and senators of Carthage were exposed to his jealousy and resentment; and all those who refused the ignominious terms which their honour and religion forbade them to accept were compelled by the Arian tyrant to embrace the condition of perpetual banishment.

XXX

(376–453 A.D.) THE CHARACTER, CONQUESTS, AND COURT OF ATTILA, KING OF THE HUNS— DEATH OF THEODOSIUS THE YOUNGER— ELEVATION OF MARCIAN TO THE EMPIRE OF THE EAST

The Western world was oppressed by the Goths and Vandals, who fled before the Huns; but the achievements of the Huns themselves were not adequate to their power and prosperity. Their victorious hordes had spread from the Volga to the Danube; but the public force was exhausted by the discord of independent chieftains; their valour was idly consumed in obscure and predatory excursions; and they often degraded their national dignity, by condescending, for the hopes of spoil, to enlist under the banners of their fugitive enemies. In the reign of ATTILA the Huns again became the terrors of the world; and I shall now describe the character and actions of that formidable barbarian, who alternately insulted and invaded the East and the West and urged the rapid downfall of the Roman Empire.

In the tide of emigration which impetuously rolled from the confines of China to those of Germany, the most powerful and populous tribes may commonly be found on the verge of the Roman provinces. The accumulated weight was sustained for a while by artificial barriers; and the easy condescension of the emperors invited, without satisfying, the insolent demands of the barbarians, who had acquired an eager appetite for the luxuries of civilised life. The Hungarians, who ambitiously insert the name of Attila among their native kings, may affirm with truth that the hordes which were subject to his uncle Roas, or Rugilas, had formed their encampments within the limits of modern Hungary, in a fertile country which liberally supplied the wants of a nation of hunters and shepherds.

Attila, the son of Mundzuk, deduced his noble, perhaps his regal, descent from the ancient Huns, who had formerly contended with the monarchs of China. His features, according to the observation of a Gothic historian, bore the stamp of his national origin; and the portrait of Attila exhibits the genuine deformity of a modern Calmuck; a large head, a swarthy complexion, small deep-seated eyes, a flat nose, a few hairs in the place of a beard, broad shoulders, and a short square body, of nervous strength, though of a disproportioned form. The haughty step and demeanour of the king of the Huns expressed the consciousness of his supe-riority above the rest of mankind; and he had a custom of fiercely rolling his eyes, as if he wished to enjoy the terror which he inspired. Yet this savage hero was not inaccessible to pity; his suppliant enemies might confide in the assurance of peace or pardon; and Attila was considered by his subjects as a just and indulgent master. He delighted in war; but, after he had ascended the throne in a mature age, his head, rather than his hand, achieved the conquest of the North; and the fame of an adventurous soldier was usefully exchanged for that of a prudent and successful general. The effects of personal valour are so inconsiderable, except in poetry or romance, that victory, even among barbarians, must depend on the degree of skill with which the passions of the multitude are combined and guided for the service of a single man. The Scythian conquerors, Attila and Zingis, surpassed their rude countrymen in art, rather than in courage; and it may be observed that the monarchies, both of the Huns and of the Moguls, were erected by their founders on the basis of popular superstition. The miraculous conception, which fraud and credulity ascribed to the virgin mother of Zingis, raised him above the level of human nature; and the naked prophet, who, in the name of the Deity, invested him with the empire of the earth, pointed the valour of the Moguls with irresistible enthusiasm. The religious arts of Attila were not less skillfully adapted to the character of his age and country. It was natural enough that the Scythians should adore, with peculiar devotion, the god of war; but as they were incapable of forming either an abstract idea or a corporeal representation, they worshipped their tutelar deity under the symbol of an iron cimeter. One of the shepherds of the Huns perceived that a heifer, who was grazing, had wounded herself in the foot, and curiously followed the track of the blood, till he discovered, among the long grass, the point of an ancient sword, which he dug out of the ground, and presented to Attila. That magnanimous, or rather that artful, prince accepted, with pious gratitude, this celestial favour;

and, as the rightful possessor of the *sword of Mars*, asserted his divine and indefeasible claim to the dominion of the earth. If the rites of Scythia were practised on this solemn occasion, a lofty altar, or rather pile of faggots, three hundred yards in length and in breadth, was raised in a spacious plain; and the sword of Mars was placed erect on the summit of this rustic altar, which was annually consecrated by the blood of sheep, horses, and of the hundredth captive. Whether human sacrifices formed any part of the worship of Attila, or whether he propitiated the god of war with the victims which he continually offered in the field of battle, the favourite of Mars soon acquired a sacred character, which rendered his conquests more easy and more permanent; and the barbarian princes confessed, in the language of devotion or flattery, that they could not presume to gaze, with a steady eye, on the divine majesty of the king of the Huns. His brother Bleda, who reigned over a considerable part of the nation, was compelled to resign his sceptre and his life. Yet even this cruel act was attributed to a supernatural impulse; and the vigour with which Attila wielded the sword of Mars convinced the world that it had been reserved alone for his invincible arm. But the extent of his empire affords the only remaining evidence of the number and importance of his victories; and the Scythian monarch, however ignorant of the value of science and philosophy, might perhaps lament that his illiterate subjects were destitue of the art which could perpetuate the memory of his exploits.

If a line of separation were drawn between the civilised and the savage climates of the globe; between the inhabitants of cities, who cultivated the earth, and the hunters and shepherds, who dwelt in tents, Attila might aspire to the title of supreme and sole monarch of the barbarians. He alone, among the conquerors of ancient and modern times, united the two mighty kingdoms of Germany and Scythia; and those vague appellations, when they are applied to his reign, may be understood with an ample latitude. Thuringia, which stretched beyond its actual limits as far as the Danube, was in the number of his provinces; he interposed, with the weight of a powerful neighbour, in the domestic affairs of the Franks; and one of his lieutenants chastised, and almost exterminated, the Burgundians of the Rhine. He subdued the islands of the ocean, the kingdoms of Scandinavia, encompassed and divided by the waters of the Baltic; and the Huns might derive a tribute of furs from that northern region, which has been protected from all other conquerors by the severity of the climate and the courage of the natives. Towards the East, it is difficult to circumscribe the dominion of Attila over the Scythian deserts; yet we may be assured that he reigned on the banks of the Volga; that the king of the Huns was dreaded, not only as a warrior, but as a magician; that he insulted and vanquished the khan of the formidable Geougen; and that he sent ambassadors to negotiate an equal alliance with the empire of China. In the proud review of the nations who acknowledged the sovereignty of Attila, and who never entertained, during his lifetime, the thought of a revolt, the Gepidæ and the Ostrogoths were distinguished by their numbers, their bravery, and the personal merit of their chiefs. The renowned Ardaric, king of the Gepidæ, was the faithful and sagacious counsellor of the monarch, who esteemed his intrepid genius, whilst he loved the mild and discreet virtues of the noble Walamir, king of the Ostrogoths. The crowd of vulgar kings, the leaders of so many martial tribes, who served under the standard of Attila, were ranged in the submissive order of guards and domestics round the person of their master. They watched his nod; they trembled at his frown; and at the first signal of his will, they executed, without murmur or hesitation, his stern and absolute commands. In time of peace, the dependent princes, with their national troops, attended the royal camp in regular succession; but when Attila collected his military force he was able to bring into the field an army of five, or, according to another account, of seven hundred thousand barbarians.

It may be affirmed with assurance that the Huns depopulated the provinces of the empire by the number of Roman subjects whom they led away into captivity. In the hands of a wise legislator such an industrious colony might have contributed to diffuse through the diserts of Scythia the rudiments of the useful and ornamental arts; but these captives, who had been taken in war, were accidentally dispersed among the hordes that obeyed the empire of Attila. The estimate of their respective value was formed by the simple judgment of unenlightened and unprejudiced barbarians. Perhaps they might not understand the merit of a theologian profoundly skilled in the controversies of the Trinity and the Incarnation; yet they respected the ministers of every religion; and the active zeal of the Christian missionaries, without approaching the person or the palace of the monarch, successfully laboured in the propagation of the gospel. The pastoral tribes, who were ignorant of the distinction of landed property, must have disregarded the use as well as the abuse of civil jurisprudence; and the skill of an eloquent lawyer could excite only their contempt or their abhorrence. The perpetual intercourse of the Huns and the Goths had communicated the familiar knowledge of the two national dialects; and the barbarians were ambitious of conversing in Latin, the military idiom even of the Eastern empire. But they disdained the language and the sciences of the Greeks; and the vain sophist or grave philosopher who had enjoyed the flattering applause of the schools, was mortified to find that his robust servant was a captive of more value and importance than himself. The mechanic arts were encouraged and esteemed, as they tended to satisfy the wants of the Huns. An architect in the service of Onegesius, one of the favourites of Attila, was employed to construct a bath: but this work was a rare example of private luxury; and the trades of the smith, the carpenter, the armourer, were much more adapted to supply a wandering people with the useful instruments of peace and war. But the merit of the physician was received with universal favour and respect: the barbarians, who despised death, might be apprehensive of disease; and the haughty conqueror trembled in the presence of a captive to whom he ascribed perhaps an imaginary power of prolonging or preserving his life. The Huns might be provoked to insult the misery of their slaves, over whom they exercised a despotic command; but their manners were not susceptible of a refined system of oppression, and the efforts of courage and diligence were often recompensed by the gift of freedom. The historian Priscus, whose embassy is a source of curious instruction, was accosted in the camp of Attila by a stranger, who saluted him in the Greek language, but whose dress and figure displayed the appearance of a wealthy Scythian. In the siege of Viminiacum he had lost, according to his own account, his fortune and liberty: he became the slave of Onegesius; but his faithful services against the Romans and the Acatzires had gradually raised him to the rank of the native Huns, to whom he was attached by the domestic pledges of a new wife and several children. The spoils of war had restored and improved his private property; he was admitted to the table of his former lord; and the apostate Greek blessed the hour of his captivity, since it had been the introduction to a happy and independent state, which he held by the honourable tenure of military service. This reflection naturally produced a dispute on the advantages and defects of the

Roman government, which was severely arraigned by the apostate, and defended by Priscus in a prolix and feeble declamation. The freedman of Onegesius exposed, in true and lively colours, the vices of a declining empire of which he had so long been the victim; the cruel absurdity of the Roman princes, unable to protect their subjects against the public enemy, unwilling to trust them with arms for their own defence; the intolerable weight of taxes, rendered still more oppressive by the intricate or arbitrary modes of collection; the obscurity of numerous and contradictory laws; the tedious and expensive forms of judicial proceedings; the partial administration of justice; and the universal corruption which increased the influence of the rich and aggravated the misfortunes of the poor. A sentiment of patriotic sympathy was at length revived in the breast of the fortunate exile, and he lamented with a flood of tears the guilt or weakness of those magistrates who had perverted the wisest and most salutary institutions.

The timid or selfish policy of the Western Romans had abandoned the Eastern empire to the Huns. The loss of armies and the want of discipline or virtue were not supplied by the personal character of the monarch. Theodosius might still affect the style as well as the title of *Invincible Augustus*, but he was reduced to solicit the clemency of Attila who imperiously dictated these harsh and humiliating conditions of peace. I. The emperor of the East resigned, by an express or tacit convention, an extensive and important territory which stretched along the southern banks of the Danube, from Singidunum, or Belgrade, as far as Novæ, in the diocese of Thrace. The breadth was defined by the vague computation of fifteen days' journey; but, from the proposal of Attila to remove the situation of the national market, it soon appeared that he comprehended the ruined city of Naissus within the limits of his dominions. II. The king of the Huns required and obtained that his tribute or subsidy should be augmented from seven hundred pounds of gold to the annual sum of two thousand one hundred; and he stipulated the immediate payment of six thousand pounds of gold to defray the expenses, or to expiate the guilt, of the war. One might imagine that such a demand, which scarcely equalled the measure of private wealth, would have been readily discharged by the opulent empire of the East; and the public distress affords a remarkable proof of the impoverished, or at least of the disorderly, state of the finances. A large proportion of the taxes extorted from the people was detained and intercepted in their passage through the foulest channels to the treasury of Constantinople. The revenue was dissipated by Theodosius and his favourites in wasteful and profuse luxury, which was disguised by the names of Imperial magnificence or Christian charity. The immediate supplies had been exhausted by the unforeseen necessity of military preparations. A personal contribution, rigorously but capriciously imposed on the members of the senatorian order, was the only expedient that could disarm without loss of time the impatient avarice of Attila: and the poverty of the nobles compelled them to adopt the scandalous resource of exposing to public auction the jewels of their wives and the hereditary ornaments of their palaces. III. The king of the Huns appears to have established as a principle of national jurisprudence, that he could never lose the property which he had once acquired in the persons who had yielded either a voluntary or reluctant submission to his authority. From this principle he concluded, and the conclusions of Attila were irrevocable laws, that the Huns who had been taken prisoners in war should be released without delay and without ransom; that every Roman captive who had presumed to escape should purchase his right to freedom at the price of twelve pieces of gold; and that all the barbarians who had deserted the standard of Attila should be restored without any promise or stipulation of pardon. In the execution of this cruel and ignominious treaty the Imperial officers were forced to massacre several loyal and noble deserters who refused to devote themselves to certain death; and the Romans forfeited all reasonable claims to the friendship of any Scythian people by this public confession that they were destitute either of faith or power to protect the suppliant who had embraced the throne of Theodosius.

The firmness of a single town, so obscure that except on this occasion it has never been mentioned by any historian or geographer, exposed the disgrace of the emperor and empire. Azimus, or Azimuntium, a small city of Thrace on the Illyrian borders, had been distinguished by the martial spirit of its youth, the skill and reputation of the leaders whom they had chosen, and their daring exploits against the innumerable host of the barbarians. Instead of tamely expecting their approach, the Azimuntines attacked, in frequent and successful sallies, the troops of the Huns, who gradually declined the dangerous neighbourhood, rescued from their hands the spoil and the captives, and recruited their domestic force by the voluntary association of fugitives and deserters. After the conclusion of the treaty Attila still menaced the empire with implacable war, unless the Azimuntines were persuaded or compelled to comply with the conditions which their sovereign had accepted. The ministers of Theodosius confessed, with shame and with truth, that they no longer possessed any authority over a society of men who so bravely asserted their natural independence; and the king of the Huns condescended to negotiate an equal exchange with the citizens of Azimus. They demanded the restitution of some shepherds, who with their cattle had been accidentally surprised. A strict though fruitless inquiry was allowed; but the Huns were obliged to swear that they did not detain any prisoners belonging to the city before they could recover two surviving countrymen whom the Azimuntines had reserved as pledges for the safety of their lost companions. Attila, on his side, was satisfied and deceived by their solemn asseveration that the rest of the captives had been put to the sword; and that it was their constant practice immediately to dismiss the Romans and the deserters who had obtained the security of the public faith. This prudent and officious dissimulation may be condemned or excused by the casuists as they incline to the rigid decree of St. Augustin, or the milder sentiment of St. Jerom and St. Chrysostom: but every soldier, every statesman, must acknowledge that, if the race of the Azimuntines had been encouraged and multiplied, the barbarians would have ceased to trample on the majesty of the empire.

The emperor Theodosius did not long survive the most humiliating circumstance of an inglorious life. As he was riding or hunting in the neighbourhood of Constantinople, he was thrown from his horse into the river Lycus: the spine of his back was injured by the fall; and he expired some days afterwards, in the fiftieth year of his age, and the forty-third of his reign. His sister Pulcheria, whose authority had been controlled both in civil and ecclesiastical affairs by the pernicious influence of the eunuchs, was unanimously proclaimed empress of the East; and the Romans, for the first time, submitted to a female reign. No sooner had Pulcheria ascended the throne than she indulged her own and the public resentment by an act of popular justice. Without any legal trial, the eunuch Chrysaphius was executed before the gates of the city; and the immense riches which had been accumulated by the rapacious favourite served only to hasten and to justify his punishment. Amidst the general acclamations of the clergy and people, the empress did not forget the prejudice and disadvantage to which her sex was exposed; and she wisely resolved to prevent their murmurs by the choice of a colleague who would always respect the superior rank and virgin chastity of his wife. She gave her hand to Marcian, a senator, about sixty years of age, and the nominal husband of Pulcheria was solemnly invested with the Imperial purple. The zeal which he displayed for the orthodox creed, as it was established by the council of Chalcedon, would alone have inspired the grateful eloquence of the catholics. But the behaviour of Marcian in a private life, and afterwards on the throne, may support a more rational belief that he was qualified to restore and invigorate an empire which had been almost dissolved by the successive weakness of two hereditary monarchs. He was born in Thrace, and educated to the profession of arms; but Marcian's youth had been severely exercised by poverty and misfortune, since his only resource, when he first arrived at Constantinople, consisted in two hundred pieces of gold which he had borrowed of a friend. He passed nineteen years in the domestic and military service of Aspar and his son Ardaburius; followed those powerful generals to the Persian and African wars; and obtained, by their influence, the honourable rank of tribune and senator. His mild disposition and useful talents, without alarming the jealousy, recommended Marcian to the esteem and favour of his patrons; he had seen, perhaps he had felt, the abuses of a venal and oppressive administration; and his own example gave weight and energy to the laws which he promulgated for the reformation of manners.

XXXI

(419–455 A.D.) INVASION OF GAUL BY ATTILA— HE IS REPULSED BY AËTIUS AND THE VISIGOTHS—ATTILA INVADES AND EVACU- ATES ITALY—DEATHS OF ATTILA, AËTIUS, AND VALENTINIAN THE THIRD

It was the opinion of Marcian, that war should be avoided as long as it is possible to preserve a secure and honourable peace; but it was likewise his opinion that peace cannot be honourable or secure, if the sovereign betrays a pusillanimous aversion to war. This temperate courage dictated his reply to the demands of Attila, who insolently pressed the payment of the annual tribute. The emperor signified to the barbarians that they must no longer insult the majesty of Rome by the mention of a tribute; that he was disposed to reward, with becoming liberality, the faithful friendship of his allies; but that, if they presumed to violate the public peace, they should feel that he possessed troops, and arms, and resolution, to repel their attacks. The same language, even in the camp of the Huns, was used by his ambassador Apollonius, whose bold refusal to deliver the presents, till he had been admitted to a personal interview, displayed a sense of dignity, and a contempt of danger, which Attila was not prepared to expect from the degenerate Romans. He threatened to chastise the rash successor of Theodosius; but he hesitated, whether he should first direct his invincible arms against the Eastern or the Western empire. While mankind awaited his decision with awful suspense, he sent an equal defiance to the courts of Ravenna and Constantinople; and his ministers saluted the two emperors with the same haughty declaration. "Attila, *my* lord, and *thy* lord, commands thee to provide a palace for his immediate reception." But as the barbarian despised, or affected to despise, the Romans of the East, whom he had so often vanquished, he soon declared his resolution of suspending the easy conquest till he had achieved a more glorious and important enterprise. In the memorable invasions of Gaul and Italy, the Huns were naturally attracted by the wealth and fertility of those provinces; but the particular motives and provocations of Attila can only be explained by the state of the Western empire under the reign of Valentinian, or, to speak more correctly, under the administration of Aëtius.

After the death of his rival Boniface, Aëtius had prudently retired to the tents of the Huns; and he was indebted to their alliance for his safety and his restoration. Instead of the suppliant language of a guilty exile, he solicited his pardon at the head of sixty thousand barbarians; and the empress Placidia confessed, by a feeble resistance, that the condescension which might have been ascribed to clemency was the effect of weakness or fear. She delivered herself, her son Valentinian, and the Western empire, into the hands of an insolent subject; nor could Placidia protect the son-in-law of Boniface, the virtuous and faithful Sebastian, from the implacable persecution which urged him from one kingdom to another, till he miserably perished in the service of the Vandals. The fortunate Aëtius, who was immediately promoted to the rank of patrician, and thrice invested with the honours of the consulship, assumed, with the title of master of the cavalry and infantry, the whole military power of the state; and he is sometimes styled, by contemporary writers, the duke, or general, of the Romans of the West. His prudence, rather than his virtue, engaged him to leave the grandson of Theodosius in the possession of the purple; and Valentinian was permitted to enjoy the peace and luxury of Italy, while the patrician appeared in the glorious light of a hero and a patriot, who supported near twenty years the ruins of the Western empire.

The kingdom established by the Visigoths in the southern provinces of Gaul had gradually acquired strength and maturity; and the conduct of those ambitious barbarians, either in peace or war, engaged the perpetual vigilance of Aëtius. After the death of Wallia, the Gothic sceptre devolved to Theodoric, the son of the great Alaric; and his prosperous reign of more than thirty years over a turbulent people may be allowed to prove that his prudence was supported by uncommon vigour, both of mind and body. Impatient of his narrow limits, Theodoric aspired to the possession of Arles, the wealthy seat of government and commerce; but the city was saved by the timely approach of Aëtius; and the Gothic king, who had raised the siege with some loss and disgrace, was persuaded, for an adequate subsidy, to divert the martial valour of his subjects in a Spanish war. Yet Theodoric still watched, and eagerly seized, the favourable moment of renewing his hostile attempts. The Goths besieged Narbonne, while the Belgic provinces were invaded by the Burgundians; and the public safety was threatened on every side by the apparent union of the enemies of Rome. On every side, the activity of Aëtius and his Scythian cavalry opposed a firm and successful resistance. Twenty thousand Burgundians were slain in battle; and the remains of the nation humbly accepted a dependent seat in the mountains of Savoy. The walls of Narbonne had been shaken by the battering engines, and the inhabitants had endured the last extremities of famine, when Count Litorius, approaching in silence, and directing each horseman to carry behind him two sacks of flour, cut his way through the entrenchments of the besiegers. The siege was immediately raised; and the more decisive victory, which is ascribed to the personal conduct of Aëtius himself, was marked with the blood of eight thousand Goths. But in the absence of the patrician, who was hastily summoned to Italy by some public or private interest, Count Litorius succeeded to the command; and his presumption soon discovered that far different talents are required to lead a wing of cavalry, or to direct the operations of an important war. At the head of an army of Huns, he rashly advanced to the gates of Toulouse, full of careless contempt for an enemy whom his misfortunes had rendered prudent, and his situation made desperate. The predictions of the augurs had inspired Litorius with the profane confidence that he should enter the Gothic capital in triumph; and the trust which he reposed in his Pagan allies encouraged him to reject the fair conditions of peace which were repeatedly proposed by the bishops in the name of Theodoric. The king of the Goths exhibited in his distress the edifying contrast of Christian piety and moderation; nor did he lay aside his sackcloth and ashes till he was prepared to arm for the combat. His soldiers, animated with martial and religious enthusiasm, assaulted the camp of Litorius. The conflict was obstinate; the slaughter was mutual. The Roman general, after a total defeat, which could be imputed only to his unskilful rashness, was actually led through the streets of Toulouse, not in his own, but in an hostile triumph; and the misery which he experienced, in a long and ignominious captivity, excited the compassion of the barbarians themselves. Such a loss, in a country whose spirit and finances were long since exhausted, could not easily be repaired; and the Goths, assuming, in their turn, the sentiments of ambition and revenge, would have planted their victorious standards on the banks of the Rhône, if the presence of Aëtius had not restored strength and discipline to the Romans. The two armies expected the signal of a decisive action; but the generals, who were conscious of each other's force, and doubtful of their own superiority, prudently sheathed their swords in the field of battle; and their reconciliation was permanent and sincere. Theodoric, king of the Visigoths, appears to have deserved the love of his subjects, the confidence of his allies, and the esteem of mankind.

The sister of Valentinian was educated in the palace of Ravenna; and as her marriage might be productive of some danger to the state, she was raised, by the title of *Augusta*, above the hopes of the most presumptuous subject. But the fair Honoria had no sooner attained the sixteenth year of her age than she detested the importunate greatness which must for ever exclude her from the comforts of honourable love: in the midst of vain and unsatisfactory pomp Honoria sighed, yielded to the impulse of nature, and threw herself into the arms of her chamberlain Eugenius. Her guilt and shame (such is the absurd language of imperious man) were soon betrayed by the appearances of pregnancy: but the disgrace of the royal family was published to the world by the imprudence of the empress Placidia, who dismissed her daughter, after a strict and shameful confinement, to a remote exile at Constantinople. The unhappy princess passed twelve or fourteen years in the irksome society of the sisters of Theodosius and their chosen virgins, to whose *crown* Honoria could no longer aspire, and whose monastic assiduity of prayer, fasting, and vigils she reluctantly imitated. Her impatience of long and hopeless celibacy urged her to embrace a strange and desperate resolution. The name of Attila was familiar and formidable at Constantinople, and his frequent embassies entertained a perpetual intercourse between his camp and the Imperial palace. In the pursuit of love, or rather of revenge, the daughter of Placidia sacrificed every duty and every prejudice, and offered to deliver her person into the arms of a barbarian of whose language she was ignorant, whose figure was scarcely human, and whose religion and manners she abhorred. By the ministry of a faithful eunuch she transmitted to Attila a ring, the pledge of her affection, and earnestly conjured him to claim her as a lawful spouse to whom he had been secretly betrothed. These indecent advances were received, however, with coldness and disdain; and the king of the Huns continued to multiply the number of his wives till his love was awakened by the more forcible passions of ambition and avarice. The invasion of Gaul was preceded and justified by a formal demand of the princess Honoria, with a just and equal share of the Imperial patrimony. His predecessors, the ancient Tanjous, had often addressed in the same hostile and peremptory manner the daughters of China; and the pretensions of Attila were not less offensive to the majesty of Rome. A firm but temperate refusal was communicated to his ambassadors. The right of female succession, though it might derive a specious argument from the recent examples of Placidia and Pulcheria, was strenuously denied, and the indissoluble engagements of Honoria were opposed to the claims of her Scythian lover. On the discovery of her connection with the king of the Huns, the guilty princess had been sent away, as an object of horror, from Constantinople to Italy: her life was spared, but the ceremony of her marriage was performed with some obscure and nominal husband before she was immured in a perpetual prison, to bewail those crimes and misfortunes which Honoria might have escaped had she not been born the daughter of an emperor.

A native of Gaul and a contemporary, the learned and eloquent Sidonius, who was afterwards bishop of Clermont, had made a promise to one of his friends that he would compose a regular history of the war of Attila. If the modesty of Sidonius had not discouraged him from the prosecution of this interesting work, the historian would have related with the simplicity of truth those memorable events to which the poet, in vague and doubtful metaphors, has concisely alluded. The kings and nations of Germany and Scythia, from the Volga perhaps to the Danube, obeyed the warlike summons of Attila. From the royal village in the plains of Hungary his standard moved towards the West, and after a march of seven or eight hundred miles he reached the conflux of the Rhine and the Neckar, where he was joined by the Franks who adhered to his ally, the elder of the sons of Clodion. A troop of light barbarians who roamed in quest of plunder might choose the winter for the convenience of passing the river on the ice, but the innumerable cavalry of the Huns required such plenty of forage and provisions as could be procured only in a milder season; the Hercynian forest supplied materials for a bridge of boats, and the hostile myriads were poured with resistless violence into the Belgic provinces. The consternation of Gaul was universal, and the various fortunes of its cities have been adorned by tradition with martyrdoms and miracles. Troyes was saved by the merits of St. Lupus; St. Servatius was removed from the world that he might not behold the ruin of Tongres; and the prayers of St. Genevieve diverted the march of Attila from the neighbourhood of Paris. But as the greatest part of the Gallic cities were alike destitute of saints and soldiers, they were besieged and stormed by the Huns, who practised, in the example of Metz, their customary maxims of war. They involved in a promiscuous massacre the priests who served at the altar and the infants who, in the hour of danger, had been providently baptised by the bishop; the flourishing city was delivered to the flames, and a solitary chapel of St. Stephen marked the place where it formerly stood. From the Rhine and the Moselle, Attila advanced into the heart of Gaul, crossed the Seine at Auxerre, and after a long and laborious march fixed his camp under the walls of Orleans.

The facility with which Attila had penetrated into the heart of Gaul may be ascribed to his insidious policy as well as to the terror of his arms. His public declarations were skilfully mitigated by his private assurances; he alternately soothed and threatened the Romans and the Goths; and the courts of Ravenna and Toulouse, mutually suspicious of each other's intentions, beheld with supine indifference the approach of their common enemy. Aëtius was the sole guardian of the public safety; but his wisest measures were embarrassed by a faction which, since the death of Placidia, infested the Imperial palace: the youth of Italy trembled at the sound of the trumpet; and the barbarians, who from fear or affection were inclined to the cause of Attila, awaited with doubtful and venal faith the event of the war. The patrician passed the Alps at the head of some troops whose strength and numbers scarcely deserved the name of an army. But on his arrival at Arles or Lyons he was confounded by the intelligence that the Visigoths, refusing to embrace the defence of Gaul, had determined to expect within their own territories the formidable invader whom they professed to despise. The senator Avitus, who after the honourable exercise of the Prætorian præfecture had retired to his estate in Auvergne, was persuaded to accept the important embassy, which he executed with ability and success. He represented to Theodoric that an ambitious conqueror who aspired to the dominion of the earth could be resisted only by the firm and unanimous alliance of the powers whom he laboured to oppress. The lively eloquence of Avitus inflamed the Gothic warriors by the description of the injuries which their ancestors had suffered from the Huns, whose implacable fury still pursued them from the Danube to the foot of the Pyrenees. He strenuously urged that it was the duty of every Christian to save from sacrilegious violation the churches of God and the relics of the saints; that it was the interest of every barbarian who had acquired a settlement in Gaul to defend the fields and vineyards, which were cultivated for his use, against the desolation of the Scythian shepherds. Theodoric yielded to the evidence of truth, adopted the measure at once the most prudent and the most honourable, and declared that as the faithful ally of Aëtius and the Romans he was ready to expose his life and kingdom for the common safety of Gaul. The Visigoths, who at that time were in the mature vigour of their fame and power, obeyed with alacrity the signal of war, prepared their arms and horses, and assembled under the standard of their aged king, who was resolved, with his two eldest sons, Torismond and Theodoric, to command in person his numerous and valiant people. The example of the Goths determined several tribes or nations that seemed to fluctuate between the Huns and the Romans. The indefatigable diligence of the patrician gradually collected the troops of Gaul and Germany, who had formerly acknowledged themselves the subjects or soldiers of the republic, but who now claimed the rewards of voluntary service and the rank of independent allies; the Læti, the Armoricans, the Breones, the Saxons, the Burgundians, the Sarmatians or Alani, the Ripuarians, and the Franks who followed Meroveus as their lawful prince. Such was the various army which, under the conduct of Aëtius and Theodoric, advanced by rapid marches to relieve Orleans, and to give battle to the innumerable host of Attila.

On their approach the king of the Huns immediately raised the siege, and sounded a retreat to recall the foremost of his troops from the pillage of a city which they had already entered. The valour of Attila was always guided by his prudence; and as he foresaw the fatal consequences of a defeat in the heart of Gaul, he repassed the Seine, and expected the enemy in the plains of Châlons, whose smooth and level surface was adapted to the operations of his Scythian cavalry. But in this tumultuary retreat the vanguard of the Romans and their allies continually pressed, and sometimes engaged, the troops whom Attila had posted in the rear; the hostile columns, in the darkness of the night and the perplexity of the roads, might encounter each other without design; and the bloody conflict of the Franks and Gepidæ, in which fifteen thousand barbarians were slain, was a prelude to a more general and decisive action. The Catalaunian fields spread themselves round Châlons, and extend, according to the vague measurement of Jornandes, to the length of one hundred and fifty, and the breadth of one hundred miles, over the whole province, which is entitled to the appellation of a *champaign* country. This spacious plain was distinguished, however, by some inequalities of ground; and the importance of an height which commanded the camp of Attila was understood and disputed by the two generals. The young and valiant Torismond first occupied the summit; the Goths rushed with irresistible weight on the Huns, who laboured to ascend from the opposite side: and the possession of this advantageous post inspired both the troops and their leaders with a fair assurance of victory. The anxiety of Attila prompted him to consult his priests and haruspices. It was reported that, after scrutinising the entrails of victims and scraping their bones, they revealed, in mysterious language, his own defeat, with the death of his principal adversary; and that the barbarian, by accepting the equivalent, expressed his involuntary esteem for the superior merit of Aëtius. The spirit of the barbarians was rekindled by the presence, the voice, and the example of their intrepid leader; and Attila, yielding to their impatience, immediately formed his order of battle. At the head of his brave and faithful Huns, he occupied in person the centre of the line. The nations subject to his empire, the Rugians, the Heruli, the Thuringians, the Franks, the Burgundians, were extended, on either hand, over the ample space of the Catalaunian fields; the right wing was commanded by Ardaric, king of the Gepidæ; and the three valiant brothers who reigned over the Ostrogoths were posted on the left to oppose the kindred tribes of the Visigoths. The disposition of the allies was regulated by a different principle. Sangiban, the faithless king of the Alani, was placed in the centre: where his motions might be strictly watched, and his treachery might be instantly punished. Aëtius assumed the command of the left, and Theodoric of the right wing; while Torismond still continued to occupy the heights which appear to have stretched on the flank, and perhaps the rear, of the Scythian army. The nations from the Volga to the Atlantic were assembled on the plain of Châlons; but many of these nations had been divided by faction, or conquest, or emigration; and the appearance of similar arms and ensigns, which threatened each other, presented the image of a civil war.

The discipline and tactics of the Greeks and Romans form an interesting part of their national manners. The attentive study of the military operations of Xenophon, or Cæsar, or Frederic, when they are described by the same genius which conceived and executed them, may tend to improve (if such improvement can be wished) the art of destroying the human species. But the battle of Châlons can only excite our curiosity by the magnitude of the object; since it was decided by the blind impetuosity of barbarians, and has been related by partial writers, whose civil or ecclesiastical profession secluded them from the knowledge of military affairs. Cassiodorus, however, had familiarly conversed with many Gothic warriors who served in that memorable engagement; "a conflict," as they informed him, "fierce, various, obstinate, and bloody; such as could not be paralleled either in the present or in past ages." The number of the slain amounted to one hundred and sixty-two thousand, or, according to another account, three hundred thousand persons; and these incredible exaggerations suppose a real and effective loss, sufficient to justify the historian's remark that whole generations may be swept away by the madness of kings in the space of a single hour. After the mutual and repeated discharge of missile weapons, in which the archers of Scythia might signalise their superior dexterity, the cavalry and infantry of the two armies were furiously mingled in closer combat. The Huns, who fought under the eyes of their king, pierced through the feeble and doubtful centre of the allies, separated their wings from each other, and wheeling, with a rapid effort, to the left, directed their whole force against the Visigoths. As Theodoric rode along the ranks to animate his troops, he received a mortal stroke from the javelin of Andages, a noble Ostrogoth, and immediately fell from his horse. The wounded king was oppressed in the general disorder and trampled under the feet of his own cavalry; and this important death served to explain the ambiguous prophecy of the haruspices. Attila already exulted in the confidence of victory, when the valiant Torismond descended from the hills, and verified the remainder of the prediction. The Visigoths, who had been thrown into confusion by the flight, or defection, of the Alani, gradually restored their order of battle; and the Huns were undoubtedly vanquished, since Attila was compelled to retreat. He had exposed his person with the rashness of a private soldier; but the intrepid troops of the centre had pushed forwards beyond the rest of the line; their attack was faintly supported; their flanks were unguarded; and the conquerors of Scythia and Germany were saved by the approach of the night from a total defeat.

The Imperial general was soon satisfied of the defeat of Attila, who still remained inactive within his entrenchments; and when he contemplated the bloody scene, he observed, with secret satisfaction, that the loss had principally fallen on the barbarians. The body of Theodoric, pierced with honourable wounds, was discovered under a heap of the slain: his subjects bewailed the death of their king and father; but their tears were mingled with songs and acclamations, and his funeral rites were performed in the face of a vanquished enemy. The Goths, clashing their arms, elevated on a buckler his eldest son Torismond, to whom they justly ascribed the glory of their success; and the new king accepted the obligation of revenge as a sacred portion of his paternal inheritance. Yet the Goths themselves were astonished by the fierce and undaunted aspect of their formidable antagonist; and their historian has compared Attila to a lion encompassed in his den and threatening his hunters with redoubled fury. The kings and nations who might have deserted his standard in the hour of distress were made sensible that the displeasure of their monarch was the most imminent and inevitable danger. All his instruments of martial music incessantly sounded a loud and animating strain of defiance; and the foremost troops, who advanced to the assault, were checked or destroyed by showers of arrows from every side of the entrenchments. It was determined in a general council of war to besiege the king of the Huns in his camp, to intercept his provisons, and to reduce him to the alternative of a disgraceful treaty or an unequal combat. But the impatience of the barbarians soon disdained these cautious and dilatory measures: and the mature policy of Aëtius was apprehensive that, after the extirpation of the Huns, the republic would be oppressed by the pride and power of the Gothic nation. The patrician exerted the superior ascendant of authority and reason to calm the passions which the son of Theodoric considered as a duty; represented, with seeming affection and real truth, the dangers of absence and delay; and persuaded Torismond to disappoint, by his speedy return, the ambitious designs of his brothers, who might occupy the throne and treasures of Toulouse. After the departure of the Goths, and the separation of the allied army, Attila was surprised at the vast silence that reigned over the plains of Châlons: the suspicion of some hostile stratagem detained him several days within the circle of his waggons, and his retreat beyond the Rhine confessed the last victory which was achieved in the name of the Western empire.

Neither the spirit, nor the forces, nor the reputation of Attila were impaired by the failure of the Gallic expedition. In the ensuing spring he repeated his demand of the princess Honoria and her patrimonial treasures. The demand was again rejected or eluded; and the indignant lover immediately took the field, passed the Alps, invaded Italy, and besieged Aquileia with an innumerable host of barbarians. Aquileia was at that period one of the richest, the most populous, and the strongest of the maritime cities of the Hadriatic coast. The Gothic auxiliaries, who appear to have served under their native princes, Alaric and Antala, communicated their intrepid spirit; and the citizens still remembered the glorious and successful resistance which their ancestors had opposed to a fierce, inexorable barbarian, who disgraced the majesty of the Roman purple. Three months were consumed without effect in the siege of Aquileia; till the want of provisions and the clamours of his army compelled Attila to relinquish the enterprise, and reluctantly to issue his orders that the troops should strike their tents the next morning, and begin their retreat. But as he rode round the walls, pensive, angry, and disappointed, he observed a stork preparing to leave her nest in one of the towers, and to fly with her infant family towards the country. He seized, with the ready penetration of a statesman, this trifling incident which chance had offered to superstition; and exclaimed, in a loud and cheerful tone, that such a domestic bird, so constantly attached to human society, would never have abandoned her ancient seats unless those towers had been devoted to impending ruin and solitude. The favourable omen inspired an assurance of victory; the siege was renewed, and prosecuted with fresh vigour; a large breach was made in the part of the wall from whence the stork had taken her flight; the Huns mounted to the assault with irresistible fury; and the succeeding generation could scarcely discover the ruins of Aquileia. After this dreadful chastisement, Attila pursued his march; and as he passèd, the cities of Altinum, Concordia, and Padua were reduced into heaps of stones and ashes. The inland towns, Vicenza, Verona, and Bergamo, were exposed to the rapacious cruelty of the Huns. Milan and Pavia submitted, without resistance, to the loss of their wealth; and applauded the unusual clemency which preserved from the flames the public as well as private buildings, and spared the lives of the captive multitude. The popular traditions of Comum, Turin, or Modena may justly be suspected; yet they concur with more authentic evidence to prove that Attila spread his ravages over the rich plains of modern Lombardy, which are divided by the Po, and bounded by the Alps and Apennine. When he took possession of the royal palace of Milan, he was surprised and offended at the sight of a picture which represented the Cæsars seated on their throne, and the princes of Scythia prostrate at their feet. The revenge which Attila inflicted on this monument of Roman vanity was harmless and ingenious. He commanded a painter to reverse the figures and the attitudes; and the emperors were delineated on the same canvas approaching in a suppliant posture to empty their bags of tributary gold before the throne of the Scythian monarch. The spectators must have confessed the truth and propriety of the alteration; and were perhaps tempted to apply, on this singular occasion, the well-known fable of the dispute between the lion and the man.

It is a saying worthy of the ferocious pride of Attila, that the grass never grew on the spot where his horse had trod. Yet the savage destroyer undesignedly laid the foundations of a republic which revived, in the feudal state of Europe, the art and spirit of a commercial industry. The celebrated name of Venice, or Venetia, was formerly diffused over a large and fertile province of Italy, from the confines of Pannonia to the river Addua, and from the Po to the Rhætian and Julian Alps. Before the irruption of the barbarians, fifty Venetian cities flourished in peace and prosperity: Aquileia was placed in the most conspicuous station: but the ancient dignity of Padua was supported by agriculture and manufactures; and the property of five hundred citizens, who were entitled to the equestrian rank, must have amounted, at the strictest computation, to one million seven hundred thousand pounds. Many families of Aquileia, Padua, and the adjacent towns, who fled from the sword of the Huns, found a safe, though obscure, refuge in the neighbouring islands. At the extremity of the Gulf, where the Hadriatic feebly imitates the tides of the ocean, near an hundred small islands are separated by shallow water from the continent, and protected from the waves by several long slips of land, which admit the entrance of vessels through some secret and narrow channels. Till the middle of the fifth century these remote and sequestered spots remained without cultivation, with few inhabitants, and almost without a name. But the manners of the Venetian fugitives, their arts and their government, were gradually formed by their new situation; and one of the epistles of Cassiodorus, which describes their condition about seventy years afterwards, may be considered as the primitive monument of the republic. The minister of Theodoric compares them, in his quaint declamatory style, to waterfowl, who had fixed their nests on the bosom of the waves; and though he allows that the Venetian provinces had formerly contained many noble families, he insinuates that they were now reduced by misfortune to the same level of humble poverty.

The Italians, who had long since renounced the exercise of arms, were surprised, after forty years' peace, by the approach of a formidable barbarian, whom they abhorred as the enemy of their religion as well as of their republic. Amidst the general consternation, Aëtius alone was incapable of fear; but it was impossible that he should achieve alone and unassisted any military exploits worthy of his former renown. The barbarians who had defended Gaul refused to march to the relief of Italy; and the succours promised by the Eastern emperor were distant and doubtful. Since Aëtius, at the head of his domestic troops, still maintained the field, and harassed or retarded the march of Attila, he never showed himself more truly great than at the time when his conduct was blamed by an ignorant and ungrateful people. If the mind of Valentinian had been susceptible of any generous sentiments, he would have chosen such a general for his example and his guide. But the timid grandson of Theodosius, instead of sharing the dangers, escaped from the sound, of war; and his hasty retreat from Ravenna to Rome, from an impregnable fortress to an open capital, betrayed his secret intention of abandoning Italy as soon as the danger should approach his Imperial person. This shameful abdication was suspended, however, by the spirit of doubt and delay which commonly adheres to pusillanimous counsels, and sometimes corrects their pernicious tendency. The Western emperor, with the senate and people of Rome, embraced the more salutary resolution of deprecating, by a solemn and suppliant embassy, the wrath of Attila. This important commission was accepted by Avienus, who, from his birth and riches, his consular dignity, the numerous train of his clients, and his personal abilities, held the first rank in the Roman senate. The specious and artful character of Avienus was admirably qualified to conduct a negotiation either of public or private interest: his colleague Trigetius had exercised the Prætorian præfecture of Italy; and Leo, bishop of Rome, consented to expose his life for the safety of his flock. The genius of Leo was exercised and displayed in the public misfortunes; and he has deserved the appellation of *Great* by the successful zeal with which he laboured to establish his opinions and his authority, under the venerable names of orthodox faith and ecclesiastical discipline. The Roman ambassadors were introduced to the tent of Attila, as he lay encamped at the place where the slow-winding Mincius is lost in the foaming waves of the lake Benacus, and trampled, with his Scythian cavalry, the farms of Catullus and Virgil. The barbarian monarch listened with favourable, and even respectful, attention; and the deliverance of Italy was purchased by the immense ransom or dowry of the princess Honoria. The state of his army might facilitate the treaty and hasten his retreat. Their martial spirit was relaxed by the wealth and indolence of a warm climate. The shepherds of the North, whose ordinary food consisted of milk and raw flesh, indulged themselves too freely in the use of bread, of wine, and of meat prepared and seasoned by the arts of cookery; and the progress of disease revenged in some measure the injuries of the Italians. When Attila declared his resolution of carrying his victorious arms to the gates of Rome, he was admonished by his friends, as well as by his enemies, that Alaric had not long survived the conquest of the eternal city. His mind, superior to real danger, was assaulted by imaginary terrors; nor could he escape the influence of superstition, which had so often been subservient to his designs. The pressing eloquence of Leo, his majestic aspect and sacerdotal robes, excited the veneration of Attila for the spiritual father of the Christians. The apparition of the two apostles of St. Peter and St. Paul, who menaced the barbarian with instant death if he rejected the prayer of their successor, is one of the noblest legends of ecclesiastical tradition. The safety of Rome might deserve the interposition of celestial beings; and some indulgence is due to a fable which has been represented by the pencil of Raphael and the chisel of Algardi.

Before the king of the Huns evacuated Italy, he threatened to return more dreadful, and more implacable, if his bride, the princess Honoria, were not delivered to his ambassadors within the term stipulated by the treaty. Yet, in the meanwhile, Attila relieved his tender anxiety, by adding a beautiful maid, whose name was Ildico, to the list of his innumerable wives. Their marriage was celebrated with barbaric pomp and festivity, at his wooden palace beyond the Danube; and the monarch, oppressed with wine and sleep, retired at a late hour from the banquet to the nuptial bed. His attendants continued to respect his pleasures or his repose the greatest part of the ensuing day, till the unusual silence alarmed their fears and suspicions; and, after attempting to awaken Attila by loud and repeated cries, they at length broke into the royal apartment. They found the trembling bride sitting by the bedside, hiding her face with her veil, and lamenting her own danger, as well as the death of the king, who had expired during the night. An artery had suddenly burst: and as Attila lay in a supine posture, he was suffocated by a torrent of blood, which, instead of finding a passage through the nostrils, regurgitated into the lungs and stomach. His body was solemnly exposed in the midst of the plain, under a silken pavilion; and the chosen squadrons of the Huns, wheeling round in measured evolutions, chanted a funeral song to the memory of a hero, glorious in his life, invincible in his death, the father of his people, the scourge of his enemies, and the terror of the world. According to their national custom, the barbarians cut off a part of their hair, gashed their faces with unseemly wounds, and bewailed their valiant leader as he deserved, not with the tears of women, but with the blood of warriors. The remains of Attila were enclosed within three coffins of gold, of silver, and of iron, and privately buried in the night: the spoils of nations were thrown into his grave; the captives who had opened the ground were inhumanly massacred; and the same Huns, who had indulged such excessive grief, feasted, with dissolute and intemperate mirth, about the recent sepulchre of their king. It was reported at Constantinople that, on the fortunate night in which he expired, Marcian beheld in a dream the bow of Attila broken asunder: and the report may be allowed to prove how seldom the image of that formidable barbarian was absent from the mind of a Roman emperor.

The revolution which subverted the empire of the Huns established the fame of Attila, whose genius alone had sustained the huge and disjointed fabric. After his death the boldest chieftains aspired to the rank of kings; the most powerful kings refused to acknowledge a superior; and the numerous sons whom so many various mothers bore to the deceased monarch divided and disputed like a private inheritance the sovereign command of the nations of Germany and Scythia. Such an event might contribute to the safety of the Eastern empire under the reign of a prince who conciliated the friendship, without forfeiting the esteem, of the barbarians. But the emperor of the West, the feeble and dissolute Valentinian, who had reached his thirty-fifth year without attaining the age of reason or courage, abused this apparent security to undermine the foundations of his own throne by the murder of the patrician Aëtius. From the instinct of a base and jealous mind, he hated the man who was universally celebrated as the terror of the barbarians and the support of the republic; and his new favourite, the eunuch Heraclius, awakened the emperor from the supine lethargy which might be disguised during the life of Placidia by the excuse of filial piety. The fame of Aëtius, his wealth and dignity, the numerous and martial train of barbarian followers, his powerful dependents who filled the civil offices of the state, and the hopes of his son Gaudentius, who was already contracted to Eudoxia, the emperor's daughter, had raised him above the rank of a subject. The ambitious designs, of which he was secretly accused, excited the fears as well as the resentment of Valentinian. Aëtius himself, supported by the consciousness of his merit, his services, and perhaps his innocence, seems to have maintained a haughty and indiscreet behaviour. The patrician offended his sovereign by an hostile declaration; he aggravated the offence by compelling him to ratify with a solemn oath a treaty of reconciliation and alliance; he proclaimed his suspicions, he neglected his safety; and from a vain confidence that the enemy whom he despised was incapable even of a manly crime, he rashly ventured his person in the palace of Rome. Whilst he urged, perhaps with intemperate vehemence, the marriage of his son, Valentinian, drawing his sword—the first sword he had ever drawn—plunged it in the breast of a general who had saved his empire: his courtiers and eunuchs ambitiously struggled to imitate their master; and Aëtius, pierced with an hundred wounds, fell dead in the royal presence. Boethius, the Prætorian præfect, was killed at the same moment; and before the event could be divulged, the principal friends of the patrician were summoned to the palace and separately murdered. The horrid deed, palliated by the specious names of justice and necessity, was immediately communicated by the emperor to his soldiers, his subjects, and his allies. The nations who were strangers or enemies to Aëtius generously deplored the unworthy fate of a hero; the barbarians who had been attached to his service dissembled their grief and resentment; and the public contempt which had been so long entertained for Valentinian was at once converted into deep and universal abhorrence. Such sentiments seldom pervade the walls of a palace; yet the emperor was confounded by the honest reply of a Roman whose approbation he had not disdained to solicit. "I am ignorant, sir, of your motives or provocations; I only know that you have acted like a man who cuts off his right hand with his left."

The luxury of Rome seems to have attracted the long and frequent visits of Valentinian, who was consequently more despised at Rome than in any other part of his dominions. A republican spirit was insensibly revived in the senate, as their authority, and even their supplies, became necessary for the support of his feeble government. The stately demeanour of an hereditary monarch offended their pride, and the pleasures of Valentinian were injurious to the peace and honour of noble families. The birth of the empress Eudoxia was equal to his own, and her charms and tender affection deserved those testimonies of love which her inconstant husband dissipated in vague and unlawful amours. Petronius Maximus, a wealthy senator of the Anician family, who had been twice consul, was possessed of a chaste and beautiful wife: her obstinate resistance served only to irritate the desires of Valentinian, and he resolved to accomplish them either by stratagem or force. Deep gaming was one of the vices of the court; the emperor, who, by chance or contrivance, had gained from Maximus a considerable sum, uncourteously exacted his ring as a security for the debt, and sent it by a trusty messenger to his wife, with an order in her husband's name that she should immediately attend the empress Eudoxia. The unsuspecting wife of Maximus was conveyed in her litter to the Imperial palace; the emissaries of her impatient lover conducted her to a remote and silent bed-chamber; and Valentinian violated, without remorse, the laws of hospitality. Her tears when she returned home, her deep affliction, and the bitter reproaches against a husband whom she considered as the accomplice of his own shame, excited Maximus to a just revenge; the desire of revenge was stimulated by ambition; and he might reasonably aspire, by the free suffrage of the Roman senate, to the throne of a detested and despicable rival. Valentinian, who supposed that every human breast was devoid like his own of friendship and gratitude, had imprudently admitted among his guards several domestics and followers of Aëtius. Two of these, of barbarian race, were persuaded to execute a sacred and honourable duty by punishing with death the assassin of their patron; and their intrepid courage did not long expect a favourable moment. Whilst Valentinian amused himself in the field of Mars with the spectacle of some military sports, they suddenly rushed upon him with drawn weapons, despatched the guilty Heraclius, and stabbed the emperor to the heart, without the least opposition from his numerous train, who seemed to rejoice in the tyrant's death. Such was the fate of Valentinian the Third, the last Roman emperor of the family of Theodosius. He faithfully imitated the hereditary weakness of his cousin and his two uncles, without inheriting the gentleness, the purity, the innocence, which alleviate in their characters the want of spirit and ability. Valentinian was less excusable, since he had passions without virtues: even his religion was questionable; and though he never deviated into the paths of heresy, he scandalised the pious Christians by his attachment to the profane arts of magic and divination.

As early as the time of Cicero and Varro it was the opinion of the Roman augurs that the *twelve vultures* which Romulus had seen, represented the *twelve centuries* assigned for the fatal period of his city. This prophecy, disregarded perhaps in the season of health and prosperity, inspired the people with gloomy apprehensions when the twelfth century, clouded with disgrace and misfortune, was almost elapsed; and even posterity must acknowledge with some surprise that the arbitrary interpretation of an accidental or fabulous circumstance has been seriously verified in the downfall of the Western empire. But its fall was announced by a clearer omen than the flight of vultures: the Roman government appeared every day less formidable to its enemies, more odious and oppressive to its subjects. The taxes were multiplied with the public distress; economy was neglected in proportion as it became necessary; and the injustice of the rich shifted the unequal burden from themselves to the people, whom they defrauded of the *indulgences* that might sometimes have alleviated their misery. The severe inquisition, which confiscated their goods and tortured their persons, compelled the subjects of Valentinian to prefer the more simple tyranny of the barbarians, to fly to the woods and mountains, or to embrace the vile and abject condition of mercenary servants. They abjured and abhorred the name of Roman citizens, which had formerly excited the ambition of mankind. The Armorican provinces of Gaul and the greatest part of Spain were thrown into a state of disorderly independence by the confederations of the Bagaudæ, and the Imperial ministers pursued with proscriptive laws and ineffectual arms the rebels whom they had made. If all the barbarian conquerors had been annihilated in the same hour, their total destruction would not have restored the empire of the West: and if Rome still survived, she survived the loss of freedom, of virtue, and of honour.

XXXII

(430–490 A.D.) SACK OF ROME BY GENSERIC, KING OF THE VANDALS—HIS NAVAL DEPREDATIONS—SUCCESSION OF THE LAST EMPERORS OF THE WEST, MAXIMUS, AVITUS, MAJORIAN, SEVERUS, ANTHEMIUS, OLYBRIUS, GLYCERIUS, NEPOS, AUGUSTULUS—TOTAL EXTINCTION OF THE WESTERN EMPIRE—REIGN OF ODOACER, THE FIRST BARBARIAN KING OF ITALY

The loss or desolation of the provinces from the Ocean to the Alps impaired the glory and greatness of Rome: her internal prosperity was irretrievably destroyed by the separation of Africa. The rapacious Vandals confiscated the patrimonial estates of the senators, and intercepted the regular subsidies which relieved the poverty and encouraged the idleness of the plebeians. The distress of the Romans was soon aggravated by an unexpected attack; and the province, so long cultivated for their use by industrious and obedient subjects, was armed against them by an ambitious barbarian. The Vandals and Alani, who followed the successful standard of Genseric, had acquired a rich and fertile territory, which stretched along the coast above ninety days' journey from Tangier to Tripoli; but their narrow limits were pressed and confined, on either side, by the sandy desert and the Mediterranean. The discovery and conquest of the Black nations, that might dwell beneath the torrid zone, could not tempt the rational ambition of Genseric; but he cast his eyes towards the sea; he resolved to create a naval power, and his bold resolution was executed with steady and active perseverance. The woods of Mount Atlas afforded an inexhaustible nursery of timber; his new subjects were skilled in the arts of navigation and shipbuilding; he animated his daring Vandals to embrace a mode of warfare which would render every maritime country accessible to their arms; the Moors and Africans were allured by the hopes of plunder; and, after an interval of six

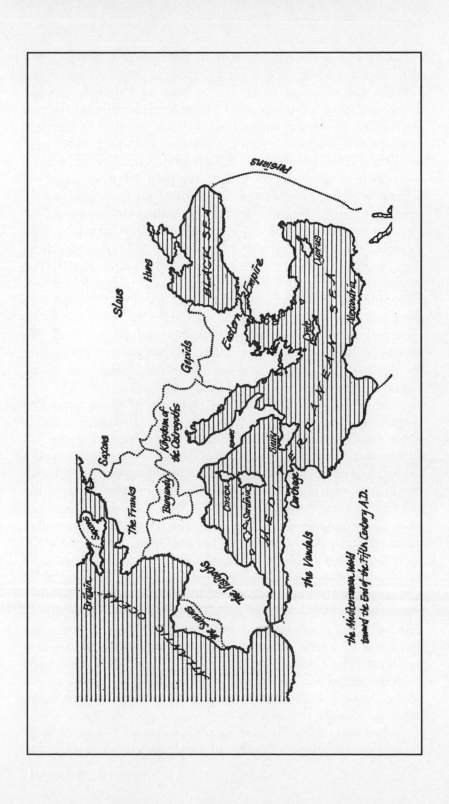

the Mediterranean World
toward the End of the Fifth Century A.D.

centuries, the fleets that issued from the port of Carthage again claimed the empire of the Mediterranean. The success of the Vandals, the conquest of Sicily, the sack of Palermo, and the frequent descents on the coast of Lucania, awakened and alarmed the mother of Valentinian and the sister of Theodosius. Alliances were formed; and armaments, expensive and ineffectual, were prepared for the destruction of the common enemy, who reserved his courage to encounter those dangers which his policy could not prevent or elude. The designs of the Roman government were repeatedly baffled by his artful delays, ambiguous promises, and apparent concessions; and the interposition of his formidable confederate, the king of the Huns, recalled the emperors from the conquest of Africa to the care of their domestic safety. The revolutions of the palace, which left the Western empire without a defender and without a lawful prince, dispelled the apprehensions and stimulated the avarice of Genseric. He immediately equipped a numerous fleet of Vandals and Moors, and cast anchor at the mouth of the Tiber, about three months after the death of Valentinian and the elevation of Maximus to the Imperial throne.

The private life of the senator Petronius Maximus was often alleged as a rare example of human felicity. His birth was noble and illustrious, since he descended from the Anician family; his dignity was supported by an adequate patrimony in land and money; and these advantages of fortune were accompanied with liberal arts and decent manners, which adorn or imitate the inestimable gifts of genius and virtue. The luxury of his palace and table was hospitable and elegant. But the day of his inauguration was the last day of his happiness. He was imprisoned (such is the lively expression of Sidonius) in the palace; and after passing a sleepless night, he sighed that he had attained the summit of his wishes, and aspired only to descend from the dangerous elevation. Oppressed by the weight of the diadem, he communicated his anxious thoughts to his friend and quæstor Fulgentius; and when he looked back with unavailing regret on the secure pleasures of his former life, the emperor exclaimed, "O fortunate Damocles, thy reign began and ended with the same dinner": a well-known allusion, which Fulgentius afterwards repeated as an instructive lesson for princes and subjects.

Whatever abilities Maximus might have shown in a subordinate station, he was found incapable of administering an empire: and

though he might easily have been informed of the naval preparations which were made on the opposite shores of Africa, he
expected with supine indifference the approach of the enemy,
without adopting any measures of defence, of negotiation, or of a
timely retreat. When the Vandals disembarked at the mouth of the
Tiber, the emperor was suddenly roused from his lethargy by the
clamours of a trembling and exasperated multitude. The only
hope which presented itself to his astonished mind was that of a
precipitate flight, and he exhorted the senators to imitate the
example of their prince. But no sooner did Maximus appear in the
streets than he was assaulted by a shower of stones: a Roman or a
Burgundian soldier claimed the honour of the first wound; his
mangled body was ignominiously cast into the Tiber; the Roman
people rejoiced in the punishment which they had inflicted on the
author of the public calamities; and the domestics of Eudoxia
signalised their zeal in the service of their mistress.

On the third day after the tumult, Genseric boldly advanced
from the port of Ostia to the gates of the defenceless city. Instead
of a sally of the Roman youth, there issued from the gates an
unarmed and venerable procession of the bishop at the head of his
clergy. The fearless spirit of Leo, his authority and eloquence,
again mitigated the fierceness of a barbarian conqueror: the king
of the Vandals promised to spare the unresisting multitude, to
protect the buildings from fire, and to exempt the captives from
torture; and although such orders were neither seriously given, nor
strictly obeyed, the mediation of Leo was glorious to himself, and
in some degree beneficial to his country. But Rome and its
inhabitants were delivered to the licentiousness of the Vandals and
Moors, whose blind passions revenged the injuries of Carthage.
The pillage lasted fourteen days and nights; and all that yet
remained of public or private wealth, of sacred or profane treasure,
was diligently transported to the vessels of Genseric. Among the
spoils, the splendid relics of two temples, or rather of two religions,
exhibited a memorable example of the vicissitudes of human and
divine things. Since the abolition of Paganism, the Capitol had been
violated and abandoned; yet the statues of the gods and heroes
were still respected, and the curious roof of gilt bronze was reserved
for the rapacious hands of Genseric. The holy instruments of the
Jewish worship, the gold table, and the gold candlestick with seven
branches, originally framed according to the particular instructions
of God himself, and which were placed in the sanctuary of his

temple, had been ostentatiously displayed to the Roman people in the triumph of Titus. They were afterwards deposited in the temple of Peace; and at the end of four hundred years, the spoils of Jerusalem were transferred from Rome to Carthage, by a barbarian who derived his origin from the shores of the Baltic. These ancient monuments might attract the notice of curiosity as well as of avarice. But the Christian churches, enriched and adorned by the prevailing superstition of the times, afforded more plentiful materials for sacrilege; and the pious liberality of pope Leo, who melted six silver vases, the gift of Constantine, each of an hundred pounds weight, is an evidence of the damage which he attempted to repair. In the forty-five years that had elapsed since the Gothic invasion, the pomp and luxury of Rome were in some measure restored; and it was difficult either to escape, or to satisfy, the avarice of a conqueror who possessed leisure to collect, and ships to transport, the wealth of the capital. The Imperial ornaments of the palace, the magnificent furniture and wardrobe, the sideboards of massy plate, were accumulated with disorderly rapine: the gold and silver amounted to several thousand talents; yet even the brass and copper were laboriously removed. Eudoxia herself, who advanced to meet her friend and deliverer, soon bewailed the imprudence of her own conduct. She was rudely stripped of her jewels; and the unfortunate empress, with her two daughters, the only surviving remains of the great Theodosius, was compelled, as a captive, to follow the haughty Vandal, who immediately hoisted sail, and returned with a prosperous navigation to the port of Carthage. Many thousand Romans of both sexes, chosen for some useful or agreeable qualifications, reluctantly embarked on board the fleet of Genseric; and their distress was aggravated by the unfeeling barbarians, who, in the division of the booty, separated the wives from their husbands, and the children from their parents. The charity of Deogratias, bishop of Carthage, was their only consolation and support. He generously sold the gold and silver plate of the church to purchase the freedom of some, to alleviate the slavery of others, and to assist the wants and infirmities of a captive multitude, whose health was impaired by the hardships which they had suffered in the passage from Italy to Africa. By his order, two spacious churches were converted into hospitals: the sick were distributed in convenient beds, and liberally supplied with food and medicines; and the aged prelate repeated his visits both in the day and night, with an assiduity that surpassed his strength, and a tender sympathy which enhanced the value of his services. Compare this scene with the field of Cannæ; and judge between Hannibal and the successor of St. Cyprian.

The season was now approaching in which the annual assembly of the seven provinces was held at Arles; their deliberations might perhaps be influenced by the presence of Theodoric and his martial brothers; but their choice would naturally incline to the most illustrious of their countrymen. Avitus, after a decent resistance, accepted the Imperial diadem from the representatives of Gaul; and his election was ratified by the acclamations of the barbarians and provincials. The formal consent of Martian, emperor of the East, was solicited and obtained; but the senate, Rome, and Italy, though humbled by their recent calamities, submitted with a secret murmur to the presumption of the Gallic usurper. Theodoric, to whom Avitus was indebted for the purple, had acquired the Gothic sceptre by the murder of his elder brother Torismond; and he justified this atrocious deed by the design which his predecessor had formed of violating his alliance with the empire. Such a crime might not be incompatible with the virtues of a barbarian; but the manners of Theodoric were gentle and humane; and posterity may contemplate without terror the original picture of a Gothic king, whom Sidonius had intimately observed in the hours of peace and of social intercourse.

When the king of the Visigoths encouraged Avitus to assume the purple, he offered his person and his forces as a faithful soldier of the republic. The exploits of Theodoric soon convinced the world that he had not degenerated from the warlike virtues of his ancestors. After the establishment of the Goths in Aquitain, and the passage of the Vandals into Africa, the Suevi, who had fixed their kingdom in Gallicia, aspired to the conquest of Spain, and threatened to extinguish the feeble remains of the Roman dominion. The provincials of Carthagena and Tarragona, afflicted by an hostile invasion, represented their injuries and their apprehensions. Count Fronto was despatched, in the name of the emperor Avitus, with advantageous offers of peace and alliance; and Theodoric interposed his weighty mediation to declare that, unless his brother-in-law, the king of the Suevi, immediately retired, he should be obliged to arm in the cause of justice and of Rome. "Tell him," replied the haughty Rechiarius, "that I despise his friendship and his arms; but that I shall soon try whether he will dare to expect my arrival under the walls of Toulouse." Such a challenge urged

Theodoric to prevent the bold designs of his enemy: he passed the Pyrenees at the head of the Visigoths; the Franks and Burgundians served under his standard; and though he professed himself the dutiful servant of Avitus, he privately stipulated, for himself and his successors, the absolute possession of his Spanish conquests. The two armies, or rather the two nations, encountered each other on the banks of the river Urbicus, about twelve miles from Astorga; and the decisive victory of the Goths appeared for a while to have extirpated the name and kingdom of the Suevi. From the field of battle Theodoric advanced to Braga, their metropolis, which still retained the splendid vestiges of its ancient commerce and dignity. His entrance was not polluted with blood; and the Goths respected the chastity of their female captives, more especially of the consecrated virgins: but the greatest part of the clergy and people were made slaves, and even the churches and altars were confounded in the universal pillage. The unfortunate king of the Suevi had escaped to one of the ports of the ocean; but the obstinacy of the winds opposed his flight: he was delivered to his implacable rival; and Rechiarius, who neither desired nor expected mercy, received, with manly constancy, the death which he would probably have inflicted. After this bloody sacrifice to policy or resentment, Theodoric carried his victorious arms as far as Merida, the principal town of Lusitania, without meeting any resistance, except from the miraculous powers of St. Eulalia; but he was stopped in the full career of success, and recalled from Spain before he could provide for the security of his conquests. In his retreat towards the Pyrenees he revenged his disappointment on the country through which he passed; and, in the sack of Polentia and Astorga, he showed himself a faithless ally, as well as a cruel enemy. Whilst the king of the Visigoths fought and vanquished in the name of Avitus, the reign of Avitus had expired; and both the honour and the interest of Theodoric were deeply wounded by the disgrace of a friend whom he had seated on the throne of the Western empire.

The successor of Avitus presents the welcome discovery of a great and heroic character, such as sometimes arise, in a degenerate age, to vindicate the honour of the human species. The emperor Majorian has deserved the praises of his contemporaries and of posterity; and these praises may be strongly expressed in the words of a judicious and disinterested historian: "That he was gentle to his subjects; that he was terrible to his enemies; and that he excelled in *every* virtue *all* his predecessors who had reigned over the Romans." Such a testimony may justify at least the panegyric of Sidonius; and we may acquiesce in the assurance that, although the obsequious orator would have flattered with equal zeal the most worthless of princes, the extraordinary merit of his object confined him, on this occasion, within the bounds of truth. Majorian derived his name from his maternal grandfather, who, in the reign of the great Theodosius, had commanded the troops of the Illyrian frontier. He gave his daughter in marriage to the father of Majorian, a respectable officer, who administered the revenues of Gaul with skill and integrity; and generously preferred the friendship of Aëtius to the tempting offers of an insidious court. His son, the future emperor, who was educated in the profession of arms, displayed, from his early youth, intrepid courage, premature wisdom, and unbounded liberality in a scanty fortune. He followed the standard of Aëtius, contributed to his success, shared, and sometimes eclipsed, his glory, and at last excited the jealousy of the patrician, or rather of his wife, who forced him to retire from the service. Majorian, after the death of Aëtius, was recalled and promoted: and his intimate connection with Count Ricimer was the immediate step by which he ascended the throne of the Western empire. During the vacancy that succeeded the abdication of Avitus, the ambitious barbarian, whose birth excluded him from the Imperial dignity, governed Italy, with the title of Patrician; resigned to his friend the conspicuous station of master-general of the cavalry and infantry, and, after an interval of some months, consented to the unanimous wish of the Romans, whose favour Majorian had solicited by a recent victory over the Alemanni. He was invested with the purple at Ravenna: and the epistle which he addressed to the senate will best describe his situation and his sentiments. "Your election, Conscript Fathers! and the ordinance of the most valiant army, have made me your emperor. May the propitious Deity direct and prosper the counsels and events of my administration to your advantage and to the public welfare! For my own part, I did not aspire, I have submitted, to reign; nor should I have discharged the obligations of a citizen if I had refused, with base and selfish ingratitude, to support the weight of those labours which were imposed by the republic. Assist, therefore, the prince whom you have made; partake the duties which you have enjoined; and may our common endeavours promote the happiness of an empire which I have accepted from your hands. Be assured that, in our times, justice shall resume her ancient vigour, and that virtue shall become not only innocent but meritorious. Let none, except the authors themselves, be apprehensive of *delations*, which, as a subject, I have always condemned, and, as a prince, will severely punish. Our own vigilance, and that of our father, the patrician Ricimer, shall regulate all military affairs and provide for the safety of the Roman world, which we have saved from foreign and domestic enemies. You now understand the maxims of my government: you may confide in the faithful love and sincere assurances of a prince who has formerly been the companion of your life and dangers, who still glories in the name of senator, and who is anxious that you should never repent of the judgment which you have pronounced in his favour." The emperor, who, amidst the ruins of the Roman world, revived the ancient language of law and liberty, which Trajan would not have disclaimed, must have derived those generous sentiments from his own heart, since they were not suggested to his imitation by the customs of his age or the example of his predecessors.

The private and public actions of Majorian are very imperfectly known: but his laws, remarkable for an original cast of thought and expression, faithfully represent the character of a sovereign who loved his people, who sympathised in their distress, who had studied the causes of the decline of the empire, and who was capable of applying (as far as such reformation was practicable) judicious and effectual remedies to the public disorders. His regulations concerning the finances manifestly tended to remove, or at least to mitigate, the most intolerable grievances. I. From the first hour of his reign he was solicitous (I translate his own words) to relieve the *weary* fortunes of the provincials, oppressed by the accumulated weight of indictions and superindictions. With this view, he granted an universal amnesty, a final and absolute discharge of all arrears of tribute, of all debts which, under any pretence, the fiscal officers might demand from the people. This wise dereliction of obsolete, vexatious, and unprofitable claims, improved and purified the sources of the public revenue; and the subject, who could now look back without despair, might labour with hope and gratitude for himself and for his country. II. In the assessment and collection of taxes Majorian restored the ordinary jurisdiction of the provincial magistrates, and suppressed the extraordinary commissions which had been introduced in the name of the emperor himself or of the Prætorian præfects. The favourite servants who obtained such irregular powers were insolent in their behaviour and arbitrary in their demands: they affected to despise the subordinate tribunals, and they were discontented if their fees and profits did not twice exceed the sum which they condescended to pay into the treasury. One instance of their extortion would appear incredible were it not authenticated by the legislator himself. They exacted the whole payment in gold: but they refused the current coin of the empire, and would accept only such ancient pieces as were stamped with the names of Faustina or the Antonines. The subject who was unprovided with these curious medals had recourse to the expedient of compounding with their rapacious demands; or, if he succeeded in the research, his imposition was doubled according to the weight and value of the money of former times. III. "The municipal corporations (says the emperor), the lesser senates (so antiquity has justly styled them), deserve to be considered as the heart of the cities and the sinews of the republic. And yet so low are they now reduced, by the injustice of magistrates and the venality of collectors, that many of their members, renouncing their dignity and their country, have taken refuge in distant and obscure exile." He urges, and even compels, their return to their respective cities; but he removes the grievance which had forced them to desert the exercise of their municipal functions. They are directed, under the authority of the provincial magistrates, to resume their office of levying the tribute; but, instead of being made responsible for the whole sum assessed on their district, they are only required to produce a regular account of the payments which they have actually received, and of the defaulters who are still indebted to the public. IV. But Majorian was not ignorant that these corporate bodies were too much inclined to retaliate the injustice and oppression which they had suffered, and he therefore revives the useful office of the *defenders of cities*. He exhorts the people to elect, in a full and free assembly, some man of discretion and integrity who would dare to assert their privileges, to represent their grievances, to protect the poor from the tyranny of the rich, and to inform the emperor of the abuses that were committed under the sanction of his name and authority.

The spectator who casts a mournful view over the ruins of ancient Rome is tempted to accuse the memory of the Goths and Vandals for the mischief which they had neither leisure, nor power, nor perhaps inclination, to perpetrate. The tempest of war might strike some lofty turrets to the pound; but the destruction which undermined the foundations of those massy fabrics was prosecuted, slowly and silently, during a period of ten centuries; and the motives of interest, that afterwards operated without shame or control, were severely checked by the taste and spirit of the emperor Majorian. The decay of the city had gradually impaired the value of the public works. The circus and theatres might still excite, but they seldom gratified, the desires of the people: the temples which had escaped the zeal of the Christians were no longer inhabited either by gods or men; the diminished crowds of the Romans were lost in the immense space of their baths and porticoes; and the stately libraries and halls of justice became useless to an indolent generation whose repose was seldom disturbed either by study or business. The monuments of consular or Imperial greatness were no longer revered as the immortal glory of the capital: they were only esteemed as an inexhaustible mine of materials, cheaper, and more convenient, than the distant quarry. Specious petitions were continually addressed to the easy magistrates of Rome which stated the want of stones or bricks for some necessary service: the fairest forms of architecture were rudely defaced for the sake of some paltry or pretended repairs; and the degenerate Romans, who converted the spoil to their own emolument, demolished, with sacrilegious hands, the labours of their ancestors.

The virtues of Majorian could not protect him from the impetuous sedition which broke out in the camp near Tortona at the foot of the Alps. He was compelled to abdicate the Imperial purple; five days after his abdication it was reported that he died of a dysentery, and the humble tomb which covered his remains was consecrated by the respect and gratitude of succeeding generations. The private character of Majorian inspired love and respect. Malicious calumny and satire excited his indignation, or, if he himself were the object, his contempt; but he protected the freedom of wit, and in the hours which the emperor gave to the familiar society of his friends he could indulge his taste for pleasantry without degrading the majesty of his rank. It was not perhaps without some regret that Ricimer sacrificed his friend to the interest of his ambition: but he resolved in a second choice to avoid the imprudent preference of superior virtue and merit. At his command the obsequious senate of Rome bestowed the Imperial title on Libius Severus, who ascended the throne of the West without emerging from the obscurity of a private condition. History has scarcely deigned to notice his birth, his elevation, his character, or his death. Severus expired as soon as his life became inconvenient to his patron; and it would be useless to discriminate his nominal reign in the vacant interval of six years between the death of Majorian and the elevation of Anthemius. During that period the government was in the hands of Ricimer alone; and although the modest barbarian disclaimed the name of king, he accumulated treasures, formed a separate army, negotiated private alliances, and ruled Italy with the same independent and despotic authority which was afterwards exercised by Odoacer and Theodoric.

The kingdom of Italy, a name to which the Western empire was gradually reduced, was afflicted, under the reign of Ricimer, by the incessant depredations of the Vandal pirates. In the spring of each year they equipped a formidable navy in the port of Carthage, and Genseric himself, though in a very advanced age, still commanded in person the most important expeditions. His designs were concealed with impenetrable secrecy till the moment that he hoisted sail. When he was asked by his pilot what course he should steer, "Leave the determination to the winds (replied the barbarian, with pious arrogance): *they* will transport us to the guilty coast whose inhabitants have provoked the divine justice;" but if Genseric himself deigned to issue more precise orders, he judged the most wealthy to be the most criminal. The Vandals repeatedly visited the coasts of Spain, Liguria, Tuscany, Campania, Lucania, Bruttium, Apulia, Calabria, Venetia, Dalmatia, Epirus, Greece, and Sicily: they were tempted to subdue the island of Sardinia, so advantageously placed in the centre of the Mediterranean; and their arms spread desolation or terror from the Columns of Hercules to the mouth of the Nile. As they were more ambitious of spoil than of glory, they seldom attacked any fortified cities, or engaged any regular troops in the open field. But the celerity of their motions enabled them almost at the same time to threaten and to attack the most distant objects which attracted their desires; and as they always embarked a sufficient number of horses, they had no sooner landed than they swept the dismayed country with a body of light cavalry. Yet, notwithstanding the example of their king, the native Vandals and Alani insensibly declined this toilsome and perilous warfare; the hardy generation of the first conquerors was almost extinguished, and their sons, who were born in Africa, enjoyed the delicious baths and gardens which had been acquired by the valour of their fathers. Their place was readily supplied by a various multitude of Moors and Romans, of captives and outlaws;

and those desperate wretches, who had already violated the laws of their country, were the most eager to promote the atrocious acts which disgraced the victories of Genseric. In the treatment of his unhappy prisoners he sometimes consulted his avarice, and sometimes indulged his cruelty; and the massacre of five hundred noble citizens of Zante or Zacynthus, whose mangled bodies he cast into the Ionian Sea, was imputed by the public indignation to his latest posterity.

The haughty Ricimer, who had long struggled with the difficulties of his situation, was at length reduced to address the throne of Constantinople in the humble language of a subject; and Italy submitted, as the price and security of the alliance, to accept a master from the choice of the emperor of the East. Leo listened to the complaints of the Italians; resolved to extirpate the tyranny of the Vandals; and declared his alliance with his colleague Anthemius, whom he solemnly invested with the diadem and purple of the West. The virtues of Anthemius have perhaps been magnified, since the Imperial descent, which he could only deduce from the usurper Procopius, has been swelled into a line of emperors. In all his public declarations the emperor Leo assumes the authority, and professes the affection of a father for his son Anthemius, with whom he had divided the administration of the universe. The situation, and perhaps the character, of Leo dissuaded him from exposing his person to the toils and dangers of an African war. But the powers of the Eastern empire were strenuously exerted to deliver Italy and the Mediterranean from the Vandals; and Genseric, who had so long oppressed both the land and sea, was threatened from every side with a formidable invasion. Basiliscus, the brother of the empress Verina, was intrusted with this important command. His sister, the wife of Leo, had exaggerated the merit of his former exploits against the Scythians. But the discovery of his guilt, or incapacity, was reserved for the African war; and his friends could only save his military reputation by asserting that he had conspired with Aspar to spare Genseric, and to betray the last hope of the Western empire.

Experience has shown that the success of an invader most commonly depends on the vigour and celerity of his operations. The strength and sharpness of the first impression are blunted by delay; the health and spirit of the troops insensibly languish in a distant climate; the naval and military force, a mighty effort which perhaps can never be repeated, is silently consumed; and every hour that is wasted in negotiation accustoms the enemy to contemplate and examine those hostile terrors which, on their first appearance, he deemed irresistible. The formidable navy of Basiliscus pursued its prosperous navigation from the Thracian Bosphorus to the coast of Africa. He landed his troops at Cape Bona, or the promontory of Mercury, about forty miles from Carthage. The army of Heraclius, and the fleet of Marcellinus, either joined or seconded the Imperial lieutenant; and the Vandals who opposed his progress by sea or land were successively vanquished. If Basiliscus had seized the moment of consternation, and boldly advanced to the capital, Carthage must have surrendered, and the kingdom of the Vandals was extinguished. Genseric beheld the danger with firmness, and eluded it with his veteran dexterity. He protested, in the most respectful language, that he was ready to submit his person and his dominions to the will of the emperor; but he requested a truce of five days to regulate the terms of his submission; and it was universally believed that his secret liberality contributed to the success of this public negotiation. Instead of obstinately refusing whatever indulgence his enemy so earnestly solicited, the guilty, or the credulous, Basiliscus consented to the fatal truce; and his imprudent security seemed to proclaim that he already considered himself as the conqueror of Africa. During this short interval the wind became favourable to the designs of Genseric. He manned his largest ships of war with the bravest of the Moors and Vandals; and they towed after them many large barks filled with combustible materials. In the obscurity of the night, these destructive vessels were impelled against the unguarded and unsuspecting fleet of the Romans, who were awakened by the sense of their instant danger. Their close and crowded order assisted the progress of the fire, which was communicated with rapid and irresistible violence; and the noise of the wind, the crackling of the flames, the dissonant cries of the soldiers and mariners, who could neither command nor obey, increased the horror of the nocturnal tumult. Whilst they laboured to extricate themselves from the fire-ships, and to save at least a part of the navy, the galleys of Genseric assaulted them with temperate and disciplined valour; and many of the Romans, who escaped the fury of the flames, were destroyed or taken by the victorious Vandals. Among the events of that disastrous night, the heroic, or rather desperate, courage of John, one of the principal officers of Basiliscus, has rescued his name from oblivion. When the ship which he had bravely defended was almost consumed, he threw himself in his armour into the sea, disdainfully rejected the esteem and pity of Genso, the son of Genseric, who pressed him to accept honourable quarter, and sunk under the waves; exclaiming, with his last breath, that he would never fall alive into the hands of those impious dogs. Actuated by a far different spirit, Basiliscus, whose station was the most remote from danger, disgracefully fled in the beginning of the engagement, returned to Constantinople with the loss of more than half of his fleet and army, and sheltered his guilty head in the sanctuary of St. Sophia, till his sister, by her tears and entreaties, could obtain his pardon from the indignant emperor.

The peaceful and prosperous reign which Anthemius had promised to the West was soon clouded by misfortune and discord. Ricimer, apprehensive or impatient of a superior, retired from Rome and fixed his residence at Milan; an advantageous situation, either to invite or to repel the warlike tribes that were seated between the Alps and the Danube. Italy was gradually divided into two independent and hostile kingdoms; and the nobles of Liguria, who trembled at the near approach of a civil war, fell prostrate at the feet of the patrician, and conjured him to spare their unhappy country. "For my own part," replied Ricimer, in a tone of insolent moderation, "I am still inclined to embrace the friendship of the Galatian; but who will undertake to appease his anger, or to mitigate the pride which always rises in proportion to our submission?" They informed him that Epiphanius, bishop of Pavia, united the wisdom of the serpent with the innocence of the dove; and appeared confident that the eloquence of such an ambassador must prevail against the strongest opposition, either of interest or passion. Their recommendation was approved; and Epiphanius, assuming the benevolent office of mediation, proceeded without delay to Rome, where he was received with the honours due to his merit and reputation. The oration of a bishop in favour of peace may be easily supposed: he argued that, in all possible circumstances, the forgiveness of injuries must be an act of mercy, or magnanimity, or prudence; and he seriously admonished the emperor to avoid a contest with a fierce barbarian, which might be fatal to himself, and must be ruinous to his dominions. Anthemius acknowledged the truth of his maxims; but he deeply felt, with grief and indignation, the behaviour of Ricimer; and his passion gave eloquence and energy to his discourse. "What favours," he warmly exclaimed, "have we refused to this ungrateful man? What provocations have we not endured? Regardless of the majesty of the purple, I gave my daughter to a Goth; I sacrificed my own blood to the safety of the republic. The liberality which ought to have secured the eternal attachment of Ricimer has exasperated him against his benefactor. What wars has he not excited against the empire? How often has he instigated and assisted the fury of hostile nations? Shall I now accept his perfidious friendship? Can I hope that he will respect the engagements of a treaty, who has already violated the duties of a son?" But the anger of Anthemius evaporated in these passionate exclamations: he insensibly yielded to the proposals of Epiphanius; and the bishop returned to his diocese with the satisfaction of restoring the peace of Italy by a reconciliation, of which the sincerity and continuance might be reasonably suspected. The clemency of the emperor was extorted from his weakness; and Ricimer suspended his ambitious designs till he had secretly prepared the engines with which he resolved to subvert the throne of Anthemius. The mask of peace and moderation was then thrown aside. The army of Ricimer was fortified by a numerous reinforcement of Burgundians and Oriental Suevi: he disclaimed all allegiance to the Greek emperor, marched from Milan to the gates of Rome, and, fixing his camp on the banks of the Anio, impatiently expected the arrival of Olybrius, his Imperial candidate.

The senator Olybrius, of the Anician family, might esteem himself the lawful heir of the Western empire. He had married Placidia, the younger daughter of Valentinian, after she was restored by Genseric, who still detained her sister Eudoxia, as the wife, or rather as the captive, of his son. The king of the Vandals supported, by threats and solicitations, the fair pretensions of his Roman ally; and assigned, as one of the motives of the war, the refusal of the senate and people to acknowledge their lawful prince, and the unworthy preference which they had given to a stranger. The friendship of the public enemy might render Olybrius still more unpopular to the Italians; but when Ricimer meditated the ruin of the emperor Anthemius, he tempted, with the offer of a diadem, the candidate who could justify his rebellion by an illustrious name and a royal alliance. The husband of Placidia, who, like most of his ancestors, had been invested with the consular dignity, might have continued to enjoy a secure and splendid fortune in the peaceful residence of Constantinople; nor does he appear to have been tormented by such a genius as cannot be amused or occupied unless by the administration of an empire. Yet Olybrius yielded to the importunities of his friends, perhaps of his wife; rashly plunged into the dangers and calamities of a civil war; and, with the secret connivance of the emperor Leo, accepted the Italian purple, which was bestowed, and resumed, at the capricious will of a barbarian. He landed without obstacle (for Genseric was master of the sea) either at Ravenna or the port of Ostia, and immediately proceeded to the camp of Ricimer, where he was received as the sovereign of the Western world.

The patrician, who had extended his posts from the Anio to the Milvian bridge, already possessed two quarters of Rome, the Vatican and the Janiculum, which are separated by the Tiber from the rest of the city; and it may be conjectured that an assembly of seceding senators imitated, in the choice of Olybrius, the forms of a legal election. But the body of the senate and people firmly adhered to the cause of Anthemius; and the more effectual support of a Gothic army enabled him to prolong his reign, and the public distress, by a resistance of three months, which produced the concomitant evils of famine and pestilence. At length Ricimer made a furious assault on the bridge of Hadrian, or St. Angelo; and the narrow pass was defended with equal valour by the Goths till the death of Gilimer, their leader. The victorious troops, breaking down every barrier, rushed with irresistible violence into the heart of the city, and Rome (if we may use the language of a contemporary pope) was subverted by the civil fury of Anthemius and Ricimer. The unfortunate Anthemius was dragged from his concealment and inhumanly massacred by the command of his son-in-law, who thus added a third, or perhaps a fourth, emperor to the number of his victims. The soldiers, who united the rage of factious citizens with the savage manners of barbarians, were indulged without control in the licence of rapine and murder: the crowd of slaves and plebeians, who were unconcerned in the event, could only gain by the indiscriminate pillage; and the face of the city exhibited the strange contrast of stern cruelty and dissolute intemperance. Forty days after this calamitous event, the subject, not of glory, but of guilt, Italy was delivered, by a painful disease, from the tyrant Ricimer, who bequeathed the command of his army to his nephew Gundobald, one of the princes of the Burgundians. In the same year all the principal actors in this great revolution were removed from the stage; and the whole reign of Olybrius, whose death does not betray any symptoms of violence, is included within the term of seven months. He left one daughter, the offspring of his marriage with Placidia; and the family of the great Theodosius, transplanted from Spain to Constantinople, was propagated in the female line as far as the eighth generation.

Whilst the vacant throne of Italy was abandoned to lawless barbarians, the election of a new colleague was seriously agitated in the council of Leo. The empress Verina, studious to promote the greatness of her own family, had married one of her nieces to Julius Nepos, who succeeded his uncle Marcellinus in the sovereignty of Dalmatia, a more solid possession than the title which he was persuaded to accept of Emperor of the West. But the measures of the Byzantine court were so languid and irresolute, that many months elapsed after the death of Anthemius, and even of Olybrius, before their destined successor could show himself, with a respectable force, to his Italian subjects. During that interval, Glycerius, an obscure soldier, was invested with the purple by his patron Gundobald; but the Burgundian prince was unable or unwilling to support his nomination by a civil war: the pursuits of domestic ambition recalled him beyond the Alps, and his client was permitted to exchange the Roman sceptre for the bishopric of Salona. After extinguishing such a competitor, the emperor Nepos was acknowledged by the senate, by the Italians, and by the provincials of Gaul; his moral virtues and military talents were loudly celebrated; and those who derived any private benefit from his government announced in prophetic strains the restoration of the public felicity. Their hopes (if such hopes had been entertained) were confounded within the term of a single year; and the treaty of peace, which ceded Auvergne to the Visigoths, is the only event of his short and inglorious reign. The most faithful subjects of Gaul were sacrificed by the Italian emperor to the hope of domestic security; but his repose was soon invaded by a furious sedition of the barbarian confederates, who, under the command of Orestes, their general, were in full march from Rome to Ravenna. Nepos trembled at their approach; and, instead of placing a just confidence in the strength of Ravenna, he hastily escaped to his ships, and retired to his Dalmatian principality, on the opposite coast of the Hadriatic. By this shameful abdication he protracted his life about five years, in a very ambiguous state between an emperor and an exile, till he was assassinated at

Salona by the ungrateful Glycerius, who was translated, perhaps as the reward of his crime, to the archbishopric of Milan.

The nations who had asserted their independence after the death of Attila were established, by the right of possession or conquest, in the boundless countries to the north of the Danube; or in the Roman provinces between the river and the Alps. But the bravest of their youth enlisted in the army of *confederates*, who formed the defence and the terror of Italy; and in this promiscuous multitude, the names of the Heruli, the Sciri, the Alani, the Turcilingi, and the Rugians, appear to have predominated. The example of these warriors was imitated by Orestes, the son of Tatullus, and the father of the last Roman emperor of the West. Orestes, who has been already mentioned in this history, had never deserted his country. His birth and fortunes rendered him one of the most illustrious subjects of Pannonia. When that province was ceded to the Huns, he entered into the service of Attila, his lawful sovereign, obtained the office of his secretary, and was repeatedly sent ambassador to Constantinople, to represent the person and signify the commands of the imperious monarch. The death of that conqueror restored him to his freedom; and Orestes might honourably refuse either to follow the sons of Attila into the Scythian desert, or to obey the Ostrogoths, who had usurped the dominion of Pannonia. He preferred the service of the Italian princes, the successors of Valentinian; and, as he possessed the qualifications of courage, industry, and experience, he advanced with rapid steps in the military profession, till he was elevated, by the favour of Nepos himself, to the dignities of patrician and mastergeneral of the troops. These troops had been long accustomed to reverence the character and authority of Orestes, who affected their manners, conversed with them in their own language, and was intimately connected with their national chieftains by long habits of familiarity and friendship. At his solicitation they rose in arms against the obscure Greek who presumed to claim their obedience; and when Orestes, from some secret motive, declined the purple, they consented, with the same facility, to acknowledge his son Augustulus as the emperor of the West. By the abdication of Nepos, Orestes had now attained the summit of his ambitious hopes; but he soon discovered, before the end of the first year, that the lessons of perjury and ingratitude which a rebel must inculcate will be retorted against himself, and that the precarious sovereign of Italy was only permitted to choose whether he would be the slave or the victim of his barbarian mercenaries. The dangerous alliance of these strangers had oppressed and insulted the last remains of Roman freedom and dignity. At each revolution their pay and privileges were augmented; but their insolence increased in a still more extravagant degree; they envied the fortune of their brethren in Gaul, Spain, and Africa, whose victorious arms had acquired an independent and perpetual inheritance; and they insisted on their peremptory demand that a *third* part of the lands of Italy should be immediately divided among them. Orestes, with a spirit which, in another situation, might be entitled to our esteem, chose rather to encounter the rage of an armed multitude than to subscribe the ruin of an innocent people. He rejected the audacious demand; and his refusal was favourable to the ambition of Odoacer, a bold barbarian, who assured his fellow-soldiers that, if they dared to associate under his command, they might soon extort the justice which had been denied to their dutiful petitions. From all the camps and garrisons of Italy the confederates, actuated by the same resentment and the same hopes, impatiently flocked to the standard of this popular leader; and the unfortunate patrician, overwhelmed by the torrent, hastily retreated to the strong city of Pavia, the episcopal seat of the holy Epiphanites. Pavia was immediately besieged, the fortifications were stormed, the town was pillaged; and although the bishop might labour, with much zeal and some success, to save the property of the church and the chastity of female captives, the tumult could only be appeased by the execution of Orestes. His brother Paul was slain in an action near Ravenna; and the helpless Augustulus, who could no longer command the respect, was reduced to implore the clemency, of Odoacer.

Royalty was familiar to the barbarians, and the submissive people of Italy was prepared to obey, without a murmur, the authority which he should condescend to exercise as the vice-gerent of the emperor of the West. But Odoacer had resolved to abolish that useless and expensive office; and such is the weight of antique prejudice, that it required some boldness and penetration to discover the extreme facility of the enterprise. The unfortunate Augustulus was made the instrument of his own disgrace; he signified his resignation to the senate; and that assembly, in their last act of obedience to a Roman prince, still affected the spirit of freedom and the forms of the constitution. An epistle was addressed, by their unanimous decree, to the emperor Zeno, the son-in-law and successor of Leo, who had lately been restored, after a short rebellion, to the Byzantine throne. They solemnly "disclaim the necessity, or even the wish, of continuing any longer the Imperial succession in Italy; since, in their opinion, the majesty of a sole monarch is sufficient to pervade and protect, at the same time, both the East and the West. In their own name, and in the name of the people, they consent that the seat of universal empire shall be transferred from Rome to Constantinople; and they basely renounce the right of choosing their master, the only vestige that yet remained of the authority which had given laws to the world. The republic (they repeat that name without a blush) might safely confide in the civil and military virtues of Odoacer; and they humbly request that the emperor would invest him with the title of Patrician, and the administration of the *diocese* of Italy." The deputies of the senate were received at Constantinople with some mark of displeasure and indignation: and when they were admitted to the audience of Zeno, he sternly reproached them with their treatment of the two emperors, Anthemius and Nepos, whom the East had successively granted to the prayers of Italy. "The first (continued he) you have murdered; the second you have expelled: but the second is still alive, and whilst he lives he is your lawful sovereign." But the prudent Zeno soon deserted the hopeless cause of his abdicated colleague. His vanity was gratified by the title of sole emperor, and by the statues erected to his honour in the several quarters of Rome; he entertained a friendly, though ambiguous, correspondence with the *patrician* Odoacer; and he gratefully accepted the Imperial ensigns, the sacred ornaments of the throne and palace, which the barbarian was not unwilling to remove from the sight of the people.

In the space of twenty years since the death of Valentinian, nine emperors had successively disappeared; and the son of Orestes, a youth recommended only by his beauty, would be the least entitled to the notice of posterity, if his reign, which was marked by the extinction of the Roman empire in the West, did not leave a memorable era in the history of mankind. The patrician Orestes had married the daughter of Count *Romulus*, of Petovio in Noricum; the name of *Augustus*, notwithstanding the jealousy of power, was known at Aquileia as a familiar surname; and the appellations of the two great founders, of the city and of the monarchy, were thus strangely united in the last of their successors.

The son or Orestes assumed and disgraced the names of Romulus Augustus; but the first was corrupted into Momyllus by the Greeks, and the second has been changed by the Latins into the contemptible diminutive Augustulus. The life of this inoffensive youth was spared by the generous clemency of Odoacer; who dismissed him, with his whole family, from the Imperial palace, fixed his annual allowance at six thousand pieces of gold, and assigned the castle of Lucullus, in Campania, for the place of his exile or retirement.

The king of Italy was not unworthy of the high station to which his valour and fortune had exalted him: his savage manners were polished by the habits of conversation; and he respected, though a conqueror and a barbarian, the institutions, and even the prejudices, of his subjects. After an interval of seven years, Odoacer restored the consulship of the West. For himself, he modestly, or proudly, declined an honour which was still accepted by the emperors of the East; but the curule chair was successively filled by eleven of the most illustrious senators; and the list is adorned by the respectable name of Basilius, whose virtues claimed the friendship and grateful applause of Sidonius, his client. The laws of the emperors were strictly enforced, and the civil administration of Italy was still exercised by the Prætorian præfect and his subordinate officers. Odoacer devolved on the Roman magistrates the odious and oppressive task of collecting the public revenue; but he reserved for himself the merit of seasonable and popular indulgence. Like the rest of the barbarians, he had been instructed in the Arian heresy; but he revered the monastic and episcopal characters; and the silence of the catholics attests the toleration which they enjoyed. The peace of the city required the interposition of his præfect Basilius in the choice of a Roman pontiff: the decree which restrained the clergy from alienating their lands was ultimately designed for the benefit of the people, whose devotion would have been taxed to repair the dilapidations of the church. Italy was protected by the arms of its conqueror; and its frontiers were respected by the barbarians of Gaul and Germany, who had so long insulted the feeble race of Theodosius. Odoacer passed the Hadriatic, to chastise the assassins of the emperor Nepos, and to acquire the maritime province of Dalmatia. He passed the Alps, to rescue the remains of Noricum from Fava, or Feletheus, king of the Rugians, who held his residence beyond the Danube. The king was vanquished in battle, and led away prisoner; a numerous colony of captives and subjects was transplanted into Italy; and Rome, after a long period of defeat and disgrace, might claim the triumph of her barbarian master.

Notwithstanding the prudence and success of Odoacer, his kingdom exhibited the sad prospect of misery and desolation. Since the age of Tiberius, the decay of agriculture had been felt in Italy; and it was a just subject of complaint that the life of the Roman people depended on the accidents of the winds and waves. In the division and the decline of the empire, the tributary harvests of Egypt and Africa were withdrawn; the numbers of the inhabitants continually diminished with the means of subsistence; and the country was exhausted by the irretrievable losses of war, famine, and pestilence. St. Ambrose has deplored the ruin of a populous district, which had been once adorned with the flourishing cities of Bologna, Modena, Rhegium, and Placentia. Pope Gelasius was a subject of Odoacer; and he affirms, with strong exaggeration, that in Æmilia, Tuscany, and the adjacent provinces, the human species was almost extirpated. The plebeians of Rome, who were fed by the hand of their master, perished or disappeared as soon as his liberality was suppressed; the decline of the arts reduced the industrious mechanic to idleness and want; and the senators, who might support with patience the ruin of their country, bewailed their private loss of wealth and luxury. One third of those ample estates, to which the ruin of Italy is originally imputed, was extorted for the use of the conquerors. Injuries were aggravated by insults; the sense of actual sufferings was embittered by the fear of more dreadful evils; and as new lands were allotted to new swarms of barbarians, each senator was apprehensive lest the arbitrary surveyors should approach his favourite villa, or his most profitable farm. The least unfortunate were those who submitted without a murmur to the power which it was impossible to resist. Since they desired to live, they owed some gratitude to the tyrant who had spared their lives; and since he was the absolute master of their fortunes, the portion which he left must be accepted as his pure and voluntary gift. The distress of Italy was mitigated by the prudence and humanity of Odoacer, who had bound himself, as the price of his elevation, to satisfy the demands of a licentious and turbulent multitude. The kings of the barbarians were fre-quently resisted, deposed, or murdered, by their *native* subjects; and the various bands of Italian mercenaries, who associated under the standard of an elective general, claimed a larger privilege of freedom and rapine. A monarchy destitute of national union and hereditary right hastened to its dissolution. After a reign of fourteen years Odoacer was oppressed by the superior genius of Theodoric, king of the Ostrogoths; a hero alike excellent in the arts of war and of government, who restored an age of peace and prosperity, and whose name still excites and deserves the attention of mankind.

XXXIII

(305–712 A.D.) MONASTICISM—CONVERSION OF THE BARBARIANS TO CHRISTIANITY AND ARIANISM

Gibbon believed that the monasticism and the sectarian squabbles within the church were important factors in weakening the fabric of the empire. The following passages from his Chapter XXXVII illustrate his reasoning on the subject.

The monastic profession of the ancients was an act of voluntary devotion. The inconstant fanatic was threatened with the eternal vengeance of the God whom he deserted; but the doors of the monastery were still open for repentance. Those monks whose conscience was fortified by reason or passion were at liberty to resume the character of men and citizens; and even the spouses of Christ might accept the legal embraces of an earthly lover. The examples of scandal, and the progress of superstition, suggested the propriety of more forcible restraints. After a sufficient trial, the fidelity of the novice was secured by a solemn and perpetual vow; and his irrevocable engagement was ratified by the laws of the church and state. A guilty fugitive was pursued, arrested, and restored to his perpetual prison; and the interposition of the magistrate oppressed the freedom and merit which had alleviated, in some degree, the abject slavery of the monastic discipline. The actions of a monk, his words, and even his thoughts, were determined by an inflexible rule or a capricious superior: the slightest offences were corrected by disgrace or confinement, extraordinary fasts, or bloody flagellation; and disobedience, murmur, or delay were ranked in the catalogue of the most heinous sins. A blind submission to the commands of the abbot, however absurd, or even criminal, they might seem, was the ruling principle, the first virtue of the Egyptian monks; and their patience was frequently exercised by the most extravagant trials. They were directed to remove an enormous rock; assiduously to water a barren staff that was planted in the ground, till, at the end of three years, it should vegetate and blossom like a tree; to walk into a fiery furnace; or to cast their infant into a deep pond: and several saints, or madmen, have been immortalised in monastic story by their thoughtless and fearless obedience. The freedom of the mind, the source of every generous and rational sentiment, was destroyed by the habits of credulity and submission; and the monk, contracting the vices of a slave, devoutly followed the faith and passions of his ecclesiastical tyrant. The peace of the Eastern church was invaded by a swarm of fanatics, incapable of fear, or reason, or humanity; and the Imperial troops acknowledged, without shame, that they were much less apprehensive of an encounter with the fiercest barbarians.

The monks were divided into two classes: the *Cænobites*, who lived under a common and regular discipline; and the *Anachorets*, who indulged their unsocial, independent fanaticism. The most devout or the most ambitious, of the spiritual brethren renounced the convent, as they had renounced the world. The fervent monasteries of Egypt, Palestine, and Syria were surrounded by a *Laura*, a distant circle of solitary cells; and the extravagant penance of the Hermits was stimulated by applause and emulation. They sunk under the painful weight of crosses and chains; and their emaciated limbs were confined by collars, bracelets, gauntlets, and greaves of massy and rigid iron. All superfluous incumbrance of dress they contemptuously cast away; and some savage saints of both sexes have been admired, whose naked bodies were only covered by their long hair. They aspired to reduce themselves to the rude and miserable state in which the human brute is scarcely distinguished above his kindred animals; and the numerous sect of Anachorets derived their name from their humble practice of grazing in the fields of Mesopotamia with the common herd. They often usurped the den of some wild beast whom they affected to resemble; they buried themselves in some gloomy cavern, which art or nature had scooped out of the rock; and the marble quarries of Thebais are still inscribed with the monuments of their penance. The most perfect Hermits are supposed to have passed many days without food, many nights without sleep, and many years without speaking; and glorious was the *man* (I abuse that name) who contrived any cell, or seat, of a peculiar construction, which might expose him, in the most inconvenient posture, to the inclemency of the seasons.

Among these heroes of the monastic life, the name and genius of Simeon Stylites have been immortalised by the singular invention of an aërial penance. At the age of thirteen the young Syrian deserted the profession of a shepherd, and threw himself into an austere monastery. After a long and painful novitiate, in which Simeon was repeatedly saved from pious suicide, he established his residence on a mountain, about thirty or forty miles to the east of Antioch. Within the space of a *mandra*, or circle of stones, to which he had attached himself by a ponderous chain, he ascended a column, which was successively raised from the height of nine, to that of sixty, feet from the ground. In this last and lofty station, the Syrian Anachoret resisted the heat of thirty summers, and the cold of as many winters. Habit and exercise instructed him to maintain his dangerous situation without fear or giddiness, and successively to assume the different postures of devotion. He sometimes prayed in an erect attitude, with his outstretched arms in the figure of a cross; but his most familiar practice was that of bending his meagre skeleton from the forehead to the feet; and a curious spectator, after numbering twelve hundred and forty-four repetitions, at length desisted from the endless account. The progress of an ulcer in his thigh might shorten, but it could not disturb, this *celestial* life; and the patient Hermit expired without descending from his column. A prince, who should capriciously inflict such tortures, would be deemed a tyrant; but it would surpass the power of a tyrant to impose a long and miserable existence on the reluctant victims of his cruelty. This voluntary martyrdom must have gradually destroyed the sensibility both of the mind and body; nor can it be presumed that the fanatics who torment themselves are susceptible of any lively affection for the rest of mankind. A cruel, unfeeling temper has distinguished the monks of every age and country; their stern indifference, which is seldom mollified by personal friendship, is inflamed by religious hatred; and their merciless zeal has strenuously administered the holy office of the Inquisition.

The monastic saints, who excite only the contempt and pity of a philosopher, were respected and almost adored by the prince and people. Successive crowds of pilgrims from Gaul and India saluted the divine pillar of Simeon; the tribes of Saracens disputed in arms the honour of his benediction; the queens of Arabia and Persia gratefully confessed his supernatural virtue; and the angelic Hermit was consulted by the younger Theodosius in the most important concerns of the church and state. His remains were transported from the mountain of Telenissa, by a solemn procession of the patriarch, the master-general of the East, six bishops, twenty-one counts or tribunes, and six thousand soldiers; and Antioch revered his bones as her glorious ornament and impregnable defence. The fame of the apostles and martyrs was gradually eclipsed by these recent and popular Anachorets; the Christian world fell prostrate before their shrines; and the miracles ascribed to their relics exceeded, at least in number and duration, the spiritual exploits of their lives. But the golden legend of their lives was embellished by the artful credulity of their interested brethren; and a believing age was easily persuaded that the slightest caprice of an Egyptian or a Syrian monk had been sufficient to interrupt the eternal laws of the universe. The favourites of Heaven were accustomed to cure inveterate diseases with a touch, a word, or a distant message; and to expel the most obstinate demons from the souls or bodies which they possessed. They familiarly accosted, or imperiously commanded, the lions and serpents of the desert; infused vegetation into a sapless trunk; suspended iron on the surface of the water; passed the Nile on the back of a crocodile; and refreshed themselves in a fiery furnace. These extravagant tales, which display the fiction, without the genius, of poetry, have seriously affected the reason, the faith, and the morals of the Christians. Their credulity debased and vitiated the faculties of the mind: they corrupted the evidence of history; and superstition gradually extinguished the hostile light of philosophy and science. Every mode of religious worship which had been practised by the saints, every mysterious doctrine which they believed, was fortified by the sanction of divine revelation, and all the manly virtues were oppressed by the servile and pusillanimous reign of the monks. If it be possible to measure the interval between the philosophic writings of Cicero and the sacred legend of Theodoret, between the character of Cato and that of Simeon, we may appreciate the memorable revolution which was accomplished in the Roman empire within a period of five hundred years.

The progress of Christianity has been marked by two glorious and decisive victories: over the learned and luxurious citizens of the Roman empire; and over the warlike barbarians of Scythia and Germany, who subverted the empire and embraced the religion of the Romans. The Goths were the foremost of these savage proselytes; and the nation was indebted for its conversion to a countryman, or at least to a subject, worthy to be ranked among the inventors of useful arts who have deserved the remembrance and gratitude of posterity. A great number of Roman provincials had been led away into captivity by the Gothic bands who ravaged Asia in the time of Gallienus; and of these captives many were Christians, and several belonged to the ecclesiastical order. Those involuntary missionaries, dispersed as slaves in the villages of Dacia, successively laboured for the salvation of their masters. The seeds which they planted of the evangelic doctrine were gradually propagated; and before the end of a century the pious work was achieved by the labours of Ulphilas, whose ancestors had been transported beyond the Danube from a small town of Cappadocia.

Ulphilas, the bishop and apostle of the Goths, acquired their love and reverence by his blameless life and indefatigable zeal, and they received with implicit confidence the doctrines of truth and virtue which he preached and practised. He executed the arduous task of translating the Scriptures into their native tongue, a dialect of the German or Teutonic language; but he prudently suppressed the four books of Kings, as they might tend to irritate the fierce and sanguinary spirit of the barbarians. The rude, imperfect idiom of soldiers and shepherds, so ill qualified to communicate any spiritual ideas, was improved and modulated by his genius; and Ulphilas, before he could frame his version, was obliged to compose a new alphabet of twenty-four letters; four of which he invented to express the peculiar sounds that were unknown to the Greek and Latin pronunciation.

Christianity, which opened the gates of Heaven to the barbarians, introduced an important change in their moral and political condition. They received, at the same time, the use of letters, so essential to a religion whose doctrines are contained in a sacred book; and while they studied the divine truth, their minds were insensibly enlarged by the distant view of history, of nature, of the arts, and of society. The version of the Scriptures into their native tongue, which had facilitated their conversion, must excite, among their clergy, some curiosity to read the original text, to understand the sacred liturgy of the church, and to examine, in the writings of the fathers, the chain of ecclesiastical tradition. These spiritual gifts were preserved in the Greek and Latin languages, which concealed the inestimable monuments of ancient learning. The immortal productions of Virgil, Cicero, and Livy, which were accessible to the Christian barbarians, maintained a silent intercourse between the reign of Augustus and the times of Clovis and Charlemagne. The emulation of mankind was encouraged by the remembrance of a more perfect state; and the flame of science was secretly kept alive, to warm and enlighten the mature age of the Western world. In the most corrupt state of Christianity the barbarians might learn justice from the *law*, and mercy from the *gospel*; and if the knowledge of their duty was insufficient to guide their actions or to regulate their passions, they were sometimes restrained by conscience, and frequently punished by remorse. But the direct authority of religion was less effectual than the holy communion, which united them with their Christian brethren in spiritual friendship. The influence of these sentiments contributed to secure their fidelity in the service or the alliance of the Romans, to alleviate the horrors of war, to moderate the insolence of conquest, and to preserve, in the downfall of the empire, a permanent respect for the name and institutions of Rome.

But the operation of these causes was checked and retarded by the unfortunate accident which infused a deadly poison into the cup of salvation. Whatever might be the early sentiments of Ulphilas, his connections with the empire and the church were formed during the reign of Arianism. The apostle of the Goths subscribed the creed of Rimini; professed with freedom, and perhaps with sincerity, that the Son was not equal or consubstantial to the FATHER, communicated these errors to the clergy and people; and infected the barbaric world with an heresy which the great Theodosius proscribed and extinguished among the Romans. The temper and understanding of the new proselytes were not adapted to metaphysical subtleties; but they strenuously maintained what they had piously received as the pure and genuine doctrines of Christianity. The advantage of preaching and expounding the Scriptures in the Teutonic language promoted the apostolic labours of Ulphilas and his successors; and they ordained a competent number of bishops and presbyters for the instruction of the kindred tribes. The Ostrogoths, the Burgundians, the Suevi, and the Vandals, who had listened to the eloquence of the Latin clergy, preferred the more intelligible lessons of their domestic teachers, and Arianism was adopted as the national faith of the warlike converts who were seated on the ruins of the Western empire. This irreconcilable difference of religion was a perpetual source of jealousy and hatred; and the reproach of *Barbarian* was embittered by the more odious epithet of *Heretic*. The heroes of the North, who had submitted with some reluctance to believe that all their ancestors were in hell, were astonished and exasperated to learn that they themselves had only changed the mode of their eternal condemnation. Instead of the smooth applause which Christian kings are accustomed to expect from their loyal prelates, the orthodox bishops and their clergy were in a state of opposition to the Arian courts; and their indiscreet opposition frequently became criminal, and might sometimes be dangerous. The pulpit, that safe and sacred organ of sedition, resounded with the names of Pharaoh and Holofernes; the public discontent was inflamed by the hope or promise of a glorious deliverance; and the seditious saints were tempted to promote the accomplishment of their own predictions. Notwithstanding these provocations, the catholics of Gaul, Spain, and Italy enjoyed, under the reign of the Arians, the free and peaceful exercise of their religion. Their haughty masters respected the zeal of a numerous people, resolved to die at the foot of their altars, and the example of their devout constancy was admired and imitated by the barbarians themselves. The conquerors evaded, however, the disgraceful reproach or confession of fear, by attributing their toleration to the liberal motives of reason and humanity; and while they affected the language, they imperceptibly imbibed the spirit, of genuine Christianity.

XXXIV

(449–582 A.D.) REIGN AND CONVERSION OF CLOVIS—HIS VICTORIES OVER THE VISI-GOTHS—ESTABLISHMENT OF THE FRENCH MONARCHY IN GAUL—LAWS OF THE BAR-BARIANS—STATE OF THE ROMANS—THE VISIGOTHS OF SPAIN—CONQUESTS OF BRITAIN BY THE SAXONS

The Gauls, who impatiently supported the Roman yoke, received a memorable lesson from one of the lieutenants of Vespasian, whose weighty sense has been refined and expressed by the genius of Tacitus. "The protection of the republic has delivered Gaul from internal discord and foreign invasions. By the loss of national independence you have acquired the name and privileges of Roman citizens. You enjoy, in common with ourselves, the permanent benefits of civil government; and your remote situation is less exposed to the accidental mischiefs of tyranny. Instead of exercising the rights of conquest, we have been contented to impose such tributes as are requisite for your own preservation. Peace cannot be secured without armies, and armies must be supported at the expense of the people. It is for your sake, not for our own, that we guard the barrier of the Rhine against the ferocious Germans, who have so often attempted, and who will always desire, to exchange the solitude of their woods and morasses for the wealth and fertility of Gaul. The fall of Rome would be fatal to the provinces, and you would be buried in the ruins of that mighty fabric which has been raised by the valour and wisdom of eight hundred years. Your imaginary freedom would be insulted and oppressed by a savage master, and the expulsion of the Romans would be succeeded by the eternal hostilities of the barbarian conquerors." This salutary advice was accepted, and this strange prediction was accomplished. In the space of four hundred years the hardy Gauls, who had encountered the arms of Cæsar, were imperceptibly melted into the general mass of citizens and subjects: the Western empire was dissolved; and the Germans who had passed the Rhine fiercely contended for the possession of Gaul, and excited the contempt or abhorrence of its peaceful and polished inhabitants. With that conscious pride which the preeminence of knowledge and luxury seldom fails to inspire, they derided the hairy and gigantic savages of the North; their rustic manners, dissonant joy, voracious appetite, and their horrid appearance, equally disgusting to the sight and to the smell. The liberal studies were still cultivated in the schools of Autun and Bordeaux, and the language of Cicero and Virgil was familiar to the Gallic youth. Their ears were astonished by the harsh and unknown sounds of the Germanic dialect, and they ingeniously lamented that the trembling muses fled from the harmony of a Burgundian lyre. The Gauls were endowed with all the advantages of art and nature, but, as they wanted courage to defend them, they were justly condemned to obey, and even to flatter, the victorious barbarians by whose clemency they held their precarious fortunes and their lives.

As soon as Odoacer had extinguished the Western empire, he sought the friendship of the most powerful of the barbarians. The new sovereign of Italy resigned to Euric, king of the Visigoths, all the Roman conquests beyond the Alps, as far as the Rhine and the Ocean; and the senate might confirm this liberal gift with some ostentation of power, and without any real loss of revenue or dominion. The lawful pretensions of Euric were justified by ambition and success, and the Gothic nation might aspire under his command to the monarchy of Spain and Gaul. Arles and Marseilles surrendered to his arms: he oppressed the freedom of Auvergne, and the bishop condescended to purchase his recall from exile by a tribute of just but reluctant praise. Sidonius waited before the gates of the palace among a crowd of ambassadors and suppliants, and their various business at the court of Bordeaux attested the power and the renown of the king of the Visigoths. The Heruli of the distant ocean, who painted their naked bodies with its cærulean colour, implored his protection; and the Saxons respected the maritime provinces of a prince who was destitute of any naval force. The tall Burgundians submitted to his authority; nor did he restore the captive Franks till he had imposed on that fierce nation the terms of an unequal peace. The Vandals of Africa cultivated his useful friendship, and the Ostrogoths of Pannonia were supported by his powerful aid against the oppression of the neighbouring Huns. The North (such are the lofty strains of the poet) was agitated or appeased by the nod of Euric, the great king of Persia consulted the oracle of the West, and the aged god of the Tiber was protected by the swelling genius of the Garonne. The fortune of nations has often depended on accidents; and France may ascribe her greatness to the premature death of the Gothic king at a time when his son Alaric was a helpless infant, and his adversary Clovis an ambitious and valiant youth.

While Childeric, the father of Clovis, lived an exile in Germany, he was hospitably entertained by the queen as well as by the king of the Thuringians. After his restoration Bafina escaped from her husband's bed to the arms of her lover, freely declaring that, if she had known a man wiser, stronger, or more beautiful than Childeric, that man should have been the object of her preference. Clovis was the offspring of this voluntary union, and when he was no more than fifteen years of age he succeeded, by his father's death, to the command of the Salian tribe. The narrow limits of his kingdom were confined to the island of the Batavians, with the ancient dioceses of Tournay and Arras; and at the baptism of Clovis the number of his warriors could not exceed five thousand. The kindred tribes of the Franks who had seated themselves along the Belgic rivers, the Scheldt, the Meuse, the Moselle, and the Rhine, were governed by their independent kings of the Merovingian race—the equals, the allies, and sometimes the enemies, of the Salic prince. But the Germans, who obeyed in peace the hereditary jurisdiction of their chiefs, were free to follow the standard of a popular and victorious general; and the superior merit of Clovis attracted the respect and allegiance of the national confederacy. When he first took the field, he had neither gold and silver in his coffers, nor wine and corn in his magazines; but he imitated the example of Cæsar, who in the same country had acquired wealth by the sword, and purchased soldiers with the fruits of conquest. After each successful battle or expedition the spoils were accumulated in one common mass; every warrior received his proportionable share, and the royal prerogative submitted to the equal regulations of military law. The untamed spirit of the barbarians was taught to acknowledge the advantages of regular discipline. At the annual review of the month of March their arms were diligently inspected, and when they traversed a peaceful territory they were prohibited from touching a blade of grass. The justice of Clovis was inexorable, and his careless or disobedient soldiers were punished with instant death. It would be superfluous to praise the valour of a

Frank, but the valour of Clovis was directed by cool and consummate prudence. In all his transactions with mankind he calculated the weight of interest, of passion, and of opinion; and his measures were sometimes adapted to the sanguinary manners of the Germans, and sometimes moderated by the milder genius of Rome and Christianity. He was intercepted in the career of victory, since he died in the forty-fifth year of his age: but he had already accomplished, in a reign of thirty years, the establishment of the French monarchy in Gaul.

Till the thirtieth year of his age Clovis continued to worship the gods of his ancestors. His disbelief, or rather disregard of Christianity, might encourage him to pillage with less remorse the churches of an hostile territory: but his subjects of Gaul enjoyed the free exercise of religious worship, and the bishops entertained a more favourable hope of the idolater than of the heretics. The Merovingian prince had contracted a fortunate alliance with the fair Clotilda, the niece of the king of Burgundy, who in the midst of an Arian court was educated in the profession of the catholic faith. It was her interest as well as her duty to achieve the conversion of a Pagan husband; and Clovis insensibly listened to the voice of love and religion. He consented (perhaps such terms had been previously stipulated) to the baptism of his eldest son; and though the sudden death of the infant excited some superstitious fears, he was persuaded a second time to repeat the dangerous experiment. In the distress of the battle of Tolbiac, Clovis loudly invoked the God of Clotilda and the Christians; and victory disposed him to hear with respectful gratitude the eloquent Remigius, bishop of Rheims, who forcibly displayed the temporal and spiritual advantages of his conversion. The king declared himself satisfied of the truth of the catholic faith; and the political reasons which might have suspended his public profession were removed by the devout or loyal acclamations of the Franks, who showed themselves alike prepared to follow their heroic leader to the field of battle or to the baptismal font. The important ceremony was performed in the cathedral of Rheims with every circumstance of magnificence and solemnity that could impress an awful sense of religion on the minds of its rude proselytes. The new Constantine was immediately baptised with three thousand of his warlike subjects, and their example was imitated by the remainder of the *gentle barbarians*, who, in obedience to the victorious prelate, adored the cross which they had burnt, and burnt the idols which they had formerly adored. The mind of Clovis was susceptible of transient fervour: he was exasperated by the pathetic tale of the passion and death of Christ; and instead of weighing the salutary consequences of that mysterious sacrifice, he exclaimed with indiscreet fury, "Had I been present at the head of my valiant Franks, I would have revenged his injuries." But the savage conqueror of Gaul was incapable of examining the proofs of a religion which depends on the laborious investigation of historic evidence and speculative theology. He was still more incapable of feeling the mild influence of the Gospel, which persuades and purifies the heart of a genuine convert. His ambitious reign was a perpetual violation of moral and Christian duties: his hands were stained with blood in peace as well as in war; and, as soon as Clovis had dismissed a synod of the Gallician church, he calmly assassinated *all* the princes of the Merovingian race.

At Paris, which he already considered as his royal seat, Clovis declared to an assembly of the princes and warriors the pretence and the motive of a Gothic war. "It grieves me to see that the Arians still possess the fairest portion of Gaul. Let us march against them with the aid of God; and, having vanquished the heretics, we will possess and divide their fertile provinces." The Franks, who were inspired by hereditary valour and recent zeal, applauded the generous design of their monarch; expressed their resolution to conquer or die, since death and conquest would be equally profitable; and solemnly protested that they would never shave their beards till victory should absolve them from that inconvenient vow. The enterprise was promoted by the public or private exhortations of Clotilda. She reminded her husband how effectually some pious foundation would propitiate the Deity and his servants: and the Christian hero, darting his battle-axe with a skilful and nervous hand, "There (said he), on that spot where my *Francisca* shall fall, will I erect a church in honour of the holy apostles." This ostentatious piety confirmed and justified the attachment of the catholics, with whom he secretly corresponded; and their devout wishes were gradually ripened into a formidable conspiracy. The people of Aquitain was alarmed by the indiscreet reproaches of their Gothic tyrants, who justly accused them of preferring the dominion of the Franks; and their zealous adherent Quintianus, bishop of Rodez, preached more forcibly in his exile than in his diocese. To resist these foreign and domestic enemies, who were fortified by the alliance of the Burgundians, Alaric collected his troops, far more numerous than the military powers of Clovis. The Visigoths resumed the exercise of arms, which they had neglected in a long and luxurious peace; a select band of valiant and robust slaves attended their masters to the field; and the cities of Gaul were compelled to furnish their doubtful and reluctant aid. Theodoric, king of the Ostrogoths, who reigned in Italy, had laboured to maintain the tranquillity of Gaul; and he assumed, or affected, for that purpose the impartial character of a mediator. But the sagacious monarch dreaded the rising empire of Clovis, and he was firmly engaged to support the national and religious cause of the Goths.

The accidental or artificial prodigies which adorned the expedition of Clovis were accepted, by a superstitious age, as the manifest declaration of the Divine favour. He marched from Paris; and as he proceeded with decent reverence through the holy diocese of Tours, his anxiety tempted him to consult the shrine of St. Martin, the sanctuary, and the oracle of Gaul. His messengers were instructed to remark the words of the Psalm which should happen to be chanted at the precise moment when they entered the church. Those words most fortunately expressed the valour and victory of the champions of Heaven, and the application was easily transferred to the new Joshua, the new Gideon, who went forth to battle against the enemies of the Lord. Orleans secured to the Franks a bridge on the Loire; but, at the distance of forty miles from Poitiers, their progress was intercepted by an extraordinary swell of the river Vigenna or Vienne; and the opposite banks were covered by the encampment of the Visigoths. Delay must be always dangerous to barbarians, who consume the country through which they march; and had Clovis possessed leisure and materials, it might have been impracticable to construct a bridge, or to force a passage, in the face of a superior enemy. But the affectionate peasants, who were impatient to welcome their deliverer, could easily betray some unknown or unguarded ford: the merit of the discovery was enhanced by the useful interposition of fraud or fiction; and a white hart, of singular size and beauty, appeared to guide and animate the march of the catholic army. The counsels of the Visigoths were irresolute and distracted. A crowd of impatient warriors, presumptuous in their strength, and disdaining to fly before the robbers of Germany, excited Alaric to assert in arms the name and blood of the conqueror of Rome. The advice of the graver chieftains pressed him to elude the first ardour of the Franks;

and to expect, in the southern provinces of Gaul, the veteran and victorious Ostrogoths, whom the king of Italy had already sent to his assistance. The decisive moments were wasted in idle deliberation; the Goths too hastily abandoned, perhaps, an advantageous post; and the opportunity of a secure retreat was lost by their slow and disorderly motions. After Clovis had passed the ford, as it is still named, of the *Hart*, he advanced with bold and hasty steps to prevent the escape of the enemy. His nocturnal march was directed by a flaming meteor suspended in the air above the cathedral of Poitiers; and this signal, which might be previously concerted with the orthodox successor of St. Hilary, was compared to the column of fire that guided the Israelites in the desert. At the third hour of the day, about ten miles beyond Poitiers, Clovis overtook, and instantly attacked, the Gothic army, whose defeat was already prepared by terror and confusion. Yet they rallied in their extreme distress, and the martial youths, who had clamorously demanded the battle, refused to survive the ignominy of flight. The two kings encountered each other in single combat. Alaric fell by the hand of his rival; and the victorious Frank was saved, by the goodness of his cuirass and the vigour of his horse, from the spears of two desperate Goths, who furiously rode against him to revenge the death of their sovereign. The vague expression of a mountain of the slain serves to indicate a cruel, though indefinite, slaughter; but Gregory has carefully observed that his valiant countryman Apollinaris, the son of Sidonius, lost his life at the head of the nobles of Auvergne. Perhaps these suspected catholics had been maliciously exposed to the blind assault of the enemy; and perhaps the influence of religion was superseded by personal attachment or military honour.

Such is the empire of Fortune (if we may still disguise our ignorance under that popular name), that it is almost equally difficult to foresee the events of war, or to explain their various consequences. A bloody and complete victory has sometimes yielded no more than the possession of the field; and the loss of ten thousand men has sometimes been sufficient to destroy, in a single day, the work of ages. The decisive battle of Poitiers was followed by the conquest of Aquitain. Alaric had left behind him an infant son, a bastard competitor, factious nobles, and a disloyal people; and the remaining forces of the Goths were oppressed by the general consternation, or opposed to each other in civil discord. The victorious king of the Franks proceeded without delay to the siege of Angoulême. At the sound of his trumpets the walls of the city imitated the example of Jericho, and instantly fell to the ground; a splendid miracle, which may be reduced to the supposition that some clerical engineers had secretly undermined the foundations of the rampart. At Bordeaux, which had submitted without resistance, Clovis established his winter quarters; and his prudent economy transported from Toulouse the royal treasures, which were deposited in the capital of the monarchy. The conqueror penetrated as far as the confines of Spain; restored the honours of the catholic church; fixed in Aquitain a colony of Franks; and delegated to his lieutenants the easy task of subduing or extirpating the nation of the Visigoths. But the Visigoths were protected by the wise and powerful monarch of Italy. While the balance was still equal, Theodoric had perhaps delayed the march of the Ostrogoths; but their strenuous efforts successfully resisted the ambition of Clovis; and the army of the Franks, and their Burgundian allies, was compelled to raise the siege of Arles, with the loss, as it is said, of thirty thousand men. These vicissitudes inclined the fierce spirit of Clovis to acquiesce in an advantageous treaty of peace. The Visigoths were suffered to retain the possession of Septimania, a narrow tract of sea-coast, from the Rhône to the Pyrenees; but the ample province of Aquitain, from those mountains to the Loire, was indissolubly united to the kingdom of France.

After the success of the Gothic war, Clovis accepted the honours of the Roman consulship. The emperor Anastasius ambitiously bestowed on the most powerful rival of Theodoric the title and ensigns of that eminent dignity; yet, from some unknown cause, the name of Clovis has not been inscribed in the *Fasti* either of the East or West. On the solemn day, the monarch of Gaul, placing a diadem on his head, was invested, in the church of St. Martin, with a purple tunic and mantle. From thence he proceeded on horseback to the cathedral of Tours; and, as he passed through the streets, profusely scattered, with his own hand, a donative of gold and silver to the joyful multitude, who incessantly repeated their acclamations of *Consul* and *Augustus*. The actual or legal authority of Clovis could not receive any new accessions from the consular dignity. It was a name, a shadow, an empty pageant; and if the conqueror had been instructed to claim the ancient prerogatives of that high office, they must have expired with the period of its annual duration. But the Romans were disposed to revere, in the person of their master, that antique title which the emperors condescended to assume: the barbarian himself seemed to contract a sacred obligation to respect the majesty of the republic; and the successors of Theodosius, by soliciting his friendship, tacitly forgave, and almost ratified, the usurpation of Gaul.

Twenty-five years after the death of Clovis this important concession was more formally declared in a treaty between his sons and the emperor Justinian. The Ostrogoths of Italy, unable to defend their distant acquisitions, had resigned to the Franks the cities of Arles and Marseilles: of Arles, still adorned with the seat of a Prætorian præfect, and of Marseilles, enriched by the advantages of trade and navigation. This transaction was confirmed by the Imperial authority; and Justinian, generously yielding to the Franks the sovereignty of the countries beyond the Alps, which they already possessed, absolved the provincials from their allegiance; and established on a more lawful, though not more solid, foundation, the throne of the Merovingians. When the last survivor of the sons of Clovis united the inheritance and conquests of the Merovingians, his kingdom extended far beyond the limits of modern France. Yet modern France, such has been the progress of arts and policy, far surpasses, in wealth, populousness, and power, the spacious but savage realms of Clotaire or Dagobert.

The Merovingians, instead of imposing a uniform rule of conduct on their various subjects, permitted each people, and each family, of their empire freely to enjoy their domestic institutions; nor were the Romans excluded from the common benefits of this legal toleration. The children embraced the *law* of their parents, the wife that of her husband, the freedman that of his patron; and in all causes where the parties were of different nations, the plaintiff or accuser was obliged to follow the tribunal of the defendant, who may always plead a judicial presumption of right or innocence. A more ample latitude was allowed, if every citizen, in the presence of the judge, might declare the law under which he desired to live, and the national society to which he chose to belong. Such an indulgence would abolish the partial distinctions of victory: and the Roman provincials might patiently acquiesce in the hardships of their condition, since it depended on themselves to assume the privilege, if they dared to assert the character, of free and warlike barbarians.

The civil and military professions, which had been separated by Constantine, were again united by the barbarians. The harsh sound of the Teutonic appellations was mollified into the Latin titles of Duke, of Count, or of Præfect; and the same officer assumed, within his district, the command of the troops and the administration of justice. But the fierce and illiterate chieftain was seldom qualified to discharge the duties of a judge, which require all of the faculties of a philosophic mind, laboriously cultivated by experience and study; and his rude ignorance was compelled to embrace some simple and visible methods of ascertaining the cause of justice. In every religion the Deity has been invoked to confirm the truth, or to punish the falsehood, of human testimony; but this powerful instrument was misapplied and abused by the simplicity of the German legislators. The party accused might justify his innocence, by producing before their tribunal a number of friendly witnesses, who solemnly declared their belief or assurance that he was not guilty. According to the weight of the charge this legal number of *compurgators* was multiplied: seventy-two voices were required to absolve an incendiary or assassin; and when the chastity of a queen of France was suspected, three hundred gallant nobles swore, without hesitation, that the infant prince had been actually begotten by her deceased husband. The sin and scandal of manifest and frequent perjuries engaged the magistrates to remove these dangerous temptations, and to supply the defects of human testimony by the famous experiments of fire and water. These extraordinary trials were so capriciously contrived, that in some cases guilt, and innocence in others, could not be proved without the interposition of a miracle. Such miracles were readily provided by fraud and credulity; the most intricate causes were determined by this easy and infallible method; and the turbulent barbarians, who might have disdained the sentence of the magistrate, submissively acquiesced in the judgment of God.

But the trials by single combat gradually obtained superior credit and authority among a warlike people, who could not believe that a brave man deserved to suffer, or that a coward deserved to live. Both in civil and criminal proceedings, the plaintiff, or accuser, the defendant, or even the witness, were exposed to mortal challenge from the antagonist who was destitute of legal proofs; and it was incumbent on them either to desert their cause or publicly to maintain their honour in the lists of battle. They fought either on foot or on horseback, according to the custom of their nation; and the decision of the sword or lance was ratified by the sanction of Heaven, of the judge, and of the people. This sanguinary law was introduced into Gaul by the Burgundians; and their legislator Gundobald condescended to answer the complaints and objections of his subject Avitus. "Is it not true," said the king of Burgundy to the bishop, "that the event of national wars and private combats is directed by the judgment of God; and that his providence awards the victory to the juster cause?" By such prevailing arguments, the absurd and cruel practice of judicial duels, which had been peculiar to some tribes of Germany, was propagated and established in all the monarchies of Europe, from Sicily to the Baltic. At the end of ten centuries the reign of legal violence was not totally extinguished; and the ineffectual censures of saints, of popes, and of synods, may seem to prove that the influence of superstition is weakened by its unnatural alliance with reason and humanity. The tribunals were stained with the blood, perhaps, of innocent and respectable citizens; the law, which now favours the rich, then yielded to the strong; and the old, the feeble, and the infirm, were condemned either to renounce their fairest claims and possessions, to sustain the dangers of an unequal conflict, or to trust the doubtful aid of a mercenary champion. This oppressive jurisprudence was imposed on the provincials of Gaul who complained of any injuries in their persons and property. Whatever might be the strength or courage of individuals, the victorious barbarians excelled in the love and exercise of arms; and the vanquished Roman was unjustly summoned to repeat, in his own person, the bloody contest which had been already decided against his country.

We are now qualified to despise the opposite, and perhaps artful, misrepresentations which have softened or exaggerated the oppression of the Romans of Gaul under the reign of the Merovingians. The conquerors never promulgated any *universal* edict of servitude or confiscation: but a degenerate people, who excused their weakness by the specious names of politeness and peace, was exposed to the arms and laws of the ferocious barbarians, who contemptuously insulted their possessions, their freedom, and their safety. Their personal injuries were partial and irregular; but the great body of the Romans survived the revolution, and still preserved the property and privileges of citizens. A large portion of their lands was exacted for the use of the Franks: but they enjoyed the remainder exempt from tribute; and the same irresistible violence which swept away the arts and manufactures of Gaul destroyed the elaborate and expensive system of Imperial despotism. The provincials must frequently deplore the savage jurisprudence of the Salic or Ripuarian laws; but their private life, in the important concerns of marriage, testaments, or inheritance, was still regulated by the Theodosian Code; and a discontented Roman might freely aspire or descend to the title and character of a barbarian. The honours of the state were accessible to his ambition: the education and temper of the Romans more peculiarly qualified them for the offices of civil government; and as soon as emulation had rekindled their military ardour, they were permitted to march in the ranks, or even at the head, of the victorious Germans. I shall not attempt to enumerate the generals and magistrates whose names attest the liberal policy of the Merovingians. The supreme command of Burgundy, with the title of Patrician, was successively intrusted to three Romans; and the last and most powerful, Mummolus, who alternately saved and disturbed the monarchy, had supplanted his father in the station of count of Autun, and left a treasure of thirty talents of gold and two hundred and fifty talents of silver. The fierce and illiterate barbarians were excluded, during several generations, from the dignities, and even from the orders, of the church. The clergy of Gaul consisted almost entirely of native provincials; the haughty Franks fell prostrate at the feet of their subjects who were dignified with the episcopal character; and the power and riches which had been lost in war were insensibly recovered by superstition. In all temporal affairs the Theodosian Code was the universal law of the clergy; but the barbaric jurisprudence had liberally provided for their personal safety: a subdeacon was equivalent to two Franks; the *antrustion* and priest were held in similar estimation; and the life of a bishop was appreciated far above the common standard, at the price of nine hundred pieces of gold. The Romans communicated to their conquerors the use of the Christian religion and Latin language; but their language and their religion had alike degenerated from the simple purity of the Augustan and Apostolic age. The progress of superstition and barbarism was rapid and universal: the worship of the saints concealed from vulgar eyes the God of the Christians, and the rustic dialect of peasants and soldiers was corrupted by a Teutonic idiom and pronunciation. Yet such intercourse of sacred and social communion eradicated the distinctions of birth and victory; and the nations of Gaul were gradually confounded under the name and government of the Franks.

The Visigoths had resigned to Clovis the greatest part of their Gallic possessions; but their loss was amply compensated by the

easy conquest and secure enjoyment of the provinces of Spain.
From the monarchy of the Goths, which soon involved the Suevic
kingdom of Gallicia, the modern Spaniards still derive national
vanity, but the historian of the Roman empire is neither invited nor
compelled to pursue the obscure and barren series of their annals.
The Goths of Spain were separated from the rest of mankind by
the lofty ridge of the Pyrenæan mountains: their manners and
institutions, as far as they were common to the Germanic tribes,
have been already explained. I have anticipated in the preceding
chapter the most important of their ecclesiastical events—the fall
of Arianism and the persecution of the Jews: and it only remains
to observe some interesting circumstances which relate to the civil
and ecclesiastical constitution of the Spanish kingdom.

After their conversion from idolatry or heresy, the Franks and
the Visigoths were disposed to embrace, with equal submission, the
inherent evils and the accidental benefits of superstition. But the
prelates of France, long before the extinction of the Merovingian
race, had degenerated into fighting and hunting barbarians. They
disdained the use of synods, forgot the laws of temperance and
chastity, and preferred the indulgence of private ambition and luxury
to the general interest of the sacerdotal profession. The bishops of
Spain respected themselves, and were respected by the public:
their indissoluble union disguised their vices, and confirmed their
authority; and the regular discipline of the church introduced peace,
order, and stability into the government of the state. From the reign
of Recared, the first catholic king, to that of Witiza, the immediate
predecessor of the unfortunate Roderic, sixteen national councils
were successively convened. The six metropolitans, Toledo, Seville,
Merida, Braga, Tarragona, and Narbonne, presided according to
their respective seniority; the assembly was composed of their
suffragan bishops, who appeared in person or by their proxies, and
a place was assigned to the most holy or opulent of the Spanish
abbots. During the first three days of the convocation, as long as
they agitated the ecclesiastical questions of doctrine and discipline,
the profane laity was excluded from their debates, which were conducted, however, with decent solemnity. But on the morning of the
fourth day the doors were thrown open for the entrance of the great
officers of the palace, the dukes and counts of the provinces, the
judges of the cities, and the Gothic nobles; and the decrees of
Heaven were ratified by the consent of the people. The same rules
were observed in the provincial assemblies, the annual synods,

which were empowered to hear complaints and to redress grievances; and a legal government was supported by the prevailing influence of the Spanish clergy. The bishops, who in each revolution were prepared to flatter the victorious and to insult the prostrate, laboured with diligence and success to kindle the flames of persecution, and to exalt the mitre above the crown. Yet the national councils of Toledo, in which the free spirit of the barbarians was tempered and guided by episcopal policy, have established some prudent laws for the common benefit of the king and people. The vacancy of the throne was supplied by the choice of the bishops and palatines; and after the failure of the line of Alaric, the regal dignity was still limited to the pure and noble blood of the Goths. The clergy, who anointed their lawful prince, always recommended, and sometimes practised, the duty of allegiance: and the spiritual censures were denounced on the heads of the impious subjects who should resist his authority, conspire against his life, or violate by an indecent union the chastity even of his widow. But the monarch himself, when he ascended the throne, was bound by a reciprocal oath to God and his people that he would faithfully execute his important trust. The real or imaginary faults of his administration were subject to the control of a powerful aristocracy; and the bishops and palatines were guarded by a fundamental privilege that they should not be degraded, imprisoned, tortured, nor punished with death, exile, or confiscation, unless by the free and public judgment of their peers.

While the kingdoms of the Franks and Visigoths were established in Gaul and Spain, the Saxons achieved the conquest of Britain, the third great diocese of the præfecture of the West. Since Britain was already separated from the Roman empire, I might without reproach decline a story familiar to the most illiterate, and obscure to the most learned, of my readers. The Saxons, who excelled in the use of the oar or the battleaxe, were ignorant of the art which could alone perpetuate the fame of their exploits; the provincials, relapsing into barbarism, neglected to describe the ruin of their country; and the doubtful tradition was almost extinguished before the missionaries of Rome restored the light of science and Christianity. The declamations of Gildas, the fragments or fables of Nennius, tie obscure hints of the Saxon laws and chronicles, and the ecclesiastical tales of the venerable Bede, have been illustrated by the diligence, and sometimes embellished by the fancy, of succeeding writers, whose works I am not ambitious either to censure or to transcribe. Yet the historian of the empire may be tempted to pursue the revolutions of a Roman province till it vanishes from his sight; and an Englishman may curiously trace the establishment of the barbarians from whom he derives his name, his laws, and perhaps his origin.

About forty years after the dissolution of the Roman government Vortigern appears to have obtained the supreme, though precarious, command of the princes and cities of Britain. That unfortunate monarch has been almost unanimously condemned for the weak and mischievous policy of inviting a formidable stranger to repel the vexatious inroads of a domestic foe. His ambassadors are despatched by the gravest historians to the coast of Germany: they address a pathetic oration to the general assembly of the Saxons, and those warlike barbarians resolve to assist with a fleet and army the suppliants of a distant and unknown island. If Britain had indeed been unknown to the Saxons, the measure of its calamities would have been less complete. But the strength of the Roman government could not always guard the maritime province against the pirates of Germany: the independent and divided states were exposed to their attacks, and the Saxons might sometimes join the Scots and the Picts in a tacit or express confederacy of rapine and destruction. Vortigern could only balance the various perils which assaulted on every side his throne and his people; and his policy may deserve either praise or excuse if he preferred the alliance of *those* barbarians whose naval power rendered them the most dangerous enemies, and the most serviceable allies. Hengist and Horsa, as they ranged along the eastern coast with three ships, were engaged by the promise of an ample stipend to embrace the defence of Britain, and their intrepid valour soon delivered the country from the Caledonian invaders. The Isle of Thanet, a secure and fertile district, was allotted for the residence of these German auxiliaries, and they were supplied according to the treaty with a plentiful allowance of clothing and provisions. This favourable reception encouraged five thousand warriors to embark with their families in seventeen vessels, and the infant power of Hengist was fortified by this strong and seasonable reinforcement. The crafty barbarian suggested to Vortigern the obvious advantage of fixing, in the neighbourhood of the Picts, a colony of faithful allies: a third fleet, of forty ships, under the command of his son and nephew, sailed from Germany, ravaged the Orkneys, and disembarked a new army on the coast of Northumberland or Lothian, at the opposite extremity of the devoted land.

It was easy to foresee, but it was impossible to prevent, the impending evils. The two nations were soon divided and exasperated by mutual jealousies. The Saxons magnified all that they had done and suffered in the cause of an ungrateful people; while the Britons regretted the liberal rewards which could not satisfy the avarice of those haughty mercenaries. The causes of fear and hatred were inflamed into an irreconcilable quarrel. The Saxons flew to arms; and if they perpetrated a treacherous massacre during the security of a feast, they destroyed the reciprocal confidence which sustains the intercourse of peace and war.

While the continent of Europe and Africa yielded, without resistance, to the barbarians, the British island, alone and unaided, maintained a long, vigorous, though an unsuccessful, struggle, against the formidable pirates who, almost at the same instant, assaulted the northern, the eastern, and the southern coasts. The cities, which had been fortified with skill, were defended with resolution; the advantages of ground, hills, forests, and morasses, were diligently improved by the inhabitants; the conquest of each district was purchased with blood; and the defeats of the Saxons are strongly attested by the discreet silence of their annalist. Hengist might hope to achieve the conquest of Britain; but his ambition, in an active reign of thirty-five years, was confined to the possession of Kent; and the numerous colony which he had planted in the North was extirpated by the sword of the Britons. The monarchy of the West Saxons was laboriously founded by the persevering efforts of three martial generations. The life of Cerdic, one of the bravest of the children of Woden, was consumed in the conquest of Hampshire and the Isle of Wight; and the loss which he sustained in the battle of Mount Badon reduced him to a state of inglorious repose. Kenric, his valiant son, advanced into Wiltshire; besieged Salisbury, at that time seated on a commanding eminence; and vanquished an army which advanced to the relief of the city. In the subsequent battle of Marlborough, his British enemies displayed their military science. Their troops were formed in three lines; each line consisted of three distinct bodies; and the cavalry, the archers, and the pikemen were distributed according to the principles of Roman tactics. The Saxons charged in one weighty column, boldly encountered with their short swords the long lances of the Britons, and maintained an equal conflict till the approach of night. Two decisive victories, the death of three British kings, and the reduction of Cirencester, Bath, and Gloucester, established the fame and power of Ceaulin, the grandson of Cerdic, who carried his victorious arms to the banks of the Severn.

After a war of an hundred years the independent Britons still occupied the whole extent of the western coast, from the wall of Antoninus to the extreme promontory of Cornwall; and the principal cities of the inland country still opposed the arms of the barbarians. Resistance became more languid, as the number and boldness of the assailants continually increased. Winning their way by slow and painful efforts, the Saxons, the Angles, and their various confederates, advanced from the North, from the East, and from the South, till their victorious banners were united in the centre of the island. Beyond the Severn the Britons still asserted their national freedom, which survived the heptarchy, and even the monarchy, of the Saxons. The bravest warriors, who preferred exile to slavery, found a secure refuge in the mountains of Wales: the reluctant submission of Cornwall was delayed for some ages; and a band of fugitives acquired a settlement in Gaul, by their own valour, or the liberality of the Merovingian kings. The western angle of Armorica acquired the new appellations of *Cornwall* and the *Lesser Britain*; and the vacant lands of the Osismii were filled by a strange people, who, under the authority of their counts and bishops, preserved the laws and language of their ancestors. To the feeble descendants of Clovis and Charlemagne, the Britons of Armorica refused the customary tribute, subdued the neighbouring dioceses of Vannes, Rennes, and Nantes, and formed a powerful, though vassal, state, which has been united to the crown of France.

In a century of perpetual, or at least implacable, war, much courage, and some skill, must have been exerted for the defence of Britain. Yet if the memory of its champions is almost buried in oblivion, we need not repine; since every age, however destitute of science or virtue, sufficiently abounds with acts of blood and military renown. The tomb of Vortimer, the son of Vortigern, was erected on the margin of the sea-shore, as a landmark formidable to the Saxons, whom he had thrice vanquished in the fields of Kent. Ambrosius Aurelian was descended from a noble family of Romans; his modesty was equal to his valour, and his valour, till the last fatal action, was crowned with splendid success. But every British name is effaced by the illustrious name of ARTHUR, the hereditary prince of the Silures, in South Wales, and the elective king or general of the nation. According to the most rational account, he defeated, in twelve successive battles, the Angles of the

North and the Saxons of the West; but the declining age of the hero was embittered by popular ingratitude and domestic misfortunes. The events of his life are less interesting than the singular revolutions of his fame. During a period of five hundred years the tradition of his exploits was preserved, and rudely embellished, by the obscure bards of Wales and Armorica, who were odious to the Saxons, and unknown to the rest of mankind. The pride and curiosity of the Norman conquerors prompted them to inquire into the ancient history of Britain; they listened with fond credulity to the tale of Arthur, and eagerly applauded the merit of a prince who had triumphed over the Saxons, their common enemies. His romance, transcribed in the Latin of Jeffrey of Monmouth, and afterwards translated into the fashionable idiom of the times, was enriched with the various, though incoherent, ornaments which were familiar to the experience, the learning, or the fancy of the twelfth century. The progress of a Phrygian colony, from the Tiber to the Thames, was easily engrafted on the fable of the Æneid; and the royal ancestors of Arthur derived their origin from Troy, and claimed their alliance with the Cæsars. His trophies were decorated with captive provinces and Imperial titles; and his Danish victories avenged the recent injuries of his country. The gallantry and superstition of the British hero, his feasts and tournaments, and the memorable institution of his Knights of the *Round Table*, were faithfully copied from the reigning manners of chivalry; and the fabulous exploits of Uther's son appear less incredible than the adventures which were achieved by the enterprising valour of the Normans. Pilgrimage, and the holy wars, introduced into Europe the specious miracles of Arabian magic. Fairies and giants, flying dragons and enchanted palaces, were blended with the more simple fictions of the West; and the fate of Britain depended on the art, or the predictions, of Merlin. Every nation embraced and adorned the popular romance of Arthur and the Knights of the Round Table: their names were celebrated in Greece and Italy; and the voluminous tales of Sir Lancelot and Sir Tristram were devoutly studied by the princes and nobles who disregarded the genuine heroes and historians of antiquity. At length the light of science and reason was rekindled; the talisman was broken; the visionary fabric melted into air; and by a natural, though unjust, reverse of the public opinion, the severity of the present age is inclined to question the *existence* of Arthur.

The independent Britons appear to have relapsed into the state of original barbarism from whence they had been imperfectly reclaimed. Separated by their enemies from the rest of mankind, they soon became an object of scandal and abhorrence to the catholic world. Christianity was still professed in the mountains of Wales; but the rude schismatics, in the *form* of the clerical tonsure, and in the *day* of the celebration of Easter, obstinately resisted the imperious mandates of the Roman pontiffs. The use of the Latin language was insensibly abolished, and the Britons were deprived of the arts and learning which Italy communicated to her Saxon proselytes. In Wales and Armorica, the Celtic tongue, the native idiom of the West, was preserved and propagated; and the *Bards*, who had been the companions of the Druids, were still protected, in the sixteenth century, by the laws of Elizabeth. Their chief, a respectable officer of the courts of Pengwern, or Aberfraw, or Caermarthen, accompanied the king's servants to war: the monarchy of the Britons, which he sung in the front of battle, excited their courage, and justified their depredations; and the songster claimed for his legitimate prize the fairest heifer of the spoil. His subordinate ministers, the masters and disciples of vocal and instrumental music, visited, in their respective circuits, the royal, the noble, and the plebeian houses; and the public poverty, almost exhausted by the clergy, was oppressed by the importunate demands of the bards. Their rank and merit were ascertained by solemn trials, and the strong belief of supernatural inspiration exalted the fancy of the poet and of his audience. The last retreats of Celtic freedom, the extreme territories of Gaul and Britain, were less adapted to agriculture than to pasturage: the wealth of the Britons consisted in their flocks and herds; milk and flesh were their ordinary food; and bread was sometimes esteemed, or rejected, as a foreign luxury. Liberty had peopled the mountains of Wales and the morasses of Armorica: but their populousness has been maliciously ascribed to the loose practice of polygamy; and the houses of these licentious barbarians have been supposed to contain ten wives, and perhaps fifty children. Their disposition was rash and choleric: they were bold in action and in speech; and as they were ignorant of the arts of peace, they alternately indulged their passions in foreign and domestic war. The cavalry of Armorica, the spearmen of Gwent, and the archers of Merioneth, were equally formidable; but their poverty could seldom procure either shields or helmets; and the inconvenient weight would have retarded the speed and agility of their desultory operations. One of the greatest of the English monarchs was requested to satisfy the curiosity of a Greek emperor concerning the state of Britain; and Henry II. could assert, from his personal experience, that Wales was inhabited by a race of naked warriors, who encountered, without fear, the defensive armour of their enemies.

By the revolution of Britain the limits of science as well as of empire were contracted. The dark cloud which had been cleared by the Phœnician discoveries, and finally dispelled by the arms of Cæsar, again settled on the shores of the Atlantic, and a Roman province was again lost among the fabulous Islands of the Ocean. One hundred and fifty years after the reign of Honorius the gravest historian of the times describes the wonders of a remote isle, whose eastern and western parts are divided by an antique wall, the boundary of life and death, or, more properly, of truth and fiction. The east is a fair country, inhabited by a civilised people: the air is healthy, the waters are pure and plentiful, and the earth yields her regular and fruitful increase. In the west, beyond the wall, the air is infectious and mortal; the ground is covered with serpents; and this dreary solitude is the region of departed spirits, who are transported from the opposite shores in substantial boats and by living rowers. Some families of fishermen, the subjects of the Franks, are excused from tribute, in consideration of the mysterious office which is performed by these Charons of the ocean. Each in his turn is summoned, at the hour of midnight, to hear the voices, and even the names, of the ghosts: he is sensible of their weight, and he feels himself impelled by an unknown, but irresistible, power. After this dream of fancy, we read with astonishment that the name of this island is *Brittia*; that it lies in the ocean, against the mouth of the Rhine, and less than thirty miles from the continent; that it is possessed by three nations, the Frisians, the Angles, and the Britons; and that some Angles had appeared at Constantinople in the train of the French ambassadors.

I have now accomplished the laborious narrative of the decline and fall of the Roman empire, from the fortunate age of Trajan and the Antonines to its total extinction in the West, about five centuries after the Christian era. At that unhappy period the Saxons fiercely struggled with the natives for the possession of Britain: Gaul and Spain were divided between the powerful monarchies of the Franks and Visigoths and the dependent kingdoms of the Suevi and Burgundians: Africa was exposed to the cruel persecution of the Vandals and the savage insults of the Moors: Rome and Italy, as far as the banks of the Danube, were afflicted by an army of barbarian mercenaries, whose lawless tyranny was succeeded by the reign of Theodoric the Ostrogoth. All the subjects of the empire, who, by the use of the Latin language, more particularly deserved the name and privileges of Romans, were oppressed by the disgrace and calamities of foreign conquest; and the victorious nations of Germany established a new system of manners and government in the western countries of Europe. The majesty of Rome was faintly represented by the princes of Constantinople, the feeble and imaginary successors of Augustus. Yet they continued to reign over the East, from the Danube to the Nile and Tigris; the Gothic and Vandal kingdoms of Italy and Africa were subverted by the arms of Justinian; and the history of the *Greek* emperors may still afford a long series of instructive lessons and interesting revolutions.

GENERAL OBSERVATIONS ON THE FALL OF THE ROMAN EMPIRE IN THE WEST

The rise of a city, which swelled into an empire, may deserve, as a singular prodigy, the reflection of a philosophic mind. But the decline of Rome was the natural and inevitable effect of immoderate greatness. Prosperity ripened the principle of decay; the causes of destruction multiplied with the extent of conquest; and as soon as time or accident had removed the artificial supports, the stupendous fabric yielded to the pressure of its own weight. The story of its ruin is simple and obvious; and instead of inquiring *why* the Roman empire was destroyed, we should rather be surprised that it had subsisted so long. The victorious legions, who, in distant wars, acquired the vices of strangers and mercenaries, first oppressed the freedom of the republic, and afterwards violated the majesty of the purple. The emperors, anxious for their personal safety and the public peace, were reduced to the base expedient of corrupting the discipline which rendered them alike formidable to their sovereign and to the enemy; the vigour of the military government was relaxed and finally dissolved by the partial institutions of Constantine; and the Roman world was overwhelmed by a deluge of barbarians.

The decay of Rome has been frequently ascribed to the translation of the seat of empire; but this history has already shown that the powers of Government were *divided* rather than *removed.* The throne of Constantinople was erected in the East; while the West was still possessed by a series of emperors who held their residence in Italy, and claimed their equal inheritance of the legions and provinces. This dangerous novelty impaired the strength and fomented the vices of a double reign: the instruments of an oppressive and arbitrary system were multiplied; and a vain emulation of luxury, not of merit, was introduced and supported between the degenerate successors of Theodosius. Extreme distress, which unites the virtue of a free people, embitters the factions of a declining monarchy. The hostile favourites of Arcadius and Honorius betrayed the republic to its common enemies; and the Byzantine court beheld with indifference, perhaps with pleasure, the disgrace of Rome, the misfortunes of Italy, and the loss of the West. Under the succeeding reigns the alliance of the two empires was restored; but the aid of the Oriental Romans was tardy, doubtful, and ineffectual; and the national schism of the Greeks and Latins was enlarged by the perpetual difference of language and manners, of interests, and even of religion. Yet the salutary event approved in some measure the judgment of Constantine. During a long period of decay his impregnable city repelled the victorious armies of barbarians, protected the wealth of Asia, and commanded, both in peace and war, the important straits which connect the Euxine and Mediterranean seas. The foundation of Constantinople more essentially contributed to the preservation of the East than to the ruin of the West.

As the happiness of a *future* life is the great object of religion, we may hear without surprise or scandal that the introduction, or at least the abuse of Christianity, had some influence on the decline and fall of the Roman empire. The clergy successfully preached the doctrines of patience and pusillanimity; the active virtues of society were discouraged; and the last remains of military spirit were buried in the cloister: a large portion of public and private wealth was consecrated to the specious demands of charity and devotion; and the soldiers' pay was lavished on the useless multitudes of both sexes who could only plead the merits of abstinence and chastity. Faith, zeal, curiosity, and more earthly passions of malice and ambition, kindled the flame of theological discord; the church, and even the state, were distracted by religious factions, whose conflicts were sometimes bloody and always implacable; the attention of the emperors was diverted from camps to synods; the Roman world was oppressed by a new species of tyranny; and the persecuted sects became the secret enemies of their country. Yet party-spirit, however pernicious or absurd, is a principle of union as well as of dissension. The bishops, from eighteen hundred pulpits, inculcated the duty of passive obedience to a lawful and orthodox sovereign; their frequent assemblies and perpetual correspondence maintained the communion of distant churches; and the benevolent temper of the Gospel was strengthened, though confirmed, by the spiritual alliance of the catholics. The sacred indolence of the monks was devoutly embraced by a servile and effeminate age; but if superstition had not afforded a decent retreat, the same vices would have tempted the unworthy Romans to desert, from baser motives, the standard of the republic. Religious precepts are easily obeyed which indulge and sanctify the natural inclinations of their votaries; but the pure and genuine influence of Christianity may be traced in its beneficial, though imperfect, effects on the barbarian proselytes of the North. If the decline of the Roman empire was hastened by the conversion of Constantine, his victorious religion broke the violence of the fall, and mollified the ferocious temper of the conquerors.

This awful revolution may be usefully applied to the instruction of the present age. It is the duty of a patriot to prefer and promote the exclusive interest and glory of his native country: but a philosopher may be permitted to enlarge his views, and to consider Europe as one great republic, whose various inhabitants have attained almost the same level of politeness and cultivation. The experience of four thousand years should enlarge our hopes and diminish our apprehensions: we cannot determine to what height the human species may aspire in their advance towards perfection; but it may safely be presumed that no people, unless the face of nature is changed, will relapse into their original barbarism. The improvements of society may be viewed under a threefold aspect. 1. The poet or philosopher illustrates his age and country by the efforts of a *single* mind; but these superior powers of reason or fancy are rare and spontaneous productions; and the genius of Homer, or Cicero, or Newton, would excite less admiration if they could be created by the will of a prince or the lessons of a preceptor. 2. The benefits of law and policy, of trade and manufactures, of arts and sciences, are more solid and permanent; and *many* individuals may be qualified, by education and discipline, to promote, in their respective stations, the interest of the community. But this general order is the effect of skill and labour; and the complex machinery may be decayed by time, or injured by violence. 3. Fortunately for mankind, the more useful, or, at least, more necessary arts, can be performed without superior talents or national subordination; without powers of *one*, or the union of *many*. Each village, each family, each individual, must always possess both ability and inclination to perpetuate the use of fire and of metals; the propagation and service of domestic animals; the methods of hunting and fishing; the rudiments of navigation; the imperfect cultivation of corn or other nutritive grain; and the simple practice of the mechanic trades. Private genius and public industry may be extirpated, but these hardy plants survive the tempest, and strike an everlasting root into the most unfavourable soil. The splendid days of Augustus and Trajan were eclipsed by a cloud of ignorance; and the barbarians subverted the laws and palaces of Rome. But the scythe, the invention or emblem of Saturn, still continued annually to mow the harvests of Italy; and the human feasts of the Læstrigons have never been renewed on the coast of Campania.

Since the first discovery of the arts, war, commerce, and religious zeal have diffused among the savages of the Old and New World these inestimable gifts: they have been successively propagated; they can never be lost. We may therefore acquiesce in the pleasing conclusion that every age of the world has increased and still increases the real wealth, the happiness, the knowledge, and perhaps the virtue, of the human race.

XXXV

BYZANTIUM EXTENT AND NATURE—THEODORA—THE FACTIONS OF THE CIRCUS—THE TRISAGION RIOTS—THE EASTERN EMPIRE IN THE TENTH CENTURY—THE SIEGE AND FALL OF CONSTANTINOPLE

The division of the Roman world between the sons of Theodosius marks the final establishment of the empire of the East, which, from the reign of Arcadius to the taking of Constantinople by the Turks, subsisted one thousand and fifty-eight years in a state of premature and perpetual decay. The sovereign of that empire assumed and obstinately retained the vain, and at length fictitious, title of Emperor of the ROMANS; and the hereditary appellations of CAESAR and AUGUSTUS continued to declare that he was the legitimate successor of the first of men, who had reigned over the first of nations. The palace of Constantinople rivalled, and perhaps excelled, the magnificence of Persia; and the eloquent sermons of St. Chrysostom celebrate, while they condemn, the pompous luxury of the reign of Arcadius. "The emperor," says he, "wears on his head either a diadem or a crown of gold, decorated with precious stones of inestimable value. These ornaments and his purple garments are reserved for his sacred person alone; and his robes of silk are embroidered with the figures of golden dragons. His throne is of massy gold. Whenever he appears in public he is surrounded by his courtiers, his guards, and his attendants. Their spears, their shields, their cuirasses, the bridles and trappings of their horses, have either the substance or the appearance of gold; and the large splendid boss in the midst of their shield is encircled with smaller bosses, which represent the shape of the human eye. The two mules that draw the chariot of the monarch are perfectly white, and shining all over with gold. The chariot itself, of pure and solid gold, attracts the admiration of the spectators, who contemplate the purple curtains, the snowy carpet, the size of the precious stones, and the resplendent plates of gold, that glitter as they are agitated by the motion of the carriage. The Imperial pictures are white, on a blue ground; the emperor appears seated on his throne, with his arms, his horses, and his guards beside him; and his vanquished enemies in chains at his feet." The successors of Constantine established their perpetual residence in the royal city which he had erected on the verge of Europe and Asia. Inaccessible to the menaces of their enemies, and perhaps to the complaints of their people, they received with each wind the tributary productions of every climate; while the impregnable strength of their capital continued for ages to defy the hostile attempts of the barbarians. Their dominions were bounded by the Hadriatic and the Tigris; and the whole interval of twenty-five days' navigation, which separated the extreme cold of Scythia from the torrid zone of Æthiopia, was comprehended within the limits of the empire of the East. The populous countries of that empire were the seat of art and learning, of luxury and wealth; and the inhabitants, who had assumed the language and manners of Greeks, styled themselves, with some appearance of truth, the most enlightened and civilised portion of the human species. The form of government was a pure and simple monarchy; the name of the ROMAN REPUBLIC, which so long preserved a faint tradition of freedom, was confined to the Latin provinces; and the princes of Constantinople measured their greatness by the servile obedience of their people. They were ignorant how much this passive disposition enervates and degrades every faculty of the mind. The subjects who had resigned their will to the absolute commands of a master were equally incapable of guarding their lives and fortunes against the assaults of the barbarians or of defending their reason from the terrors of superstition.

In the exercise of supreme power, the first act of Justinian was to divide it with the woman whom he loved, the famous Theodora, whose strange elevation cannot be applauded as the triumph of female virtue. Under the reign of Anastasius, the care of the wild beasts maintained by the great faction at Constantinople was intrusted to Acacius, a native of the isle of Cyprus, who, from his employment, was surnamed the master of the bears. This honourable office was given after his death to another candidate, notwithstanding the diligence of his widow, who had already provided a husband and a successor. Acacius had left three daughters, Comito, THEODORA, and Anastasia, the eldest of whom did not then exceed the age of seven years. On a solemn festival, these helpless orphans

were sent by their distressed and indignant mother, in the garb of
suppliants, into the midst of the theatre: the green faction received
them with contempt, the blues with compassion; and this difference, which sunk deep into the mind of Theodora, was felt long
afterwards in the administration of the empire. As they improved
in age and beauty, the three sisters were successively devoted to
the public and private pleasures of the Byzantine people; and
Theodora, after following Comito on the stage, in the dress of a
slave, with a stool on her head, was at length permitted to exercise
her independent talents. She neither danced, nor sung, nor played
on the flute; her skill was confined to the pantomime art; she
excelled in buffoon characters; and as often as the comedian
swelled her cheeks, and complained with a ridiculous tone and
gesture of the blows that were inflicted, the whole theatre of Constantinople resounded with laughter and applause. The beauty of
Theodora was the subject of more flattering praise, and the source
of more exquisite delight. Her features were delicate and regular;
her complexion, though somewhat pale, was tinged with a natural
colour; every sensation was instantly expressed by the vivacity of
her eyes; her easy motions displayed the graces of a small but elegant
figure; and either love or adulation might proclaim that painting
and poetry were incapable of delineating the matchless excellence
of her form. But this form was degraded by the facility with which
it was exposed to the public eye, and prostituted to licentious
desire. Her venal charms were abandoned to a promiscuous crowd
of citizens and strangers, of every rank and of every profession: the
fortunate lover who had been promised a night of enjoyment was
often driven from her bed by a stronger or more wealthy favourite;
and when she passed through the streets, her presence was avoided
by all who wished to escape either the scandal or the temptation.
The satirical historian has not blushed to describe the naked scenes
which Theodora was not ashamed to exhibit in the theatre. After
exhausting the arts of sensual pleasure, she most ungratefully
murmured against the parsimony of Nature; but her murmurs, her
pleasures, and her arts, must be veiled in the obscurity of a learned
language. After reigning for some time the delight and contempt
of the capital, she condescended to accompany Ecebolus, a native
of Tyre, who had obtained the government of the African Pentapolis.
But this union was frail and transient; Ecebolus soon rejected an
expensive or faithless concubine; she was reduced at Alexandria to
extreme distress; and in her laborious return to Constantinople,

every city of the East admired and enjoyed the fair Cyprian, whose merit appeared to justify her descent from the peculiar island of Venus. The vague commerce of Theodora, and the most detestable precautions, preserved her from the danger which she feared; yet once, and once only, she became a mother. The infant was saved and educated in Arabia by his father, who imparted to him on his deathbed that he was the son of an empress. Filled with ambitious hopes, the unsuspecting youth immediately hastened to the palace of Constantinople, and was admitted to the presence of his mother. As he was never more seen, even after the decease of Theodora, she deserves the foul imputation of extinguishing with his life a secret so offensive to her imperial virtue.

In the most abject state of her fortune and reputation, some vision, either of sleep or of fancy, had whispered to Theodora the pleasing assurance that she was destined to become the spouse of a potent monarch. Conscious of her approaching greatness, she returned from Paphlagonia to Constantinople; assumed, like a skilful actress, a more decent character; relieved her poverty by the laudable industry of spinning wool; and affected a life of chastity and solitude in a small house, which she afterwards changed into a magnificent temple. Her beauty, assisted by art or accident, soon attracted, captivated, and fixed, the patrician Justinian, who already reigned with absolute sway under the name of his uncle. Perhaps she contrived to enhance the value of a gift which she had so often lavished on the meanest of mankind; perhaps she inflamed, at first by modest delays, and at last by sensual allurements, the desires of a lover who, from nature or devotion, was addicted to long vigils and abstemious diet. When his first transports had subsided, she still maintained the same ascendant over his mind by the more solid merit of temper and understanding. Justinian delighted to ennoble and enrich the object of his affection: the treasures of the East were poured at her feet, and the nephew of Justin was determined, perhaps by religious scruples, to bestow on his concubine the sacred and legal character of a wife. But the laws of Rome expressly prohibited the marriage of a senator with any female who had been dishonoured by a servile origin or theatrical profession: the empress Lupicina or Euphemia, a barbarian of rustic manners, but of irreproachable virtue, refused to accept a prostitute for her niece; and even Vigilantia, the superstitious mother of Justinian, though she acknowledged the wit and beauty of Theodora, was seriously apprehensive lest the levity and arrogance of that artful paramour might corrupt the piety and happiness of her son. These obstacles were removed by the inflexible constancy of Justinian. He patiently expected the death of the empress; he despised the tears of his mother, who soon sunk under the weight of her affliction; and a law was promulgated, in the name of the emperor Justin, which abolished the rigid jurisprudence of antiquity. A glorious repentance (the words of the edict) was left open for the unhappy females who had prostituted their persons on the theatre, and they were permitted to contract a legal union with the most illustrious of the Romans. This indulgence was speedily followed by the solemn nuptials of Justinian and Theodora; her dignity was gradually exalted with that of her lover; and, as soon as Justin had invested his nephew with the purple, the patriarch of Constantinople placed the diadem on the heads of the emperor and empress of the East. But the usual honours which the severity of Roman manners had allowed to the wives of princes could not satisfy either the ambition of Theodora or the fondness of Justinian. He seated her on the throne as an equal and independent colleague in the sovereignty of the empire, and an oath of allegiance was imposed on the governors of the provinces in the joint names of Justinian and Theodora. The Eastern world fell prostrate before the genius and fortune of the daughter of Acacius. The prostitute who, in the presence of innumerable spectators, had polluted the theatre of Constantinople, was adored as a queen in the same city, by grave magistrates, orthodox bishops, victorious generals, and captive monarchs.

But the reproach of cruelty, so repugnant even to her softer vices, has left an indelible stain on the memory of Theodora. Her numerous spies observed and zealously reported every action, or word, or look, injurious to their royal mistress. Whomsoever they accused were cast into her peculiar prisons, inaccessible to the inquiries of justice; and it was rumoured that the torture of the rack or scourge had been inflicted in the presence of a female tyrant, insensible to the voice of prayer or of pity. Some of these unhappy victims perished in deep unwholesome dungeons, while others were permitted, after the loss of their limbs, their reason, or their fortune, to appear in the world, the living monuments of her vengeance, which was commonly extended to the children of those whom she had suspected or injured. The senator or bishop whose death or exile Theodora had pronounced, was delivered to a trusty messenger, and his diligence was quickened by a menace from her own mouth. "If you fail in the execution of my commands, I swear by him who liveth for ever that your skin shall be flayed from your body."

If the creed of Theodora had not been tainted with heresy, her exemplary devotion might have atoned, in the opinion of her contemporaries, for pride, avarice, and cruelty; but if she employed her influence to assuage the intolerant fury of the emperor, the present age will allow some merit to her religion, and much indulgence to her speculative errors. The name of Theodora was introduced, with equal honour, in all the pious and charitable foundations of Justinian; and the most benevolent institution of his reign may be ascribed to the sympathy of the empress for her less fortunate sisters, who had been seduced or compelled to embrace the trade of prostitution. A palace, on the Asiatic side of the Bosphorus, was converted into a stately and spacious monastery, and a liberal maintenance was assigned to five hundred women who had been collected from the streets and brothels of Constantinople. In this safe and holy retreat they were devoted to perpetual confinement; and the despair of some, who threw themselves headlong into the sea, was lost in the gratitude of the penitents who had been delivered from sin and misery by their generous benefactress. The prudence of Theodora is celebrated by Justinian himself; and his laws are attributed to the sage counsels of his most reverend wife, whom he had received as the gift of the Deity. Her courage was displayed amidst the tumult of the people and the terrors of the court. Her chastity, from the moment of her union with Justinian, is founded on the silence of her implacable enemies; and although the daughter of Acacius might be satiated with love, yet some applause is due to the firmness of a mind which could sacrifice pleasure and habit to the stronger sense either of duty or interest. The wishes and prayers of Theodora could never obtain the blessing of a lawful son, and she buried an infant daughter, the sole offspring of her marriage. Notwithstanding this disappointment, her dominion was permanent and absolute; she preserved, by art or merit, the affections of Justinian; and their seeming dissensions were always fatal to the courtiers who believed them to be sincere. Perhaps her health had been impaired by the licentiousness of her youth; but it was always delicate, and she was directed by her physicians to use the Pythian warm-baths. In this journey the empress was followed by the Prætorian præfect, the great treasurer, several counts and patricians, and a splendid train of four thousand attendants: the highways were repaired at her approach; a palace was erected for her reception; and as she passed through Bithynia she distributed liberal alms to the churches, the monasteries, and the hospitals, that they might implore Heaven for the restoration of her health. At length, in the twenty-fourth year of her marriage, and the twenty-second of her reign, she was consumed by a cancer; and the irreparable loss was deplored by her husband, who, in the room of a theatrical prostitute, might have selected the purest and most noble virgin of the East.

A material difference may be observed in the games of antiquity: the most eminent of the Greeks were actors, the Romans were merely spectators. The Olympic stadium was open to wealth, merit, and ambition; and if the candidates could depend on their personal skill and activity, they might pursue the footsteps of Diomede and Menelaus, and conduct their own horses in the rapid career. Ten, twenty, forty chariots, were allowed to start at the same instant; a crown of leaves was the reward of the victor, and his fame, with that of his family and country, was chanted in lyric strains more durable than monuments of brass and marble. But a senator, or even a citizen, conscious of his dignity, would have blushed to expose his person or his horses in the circus of Rome. The games were exhibited at the expense of the republic, the magistrates, or the emperors; but the reins were abandoned to servile hands; and if the profits of a favourite charioteer sometimes exceeded those of an advocate, they must be considered as the effects of popular extravagance, and the high wages of a disgraceful profession. The race, in its first institution, was a simple contest of two chariots, whose drivers were distinguished by *white* and *red* liveries: two additional colours, a light *green* and a cærulean *blue*, were afterwards introduced; and, as the races were repeated twenty-five times, one hundred chariots contributed in the same day to the pomp of the circus. The four *factions* soon acquired a legal establishment and a mysterious origin, and their fanciful colours were derived from the various appearances of nature in the four seasons of the year; the red dog-star of summer, the snows of winter, the deep shades of autumn, and the cheerful verdure of the spring. Another interpretation preferred the elements of the seasons, and the struggle of the green and blue was supposed to represent the conflict of the earth and sea. Their respective victories announced either a plentiful harvest or a prosperous navigation, and the hostility of the husbandmen and mariners was somewhat less absurd than the blind ardour of the Roman people, who devoted their lives and fortunes to the colour which they had espoused. Such folly was disdained and indulged by the wisest princes; but the names of Caligula, Nero, Vitellius, Verus, Commodus, Caracalla, and Elagabalus, were enrolled in the blue or green factions of the circus: they frequented their stables, applauded their favourites, chastised their antagonists, and deserved the esteem of the populace by the natural or affected imitation of their manners. The bloody and tumultuous contest continued to disturb the public festivity till the last age of the spectacles of Rome; and Theodoric, from a motive of justice or affection, interposed his authority to protect the greens against the violence of a consul and a patrician who were passionately addicted to the blue faction of the circus.

Constantinople adopted the follies, though not the virtues, of ancient Rome; and the same factions which had agitated the circus raged with redoubled fury in the hippodrome. Under the reign of Anastasius, this popular frenzy was inflamed by religious zeal; and the greens, who had treacherously concealed stones and daggers under baskets of fruit, massacred at a solemn festival three thousand of their blue adversaries. From the capital this pestilence was diffused into the provinces and cities of the East, and the sportive distinction of two colours produced two strong and irreconcilable factions, which shook the foundations of a feeble government. The popular dissensions, founded on the most serious interest or holy pretence, have scarcely equalled the obstinacy of this wanton discord, which invaded the peace of families, divided friends and brothers, and tempted the female sex, though seldom seen in the circus, to espouse the inclinations of their lovers, or to contradict the wishes of their husbands. Every law, either human or divine, was trampled under foot; and as long as the party was successful, its deluded followers appeared careless of private distress or public calamity. The licence, without the freedom, of democracy, was revived at Antioch and Constantinople, and the support of a faction became necessary to every candidate for civil or ecclesiastical honours. A secret attachment to the family or sect of Anastasius was imputed to the greens; the blues were zealously devoted to the cause of orthodoxy and Justinian, and their grateful patron protected, above five years, the disorders of a faction whose seasonable tumults overawed the palace, the senate, and the capitals of the East. Insolent with royal favour, the blues affected to strike tenor by a peculiar and barbaric dress—the long hair of the Huns, their close sleeves and ample garments, a lofty step, and a sonorous voice. In the day they concealed their two-edged poniards, but in the night they boldly assembled in arms and in numerous bands, prepared for every act of violence and rapine. Their adversaries of the green faction, or even inoffensive citizens, were stripped and often murdered by these nocturnal robbers, and it became dangerous to wear any gold buttons or girdles, or to appear at a late hour in the streets of a peaceful capital. A daring spirit, rising with impunity, proceeded to violate the safeguard of private houses; and fire was employed to facilitate the attack, or to conceal the crimes, of these factious rioters. No place was safe or sacred from their depredations; to gratify either avarice or revenge they profusely spilt the blood of the innocent; churches and altars were polluted by atrocious murders, and it was the boast of the assassins that their dexterity could always inflict a mortal wound with a single stroke of their dagger.

A sedition, which almost laid Constantinople in ashes, was excited by the mutual hatred and momentary reconciliation of the two factions. In the fifth year of his reign Justinian celebrated the festival of the ides of January: the games were incessantly disturbed by the clamorous discontent of the greens; till the twenty-second race the emperor maintained his silent gravity; at length, yielding to his impatience, he condescended to hold, in abrupt sentences, and by the voice of a crier, the most singular dialogue that ever passed between a prince and his subjects. Their first complaints were respectful and modest; they accused the subordinate ministers of oppression, and proclaimed their wishes for the long life and victory of the emperor. "Be patient and attentive, ye insolent railers!" exclaimed Justinian; "be mute, ye Jews, Samaritans, and Manichæans!" The greens still attempted to awaken his compassion. "We are poor, we are innocent, we are injured, we dare not pass through the streets: a general persecution is exercised against our name and colour. Let us die, O emperor! but let us die by your command, and for your service!" But the repetition of partial and passionate invectives degraded, in their eyes, the majesty of the purple; they renounced allegiance to the prince who refused justice to his people, lamented that the father of Justinian had been born, and branded his son with the opprobrious names of a homicide, an ass, and a perjured tyrant. "Do you despise your lives?" cried the indignant monarch. The blues rose with fury from their seats, their hostile clamours thundered in the hippodrome, and their adversaries, deserting the unequal contest, spread terror and despair through the streets of Constantinople. At this dangerous moment, seven notorious assassins of both factions, who had been condemned by the præfect, were carried round the city, and afterwards transported to the place of execution in the suburb of Pera. Four were immediately beheaded; a fifth was hanged; but, when the same punishment was inflicted on the remaining two, the rope broke, they fell alive to the ground, the populace applauded their escape, and the monks of St. Conon, issuing from the neighbouring convent, conveyed them in a boat to the sanctuary of the church. As one of these criminals was of the blue, and the other of the green, livery, the two factions were equally provoked by the cruelty of their oppressor or the ingratitude of their patron, and a short truce was concluded till they had delivered their prisoners and satisfied their revenge. The palace of the præfect, who withstood the seditious torrent, was instantly burnt, his officers and guards were massacred, the prisons were forced open, and freedom was restored to those who could only use it for the public destruction. A military force which had been despatched to the aid of the civil magistrate was fiercely encountered by an armed multitude, whose numbers and boldness continually increased: and the Heruli, the wildest barbarians in the service of the empire, overturned the priests and their relics, which, from a pious motive, had been rashly interposed to separate the bloody conflict. The tumult was exasperated by this sacrilege; the people fought with enthusiasm in the cause of God; the women, from the roofs and windows, showered stones on the heads of the soldiers, who darted firebrands against the houses; and the various flames, which had been kindled by the hands of citizens and strangers, spread without control over the face of the city. The conflagration involved the cathedral of St. Sophia, the baths of Zeuxippus, a part of the palace from the first entrance to the altar of Mars, and the long portico from the palace to the forum of Constantine: a large hospital, with the sick patients, was consumed; many churches and stately edifices were destroyed; and an immense treasure of gold and silver was either melted or lost. From such scenes of horror and distress the wise and wealthy citizens escaped over the Bosphorus to the Asiatic side, and during five days Constantinople was abandoned to the factions, whose watchword, NIKA, *vanquish*! has given a name to this memorable sedition.

The obstinacy of the tumult was now imputed to a secret and ambitious conspiracy, and a suspicion was entertained that the insurgents, more especially the green faction, had been supplied with arms and money by Hypatius and Pompey, two patricians who could neither forget with honour, nor remember with safety, that they were the nephews of the emperor Anastasius. Capriciously trusted, disgraced, and pardoned by the jealous levity of the monarch, they had appeared as loyal servants before the throne, and, during five days of the tumult, they were detained as important hostages; till at length, the fears of Justinian prevailing over his prudence, he viewed the two brothers in the light of spies, perhaps of assassins, and sternly commanded them to depart from the palace. After a fruitless representation that obedience might lead to involuntary treason, they retired to their houses, and in the morning of the sixth day Hypatius was surrounded and seized by the people, who, regardless of his virtuous resistance and the tears of his wife, transported their favourite to the forum of Constantine, and, instead of a diadem, placed a rich collar on his head. If the usurper, who afterwards pleaded the merit of his delay, had complied with the advice of his senate, and urged the fury of the multitude, their first irresistible effort might have oppressed or expelled his trembling competitor. The Byzantine palace enjoyed a free communication with the sea, vessels lay ready at the garden-stairs, and a secret resolution was already formed to convey the emperor with his family and treasures to a safe retreat at some distance from the capital.

Justinian was lost, if the prostitute whom he raised from the theatre had not renounced the timidity as well as the virtues of her sex. In the midst of a council where Belisarius was present, Theodora alone displayed the spirit of a hero, and she alone, without apprehending his future hatred, could save the emperor from the imminent danger and his unworthy fears. "If flight," said the consort of Justinian, "were the only means of safety, yet I should disdain to fly. Death is the condition of our birth, but they who have reigned should never survive the loss of dignity and dominion. I implore Heaven that I may never be seen, not a day, without my diadem and purple; that I may no longer behold the light when I cease to be saluted with the name of queen. If you resolve, O Cæsar! to fly, you have treasures; behold the sea, you have ships; but tremble lest the desire of life should expose you to wretched exile and ignominious death. For my own part, I adhere to the maxim of antiquity, that the throne is a glorious sepulchre." The firmness of a woman restored the courage to deliberate and act, and courage soon discovers the resources of the most desperate situation. It was an easy and a decisive measure to revive the animosity of the factions; the blues were astonished at their own guilt and folly, that a trifling injury should provoke them to conspire with their implacable enemies against a gracious and liberal benefactor; they again proclaimed the majesty of Justinian; and the greens, with their upstart emperor, were left alone in the hippodrome. The fidelity of the guards was doubtful; but the military force of Justinian consisted in three thousand veterans, who had been trained to valour and discipline in the Persian and Illyrian wars. Under the command of Belisarius and Mundus, they silently marched in two divisions from the palace, forced their obscure way through narrow passages, expiring flames, and falling edifices, and burst open at the same moment the two opposite gates of the hippodrome. In this narrow space the disorderly and affrighted crowd was incapable of resisting on either side a firm and regular attack; the blues signalised the fury of their repentance, and it is computed that above thirty thousand persons were slain in the merciless and promiscuous carnage of the day. Hypatius was dragged from his throne, and conducted with his brother Pompey to the feet of the emperor; they implored his clemency, but their crime was manifest, their innocence uncertain, and Justinian had been too much terrified to forgive. The next morning the two nephews of Anastasius, with eighteen *illustrious* accomplices, of patrician or consular rank, were privately executed by the soldiers, their bodies were thrown into the sea, their palaces razed, and their fortunes confiscated. The hippodrome itself was condemned, during several years, to a mournful silence; with the restoration of the games the same disorders revived, and the blue and green factions continued to afflict the reign of Justinian, and to disturb the tranquillity of the Eastern empire.

In the fever of the times the sense, or rather the sound of a syllable, was sufficient to disturb the peace of an empire. The TRISAGION (thrice holy), "Holy, holy, holy, Lord God of Hosts!" is supposed by the Greeks to be the identical hymn which the angels and cherubim eternally repeat before the throne of God, and which, about the middle of the fifth century, was miraculously revealed to the church of Constantinople. The devotion of Antioch soon added, "who was crucified for us!" and this grateful address, either to Christ alone, or to the whole Trinity, may be justified by the rules of theology, and has been gradually adopted by the Catholics of the East and West. But it had been imagined by a

Monophysite bishop; the gift of an enemy was at first rejected as a dire and dangerous blasphemy, and the rash innovation had nearly cost the emperor Anastasius his throne and his life. The people of Constantinople were devoid of any rational principles of freedom; but they held, as a lawful cause of rebellion, the colour of a livery in the races, or the colour of a mystery in the schools. The Trisagion, with and without this obnoxious addition, was chanted in the cathedral by two adverse choirs, and, when their lungs were exhausted, they had recourse to the more solid arguments of sticks and stones; the aggressors were punished by the emperor, and defended by the patriarch; and the crown and miter were staked on the event of this momentous quarrel. The streets were instantly crowded with innumerable swarms of men, women, and children; the legions of monks, in regular array, marched, and shouted, and fought at their head. "Christians! this is the day of martyrdom: let us not desert our spiritual father; anathema to the Manichæan tyrant! he is unworthy to reign." Such was the Catholic cry; and the galleys of Anastasius lay upon their oars before the palace, till the patriarch had pardoned his penitent, and hushed the waves of the troubled multitude. The triumph of Macedonius was checked by a speedy exile; but the zeal of his flock was again exasperated by the same question, "Whether one of the Trinity had been crucified?" On this momentous occasion the blue and green factions of Constantinople suspended their discord, and the civil and military powers were annihilated in their presence. The keys of the city, and the standards of the guards, were deposited in the forum of Constantine, the principal station and camp of the faithful. Day and night they were incessantly busied either in singing hymns to the honour of their God, or in pillaging and murdering the servants of their prince. The head of his favourite monk, the friend, as they styled him, of the enemy of the Holy Trinity, was borne aloft on a spear; and the fire-brands, which had been darted against heretical structures, diffused the undistinguishing flames over the most orthodox buildings. The statues of the emperor were broken, and his person was concealed in a suburb, till, at the end of three days, he dared to implore the mercy of his subjects. Without his diadem, and in the posture of a suppliant, Anastasius appeared on the throne of the circus. The Catholics, before his face, rehearsed their genuine Trisagion; they exulted in the offer which he proclaimed by the voice of a herald of abdicating the purple; they listened to the admonition, that, since *all* could not reign, they should previously agree in the choice of a sovereign: and they accepted the blood of two unpopular ministers, whom their master without hesitation condemned to the lions. These furious but transient seditions were encouraged by the success of Vitalian, who, with an army of Huns and Bulgarians, for the most part idolaters, declared himself the champion of the Catholic faith. In this pious rebellion he depopulated Thrace, besieged Constantinople, exterminated sixty-five thousand of his fellow-Christians, till he obtained the recall of the bishops, the satisfaction of the pope, and the establishment of the council of Chalcedon, an orthodox treaty, reluctantly signed by the dying Anastasius, and more faithfully performed by the uncle of Justinian. And such was the event of the *first* of the religious wars which have been waged in the name and by the disciples of the God of Peace.

A ray of historic light seems to beam from the darkness of the tenth century. We open with curiosity and respect the royal volumes of Constantine Porphyrogenitus, which he composed at a mature age for the instruction of his son, and which promise to unfold the state of the Eastern empire, both in peace and war, both at home and abroad. In the first of these works he minutely describes the pompous ceremonies of the church and palace of Constantinople, according to his own practice and that of his predecessors. In the second he attempts an accurate survey of the provinces, the *themes*, as they were then denominated, both of Europe and Asia. The system of Roman tactics, the discipline and order of the troops, and the military operations by land and sea, are explained in the third of these didactic collections, which may be ascribed to Constantine or his father Leo. In the fourth, of the administration of the empire, he reveals the secrets of the Byzantine policy, in friendly or hostile intercourse with the nations of the earth. The literary labours of the age, the practical systems of law, agriculture, and history, might redound to the benefit of the subject, and the honour of the Macedonian princes. The sixty books of the *Basilics*, the code and pandects of civil jurisprudence, were gradually framed in the three first reigns of that prosperous dynasty. The art of agriculture had amused the leisure, and exercised the pens, of the best and wisest of the ancients; and their chosen precepts are comprised in the twenty books of the *Geoponics* of Constantine. At his command the historical examples of vice and virtue were methodised in fifty-three books, and every citizen might apply to his contemporaries or himself the lesson or the warning of past times. From the august character of a legislator, the sovereign of the East descends to the more humble office of a teacher and a scribe; and if his successors and subjects were regardless of his paternal cares, we may inherit and enjoy the everlasting legacy.

After the final division between the sons of Theodosius, the swarms of barbarians from Scythia and Germany overspread the provinces and extinguished the empire of ancient Rome. The weakness of Constantinople was concealed by extent of dominion; her limits were inviolate, or at least entire; and the kingdom of Justinian was enlarged by the splendid acquisition of Africa and Italy. But the possession of these new conquests was transient and precarious, and almost a moiety of the Eastern empire was torn away by the arms of the Saracens. Syria and Egypt were oppressed by the Arabian caliphs, and, after the reduction of Africa, their lieutenants invaded and subdued the Roman province which had been changed into the Gothic monarchy of Spain. The islands of the Mediterranean were not inaccessible to their naval powers; and it was from their extreme stations, the harbours of Crete and the fortresses of Cilicia, that the faithful or rebel emirs insulted the majesty of the throne and capital. The remaining provinces, under the obedience of the emperors, were cast into a new mould; and the jurisdiction of the presidents, the consulars, and the counts was superseded by the institution of the *themes*, or military governments, which prevailed under the successors of Heraclius, and are described by the pen of the royal author. Of the twenty-nine themes, twelve in Europe and seventeen in Asia, the origin is obscure, the etymology doubtful or capricious, the limits were arbitrary and fluctuating; but some particular names that sound the most strangely to our ear were derived from the character and attributes of the troops that were maintained at the expense and for the guard of the respective divisions. The vanity of the Greek princes most eagerly grasped the shadow of conquest and the memory of lost dominion. A new Mesopotamia was created on the western side of the Euphrates; the appellation and prætor of Sicily were transferred to a narrow slip of Calabria; and a fragment of the duchy of Beneventum was promoted to the style and title of the theme of Lombardy. In the decline of the Arabian empire the successors of Constantine might indulge their pride in more solid advantages. The victories of Nicephorus, John Zimisces, and Basil the Second, revived the fame, and enlarged the boundaries, of the Roman name; the province of Cilicia, the metropolis of Antioch, the islands of Crete and Cyprus were restored to the allegiance of Christ and Cæsar; one-third of Italy was annexed to the throne of Constantinople, the kingdom of Bulgaria was destroyed, and the last sovereigns of the Macedonian dynasty extended their sway from the sources of the Tigris to the neighbourhood of Rome. In the eleventh century the prospect was again clouded by new enemies and new misfortunes; the relics of Italy were swept away by the Norman adventurers, and almost all the Asiatic branches were dissevered from the Roman trunk by the Turkish conquerors. After these losses the emperors of the Comnenian family continued to reign from the Danube to Peloponnesus, and from Belgrade to Nice, Trebizond, and the winding stream of the Mcander. The spacious provinces of Thrace, Macedonia, and Greece were obedient to their sceptre; the possession of Cyprus, Rhodes, and Crete was accompanied by the fifty islands of the Ægean or Holy Sea, and the remnant of their empire transcends the measure of the largest of the European kingdoms.

The same princes might assert, with dignity and truth, that of all the monarchs of Christendom they possessed the greatest city, the most ample revenue, the most flourishing and populous state. With the decline and fall of the empire the cities of the West had decayed and fallen; nor could the ruins of Rome, or the mud walls, wooden hovels, and narrow precincts of Paris and London, prepare the Latin stranger to contemplate the situation and extent of Constantinople, her stately palaces and churches, and the arts and luxury of an innumerable people.

I must repeat the complaint that the vague and scanty memorials of the times will not afford any just estimate of the taxes, the revenue, and the resources of the Greek empire. From every province of Europe and Asia the rivulets of gold and silver discharged into the Imperial reservoir a copious and perennial stream. The separation of the branches from the trunk increased the relative magnitude of Constantinople; and the maxims of despotism contracted the state to the capital, the capital to the palace, and the palace to the royal person. A Jewish traveller, who visited the East in the twelfth century, is lost in his admiration of the Byzantine riches. "It is here," says Benjamin of Tudela, "in the queen of cities, that the tributes of the Greek empire are annually deposited, and the lofty towers are filled with precious magazines of silk, purple, and gold. It is said that Constantinople pays each day to her sovereign twenty thousand pieces of gold, which are levied on the shops, taverns, and markets, on the merchants of Persia and Egypt, of Russia and Hungary, of Italy and Spain, who frequent the capital by sea and land." In all pecuniary matters the authority of a Jew is doubtless respectable; but as the three hundred and sixty-five days would produce a yearly income exceeding seven millions sterling, I am tempted to retrench at least the numerous festivals of the Greek calendar. The mass of treasure that was saved by Theodora and Basil the Second will suggest a splendid, though indefinite, idea of their supplies and resources. The mother of Michael, before she retired to a cloister, attempted to check or expose the prodigality of her ungrateful son by a free and faithful account of the wealth which he inherited; one hundred and nine thousand pounds of gold and three hundred thousand of silver, the fruits of her own economy and that of her deceased husband. The avarice of Basil is not less renowned than his valour and fortune: his victorious armies were paid and rewarded without breaking into the mass of two hundred thousand pounds of gold (about eight millions sterling), which he had buried in the subterraneous vaults of the palace. Such accumulation of treasure is rejected by the theory and practice of modern policy; and we are more apt to compute the national riches by the use and abuse of the public credit. Yet the maxims of antiquity are still embraced by a monarch formidable to his enemies; by a republic respectable to her allies; and both have attained their respective ends of military power and domestic tranquillity.

Whatever might be consumed for the present wants or reserved for the future use of the state, the first and most sacred demand was for the pomp and pleasure of the emperor; and his discretion only could define the measure of his private expense. The princes of Constantinople were far removed from the simplicity of nature; yet, with the revolving seasons, they were led by taste or fashion to withdraw to a purer air from the smoke and tumult of the capital. They enjoyed, or affected to enjoy, the rustic festival of the vintage: their leisure was amused by the exercise of the chase and the calmer occupation of fishing; and in the summer heats they were shaded from the sun, and refreshed by the cooling breezes from the sea. The coasts and islands of Asia and Europe were covered with their magnificent villas; but instead of the modest art which secretly strives to hide itself and to decorate the scenery of nature, the marble structure of their gardens served only to expose the

riches of the lord and the labours of the architect. The successive
casualties of inheritance and forfeiture had rendered the sovereign
proprietor of many stately houses in the city and suburbs, of which
twelve were appropriated to the ministers of state; but the great
palace, the centre of the Imperial residence, was fixed during
eleven centuries to the same position, between the hippodrome,
the cathedral of St. Sophia, and the gardens, which descended by
many a terrace to the shores of the Propontis. The primitive edifice
of the first Constantine was a copy, or rival, of ancient Rome; the
gradual improvements of his successors aspired to emulate the wonders of the old world, and in the tenth century the Byzantine palace
excited the admiration, at least of the Latins, by an unquestionable
pre-eminence of strength, size, and magnificence. But the toil and
treasure of so many ages had produced a vast and irregular pile:
each separate building was marked with the character of the times
and of the founder; and the want of space might excuse the reigning monarch who demolished, perhaps with secret satisfaction, the
works of his predecessors. The economy of the emperor Theophilus
allowed a more free and ample scope for his domestic luxury and
splendour. A favourite ambassador, who had astonished the Abbassides themselves by his pride and liberality, presented on his return
the model of a palace which the caliph of Bagdad had recently
constructed on the banks of the Tigris. The model was instantly
copied and surpassed: the new buildings of Theophilus were
accompanied with gardens and with five churches, one of which
was conspicuous for size and beauty: it was crowned with three
domes, the roof of gilt brass reposed on columns of Italian marble,
and the walls were incrusted with marbles of various colours. In
the face of the church a semicircular portico, of the figure and
name of the Greek *sigma*, was supported by fifteen columns of
Phrygian marble, and the subterraneous vaults were of a similar
construction. The square before the sigma was decorated with a
fountain, and the margin of the basin was lined and encompassed
with plates of silver. In the beginning of each season the basin, instead
of water, was replenished with the most exquisite fruits, which were
abandoned to the populace for the entertainment of the prince. He
enjoyed this tumultuous spectacle from a throne resplendent with
gold and gems, which was raised by a marble staircase to the height
of a lofty terrace. Below the throne were seated the officers of his
guards, the magistrates, the chiefs of the factions of the circus; the
inferior steps were occupied by the people, and the place below

was covered with troops of dancers, singers, and pantomimes. The square was surrounded by the hall of justice, the arsenal, and the various offices of business and pleasure; and the *purple* chamber was named from the annual distribution of robes of scarlet and purple by the hand of the empress herself. The long series of the apartments was adapted to the seasons, and decorated with marble and porphyry, with painting, sculpture, and mosaics, with a profusion of gold, silver, and precious stones. His fanciful magnificence employed the skill and patience of such artists as the times could afford; but the taste of Athens would have despised their frivolous and costly labours; a golden tree, with its leaves and branches, which sheltered a multitude of birds warbling their artificial notes, and two lions of massy gold, and of the natural size, who looked and roared like their brethren of the forest. The successors of Theophilus, of the Basilian and Comnenian dynasties, were not less ambitious of leaving some memorial of their residence; and the portion of the palace most splendid and august was dignified with the title of the golden *triclinium*. With becoming modesty the rich and noble Greeks aspired to imitate their sovereign, and when they passed through the streets on horseback, in their robes of silk and embroidery, they were mistaken by the children for kings.

In an absolute government, which levels the distinctions of noble and plebeian birth, the sovereign is the sole fountain of honour; and the rank, both in the palace and the empire, depends on the titles and offices which are bestowed and resumed by his arbitrary will. Above a thousand years, from Vespasian to Alexius Comnenus, the *Cæsar* was the second person, or at least the second degree, after the supreme title of *Augustus* was more freely communicated to the sons and brothers of the reigning monarch. To elude without violating his promise to a powerful associate, the husband of his sister, and, without giving himself an equal, to reward the piety of his brother Isaac, the crafty Alexius interposed a new and supereminent dignity. The happy flexibility of the Greek tongue allowed him to compound the names of Augustus and Emperor (Sebastos and Autocrator), and the union produced the sonorous title of *Sebastocrator.* He was exalted above the Cæsar on the first step of the throne: the public acclamations repeated his name; and he was only distinguished from the sovereign by some peculiar ornaments of the head and feet. The emperor alone could assume the purple or red buskins, and the close diadem or tiara, which imitated the fashion of the Persian kings. It was a high pyramidal cap of cloth or silk, almost concealed by a profusion of pearls and jewels: the crown was formed by a horizontal circle and two arches of gold: at the summit, the point of their intersection, was placed a globe or cross, and two strings or lappets of pearl depended on either cheek. Instead of red, the buskins of the Sebastocrator and Cæsar were green; and on their *open* coronets, or crowns, the precious gems were more sparingly distributed. Beside and below the Cæsar the fancy of Alexius created the *Panhypersebastos* and the *Protosebastos*, whose sound and signification will satisfy a Grecian ear. They imply a superiority and a priority above the simple name of Augustus; and this sacred and primitive title of the Roman prince was degraded to the kinsmen and servants of the Byzantine court. The daughter of Alexius applauds with fond complacency this artful gradation of hopes and honours; but the science of words is accessible to the meanest capacity; and this vain dictionary was easily enriched by the pride of his successors. To their favourite sons or brothers they imparted the more lofty appellation of Lord or *Despot*, which was illustrated with new ornaments and prerogatives, and placed immediately after the person of the emperor himself. The five titles of, 1. *Despot*; 2. *Sebastocrator*; 3. *Cæsar*; 4. *Panhypersebastos*; and 5. *Protosebastos*; were usually confined to the princes of his blood: they were the emanations of his majesty; but as they exercised no regular functions, their existence was useless, and their authority precarious.

But in every monarchy the substantial powers of government must be divided and exercised by the ministers of the palace and treasury, the fleet and army. The titles alone can differ; and in the revolution of ages, the counts and præfects, the prætor and quæstor, insensibly descended, while their servants rose above their heads to the first honours of the state. 1. In a monarchy, which refers every object to the person of the prince, the care and ceremonies of the palace form the most respectable department. The *Curopalata*, so illustrious in the age of Justinian, was supplanted by the *Protovestiare*, whose primitive functions were limited to the custody of the wardrobe. From thence his jurisdiction was extended over the numerous menials of pomp and luxury; and he presided with his silver wand at the public and private audience. 2. In the ancient system of Constantine, the name of *Logothete*, or accountant, was applied to the receivers of the finances: the principal officers were distinguished as the Logothetes of the domain, of the posts, the army, the private and public treasure; and the *great Logothete*, the supreme guardian of the laws and revenues, is compared with the chancellor of the Latin monarchies. His discerning eye pervaded the civil administration; and he was assisted, in due subordination, by the eparch or præfect of the city, the first secretary, and the keepers of the privy seal, the archives, and the red and purple ink which was reserved for the sacred signature of the emperor alone. The introductor and interpreter of foreign ambassadors were the great *Chiauss* and the *Dragoman*, two names of Turkish origin, and which are still familiar to the Sublime Porte. 3. From the humble style and service of guards, the *Domestics* insensibly rose to the station of generals; the military themes of the East and West, the legions of Europe and Asia, were often divided, till the *great Domestic* was finally invested with the universal and absolute command of the land forces. The *Protostrator*, in his original functions, was the assistant of the emperor when he mounted on horseback: he gradually became the lieutenant of the great Domestic in the field; and his jurisdiction extended over the stables, the cavalry, and the royal train of hunting and hawking. The *Stratopedarch* was the great judge of the camp: the *Protospathaire* commanded the guards; the *Constable*, the great *Æteriarch*, and the *Acolyth*, were the separate chiefs of the Franks, the barbarians, and the Varangi, or English, the mercenary strangers, who, in the decay of the national spirit, formed the nerve of the Byzantine armies. 4. The naval powers were under the command of the *great Duke*; in his absence they obeyed the *great Drungaire* of the fleet; and, in *his* place, the *Emir*, or *Admiral*, a name of Saracen extraction, but which has been naturalised in all the modern languages of Europe. Of these officers, and of many more whom it would be useless to enumerate, the civil and military hierarchy was framed. Their honours and emoluments, their dress and titles, their mutual salutations and respective pre-eminence, were balanced with more exquisite labour than would have fixed the constitution of a free people; and the code was almost perfect when this baseless fabric, the monument of pride and servitude, was for ever buried in the ruins of the empire.

The most lofty titles, and the most humble postures, which devotion has applied to the Supreme Being, have been prostituted by flattery and fear to creatures of the same nature with ourselves. The mode of *adoration*, of falling prostrate on the ground and kissing the feet of the emperor, was borrowed by Diocletian from Persian servitude; but it was continued and aggravated till the last age of the Greek monarchy. Excepting only on Sundays, when it was waived, from a motive of religious pride, this humiliating reverence was exacted from all who entered the royal presence, from the princes invested with the diadem and purple, and from the ambassadors who represented their independent sovereigns, the caliphs of Asia, Egypt, or Spain, the kings of France and Italy, and the Latin emperors of ancient Rome. In his transactions of business, Liutprand, bishop of Cremona, asserted the free spirit of a Frank and the dignity of his master Otho. Yet his sincerity cannot disguise the abasement of his first audience. When he approached the throne, the birds of the golden tree began to warble their notes, which were accompanied by the roarings of the two lions of gold. With his two companions Liutprand was compelled to bow and to fall prostrate; and thrice he touched the ground with his forehead. He arose; but in the short interval the throne had been hoisted by an engine from the floor to the ceiling, the Imperial figure appeared in new and more gorgeous apparel, and the interview was concluded in haughty and majestic silence. In this honest and curious narrative the bishop of Cremona represents the ceremonies of the Byzantine court, which are still practised in the Sublime Porte, and which were preserved in the last age of the dukes of Muscovy or Russia. After a long journey by the sea and land, from Venice to Constantinople, the ambassador halted at the golden gate, till he was conducted by the formal officers to the hospitable palace prepared for his reception; but this palace was a prison, and his jealous keepers prohibited all social intercourse either with Strangers or natives. At his first audience he offered the gifts of his master— slaves, and golden vases, and costly armour. The ostentatious payment of the officers and troops displayed before his eyes the riches of the empire: he was entertained at a royal banquet, in which the ambassadors of the nations were marshalled by the esteem or contempt of the Greeks: from his own table, the emperor, as the most signal favour, sent the plates which he had tasted; and his favourites were dismissed with a robe of honour. In the morning and evening of each day his civil and military servants attended their duty in the palace; their labour was repaid by the sight, perhaps by the smile, of their lord; his commands were signified by a nod or a sign: but all earthly greatness *stood* silent and submissive in his presence. In his regular or extraordinary processions through the capital, he unveiled his person to the public view: the rites of policy were connected with those of religion, and his visits to the principal churches were regulated by the festivals of the Greek calendar.

On the eve of these processions the gracious or devout intention of the monarch was proclaimed by the heralds. The streets were cleared and purified; the pavement was strewed with flowers; the most precious furniture, the gold and silver plate and silken hangings, were displayed from the windows and balconies; and a severe discipline restrained and silenced the tumult of the populace. The march was opened by the military officers at the head of their troops: they were followed in long order by the magistrates and ministers of the civil government: the person of the emperor was guarded by his eunuchs and domestics, and at the church door he was solemnly received by the patriarch and his clergy. The task of applause was not abandoned to the rude and spontaneous voices of the crowd. The most convenient stations were occupied by the bands of the blue and green factions of the circus; and their furious conflicts, which had shaken the capital, were insensibly sunk to an emulation of servitude. From either side they echoed in responsive melody the praises of the emperor; their poets and musicians directed the choir, and long life and victory were the burden of every song. The same acclamations were performed at the audience, the banquet, and the church; and as an evidence of boundless sway, they were repeated in the Latin, Gothic, Persian, French, and even English language, by the mercenaries who sustained the real or fictitious character of those nations. By the pen of Constantine Porphyrogenitus this science of form and flattery has been reduced into a pompous and trifling volume, which the vanity of succeeding times might enrich with an ample supplement.

In the Byzantine palace the emperor was the first slave of the ceremonies which he imposed, of the rigid forms which regulated each word and gesture, besieged him in the palace, and violated the leisure of his rural solitude. But the lives and fortunes of millions hung on his arbitrary will; and the firmest minds, superior to the allurements of pomp and luxury, may be seduced by the more active pleasure of commanding their equals. The legislative and executive powers were centred in the person of the monarch, and the last remains of the authority of the senate were finally eradicated by Leo the Philosopher. A lethargy of servitude had benumbed the minds of the Greeks: in the wildest tumults of rebellion they never aspired to the idea of a free constitution; and the private character of the prince was the only source and measure of their public happiness. Superstition riveted their chains; in the church of St. Sophia he was solemnly crowned by the patriarch; at the foot of the altar they pledged their passive and unconditional obedience to his government and family. On his side he engaged to abstain as much as possible from the capital punishments of death and mutilation; his orthodox creed was subscribed with his own hand, and he promised to obey the decrees of the seven synods and the canons of the holy church. But the assurance of mercy was loose and indefinite: he swore, not to his people, but to an invisible judge; and except in the inexpiable guilt of heresy, the ministers of heaven were always prepared to preach the indefeasible right, and to absolve the venial transgressions, of their sovereign. The Greek ecclesiastics were themselves the subjects of the civil magistrate: at the nod of a tyrant the bishops were created, or transferred, or deposed, or punished with an ignominious death; whatever might be their wealth or influence, they could never succeed like the Latin clergy in the establishment of an independent republic; and the patriarch of Constantinople condemned, what he secretly envied, the temporal greatness of his Roman brother. Yet the exercise of boundless despotism is happily checked by the laws of nature and necessity. In proportion to his wisdom and virtue, the master of an empire is confined to the path of his sacred and laborious duty. In proportion to his vice and folly, he drops the sceptre too weighty for his hands; and the motions of the royal image are ruled by the imperceptible thread of some minister or favourite, who undertakes for his private interest to exercise the task of the public oppression. In some fatal moment the most absolute monarch may dread the reason or the caprice of a nation of slaves; and experience has proved that whatever is gained in the extent is lost in the safety and solidity of regal power.

While the government of the East was transacted in Latin, the Greek was the language of literature and philosophy, nor could the masters of this rich and perfect idiom be tempted to envy the borrowed learning and imitative taste of their Roman disciples. After the fall of Paganism, the loss of Syria and Egypt, and the extinction of the schools of Alexandria and Athens, the studies of the Greeks insensibly retired to some regular monasteries, and, above all, to the royal college of Constantinople, which was burnt in the reign of Leo the Isaurian. In the pompous style of the age, the president of that foundation was named the Sun of Science; his twelve associates, the professors in the different arts and faculties, were the twelve signs of the zodiac; a library of thirty-six thousand five hundred volumes was open to their inquiries; and they could show an ancient manuscript of Homer, on a roll of parchment one hundred and twenty feet in length, the intestines, as it was fabled, of a prodigious serpent. But the seventh and eighth centuries were a period of discord and darkness; the library was burnt, the college was abolished, the Iconoclasts are represented as the foes of antiquity, and a savage ignorance and contempt of letters has disgraced the princes of the Heraclean and Isaurian dynasties.

In the ninth century we trace the first dawnings of the restoration of science. After the fanaticism of the Arabs had subsided, the caliphs aspired to conquer the arts, rather than the provinces, of the empire: their liberal curiosity rekindled the emulation of the Greeks, brushed away the dust from their ancient libraries, and taught them to know and reward the philosophers, whose labours had been hitherto repaid by the pleasure of study and the pursuit of truth. The Cæsar Bardas, the uncle of Michael the Third, was the generous protector of letters, a title which alone has preserved his memory and excused his ambition. A particle of the treasures of his nephew was sometimes diverted from the indulgence of vice and folly; a school was opened in the palace of Magnaura, and the presence of Bardas excited the emulation of the masters and students. At their head was the philosopher Leo, archbishop of Thessalonica; his profound skill in astronomy and the mathematics was admired by the strangers of the East, and this occult science was magnified by vulgar credulity, which modestly supposes that all knowledge superior to its own must be the effect of inspiration or magic. At the pressing entreaty of the Cæsar, his friend, the celebrated Photius, renounced the freedom of a secular and studious life, ascended the patriarchal throne, and was alternately excommunicated and absolved by the synods of the East and West. By the confession even of priestly hatred, no art or science, except poetry, was foreign to this universal scholar, who was deep in thought, indefatigable in reading, and eloquent in diction. Whilst he exercised the office of protospathaire, or captain of the guards, Photius was sent ambassador to the caliph of Bagdad. The tedious hours of exile, perhaps of confinement, were beguiled by the hasty composition of his *Library*, a living monument of erudition and criticism. Two hundred and fourscore writers, historians, orators, philosophers, theologians, are reviewed without any regular method; he abridges their narrative or doctrine, appreciates their style and character, and judges even the fathers of the church with a discreet freedom which often breaks through the superstition of the times. The emperor Basil, who lamented the defects of his own education, intrusted to the care of Photius his son and successor Leo the Philosopher, and the reign of that prince and of his son Constantine Porphyrogenitus forms one of the most prosperous eras of the Byzantine literature. By their munificence the treasures of antiquity were deposited in the Imperial library; by their pens, or those of their associates, they were imparted in such extracts and abridgments as might amuse the curiosity, without oppressing the indolence, of the public. Besides the *Basilics*, or code of laws, the arts of husbandry and war, of feeding or destroying the human species, were propagated with equal diligence; and the history of Greece and Rome was digested into fifty-three heads or titles, of which two only (of embassies, and of virtues and vices) have escaped the injuries of time. In every station the reader might contemplate the image of the past world, apply the lesson or warning of each page, and learn to admire, perhaps to imitate, the examples of a brighter period. I shall not expatiate on the works of the Byzantine Greeks, who, by the assiduous study of the ancients, have deserved, in some measure, the remembrance and gratitude of the moderns. The scholars of the present age may still enjoy the benefit of the philosophical commonplace-book of Stobæus, the grammatical and historic lexicon of Suidas, the Chiliads of Tzetzes, which comprise six hundred narratives in twelve thousand verses, and the commentaries on Homer of Eustathius archbishop of Thessalonica, who, from his horn of plenty, has poured the names and authorities of four hundred writers. From these originals, and from the numerous tribe of scholiasts and critics, some estimate may be formed of the literary wealth of the twelfth century. Constantinople was enlightened by the genius of Homer and Demosthenes, of Aristotle and Plato; and in the enjoyment or neglect of our present riches we must envy the generation that could still peruse the history of Theopompus, the orations of Hyperides, the comedies of Menander, and the odes of Alcæus and Sappho. The frequent labour of illustration attests not only the existence but the popularity of the Grecian classics; the general knowledge of the age may be deduced from the example of two learned females, the empress Eudocia and the princess Anna Comnena, who cultivated, in the purple, the arts of rhetoric and philosophy. The vulgar dialect of the city was gross and barbarous: a more correct and elaborate style distinguished the discourse, or at least the compositions, of the church and palace, which sometimes affected to copy the purity of the Attic models.

In our modern education, the painful though necessary attainment of two languages which are no longer living may consume the time and damp the ardour of the youthful student. The poets and orators were long imprisoned in the barbarous dialects of our Western ancestors, devoid of harmony or grace; and their genius, without precept or example, was abandoned to the rude and native powers of their judgment and fancy. But the Greeks of Constantinople, after purging away the impurities of their vulgar speech, acquired the free use of their ancient language, the most happy composition of human art, and a familiar knowledge of the sublime masters who had pleased or instructed the first of nations. But these advantages only tend to aggravate the reproach and shame of a degenerate people. They held in their lifeless hands the riches of their fathers, without inheriting the spirit which had created and improved that sacred patrimony: they read, they compiled, but their languid souls seemed alike incapable of thought and action. In the revolution of ten centuries, not a single discovery was made to exalt the dignity or promote the happiness of mankind. Not a single idea has been added to the speculative systems of antiquity, and a succession of patient disciples became in their turn the dogmatic teachers of the next servile generation. Not a single composition of history, philosophy, or literature, has been saved from oblivion by the intrinsic beauties of style or sentiment, or original fancy, or even of successful imitation. In prose, the least offensive of the Byzantine writers are absolved from censure by their naked and unpresuming simplicity: but the orators, most eloquent in their own conceit, are the farthest removed from the models whom they affect to emulate. In every page our taste and reason are wounded by the choice of gigantic and obsolete words, a stiff and intricate phraseology, the discord of images, the childish play of false or unseasonable ornament, and the painful attempt to elevate themselves, to astonish the reader, and to involve a trivial meaning in the smoke of obscurity and exaggeration. Their prose is soaring to the vicious affectation of poetry: their poetry is sinking below the flatness and insipidity of prose. The tragic, epic, and lyric muses were silent and inglorious: the bards of Constantinople seldom rose above a riddle or epigram, a panegyric or tale; they forgot even the rules of prosody; and with the melody of Homer yet sounding in their ears, they confound all measure of feet and syllables in the impotent strains which have received the name of *political* or city verses. The minds of the Greeks were bound in the fetters of a base and imperious superstition, which extends her dominion round the circle of profane science. Their understandings were bewildered in metaphysical controversy: in the belief of visions and miracles they had lost all principles of moral evidence, and their taste was vitiated by the homilies of the monks, an absurd medley of declamation and Scripture. Even these contemptible studies were no longer dignified by the abuse of superior talents: the leaders of the Greek church were humbly content to admire and copy the oracles of antiquity, nor did the schools or pulpit produce any rivals of the fame of Athanasius and Chrysostom.

In all the pursuits of active and speculative life, the emulation of states and individuals is the most powerful spring of the efforts and improvements of mankind. The cities of ancient Greece were cast in the happy mixture of union and independence, which is repeated on a larger scale, but in a looser form, by the nations of modern Europe: the union of language, religion, and manners, which renders them the spectators and judges of each other's merit: the independence of government and interest, which asserts their separate freedom, and excites them to strive for pre-eminence in the career of glory. The situation of the Romans was less favourable; yet in the early ages of the republic, which fixed the national character, a similar emulation was kindled among the states of Latium and Italy; and in the arts and sciences they aspired to equal or surpass their Grecian masters. The empire of the Cæsars undoubtedly checked the activity and progress of the human mind: its magnitude might indeed allow some scope for domestic competition; but when it was gradually reduced, at first to the East, and at last to Greece and Constantinople, the Byzantine subjects were degraded to an abject and languid temper, the natural effect of their solitary and insulated state. From the North they were oppressed by nameless tribes of barbarians, to whom they scarcely imparted the appellation of men. The language and religion of the more polished Arabs were an insurmountable bar to all social intercourse. The conquerors of Europe were their brethren in the Christian faith; but the speech of the Franks or Latins was unknown, their manners were rude, and they were rarely connected, in peace or war, with the successors of Heraclius. Alone in the universe, the self-satisfied pride of the Greeks was not disturbed by the comparison of foreign merit; and it is no wonder if they fainted in the race, since they had neither competitors to urge their speed, nor judges to crown their victory. The nations of Europe and Asia were mingled by the expeditions to the Holy Land; and it is under the Comnenian dynasty that a faint emulation of knowledge and military virtue was rekindled in the Byzantine empire.

The Mohammedan, and more especially the Turkish casuists, have pronounced that no promise can bind the faithful against the interest and duty of their religion, and that the sultan may abrogate his own treaties and those of his predecessors. The justice and magnanimity of Amurath had scorned this immoral privilege; but his son, though the proudest of men, could stoop from ambition to the basest arts of dissimulation and deceit. Peace was on his lips while war was in his heart: he incessantly sighed for the possession of Constantinople; and the Greeks, by their own indiscretion, afforded the first pretence of the fatal rupture. Instead of labouring to be forgotten, their ambassadors pursued his camp to demand the payment, and even the increase, of their annual stipend: the divan was importuned by their complaints; and the vizir, a secret friend of the Christians, was constrained to deliver the sense of his brethren. "Ye foolish and miserable Romans," said Calil, "we know your devices, and ye are ignorant of your own danger! the scrupulous Amurath is no more; his throne is occupied by a young conqueror whom no laws can bind, and no obstacles can resist: and if you escape from his hands, give praise to the divine clemency, which yet delays the chastisement of your sins. Why do you seek to affright us by vain and indirect menaces? Release the fugitive Orchan, crown him sultan of Romania, call the Hungarians from beyond the Danube, arm against us the nations of the West, and be assured that you will only provoke and precipitate your ruin." But if the fears of the ambassadors were alarmed by the stern language of the vizir, they were soothed by the courteous audience and friendly speeches of the Ottoman prince; and Mohammed assured them that on his return to Adrianople he would redress the grievances, and consult the true interests of the Greeks. No sooner had he repassed the Hellespont than he issued a mandate to suppress their pension, and to expel their officers from the banks of the Strymon: in this measure he betrayed a hostile mind; and the second order announced, and in some degree commenced, the siege of Constantinople. In the narrow pass of the Bosphorus an Asiatic fortress had formerly been raised by his grandfather; in the opposite situation, on the European side, he resolved to erect a more formidable castle, and a thousand masons were commanded to assemble in the spring on a spot named Asomaton, about five miles from the Greek metropolis. Persuasion is the resource of the feeble; and the feeble can seldom persuade: the ambassadors of the emperor attempted, without success, to divert Mohammed from the execution of his design. They represented that his grandfather had solicited the permission of Manuel to build a castle on his own territories; but that this double fortification, which would command the strait, could only tend to violate the alliance of the nations, to intercept the Latins who traded in the Black Sea, and perhaps to annihilate the subsistence of the city. "I form no enterprise," replied the perfidious sultan, "against the city; but the empire of Constantinople is measured by her walls. Have you forgot the distress to which my father was reduced when you formed a league with the Hungarians, when they invaded our country by land, and the Hellespont was occupied by the French galleys? Amurath was compelled to force the passage of the Bosphorus; and your strength was not equal to your malevolence. I was then a child at Adrianople, the Moslems trembled, and for a while the *Gabours* insulted our disgrace. But when my father had triumphed in the field of Varna, he vowed to erect a fort on the western shore, and that vow it is my duty to accomplish. Have ye the right, have ye the power, to control my actions on my own ground? For that ground *is* my own: as far as the shores of the Bosphorus Asia is inhabited by the Turks, and Europe is deserted by the Romans. Return, and inform your king that the present Ottoman is far different from his predecessors, that *his* resolutions surpass *their* wishes, and that *he* performs more than *they* could resolve. Return in safety; but the next who delivers a similar message may expect to be flayed alive." After this declaration, Constantine, the first of the Greeks in spirit as in rank, had determined to unsheathe the sword, and to resist the approach and establishment of the Turks on the Bosphorus. He was disarmed by the advice of his civil and ecclesiastical ministers, who recommended a system less generous, and even less prudent, than his own, to approve their patience and longsuffering, to brand the Ottoman with the name and guilt of an aggressor, and to depend on chance and time for their own safety, and the destruction of a fort which could not long be maintained in the neighbourhood of a great and populous city. Amidst hope and fear, the fears of the wise and the hopes of the credulous, the winter rolled away; the proper business of each man and each hour was postponed; and the Greeks shut their eyes against the impending danger, till the arrival of the spring and the sultan decided the assurance of their ruin.

Of a master who never forgives, the orders are seldom disobeyed. On the twenty-sixth of March the appointed spot of Asomaton was covered with an active swarm of Turkish artificers; and the materials by sea and land were diligently transported from Europe and Asia. The lime had been burnt in Cataphrygia, the timber was cut down in the woods of Heraclea and Nicomedia, and the stones were dug from the Anatolian quarries. Each of the thousand masons was assisted by two workmen; and a measure of two cubits was marked for their daily task. The fortress was built in a triangular form; each angle was flanked by a strong and massy tower, one on the declivity of the hill, two along the sea-shore; a thickness of twenty-two feet was assigned for the walls, thirty for the towers; and the whole building was covered with a solid platform of lead. Mohammed himself pressed and directed the work with indefatigable ardour: his three viziers claimed the honour of finishing their respective towers; the zeal of the cadhis emulated that of the Janizaries; the meanest labour was ennobled by the service of God and the sultan; and the diligence of the multitude was quickened by the eye of a despot whose smile was the hope of fortune, and whose frown was the messenger of death. The Greek emperor beheld with terror the irresistible progress of the work, and vainly strove by flattery and gifts to assuage an implacable foe, who sought, and secretly fomented, the slightest occasion of a quarrel. Such occasions must soon and inevitably be found. The ruins of stately churches, and even the marble columns which had been consecrated to Saint Michael the archangel, were employed without scruple by the profane and rapacious Moslems; and some Christians, who presumed to oppose the removal, received from their hands the crown of martyrdom. Constantine had solicited a Turkish guard to protect the fields and harvests of his subjects: the guard was fixed; but their first order was to allow free pasture to the mules and horses of the camp, and to defend their brethren if they should be molested by the natives. The retinue of an Ottoman chief had left their horses to pass the night among the ripe corn: the damage was felt, the insult was resented, and several of both nations were slain in a tumultuous conflict. Mohammed listened with joy to the complaint; and a detachment was commanded to exterminate the guilty village: the guilty had fled; but forty innocent and unsuspecting reapers were massacred by the soldiers. Till this provocation

Constantinople had been open to the visits of commerce and curiosity: on the first alarm the gates were shut; but the emperor, still anxious for peace, released on the third day his Turkish captives, and expressed, in a last message, the firm resignation of a Christian and a soldier. "Since neither oaths, nor treaty, nor submission can secure peace, pursue," said he to Mohammed, "your impious warfare. My trust is in God alone: if it should please him to mollify your heart, I shall rejoice in the happy change; if he delivers the city into your hands, I submit without a murmur to his holy will. But until the Judge of the earth shall pronounce between us, it is my duty to live and die in the defence of my people." The sultan's answer was hostile and decisive: his fortifications were completed; and before his departure for Adrianople he stationed a vigilant Aga and four hundred Janizaries to levy a tribute on the ships of every nation that should pass within the reach of their cannon. A Venetian vessel, refusing obedience to the new lords of the Bosphorus, was sunk with a single bullet. The master and thirty sailors escaped in the boat; but they were dragged in chains to the *Porte*: the chief was impaled, his companions were beheaded; and the historian Ducas beheld, at Demotica, their bodies exposed to the wild beasts. The siege of Constantinople was deferred till the ensuing spring; but an Ottoman army marched into the Morea to divert the force of the brothers of Constantine. At this era of calamity one of these princes, the despot Thomas, was blessed or afflicted with the birth of a son—"the last heir," says the plaintive Phranza, "of the last spark of the Roman empire."

While Mohammed threatened the capital of the East, the Greek emperor implored with fervent prayers the assistance of earth and Heaven. But the invisible powers were deaf to his supplications; and Christendom beheld with indifference the fall of Constantinople, while she derived at least some promise of supply from the jealous and temporal policy of the sultan of Egypt. Some states were too weak, and others too remote; by some the danger was considered as imaginary, by others as inevitable: the Western princes were involved in their endless and domestic quarrels; and the Roman pontiff was exasperated by the falsehood or obstinacy of the Greeks. Instead of employing in their favour the arms and treasures of Italy, Nicholas the Fifth had foretold their approaching ruin; and his honour was engaged in the accomplishment of his prophecy. Perhaps he was softened by the last extremity of their distress; but his compassion was tardy; his efforts were faint and unavailing; and Constantinople had fallen before the squadrons of Genoa and Venice could sail from their harbours. Even the princes of the Morea and of the Greek islands affected a cold neutrality: the Genoese colony of Galata negotiated a private treaty; and the sultan indulged them in the delusive hope that by his clemency they might survive the ruin of the empire. A plebeian crowd and some Byzantine nobles basely withdrew from the danger of their country; and the avarice of the rich denied the emperor, and reserved for the Turks, the secret treasures which might have raised in their defence whole armies of mercenaries. The indigent and solitary prince prepared however to sustain his formidable adversary; but if his courage were equal to the peril, his strength was inadequate to the contest. In the beginning of the spring the Turkish vanguard swept the towns and villages as far as the gates of Constantinople: submission was spared and protected; whatever presumed to resist was exterminated with fire and sword. The Greek places on the Black Sea, Mesembria, Acheloum, and Bizon, surrendered on the first summons; Selymbria alone deserved the honours of a siege or blockade; and the bold inhabitants, while they were invested by land, launched their boats, pillaged the opposite coast of Cyzicus, and sold their captives in the public market. But on the approach of Mohammed himself all was silent and prostrate: he first halted at the distance of five miles; and, from thence advancing in battle array, planted before the gate of St. Romanus the Imperial standard; and on the sixth day of April formed the memorable siege of Constantinople.

The troops of Asia and Europe extended on the right and left from the Propontis to the harbour; the Janizaries in the front were stationed before the sultan's tent; the Ottoman line was covered by a deep intrenchment; and a subordinate army enclosed the suburb of Galata, and watched the doubtful faith of the Genoese. The inquisitive Philelphus, who resided in Greece about thirty years before the siege, is confident that all the Turkish forces of any name or value could not exceed the number of sixty thousand horse and twenty thousand foot; and he upbraids the pusillanimity of the nations who had tamely yielded to a handful of barbarians. Such indeed might be the regular establishment of the *Capiculi*, the troops of the Porte who marched with the prince, and were paid from his royal treasury. But the bashaws, in their respective governments, maintained or levied a provincial militia; many lands were held by a military tenure; many volunteers were attracted by the hope of spoil; and the sound of the holy trumpet invited a swarm of hungry and fearless fanatics, who might contribute at least to multiply the terrors, and in a first attack to blunt the swords of the Christians. The whole mass of the Turkish powers is magnified by Ducas, Chalcocondyles, and Leonard of Chios, to the amount of three or four hundred thousand men; but Phranza was a less remote and more accurate judge; and his precise definition of two hundred and fifty-eight thousand does not exceed the measure of experience and probability. The navy of the besiegers was less formidable: the Propontis was overspread with three hundred and twenty sail; but of these no more than eighteen could be rated as galleys of war; and the far greater part must be degraded to the condition of store-ships and transports, which poured into the camp fresh supplies of men, ammunition, and provisions. In her last decay Constantinople was still peopled with more than a hundred thousand inhabitants; but these numbers are found in the accounts, not of war, but of captivity; and they mostly consisted of mechanics, of priests, of women, and of men devoid of that spirit which even women have sometimes exerted for the common safety. I can suppose, I could almost excuse, the reluctance of subjects to serve on a distant frontier, at the will of a tyrant; but the man who dares not expose his life in the defence of his children and his property has lost in society the first and most active energies of nature. By the emperor's command a particular inquiry had been made through the streets and houses, how many of the citizens, or even of the monks, were able and willing to bear arms for their country. The lists were intrusted to Phranza; and after a diligent addition he informed his master, with grief and surprise, that the national defence was reduced to four thousand nine hundred and seventy *Romans*. Between Constantine and his faithful minister this comfortless secret was preserved; and a sufficient proportion of shields, cross-bows, and muskets, was distributed from the arsenal to the city bands. They derived some accession from a body of two thousand strangers, under the command of John Justiniani, a noble Genoese; a liberal donative was advanced to these auxiliaries; and a princely recompense, the isle of Lemnos, was promised to the valour and victory of their chief. A strong chain was drawn across the mouth of the harbour: it was supported by some Greek and Italian vessels of war and merchandise; and the ships of every Christian nation, that successively arrived from Candia and the Black Sea, were detained for the public service. Against the powers of the Ottoman empire, a city of the extent of thirteen, perhaps of sixteen, miles was defended by a scanty garrison of seven or eight thousand soldiers. Europe and Asia were open to the besiegers; but the strength and provisions of the Greeks must sustain a daily decrease; nor could they indulge the expectation of any foreign succour or supply.

The primitive Romans would have drawn their swords in the resolution of death or conquest. The primitive Christians might have embraced each other, and awaited in patience and charity the stroke of martyrdom. But the Greeks of Constantinople were animated only by the spirit of religion, and that spirit was productive only of animosity and discord. Before his death the emperor John Palæologus had renounced the unpopular measure of a union with the Latins; nor was the idea revived till the distress of his brother Constantine imposed a last trial of flattery and dissimulation. With the demand of temporal aid his ambassadors were instructed to mingle the assurance of spiritual obedience: his neglect of the church was excused by the urgent cares of the state; and his orthodox wishes solicited the presence of a Roman legate. The Vatican had been too often deluded; yet the signs of repentance could not decently be overlooked; a legate was more easily granted than an army; and about six months before the final destruction, the cardinal Isidore of Russia appeared in that character with a retinue of priests and soldiers. The emperor saluted him as a friend and father; respectfully listened to his public and private sermons; and with the most obsequious of the clergy and laymen subscribed the act of union, as it had been ratified in the council of Florence. On the twelfth of December the two nations, in the church of St. Sophia, joined in the communion of sacrifice and prayer; and the names of the two pontiffs were solemnly commemorated; the names of Nicholas the Fifth, the vicar of Christ, and of the patriarch Gregory, who had been driven into exile by a rebellious people.

But the dress and language of the Latin priest who officiated at the altar were an object of scandal; and it was observed with horror that he consecrated a cake or wafer of *unleavened* bread, and poured cold water into the cup of the sacrament. A national historian acknowledges with a blush that none of his countrymen, not the emperor himself, were sincere in this occasional conformity. Their hasty and unconditional submission was palliated by a promise of future revisal; but the best, or the worst, of their excuses was the confession of their own perjury. When they were pressed by the reproaches of their honest brethren, "Have patience," they whispered, "have patience till God shall have delivered the city from the great dragon who seeks to devour us. You shall then perceive whether we are truly reconciled with the Azymites." But patience is not the attribute of zeal; nor can the arts of a court be adapted to the freedom and violence of popular enthusiasm. From the dome of St. Sophia the inhabitants of either sex, and of every degree, rushed in crowds to the cell of the monk Gennadius, to consult the oracle of the church. The holy man was invisible; entranced, as it should seem, in deep meditation, or divine rapture: but he had exposed on the door of his cell a speaking tablet; and they successively withdrew, after reading these tremendous words: "O miserable Romans, why will ye abandon the truth; and why, instead of confiding in God, will ye put your trust in the Italians? In losing your faith you will lose your city. Have mercy on me, O Lord! I protest in thy presence that I am innocent of the crime. O miserable Romans, consider, pause, and repent. At the same moment that you renounce the religion of your fathers, by embracing impiety, you submit to a foreign servitude." According to the advice of Gennadius, the religious virgins, as pure as angels, and as proud as demons, rejected the act of union, and abjured all communion with the present and future associates of the Latins; and their example was applauded and imitated by the greatest part of the clergy and people. From the monastery the devout Greeks dispersed themselves in the taverns; drank confusion to the slaves of the pope; emptied their glasses in honour of the image of the holy Virgin; and besought her to defend against Mohammed the city which she had formerly saved from Chosroes and the Chagan. In the double intoxication of zeal and wine, they valiantly exclaimed, "What occasion have we for succour, or union, or Latins? far from us be the worship of the Azymites!" During the winter that preceded the Turkish conquest the nation was distracted by this epidemical frenzy; and the season of Lent, the approach of Easter, instead of breathing charity and love, served only to fortify the obstinacy and influence of the zealots. The confessors scrutinised and alarmed the conscience of their votaries, and a rigorous penance was imposed on those who had received the communion from a priest who had given an express or tacit consent to the union. His service at the altar propagated the infection to the mute and simple spectators of the ceremony: they forfeited, by the impure spectacle, the virtue of the sacerdotal character; nor was it lawful, even in danger of sudden death, to invoke the assistance of their prayers or absolution. No sooner had the church of St. Sophia been polluted by the Latin sacrifice than it was deserted as a Jewish synagogue, or a heathen temple, by the clergy and people; and a vast and gloomy silence prevailed in that venerable dome, which had so often smoked with a cloud of incense, blazed with innumerable lights, and resounded with the voice of prayer and thanksgiving. The Latins were the most odious of heretics and infidels; and the first minister of the empire, the great duke, was heard to declare that he had rather behold in Constantinople the turban of Mohammed than the pope's tiara or a cardinal's hat. A sentiment so unworthy of Christians and patriots was familiar and fatal to the Greeks: the emperor was deprived of the affection and support of his subjects; and their native cowardice was sanctified by resignation to the divine decree or the visionary hope of a miraculous deliverance.

Of the triangle which composes the figure of Constantinople the two sides along the sea were made inaccessible to an enemy; the Propontis by nature, and the harbour by art. Between the two waters, the basis of the triangle, the land side was protected by a double wall and a deep ditch of the depth of one hundred feet. Against this line of fortification, which Phranza, an eye-witness, prolongs to the measure of six miles, the Ottomans directed their principal attack; and the emperor, after distributing the service and command of the most perilous stations, undertook the defence of the external wall. In the first days of the siege the Greek soldiers descended into the ditch, or sallied into the field; but they soon discovered that, in the proportion of their numbers, one Christian was of more value than twenty Turks; and, after these bold preludes, they were prudently content to maintain the rampart with their missile weapons. Nor should this prudence be accused of pusillanimity. The nation was indeed pusillanimous and base; but the last Constantine deserves the name of a hero: his noble band of volunteers was inspired with Roman virtue; and the foreign auxiliaries supported the honour of the Western chivalry. The incessant volleys of lances and arrows were accompanied with the smoke, the sound, and the fire of their musketry and cannon. Their small arms discharged at the same time either five, or even ten, balls of lead, of the size of a walnut; and, according to the closeness of the ranks and the force of the powder, several breastplates and bodies were transpierced by the same shot. But the Turkish approaches were soon sunk in trenches or covered with ruins. Each day added to the

science of the Christians; but their inadequate stock of gunpowder
was wasted in the operations of each day. Their ordnance was not
powerful either in size or number; and if they possessed some heavy
cannon, they feared to plant them on the walls, lest the aged structure should be shaken and overthrown by the explosion. The same
destructive secret had been revealed to the Moslems; by whom it was
employed with the superior energy of zeal, riches, and despotism.
The great cannon of Mohammed has been separately noticed; an
important and visible object in the history of the times: but that
enormous engine was flanked by two fellows almost of equal magnitude: the long order of the Turkish artillery was pointed against
the walls; fourteen batteries thundered at once on the most accessible places; and of one of these it is ambiguously expressed that
it was mounted with one hundred and thirty guns, or that it
discharged one hundred and thirty bullets. Yet in the power and
activity of the sultan we may discern the infancy of the new science.
Under a master who counted the moments the great cannon could
be loaded and fired no more than seven times in one day. The
heated metal unfortunately burst; several workmen were destroyed,
and the skill of an artist was admired who bethought himself of
preventing the danger and the accident, by pouring oil, after each
explosion, into the mouth of the cannon.

The first random shots were productive of more sound than
effect; and it was by the advice of a Christian that the engineers
were taught to level their aim against the two opposite sides of the
salient angles of a bastion. However imperfect, the weight and
repetition of the fire made some impression on the walls; and the
Turks, pushing their approaches to the edge of the ditch, attempted
to fill the enormous chasm and to build a road to the assault.
Innumerable fascines, and hogsheads, and trunks of trees, were
heaped on each other; and such was the impetuosity of the throng,
that the foremost and the weakest were pushed headlong down the
precipice and instantly buried under the accumulated mass. To fill
the ditch was the toil of the besiegers; to clear away the rubbish
was the safety of the besieged; and, after a long and bloody conflict,
the web that had been woven in the day was still unravelled in the
night. The next resource of Mohammed was the practice of mines;
but the soil was rocky; in every attempt he was stopped and
undermined by the Christian engineers; nor had the art been yet
invented of replenishing those subterraneous passages with gunpowder and blowing whole towers and cities into the air. A circumstance

that distinguishes the siege of Constantinople is the reunion of the ancient and modern artillery. The cannon were intermingled with the mechanical engines for casting stones and darts; the bullet and the battering-ram were directed against the same walls; nor had the discovery of gunpowder superseded the use of the liquid and unextinguishable fire. A wooden turret of the largest size was advanced on rollers: this portable magazine of ammunition and fascines was protected by a threefold covering of bulls' hides; incessant volleys were securely discharged from the loopholes; in the front three doors were contrived for the alternate sally and retreat of the soldiers and workmen. They ascended by a staircase to the upper platform, and, as high as the level of that platform, a scaling-ladder could be raised by pulleys to form a bridge and grapple with the adverse rampart. By these various arts of annoyance, some as new as they were pernicious to the Greeks, the tower of St. Romanus was at length overturned: after a severe struggle the Turks were repulsed from the breach and interrupted by darkness; but they trusted that with the return of light they should renew the attack with fresh vigour and decisive success. Of this pause of action, this interval of hope, each moment was improved by the activity of the emperor and Justiniani, who passed the night on the spot, and urged the labours which involved the safety of the church and city. At the dawn of day the impatient sultan perceived, with astonishment and grief, that his wooden turret had been reduced to ashes: the ditch was cleared and restored, and the tower of St. Romanus was again strong and entire. He deplored the failure of his design, and uttered a profane exclamation, that the word of the thirty-seven thousand prophets should not have compelled him to believe that such a work, in so short a time, could have been accomplished by the infidels.

The generosity of the Christian princes was cold and tardy; but in the first apprehension of a siege Constantine had negotiated, in the isles of the Archipelago, the Morea, and Sicily, the most indispensable supplies. As early as the beginning of April, five great ships, equipped for merchandise and war, would have sailed from the harbour of Chios, had not the wind blown obstinately from the north. One of these ships bore the Imperial flag; the remaining four belonged to the Genoese; and they were laden with wheat and barley, with wine, oil, and vegetables, and, above all, with soldiers and mariners, for the service of the capital. After a tedious delay a gentle breeze, and on the second day a strong gale from the south,

carried them through the Hellespont and the Propontis; but the
city was already invested by sea and land, and the Turkish fleet, at
the entrance of the Bosphorus, was stretched from shore to shore,
in the form of a crescent, to intercept, or at least to repel, these
bold auxiliaries. The reader who has present to his mind the geo-
graphical picture of Constantinople will conceive and admire the
greatness of the spectacle. The five Christian ships continued to
advance with joyful shouts, and a full press both of sails and oars,
against the hostile fleet of three hundred vessels; and the rampart,
the camp, the coasts of Europe and Asia, were lined with innumerable spectators, who anxiously awaited the event of this
momentous succour. At the first view that event could not appear
doubtful; the superiority of the Moslems was beyond all measure
or account, and, in a calm, their numbers and valour must
inevitably have prevailed. But their hasty and imperfect navy had
been created, not by the genius of the people, but by the will of
the sultan: in the height of their prosperity the Turks have
acknowledged that, if God had given them the earth, he had left
the sea to the infidels; and a series of defeats, a rapid progress of
decay, had established the truth of their modest confession. Except
eighteen galleys of some force, the rest of their fleet consisted of
open boats, rudely constructed and awkwardly managed, crowded
with troops, and destitute of cannon; and since courage arises in a
great measure from the consciousness of strength, the bravest of the
Janizaries might tremble on a new element. In the Christian
squadron five stout and lofty ships were guided by skilful pilots, and
manned with the veterans of Italy and Greece, long practised in
the arts and perils of the sea. Their weight was directed to sink or
scatter the weak obstacles that impeded their passage: their artillery
swept the waters; their liquid fire was poured on the heads of the
adversaries, who, with the design of boarding, presumed to
approach them; and the winds and waves are always on the side of
the ablest navigators. In this conflict the Imperial vessel, which had
been almost overpowered, was rescued by the Genoese; but the Turks,
in a distant and a closer attack, were twice repulsed with considerable loss. Mohammed himself sat on horseback on the beach, to
encourage their valour by his voice and presence, by the promise
of reward, and by fear more potent than the fear of the enemy. The
passions of his soul, and even the gestures of his body, seemed to
imitate the actions of the combatants; and, as if he had been the
lord of nature, he spurred his horse with a fearless and impotent

effort into the sea. His loud reproaches, and the clamours of the camp, urged the Ottomans to a third attack, more fatal and bloody than the two former; and I must repeat, though I cannot credit, the evidence of Phranza, who affirms, from their own mouth, that they lost above twelve thousand men in the slaughter of the day. They fled in disorder to the shores of Europe and Asia, while the Christian squadron, triumphant and unhurt, steered along the Bosphorus, and securely anchored within the chain of the harbour. In the confidence of victory, they boasted that the whole Turkish power must have yielded to their arms; but the admiral, or captain bashaw, found some consolation for a painful wound in his eye, by representing that accident as the cause of his defeat. Baltha Ogli was a renegade of the race of the Bulgarian princes: his military character was tainted with the unpopular vice of avarice; and under the despotism of the prince or people, misfortune is a sufficient evidence of guilt. His rank and services were annihilated by the displeasure of Mohammed. In the royal presence, the captain bashaw was extended on the ground by four slaves, and received one hundred strokes with a golden rod: his death had been pronounced, and he adored the clemency of the sultan, who was satisfied with the milder punishment of confiscation and exile. The introduction of this supply revived the hopes of the Greeks, and accused the supineness of their Western allies. Amidst the deserts of Anatolia and the rocks of Palestine, the millions of the crusades had buried themselves in a voluntary and inevitable grave; but the situation of the Imperial city was strong against her enemies, and accessible to her friends; and a rational and moderate armament of the maritime states might have saved the relics of the Roman name, and maintained a Christian fortress in the heart of the Ottoman empire. Yet this was the sole and feeble attempt for the deliverance of Constantinople: the more distant powers were insensible of its danger; and the ambassador of Hungary, or at least of Huniades, resided in the Turkish camp, to remove the fears and to direct the operations of the sultan.

It was difficult for the Greeks to penetrate the secret of the divan; yet the Greeks are persuaded that a resistance so obstinate and surprising had fatigued the perseverance of Mohammed. He began to meditate a retreat; and the siege would have been speedily raised, if the ambition and jealousy of the second vizir had not opposed the perfidious advice of Calil Bashaw, who still maintained a secret correspondence with the Byzantine court. The reduction of the city appeared to be hopeless, unless a double attack could be made from the harbour as well as from the land; but the harbour was inaccessible: an impenetrable chain was now defended by eight large ships, more than twenty of a smaller size, with several galleys and sloops; and, instead of forcing this barrier, the Turks might apprehend a naval sally and a second encounter in the open sea. In this perplexity the genius of Mohammed conceived and executed a plan of a bold and marvellous cast, of transporting by land his lighter vessels and military stores from the Bosphorus into the higher part of the harbour. The distance is about ten miles; the ground is uneven, and was overspread with thickets; and, as the road must be opened behind the suburb of Galata, their free passage or total destruction must depend on the option of the Genoese. But these selfish merchants were ambitious of the favour of being the last devoured, and the deficiency of art was supplied by the strength of obedient myriads. A level way was covered with a broad platform of strong and solid planks; and to render them more slippery and smooth, they were anointed with the fat of sheep and oxen. Four-score light galleys and brigantines of fifty and thirty oars were disembarked on the Bosphorus shore, arranged successively on rollers, and drawn forwards by the power of men and pulleys. Two guides or pilots were stationed at the helm and the prow of each vessel: the sails were unfurled to the winds, and the labour was cheered by song and acclamation. In the course of a single night this Turkish fleet painfully climbed the hill, steered over the plain, and was launched from the declivity into the shallow waters of the harbour, far above the molestation of the deeper vessels of the Greeks. The real importance of this operation was magnified by the consternation and confidence which it inspired; but the noto-rious, unquestionable fact was displayed before the eyes, and is recorded by the pens, of the two nations. A similar stratagem had been repeatedly practised by the ancients; the Ottoman galleys (I must again repeat) should be considered as large boats; and, if we compare the magnitude and the distance, the obstacles and the means, the boasted miracle has perhaps been equalled by the industry of our own times. As soon as Mohammed had occupied the upper harbour with a fleet and army, he constructed in the narrowest part a bridge, or rather mole, of fifty cubits in breadth and one hundred in length: it was formed of casks and hogsheads, joined with rafters, linked with iron, and covered with a solid floor. On this floating battery he planted one of his largest cannon, while the fourscore galleys, with troops and scaling-ladders, approached the most accessible side, which had formerly been stormed by the Latin conquerors. The indolence of the Christians has been accused for not destroying these unfinished works; but their fire, by a superior fire, was controlled and silenced; nor were they wanting in a nocturnal attempt to burn the vessels as well as the bridge of the sultan. His vigilance prevented their approach: their foremost galliots were sunk or taken; forty youths, the bravest of Italy and Greece, were inhumanly massacred at his command; nor could the emperor's grief be assuaged by the just though cruel retaliation of exposing from the walls the heads of two hundred and sixty Musulman captives. After a siege of forty days the fate of Constantinople could no longer be averted. The diminutive garrison was exhausted by a double attack: the fortifications, which had stood for ages against hostile violence, were dismantled on all sides by the Ottoman cannon; many breaches were opened, and near the gate of St. Romanus four towers had been levelled with the ground. For the payment of his feeble and mutinous troops, Constantine was compelled to despoil the churches with the promise of a fourfold restitution; and his sacrilege offered a new reproach to the enemies of the union. A spirit of discord impaired the remnant of the Christian strength: the Genoese and Venetian auxiliaries asserted the pre-eminence of their respective service; and Justiniani and the great duke, whose ambition was not extinguished by the common danger, accused each other of treachery and cowardice.

During the siege of Constantinople the words of peace and capitulation had been sometimes pronounced; and several embassies had passed between the camp and the city. The Greek emperor was humbled by adversity; and would have yielded to any terms compatible with religion and royalty. The Turkish sultan was desirous of sparing the blood of his soldiers; still more desirous of securing for his own use the Byzantine treasures; and he accomplished a sacred duty in presenting to the Gabours the choice of circumcision, of tribute, or of death. The avarice of Mohammed might have been satisfied with an annual sum of one hundred thousand ducats; but his ambition grasped the capital of the East: to the prince he offered a rich equivalent, to the people a free toleration, or a safe departure: but after some fruitless treaty, he declared his resolution of finding either a throne or a grave under the walls of Constantinople. A sense of honour, and the fear of universal reproach, forbade Palæologus to resign the city into the hands of the Ottomans; and he determined to abide the last extremities of war. Several days were employed by the sultan in the preparations of the assault; and a respite was granted by his favourite science of astrology, which had fixed on the twenty-ninth of May as the fortunate and fatal hour. On the evening of the twenty-seventh he issued his final orders; assembled in his presence the military chiefs; and dispersed his heralds through the camp to proclaim the duty and the motives of the perilous enterprise. Fear is the first principle of a despotic government; and his menaces were expressed in the Oriental style, that the fugitives and deserters, had they the wings of a bird, should not escape from his inexorable justice. The greatest part of his bashaws and Janizaries were the off-spring of Christian parents: but the glories of the Turkish name were perpetuated by successive adoption; and in the gradual change of individuals, the spirit of a legion, a regiment, or an *oda*, is kept alive by imitation and discipline. In this holy warfare the Moslems were exhorted to purify their minds with prayer, their bodies with seven ablutions; and to abstain from food till the close of the ensuing day. A crowd of dervishes visited the tents, to instil the desire of martyrdom, and the assurance of spending an immortal youth amidst the rivers and gardens of paradise, and in the embraces of the black-eyed virgins. Yet Mohammed principally trusted to the efficacy of temporal and visible rewards. A double pay was promised to the victorious troops; "The city and the buildings," said Mohammed, "are mine; but I resign to your valour the captives and the spoil, the treasures of gold and beauty; be rich and be happy. Many are the provinces of my empire: the intrepid soldier who first ascends the walls of Constantinople shall be rewarded with the government of the fairest and most wealthy; and my gratitude shall accumulate his honours and fortunes above the measure of his own hopes." Such various and potent motives diffused among the Turks a general ardour, regardless of life and impatient for action: the camp re-echoed with the Moslem shouts of "God is God: there is but one God, and Mohammed is the apostle of God"; and the sea and land, from Galata to the seven towers, were illuminated by the blaze of their nocturnal fires.

Far different was the state of the Christians; who, with loud and impotent complaints, deplored the guilt, or the punishment, of their sins. The celestial image of the Virgin had been exposed in solemn procession; but their divine patroness was deaf to their entreaties: they accused the obstinacy of the emperor for refusing a timely surrender; anticipated the horrors of their fate; and sighed for the repose and security of Turkish servitude. The noblest of the Greeks, and the bravest of the allies, were summoned to the palace, to prepare them, on the evening of the twenty-eighth, for the duties and dangers of the general assault. The last speech of Palæologus was the funeral oration of the Roman empire: he promised, he conjured, and he vainly attempted to infuse the hope which was extinguished in his own mind. In this world all was comfortless and gloomy; and neither the Gospel nor the church have proposed any conspicuous recompense to the heroes who fall in the service of their country. But the example of their prince, and the confinement of a siege, had armed these warriors with the courage of despair; and the pathetic scene is described by the feelings of the historian Phranza, who was himself present at this mournful assembly. They wept, they embraced: regardless of their families and fortunes, they devoted their lives; and each commander, departing to his station, maintained all night a vigilant and anxious watch on the rampart. The emperor, and some faithful companions, entered the dome of St. Sophia, which in a few hours was to be converted into a mosque; and devoutly received, with tears and prayers, the sacrament of the holy communion. He reposed some moments in the palace, which resounded with cries and lamentations; solicited the pardon of all whom he might have injured; and mounted on horseback to visit the guards, and explore the motions of the enemy. The distress and fall of the last Constantine are more glorious than the long prosperity of the Byzantine Cæsars.

In the confusion of darkness an assailant may sometimes succeed; but in this great and general attack, the military judgment and astrological knowledge of Mohammed advised him to expect the morning, the memorable twenty-ninth of May, in the fourteen hundred and fifty-third year of the Christian era. The preceding night had been strenuously employed: the troops, the cannon, and the fascines were advanced to the edge of the ditch, which in many parts presented a smooth and level passage to the breach; and his fourscore galleys almost touched, with the prows and their scaling ladders, the less defensible walls of the harbour. Under pain of death, silence was enjoined; but the physical laws of motion and sound are not obedient to discipline or fear: each individual might suppress his voice and measure his footsteps; but the march and labour of thousands must inevitably produce a strange confusion of dissonant clamours, which reached the ears of the watchmen of the towers. At daybreak, without the customary signal of the morning gun, the Turks assaulted the city by sea and land; and the similitude of a twined or twisted thread has been applied to the closeness and continuity of their line of attack. The foremost ranks consisted of the refuse of the host, a voluntary crowd who fought without order or command; of the feebleness of age or childhood, of peasants and vagrants, and of all who had joined the camp in the blind hope of plunder and martyrdom. The common impulse drove them onwards to the wall; the most audacious to climb were instantly precipitated; and not a dart, not a bullet, of the Christians, was idly wasted on the accumulated throng. But their strength and ammunition were exhausted in this laborious defence: the ditch was filled with the bodies of the slain; they supported the footsteps of their companions; and of this devoted vanguard the death was more serviceable than the life. Under their respective bashaws and sanjaks, the troops of Anatolia and Romania were successively led to the charge: their progress was various and doubtful; but, after a conflict of two hours, the Greeks still maintained and improved their advantage; and the voice of the emperor was heard, encouraging his soldiers to achieve, by a last effort, the deliverance of their country. In that fatal moment the Janizaries arose, fresh, vigorous, and invincible. The sultan himself on horseback, with an iron mace in his hand, was the spectator and judge of their valour; he was surrounded by ten thousand of his domestic troops, whom he reserved for the decisive occasion; and the tide of battle was directed and impelled by his voice and eye. His numerous ministers of justice were posted behind the line, to urge, to restrain, and to punish; and if danger was in the front, shame and inevitable death were in the rear, of the fugitives. The cries of fear and of pain were drowned in the martial music of drums, trumpets, and attaballs; and experience has proved that the mechanical operation of sounds, by quickening the circulation of the blood and spirits, will act on the human machine more forcibly than the eloquence of reason and honour. From the lines, the galleys, and the bridge, the Ottoman artillery thundered on all sides; and the camp and city, the Greeks and the Turks, were involved in a cloud of smoke, which could only be dispelled by the final deliverance or destruction of the Roman empire. The single combats of the heroes of history or fable amuse our fancy and engage our affections: the skilful evolutions of war may inform the mind, and improve a necessary, though pernicious, science. But in the uniform and odious pictures of a general assault, all is blood, and horror, and confusion; nor shall I strive, at the distance of three centuries and a thousand miles, to delineate a scene of which there could be no spectators, and of which the actors themselves were incapable of forming any just or adequate idea.

The immediate loss of Constantinople may be ascribed to the bullet, or arrow, which pierced the gauntlet of John Justiniani. The sight of his blood, and the exquisite pain, appalled the courage of the chief, whose arms and counsels were the firmest rampart of the city. As he withdrew from his station in quest of a surgeon, his flight was perceived and stopped by the indefatigable emperor. "Your wound," exclaimed Palæologus, "is slight; the danger is pressing: your presence is necessary; and whither will you retire?"—"I will retire," said the trembling Genoese, "by the same road which God has opened to the Turks"; and at these words he hastily passed through one of the breaches of the inner wall. By this pusillanimous act he stained the honours of a military life; and the few days which he survived in Galata, or the isle of Chios, were embittered by his own and the public reproach. His example was imitated by the greatest part of the Latin auxiliaries, and the defence began to slacken when the attack was pressed with redoubled vigour. The number of the Ottomans was fifty, perhaps a hundred, times superior to that of the Christians; the double walls were reduced by the cannon to a heap of ruins: in a circuit of several miles some places must be found more easy of access, or more feebly guarded; and if the besiegers could penetrate in a single point, the whole city was irrecoverably lost. The first who deserved the sultan's reward was Hassan the Janizary, of gigantic stature and strength. With his scimitar in one hand and his buckler in the other, he ascended the outward fortification: of the thirty Janizaries who were emulous of his valour, eighteen perished in the bold adventure. Hassan and his twelve companions had reached the summit: the giant was precipitated from the rampart: he rose on one knee, and was again oppressed by a shower of darts and stones. But his success had proved that the achievement was possible: the walls and towers were instantly covered with a swarm of Turks; and the Greeks, now driven from the vantage ground, were overwhelmed by increasing multitudes. Amidst these multitudes, the emperor, who accomplished all the duties of a general and a soldier, was long seen and finally lost. The nobles, who fought round his person, sustained, till their last breath, the honourable names of Palæologus and

Cantacuzene: his mournful exclamation was heard, "Cannot there be found a Christian to cut off my head?" and his last fear was that of falling alive into the hands of the infidels. The prudent despair of Constantine cast away the purple: amidst the tumult he fell by an unknown hand, and his body was buried under a mountain of the slain. After his death resistance and order were no more: the Greeks fled towards the city; and many were pressed and stifled in the narrow pass of the gate of St. Romanus. The victorious Turks rushed through the breaches of the inner wall; and as they advanced into the streets, they were soon joined by their brethren, who had forced the gate Phenar on the side of the harbour. In the first heat of the pursuit about two thousand Christians were put to the sword; but avarice soon prevailed over cruelty; and the victors acknowledged that they should immediately have given quarter, if the valour of the emperor and his chosen bands had not prepared them for a similar opposition in every part of the capital. It was thus, after a siege of fiftythree days, that Constantinople, which had defied the power of Chosroes, the Chagan, and the caliphs, was irretrievably subdued by the arms of Mohammed the Second. Her empire only had been subverted by the Latins: her religion was trampled in the dust by the Moslem conquerors.

The tidings of misfortune fly with a rapid wing; yet such was the extent of Constantinople, that the more distant quarters might prolong, some moments, the happy ignorance of their ruin. But in the general consternation, in the feelings of selfish or social anxiety, in the tumult and thunder of the assault, a *sleepless* night and morning must have elapsed; nor can I believe that many Grecian ladies were awakened by the Janizaries from a sound and tranquil slumber. On the assurance of the public calamity, the houses and convents were instantly deserted; and the trembling inhabitants flocked together in the streets, like a herd of timid animals, as if accumulated weakness could be productive of strength, or in the vain hope that amid the crowd each individual might be safe and invisible. From every part of the capital they flowed into the church of St. Sophia: in the space of an hour, the sanctuary, the choir, the nave, the upper and lower galleries, were filled with the multitudes of fathers and husbands, of women and children, of priests, monks, and religious virgins: the doors were barred on the inside, and they sought protection from the sacred dome which they had so lately abhorred as a profane and polluted edifice. Their confidence was founded on the prophecy of an enthusiast or impostor, that one day the Turks would enter Constantinople, and pursue the Romans as far as the column of Constantine in the square before St. Sophia: but that this would be the term of their calamities; that an angel would descend from heaven with a sword in his hand, and would deliver the empire, with that celestial weapon, to a poor man seated at the foot of the column. "Take this sword," would he say, "and avenge the people of the Lord." At these animating words the Turks would instantly fly, and the victorious Romans would drive them from the West, and from all Anatolia, as far as the frontiers of Persia. It is on this occasion that Ducas, with some fancy and much truth, upbraids the discord and obstinacy of the Greeks. "Had that angel appeared," exclaims the historian, "had he offered to exterminate your foes if you would consent to the union of the church, even then, in that fatal moment, you would have rejected your safety, or have deceived your God."

While they expected the descent of the tardy angel, the doors were broken with axes; and as the Turks encountered no resistance, their bloodless hands were employed in selecting and securing the multitude of their prisoners. Youth, beauty, and the appearance of wealth, attracted their choice; and the right of property was decided among themselves by a prior seizure, by personal strength, and by the authority of command. In the space of an hour the male captives were bound with cords, the females with their veils and girdles. The senators were linked with their slaves; the prelates with the porters of the church; and young men of a plebeian class with noble maids whose faces had been invisible to the sun and their nearest kindred. In this common captivity the ranks of society were confounded; the ties of nature were cut asunder; and the inexorable soldier was careless of the father's groans, the tears of the mother, and the lamentations of the children. The loudest in their wailings were the nuns, who were torn from the altar with naked bosoms, outstretched hands, and dishevelled hair; and we should piously believe that few could be tempted to prefer the vigils of the harem to those of the monastery. Of these unfortunate Greeks, of these domestic animals, whole strings were rudely driven through the streets; and as the conquerors were eager to return for more prey, their trembling pace was quickened with menaces and blows. At the same hour a similar rapine was exercised in all the churches and monasteries, in all the palaces and habitations, of the capital; nor could any place, however sacred or sequestered, protect the persons or the property of the Greeks. Above sixty thousand of this devoted people were transported from the city to the camp and fleet; exchanged or sold according to the caprice or interest of their masters, and dispersed in remote servitude through the provinces of the Ottoman empire. Among these we may notice some remarkable characters. The historian Phranza, first chamberlain and principal secretary, was involved with his family in the common lot. After suffering four months the hardships of slavery, he recovered his freedom: in the ensuing winter he ventured to Adrianople, and ransomed his wife from the *mir bashi*, or master of the horse; but his two children, in the flower of youth and beauty, had been seized for the use of Mohammed himself. The daughter of Phranza died in the seraglio, perhaps a virgin: his son, in the fifteenth year of his age, preferred death to infamy, and was stabbed by the hand of the royal lover. A deed thus inhuman cannot surely be expiated by the taste and liberality with which he released a Grecian matron and her two daughters, on receiving a Latin ode from Philelphus, who had chosen a wife in that noble family. The pride or cruelty of Mohammed would have been most sensibly gratified by the capture of a Roman legate; but the dexterity of Cardinal Isidore eluded the search, and he escaped from Galata in a plebeian habit. The chain and entrance of the outward harbour was still occupied by the Italian ships of merchandise and war. They had signalised their valour in the siege: they embraced the moment of retreat, while the Turkish mariners were dissipated in the pillage of the city. When they hoisted sail, the beach was covered with a suppliant and lamentable crowd; but the means of transportation were scanty; the Venetians and Genoese selected their countrymen; and, notwithstanding the fairest promises of the sultan, the inhabitants of Galata evacuated their houses, and embarked with their most precious effects.

In the fall and the sack of great cities an historian is condemned to repeat the tale of uniform calamity: the same effects must be produced by the same passions; and when those passions may be indulged without control, small, alas! is the difference between civilised and savage man. Amidst the vague exclamations of bigotry and hatred, the Turks are not accused of a wanton or immoderate effusion of Christian blood: but according to their maxims (the maxims of antiquity), the lives of the vanquished were forfeited; and the legitimate reward of the conqueror was derived from the service, the sale, or the ransom of his captives of both sexes. The wealth of Constantinople had been granted by the sultan to his victorious troops; and the rapine of an hour is more productive than the industry of years. But as no regular division was attempted of the spoil, the respective shares were not determined by merit; and the rewards of valour were stolen away by the followers of the camp, who had declined the toil and danger of the battle. The narrative of their depredations could not afford either amusement or instruction: the total amount, in the last poverty of the empire, has been valued at four millions of ducats; and of this sum a small part was the property of the Venetians, the Genoese, the Florentines, and the merchants of Ancona. Of these foreigners the stock was improved in quick and perpetual circulation: but the riches of the Greeks were displayed in the idle ostentation of palaces and wardrobes, or deeply buried in treasures of ingots and old coin, lest it should be demanded at their hands for the defence of their country. The profanation and plunder of the monasteries and churches excited the most tragic complaints. The dome of St. Sophia itself, the earthly heaven, the second firmament, the vehicle of the cherubim, the throne of the glory of God, was despoiled of the oblations of ages; and the gold and silver, the pearls and jewels, the vases and sacerdotal ornaments, were most wickedly converted to the service of mankind. After the divine images had been stripped of all that could be valuable to a profane eye, the canvas, or the wood, was torn, or broken, or burnt, or trod under foot, or applied, in the stables or the kitchen, to the vilest uses. The example of sacrilege was imitated, however, from the Latin conquerors of Constantinople; and the treatment which Christ, the Virgin, and the saints had sustained from the guilty Catholic, might be inflicted by the zealous Musulman on the monuments of idolatry. Perhaps, instead of joining the public clamour, a philosopher will observe that in the decline of the arts the workmanship could not be more valuable than the work, and that a fresh supply of visions and miracles would speedily be renewed by the craft of the priest and the credulity of the people. He will more seriously deplore the loss of the Byzantine libraries, which were destroyed or scattered in the general confusion: one hundred and twenty thousand manuscripts are said to have disappeared; ten volumes might be purchased for a single ducat; and the same ignominious price, too high perhaps for a shelf of theology, included the whole works of Aristotle and Homer, the noblest productions of the science and literature of ancient Greece. We may reflect with pleasure that an inestimable portion of our classic treasures was safely deposited in Italy; and that the mechanics of a German town had invented an art which derides the havoc of time and barbarism.

From the first hour of the memorable twenty-ninth of May, disorder and rapine prevailed in Constantinople till the eighth hour of the same day, when the sultan himself passed in triumph through the gates of St. Romanus. He was attended by his vizirs, bashaws, and guards, each of whom (says a Byzantine historian) was robust as Hercules, dexterous as Apollo, and equal in battle to any ten of the race of ordinary mortals. The conqueror gazed with satisfaction and wonder on the strange though splendid appearance of the domes and palaces, so dissimilar from the style of Oriental architecture. In the hippodrome, or *atmeidan*, his eye was attracted by the twisted column of the three serpents; and, as a trial of his strength, he shattered with his iron mace or battle-axe the under jaw of one of these monsters, which in the eyes of the Turks were the idols or talismans of the city. At the principal door of St. Sophia he alighted from his horse and entered the dome; and such was his jealous regard for that monument of his glory, that, on observing a zealous Musulman in the act of breaking the marble pavement, he admonished him with his scimitar that, if the spoil and captives were granted to the soldiers, the public and private buildings had been reserved for the prince. By his command the metropolis of the Eastern church was transformed into a mosque: the rich and portable instruments of superstition had been removed; the crosses were thrown down; and the walls, which were covered with images and mosaics, were washed and purified, and restored to a state of naked simplicity. On the same day, or on the ensuing Friday, the *muezin*, or crier, ascended the most lofty turret, and proclaimed the *ezan*, or public invitation, in the name of God and his prophet; the imam preached; and Mohammed the Second performed the *namaz* of prayer and thanksgiving on the great altar, where the Christian mysteries had so lately been celebrated before the last of the Cæsars. From St. Sophia he proceeded to the august but desolate mansion of a hundred successors of the great Constantine, but which in a few hours had been stripped of the pomp of royalty. A melancholy reflection on the vicissitudes of human greatness forced itself on his mind, and he repeated an elegant distich of Persian poetry: "The spider has wove his web in the Imperial palace, and the owl hath sung her watch-song on the towers of Afrasiab."

XXXVI

EPILOGUE
PROSPECT OF THE RUINS OF ROME IN THE FIFTEENTH CENTURY—FOUR CAUSES OF DECAY AND DESTRUCTION—EXAMPLE OF THE COLISEUM—RENOVATION OF THE CITY—CONCLUSION OF THE WHOLE WORK

In the last days of Pope Eugenius the Fourth, two of his servants, the learned Poggius and a friend, ascended the Capitoline hill, reposed themselves among the ruins of columns and temples, and viewed from that commanding spot the wide and various prospect of desolation. The place and the object gave ample scope for moralising on the vicissitudes of fortune, which spares neither man nor the proudest of his works, which buries empires and cities in a common grave; and it was agreed that, in proportion to her former greatness, the fall of Rome was the more awful and deplorable. "Her primeval state, such as she might appear in a remote age, when Evander entertained the stranger of Troy, has been delineated by the fancy of Virgil. This Tarpeian rock was then a savage and solitary thicket: in the time of the poet it was crowned with the golden roofs of a temple; the temple is overthrown, the gold has been pillaged, the wheel of fortune has accomplished her revolution, and the sacred ground is again disfigured with thorns and brambles. The hill of the Capitol, on which we sit, was formerly the head of the Roman empire, the citadel of the earth, the terror of kings; illustrated by the footsteps of so many triumphs, enriched with the spoils and tributes of so many nations. This spectacle of the world, how is it fallen! how changed! how defaced! the path of victory is obliterated by vines, and the benches of the senators are concealed by a dunghill. Cast your eyes on the Palatine hill, and seek among the shapeless and enormous fragments the marble theatre, the obelisks, the colossal statues, the porticoes of Nero's palace: survey the other hills of the city, the vacant space is interrupted only by ruins and gardens. The forum of the Roman people, where they assembled to enact their laws and elect their magistrates, is now enclosed for the cultivation of potherbs, or thrown open for the reception of swine and buffaloes. The public and private edifices, that were founded for eternity, lie prostrate, naked, and broken, like the limbs of a mighty giant; and the ruin is the more visible, from the stupendous relics that have survived the injuries of time and fortune."

After a diligent inquiry I can discern four principal causes of the ruin of Rome, which continued to operate in a period of more than a thousand years. I. The injuries of time and nature. II. The hostile attacks of the barbarians and Christians. III. The use and abuse of the materials. And, IV. The domestic quarrels of the Romans.

I. The art of man is able to construct monuments far more permanent than the narrow span of his own existence: yet these monuments, like himself, are perishable and frail; and in the boundless annals of time his life and his labours must equally be measured as a fleeting moment. Of a simple and solid edifice it is not easy however to circumscribe the duration. As the wonders of ancient days, the pyramids attracted the curiosity of the ancients: a hundred generations, the leaves of autumn, have dropped into the grave; and after the fall of the Pharaohs and Ptolemies, the Cæsars and caliphs, the same pyramids stand erect and unshaken above the floods of the Nile. A complex figure of various and minute parts is more accessible to injury and decay; and the silent lapse of time is often accelerated by hurricanes and earthquakes, by fires and inundations. The air and earth have doubtless been shaken; and the lofty turrets of Rome have tottered from their foundations; but the seven hills do not appear to be placed on the great cavities of the globe; nor has the city, in any age, been exposed to the convulsions of nature, which, in the climate of Antioch, Lisbon, or Lima, have crumbled in a few moments the works of ages into dust. Fire is the most powerful agent of life and death: the rapid mischief may be kindled and propagated by the industry or negligence of mankind; and every period of the Roman annals is marked by the repetition of similar calamities. A memorable conflagration, the guilt or misfortune of Nero's reign, continued, though with unequal fury, either six or nine days. Innumerable buildings, crowded in close and crooked streets, supplied perpetual fuel for the flames; and when they ceased, four only of the fourteen regions were left entire; three were totally destroyed, and seven were deformed by the relics of smoking and lacerated edifices. In the full meridian of empire the metropolis arose with fresh beauty from her ashes; yet the memory of the old deplored their irreparable losses, the arts of Greece, the trophies of victory, the monuments of primitive or fabulous antiquity. In the days of distress and anarchy every wound is mortal, every fall irretrievable; nor can the damage be restored either by the public care of government, or the activity of private interest. Yet two causes may be alleged which render the calamity of fire more destructive to a flourishing than a decayed city. 1. The more combustible materials of brick, timber, and metals, are first melted or consumed; but the flames may play without injury or effect on the naked walls and massy arches that have been despoiled of their ornaments. 2. It is among the common and plebeian habitations that a mischievous spark is most easily blown to a conflagration; but as soon as they are devoured, the greater edifices which have resisted or escaped are left as so many islands in a state of solitude and safety. From her situation, Rome is exposed to the danger of frequent inundations. Without excepting the Tiber, the rivers that descend from either side of the Apennine have a short and irregular course; a shallow stream in the summer heats; an impetuous torrent when it is swelled in the spring or winter, by the fall of rain and the melting of the snows. When the current is repelled from the sea by adverse winds, when the ordinary bed is inadequate to the weight of waters, they rise above the banks, and overspread, without limits or control, the plains and cities of the adjacent country. Soon after the triumph of the first Punic war the Tiber was increased by unusual rains; and the inundation, surpassing all former measure of time and place, destroyed all the buildings that were situate below the hills of Rome. According to the variety of ground, the same mischief was produced by different means; and the edifices were either swept away by the sudden impulse, or dissolved and undermined by the long continuance, of the flood. Under the reign of Augustus the same calamity was renewed: the lawless river overturned the palaces and temples on its banks; and, after the labours of the emperor in cleansing and widening the bed that was encumbered with ruins, the vigilance of his successors was exercised by similar dangers and designs. The project of diverting into new channels the Tiber itself, or some of the dependent streams, was long opposed by superstition and local interests; nor did the use compensate the toil and cost of the tardy and imperfect execution. The servitude of rivers is the noblest and most important victory which man has obtained over the licentiousness of nature; and if such were the ravages of the Tiber under a firm and active government, what could oppose, or who can enumerate, the injuries of the city after the fall of the Western empire? A remedy was at length produced by the evil itself: the accumulation of rubbish and the earth that has been washed down from the hills is supposed to have elevated the plain of Rome fourteen or fifteen feet, perhaps, above the ancient level; and the modern city is less accessible to the attacks of the river.

II. The crowd of writers of every nation, who impute the destruction of the Roman monuments to the Goths and the Christians, have neglected to inquire how far they were animated by a hostile principle, and how far they possessed the means and the leisure to satiate their enmity. In the preceding volumes of this History I have described the triumph of barbarism and religion; and I can only resume, in a few words, their real or imaginary connection with the ruin of ancient Rome. Our fancy may create, or adopt, a pleasing romance, that the Goths and Vandals sallied from Scandinavia, ardent to avenge the flight of Odin; to break the chains, and to chastise the oppressors, of mankind; that they wished to burn the records of classic literature, and to found their national architecture on the broken members of the Tuscan and Corinthian orders. But in simple truth, the northern conquerors were neither sufficiently savage, nor sufficiently refined, to entertain such aspiring ideas of destruction and revenge. The shepherds of Scythia and Germany had been educated in the armies of the empire, whose discipline they acquired, and whose weakness they invaded: with the familiar use of the Latin tongue they had learned to reverence the name and titles of Rome; and, though incapable of emulating, they were more inclined to admire than to abolish the arts and studies of a brighter period. In the transient possession of a rich and unresisting capital, the soldiers of Alaric and Genseric were stimulated by the passions of a victorious army; amidst the wanton indulgence of lust or cruelty, portable wealth was the object of their search: nor could they derive either pride or pleasure from the unprofitable reflection that they had battered to the ground the works of the consuls and Cæsars. Their moments were indeed precious: the Goths evacuated Rome on the sixth, the Vandals on the fifteenth day; and, though it be far more difficult to build than to destroy, their hasty assault would have made a slight impression on the solid piles of antiquity. We may remember that both Alaric and Genseric affected to spare the buildings of the city; that they subsisted in strength and beauty under the auspicious government of Theodoric; and that the momentary resentment of Totila was disarmed by his own temper and the advice of his friends and enemies. From these innocent barbarians the reproach may be transferred to the Catholics of Rome. The statues, altars, and houses of the demons were an abomination in their eyes; and in the absolute command of the city, they might labour with zeal and perseverance to erase the idolatry of their ancestors. The demolition of the temples in the East affords to *them* an example of conduct, and to *us* an argument of belief; and it is probable that a portion of guilt or merit may be imputed with justice to the Roman proselytes. Yet their abhorrence was confined to the monuments of heathen superstition; and the civil structures that were dedicated to the business or pleasure of society might be preserved without injury or scandal. The change of religion was accomplished, not by a popular tumult, but by the decrees of the emperors, of the senate, and of time. Of the Christian hierarchy, the bishops of Rome were commonly the most prudent and least fanatic; nor can any positive charge be opposed to the meritorious act of saving and converting the majestic structure of the Pantheon.

III. The value of any object that supplies the wants or pleasures of mankind is compounded of its substance and its form, of the materials and the manufacture. Its price must depend on the number of persons by whom it may be acquired and used; on the extent of the market; and consequently on the ease or difficulty of remote exportation, according to the nature of the commodity, its local situation, and the temporary circumstances of the world. The barbarian conquerors of Rome usurped in a moment the toil and treasure of successive ages; but, except the luxuries of immediate consumption, they must view without desire all that could not be removed from the city in the Gothic waggons or the fleet of the Vandals. Gold and silver were the first objects of their avarice; as in every country, and in the smallest compass, they represent the most ample command of the industry and possessions of mankind. A vase or a statue of those precious metals might tempt the vanity of some barbarian chief; but the grosser multitude, regardless of the form, was tenacious only of the substance; and the melted ingots might be readily divided and stamped into the current coin of the empire. The less active or less fortunate robbers were reduced to the baser plunder of brass, lead, iron, and copper:

whatever had escaped the Goths and Vandals was pillaged by the Greek tyrants; and the emperor Constans, in his rapacious visit, stripped the bronze tiles from the roof of the Pantheon. The edifices of Rome might be considered as a vast and various mine; the first labour of extracting the materials was already performed; the metals were purified and cast; the marbles were hewn and polished; and after foreign and domestic rapine had been satiated, the remains of the city, could a purchaser have been found, were still venal. The monuments of antiquity had been left naked of their precious ornaments; but the Romans would demolish with their own hands the arches and walls, if the hope of profit could surpass the cost of the labour and exportation. If Charlemagne had fixed in Italy the seat of the Western empire, his genius would have aspired to restore, rather than to violate, the works of the Cæsars; but policy confined the French monarch to the forests of Germany; his taste could be gratified only by destruction; and the new palace of Aix-la-Chapelle was decorated with the marbles of Ravenna and Rome. Five hundred years after Charlemagne, a king of Sicily, Robert, the wisest and most liberal sovereign of the age, was supplied with the same materials by the easy navigation of the Tiber and the sea; and Petrarch sighs in indignant complaint, that the ancient capital of the world should adorn from her own bowels the slothful luxury of Naples. But these examples of plunder or purchase were rare in the darker ages; and the Romans, alone and unenvied, might have applied to their private or public use the remaining structures of antiquity, if in their present form and situation they had not been useless in a great measure to the city and its inhabitants. The walls still described the old circumference, but the city had descended from the seven hills into the Campus Martius; and some of the noblest monuments which had braved the injuries of time were left in a desert far remote from the habitations of mankind. The palaces of the senators were no longer adapted to the manners or fortunes of their indigent successors: the use of baths and porticoes was forgotten: in the sixth century the games of the theatre, amphitheatre, and circus had been interrupted: some temples were devoted to the prevailing worship; but the Christian churches preferred the holy figure of the cross; and fashion, or reason, had distributed after a peculiar model the cells and offices of the cloister. Under the ecclesiastical reign the number of these pious foundations was enormously multiplied; and the city was crowded with forty monasteries of men, twenty of women, and sixty chapters and colleges of canons and priests, who aggravated, instead of relieving, the depopulation of the tenth century. But if the forms of ancient architecture were disregarded by a people insensible of their use and beauty, the plentiful materials were applied to every call of necessity or superstition; till the fairest columns of the Ionic and Corinthian orders, the richest marbles of Paros and Numidia, were degraded, perhaps to the support of a convent or a stable. The daily havoc which is perpetrated by the Turks in the cities of Greece and Asia may afford a melancholy example; and in the gradual destruction of the monuments of Rome, Sixtus the Fifth may alone be excused for employing the stones of the Septizonium in the glorious edifice of St. Peter's. A fragment, a ruin, howsoever mangled or profaned, may be viewed with pleasure and regret; but the greater part of the marble was deprived of substance, as well as of place and proportion; it was burnt to lime for the purpose of cement. Since the arrival of Poggius the temple of Concord and many capital structures had vanished from his eyes; and an epigram of the same age expresses a just and pious fear that the continuance of this practice would finally annihilate all the monuments of antiquity. The smallness of their numbers was the sole check on the demands and depredations of the Romans. The imagination of Petrarch might create the presence of a mighty people; and I hesitate to believe that, even in the fourteenth century, they could be reduced to a contemptible list of thirty-three thousand inhabitants. From that period to the reign of Leo the Tenth, if they multiplied to the amount of eighty-five thousand, the increase of citizens was in some degree pernicious to the ancient city.

IV. I have reserved for the last the most potent and forcible cause of destruction, the domestic hostilities of the Romans themselves. Under the dominion of the Greek and French emperors the peace of the city was disturbed by accidental, though frequent, seditions: it is from the decline of the latter, from the beginning of the tenth century, that we may date the licentiousness of private war, which violated with impunity the laws of the Code and the Gospel, without respecting the majesty of the absent sovereign, or the presence and person of the vicar of Christ. In a dark period of five hundred years Rome was perpetually afflicted by the sanguinary quarrels of the nobles and the people, the Guelphs and Ghibelines, the Colonna and Ursini; and if much has escaped the knowledge, and much is unworthy of the notice, of history, I have exposed in the two preceding chapters the causes and effects of the public disorders. At such a time, when every quarrel was decided by the sword, and none could trust their lives or properties to the impotence of law, the powerful citizens were armed for safety, or offence, against the domestic enemies whom they feared or hated. Except Venice alone, the same dangers and designs were common to all the free republics of Italy; and the nobles usurped the prerogative of fortifying their houses, and erecting strong towers that were capable of resisting a sudden attack. The cities were filled with these hostile edifices; and the example of Lucca, which contained three hundred towers; her law, which confined their height to the measure of fourscore feet, may be extended with suitable latitude to the more opulent and populous states. The first step of the senator Brancaleone in the establishment of peace and justice was to demolish (as we have already seen) one hundred and forty of the towers of Rome; and, in the last days of anarchy and discord, as late as the reign of Martin the Fifth, forty-four still stood in one of the thirteen or fourteen regions of the city. To this mischievous purpose the remains of antiquity were most readily adapted: the temples and arches afforded a broad and solid basis for the new structures of brick and stone; and we can name the modern turrets that were raised on the triumphal monuments of Julius Cæsar, Titus, and the Antonines. With some slight alterations, a theatre, an amphitheatre, a mausoleum, was transformed into a strong and spacious citadel. I need not repeat that the mole of Hadrian had assumed the title and form of the castle of St. Angelo; the Septizonium of Severus was capable of standing against a royal army; the sepulchre of Metella has sunk under its outworks; the theatres of Pompey and Marcellus were occupied by the Savelli and Ursini families; and the rough fortress has been gradually softened to the splendour and elegance of an Italian palace. Even the churches were encompassed with arms and bulwarks, and the military engines on the roof of St. Peter's were the terror of the Vatican and the scandal of the Christian world. Whatever is fortified will be attacked; and whatever is attacked may be destroyed. Could the Romans have wrested from the popes the castle of St. Angelo, they had resolved by a public decree to annihilate that monument of servitude. Every building of defence was exposed to a siege; and in every siege the arts and engines of destruction were laboriously employed. After the death of Nicholas the Fourth, Rome, without a sovereign or a senate, was abandoned six months to the fury of civil war. "The houses," says a cardinal and poet of the times, "were crushed by the weight and velocity of enormous stones; the walls were perforated by the strokes of the battering-ram; the towers were involved in fire and smoke; and the assailants were stimulated by rapine and revenge." The work was consummated by the tyranny of the laws; and the factions of Italy alternately exercised a blind and thoughtless vengeance on their adversaries, whose houses and castles they razed to the ground. In comparing the *days* of foreign with the *ages* of domestic hostility, we must pronounce that the latter have been far more ruinous to the city; and our opinion is confirmed by the evidence of Petrarch. "Behold," says the laureate, "the relics of Rome, the image of her pristine greatness! neither time nor the barbarian can boast the merit of this stupendous destruction: it was perpetrated by her own citizens, by the most illustrious of her sons; and your ancestors (he writes to a noble Annibaldi) have done with the battering-ram what the Punic hero could not accomplish with the sword." The influence of the two last principles of decay must in some degree be multiplied by each other; since the houses and towers which were subverted by civil war required a new and perpetual supply from the monuments of antiquity.

These general observations may be separately applied to the amphitheatre of Titus, which has obtained the name of the COLISEUM, either from its magnitude, or from Nero's colossal statue: an edifice, had it been left to time and nature, which might perhaps have claimed an eternal duration. The curious antiquaries, who have computed the numbers and seats, are disposed to believe that above the upper row of stone steps the amphitheatre was encircled and elevated with several stages of wooden galleries, which were repeatedly consumed by fire, and restored by the emperors. Whatever was precious, or portable, or profane, the statues of gods and heroes, and the costly ornaments of sculpture, which were cast in brass, or overspread with leaves of silver and gold, became the first prey of conquest or fanaticism, of the avarice of the barbarians or the Christians. In the massy stones of the Coliseum many holes are discerned; and the two most probable conjectures represent the various accidents of its decay. These stones were connected by solid links of brass or iron, nor had the eye of rapine overlooked the value of the baser metals; the vacant space was converted into a fair or market; the artisans of the Coliseum are mentioned in an ancient survey; and the chasms were perforated or enlarged to receive the poles that supported the shops or tents of the mechanic trades. Reduced to its naked majesty, the Flavian amphitheatre was contemplated with awe and admiration by the pilgrims of the North; and their rude enthusiasm broke forth in a sublime proverbial expression, which is recorded in the eighth century, in the fragments of the venerable Bede: "As long as the Coliseum stands, Rome shall stand; when the Coliseum falls, Rome will fall; when Rome falls, the world will fall." In the modern system of war, a situation commanded by three hills would not be chosen for a fortress; but the strength of the walls and arches could resist the engines of assault; a numerous garrison might be lodged in the enclosure; and while one faction occupied the Vatican and the Capitol, the other was intrenched in the Lateran and the Coliseum.

The abolition at Rome of the ancient games must be understood with some latitude; and the carnival sports, of the Testacean mount and the Circus Agonalis, were regulated by the law or custom of the city. The senator presided with dignity and pomp to adjudge and distribute the prizes, the gold ring, or the *pallium*, as it was styled, of cloth or silk. A tribute on the Jews supplied the annual expense; and the races, on foot, on horseback, or in chariots, were ennobled by a tilt and tournament of seventy-two of the Roman youth. This use of the amphitheatre was a rare, perhaps a singular, festival: the demand for the materials was a daily and continual want, which the citizens could gratify without restraint or remorse. In the fourteenth century a scandalous act of concord secured to both factions the privilege of extracting stones from the free and common quarry of the Coliseum; and Poggius laments that the greater part of these stones had been burnt to lime by the folly of the Romans. To check this abuse, and to prevent the nocturnal crimes that might be perpetrated in the vast and gloomy recess, Eugenius the Fourth surrounded it with a wall; and, by a charter, long extant, granted both the ground and edifice to the monks of an adjacent convent. After his death the wall was overthrown in a tumult of the people; and had they themselves respected the noblest monument of their fathers, they might have justified the resolve that it should never be degraded to private property. The inside was damaged; but in the middle of the sixteenth century, an era of taste and learning, the exterior circumference of one thousand six hundred and twelve feet was still entire and inviolate; a triple elevation of fourscore arches, which rose to the height of one hundred and eight feet. Of the present ruin the nephews of Paul the Third are the guilty agents; and every traveller who views the Farnese palace may curse the sacrilege and luxury of these upstart princes. A similar reproach is applied to the Barberini; and the repetition of injury might be dreaded from every reign, till the Coliseum was placed under the safeguard of religion by the most liberal of the pontiffs, Benedict the Fourteenth, who consecrated a spot which persecution and fable had stained with the blood of so many Christian martyrs.

But the clouds of barbarism were gradually dispelled; and the peaceful authority of Martin the Fifth and his successors restored the ornaments of the city as well as the order of the ecclesiastical state. The map, the description, the monuments of ancient Rome, have been elucidated by the diligence of the antiquarian and the student; and the footsteps of heroes, the relics, not of superstition, but of empire, are devoutly visited by a new race of pilgrims from the remote and once savage countries of the North.

Of these pilgrims, and of every reader, the attention will be excited by a History of the Decline and Fall of the Roman Empire; the greatest, perhaps, and most awful scene in the history of mankind. The various causes and progressive effects are connected with many of the events most interesting in human annals: the artful policy of the Cæsars, who long maintained the name and image of a free republic; the disorders of military despotism; the rise, establishment, and sects of Christianity; the foundation of Constantinople; the division of the monarchy; the invasion and settlements of the barbarians of Germany and Scythia; the institutions of the civil law; the character and religion of Mohammed; the temporal sovereignty of the popes; the restoration and decay of the Western empire of Charlemagne; the crusades of the Latins in the East; the conquests of the Saracens and Turks; the ruin of the Greek empire; the state and revolutions of Rome in the middle age. The historian may applaud the importance and variety of his subject; but, while he is conscious of his own imperfections, he must often accuse the deficiency of his materials. It was among the ruins of the Capitol that I first conceived the idea of a work which has amused and exercised near twenty years of my life, and which, however inadequate to my own wishes, I finally deliver to the curiosity and candour of the public.

LAUSANNE,
    June 27, 1787

EMPERORS OF THE ROMAN EMPIRE UNTIL THE DIVISION INTO WESTERN AND EASTERN EMPIRES

EMPERORS OF THE ROMAN EMPIRE UNTIL THE DIVISION INTO WESTERN AND EASTERN EMPIRES

(Where there is more than one regnant emperor, the senior partner is in capitals, the junior partner or partners are indented and in upper and lower case.)

AUGUSTUS	23 B.C.–14 A.D.
TIBERIUS	14–37
CALIGULA	37–41
CLAUDIUS I	41–54
NERO	54–68
GALBA	68–69
OTHO	69
VITELLIUS	69
VESPASIAN	69–79
TITUS	79–81
DOMITIAN	81–96
NERVA	96–98
TRAJAN	98–117
HADRIAN	117–138
ANTONINUS PIUS	138–161
MARCUS AURELIUS	161–180
Lucius Verus	161–169
Commodus	176–180
COMMODUS	180–192
PERTINAX	193
DIDIUS JULIANUS	193
SEPTIMIUS SEVERUS	193–211
Caracalla	198–211
Geta	209–211
CARACALLA	211–217
Geta	211–212
MACRINUS	217–218
ELAGABALUS	218–222
SEVERUS ALEXANDER	222–235
MAXIMINUS	235–238
GORDIAN I	238
GORDIAN II	238

BALBINUS 238
PUPIENIUS 238
GORDIAN III 238–244
PHILIP 244–249
DECIUS 249–251
TREBONIANUS GALLUS 251–253
AEMILIANUS 253
VALERIANUS 253–259
    Gallienus 253–259
GALLIENUS 259–268
    Postumus (in Gaul) 258–267
CLAUDIUS II 268–270
    Tetricus (in Gaul) 268–273
QUINTILLUS 270
AURELIAN 270–275
TACITUS 275–276
FLORIANUS 276
PROBUS 276–282
CARUS 282–283
CARINUS 283–285
    Numerianus 283–284
DIOCLETIAN 284–305
    Maximian 286–305
GALERIUS and CONSTANTIUS 305
GALERIUS and SEVERUS 306
GALERIUS, LICINIUS, CONSTANTINE,
    DAIA, and MAXENTIUS 307–
    (Galerius d. 311, Maxentius d. 312,
        Daia d. 313, Licinius defeated 324)
CONSTANTINE I 324–337
CONSTANTINE II 337–340
    Constans 337–340
    Constantius 337–340
CONSTANS 340–350
CONSTANTIUS 340–361
JULIAN 360–363
JOVIAN 363–364
VALENTINIAN I 364–375
    Valens 364–375
    Gratian 367–375
VALENS 375–378

GRATIAN	378–383
VALENTINIAN II	375–392
Theodosius I	379–392
THEODOSIUS I	392–395
Arcadius	383–395
Honorius	394–395

EMPERORS OF THE WESTERN EMPIRE AFTER THEODOSIUS I

HONORIUS	394–423
VALENTINIAN III	423–455
MAXIMUS	455
AVITUS	455–456
MAJORIAN	457–461
SEVERUS	461–465
No emperor	465–467
ANTHEMIUS	467–472
OLYBRIUS	472
GLYCERIUS	473–474
NEPOS	474–475
ROMULUS AUGUSTULUS	475–476

End of Western Empire: Odovacar, King of Italy

EMPERORS OF THE EASTERN EMPIRE AFTER THEODOSIUS I

ARCADIUS	395–408
THEODOSIUS II	408–450
MARCIAN	450–457
LEO I	457–474
LEO II	474
ZENO	474–491
ANASTASIUS I	491–518
JUSTIN I	518–527
JUSTINIAN I	527–565
JUSTIN II	565–578
TIBERIUS II	578–582
MAURICE	582–602
Theodosius III	590–602
PHOCAS	602–610
HERACLIUS I	610–641
Constantine III	613–641
Heracleonas	638–641
CONSTANTINE III	641

HERACLEONAS 641
CONSTANS II 641–668
   Constantine IV 659–668
   Heraclius 659–681
   Tiberius 659–681
CONSTANTINE IV, Pogonatus 668–685
JUSTINIAN II, Rhinotmetus 685–695
LEONTIUS 695–698
TIBERIUS III, Apsimar 698–705
JUSTINIAN II, Rhinotmetus 705–711
   Tiberius 706–711
PHILIPPICUS, Bardanes 711–713
ANASTASIUS II, Artemius 713–715
THEODOSIUS III 715–717
LEO III, the Isaurian 717–740
   Constantine V 720–740
CONSTANTINE V, Copronymus 740–775
   Leo IV 750–775
LEO IV, the Chazar 775–780
   Constantine VI 776–780
CONSTANTINE VI 780–797
IRENE 797–802
NICEPHORUS I 802–811
STAURACIUS 811
MICHAEL I, Rhangabe 811–813
LEO V, the Armenian 813–820
MICHAEL II, the Amorian 820–829
   Theophilus 821–829
THEOPHILUS 829–842
MICHAEL III, the Drunkard 842–867
   Basil I 866–867
BASIL I, the Macedonian 867–886
   Constantine 869–880
   Leo VI 870–886
   Alexander 871–912
LEO VI, the Wise 886–912
   Constantine VII 911–913
ALEXANDER 912–913
CONSTANTINE VII, Porphyrogenetus 913–919
ROMANUS I, Lecapenus 919–944
   Constantine VII 919–944

Christopher Lecapenus	921–931
Stephen Lecapenus	924–945
Constantine Lecapenus	924–945
CONSTANTINE VII, Porphyrogenetus	944–959
Romanus II	ca. 950–959
ROMANUS II	959–963
Basil II	960–963
Constantine VIII	961–1025
BASIL II, Bulgaroctonus	963
NICEPHORUS II, Phocas	963–969
Basil II	963–976
JOHN I, Tzimisces	969–976
BASIL II, Bulgaroctonus	976–1025
CONSTANTINE VIII	1025–1028
ROMANUS III, Argyrus	1028–1034
MICHAEL IV, the Paphlagonian	1034–1041
MICHAEL V, the Calfat	1041–1042
ZOE and THEODORA, Porphyrogennetae	1042
CONSTANTINE IX, Monomachus	1042–1055
THEODORA, Porphyrogenneta	1055–1056
MICHAEL VI, Stratioticus	1056–1057
ISAAC I, Comnenus	1057–1059
CONSTANTINE X, Ducas	1059–1067
Michael VII	ca. 1060–1067
MICHAEL VII, Parapinaces	1067–1068
ROMANUS IV, Diogenes	1068–1071
Michael VII	1068–1071
MICHAEL VII, Parapinaces	1071–1078
NICEPHORUS III, Botaniates	1078–1081
ALEXIUS I, Comnenus	1081–1118
Constantine Ducas	1081–1090
John II	1092–1118
JOHN II, Calojohannes	1118–1143
Alexius	1119–1142
MANUEL I	1143–1180
Alexius II	1172–1180
ALEXIUS II	1180–1183
Andronicus I	1182–1183
ANDRONICUS I	1183–1185
ISAAC II, Angelus	1185–1195
ALEXIUS III	1195–1203

ALEXIUS IV	1203–1204
Isaac II	1203–1204
ALEXIUS V, Murtzuphlus	1204
THEODORE I, Lascaris	1204–1222
JOHN III, Ducas Vatatzes	1222–1254
THEODORE II, Lascaris Vatatzes	1254–1258
JOHN IV, Ducas Vatatzes	1258
MICHAEL VIII, Palaeologus	1258–1282
Andronicus II	1272–1282
ANDRONICUS II	1282–1328
Michael	1295–1320
Andronicus III	1325–1328
ANDRONICUS III	1328–1341
JOHN V	1341–1347
JOHN VI, Cantacuzene	1347–1355
John V	1347–1355
Matthew Cantacuzene	1348–1355
JOHN V	1355–1376
ANDRONICUS IV	1376–1379
John VII	1376–1390
JOHN V	1379–1390
Andronicus IV	1379–1385
Manuel II	1386–1391
JOHN VII	1390
JOHN V	1390–1391
MANUEL II	1391–1425
John VII	1399–1412
John VIII	1423–1425
JOHN VIII	1425–1448
CONSTANTINE XI, Dragases	1448–1453

INDEX

Abbassides, 612
Ablavius, 296, 297
Acacius, master of the bears, 596
Academics, 18
Academy, 333
Achaia, 272
Acheloum, 627
Acolyth, 615
Adauctus, 257
Admiral, 615
Adolphus, king of the Goths, 486, 488, 490, 493–99
Adventus, 79, 80
Ælia Capitolina, 192
Ælius Verus, 42–43
Æmilianus, the emperor, 106, 107
Æmona, 475
Æsculapius, 18, 20
Æteriarch, 615
Æthiopia, 3, 53, 321
Aëtius, 481, 506–7, 510, 523–29, 534, 536–37
Africa, province of, 14, 27, 29, 92–94, 257, 331–32, 347–48, 489–90, 508–12, 609
agapæ, 220
Agathyrsi, 418
agentes in rebus. See informers
agriculture, 29–31, 283, 562, 589
Agrippina the younger, 85
Aguileia, 463
Alani, 418–19, 437, 442, 469, 470, 558
Alaric, king of the Visigoths, 576–77
Alaric, the Goth, 437, 461–67, 475, 476, 481–93
Alatheus, the Ostrogoth, 423, 425, 431
Alavivus, the Visigoth, 420, 425–26
Albania, 5
Alcæus, 620
Alemanni, 108, 109, 128, 169, 314–19, 430
Aleppo, Syria, 192
Alexander Severus, the emperor, 84, 88, 109, 219, 248–49
Alexander the Great, 5, 12, 16
Alexandria, 28, 32, 78, 191, 219, 415
Alexius I Comnenus, the emperor, 613–14
Alsace, 314
Altinum, 482, 532
Amali, 438, 461
Amandus, 184
Amazons, 135
Ambrose, 403, 446–48, 455–56, 470–71
Ambrosius Aurelian, 587–88

America, 13, 27
Amida, 311–13, 313
Amiens, 473
Ammianus Marcellinus, 349, 370–71, 398, 403–4
Amurath, Turkish sultan, 623–24
Anachorets, 565–67
Anastasia, 290
Anastasia, daughter of Acacius, 596–97
Anastasius I, the emperor, 578, 607–8
Anatolius, 384, 385
Ancilia, 83
Ancyra, 133, 222
Andages, 530
Andalusia, 9
Angles, 587, 590
Anna Comnena, 620
Annibaldi, 655
Annibalianus, 143
Anthemius, the emperor, 552, 554–56
Antioch, 28, 115, 133, 191, 219, 305, 306, 376
Antiochus, 187–88, 461
Antoninus of Syria, 311
Antoninus Pius, the emperor, 1, 6–7, 10, 33, 43–44
Anulinus, 96, 152, 171
Apamaea, 111–12
Apollonius, 522
Aquileia, 95–96, 482, 532
Aquitaine, 130
Aquitania, 501
Arabia, 3, 5, 31, 32, 134, 321
Arabs, 13, 298
Araric, king of the Goths, 294
Arbela, 380
Arbogastes, 442
Arcadius, the emperor, 442, 448–49, 459, 461–63, 477
Ardaburius, son of Aspar, 521
Ardaric, king of the Gepidæ, 516, 529
Argonauts, 110
Argos, 113
Arianism, 333, 341, 569
Arians, 336–39, 344, 349
Arinthæus, Roman general, 386, 388
Aristides, 227
Aristobulus, 153
Aristotle, 34, 227, 360, 362, 620
Arius, 334–40
Arles, council of, 328, 332, 465
Armenia, 5, 114, 310, 321, 388, 409

Armorica, 502–3, 528, 588
army, Roman. *See also* Prætorian Guards
    attacks Gaul, 356–58
    barbarians in, 277–78
    Caracalla and, 77–79
    conditions sustained by, 92, 394–95
    discipline of, 145–46, 273–77, 529–30
    formations of, 7–8, 86–87
    Gothic wars fought by, 103–6, 123–25
    Persian wars and, 276–384
    ranks in, 35–36
Arras, 473
Arrius Antoninus, 246
Arrius Aper, 149–50
Artaxerxes I, Persian emperor, 100, 114
Arthur, 588–89
Asclepiodatus, 143
Asia, province of, 12–13, 27–28, 214–15, 258, 339, 433–36
Asiatics, 362
Asomaton, 623–25
Aspacuras, 409–10
Aspar, 521, 552
Assyria, province of, 5, 198, 377, 378
Asta, 465–66
Astarte, 83
Asterius, Count, 508
Astingi, 294
Astorga, 546
Asturians, 9
Athanaric, judge of the Visigoths, 420, 438–39
Athanasians, 349
Athanasius, 337, 338
Athanasius of Alexandria, 341–43
Athens, 20, 32–33, 112, 113, 308
atmeidan, 646
Attacotti, 408
Attalus, Roman usurper, 488–90, 496, 497
Attila, king of the Huns, 506, 513–20, 522, 525–36
Augusti, 162
Augustin, 381, 471, 492
Augustulus, the emperor, 558–59
Augustus, the emperor
    Christianity and, 188
    death of, 4
    games revived by, 99
    military government of, 35–41
    provinces divided by, 9, 10–11
    public elections and, 278–79
    strategies of, 1, 3, 153
Aurelian, the emperor, 122, 125–30, 129, 133–37, 138–39, 251
Aurelian's Wall, 129
Aureolus, 122–23
Austin, 326
Austria, 11
Autun, 315

Avidius Cassius, 44
Avienus, senator, 534
Avitus, the emperor, 527, 545, 581
Azimus, 519–20
Azymites, 630

Babylon, 381
Bacurius the Iberian, 431
Bagai, 348
Bagdad, 382
Balbinus, the emperor, 95, 96–97
Baltha Ogli, 635
Balti, 461
Banners of the Mongous, 416
barbarians. *See also* Alani; Alemanni;
        Angles; Asturians; Bastarnæ; Belgæ;
        Brigantes; Burgundians; Cantabrians;
        Carpi; Celtiberians; Franks; Gepidæ;
        Goths; Heruli; Huns; Iceni; Isaurians;
        Marcomanni; Ostrogoths; Quadi;
        Sarmatians; Saxons; Scythians; Silures;
        Suevi; Vandals; Visigoths
    attacks by, 293–94, 650–51
    Augustus's friendship with, 6
    in Britain, 10
    British invasion by, 74–75
    Christianity and, 321, 568–70
    Persian wars of, 308–19
    in Roman army, 277–78
    in Spain, 9
Barbatio, 307, 316
Barcelona, 499
Bards, 588, 621
Basel, 356
Basil I, the emperor, 316, 619–20
Basil II, the emperor, 609–10
Basilics, 608, 620
Basilidians, 194
Basiliscus, 552–54
Basilius, 484–85, 561
Bassianus. *See* Elagabalus
Bastarnæ, 145, 157
Batavia, 314
Batavians, 352
Bætica, 9
Belgæ, 10
Belisarius, 605, 606
Benedict XIV, bishop of Rome, 657
Beneventum, 609
Bezabde, 313
bishops, 215–16, 219–20, 248, 252, 322, 328, 335
Bithynia, 13, 111, 133, 242, 305
Bizon, 627
Black nations, 540
Bleda, brother of Attila, 515
Blemmyes, 143
blue faction, 601–6, 617
Boethius, Prætorian præfect, 537

Bologna, 478
Boniface, Count, 494, 506–8, 510
Bœotia, 462
Bordeaux, 494, 501, 578
Borderers, 275
Borysthenes, 103
Bosnia, 11–12
Bosphorus, Cimmerian, 5, 112
Botheric, 444–45
Boulogne, 474
Bracara, 497
Braga, 546
Brancaleone, senator, 654
Bregetio, 412, 414
Breones, 528
Brigantes, 10
Britain, 3–4, 10, 27, 74–75, 144–45, 272, 405–9, 502–3, 584–90
Brutus, 443
Burgundians, 469, 473, 515, 524, 528, 569, 572, 591
Burgundy, 501
Burrhus, 85
Byzacium, 512
Byzantine Empire, 591, 595–97, 606–8, 614–46
Byzantium, 184. See also Constantinople

Cæcilian, 331, 332
Cænobites, 565
Cæsars, 162
Cæsar Bardas, 619
Cæsarea, 305, 373–74
Calabria, 609
Caledonia, 6, 75, 168, 408, 502. See also Picts
Caligula, the emperor, 39, 40, 45, 91, 160, 188, 277
Calil, Turkish vizir, 622, 635
Callinicum, 446, 562
Calmuck, 514
Camillus, 21, 470
Campania, 242
cannibalism, 408, 418–19
canonical jurisprudence, 326–27
Cantabrians, 9
Cantacuzene, 641–42
Capelianus, 94
Capiculi, 627
Capitol, 5, 103, 647, 656
Capitoline games, 97
Capitoline Jupiter, 241
Cappadocia, 13, 279
Caracalla, the emperor, 74–79, 88, 89, 109, 248
Carinus, the emperor, 147, 148, 150–51
Carpi, 104, 157.
Carpocratians, 236–37
Carrhæ, 114

Carthage, 14, 27, 94, 176, 219, 511–12
Carthagena, 508
Carus, the emperor, 143, 146–49
Cassian, duke of Mesopotamia, 310
Cassiodorus, 530, 533
Castinus, 508
catastrophes, natural, 415–16, 648–50
Catholic Church. See Christian Church
Caucaland, 438
Cedrenus, 266
celibacy, 323
Celtæ, 352
Celtiberians, 9
Celtic Gaul. See Gaul
censorship, 37
census, 6, 282
Ceylon, 32, 375
Chalcedon, 111
Chalcocondyles, 628
Châlons, Battle of, 529–31
Charlemagne, 405, 652
Chiauss, 615
Childeric, king of the Franks, 566, 573
chiliarchs, 509
China, 416–19
Chnodomar, king of Alemanni, 316, 317–18
Christian Church
    administration of, 401–4
    constitution of, 320–29
    divisions of, 330–50
    progression of, 186, 188–96, 198–205, 211–30, 567–70
    standards of, 393–94
    theology of, 606–8
Christians
    Goths and, 567–68, 650–51
    persecution of, 369–74
    primitive, 186, 205–11, 457
    Roman government and, 231–61
Chrosroes, king of Armenia, 114
Chrysaphius, 520
Chrysopolis, 185
Chrysostom, 328
Cibalis, Pannonia, 396
Cicero, 18, 21, 196, 224
Cilicia, 12, 115, 610
Cinna, 443
Circesium, 377
Circumcellions, 347–48
circus. See games
Cirta, 511
Cirtha, 176
citizen of Rome, 20–21, 88–89, 322, 473
Cius, 111–12
Claudius I, the emperor, 4, 19, 25, 45, 99
Claudius II, the emperor, 122–25, 129, 132
Claudius Pompeianus, 50, 54, 56
Cleander, 51

Clemens of Alexandria, 227
Cleodamus, 112–13
Cleopatra, 131
clergy, Latin, 325
Clodion, 526
Clodius Albinus, 63–64, 69–70
Clotilda, 574, 575
Clovis, king of the Franks, 573–79, 583
Cniva, 104
Cocaba, 241
Colchis, 110
Colchos, 5
Colias, 427–28
Coliseum, 655–57
Cologne, 314
Colonna, 653–54
Comito, daughter of Acacius, 596–97
Commodus, the emperor, 44, 48–59, 64,
      91, 248, 602
Comnenian dynasty, 610, 613, 622–23
Concordia, 482, 532
confederates, 558
Constable, 615
Constans, the emperor, 290, 292, 293, 298,
      300–301, 347, 407
Constantia, wife of Licinius, 290, 411
Constantina, 305, 306, 307
Constantine I, the emperor, 167–70, 173,
      174, 176–85, 256–59, 262, 264–68,
      270–81, 287–301, 320–25, 328–32,
      339–41, 345
Constantine II, the emperor, 182, 290, 292,
      293, 298
Constantine, Roman usurper, 474–75
Constantine VII Porphyrogenitus, the
      emperor, 608–9, 617
Constantine XI Dragases, the emperor,
      633, 637, 639, 642–43
Constantinople, 185, 264–68, 321, 344–45,
      364, 610–11, 623–46
Constantius Chlorus, the emperor, 143,
      155–56, 166–69, 173, 252, 256–57
Constantius, husband of Placidia, 504
Constantius, the emperor, 290–91, 292, 293,
      296–98, 300–314, 345–47, 351–54,
      358–60
Consubstantialists, 338
consulars, 273
consulship, 36–37, 269, 277, 578
convivial meetings, 453
copiatæ, 324
Coptos, 143
Corduba, 497
Corduene, 382–83, 388
Corea, 416
Corinth, 113, 191
coronary gold, 285
correctors, 273
Corsica, 14

Council of Ancyra, 222
      Arles, 328, 332, 465
      Chalcedon, 608
      Illiberis, 222
      Nicæa, 325–26, 370, 394
      Rome, 332
      Seleucia, 338
Count Lucilianus, 299
count of the domestics, 279
count of the sacred largesses, 279
count, ranks of, 274
County, 501
court, imperial, 38–39, 159, 278–80, 361–62,
      611–18
Cremona, 482
Crete, 14, 610
Crispus, 125, 182, 184, 290–92
Croatia, 11–12
Crocus, 169
Ctesiphon, 148, 311, 379, 380
curiæ, 319
Curopalata, 614
Cybele, 20
Cynegius, Prætorian præfect, 452
Cyprian, 217, 227
Cyprus, 610
Cyrene, 13
Cyriades, Roman usurper, 115
Cyrus, 198
Cyzicus, 112, 627

Dacia, 4, 11, 103, 127–28, 272
Dacians, 4
Dadastana, 395
Dagalaiphus, 357, 386
Dalmatia, 11–12, 65–66, 152, 415
Dalmatius, 290, 292, 296, 297, 300
Damasus, bishop of Rome, 402–4
Dardania, 124, 155
Dardanus, 496
Darius, 128, 362, 422–23
Darius Hystaspes, 310
Datianus, 256
Decebalus, 4
Decius, the emperor, 102, 104–5, 218–19,
      250
Decurions, 282
defenders of cities, 549
defensors, 401, 549
Deity, 333, 368, 415–16, 580
Delators, 50, 57, 176. See also informers
Demosthenes, 266, 372, 620
Deogratias, bishop of Carthage, 544–45
Despot, 614
Dexippus, 112–13
Diadumenianus, 80
Didius Julianus, the emperor, 61–63,
      66–68
dioceses, 272, 322

Diocletian, the emperor, 122, 143, 150–51, 152–66, 251–56, 264, 331
Diodorus, 343
Diogenes, 362
Diomede, 601
Divine Trinity, 328, 335–36
Domestics, 615
Domitian, the emperor, 4, 39, 40, 41, 44, 77, 99, 242
Domitilla, 242
Donatists, 332, 347, 348, 370, 510
Donatus, 331
doxology, 343
Dragoman, 615
Druids, 19
Ducas, 626, 628
Duchy, 501
Dukes, 274, 614
Dyrrachium, 471

Ebionites, 192, 193, 336
Ecbatana, 382, 389, 409
ecclesiastical ministers, 322–29. *See also* bishops
Ecebolus of Tyre, 597
Eclectus, 54–55
Edessa, 313, 394
Edict of Milan, 324, 331
education, 372, 400, 618–21
Egypt, 6, 13–14, 145, 198, 258, 339, 415
Elagabalus, the emperor, 81–85
Emesa, 115, 133
Emir, 615
emperors
    deification of, 39–40, 52, 154–55, 160–61
    succession of, 41–44
England, 10
Ephesus, 191
Epictetus, 229
Epicureans, 18
Epicurus, 34
Epiphanius, bishop of Pavia, 554–55
Epirus, 12, 412, 475
Episcopal Churches, 322–23
Equitius, Roman general, 410, 411, 412, 414
Essenes, 218
Eternal Cause, 368–69
Etruria, 21
Eucherius, 477, 479–80
Euclid, 227
Eudocia, 506, 620
Eudoxia, 506, 537, 538, 544
Eugenius IV, bishop of Rome, 647, 656
Eugenius, Roman usurper, 442, 448
Eunomians, 370
eunuchs, 161, 304–5, 308–9, 312–13, 359
Euric, king of the Visigoths, 572–73
Eusebia, the empress, 308, 309, 310

Eusebius of Cæsarea, 252, 260, 305, 307, 310, 335, 340, 342, 359
Eusebius of Nicomedia, 335, 337, 340–41, 367
Eustathius of Antioch, 341, 343
Eutropia, 290
Eutropius, 155, 459
excommunication, 220–22
ezan, 646
Ezra, 198

Fœderati, 440
Fadilla, 51
famine, 120–21, 318, 483–85, 498
fanaticism, religious, 373–74
Fano, 128
Farnese Palace, 656–57
Fausta, 174, 175, 290, 292
Faustina, 43, 47–48
Fava, king of the Rugians, 561–62
feudal tenures, 276
Firmus, 143, 411
Flavianus, 343
Flavius Clemens, 242
Flavius Sabinus, 242
flax, cultivation of, 30
Florence, 470–72
France, 576–79
Franks, 108, 130, 145, 174, 277, 314, 472–73, 501–2, 515, 528, 529. *See also* Gaul
fraud, 297
Fravitta, 441
Frigerid, 429
Fritigern, 420, 425–31, 437
Fronto, Count, 545
Frumentius, 321
Fulgentius, 542

Gabinius, king of the Quadi, 410, 412
Gabours, 624, 637
Galata, 627
Galba, 41
Galen, 33–34, 227
Galerius, the emperor, 143, 155–56, 166–76, 252, 253–59, 390
Galilæans, 371, 372
Gallicia, 498, 508
Gallienus, the emperor, 101, 107–10, 113, 117–23, 251
Gallus, 290, 297, 305–7, 367–68
games
    abolition of, 656
    barbarians and, 511–12
    Capitoline, 97
    emperors' involvement in, 361, 364
    factions of, 601–6
    public devotion to, 358
    secular, 52–57, 99, 149
    in Thessalonica, 444–45

Gætulia, 512
Gaudentius, Count, 452, 537
Gaul, 9–10, 27, 30, 108, 109, 129, 198, 272, 308–9, 314–19, 352–53, 405–6, 495–96, 525–29. *See also* Franks
Geberic, king of the Goths, 294
Gelasius, bishop of Rome, 562
Geloni, 418
Genii, 360
Gennadius, the monk, 630
Genoa, 10, 627, 634, 636, 637, 644
Genseric, king of the Vandals, 508–12, 540, 541–44, 551–53, 555
Genso, son of Genseric, 554
Geoponics, 608
Geougen, 516
Gepidæ, 145, 516
Germanicus, 41
Germany, 3, 7, 9, 100, 108, 143–44, 277, 321, 572–74, 591
Gerontius, 461
Geta, the emperor, 74–77
Ghibelines, 653–54
Gibraltar, 500
Gilimer, 556
Glasgow, 408
Glycerius, the emperor, 557
Gnostics, 193–94, 236–37, 331
Goar, king of the Alani, 496–97
God of Emesa, 82–83
Godigisclus, king of the Vandals, 472
golden triclinium, 613
Gonderic, king of the Vandals, 507–8
Gordian I, 93–94
Gordian II, 93–94
Gordian III, 96–98
Goths. *See also* Ostrogoths; Visigoths
    attacks by, 102–6, 110–14, 460–71
    Christianity and, 321, 567–68, 650–51
    defeats of, 124–29, 419–41
    revolts by, 460–71
    Sarmatians and, 293–94
    standards of, 295
governors of provinces, 273–74
grapes, cultivation of, 30
grass, artificial, 30
Gratian, Roman usurper, 396, 442
Gratian, the emperor, 413–14, 428–29, 434–35
great Æteriarch, 615
great Domestic, 615
great Drungaire, 615
great Duke, 615
Greece, 12, 21, 111, 214–15, 266, 415, 461–63
Greek language, spread of, 23–24, 618
green faction, 601–6, 617
Gregory, bishop, 381
Gregory Nazianzen, 337, 349, 367
Grenada, 9

Grotius, 261
Guelphs, 653–54
Gundobald, 556, 557, 581
Guntiarius, king of the Burgundians, 496–97
gymnasia, 511

Hadrian, the emperor, 1, 5–6, 7, 33, 42–43, 75, 110, 192, 199, 227
Hadrianople, Battle of, 427–32
Hannibal, 145, 217
Hannibalianus, 290, 292, 293, 296, 297
Hassan the Janizary, 641
Helena, sister of Constantius, 309, 359
Helion, 505
Helots, 462
Hengist, 585–86
Heraclea, 359
Heraclian, Count, 479, 490
Heraclius, 536–37
heresies. *See* Arianism; Basilidians; Carpocratians; Circumcellions; Donatists; Ebionites; Gnostics; Manichæans; Marcionites; Montanists; Nazarenes; Novatians; Sabellians; Trinitarian controversy; Ulphilas; Valentinians
heretics, 330, 569
Hermanric, king of the Suevi, 419, 508
Hermes, 229–30
Hermogenes, 344–45, 346
Herod, 132, 187–88
Heruli, 352, 408, 529, 558
highways, 28–29
Hilary, 339
Hippo Regius, 511
Holstein, 405
Homer, 33, 113, 131, 266, 372, 620
Homoousians, 337–39, 346, 394
Honoria, 504, 525–26, 531–32, 535
Honorius, the emperor, 442, 448–49, 459, 463–70, 477–78, 487–90, 497, 502, 504–5
Honourable, 268, 272, 273
Horace, 21
Hormisdas, 380
Horsa, 585
Hostilianus, 105–6
Huldin, 470
Hume, David, 408
Hungary, 12, 513
Huniades, 635
Huns, 416–21, 437, 469, 470, 513–20, 522–34
Hypatius, Byzantine usurper, 605, 606
Hyperides, 620
Hyrcania, 382

Iberia, 5, 321, 409
Iceni, 10

idolatry, 452–54
Igenuus, 495
Ignatius, 245
Igours, 417
Ildico, wife of Attila, 534, 535–36
Illiberis, 222
Illustrious, 268–69, 272, 278
Illyricum, 11, 412
Imaus, 416–17
immolation, 452
Imperial treasury, 92, 163, 276, 610–11
India, 5, 31, 53, 198, 321
indictions, 281–82, 548
Infidels, 344
informers, 50, 362–63, 398–99, 599
Ingenuus, 120
Innocent, bishop of Rome, 484
Ionia, 305, 308
Iphicles, 412
Ireland, 502
Irenæus, 200
Irtish, 416–17
Isaac, brother of Alexius, 613
Isaurians, 143, 309
Isidore of Russia, 629
Israelite, 348
Ister, 12
Istria, 10–11, 307, 463
Italy, 6, 10–11, 20–21, 22, 25–26, 95–96, 257, 267, 463–72, 492–95

Janizaries, 625, 626, 627, 634, 640
Jerom, 403, 433, 455–56
Jerusalem, 188
Jesus of Nazareth, 333–34, 336
Jews, 187–92, 198–99, 218, 225–26, 232–33, 238–39, 241, 321, 446, 544–45
John Justiniani, 628, 633, 637, 641
John VIII Palæologus, the emperor, 629
John Zimisces, 609–10
Jornandes, 495
Jovian, the emperor, 387–89, 393–96, 408
Jovinus, 356, 408, 495–96, 497, 501
Jovius, 356, 452, 487, 489, 490
Jude, grandsons of, 241
Julia Domna, 76, 81
Julia Mamæa, 81, 84, 85–86, 249
Julia Mæsa, 81–82, 84, 85
Julia Soæmias, 81, 85–86
Julian, the emperor, 290–91, 297, 305–10, 313–19, 351–86, 390–92
Julius Africanus, 227
Julius Cæsar, 3, 39, 285
Julius Constantius, 290, 297
Julius, master-general of troops, 434
Julius Nepos, the emperor, 557–58
Justin I, the emperor, 598–99, 608
Justin Martyr, 192–93, 200, 227
Justina, empress, 413, 414

Justinian I, the emperor, 325, 477, 579, 598–600, 605–6
Justiniani, 633, 637

Kaoti, Chinese emperor, 417

Labarum, 393
Lacedæmonians, 462
Lactantius, 200, 224, 227, 291
Lancearii, 431–32
language, influences of, 23–24
Læta, wife of Gratian, 483
Læti, 528
Latin language, spread of, 23–24, 226, 618
Latium, 129
Lætus, 54–55, 59, 61
Laura, 565
laureate, 655
Lemnos, 628
Leo, archbishop of Thessalonica, 618, 619
Leo, bishop of Rome, 534–35, 543, 544
Leo I, the emperor, 552, 556
Leo VI, the emperor, 617, 619
Leonard of Chios, 628
Leonidas, 461–62
Libanius, 391
Libius Serverus, the emperor, 550
Libyans, 14
Licinius Crassus, Marcus, 3
Licinius, the emperor, 173, 174–76, 180–85, 258–59, 262
Licinius the younger, 182, 292
Ligigantes, 295
Liguria, 554
Lipari, 497
literature, 33–34, 608–9, 619–21
Litorius, Count, 524
Liutprand, bishop of Cremona, 616
Loaodicea, 28
Logos, 333–36, 369
Logothete, 614–15
Lombardy, 10, 609
London, 408–9
Longinus, 34, 131
Lorraine, 314
Lucca, 654
Lucian, 18, 33–34, 224
Lucilian, Roman general, 357–58
Lucilla, 50
Lucillian, Count, 394–95
Lucius Verus, 50
Lupicina, 598
Lupicinus, 353, 424–25
Lusitania, 9, 546
Lustral Contribution, 284
Lyceum, 333
Lydia, 439

Macedonia, 11, 12, 170, 272, 295, 370
Macedonius, Roman usurper, 344, 345, 346, 607
Macellum, 305
Macrinus, the emperor, 79–81, 114
Magi, 321
magic, art of, 402
Magnentius, Roman usurper, 301–3
Majorca, 508
Majorian, the emperor, 546–50
Majorinus, 331
Malarich, 394–95
Malta, 15
Mamertinus, 364
mandra, 566
Manichæans, 194, 331, 603, 607
Mantinium, 346
Manuel II, the emperor, 624
Maogamalcha, 378–79
Mæonius, 131–32
Marcellinus, 410–11, 471
Marcellus, 363
Marcia, concubine of Commodus, 51, 54–55, 248
Marcian, the emperor, 521, 522, 538, 547
Marcianopolis, 103, 425–26
Marcionites, 194, 236–37, 331
Marcomanni, 49
Marcus Aurelius, the emperor, 1, 7, 33, 43, 44, 47, 48, 77, 229, 248
Marcus, Roman usurper, 474
Margus, 151, 463
Marinus, 101, 102
Marius, Roman usurper, 21, 118–19, 130, 443
Marseilles, 494, 579
Martialis, 79
Martin, bishop of Tours, 453
Martin V, bishop of Rome, 654, 657
martyrdom, 348–49, 456–58, 566
Mæsia, 11, 101, 102, 105, 106
master of respectable, 278
master of the offices, 278
Mattiarii, 431–32
Mauritania, 14, 108, 347
Maxentius, the emperor, 170–74, 176–80, 257, 289
Maximian, the emperor, 143, 152, 154–59, 163–64, 170–72, 174–76, 252, 256, 257, 289
Maximin, præfect of Gaul, 399, 410
Maximin, the emperor, 90–96, 167, 173, 175, 181–82, 249–50, 259
Maximus, philosopher, 385
Maximus, the emperor, 95–97, 424–27
Mediana, 397
Mellobaudes, 414
Menander, 620
Menelaus, 601
Mentz, 473

Meranes, general, 384
Merida, 497, 546
Merovingians, 579–83
Mesembria, 627
Mesopotamia, 5, 98, 148, 310, 375–76
Messalla, 411
Metaphysics, 197
Metius Falconius, 141
Metropolitans, 216, 322
Milan, 122, 158, 219, 308, 324, 330, 465, 532–33
Minerva, 309, 369
Minervina, 290
Minorca, 508
Misitheus, 98
Misopogon, 361
Mistrianus, 182
Mithridates of Pontus, 22
Modar, 438
Modena, 429
Mohammed II, Turkish sultan, 623–27, 630–32, 634–46
Mohammedan, 623
monarchy, definition of, 35
monasticism, 564–67
monks, 324, 343, 403
Montanists, 246, 330–31
Montesquieu, 448
Moon deity, 83
Moors, 171, 388, 509–10, 540, 542, 543
Morocco, 14
Moslems, 624–25, 632, 634, 638
Mucapor, 137
muezin, 646
Mundus, 606
Mundzuk, father of Attila, 513–14
Mursa, 302–3
Musonian, 310

Naissus, Dardania, 124, 359, 397, 463
namaz, 646
Narbonne, 494, 523–24
Narni, 482
Narses, 310–11
Naulobatus, 113
Nazarenes, 191–92, 238
Nepotianus, 290
Nero, 3, 40, 41, 52, 77, 91, 239–40
Nerva, the emperor, 1, 41–42, 242
Netherlands, 261
Nevitta, 356, 358, 364, 386
New Zealand, 408
Nice, 111–12, 340
Nicene, council of, 325–26, 370, 394
Nicephorus, 609–10
Nicholas IV, 654
Nicholas V, bishop of Rome, 626–27
Nicomedia, 111–12, 158, 163, 255
Nicopolis, 104

Nisibis, 114, 298–300, 388
Nobilissimus, 292, 505
Nohordates, general, 384
Noricum, 11
Normans, 610
Notitia, 268
Novatians, 330–31, 346, 370
Numa, 43, 83
Numerian, the emperor, 147, 148–50
Numidia, 14, 331, 347, 512

oda, 638
Odenathus, 116, 131–32, 135
Odoacer, 559–63, 572
olives, cultivation of, 30
Olybrius, the emperor, 555–57
Olympius, 477–79
Onegesius, 517–18
Optatus, 290
orators, sacred, 327–28, 621
Orestes, 557–60
oriental depotism, 363–64
Origen, 226, 227, 249, 250
Orkneys, 586
Orleans, 527
Orosius, 108, 471, 494
Orpheus, 229–30
Osius, 332, 340
Osrhoene, 5
Ossian, 408
Ostia, 487–88
Ostrogoths, 423, 425, 437–39, 516.
      See also Goths
Otho, the emperor, 41, 616

Pacatus, 443
Padua, 21, 532, 533
Paganism, 17, 19, 188, 194–95, 234, 349–50,
      368, 369–70, 451–54. See also religion
palace, administration of, 278–79
Palæologus, 637–38, 639, 641–42
Palatines, 275
Palestine, 13, 258
Palladium, 83
pallium, 656
Palmyra, 116, 130–32
Panhypersebastos, 614
Pannonia, 11, 65–66, 106, 272, 295, 411
papacy, 217–18, 260–61
Paphlagonia, 346
Papinian, 72, 73
Para, 410
parabolani, 324
Paris, 575
Parma, 429
Parthians, 3, 5, 7, 13
Patrician Opatus, 297
Patricians, 269–70
Paul of Constantinople, 341, 344–45

Paul of Samosata, 330–31
Paulus, 9–10, 21, 54, 73
Pavia, 123, 128, 470, 478
Pelagian controversy, 473–74
penance, 326–27, 447–48
Pera, 604
Persian Empire, 100, 108, 298–300, 375–89
Pertinax, the emperor, 55–60, 68
Pescennius Niger, 63, 64–65, 69
Pessinus, 373–74
Petovio, Pannonia, 307
Petrarch, 652
Petronius Maximus, the emperor, 538, 542–43
Petulants, 352
Pharisees, 198–99
Philelphus, 627, 644
Philip, the emperor, 36–38, 98–102, 103, 250
Philip, the Prætorian præfect, 345
Philippopolis, 104
philosophy, Græco-Roman, 17–18, 196–97,
      227–28, 402
Phocis, 462
Phœnicia, 13
Photius, 619
Phranza, George, 628, 631, 634, 639, 644
Phrygia, 439
Picts, 353, 407–8. See also Caledonia
Piræus, 112
Pityus, 110
Placentia, 128
Placidia, 495 96, 499, 504–10, 523, 525, 527
Plato, 34, 131, 218, 333, 360, 620
Platonists, 17–18, 197, 334, 368–69
Plautianus, 72
Plebeians, 269–70
Pliny the elder, 230
Pliny the younger, 228–30, 235, 242–43
Plotina, 42
Plotinus, 117
Plutarch, 229
Poggius, 647, 656
Pola, Istria, 307
Pompeianus, 484
Pompey, 605
pontiffs, 19, 37
Pontius Pilate, 240
Pontus, 13, 242, 272
Porch, 333
Porphyrians, 340
Portugal, 9
Posthumus, Roman usurper, 108, 129
præpositus, 278
Prætextatus, 402, 404
Prætorian Guards, 41, 51, 55–56, 59–62,
      67–69, 71–72, 87–88, 170, 178–79.
      See also army, Roman
Prætorian Præfect, 72, 78–79, 80, 98, 114,
      270–73
prætorship, 38

Presburg, 412
presbyters, 213–16, 219–20
presidents, 273
Primates, 216
principate, 35–46
Prisca, 251
Priscus, brother of Philip, 104
Priscus, philosopher, 385, 517–18
Priulf, 441
Probus, the emperor, 122, 129, 133–35,
    142–46, 411, 412
Proconnesus, 265
proconsuls, 273
Procopius, 379, 389
prophets, 213
Propontis, 265
Prosper, 471
prostitution, 51–52
protectors, 280
Protosebastos, 614
Protospathaire, 615
Protostrator, 615
Protovestiare, 614
Prusa, 111–12
Ptolemais, 143
Ptolemy, 33–34
Pulcheria, 506, 520–21
Pythagoras, 227

Quadi, 49, 295, 410–13
quæstor, 278–79

Radagaisus, 469–72, 475–76
Ratiaria, 463
Ravenna, 171, 467–68, 505
Rechiarius, 545–46
relics, holy, 456
religion
    fanatics of, 373–74
    government and, 232–34
    Huns respect for, 516–17
    policies surrounding, 16–20
    Roman, 39–40, 92
    toleration of, 366–74
Remigius, bishop of Rheims, 574
Respectable, 268–69, 272
Rhætia, 11, 122, 143, 410
Rheims, 473
Richomer, Count, 430, 431, 432, 434–35
Ricimer, Count, 547, 551, 552–56
Rimini, council of, 325, 482
Ripuarians, 528
roads. See highways
Robert, king of Sicily, 652
Roman Empire
    administration of, 20–26, 35–46, 57–58,
        89, 117–18, 144–45, 154, 158–59, 160–63,
        268–73, 278–79, 397–401, 449–50, 539,
        548–50, 579–83, 595–96, 610–18

Christians and, 231–61
    extent of, 8–15, 26–34, 99–100
    maps of, 2, 263, 541
    population of, 25–26, 121, 144, 157,
        266–67
Rome
    attacks on, 128–29
    citizens of, 20–21, 88–89, 322, 473,
        653–57
    city of, 10, 191, 262, 267–68
    councils of, 332
    decline of, 591–92, 647–57
    invasions of, 482–88, 491–92, 540, 542–44
    protection by, 157
    religious practices in, 19–20, 219, 233,
        239–40
Romulus Agustulus, the emperor, 21, 99,
    128, 539
Rorum Terebronii, 105
Roumelia, 12
Rufinus, 445, 459, 461
Rugians, 529, 558

Sabellians, 336
Sabinian, 312–13
Sabinus, 259
Sadducees, 198
saints, worship of, 455–58
Sallust, 353, 384–88
Salona, 164
Salonius, 108
Salvian, 512
Sandwich, 408
Sangiban, king of the Alani, 529
Saphrax, 423, 425, 431
Sapor, Persian emperor, 114–17, 134,
    298–300, 310–12, 375–77, 379–80,
    382, 387–88, 390, 409
Sappho, 620
Saracens, 376, 609
Sardinia, 15, 551
Sarmatians, 143, 157, 293–95, 309, 411, 412
Sarus, 470, 478, 490–91, 496
Saturnalia, 195
Saturninus, Roman usurper, 119
Sauromaces, 409–10
Savelli, 654
Saverne, 315–16
Saxons, 405–7, 502, 528, 584–90
Scandinavia, 515
Schleswig, 405
schools, 161, 265–66, 278, 280, 372, 396,
    400–401, 511, 517, 622
Scipio, 470
Sciri, 558
Scotland, 10. See also Caledonia
Scots, 353, 407–8
scrinia, 278
Scudilo, 307

Scutari, 185
Scythians, 103, 144, 277
Sebastian, master-general of infantry, 379,
   389, 429–30, 432
Sebastian, Roman usurper, 496–99, 523
Sebastocrator, 613–14
secular games, 53–57, 99, 149
Seleucia, 148, 309, 338
Selymbria, 627
Semiramis, 130–31
senate, Roman, 1, 5, 268–69
Senators, 364
Seneca, 85, 229
Septimius Severus, the emperor, 63–73, 78,
   99, 248–49
Serena, wife of Stilicho, 480, 483
Serverus, Roman general, 416
Serveus, the emperor, 167, 169, 171–72
Servius Tullius, 20, 74–77
Sesostris, 128
Severa, empress, 413
Severus, count of the domestics, 408
Seville, 497, 508
Siberia, 417, 418–19
Sibyls, 229–30
Sicily, 15, 30, 178, 415, 493
Sidonius, 526, 545, 547, 561, 572
Silingi, 498, 500
Silures, 10
Simeon Stylites, 565–67
Singara, 388
Singeric, king of the Goths, 499–500
Sirmium, 145, 146, 302, 356–58, 411, 412
Siscia, 302
Sixtus V, bishop of Rome, 653
slaves, domestic, 25, 46, 363, 421
soldiers, 8, 352–56, 450
Sosius Falco, 59
Sovou, 417
Spain, 8–9, 27, 30, 108, 272, 497–501,
   583–84
Spalatro, 164
Sparta, 20, 113
Spartans, 461–62
spies, 280–81, 306
Spires, 314, 473
Stilicho, 459, 464–67, 470–72, 475–80
Stobæus, 620
Stoic philosophy, 17–18, 44, 201
Strabo, 112
Strasburg, 314, 316, 317, 473
Stratopedarch, 615
Strymon, 623
Successianus, 110
Suerid, 427–28
Suevi, 109, 469, 500, 546
Suidas, 620
Sulpicianus, 61, 62
Sulpicius Severus, 245

Sun deity, 82, 150, 369
superindiction, 282, 548
Surenas, 378–79
Susa, 382, 389
sword of Mars, 514–15
sycophants, 176, 352
Sylla, 112, 443
Symmachus, 406–7
Synesius, 462
synods, 214–15, 328–29, 335
Syria, 13, 115, 258, 306

Tacitus, the emperor, 139–42, 229, 398, 405
Tacitus, the historian, 240
Taifalæ, 429
Tamsapor, 310
Tanjou, 416–18
Targeteers, 396
Tarraconensis, 9
Tarragona, 108, 497
Tarsus, 115, 391–92
Tartar race, 417, 418, 419
Tatullus, father of Orestes, 558
taxes, 88, 96, 162–63, 170, 241, 281–85, 401,
   424, 518–19, 548–49
temples, 372–73, 550
Termini, 420
Terminus, the God, 5
Tertullian, 202, 224, 227, 228, 334
Tetricus, Roman usurper, 123, 125, 130,
   135–36
Thebes, 113, 462
themes, 609
Theodora, 596–601
Theodoric I, king of the Visigoths, 523–25,
   527–28
Theodoric II, king of the Visigoths, 528,
   530–31, 545–46
Theodoric, king of the Ostrogoths, 545–46,
   591, 602, 651
Theodosian code, 268, 454–55, 582
Theodosius I, the emperor, 162–63, 326,
   391, 408–9, 411, 435–41, 442–50, 460
Theodosius II, the emperor, 477, 499,
   505–6, 518–19
Theophilus, the emperor, 204, 612
Theophrastus, 227
Theopompus, 620
Thermantia, 479
Thessalonica, 345, 436, 444–46, 463
Thessaly, 12, 475
Thrace, 11, 12, 258, 272, 295, 421, 438
Thuringians, 515, 529, 573
Tiber river, 649–50
Tiberius, the emperor, 19, 41, 45, 77, 240
Tiranus, 409
Tiridates of Armenia, 114
Titus, the emperor, 41
Tongres, 314

Torismond, king of the Visigoths, 528–31, 545
Totila, 651
Toulouse, 494, 501
Toulun, Khan of the Geougen, 469
Tournay, 473
Tours, 456
Toxandria, 314, 501–2
trade, international, 31–32, 265, 651
Traditors, 332
Trajan, Roman general, 432
Trajan, the emperor, 1, 4–5, 6, 12, 23, 42, 77, 93, 103, 242–43
treasurer-general. *See count of the sacred largesses*
Trebizond, 110–11
Trebonianus Gallus, the emperor, 105, 106
Trèves, 314, 412, 414, 501
tribunate, 36–38
Trigetius, Prætorian præfcct, 534
Trinitarian controversy, 332–40
Trisagion, 606–8
Troy, 113
Turcilingi, 558
Turks, 624–25, 632
Tuscan Haruspices, 383, 402
Tuscany, 471, 485–86
two counts of the domestics, 280
Tyana, 133, 395
Tyrants, the Thirty, 117–20
Tzetzes, 620

Ukraine, 103, 110
Ulphilas, bishop of the Goths, 568, 569
Ulpian, 73, 86, 87–88
Umbria, 467
Ursicinus, 312–13
Ursini, 653–54
Ursinus, 404

Valens, the emperor, 162–63, 396–401, 414, 416, 421–23, 428–32
Valentia, 409, 497
Valentinian I, the emperor, 395–413
Valentinian II, the emperor, 414
Valentinian III, the emperor, 504–6, 523, 536–39
Valentinians, 194, 331, 446
Valeria, 251
Valerian, the emperor, 106–8, 109, 110, 114–19, 142, 251

Vandals, 127, 144–45, 294, 469, 508–11, 572–73, 591, 650
Varanes, Persian emperor, 147
Varronian, Count, 387
Vatican, 629
Vegetius, 450
Venetia, 463, 533–34, 654
Venus, 369
Verina, empress, 552, 557
Verona, 102, 466–67
Vespasian, the emperor, 41, 199
Victor, Roman general, 386, 430, 432, 434–35
Victoria, 130
Victorinus, Roman usurper, 129, 130
Victors, 408
Vienna, 315
Vigilanti, mother of Justinian, 598–99
Viminiacum, 517
Virgil, 21, 33
Visigoths, 423, 425, 427–28, 437–39, 523, 527–28, 576–78, 583–84. *See also* Goths
Vitalian, 608
Vitellius, the emperor, 41, 45, 602
Volusianus, 106
Vortigern, 585–86
Vortimer, 587

Walamir, king of the Ostrogoths, 516
Wales, 10, 588
Wallachia, 420
Wallia, king of the Visigoths, 499–501
Wisumar, Vandal king, 295
Worms, 314, 473
worship, public, 455

Xerxes, 422–23

Zabdas, 132
Zamolxis, 128
Zante, 552
Zeno, 34, 44, 227, 559–60
Zenobia, 123, 125, 130–36
Zephaniah, 433
Zeuxippus, 345
Zingis, 16, 514
Zoroaster, 115, 193–94
Zoroastrianism, 100
Zosimus, 284, 471